MUSLIM SOCIETIES IN AFRICA

A Historical Anthropology

Roman Loimeier

Indiana University Press

Bloomington and Indianapolis

This book is a publication of

Indiana University Press
Office of Scholarly Publishing
Herman B Wells Library 350
1320 E. 10th Street
Bloomington, IN 47405-3907

iupress.indiana.edu

Telephone orders 800-842-6796
Fax orders 812-855-7931

∞ The paper used in this publication meets the minimum requirements of the American National Standard for Information Sciences—Permanence of Paper for Printed Library Materials, ANSI Z39.48–1992.

Manufactured in the United States of America

Library of Congress Cataloging-in-Publication Data
Loimeier, Roman.
Muslim societies in Africa : a historical anthropology / Roman Loimeier. — 1st ed.
p. cm.
Includes bibliographical references and index.
ISBN 978-0-253-00788-9 (cl : alk. paper) —
ISBN 978-0-253-00797-1 (eb) 1. Muslims—Africa—History. 2. Islam—Africa—History. 3. Africa—Civilization—Islamic influences. I. Title.
BP64.A1L65 2013
305.697096—dc23 2012050899

1 2 3 4 5 17 16 15 14 13

This book is dedicated to my parents,
Therese and Georg Loimeier

Contents

Preface and Acknowledgments *ix*

List of Abbreviations *xv*

Introduction: The Geographical and Anthropological Setting *1*

1 Is There an "African" Islam? *11*

2 The Bilād al-Maghrib: Rebels, Saints, and Heretics *35*

3 The Sahara as Connective Space *54*

4 Dynamics of Islamization in the Bilād al-Sūdān *77*

5 Dynamics of Jihād in the Bilād al-Sūdān *108*

6 Islam in Nubia and Funj *135*

7 Egyptian Colonialism and the Mahdī in the Sudan *154*

8 Ethiopia and Islam *172*

9 Muslims on the Horn of Africa *196*

10 The East African Coast *210*

11 Muslims on the Cape: Community and Dispute *248*

12 Muslims under Colonial Rule *267*

Conclusion *295*

Appendix *299*

Glossary of Arabic Terms *309*

Sources for Further Reading *315*

Index *337*

Preface and Acknowledgments

"Europeans have tended to read the rest of world history as a function of European history."

THE ABOVE QUOTATION from Marshall G. S. Hodgson's 1974 work *The Venture of Islam* (3: 22) points to an important purpose of the present book, namely to see the history and development of African Muslim societies within African historical contexts. I do not propose, of course, to dissociate African Muslim history from European history, but I would like to look at African-European relations from a southern perspective. In such a perspective, Europe is only one of several points of reference; others are the territories of the Ottoman empire, Arabia, India, the Indian Ocean, Southeast Asia, and the Atlantic.

But why should Islam be identified as a major defining factor for the analysis of societies and history in Africa? In fact, I do not claim that the analysis of the historical and societal development of Muslim and non-Muslim societies in Africa can be based on the single criteria of religious affiliation. Such an assumption would amount to crude Huntingtonian essentialism. I would rather contend that Africa and its adjoining regions, in particular the Mediterranean, the Arabian Peninsula, and the Indian Ocean can look back on a history of multiple entanglements. Yet in general histories of Africa, Muslim Africa has often been neglected and has not been seen as forming part of a larger Muslim ecumene. Also, sub-Saharan Africa including Muslim Africa has often been seen as belonging to the domain of anthropology, due to an alleged lack of written sources and texts in Arabic or vernacular languages. The publication of four volumes to date in the *Arabic Literature in Africa* (ALA) series, edited by John Hunwick and Sean R. O'Fahey or Ulrich Rebstock's *Maurische Literaturgeschichte* should have corrected such misrepresentations of African history. And yet knowledge of the existence of a multitude of traditions of Islamic learning has so far not been translated into a broader perception of African Muslim societies as core societies of Islam, although Arabic sources give access to a much deeper history of Muslim Africa: other parts of Africa (with the exception of Ethiopia) still have to rely on often scant archaeological evidence from before the sixteenth century, when European sources start to complement African oral traditions.

The present book thus tries to redress the periphery bias in the academic analysis of African Muslim societies. Such an approach is overdue: after all, Islam has, as of today, more than 450 million followers in Africa, constituting about half the population of the continent. In other words, Africa is home to one of the largest agglomerations of Muslims in the world, second only to the number of Muslims on the Indian subcontinent. Due to their undeniable importance in numerical strength as well as political potential, Muslim societies in Africa deserve a thorough study that does justice to the complexity of Africa's historical and societal development.

Considering these facts, it may appear foolish to attempt to write a comprehensive history of African Muslim societies: not only is the time period too vast for a single scholar, but the geographical scope of such a book is also daunting. Edited volumes have consequently dominated the presentation of African Muslim history, uniting the expertise of eminent scholars such as Louis Brenner, Joseph Cuoq, James Kritzeck, William H. Lewis, Donal Cruise O'Brien, Christian Coulon, Nehemia Levtzion, Randall Pouwels, and Ioan Lewis. At the same time, authoritative texts on Muslim societies in Africa and their history or specific regions within Africa have been written by individual scholars such as Jamil M. Abun-Nasr, Peter Clarke, François Constantin, Mervyn Hiskett, B. G. Martin, Vincent Monteil, Charlotte and Frederick Quinn, David Robinson, John Spencer Trimingham, and John Ralph Willis. Each of these authors has identified one or several central themes that seem to pervade African Muslim history. At the same time, their work, as well as my own, has been built upon the efforts of a large community of scholars. For readability's sake and to avoid too many quotations, their contributions are acknowledged in the "Sources for Further Reading" section for each chapter at the end of this book.

This book proposes to venture into a study of African Muslim societies across times and places. The aim, however, is not to present an exhaustive overview of the history of all African Muslim societies from the beginning of the process of Islamization to the contemporary period, but to present the major regions of Islam in Africa through the lens of historical key periods, concentrating on local dynamics of societal development as well as relations with the larger world mentioned above. I specifically explore the dynamics of historical change and identify a number of key themes in the development of African Muslim societies, such as the legitimacy of political rule, the role of outsiders in religio-political movements, the relationship between center and periphery in African Muslim empires, and the pervading importance of trade and the struggle for control of long-distance trade routes. The volume stresses the agency of African Muslims as traders and scholars, as leaders of states and movements of jihād, but also as both organizers and victims of Africa's different slave trades, and it shows how Africans have developed multiple ways of "being Muslim" (Osella and Soares 2010: 12). Another basic argument of this book is that African Muslim societies have evolved in a dialogue with their respective geographical and ecological settings, and that African Muslim societies have to be understood as being informed, to this day, by multiple historical legacies that have given individual societies their specific social, economic, political, and religious role and position. For these reasons, I describe this book as a historical anthropology of African Muslim societies.

The book thus views the history of Muslim societies in Africa as part of a larger world. Consequently, I focus on those regions and societies that have been influenced, in one way or another, by Islam, and have become, over time, Muslim in many different ways. In an introductory chapter, I present the geographical and anthropological setting for the development of Muslim societies in Africa. Both geography and anthropology offer key perspectives for a study of the history of Muslim societies in Africa. In addition, I discuss some basic themes and problems, such as whether we may talk of an African Islam or regard Muslim societies in Africa as a broad array of different realizations of Islam in distinct historical contexts, characterized by their different interfaces with Christianity, Judaism, and African indigenous religions. I also discuss historical patterns and peculiarities, continuities and discontinuities, and I point out where certain patterns of explanation apply and where they do not. Despite a large variety of societal development, historical experience, and regional and economic variation across Africa (and beyond), Islam over time has come to constitute a unifying force, a common denominator for many Africans. This is due not only to the development of traditions of learning based on a corpus of key Islamic texts, but also to the binding forces of trade, pilgrimage, and cultural exchange with the larger world of Islam, and, last but not least, the normative power of Islam in contexts of state building, especially in times of conflict. In a series of thematic chapters, I present distinct regions of Islam in Africa and focus on a number of historical key periods for the development of Muslims in these regions. By "key period" I refer to a period of time during which Muslim societies in a specific region were shaped in a decisive way. Such key periods are often remembered to this day, and are quoted as historical moments that define the "Islamicité" of a specific Muslim community or society. Finally, I look at the development of Muslim societies in Africa under colonial rule. The early twentieth century is treated from a historical "longue durée" perspective, focusing on the way in which the colonial period challenged established ways of "being Muslim" in Africa.

This book does not include two major historical periods, namely, the pre-Islamic history of Muslim societies in Africa and the postcolonial development of Muslim societies in Africa. Equally, while Egypt has received copious attention in academic research, it is presented here in marginal ways only. This is not meant to be a denial of pre-Islamic, Egyptian, and/or postcolonial histories, but reflects the fact that a thorough discussion of pre-Islamic history and postcolonial developments would exceed the limits of this volume. While pre-Islamic (and Egyptian) history are mentioned briefly where appropriate, the analysis of postcolonial history will be reserved for another time and another book. Even so, many relevant themes can be addressed only briefly and in passing. Such issues, which are central to the understanding of the larger context yet do not fit into the focus of a specific chapter, are discussed in a series of thematic insets.

I offer students and enthusiasts of African history an analysis of the dynamics of historical developments in Muslim Africa, but in addition I stress the necessity of multilingual research. Thus, in individual bibliographies at the end of each chapter that also serve as guides to the interested reader for additional source material, I have not confined recommendations to titles in English. Any serious study of the history and development of Muslim societies in Africa has to consider sources in Arabic, as well as in a number of African languages, such as Kiswahili or Hausa, in which local sources such as the Kano, Pate, or Kilwa chronicles have been produced. In addition, valuable work on Islam and Muslim societies in Africa has been done and is still being done in languages such as French, German, and Italian.

With regard to the transliteration of Arabic terms, I follow the system of the *Encyclopaedia of Islam* (with the exception of 'q' which replaces 'ḳ', and 'j' which replaces 'dj'). The Amharic 'ä' corresponds to 'a' in the Anglo-American 'Jack'. It has been claimed that the transliteration of Arabic terms can be confusing for the uninitiated, while scholars of Islam would have no problem in recognizing the proper Arabic root behind non-transliterated terms. I would like to hold against this opinion that a proper transliteration does not hurt and often helps to identify technical terms and, even more so, names and places.

For inspiration in the last twenty-five years and for constructive comments on my work during this period, including on this book, I would like to thank (in alphabetical order) Jamil M. Abun-Nasr, Chanfi Ahmed, Anne Bang, Anke Bosaller, Ulrich Braukämper, Louis Brenner, Patrick Desplat, Mamadou Diouf, the late ʿAbd al-Raḥmān Doi, the late Humphrey Fisher, Ulrike Freitag, John Hanson, Zulfiqar Hirji, Albrecht Hofheinz, Valerie Hoffman, Albert Hourani, John Hunwick, Ousmane Kane, Franz Kogelmann, Kai Kresse, Murray Last, Robert Launay, the late John Lavers, the late Nehemia Levtzion, Christoph Marx, Gottfried Müller, Hassan Mwakimako, Terje Østebø, Réné Otayek, Scott Reese, Stephan Reichmuth, David Robinson, Rüdiger Seesemann, Abdul Sheriff, Benjamin Soares, Gerd Spittler, Abdulkader Tayob, Farouk Topan, Muhammad Sani Umar, Leonardo Villalon, Holger Weiss, and David Westerlund, as well as my students at the Universities of Bayreuth, Göttingen, and Florida and also at the École des Hautes Études en Sciences Sociales in Paris, who, with their critical questions and inspired comments, have helped me to focus on the important and basic questions of societal development. I would like to thank in particular Cornelia and Josefine, who have reminded me to not forget about the realities of life. Finally, Ruth Schubert, who has worked on the language in this book and tried hard to eradicate my Germanisms, as well as the editorial team at Indiana University Press, in particular Dee Mortensen, Darja Malcolm-Clarke, and Eric Schramm, deserve my unlimited gratitude.

Sources for Further Reading

As mentioned, a number of major studies have been written on the history of Muslim societies in Africa or major regions of Africa. Most prominent are, in alphabetical order by author, Jamil M. Abun-Nasr, *A History of the Maghrib in the Islamic Period,* Cambridge, 1987; J.F.A. Ajayi and M. Crowder, *History of West Africa,* Burnt Mill, 1976; Rene Bravmann, *African Islam,* London, 1983; Louis Brenner, *Muslim Identity and Social Change in Sub-Saharan Africa,* London, 1993; Peter B. Clarke, *West Africa and Islam,* London, 1982; François Constantin, *Les voies de l'islam en Afrique orientale,* Paris, 1987; Christian Coulon, *Les musulmans et le pouvoir,* Paris, 1983; Donal B. Cruise O'Brien and Christian Coulon, *Charisma and Brotherhood in African Islam,* Oxford, 1988; Joseph M. Cuoq, *Les Musulmans en Afrique,* Paris, 1975; Mervyn Hiskett, *The Development of Islam in West Africa,* London, 1984; Mervyn Hiskett, *The Course of Islam in Africa,* Edinburgh, 1994; James Kritzeck and W. H. Lewis, *Islam in Africa,* New York, 1969; Nehemia Levtzion and H. Fisher, *Rural and Urban Islam in West Africa,* Boulder, 1987; Nehemia Levtzion and Randall L. Pouwels, *The History of Islam in Africa,* Oxford, 2000; Ioan M. Lewis, *Islam in Tropical Africa,* London, 1980; B. G. Martin, *Muslim Brotherhoods in Nineteenth Century Africa,* Cambridge, 1976; Vincent Monteil, *L'Islam Noir: Une religion à la conquête de l'Afrique,* Paris, 1980; David Robinson, *Muslim Societies in African History: New Approaches to African History,* Cambridge, 2004; Charlotte A. Quinn and Frederick Quinn, *Pride, Faith, and Fear: Islam in Sub-Saharan Africa,* Oxford, 2003; Eva Evers-Rosander and David Westerlund (eds.), *African Islam and Islam in Africa: Encounters between Sufis and Islamists,* London, 1997; several works by John Spencer Trimingham, in particular *Islam in West Africa,* Oxford, 1959, *Islam in East Africa,* Oxford, 1964, *Islam in the Sudan,* London, 1965, *Islam in Ethiopia,* London, 1976, and *The Influence of Islam upon Africa,* London, 1980; and John Ralph Willis, *Studies in West African Islamic History, I: The Cultivators of Islam,* London, 1979.

For general reading on the history of Islam, Marshall G.S. Hodgson's work is still most recommendable: *The Venture of Islam: Conscience and History in a World Civilization,* 3 vols., Chicago, 1974; an excellent overview of the development of Arabic (and vernacular) writing is provided by the four volumes published to date in the Arabic Literature in Africa (ALA) series, edited by John Hunwick and Sean R. O'Fahey, Leiden, 1994–, as well as by Ulrich Rebstock's *Maurische Literaturgeschichte,* 3 vols., Würzburg, 2001.

For a general history of Africa, I recommend John Iliffe, *Africans: History of a Continent,* Cambridge, 1995.

An excellent introduction into the "anthropology of Islam" is provided by Filippo Osella and Benjamin Soares, *Islam, Politics, Anthropology,* Milton Keynes, 2010.

Abbreviations

Afr.	Afrikaans
Amh.	Amharic
Arab.	Arabic
Ful.	FulFulde
Hau.	Hausa
Ind.	Bahasa Indonesia
Som.	Somaal
Swa.	Swahili
Tam.	Tamazight (Berber languages)
Wol.	Wolof

BSOAS	Bulletin of the School of Oriental and African Studies
CHA	Cambridge History of Africa
IJAHS	International Journal of African Historical Studies
IJMES	International Journal of Middle East Studies
ISSS	Islam et sociétés au sud du Sahara
JAH	Journal of African History
JHSN	Journal of the Historical Society of Nigeria
JIMMA	Journal (of the) Institute of Muslim Minority Affairs
JRA	Journal of Religion in Africa
SA	Sudanic Africa

MUSLIM SOCIETIES
IN AFRICA

Introduction

The Geographical and Anthropological Setting

Africa's different habitats and ecosystems, as well as its surrounding seas and oceans, have been major formative forces in the development of societies on the continent. Before delving into the analysis of the history of Muslims in Africa, it may be helpful to have a look at the anthropo-geographic context in which Africa's Muslim societies have developed since the mid-seventh century.

Anyone coming from western Asia and entering Africa from the northeast will inevitably encounter the Nile. The "nīl miṣr" (Egyptian Nile) of the Arab geographers, with its huge delta and densely settled valley, has been a major center of cultural and political development for more than 6,000 years. The Nile was of major formative importance for a whole series of cultures in the Nile valley, not only Egypt but also the countries upstream, in particular Nubia, the land between the first cataract south of Aswan and the sixth cataract north of the confluence of the Blue Nile and the White Nile. Despite these natural obstacles, especially the "baṭn al-ḥajar," the "belly of stones" between the second and the third cataracts, the Nile constituted a major highway of exchange between the Mediterranean and the lands of the Upper Nile valley, with the adjacent steppes and savannahs. Due to their dependence on its waters, the societies on the Nile developed intricate and in many ways unique strategies of calculation, technologies of irrigation and storage, administration of surplus and scarcity, defense and warfare, which subsequently informed the formation of states, principalities, and empires in the Nile valley. The empires on the Nile exerted a major influence on the surrounding regions, attracting people across Africa and Asia to come to Egypt as traders, conquerors, pilgrims, or students.

The development of a distinct, irrigation-based Nile valley civilization has been directly linked with an important ecological process of longue durée, namely the desertification of the Sahara in the Mesolithic period (c. 10,000–4,000), which almost stopped movement across the Sahara entirely. Only the introduction of the camel in the first century BCE and the subsequent emergence of a camel-based economy, first in North Africa and later in the Saharan oases, made large-scale transport and movement across the Sahara possible again. The lands north of the Sahara, the Roman provinces of Africa and Numidia, which came to be called "Ifrīqiyya" after the Arab conquest, or simply the "lands of the sunset" (Arab. bilād al-maghrib), were characterized by three major features: they constituted the southern shore of the Mediterranean and thus connected Africa with Europe; at the same time, they constituted the northern shore of the Sahara, and thus connected the Mediterranean with the lands south of the Sahara; and finally, they constituted a cosmos of mountains and valleys, high plateaus, mountain deserts and river valleys, most often small floodplains, in sum, a rather rugged and difficult terrain, ideal for transhumant pastoralism, precarious for farmers, the home of a multitude of "Imasighen" (sing. Amasigh, colloquially known as Berber) tribes, fragmented politically, seldom under the control of one empire for an extended period of time, home to a few urban centers only.

To the south of the bilād al-maghrib lay the great desert (Arab. al-ṣaḥrā' al-kubrā), stretching 5,000 kilometers from the Atlantic to the Red Sea, as well as 2,000 kilometers from its northern shores, the Atlas Mountains and the Mediterranean, to its southern rim (Arab.: sāḥil) in sub-Saharan West and Central Africa. The Sahara was not a monotonous wasteland of sand, but an ever-changing array of sand dunes (in Imasighen languages, iguīdi), sands (erg), stony plateaus (reg), high plateaus (tassili), flat bedrock plains (hammada), and mountains (ādrār), interrupted by dry wādīs and oases. During the winter rains in the bilād al-maghrib in the north (November–March), as well as the summer rains in the bilād al-sūdān in the south (May–August), erratic rains could create not only fine pastures in the midst of the desert but also flash floods in wādīs, which, besides sandstorms, were the most dangerous feature of life and trade in the Sahara (see map 1).

The growth of the Sahara in the Mesolithic period forced Saharan populations apart. In the north, Mediterranean peoples came to dominate, including a multitude of Imasighen tribes, but also Greek, Phoenician, Jewish, Roman, and, later, Arab settlers, while the south turned increasingly black. Islets of black populations inhabited Saharan oases far north, such as Ghāt and Ghadāmis until fairly recent times; but only the Tibesti mountains and the oases of Bilma still have black populations today. Labeled Tubu (mountain people) by the Kanuri in the south, and Goran (Qoran) by the Arabs in the north, the Teda in the Tibesti mountains and the Daza in the Ennedi and Borku regions were able to retain control over trans-Saharan routes in this central part of the Sahara. In other parts of the Sahara, Imasighen (Tuareg) as well as Arab populations, often organized in tribes of warriors and scholars, gained the upper hand. While the warrior tribes protected the scholars (Tam. ineslemen, lit. Muslims; Arab. zawāya, lit. those who live in a Sufi-center), the scholarly tribes organized trade and maintained Islamic education. Together, warriors and zawāya formed the social, political, and religious elites of the Sahara. The most famous warrior tribes were the Banū Ḥasan groups in the Western Sahara, but also a number of Tuareg tribes such as the Kel Tadamakkat, who came to dominate Timbuktu in the early eighteenth century. Famous zawāya/ineslemen tribes were the Kunta in the central Sahara, as well as the Awlād Ibirri and Awlād Daymān in the western Sahara. Subordinated to warrior and zawāya/ineslemen tribes were client (Tam. imgad, Arab. laḥma, lit. meat, or talāmīdh, disciples) groups, craft (smiths, weavers, etc., Tam. inaden) groups as well as the ḥaratīn (Arab. former slaves, who were still part of their respective households) and ʿabīd (Arab. full slaves;

Tam. iklan), which were of paramount importance for the Saharan oases and were set to work to dig wells and to maintain irrigation systems. These Imasighen and Arab tribal populations not only gained control over a multitude of Saharan oases such as Tuwāt, Ghadāmis, Ghāt, Fazzān, Kufra, and the Ādrār and Ahīr (Aïr) mountains, as entrepôts for the trans-Saharan trade, but were also the major intermediaries between the bilād al-maghrib, the lands north of the Sahara, and the lands of the blacks (Arab. bilād al-sūdān) south of the Sahara.

Saharan and North African populations (as well as the Bīja and Somaal in Ethiopia and in the Horn of Africa) have often been classified by anthropologists as segmentary societies based on extended family groups (tents, Arab. buyūt), tribal subdivisions and tribes (Tam. kel, Arab. qabīla). Evans-Pritchard has characterized segmentary societies as "a system of balanced opposition between tribes and tribal sections from the largest to the smallest divisions" (Evans-Pritchard 1949: 56–59), marked by a lack of absolute authority but the acceptance of rules of group solidarity in case of conflict. The logic of segmentation that stresses conflict as a major driving force of social formation should not be seen as an automatism, however. Segmentary societies are keen to prevent conflict and feud, as "a feud knows no beginning and has no end" (Peters 1969: 268). Segmentary societies have thus formed so-called diya groups that accept "blood money" (Arab. diya) as compensation for a murder in order to prevent escalation of a conflict into a feud. Segmentary societies have also developed a tradition of accepting the mediation of neutral outsiders, such as holy men, in order to prevent conflict and to form leagues (Tam., Arab. leff, reff, or saff) and alliances that transcend the logic of segmentation and provide venues of social and political integration. Steven Caton has thus concluded that (Middle Eastern) "tribesmen . . . are talking to each other probably more than they are fighting" (Caton 1987: 83).

The lands to the south of the Sahara, the lands of the blacks, can be divided into four distinct ecological regions, all oriented toward a major system of rivers or lakes: the lands in the Atlantic west, oriented toward the rivers Senegal and Gambia, which we refer to here as the Senegambian Sudan; the lands converging on the Niger, the nīl ghāna of the Arab geographers, referred to here as the Niger Sudan; the lands converging on Lake Chad and the Shari, called here Chad-Sudan, and, finally, the lands converging on the Nile, called here Nile-Sudan. Like the Nile, the rivers and lakes of the Sudanic regions had paramount importance for the development of riverine civilizations and trade and equally stimulated the emergence of river-based empires such as Mālī and Songhay. In addition, the centers of settlement on the southern shores of the Sahara became harbors for a multitude of trans-Saharan trade routes and tried to gain control over trans-Saharan trade, often in competition with Saharan populations. The bilād al-sūdān were thus direct partners of the trading regions north of the Sahara, the Saharan populations acting as the transmission belt. The ecology of the bilād al-sūdān informed the nature of the trading networks in the region: when they reached the southern shores of the Sahara, goods had to be reloaded from camels to boats, oxen and donkeys, which were more viable in the increasingly humid regions of the south, where sleeping sickness was widely spread. The ecology and the resulting logistics of transport in the Sahara and the bilād al-sūdān explains both the emergence of distinct regional trade networks and the fact that North African and Saharan traders never gained control over Sudanic trade routes and vice versa: Sudanic traders were never able to establish control over the Saharan or North African trade routes. The vast stretches of the bilād al-sūdān and their major axes of transport, the rivers, did, however, support the emergence of "Sudanic" trading empires and trading emporia, as well as urban centers such as Kano, Katsina, Timbuktu, and Jenné. These emporia in turn acted as transmission belts for trade further south, into the tropical lands of the Guinea coast.

The tropical forests of the Guinea coast constituted another distinct ecological region, connected by a multitude of rivers and rivulets, subdivided by mountain ranges and marked by swampy lowlands, as well as dry and temperate plateaus, such as those of Fuuta Jalon in Guinea, Jos (Nigeria), and Adamawa (Cameroons). Both savannahs and tropical forests were settled by a multitude of populations, the Wolof, Serer, the different Mande groups (Sarakolle, Soninke, Malinke, Bambara, Marka, Juula), the Mossi and Hausa, the Kanuri and Jerma-Songhay, the Senufo, Dogon, and Nupe, as well as the Yoruba and Akan groups that fought for control over trade routes and resources, especially gold. In their endeavors to master a difficult tropical environment, they developed a plethora of local and regional chiefdoms and kingdoms. The populations of the savannah and the tropical forest regions represent a broad array of social systems, from highly centralized to highly fragmented societies, from highly egalitarian to highly stratified, organized in both patrilineal and matrilineal descent systems. Apart from nobles and free peasant populations, as well as slaves, many stratified societies knew endogamous casted groups, identified by their specific crafts, such as smiths, leatherworkers, weavers, or potters, in addition to griots who transmitted family genealogies, sang the praises of the nobles, and could thus be regarded as word workers, indispensable transmitters of local traditions and history.

Colonial historiography and academic research has granted one linguistic group in the bilād al-sūdān particular attention, namely the so-called FulBe (sing. Pulo; Fulani/Peulh in British and French sources; or, more neutrally, Halpulaaren, those who speak the language of the FulBe, FulFulde). The fact that FulFulde-speaking groups played a major role in certain jihād movements in the eighteenth and nineteenth centuries was seen by colonial historians as a sign of the "racial superiority" of these pastoralists, who sometimes tended to be light-skinned. They were seen as the rulers of empires that were then, in an evolutionary analogy, taken over in due course by even lighter-skinned Europeans. These theories ignore the fact that FulBe pastoralists had no share in the earlier formation of the great trading empires of the bilād al-sūdān, and that the leaders of the jihād movements were not FulBe pastoralists but a class of FulFulde-speaking TorodBe scholars, who often represented larger, marginalized, and disaffected populations, even if FulBe pastoralists were among their chief supporters. The remarkable expansion of FulBe pastoralists from the Senegal in the west to the east can be explained in ecological terms: in pre-recorded times, when pastures for the cattle of the sedentary FulFulde-speaking populations (Tukulóór) in the Senegal valley started to become scarce, their herdsmen, the FulBe, started to move to new pastures in the east. The west, the north, and the south were not viable for obvious reasons: the Atlantic, the Sahara, and the tropical forests of the Guinea coast prevented expansion into these directions. On their way east, FulBe herdsmen moved within a strip of cattle-viable steppes, savannahs, and highlands, intermarrying with Arabs and Berber from the north and thus gradually becoming lighter along the way (or darker in regions where they intermarried with sedentary black populations): The FulBe reached Masina in the fourteenth century, Hausaland in the sixteenth century, Adamawa in the nineteenth century, and the Nile in the twentieth century. The example of the FulBe shows that African (Islamic) history was often informed by movements of migration that transformed geographical regions: the expansion of Berber populations across the Sahara; the settlement of Arab tribes in North Africa, on the Nile, in the Lake Chad region, and in the western Sahara; the expansion of the FulBe pastoralists across the Sudanic savannahs from the Atlantic to the Red Sea; and the migrations of the Bīja, Oromo, and Somaal in the mountains and deserts of northeastern Africa.

As in the western and central Sudanic savannahs, open steppes also facilitated trade, migration, and exchange further east in the lands bordering on the Nile. The steppes and savannahs of the Nile Sudan, both to the north and south of the confluence of the White Nile and Blue Nile, as well as a number of lesser confluents, such as the ʿAtbara, became a theater of exchanges for both camel and cattle nomads. The history of these lands on the Nile were characterized by efforts to maintain a precarious peace between mostly Arab herdsmen and sedentary populations, a situation complicated, as in the western bilād al-sūdān, by recurring droughts. The Arab populations in the Sudan were divided into numerous tribal groups. The oldest and most important group was that of the Jaʿaliyyīn, who were split into the Shāʾiqiyya, the Rubātāb, the Manāṣīr, the Mirāfāb, and the Jaʿaliyyīn proper. These tribal groups have largely merged over time with the sedentary Nubian populations of the Nile valley and become farmers. Another Arab tribal federation, the Juhayna, has kept its nomadic character and continues to own large herds of either cattle (Arab. baqqāra, Sudan Arab. baggāra) or camels (Arab. abbāla). The Juhayna are again split today into the Kabābīsh, the Rizayqāt, the Shukriyya, and the Kawāhla tribes. Depending on rainfall patterns and the long-term development of pastures, northern sections of these tribes have specialized in camel breeding, while southern sections have become cattle herders, often in symbiotic relations with the sedentary populations of Kordofan and Dārfūr, and have developed an intricate system of passageways from northern to southern pastures in an annual transhumant rhythm. These conventions of exchange collapsed, however, in situations of crisis such as drought, epidemics, or continual raiding of sedentary populations by slave traders in the nineteenth century. The so-called baggāra belt, the rich cattle grazing lands of Kordofan stretching from the Nile to Dārfūr, and beyond Dārfūr and Wadai to Lake Chad, has thus become home to numerous cattle tribes, such as the Rizayqāt, the Taʿāīsha, the Missiriyya, and the Awlād Rashīd. The westernmost Baggāra, the Shūwa, reached the Shari in the eighteenth century and today have established settlements in Borno (northeastern Nigeria). On their way west, the Baggāra met FulBe cattle herders drifting east. Today, FulBe cattle herders have reached and crossed the Nile.

While the lands on the Nile and the savannahs of Kordofan to the west came to be dominated by Arab tribes, the lands toward the east and on the Red Sea coast were dominated by the Bīja. The Bīja (Beja) consisted of a large number of mostly nomadic tribes of herdsmen and families of traders in the mountainous regions on the western shores of the Red Sea, speaking a language related to Oromo and Somaal. Possibly due to processes of desertification, Bīja tribes migrated south and reached the confines of Axum in Ethiopia by the sixth century CE. Bīja tribes not only resisted political domination by Mamlūk Egypt or Nubia, but also Christian Ethiopia, and in fact

> Epidemics and diseases are major yet often neglected features of African history, including the history of Muslim societies. In the late nineteenth century, an epidemic of rinderpest thus annihilated a major part of Africa's cattle. Imported in 1887 from India to Massawa by the Italian navy, a harbor on the coast of Eritrea, this disease killed most of Ethiopia's cattle in 1888 and then spread into the lands on the Nile and the bilād al-sūdān in the north and west, as well as to the Horn of Africa and the East African interior in the south, finally reaching South Africa, killing more than 90 percent of all African cattle and wild animals until 1898: "The epidemic spread like fire: when cattle were counted in the evening, all animals were still healthy. On the next morning, they were sick and all were dead on the second or third day" (Weiss 1995: 51). In Ethiopia, 90–100 percent of all cattle died and not only deprived farmers of their chief means of production, but also led to hunger and instability. This crisis paved the way for the Italian occupation of Eritrea in 1889. The rinderpest epidemic led to the temporary collapse of most transhumant or nomadic populations in sub-Saharan Africa in the late nineteenth century and allowed European colonial powers the almost unobstructed occupation of vast steppe and savannah regions in both West and East Africa. Only Ethiopia was able to overcome the shock of the rinderpest in time to defeat an Italian invasion in 1896.

have controlled the Red Sea region up to present times, including trade and pilgrimage routes (see map 2).

The Ethiopian highlands to the south and east of the Nile-Sudan constitute an abrupt change in geography, the lands rising from a level of a few hundred meters to elevations of more than 2,000 or 3,000 meters, and continuing to rise, in mountain blocks such as the Semien in northern Ethiopia, to almost 5,000 meters. Ethiopia has thus always been seen, by the surrounding lowlanders and by the inhabitants of the mountains, as an island. In truth, Ethiopia should be seen as a series of highlands, separated by the great African Rift Valley. Both the northwestern and the southeastern highlands are interrupted by deep gorges and divided by high mountain ranges and plateaus (Amh. amba), which were often difficult to cross. From each highland region, a number of mountain ranges branch out into western and southeastern directions, forming plateaus and fertile lake basins such as the Lake Tana basin. In the south, hilly and fertile regions such as Kaffa form Ethiopia's southern marches, which eventually drop into the deserts and dry steppes of the Horn and the Omo-Turkana region. However, Ethiopia is not only structured as a multitude of mountain ranges and highlands divided by deep gorges, it is also differentiated in vertical terms: the lower reaches of the mountains up to an elevation of about 1,700 meters are called qolla. Qolla lands are hot and humid, in particular in the rainy seasons, yet fertile, and were thus, where possible, intensively farmed. The temperate woyna dega regions up to elevations of about 2,500 meters have been major regions of settlement and intensive agriculture. The cool dega lands up to elevations of about 3,700 meters have been settled and farmed less but have also provided niches for specific crops. Due to their elevation, Ethiopian mountain ranges catch the tropical summer rains of equatorial Africa, and Ethiopia has thus come to form a green island in an otherwise rather arid climatic zone. The heart of the western highlands of Ethiopia, Lake Tana, is the source of the Blue Nile that annually transports fertile soil down the Nile to Egypt. Colonized by immigrants from southwestern Arabia, the Ethiopian highlands are in many ways related to neighboring Yemen. In contrast to Yemen, Ethiopia has become a domain of orthodox Christianity, in particular among the Tigre, Tigriña, and Amharic-speaking populations of the northern, central, and southwestern highlands, while other major groups, such as the Oromo, have turned to either Christianity or Islam or have remained loyal to their own religions. The Afar and Somaal populations in the Danakil lowlands and the Ogaden region in the east are mostly Muslim today.

Toward the east and south of the Ethiopian mountain ranges, the Horn of Africa, like the Sahara, forms a vast and arid region, devoid of major oases, crossed by two major rivers only, the Shebelle and the Juba. Few harbors (Persian: banādir, sing. bandar), such as Mogadishu, Brawa, and Marka, opened the hinterland to the Indian Ocean. The coastal settlements on the Horn may be seen as an extension of either the East African coast, as in the case of Brawa, Kismayu, Marka, Mogadishu, or as an extension of Ḥaḍramawt across the Gulf of Aden, as in the case of Berbera and

Zaylaʿ. The interior of the Horn knew no urban settlements at all in historical times. Only the lower reaches of two rivers, the Shebelle and the Juba, constituted a particular ecological niche. Between Mogadishu and its confluence with the lower Juba, the lower Shebelle runs parallel to the Indian Ocean for a length of about 400 kilometers before breaking through the coastal dunes. The lower Shebelle and Juba rivers thus formed a rich alluvial valley that stimulated the emergence of an agricultural tradition in the southern Horn, dominated by the black Bimaal Somaal tribal federation, which fed coastal trading centers such as Mogadishu. The arid and semi-arid deserts of the Horn, as well as the few ports of the Horn, were settled almost exclusively by Somaal clans that competed for access to water and pastures, as well as for control over trade routes. Like the Oromo and the Bīja, the Somaal form part of the Cushitic linguistic family. Like the Imasighen of the bilād al-maghrib, or the Arab nomads of the western Sahara and the Sudan, they were organized in clans, sub-clans, and family groups (Som. reer; lit. herd, lineage), united by the use of wells and pastures and through marriage alliances, as well as so-called diya groups, social units of several reer bound by a contract, a ḥeer (Som. custom). Such contracts usually stipulated that crimes such as homicide should not be answered by physical retaliation and subsequent feuds, but by the payment of blood money), often in the guise of cattle, in particular, highly esteemed camels. For mediation in cases of conflict, the Somaal and their diya groups accepted religious scholars (Som. wadaad). In terms of ethnic organization, the Somaal were roughly split into six major clans, the Dir, Isaaq, Hawiye, Darood, Digil, and Rahanwiin, who settled across the Horn of Africa but did not constitute or form political federations. Apart from the agricultural zones on the lower Juba and Shebelle, which were cultivated by the Bimaal, the Somaal tried to survive as transhumant pastoralists, competing for scarce resources. Ioan Lewis has characterized the Somaal as a warlike people driven by the poverty of their resources to intense competition for access to water and grazing (Lewis 1988: 11), a context that led to a Somaal saying: "If you love a person, love him moderately, for you do not know whether you will hate him one day; on the other hand, if you hate someone, hate him moderately also, for you do not know whether you will love him one day" (Cassanelli 1982: 21).

The port cities of the Horn, such as Mogadishu, Brawa, or Marka, formed part of the larger ecosystem of the East African coast, which stretched from the Banādir port cities of the southern Horn for a distance of more than 2,000 kilometers to the south, to the coasts of Mozambique. An important and defining factor for the development of a distinct Muslim East African coastal culture was the fact that the different sections of the East African coast, namely, the Banādir coast in the north (Mogadishu, Brawa, Marka), the Mrima coast in the center (Lamu, Pate, Faza, Mombasa, Malindi, Pemba, Zanzibar, and Kilwa), and the Sofala coast in the south (contemporary northern Mozambique to the delta of the Zambezi) were linked by a system of seasonal monsoons with other coasts of the Indian Ocean: from April to June/July a mild southwest monsoon (Swa. kusi) would blow in a northeasterly direction across the Indian Ocean, while the northeast monsoon (Swa. kaskasi) reversed the direction of the winds (and rainfall) and ruled the East African coast from November/December to March. From Mombasa or Lamu it was possible in a single monsoon season to reach the western coasts of India, the southern coasts of Persia and the coasts of southern Arabia, and to sail back home with the next monsoon that blew in the opposite direction. The stability of these trade winds led to the emergence of a highly integrated circum–Indian Ocean network of exchanges and to the establishment of similar patterns of ship-building, as expressed in the different types of Indian Ocean dhows, in an architecture that relied on East African mangrove poles for the construction of roofs, in similar agriculture and fishing activities, or in the adoption of the Shāfiʿī school of law by most Muslims in the region. The seasonal character of the monsoon wind system also "gridlocked" (Sheriff 2010: 22) the movement of dhows and their crews, forcing them to spend the time between the monsoons in their ports of destination, stimulating social interaction between sailors, traders, and local populations. At the same time, the northwestern Indian Ocean was linked by way of the Red Sea with Egypt, by way of the Gulf with lower Mesopotamia and Iran, by way of Southern India and Sri Lanka with the Sea of Bengal, and ultimately through the Straits of Malacca with the Chinese trading emporium. These far-reaching contacts were expressed in many ways in East African coastal culture: not only in terms of being an Muslim culture, with multiple calendars and a plethora of Indian Ocean technologies, but also in terms of language: Kiswahili, for instance, contains not only numerous Arabic loanwords, but also words from Persian and Gujarati (see map 3).

In contrast to the Saharan sāḥil, which formed a transmission belt for trade with the tropical lands of the Guinea coast further south, the East African coast and its islands has remained aloof from the African interior. Old trading cities on the East African coast such as Mombasa, Lamu, Pate, Malindi, or Kilwa, which were located almost exclusively on peninsulas or islands off the coast, turned toward the sea rather than toward the hinterland or bush (Swa.: nyika), which was seen as a place of danger. The interior was consequently neither explored nor crossed, except by trading peoples from the African interior, the Yao, Nyamwesi, and Kamba, who established trading routes to the coast, yet remained, until the nineteenth century, foreign to the Muslim coastal culture. The upcountries of East Africa were characterized by the fact that the establishment of Islam was a fairly recent historical development, which started in most East African upcountry areas not before the mid-nineteenth century. In contrast to the bilād al-sūdān in sub-Saharan (West) Africa, which formed a broad belt of Muslim cultures, expanding gradually toward the tropical belt of the Guinea Coast, Muslim societies on the East African coast thus remained confined for about 1,000 years to a chain of settlements on the shores of the Indian Ocean and the islands off the coast. Exchange between the coast and the East African interior was complicated by the fact that the immediate hinterlands of the East African coast, in contrast to the densely settled hinterlands of the bilād al-sūdān of sub-Saharan West Africa, were only sparsely populated. On the northern coast, only the lower Juba and Shebelle, as well as the lower Tana valley, provided fertile land for cultivation and were able to feed coastal settlements like Mogadishu, Brawa, Marka, and the Lamu archipelago. Otherwise, the hinterlands of the northern coast were the vast and arid regions of the Horn, which did not offer much incentive for trade. On the central Mrima coast, only the Pare-Usambara mountain chain, the (small) Pangani, and the (larger) Rufiji valleys broke through the otherwise semi-arid hinterlands of the coast. In the northern and central stretches of the coast, travelers had to cross hundreds of kilometers of arid and semi-arid highlands and steppes before eventually reaching the fertile lands around Lake (nyanza) Victoria and the Great Lakes. Only the southern stretches of the coast were in direct contact with the more densely settled regions of the Makonde plateau, the Ruvuma valley and Lake Malawi (Nyassa). Major regions of the East African interior were settled in comparatively late times, in some cases in the eighteenth century only, and until the nineteenth century experienced raids from invading populations such as the Ngoni. Widespread occurrence of sleeping sickness also made animal-based trade impossible in large parts of the East African interior (except the dry regions of the Horn). As a result, transport of goods relied on human porterage, which was difficult to organize in regions with sparse populations characterized by the absence of major navigable rivers.

To the south of the East African coast, Muslim traders eventually reached the islands off the coast, the Comoros in particular, and northern Madagascar, but also a major river in the south, the Zambezi, which provided access to the realm of the Mwene Motapa in Zimbabwe. The establishment of the Portuguese and the disintegration of Greater Zimbabwe in the sixteenth century led to the collapse of an emerging Muslim community on the Zambezi, however, and to a withdrawal of Swahili culture from northern Mozambique. The southernmost tip of the African continent, the Cape of Good Hope, was beyond the trade winds of the Indian Ocean. It was settled, in ancient times, by Khoi-Khoi and San herdsmen and hunter-gatherers, until 1652, when the Cape became a colony of the Dutch East India Company, which also brought the first Muslims from India and Indonesia to the Cape. From the mid-seventeenth century, these Muslims started to form another distinct Muslim community in Africa.

In general, it has to be kept in mind that Africa's population was fairly small in historical times: the continent (30.3 million square kilometers) had 230 million people in 1950. This number was estimated to be only 133 million in 1900, 111 million in 1850, and 107 million in 1800 (i.e., three inhabitants per square kilometer in 1800). Control over people in African history was thus always more important than control over land.

1 Is There an "African" Islam?

The Diversity of Islam in Africa

Sometimes, old patterns of thought die hard. Even in the most recent literature on Muslim societies in Africa, such as Coulon and Cruise O'Brien (1988), Evers-Rosander and Westerlund (1997), or Quinn and Quinn (2003), it is possible to find the concept of an "African" Islam or, in French, *Islam "Noir."* This African Islam is presented as peaceful and syncretistic, accommodating, and less orthodox than "militant Arab Islam." The discussion of Muslim societies and Islam in Africa has to take into account, however, that there is no uniform and singularly "orthodox" form of Islam, either in Africa or in the Islamic world as a whole. The continent is not only much too vast to harbor just one continental expression of Islam, but African historical experiences with Islam have also been much too diverse to support the notion of a single, African Islam. When visualizing the expansion of Muslim societies in Africa in geographical terms and their multiple entanglements, the force of this argument becomes immediately clear.

Traveling counter-clockwise through Africa from the north to the south, we encounter at first Egypt (Miṣr), which has always had, due to her central position in the Islamic world, an important role as a broker for many Muslim societies. Egypt has consequently been in contact with many interpretations of Islam. The famous al-Azhar University in Cairo was established in 988 by the Fāṭimid Caliph ʿAbd al-ʿAzīz as a center of Ismāʿīlī learning, yet became a center of Sunni teaching after 1171. Since the thirteenth century, al-Azhar has been home to dozens of student convents, arwiqa (sing. riwāq), and among these were three arwiqa housing students from sub-Saharan Africa, namely Bornu, Ethiopia, and Funj. Apart from her importance for the Muslim world, Egypt has also always been a major center of Orthodox Christianity, forming, from the sixth to the sixteenth century, a belt of Orthodox churches stretching from Armenia via Lesser Armenia, Palestine, Egypt, and the Nile Sudan to Ethiopia.

This strong Christian influence was largely absent in the Islamic west, the bilād al-maghrib. Yet the bilād al-maghrib were influenced by numerous Jewish communities of considerable size that settled as far south as the oasis of Tuwāt in the central Sahara. After the demise of the great Berber empires of the Almoravids and Almohads that dominated the bilād al-maghrib and large parts of the Sahara as well as al-Andalus (Spain) from the eleventh to the thirteenth centuries, the bilād al-maghrib disintegrated into essentially two zones of political organization: the lands administered by a central government (the bilād al-makhzan) and the lands beyond government control (the bilād al-sība). These political frame conditions favored the emergence of religious brokers and thus specific forms of saint veneration and Sufism that later spread, through trans-Saharan trade, to sub-Saharan West Africa. The development of Muslim societies in the bilād al-maghrib as well as the oasis of the Sahara and sub-Saharan West Africa has to be understood as being connected through the trans-Saharan trade. Saharan as well as sub-Saharan Islamic scholarship were consequently interwoven with the important centers of Islamic learning in the bilād al-maghrib, such as the Zaytūna in Tunisia, the Qarawiyyīn in Fes, and other schools in Tilimsān (Tlemçen) and Marrākish.

The most important transmission belt for the spread of Islam south of the Sahara into sub-Saharan West Africa was, as has been mentioned above, trans-Saharan trade. It would be easy to pass over this sea of sand and to move on to the next region of Islam, yet such a move would underestimate the importance of the Sahara as a major space for the development of independent centers of Islamic learning, such as the western "Mauritanian" Ādrār, the central "Malian" Ādrār, the oasis of Tuwāt, Ghāt, Ghadāmis, the Aïr mountains and Agadez, Kufra, and numerous other Saharan centers of settlement that were of paramount importance for the maintenance of the trans-Saharan trade for more than one thousand years. Muslim states and empires both north and south of the Sahara have tried to gain control over these Saharan centers of trade and scholarship, yet more often these islands in the desert were able to maintain their autonomy, often in alliance with the populations of the Sahara that also fought for the control of the trade routes. Due to its mediating role in long-distance trade, the Sahara (as well as the East African coast) has been called a "gateway" (Robinson 2004: 32ff., Levtzion/Pouwels 2000: 1). This term suggests a one-sided direction of agency into some other place, however, and does not explicitly address the mutuality of exchanges between the northern and the southern shores of the Sahara (or the different shores of the Indian Ocean). It would be more appropriate to stress the role of the Sahara as a connective space, linking both shores, the bilād al-maghrib in the north and sub-Saharan West Africa in the south, in interfacing and mutual ways.

Probably from the eighth century, and possibly earlier, networks of trade, scholarship, and pilgrimage connected sub-Saharan West Africa, the "lands of the blacks" (arab.: bilād al-sūdān) across the Sahara with the bilād al-maghrib. As a consequence, Islam was presented to the countries of sub-Saharan West Africa primarily as a religion of traders. Muslims were highly esteemed at the courts of the Sudanese kings as representatives of the most advanced civilization of the time. The rulers of the kingdoms of the bilād al-sūdān such as Takrūr, Ghāna, Mālī, Gao-Songhay, or Kānim-Bornu converted to Islam in order to become part of this civilization and supported the development of Islamic teaching. At the courts of the Sudanic kings, Muslim scholars were appreciated as experts in administrative, legal, and financial matters, as scribes and interpreters. New centers of Islamic learning such as Jenné, Timbuktu, Gao, Kano, or Katsina developed, and in the late sixteenth century Aḥmad Bābā, a scholar from Timbuktu, could remark that Islamic learning in the bilād al-sūdān had not only reached the same quality as in the famous schools of the bilād al-maghrib but surpassed these schools, in particular in the sphere of jurisprudence (Arab. fiqh). Yet, although the new religion found quick acceptance among sub-Saharan rulers and traders, Islam did not become, until the eighteenth and nineteenth centuries, the religion of the vast majority of the population. Peasant farmers and artisan groups, in particular, remained attached to communal religions, and local cults continued to coexist with Islam at the courts of the Sudanese rulers, even if most people in the bilād al-sūdān, including non-Muslims, recognized Islam as a powerful source of blessing.

The paradigm of the peaceful spread of Islam in sub-Saharan Africa by traders was equally valid for the areas of tropical West Africa south of the Sudanic belt. Here, Muslim traders did not come from the bilād al-maghrib anymore, but from the trading centers of the bilād al-sūdān: since the fourteenth and fifteenth centuries, Hausa and Mande traders started to establish Muslim trading entrepôts in the forest regions. And although these traders gained considerable influence in the eighteenth and nineteenth centuries at the courts of the states in the tropical forest regions, such as Asante or Yoruba, Islam has remained until today a religion of a minority in contemporary Ghana, Togo, or Benin. At the same time, Muslim societies in tropical West Africa have acquired multiple experiences of interaction with Christian missions and churches of different orientations as well as an array of African religions.

Whereas Islam reached sub-Saharan West Africa by way of the trans-Saharan trade routes, the lands of the Nile came into contact with Islam through Arab tribes migrating south from Upper Egypt along the axis of the Nile. Again, Islam was to develop in a different way in these regions of sub-Saharan Africa: Nile Sudan was dominated until the thirteenth century by Nubian kingdoms, such as Dongola and 'Alwa, that, like Egypt, Ethiopia, and Armenia, formed part of a string of Christian orthodox churches. Until the fourteenth century, Greek was, in fact, the language of the church in Nubia, and last vestiges of Christianity continued to exist in Nubia until the late fifteenth century. In the twelfth and thirteenth centuries, the Nubian kingdoms started to disintegrate, however, and were replaced by Muslim Arab-Nubian principalities that fought for regional predominance until the early sixteenth century. Their constant rivalry enabled the rise of another power, the Funj-federation. Since 1505, the lands of the Nile Sudan were ruled by the Funj-empire of Sinnār, and although the rulers of Sinnār were nominal Muslims, the court of Sinnār as well as the majority of the sedentary population continued to practice pre-Islamic communal cults. The process of Islamization gained impact in the eighteenth century only and was connected with the establishment of Muslim traders and local saints who came to form new local centers of power and blessing.

Islam was again expressed in different terms in the highlands of Ethiopia. Here, Muslims had first appeared as refugees from heathen Mecca, in 615, seven years before the hijra of the Prophet Muḥammad from Mecca to Medina. Their short stay at the court of Axum, Ethiopia's ancient capital city, did not have any consequences, however,

> I rather prefer the term indigenous or communal (or even communitarian) when talking about African religions which have often been labeled as African traditional religions (ATR) or even as ethnic, tribal, or primal religions, to denote their lack of "motivation to broaden their appeal outside their own community" (ter Haar 2000: 3). It is also important to stress here that Islam, Christianity, and Judaism have, of course, become African religions in the course of time, yet neither Islam nor Christianity nor Judaism is indigenous to Africa. Established umbrella terms for African religions such as those mentioned above are quite misleading, as there are major differences among African religions, such as the religion of the San of the Kalahari and the religion of the Yoruba. "Yoruba" religion or philosophy in fact seems to be about to turn into a world religion by transcending the communal context, not only due to a growing Yoruba diaspora, particularly in the Americas, but also due to an intensifying movement of conversion from outside the Yoruba ethnic context. At the same time, Yoruba priests have started to translate Yoruba religious texts into vernacular languages, in particular Spanish and English, and are engaging in disputes over the interpretation of religious tenets of Yoruba religion. These disputes over the interpretation of Yoruba religion are set in the context of a movement of reform within Yoruba religion, which is informed by debates within the Yoruba Diaspora in the Americas (communication, Claudia Rauhut, Leipzig, 5 January 2007).

and Ethiopia remained an orthodox Christian empire. Ethiopian Muslim communities that started to form in the ninth century traced their ancestry to these early migrants, however, and Ethiopia was often seen, in Muslim historical traditions, as a "dār al-ḥiyād," a neutral land, a sanctuary even, that according to a prophetic tradition (Arab. ḥadīth) was exempt from jihād. After a long history of ups and downs between the seventh and thirteenth centuries, Ethiopia's Christian emperors were able to conquer vast territories in the central, western, and southern highlands. Ethiopia's efforts to gain control over the eastern highlands as well as to gain access to the rich markets of the south led to a series of wars with the Muslim trading principalities of the eastern highlands that had developed in these regions since the ninth century. In the early sixteenth century, Imām Aḥmad b. Ibrāhīm al-Ghāzī united these Muslim emirates and subsequently inflicted a number of defeats on the Ethiopian armies. Between 1528 and 1542, Muslim armies conquered almost all of Ethiopia and were defeated only in 1542, when Imām Aḥmad was killed in a battle with the reorganized Ethiopian army. The century-old struggle between Muslim and Christian Ethiopia continues to inform

Ethiopia's historiography until today: while Ethiopia's Christian elites portray Ethiopia as being "surrounded by a sea of Islam," Ethiopia's Muslims point out their marginal role in Ethiopia.

While Ethiopian history came to be marked by the influence of the Christian orthodox church as well as a history of rivalry between Christian and Muslim states and principalities, the arid lowlands of the Horn of Africa could be seen, like the Sahara, as a region marked by stateless societies, mostly Somaal nomads. In the port cities of Berbera, Mogadishu, Marka, and Brawa, traditions of Islamic learning developed since at least the early fourteenth century, as attested by the famous traveler Ibn Baṭṭūṭa, who visited Mogadishu in this period of time.

Whereas a sea of sand connected the northern and southern coast (Arab. sāḥil) of the Sahara, the Indian Ocean and the monsoon winds of the Indian Ocean connected the East African coast with the coasts of India and Arabia. This regional orientation toward India as well as Southern Arabia and even Persia also characterized the specific development of East Africa's Muslim societies since probably the eighth or ninth centuries. Thus, the Shāfiʿī school of law came to predominate in East Africa, whereas the Nile Sudan as well as sub-Saharan Western Africa, the Sahara, and the bilād al-maghrib joined the Mālikī school of law. In contrast to North and West Africa, Islam in East Africa also remained confined to the littoral zones. Muslim traders started to penetrate into the East African interior only in the eighteenth and nineteenth centuries. At this point in time, an old Islamic culture had come into existence on the coast, characterized by a common language (Kiswahili) and a culture of seafaring and long-distance trade. In contrast to the bilād al-sūdān, however, the trading centers of the East African coast never formed empires until they were united in the nineteenth century by the Sulṭānate of Oman. Thus the history of the East African coast has to be viewed as a history of competing trading centers that were rather oriented toward the sea than toward the bush (Swa. nyika). In fact, it is possible to differentiate between a long history of the Muslim societies on the coast and a short history of Islam in the East African interior. The East African upcountry regions are informed today by a multitude of interfaces between Islam, Christianity, and African religions.

Another historical tradition, again different from other contextualizations of Islam in sub-Saharan Africa, may be found in South Africa. In 1658, only six years after the establishment of a Dutch colony in Cape Town, first Muslims from India and the East Indies arrived in Cape Town on board of Dutch ships. These Cape Muslims started to form a community that developed, due to the rigid policies of the "Nederduitse Gereformeerde Kerk," as an underground community. Constant growth connected with the ongoing settlement of political prisoners from India as well as the East Indies, but also conversion of black slaves, allowed the Cape Muslim community to grow to considerable strength in the nineteenth century. In 1850, about 40 percent of Cape Town's population was Muslim, among them a considerable number of marginalized European immigrants. Under British rule, the Cape Muslim population gained religious freedom and the number of mosques increased. The growing size of the Cape Muslim community triggered, however, a number of communal disputes that were often connected with the question as to who would be entitled to lead a specific mosque community. As a result, the Cape Muslim community was never able to achieve the kind of political unity that would have been necessary to influence Cape Town's political development in decisive ways in the late nineteenth century.

Unity within Diversity

Muslim communities and societies in Africa thus can be viewed as characterized by variegated historical experiences, their integration into different geographic settings as well as varying modes of interaction with Christianity, Judaism, and a multitude of African religions and communal cults. These trans-religious interfaces have influenced the development of local traditions of Islam and are reflected in the way in which Muslim traditions are integrated (or not) into respective Christian, Jewish, or African religious traditions or, vice versa, the way in which Muslims have integrated non-Muslim social and religious customs into their own religious and social traditions. In some regions such as the bilād al-maghrib, Egypt, or Ethiopia, Muslims share the cult of Jewish or Christian saints (and vice versa) and have adopted, in varying ways and degrees, aspects of Christian, Jewish, or African cosmologies. Such influences are particularly clear in the development of the disciplines and sciences of astrology, astronomy, numerology, and/or divination, often subsumed under the term ʿilm al-falak, where references to Jewish traditions (Kabbalah) have been important.

However, the differences among the Muslim communities in Africa are to be explained not only by these historical, regional, geographical, or cultural forces or their respective modes of interaction with other religious traditions. Their diversity is also connected with the fact that the acceptance of "Islam" as a religion is and has always been a selective process. In this process of selective and situational adoption and enculturation of Islam, specific elements of the faith have been taken over completely in some regions but were stressed less in others. Thus, the Imasighen tribes of the western Sahara accepted the norms of Islamic law as a program of reform under the influence of the Almoravid movement in the eleventh century, whereas they have found less or only marginal acceptance in other parts of Africa. Local (pre-)Islamic customs have also been incorporated, in the context of processes of conversion, into local practices of Islam as customary law and practice (Arab. ʿurf or ʿādat) in particular, when these customs did not contradict the prescriptions of the sharīʿa. Numerous local practices thus came to form part of Islamic ʿurf. This explains the formation of multiple ways of living "Islam" in Africa and Asia, which came to be challenged, from time to time, by Muslim reformers who questioned the normativity of local customs, attacking them as "un-Islamic innovations" (Arab. bidaʿ, sg. bidʿa). As often, local scholars have risen to defend local practices. Cyclical debates about the Islamic or un-Islamic

> The Wahhābiyya was a movement of reform in Arabia established by Muḥammad b. ʿAbd al-Wahhāb (d. 1792). Wahhābis stress the central doctrine of the unicity of God (tawḥīd) and consequently call themselves al-muwaḥḥidūn (unitarians). Wahhābis are Sunni Muslims and follow the Ḥanbalī school of law. They reject all forms of saint veneration and other un-Islamic innovations (bidaʿ), such as the visiting of tombs or veneration of the Prophet, and propagate a literalistic reading of the Qurʾān. In an alliance with the Āl Saʿūd family of central Najd (Darʿiyya) in Arabia, Muḥammad b. ʿAbd al-Wahhāb defeated all opponents to the movement in central Arabia by 1773, when the Wahhābī movement conquered Riyādh. In the following years, the movement took control of the al-Ḥasā region on the Gulf, finally conquering Medina (1804/1805) and Mecca (1806), and taking control of the Islamic pilgrimage and the holy cities of Islam. In 1811 the Ottoman sulṭān authorized the ruler of Egypt, Muḥammad ʿAlī, to invade Arabia and to recover Mecca and Medina. By 1818 Egyptian troops had conquered most of the Arabian Peninsula, including Darʿiyya, and terminated the first empire of the Wahhābiyya.

character of local ʿurf practices are thus part of an ongoing history of disputes which has characterized the development of Muslim societies since the time of the Prophet.

Yet, even when the norms of the sharīʿa (the principles of Islamic law) were adopted by Muslims as legal foundations of their societies, unusual interpretations of the sharīʿa could occur. After a successful jihād against the "pagan" Bambara state of Segu in sub-Saharan West Africa that led to the establishment of the imāmate of Masina in 1818, the sharīʿa became the exclusive legal foundation of this Muslim empire. Masina society was characterized, however, by a comparatively strong position of Halpulaaren women. As a consequence, the Muslim scholars of Masina did not dare to fully implement the legal norms of the sharīʿa, particularly with respect to the so-called ḥadd (pl. ḥudūd) regulations, punishments commanded by the Qurʾān. When a woman was found guilty of a crime punishable according to ḥudūd regulations, it was not the woman who was punished, but, according to the rules of legal procedure as practiced in Masina, an item in her possession. According to Amadou Hampaté Bā, the prescribed flogging was enforced "on the roof of her house or on an object belonging to her that was dear to her heart. This public replacement-punishment was as humiliating for the culprit as if the punishment would have been enforced on her in person" (Bā 1955: 49, my translation).

The process of Islamization has to be characterized thus, on the one side, as a process of gradual and selective adoption and in-culturation of the greater framework of Islam by communities of Muslims. This process was accompanied by processes of contestation and reconfiguration of an established consensus and consequently never came to an end. A major element of the discourse of Wahhābī scholars in Arabia in the eighteenth century, for instance, was that the Bedouins of the Arabian peninsula had allegedly fallen back, as far as their faith was concerned, into the times of pre-Islamic "jāhiliyya" (ignorance, heathendom), an argument taken up by Sayyid Quṭb, the twentieth-century Egyptian thinker of radical Islam in his analysis of contemporary Muslim society. Both Wahhābīs and Quṭb accordingly advocated a movement of "iṣlāḥ" (purification of the faith). On the other side, the process of Islamization has to be understood as one of localization, in which elements of the faith and religious practice were incorporated into a multitude of local contexts and thus came to form local traditions of Islam. It is not possible, therefore, to talk about an Africanization (or Asianization) of Islam, as Africa (likewise Asia) cannot be seen as homogenous geographical, cultural, or historical entities which would be informed by one single, essential "Africanité." Rather, Africa should be seen, as mentioned above, as a huge continent that forms a geographical and cultural continuum with Mediterranean Europe as well as Western Asia and the Indian Ocean. Islam could thus acquire, perhaps, a distinct Moroccan, Senegalese, or Somaal notion, but not an African (or Asian) character. Items and practices that are presented as typically African, such as amulets (Arab. ḥijāb), practices of numerology, or "ecstatic Sufi rituals" (Robinson 2004: 27–58) can in fact be found in virtually every part of the Islamic world in one form or the other. The best market for amulets from both Northern Nigeria and Senegal is Saudi Arabia, and the annual pilgrimage has become an important market for the trade in these items. Equally, spiritual healers (Swa. waganga) from the East African coast have become highly sought practitioners of "kusoma Kurani" (healing by Qur'ānic recitation) ceremonies in Saudi Arabia, although their very residence in Saudi Arabia is regarded as being illegal.

Islam as a Discursive Tradition

Despite their differences in regional, historical, and cultural terms, Muslim communities and societies in Africa (as well as in Asia) are still viewed as "Islamic," and Islam indeed constitutes a frame of reference common to all Muslims. In order to explain this paradoxical notion of unity within diversity we should visualize Islam as a great pool or corpus of texts, of prescriptions concerning the faith and/or everyday life, of shared rituals and festivals, of norms and values, as well as teaching traditions that were based on a number of key texts such as the Qur'ān, the compilations of the sunna of the Prophet, as well as a large number of legal and theological texts. In addition, all Muslim societies share one single concept of "Prophetic" time that unites Muslims across continents as well as through times. This canon has always been interpreted and reinterpreted, however. Due to its immensity it has been adopted only partially and selectively, and even religious scholars were usually familiar with only parts of the corpus of Islamic teachings. They specialized on specific aspects such as jurisprudence (fiqh) and granted "ijāzāt" (authorizations) of teaching to their students for a specific text only. Beyond the scholars' circles, knowledge about specific theological positions or aspects of the law, of Islamic history or philosophy, was even smaller. In addition, not all aspects or components of the canon were stressed equally in Muslim societies at all times: in one scholarly tradition, Sufism (Arab. taṣawwuf) could be particularly stressed, while another tradition would focus on fiqh. This could change, of course, in the course of time. In Zanzibar, the syllabus of Islamic education has moved from a stress on jurisprudence in the late nineteenth century to a stress on ʿaqīda-literature (catechisms) and ḥadīth in the late twentieth century. At the same time, the corpus of texts taught in madāris in Zanzibar has decreased from about 235 texts in the different disciplines of Islamic learning until the 1950s to about 85 texts since the 1970s and 1980s. Also, many texts, including the Qur'ān, have been translated into Kiswahili and are taught in Kiswahili.

The partial, situational, and selective realization of the canon of Islam does not imply, however, that Islam was perceived and discussed, in a specific society and a

Islam has often been characterized as an orthopraxy due to its insistence on correct ritual. This idea fails to appreciate the fact that each orthopraxy is based on an orthodoxy. Orthodoxies are not given, but formed by processes of negotiation that have led to a temporary consensus on matters of religion in a specific community. In Islam, as in Christianity and Judaism, such processes of negotiation refer to key texts. In the case of Islam, these key texts are the Qur'ān and the collections of traditions (ḥadīth) of what the Prophet Muḥammad has done and said, as well as a series of exegetical texts in religious disciplines such as tafsīr (exegesis of the Qur'ān) or tawḥīd (dogmatic theology). This canon of texts is consulted and interpreted in matters of ritual, as, for instance, in disputes over the rules for prayer (ṣalāt): each physical component of the act of prayer is defined, in fact, by a set of rules that have to be followed in order to make a prayer considered valid. Deviation from the accepted norm can be interpreted, if need arises, as a conscious break with the established tradition, both in terms of the orthopraxy of a specific community and its consensus regarding the interpretation of the canon of core texts. Changes in ritual practice can signal opposition to established authorities and can consequently be branded as unbelief (kufr). Due to the tremendous importance of the proper ritual, ritual procedure has often been at the center of disputes in Muslim communities that often touch on questions of authority.

specific period of time, in small, disconnected, or even distorted bits and pieces. Each Muslim society should rather be seen, as Talal Asad has pointed out, as a distinctive and coherent set of "discursive traditions," even if these traditions were not the same in all Muslim societies. All of them, however, referred to a corpus of "Islamic general knowledge," a pool of widely accepted and known core "sites" such as Mecca, Medina, or al-Quds/Jerusalem; core icons and symbols such as the hand of Fāṭima; core festivals such as the ʿīd al-fiṭr at the end of the month of fasting, Ramaḍān, or the ʿīd al-aḍḥā (also ʿīd al-ḥajj, ʿīd al-kabīr) on tenth Dhū l-ḥijja, the month of the pilgrimage; but also the calligraphic representation of the name of the Prophet Muḥammad, of the "shahāda" or of the "takbīr" on walls, flags, or calendars; the iconic representation of saints like Aḥmad Bamba or ʿAbd al-Qādir al-Jīlānī; as well as amulets and visualizations of the holy mosque of Mecca on carpets and prayer mats; and last but not least, core events and discourses that were and are familiar to most Muslims until today and that form, as such, a frame of reference that we may call, with Robert Redfield, a "greater tradition." Due to the fact that Muslims are still able to refer to and to quote from this canon, brokers such as religious scholars, writers, or politicians are able to conduct meaningful discourses on questions of everyday life or politics and to sanctify these discourses by establishing references to religion. The basic corpus of symbols, icons, and discourses may consequently be activated in political conflicts, when Muslim politicians or religious scholars point out, for instance, the trans-temporal importance of historical events related to the time of the Prophet Muḥammad, such as the battles of Badr (a small group of Muslims wins a surprising but decisive victory in a war against infidels) or Uḥud (Muslims suffer a serious defeat against an enemy as a form of punishment for previous disobedience but recover from the defeat). Trans-temporal references to the canon of basic texts, "lieux de mémoire" (places of memory), symbols or icons of Muslim history, may thus be cultivated for the legitimization of claims of religious superiority of one tradition over another or for the legitimization of a jihād against both non-Muslims and Muslims.

The greater tradition of Islam thus does not exist as an autonomous and never-ever changing social or religious entity. Rather, local actors, often religious scholars, who are familiar with the discursive traditions of Islam as well as locally established concepts of the ritual and Islamic teaching, seize the initiative and refer to the greater tradition of Islam in order to call for changes in the local context. In the course of these scholarly discourses, established local practices are criticized or even condemned as un-Islamic innovations, bidaʿ, with reference to the reformers' own and peculiar interpretation of the greater tradition of Islam. Interaction between the greater tradition of Islam and local communities is thus realized only when "hard" references are established by, for instance, local scholars: otherwise, the greater tradition of Islam would remain a residual category, activated, quoted, and interpreted only selectively and with respect to a specific context at a specific point of time. The Qurʾān and other texts and

> The debate on the anthropology of Islam has been informed to a large extent by Robert Redfield's work (1956) and the reactions to his argumentation (see Resources for Further Study). In contrast to Redfield, I think that a great(er) tradition (of Islam) is not confined to elites of the "reflective (urban) few" but is shared by the "un-reflective (rural) many" as mediated by a multitude of brokers. In addition, I would argue that communal/local or little traditions are scriptural in the sense of accepting the authority of texts, even if approaches to texts may differ: while Sufis stress the esoteric dimension of texts, Wahhābī-oriented scholars tend to reject the esoteric dimension of texts and stress, in contrast, a different episteme characterized by a literalist interpretation of the texts (see Brenner 2001). I do share, however, Redfield's idea of processes of universalization and parochialization that link greater traditions with little (local, communal) traditions in multiple forms of negotiation.

parts of the canon are not self-explanatory, therefore, or "inherently central" (Eickelman and Piscatori 1990: 14) for any Muslim society or time, even if they are indispensable points of reference in theological disputes. If not activated or quoted, and translated into ever changing contexts, they would remain dormant. Specific aspects of the greater tradition, in particular, those that are less quotidian than, for instance, daily prayers, acquire meaning and relevance for a specific society only through a process of negotiation as mediated by a multitude of brokers, scholars, students, traders, and pilgrims, or, today, the virtual travelers of the Worldwide Web. In this process of negotiation, specific aspects and interpretations of the canon have to be linked with the respective realities of a Muslim society to acquire social, political, and religious relevance. As contexts and frame conditions change, however, the interpretation of the texts changes as well, and texts and their interpretation have to be situated anew: The "contested nature of interpretation is a constitutive part of any Islamic tradition" (Asad 1986: 14). The basic interpretability of traditions and texts, and thus the "disponabilité" of the canon of Islam also disproves essentialist reductions of one static Islam and timeless Muslim societies. This logic extends to radical and activist (Islamist) Muslims who have tried to essentialize traditions and texts and have advocated a selective reading and interpretation of these traditions and texts in order to instrumentalize such readings for their own purposes. Yet instrumentalizations of traditions and texts are again embedded in specific political contexts. As soon as contexts change, essentializations have to be revised and adapted to new situations: even essentialistic readings of Islam do not escape the dynamics of negotiation and change.

Agents and Institutions of Brokerage

The question now arises as to how different local contextualizations of Islam are actually connected with the greater tradition of Islam beyond the obvious reference to the generally accepted canon and corpus of texts. Despite their differences, Muslim thinkers and societies are not only interwoven across time and space due to their ongoing dialogue with the texts of the canon, even though these texts are interpreted and enacted in different and often conflicting ways. They are also linked by a number of trans-local institutions and groups that act as brokers between the different local traditions in Africa (as well as in the other parts of the Islamic ecumene) and thus connect Muslim societies over space and time. The most prominent of these institutions or groups, namely scholars and schools, traders and trade, as well as pilgrims and the pilgrimage, are presented below. Yet this list is not exhaustive: regional shrine pilgrimages (Arab. ziyāra), festivals, the ritual itself, as well as the networks of the Sufi-orders and their institutions such as the zāwiya, also create community and interconnect Muslim communities.

Scholars and their institutions: In all Islamic societies in Africa (as well as in Asia), numerous local traditions of learning have developed in the course of time that have produced highly developed cultures of scholarship, schools (Arab. madāris), and mosque-colleges: Cairo, Qayrawān, Fes, Tilimsān, Marrākish, Shinqīṭ, Timbuktu, Jenné, Kano, Mombasa, Lamu, or Mogadishu, to name just a few. These traditions of learning were not isolated in their respective regions but connected through traveling scholars and their students. Through the practice of ṭalab al-ʿilm, the "journey in search of knowledge," not only the Qurʾān but all kinds of scholarly writings were spread in the Islamic oikumene. Thus, we find a major theological treatise written by the Maghribinian scholar Abū ʿAbdallāh Muḥammad b. Yūsuf al-Sanūsī (d. 1486), *ʿaqīdat ahl al-tawḥīd al-ṣughra* (also called *al-sanūsiyya* or *umm al-barāhin*, "mother of proofs"), not only in the bilād al-maghrib or the bilād al-sūdān, but also on the East African coast, in Indonesia, and in Kasan in central Russia, where this treatise still constitutes an essential feature of Islamic education.

Trade and traders: Apart from scholarly traditions and journeys as well as Islamic schools, trade and the institutions of trade such as the caravanserai-khans (Arab. funduq) were a major feature of Muslim societies that connected the different regions of the Islamic world. Centers of trade in the bilād al-sūdān have been trading with the bilād al-maghrib as well as Egypt and the regions beyond for a long period of time. It would even be possible to characterize the history of the north Saharan as well as the sub-Saharan states between the ninth and the nineteenth century as a history of their efforts to gain control over as large as possible a section of the trans-Saharan trade. At the same time, the East African coast has been connected across the Indian Ocean with the trading centers of India, Arabia, and the countries of the Gulf and the important trading regions beyond. As a consequence, archaeologists have found fifteenth-century Chinese porcelain at the court of the Mwene Motapa in Zimbabwe and gold of West African origin in northern Scandinavia.

The pilgrimage (ḥajj): The ḥajj constituted another important element of connection between the different regions of the Islamic world. In Mecca, pilgrims from Java met pilgrims from Egypt, Senegal, or central Asia and were able, by means of the common language of scholarship, Arabic, to discuss the news of the world or to dispute theological treatises. Information spread in fact quite fast among pilgrims, scholars, and traders and Muslim rulers were, as a consequence, often better informed about specific events in the world than European travelers who were cut off from all sources of information after weeks and months in the African interior. The British traveler Clapperton thus recorded, in 1824, "that he was regarded as a spy in Sokoto and that it was the common talk of the town that Europeans intended to take Hausaland as they had taken India" (Adeleye 1977: 120). Apart from the ḥajj to the holy places of Islam, a journey that was often linked with the visit of other "lieux de mémoire" (and trade) such as Cairo or Baghdad, shrine visits to local sacred places such as the graves of saints should also be mentioned here. Shrine visits not only tended to be more feasible for a majority of Muslim populations in historical times, but they were also important for the regional (religious, spiritual, economic, social) integration of Muslim societies. The experience of the ḥajj (and, to a lesser degree, of shrine visits) was not always an easy one, however. Often, the ḥajj was a long and dangerous journey that led pilgrims not only to Mecca but to other important places of Islamic learning such as Medina, Jerusalem, Cairo, or Damascus. These travel experiences were often recorded in travel accounts and books, a kind of literature that formed one of the oldest features of both non-religious and pious literature in Muslim societies. The experience of the ḥajj also became, from time to time, an issue in local disputes, as pilgrims returning from the holy cities of Islam started to criticize local customs that in their eyes were not in accordance with the norms of Islam as experienced in Mecca.

Questions of Authority

The trans-local experiences of scholars and students, travelers, traders, and pilgrims stimulated processes of reform, dissidence, protest, and dispute. Often, these conflicts were of a rather quotidian nature but sometimes they could acquire major social significance, as in the "qabḍ-sadl" disputes in the bilād as-sūdān in the early twentieth century over the question of the proper position of the arms during ritual prayers, either "sadl" (arms outstretched), as recommended by the Mālikī school of law, or "qabḍ" (arms folded over the chest), as accepted by the three other Sunni schools of law. The qabḍ-sadl disputes of the 1930s through the 1970s in sub-Saharan West Africa were informed by conflicts between a reformist movement of the Tijāniyya Sufi order as led by Ibrāhīm Niass, who insisted on qabḍ, and other branches of the Tijāniyya, as well as the Qādiriyya, who insisted on sadl. While this dispute could still be interpreted as a conflict set within the Mālikī school of law, new Muslim movements of reform affiliated with both the Saudi-oriented Wahhābiyya and the Indo-Pakistani-Tablīghi Jamā'at have recently added new aspects to this dispute. In contrast to the 'Tijānī'-qabḍ of the 1930s through the 1970s, which was identical with the qabḍ of the Shāfi'ī, Ḥanafī, and Ḥanbalī schools of law, the qabḍ of both Wahhābis and Tablīghis was characterized by the fact that hands were folded much higher on the chest. These dynamics of religious conflict point to the symbolic importance of seemingly quotidian features of the ritual, namely, to provide movements of reform with a marker of religious and/or social identity.

Reformers indeed often tried to discredit existing local traditions by attacking them as being un-Islamic innovations (Arab. bida' makrūha) that had nothing to do with their own interpretation of Islam, perceived to be much more authentic than a local interpretation of Islam. The local scholarly establishment rejected this kind of argument by accusing the reformers of trying to introduce bida' themselves and to represent a less authentic interpretation of the faith. Established scholars could also rely in their counter-argument on their own interpretation of the canon. The ultimate success or failure of a movement of reform was consequently much less connected with a convincing theological argumentation, although such an argumentation was still important for the development of the theological legitimization of respective religious and/or political positions, but with the capability of the rebels (or the representatives of the establishment) to respond to existing social, economic, or political grievances and to win, for their program of reform, acceptance as leaders of the marginalized, the poor, and the oppressed.

Thus, a whole series of religiously legitimated rebellions, often directed against slave trading, arbitrary rule, and widespread exploitation of traders as well as farming populations, have occurred in the bilād al-sūdān in the course of the eighteenth and nineteenth centuries. The Islamic revolutions brought about the foundation of new states, led by scholarly elites that sought to legitimize their newly acquired power within the framework of Islam. Islam thus became, in the eighteenth and nineteenth centuries, the only source of legitimate rule in the bilād al-sūdān. This instrumentalization of Islam for the legitimization of political power by the victorious scholarly elite, as, for instance, in the imāmate of Masina, in the Sokoto caliphate, in the empire of al-Ḥājj 'Umar Taal al-Fūtī (all in sub-Saharan West Africa), in the empire of the Mahdī in the Sudan, or in the realm of Sayyid Muḥammad 'Abdille Ḥasan in Somalia, however, also led to a new dialectic of rule and oppression that triggered resistance, rebellion, and a renewed struggle for power and domination. At the same time, the religiously legitimized rebellions of the eighteenth and nineteenth centuries were not subject to an automatism of jihād, as shown by the history of the jihād in Hausaland. In the ancient Muslim kingdom of Gobir, considerable unrest and protest had formed against high taxation, the slave raids of the aristocracy, and acts of arbitrariness against both peasant farmers and herdsmen. In the late eighteenth century, a Muslim scholar, Usman dan Fodio (1754–1817), started to criticize these policies and to condemn the practices of the government of local rulers as "un-Islamic." In 1787, the escalation of the conflict between rulers and the Islamic opposition came to a halt, however, when the Sarkin Gobir (Hau. ruler, king of Gobir) accepted a number of demands of the religious opposition. Usman dan Fodio even rose to become a councilor at the court of Gobir. Sarkin Gobir's successor, Yakuba (1790–94), continued this policy of de-escalation. Only when Sarkin Gobir Nafata came to power in 1794/95, rejected this policy, and issued a number of "anti-Islamic" decrees did dialectics of escalation start, which led from the "takfīr" (expiation) of the "un-Islamic" ruler to the theological legitimation of jihād to jihād. In a war of four years, almost all Hausa kingdoms were conquered and the Sokoto caliphate, the largest Muslim empire in nineteenth-century Sudanic West Africa, was established.

The Islamic revolutions of the eighteenth and nineteenth centuries were also linked, however, with processes of social, religious, and political change, and these processes of change continued in the twentieth century. From the 1890s to the 1960s, Islam became an ideology of resistance against mostly French and British, sometimes German and Italian, colonial rule. As David Robinson (2000) has shown, Muslim scholars at the same time developed paths of accommodation, modes of cooperation with the colonial powers that could strengthen the social and political role of Islam. However, the Muslim populations of sub-Saharan Africa also experienced a serious social crisis as the processes of colonial modernization had a strong secularizing character and were represented by non-Muslims, often Christian elites that stressed their orientation toward Europe. In many sub-Saharan African colonies and, later, independent states, formerly dominant Muslim populations and elites, as in Northern Nigeria, lost their privileged social and political position or were reduced, as in Kenya or Tanzania, to marginalized minorities in new nation-states dominated by mission-educated Christians: In the course of these developments, new forms and dynamics of interaction between Muslims and Christians have emerged, in particular, when looking at the interfaces between contemporary Muslim "missionary" movements such as the "Muslim Bible Preachers" of Tanzania and Pentecostal churches and their respective ways of approaching audiences.

In the context of these processes of modernization, a new series of Islamic reform movements developed in many parts of sub-Saharan Africa since the 1930s. In their endeavors of reform, Muslim reformers established reference to the sources of inspiration of the time, in particular the texts and teachings of the Salafiyya movement of reform, as represented by Muḥammad ʿAbdūh and Rashīd Riḍā, the movement of the Ikhwān al-Muslimīn, the Wahhābiyya of Arabia, or, more recently, the writings of Abū Āʿlā Maudūdī and Sayyid Quṭb. In the context of these renewed efforts of reform, the greater tradition of Islam was activated again and reinterpreted in order to discredit established paradigms of explanation as well as existing claims to irshād (correct guidance) with respect to the question, for instance, as to who would provide the most acceptable interpretation of the canon, who would be entitled to speak for Muslims. In their efforts of reform, recent movements of Islamic renewal were particularly successful among disgruntled urban youth as well as women. In fact, many Islamic reform movements in sub-Saharan Africa (but not only there) can be seen as an effort of the young and the women to fight against existing social and cultural limitations and to achieve some sort of religiously legitimated emancipation. These movements of reform stimulated the reemergence of other, often conservative and status-quo oriented social and political movements that rejected the reformist and sometimes modernist interpretations of Islam. Many leading representatives of recent Islamic reform movements have not acquired qualifications as religious scholars (Arab. ʿulamāʾ), however, but were trained as doctors or computer experts and consequently regarded themselves as Muslim thinkers (Arab. mufakkirūn muslimūn) or professors (Arab. asātidha, sg. ustādh). The argumentation of these reformers has acquired a decisively political connotation that has been criticized by their opponents as a distortion of the spiritual message of Islam. At the same time, established religious scholars felt threatened by their claims to hegemonic interpretation of the faith.

When looking at the history of Muslim societies in Africa (and beyond) and the impact of Muslim movements of reform that have attacked local interpretations of Islam over centuries as seemingly un-Islamic bidaʿ, the question arises again as to why we still encounter differences among Muslims, in particular when considering the importance of the unifying forces of Islam—such as pilgrimage, the canon of texts such as the Qurʾān, or contemporary means of communication, especially the internet—that seem to enhance processes of unification. The differences between Muslim societies in Africa (and beyond) may be explained by diverging geographical settings, different historical experiences, and modes of interaction with other religious cultures and traditions. At the same time, the greater tradition of Islam has been accepted and interpreted selectively in different societies, contexts, and times. Local contexts have remained important defining frameworks and spaces of reference for the realization of the greater tradition of Islam. Equally, established and seemingly obsolete social and religious practices may show astonishing persistence, despite the onslaught of generations of reformers. Muslims have shown remarkable resilience, for instance, with respect to the reformist critique of the celebration of the mawlid, the birthday of the Prophet, which has remained a popular festival despite centuries of scholarly critique.

The multiple character of Muslim societies and the persistence of local traditions of learning may thus be explained, at least to some extent, by the very vitality of local traditions of learning. The interaction between the local context and the greater tradition of Islam must not necessarily lead to greater uniformity in expression and interpretation, precisely due to the fact that the reference to the canon usually comes from the local context and is linked with its particularities. The interaction between the local and the canon can even stimulate the further accentuation of the local and lead to a further expansion of the interpretative framework of the canon. After all, even the most trans-local religious scholar is still rooted in a local context and the success of each movement of reform is equally linked with its capability to translate a program of reform into multiple local settings and their respective realities. Despite the undisputed importance of the "unifying forces" of Islam, differences in interpretation thus persist. As a consequence, we are not confronted with a single (African) Islam nor an archipelago of seemingly autonomous Muslim communities and societies but with both: the unifying framework of Islam as well as the diversifying and seemingly fragmentizing forces of change as experienced by Muslim communities and societies in their quest to negotiate and to define ever again their "Islamicité," their "Islamic identity," their ways of "being" Muslim. This dialectic has continued into times of globalization. Contemporary movements of reform have not generated more unity in Muslim societies but rather stimulated differentiation and accentuation of multiple expressions and interpretations of Islam. This process was enhanced by the fact that no church has blocked or channeled theological discussions and disputes and that many traditions of learning and traditions of reform continue to compete over questions of authority and interpretation. The spectrum of interpretation of Islam in Africa as well as in the Muslim world as such has thus grown considerably in the twentieth century and provides departments of religion, history, anthropology, and Islamics with an ever-growing array of research themes.

Theories of Conversion and the Evolution of Muslim Societies

A final core issue still has to be addressed here, namely, the question as to how and why African populations converted to Islam. This question has produced a large body of literature in the past and continues to do so until today. Europeans, often missionaries, particularly wanted to explain why major parts of Africa which had come under European control by the early twentieth century had turned Muslim only recently or were about to convert to Islam under European control, while other regions had been Muslim for hundreds of years. Missionaries and colonial officers tried to rationalize Islam in an evolutionary concept of social development and claimed that Islam was closer to supposedly simple African religious traditions than "sophisticated" Christianity. By accepting polygamous marriage and pre-Islamic ritual—in particular, spirit possession cults—conversion to Islam was allegedly easier than conversion to Christianity, which condemned these practices. In this worldview, Islam was often seen as a necessary evolutionary step from heathendom to Christianity. Based on Arabic accounts as well as the experiences of missionaries and colonial officers, colonial historians started to formulate theories on African conversion to Islam. The first influential paradigm was developed by a British missionary and historian, John Spencer Trimingham, since the late 1940s. His assumption was that Islam developed in sub-Saharan Africa in three major stages: in a first stage, Islam was introduced as a religion of North African traders and became prominent in trading centers as well as at courts: Muslim traders from North Africa were regarded as carriers of "cultural prestige," representing the "civilized world of the Mediterranean," and had, as scholars, superior knowledge of many things such as medicine, astronomy, or writing. Still, Islam was adopted slowly and selectively only and remained confined to trading centers and courts, coexisting with pagan cults. Trimingham then identified a second stage in the development of Islam in sub-Saharan Africa, an "interregnum of eclipse in the fortunes of Islam": after the collapse of the large trading empires in the fifteenth and sixteenth centuries, Islam lost its institutional backing, non-Islamic states replaced the Islamic empires, local cults reemerged, and Muslim minorities compromised and mixed originally pure and orthodox Islam with African religions. This was a period of stagnation. A third stage was characterized by the recrudescence of Islam and movements of jihād as a reaction against accommodationist rulers and the mixing of orthodox Islam with African indigenous religions and communal cults.

Although Trimingham's model of development in stages sounded quite convincing at the time, it suffered from three major problems: First, the assumption that North African traders represented pure and orthodox Islam is misleading when looking at the rather variegated development of Muslim societies in the bilād al-maghrib since the eighth century. Second, the focus on the courts, important as it may have been, ignores the fact that Islam was also represented by traders, including an increasing number of local traders, outside the courts and that local traditions of Islamic learning developed beyond the control of courts. Third, the collapse of Islam and the "mixing" of Islam with African communal cults fails to explain the emergence of Muslim reformist movements in the bilād al-sūdān in the eighteenth and nineteenth centuries: where did these scholars come from? Movements of reform did in fact originate in interaction between a multitude of small rural centers of Islamic learning as well as the urban centers and the courts. Islam had survived the collapse of the imperial courts.

In the early 1970s, a British anthropologist, Robin Horton, proposed a new approach to conversion which was structured differently and took a theological stance. Horton in particular pointed out the existence, in African indigenous religions and communal cults, of a two-tier concept of religion: "In the first tier we find the lesser spirits which are in the main concerned with the affairs of the local community and its environment. . . . In the second we find a supreme being concerned with the world as a whole" (Horton 1971: 101). Lesser spirits dominated local cults to a large extent: they were linked with mountains, wells, sacred groves, trees, and springs, and they granted order, stability, well-being, rain, and good harvests in a specific environment and area. The ancestors formed the link between these spirits and the living, in particular the priests of the different cults which required ritual and sacrifice. In times of crisis (such as natural disasters, war, and colonization) local microcosms could face destabilization and collapse. People would search for new answers in a new macrocosm, and Islam (or Christianity) would get a chance. Also, when trans-local (trans-Saharan) trade developed and traders started to move out of purely local contexts, local cults and their "lesser spirits" not only lost their function but also their meaning.

Soon after the death of the Prophet Muḥammad in 632, Muslims started to quarrel over a number of religious and political issues such as the question of the succession to the Prophet, the Caliphate (Arab. khilāfa). In these disputes three major religious orientations emerged: the Shī'at 'Alī, those who stressed the claim of the Prophet's nephew and son-in-law 'Alī to the caliphate on account of his closeness (qarāba) to the Prophet; those who opposed the idea that the caliphate should become a family dynasty and supported, in 632, 634, and 644, the succession of Abūbakar (d. 634), 'Umar (d. 644), and 'Uthmān (d. 656) on grounds of their merits and priority (sābiqa) as companions (ṣaḥāba) of the Prophet; and finally, those "people of uprightness" (ahl al-istiqāma) who supported 'Alī's claims to the caliphate in 656, yet abandoned his camp in 657 when he started to negotiate the caliphate with his major Umayyad opponent Mu'wiya. The ahl al-istiqāma (or dissenters, Khārijites) split into three competing fractions, the Ibāḍites, Ṣufrites, and Azraqites, of which only one group, the Ibāḍites, survive to this day in Oman and small communities in Libya, Tunisia, and Algeria. The Shī'at 'Alī, in contrast, started to turn into a major religious orientation in 680 when Umayyad troops massacred 'Alī's son al-Ḥusayn and his entourage near Karbalā' in 'Irāq in order to stop Shī'ite claims to the caliphate. Although the Shī'at 'Alī had lost its leader (imām), Shī'ites continued to challenge the Umayyad (and later, the 'Abbāsid) caliphate. A majority of Muslims rejected Shī'ite claims to the caliphate, however, and stressed the paramount role of the tradition (sunna) of the Prophet as a model for the social, religious, and political life of the community (jamā'a) of Muslims. In the decades to come each group developed its own tradition of legal reasoning. Among the ahl al-sunna wa-l-jamā'a, four Sunni legal traditions have survived until today, the Mālikī, Ḥanafī, Shāfi'ī, and Ḥanbalī schools of law.

As a consequence, traders looked for a more powerful "general" spirit and found this supreme deity in Allāh. On the local level, Islam and communal cults could continue to coexist, however, for a long period of time.

A British historian, Humphrey Fisher, responded to Horton's crisis theory and Trimingham's stages model and proposed, in the 1970s and early 1980s, a third approach to conversion which reactivated Trimingham's three-stage model: in a first, quarantine stage, Islam was introduced by outsiders in an orthodox mode, Muslims did not mingle, Islam was not mixed, and Muslims remained a minority. Mixing occurred in a second stage, when original Muslim enclaves dissolved: "As local people converted in increasing numbers, a stage of mixing followed, in which people combined the profession of Islam . . . with many pagan survivals. Finally, often after a lapse of centuries, the candle of reform, kept alight by the written word, and perhaps also by the devotion of some clerics who succeeded in maintaining an element of quarantine against the mixing all around them, burst into a conflagration and established the rule of the saint" (Fisher 1973: 31). Fisher's model obviously had similar problems as Trimingham's. Besides the fact that stage models suffer from the fact that they are too ahistorical and rely on the assumption of rather rigid dialectics of evolution, Fisher's model ignored the emergence of a multitude of local centers of Islamic learning, where the "written word" was actually studied and applied to local contexts. In addition, centers of Islamic learning never existed in total isolation or quarantine, but were in constant exchange amongst each other as well as with the centers of Islamic learning in the Sahara, in Egypt, and in the bilād al-maghrib. The assumption that Islam came to sub-Saharan West Africa in an orthodox form again belies realities of historical development in the bilād al-maghrib, where we find a long history of sectarian development. Before the establishment of the Mālikī school of law in major parts of the bilād al-maghrib in the eleventh and twelfth centuries, both Shīʿī and two different Khārijī orientations, the Ibāḍiyya and the Ṣufriyya, had been quite vibrant, and the establishment of something like orthodox Islam among the Imasighen populations in the Sahara took probably still longer. The "orthodox Islam from outside" perspective reflected, in fact, a colonial perspective on Muslim societies, when Arab Islam was presented as orthodox, pure, clean, undiluted, militant, and dogmatic as well as anti-European, whereas African Islam was presented as unorthodox, mixed, tolerant, and pro-European.

These models of conversion have been modified since by other historians of African history, such as John Hunwick, Robert Launay, Nehemia Levtzion, and David Robinson, who developed, since the 1970s, more sophisticated approaches to conversion to Islam in sub-Saharan Africa. Levtzion (1979) thus distinguished between "communal" and "individual" conversion. In the history of Islam, whole communities such as the Bedouin tribal groups of the Arabian peninsula or the Imasighen populations of the bilād al-maghrib converted to Islam as a group while maintaining their cultural identity as bedouin Arabs or as Imasighen: "There was hardly a break with past traditions and pre-Islamic customs and beliefs survived. In this process more and more people came under the influence of Islam, but they took longer to cover the distance from their former religion to Islam, viewed as a continuum from nominal acceptance of Islam to greater conformity and commitment" (Levtzion 1979: 19). Communal conversion, often linked with defeat and/or (voluntary) submission as sealed by an "oath" (Arab. bayʿa) of allegiance and loyalty, only started a long process of Islamization. In many regions, such as the bilād al-maghrib and the bilād al-sūdān, "initial demands on Muslims were minimal. Only after Islam had gained a foothold in a society did the exclusive nature of the Prophetic religion gradually become more manifest" (Levtzion

1979: 21). The gradual move of a community toward greater conformity and orthodoxy was marked by crises and subsequent movements of reform against allegedly lenient Muslims. Still, pre-Islamic heritage survived and was incorporated into local Islamic traditions as ʿurf. In some regions such as Egypt and Syria, conversion to Islam was not even encouraged by Muslim rulers, in particular in the early times of Islam, as ruling elites wanted to keep privileges confined to a small (Arab) Muslim elite while consolidating tax-income from "protected" (Arab. dhimmī) Christian and Jewish populations. On the other side, there has been individual conversion driven by a cocktail of motivations, both external and internal. Individual conversion was "more meaningful, a reorientation of the soul" (Levtzion 1979: 19), and implied a radical break with the past and unqualified commitment to Islam, often linked with efforts to not only internalize the ritual obligations but to also study the texts.

According to Levtzion and Hunwick, the establishment of Islam in the bilād al-sūdān can be imagined historically as the "dispersion" of Muslims (as traders), since a period of initial contact in the seventh and eighth centuries, and the emergence of small "islands" of Islam in a "sea of paganism" (Hunwick 1996: 181). Muslims were living in separate quarters, and such situations could last decades or even centuries. From the tenth and eleventh centuries, conversion to Islam became increasingly frequent. Islam was seen, in particular, in the centers of trans-Saharan trade, as being a supreme "source of blessing" (Arab. baraka), as expressed, for instance, in the story of the conversion of the king of Malal to Islam. At the courts and in trading centers, Muslims were esteemed as translators in many respects: they knew how to write, they became clerks and archivists but also experts in many trades, they were a knowledgeable elite and, with time, local centers of Islamic learning developed, often supported by the rulers in the bilād al-sūdān who wanted to profit from Muslim scholars and traders. Due to first "royal pilgrimages" as well as trade, knowledge in the bilād al-sūdān about the lands of the Muslims in the north increased, and the Muslim empires of the north and their metropolitan cities, in particular Cairo, became poles of attraction. At the same time, the islands of Islam started to expand and to form archipelagos of Islam in a shrinking sea of paganism. The increasing importance of Islam in the bilād al-sūdān created a dilemma for the rulers as they still had to respect local cults while recognizing the increasing strength of Islam: "The adoption of Islam as the official religion of the court, in Mali for example, was intended to supplement rather than to replace other principles on which the rulers based their legitimacy" (Launay 1992: 17). Coexistence of both Islam and local cults thus characterized most of the period between the tenth/eleventh and the eighteenth/nineteenth centuries, even after the demise of the great trading empires, due to the fact that the majority of rulers in the smaller kingdoms and principalities of the bilād al-sūdān, which emerged after the fifteenth and sixteenth centuries, were still involved in the trans-Saharan trade and thus linked with the Muslim emirates and empires in the north. Also, Islam continued to constitute a supreme source of legitimization of political rule in all empires and states of sub-Saharan West Africa, as rulers had to address a large array of different local communities and societies: Islam was an important common denominator, a platform uniting diverse populations with different communal cults.

Rulers, both of empires as well as smaller kingdoms, thus pampered Muslim scholars, granted privileges, donated to centers of learning, gave protection, exempted Muslim scholars from taxation or custom fees, and gave them land or cattle. This led, since the eleventh/twelfth century, to the development of two major categories of Muslim scholars in the bilād al-sūdān: those who worked at the courts and those who had their own schools and trades beyond the immediate control of the rulers. The emergence of a large number of principalities and kingdoms in the bilād al-sūdān after the collapse of the great trading empires in the fifteenth and sixteenth centuries, however, started a period of crisis, warfare, disruption, anarchy, and constant competition for resources for the maintenance of courts and the defense of local and regional fiefs. As a consequence, rulers and warlords in the bilād al-sūdān started to raid each other's territories in order to gain control over trade and resources. They started to sell captive enemies, but even more often farmers and pastoralists into slavery in increasing numbers. Since the sixteenth century we can observe the development of predatorial states in the bilād al-sūdān (as well as on the Nile and in Ethiopia) which were increasingly linked with the trans-Saharan and transoceanic (Atlantic, Indian Ocean, and Red Sea) slave trades. In this situation, Muslim scholars, often those in rural communities, started to speak up against unjust rulers (an old theme in Islamic theology), to defend the oppressed and marginalized, and condemned the slave trade of Muslims in particular. As a result, movements of opposition against the "predatorial lords" of the bilād al-sūdān started in the eighteenth and nineteenth centuries, which eventually led, in most parts of the bilād al-sūdān, to the establishment of Muslim states led

According to the Arab geographer al-Bakrī (d. 1094 in Cordoba) (*Kitāb al-masālik wa-l-mamālik,* chapter 1464, p. 875/876), the king of Malal was called al-musulmānī. His country had been plagued by a drought for years. Finally, the king asked a guest, a Muslim, who read the Qur'ān, what could be done. The Muslim asked the king to convert to Islam and to have faith in Allah, and in that case he would pray for rain on the king's behalf. The king followed his advice, his guest taught him the religious and ritual obligations of Islam, asked him to perform the prescribed ablutions, and gave him a simple cotton dress, then the Muslim climbed a hill nearby and they both prayed, on the next Friday, for rain, during most of the day and the night. In the morning, abundant rain came. Thereupon the king commanded all statues of local deities to be destroyed and both he and his successors remained Muslim.

by religious scholars. In these states, Islam became, in the eighteenth, nineteenth, and twentieth centuries, the one and only source of power and legitimization, and a sea of paganism was turned into a sea of Islam which harbored some heathen islands. Some of these islands of heathendom, such as the Maguzawa and Azna communities of northern Nigeria and southern Niger or the Boni of the northern Kenyan coast, continue to exist today and practice rituals such as the bori-spirit possession cult in Hausaland, the zār-cult in Ethiopia, Sudan, and Egypt, or varieties of the East African pepo-cult, although most pre-Islamic cult sites have disappeared and been replaced by mosques. Some religious beliefs, such as the concept of the spirits (Hau. iskoki), have been incorporated into local traditions of Islam, however, and have found acceptance as Muslim jinns (demons).

In recent years, scholars have emphasized the need to look at the many specific ways in which Africans have "made Islam their own" (Robinson 2004: 42) and incorporated "Islam" into local traditions. Their considerations have been supported by a number of field studies on processes of conversion, such as Searing (2006) on the Sereer of Siin-Saalum (Senegal) in the early 1900s, Faulkner (2006) for the Boni in the hinterlands of Lamu (Kenya) in the postcolonial period, Becker (2008) for the hinterlands of Kilwa, Mtwara, and Lindi (Tanzania) in the 1920s and 1930s, or Bunger (1979) for the Pokomo (Kenya) in the 1940s and 1950s. These studies as well as other historical research (Glassman 1995) have identified a cocktail of motivations for conversion to Islam which applies to different local contexts in different periods of time. This allows us to assume that processes of conversion to Islam may have followed similar patterns and similar motivations in earlier times, even if the cocktail of motivations for conversion may have been different in each case and varied in each local context. Such motivations for conversion can be seen to fall into two major categories: external and internal. External factors which stimulated or triggered conversion could have been experiences of war, coercion, disaster, colonization, Christian missionary pressure, or disruptive modernization. War, in particular, has to be seen as being a rather ambiguous driving force for conversion, in particular when Muslims themselves came to be seen, as in the case of the Sereer in Siin (Senegal) in the late nineteenth century or the populations of the Jos plateau (contemporary Northern Nigeria) in the nineteenth century, as the enemies who brought instability and enslavement. Among the internal factors for conversion were dissatisfaction with existing traditions which were seen as being increasingly obsolete in contexts of social change; protest against existing political elites; rebellion against an older generation or the elders as such; and the effort to establish new religious authority. Sub-Saharan African populations characterized by traditions of matrilineal inheritance and descent (ancient Nubia, for instance, but also the Sereer in Senegal, and a number of societies in East Africa) viewed conversion to Islam as a way to secure inheritance and thus control over the means of production in the patrilineage. Recent case studies (Becker 2008, Faulkner 2006, Searing 2006) show that converts were often young men who married Muslim women and wanted to make sure that their children would inherit from them, not their maternal uncle. In addition, conversion could be seen as a way to achieve social emancipation and to gain privileges confined to Muslims, a share of the booty in war, a way out of slavery, a gate toward integration into a powerful, prosperous, successful, and prestigious (civilized) community (as on the East African coast), and thus a strategy to acquire a new identity and recognition, to rise in status and to escape oppressive and obsolete local customs. In her study of conversion among the Mawri in Niger, Adeline Masquelier was for instance told by one of her local interlocutors that "people had turned to Islam because, once (colonial) peace was established, they just wanted to get on with their lives and take advantage of new opportunities" (Masquelier 2001: 60). Processes of conversion were also often characterized by a critique of existing traditions as with respect to (costly) burial rites, initiation, and marriage ceremonies. These motivations can be observed not only for processes of conversion to Islam, but also for processes of re-affiliation within Islam, as in the context of movements of reform.

Processes of conversion have thus always been situational and selective, and specific aspects of Islam were incorporated more easily than others. Equally, local traditions were not discarded completely in processes of conversion: they could be incorporated as non-objectable 'urf (and come under attack only later in a movement of reform) and they could continue to coexist with Islam (even if recognized as non-Islamic). This process of incorporation (or enculturation) should be seen as representing a cocktail of variations in different contexts. At the same time, individual conversion could take different forms: it could come as an abrupt and complete shift to Islam, a radical reorientation which has been described in recent times as "born again Islam" (Diouf and Leichtman 2008: 8f.). Or it could evolve slowly by adopting ritual aspects of Islam, in particular prayer and fasting, in multiple steps. After some time of becoming acquainted with Muslims and their variegated practices of Islam, perhaps even after generations, local traditions of learning could emerge, a process which would lead to a more reflexive view of Islam, as well as pre-Islamic religious traditions, by studying the books. This process has been described by Humphrey Fisher as a "second conversion" to Islam (Fisher 1985: 166). Recent models of conversion are thus not characterized by a concept of development in historical stages so much as by a focus on local dynamics of conversion and variegated speeds of development, different from region to region, as well as a focus on the agency of the converts and those who did not convert.

2 The Bilād al-Maghrib

Rebels, Saints, and Heretics

Historical Themes and Patterns

Between the late seventh and thirteenth centuries, the bilād al-maghrib saw a bewildering variety of religious and political developments, including a series of efforts toward religio-political hegemony. In the thirteenth century, the last efforts to unite the bilād al-maghrib came to an end and particularistic forces prevailed. The bilād al-maghrib remained politically divided into the four major regions that we know today, namely Morocco in the west, Algeria in the center, and Tunisia as well as Tripolitania (Libya) in the east. Not only the political divisions have remained the same since the thirteenth century, but major religious features which today still characterize Muslim society in the bilād al-maghrib were also defined conclusively at that time.

These features include adherence within the bilād al-maghrib as a whole to Sunni Islam and the Mālikī school of law. Shīʿī efforts to gain a foothold in the bilād al-maghrib eventually failed, despite the successful beginnings of the Fāṭimid caliphate in the tenth century. Since the thirteenth century, a few Ibāḍī minorities have been the only non-Sunni communities in the region. As such, the bilād al-maghrib are characterized today by a far greater religious homogeneity than many other regions of the Islamic world. The solid foundation of Islam in its Sunni-Mālikī orientation has, at the same time, contributed decisively to the establishment of this religious orientation in the Sahara as well as in the bilād al-sūdān to the south.

By the thirteenth century, Sufi thought had gained a foothold in the bilād al-maghrib, in particular in the regions beyond the immediate influence of the rulers. Sufi scholars, the so-called marabouts (from the Arabic term murābiṭūn, "those who live in a ribāṭ," a fortification built to defend Islam), came to represent a major social, religious, and political force as religious scholars, legal experts, mediators, sages, saints, and medical experts in local communities. The symbiosis of a number of disciplines of Islamic learning, in particular, fiqh (jurisprudence), ṭibb (medicine), tawḥīd (dogmatic theology) and taṣawwuf (Sufism), came to form a second major trait of Islam in the bilād al-maghrib which again spread into the Sahara and the bilād al-sūdān to the south. From the thirteenth century onward, all these territories came to form a vast Sunni-Mālikī realm that was strongly influenced by the legacy of Sufi saints and scholars, the marabouts and their schools and traditions of learning. And although Sufi orders (Arab. ṭuruq, sg. ṭarīqa) as organized religio-political bodies only played a central role in society from the eighteenth century onward, they again spread from the bilād al-maghrib through the Sahara to the bilād al-sūdān in the south.

Between the eighth and the thirteenth centuries, the political history of the bilād al-maghrib was characterized by three major tropes:

(a) rebellion in the name of Islam and the religious legitimization of rebellion and resistance against unjust rule;
(b) the role of outsiders as both religious and political leaders; and
(c) fluctuating center-periphery relations, with constantly changing relationships between the "lands of the treasury," the bilād al-makhzan, and the lands of those who "roamed freely," the bilād al-sība.

These themes can also be identified as themes in the history of other parts of Muslim Africa. Thus, rebellion in the name of Islam has been a leitmotif of the jihād movements in the bilād al-sūdān since the eighteenth century, as well as the Mahdiyya in the Sudan in the nineteenth century. Outsiders and legitimate references to outsiders and/or cultural heroes have equally been important in the history of other African societies, as seen, for instance, in the role of Wangarawa traders in Kano history, the Solomonic origins of the Ethiopian emperors, or the Shirazi founders of dynasties on the East African coast. References to outsiders and/or cultural heroes have also been important in the history of African Muslim societies in the context of dynastic changes or have provided legitimate background for the foundation of a new dynasty. Finally, the dynamics of center-periphery relations have marked the history of all trading empires of the bilād al-sūdān, the imperial histories of both Sinnār-Funj and Ethiopia, as well as the development of Ottoman rule in North Africa since the sixteenth century. States in these parts of Africa, in fact, consisted of "a core comprising either a homogeneous population or a fairly stable articulation of different ethnic groups. . . . This core was encircled by tributary zones with fluctuating boundaries . . . which required periodic reconquest, reinforcing the military expression of the state" (Roberts 1987: 10). In many cases, tributary zones passed into slave-hunting peripheries. This applied again not only to the Muslim trading empires of the bilād al-sūdān and the empire of Sinnār-Funj on the Nile, but also to the Christian empire of Ethiopia. Before discussing these themes in greater detail, it is necessary, however, to sketch the basic outlines of the historical development of the bilād al-maghrib from the period of conquest in the seventh century to the thirteenth century, which was characterized by the emergence and consolidation of distinct regional political centers. As the bilād al-maghrib were closely linked with the bilād al-sūdān south of the Sahara by way of the trans-Saharan trade, historical dynamics in the north tended to have influence on political, religious, economic, and social development in the south and vice versa: knowledge of the history of the bilād al-maghrib is thus essential to understand the history of sub-Saharan West Africa.

In broad terms, the history of the lands of the west in Islamic times can be divided into seven major periods: the time of conquest by Arab Muslim armies from 644 to

697; the period of Islamization and rebellion in the name of Islam from 697 to c. 909; the quest for unity from c. 909 to 1248 under the Fāṭimid, Almoravid, and Almohad dynasties; the post-Almohad dynasties from c. 1248 to 1510; the Ottoman period from c. 1510 to 1830; European (French, Spanish, and Italian) colonization from 1830 to 1974; and finally, independence from the 1950s onward. The history of the bilād al-maghrib has been discussed extensively in many scholarly works and this discussion need not be repeated here. I focus instead on the first three periods of Maghribinian history which were of formative importance not only for later periods, but also for the development of Muslim communities and societies in the Sahara and in the bilād al-sūdān. As this period of time is still too long to be covered in one chapter, I concentrate on those key themes of the history of the bilād al-maghrib which became relevant for the development of Muslim societies in other parts of Africa.

The Era of Conquest (644–697)

The conquest of the bilād al-maghrib by Arab-Muslim armies started in 644 in the guise of a first Arab-Muslim raid into Tripolitania and the Fazzān. In 670, Qayrawān in present-day southern Tunisia was founded as a permanent camp of the Arab-Muslim armies and in 697 the last resistance of local populations was suppressed. The bilād al-maghrib came under Umayyad control and were administered from Qayrawān as the wilāya (province) of Ifrīqiyya. When comparing the conquest of the bilād al-maghrib with the conquest of the bilād al-mashriq ("the lands of the east, Egypt, Syria, Mesopotamia, the Arabian peninsula, and Persia), the question arises as to why the conquest of the west took such a long time (about fifty-five years), in comparison to the conquest of the east (fifteen to twenty years). The west, after all, was only thinly populated and much smaller in geographical terms than the east, which stretched from Egypt to Transoxania. The difficulties of the Arab Muslim armies in conquering the west can be explained in several ways.

By the 630s, the Byzantine and Sassanid (Persian) empires, which had controlled most of the east, were exhausted due to decades of indecisive warfare. Once their armies were defeated, the empires collapsed. The Sassanid empire made way for the Arab-Muslim armies to cross the Iranian high plateaus to the territories further east and northeast, while the Byzantine empire managed to recover behind the Taurus mountains, yet lost its Syrian, Egyptian, and later North African peripheries. In the bilād al-maghrib, by contrast, major empires and imperial administrations did not exist. The Byzantine empire had a few coastal strongholds that were quickly evacuated, while the majority of the population represented a vast spectrum of Imasighen tribal groups and federations characterized by competition for scarce resources. Victory over one tribe did not mean automatic control over a large area, and even control of the territory of a specific tribe was often lost as soon as it was gained, when a raiding force had passed through. Due to the fact that Imasighen rebellions forced Arab troops to evacuate the bilād al-maghrib several times, Muslim traditions later claimed that "the Berbers had apostasized twelve times before they accepted Islam" (Levtzion 2007: 6).

> At the council of Chalcedon in 451, the Latin/Greek Church (later Churches) in Rome and Byzantium accepted the doctrine of diophysis, the idea that Christ, the second figure of the Trinity (God the father, Christ the son, and the Holy Spirit), united in his single, divine person two natures, one human (Jesus) and one divine (logos). At the council of Ephesus in 431, a majority of Eastern Christians had declared allegiance to the doctrine that Christ as a (divine) person had only one nature (monophysis), the human subsumed in the divine. At the same time, the council of Ephesus had condemned the Nestorian idea that Christ represented a divine nature in a divine physis (body) as well as a human nature in a human physis. The Nestorians, who, from 486, came to form the Assyrian Church, also rejected (as did Muslims) the idea of Mary as the mother of God and stressed the idea of Mary as mother of Christ. While Nestorians remained influential in 'Irāq, Iran, and central Asia until the fourteenth and fifteenth centuries, the Monophysites became the dominant Christian faith in Armenia, Egypt, Nubia, and Ethiopia. The Diophysite orientation developed into the Catholic and Protestant Churches as well as the Greek and Russian Orthodox Churches.

A considerable part of the Christian populations of the east did not follow the dominant faith of the Byzantine or Sassanid empires, namely the Byzantine (Latin, later Greek) Church or the Zoroastrian faith of the Sassanids. Rather, they followed other orientations of Christianity and perceived the conquest of their lands as liberation from Byzantine and Sassanid tyranny. As ahl al-kitāb, "people of the book," the Christian populations of the east were not only tolerated by the Muslim-Arab conquerors, but pampered, at least initially, as welcome allies, taxpayers, and administrators of the new empire. As a consequence, a majority of the populations of the east remained Christian until the eleventh to thirteenth centuries (depending on the region), and sizable Christian minorities have survived until today in Egypt, Syria, Lebanon, Palestine, Jordan, and 'Irāq. The Imasighen populations of the west, by contrast, mostly adhered to local, pre-Christian cults. Consequently, the Imasighen were not regarded by the Arab-Muslim armies as ahl al-kitāb who had to be respected, but as booty (Arab.: fay') that could be killed or enslaved. As a consequence, the resistance of the Imasighen peoples of the west against Arab-Muslim conquest was much harder, as the vanquished had to fear enslavement, or at least paying the khums, a tribute which was much higher than the jizyā (head tax) that Christian and Jewish subjects had to pay under Arab-Muslim rule. As soon as conquest was achieved, Imasighen populations converted to Islam in large numbers, and within a few years the whole region had become nominally Muslim. The armies which started to conquer Spain, "al-Andalus," in 711, consisted mostly of converted Imasighen troops under Arab command. Conversion to Islam seems to have been seen by many Imasighen leaders and their peoples as a way to gain quick emancipation and equality in status, as well as exemption from taxes, but also as a way to acquire the privilege of taking part in the war of the Arab Muslims and of claiming parts of the booty. However, conversion to Islam seems to have remained rather superficial, and indigenous centers of Islamic learning were to develop only slowly in the bilād al-maghrib. Traditions of Islamic learning remained largely confined to a few urban centers, in particular Qayrawān (from the eighth century), and later Tunis, Fes, and Tilimsān (from the tenth century). While early Umayyad caliphs refused to accept the religious, political, and legal equality of Muslims of non-Arab descent, the status of the Muslim Imasighen populations of the bilād al-maghrib improved when the Umayyad caliph ʿUmar II. ʿAbd al-ʿAzīz (r. 717–720) decreed the equality of all Muslims, Arab or non-Arab, in 717. This revolutionary decree was revoked by his successor and the status quo ante was reintroduced, which granted Arab Muslims a privileged political status. This led to widespread

> After the collapse of the Roman Empire in the fifth century, the bilād al-maghrib fell under the sway of five large Imasighen tribal groups, which were again subdivided into numerous smaller tribes. Sometimes these tribes formed federations, often competing against each other, supporting strategic alliances with different dynasties. Areas of settlement shifted, however, depending on victory or defeat in tribal wars and dynastic feuds. In the northwest, the Awrāba dominated and formed the social basis of the Idrīsid dynasty in Fes; to the south of them, numerous Maṣmūda tribes, such as the Hintata, controlled most of the western Atlas. The western Sahara, the mountains of Kabylia, and the central Atlas regions were dominated by a plethora of Ṣanhāja tribes such as the Kutāma (which came to support the Fāṭimid dynasty), or the Saharan Ṣanhāja tribal federations of the Lamṭūna, Masūfa, and Judāla, which came to form the core of the Almoravid armies; other parts of the central Atlas, as well as the eastern Maghrib, were controlled by the Ḥawwāra federation which supported the Rustamid dynasty. The Zanāta tribal family was finally split into many different regional tribal groups such as the Maghrāwa or the Miknāsa, who came to dominate the Banū Midrār dynasty in Sijilmāsa. Zanāta tribes also formed the core of the Zayyānid dynasty, but many Zanāta had to leave the central bilād al-maghrib in the eleventh century and resettle in northern Morocco. In the fifteenth century, the Banū Marīn, another Zanāta group, formed the core of the Marīnid dynasty in Morocco.

unrest and protest among the Imasighen Muslim populations in the bilād al-maghrib and to the outbreak of large-scale rebellions in 739/740, which brought about the collapse of the Umayyad administration in the bilād al-maghrib.

Rebellion in the Name of Islam (697–909)

Due to the discrimination of recently converted Imasighen populations, rebellions against the Umayyad dynasty took place in the name of Islam, "fi-sabīl Allāh." This rebellion did not aspire to reestablish old, pre-Islamic concepts of society and polity, but were formulated in Islamic theological terms. The argument of the rebels acquired two major forms:

Descent: By establishing a genealogical link to the house and family of the Prophet (Banū Ḥāshim), rebels could brand the Umayyad caliphate as the rule of Banū Umāyya upstarts who had actually fought the Prophet until the very last moment. A genealogical link and closeness (Arab. qarāba) to the family of the Prophet had both a delegitimizing as well as a legitimizing dimension and was formulated most clearly in a dynasty which emerged in the late eighth century (788) in the region of Fes. The founder of this dynasty, which existed until 958, was Idrīs b. ʿAbdallāh, an Arab who claimed descent from the house of the Prophet through al-Ḥasan, ʿAlī's eldest son. Al-Ḥasan as well as his younger brother al-Ḥusayn came to form the nucleus of the highly respected ahl al-bayt, "the people of the house" (the family of the Prophet Muḥammad), who are regarded until today as sharīf (noble, respected; pl. shurafāʾ or ashrāf), not only in the bilād al-maghrib, but in all other parts of the Islamic world. The shurafāʾ/ashrāf have consequently come to form a class of religious nobility in Muslim societies. In local communities they were represented by leaders from their own ranks, the "naqīb al-ashrāf" (the head of the ashrāf).

Egalitarian theology: By claiming that all Muslims, regardless of their ethnic origin, were equal in their faith, rebels could brand Umayyad rule as exclusivist and even anti-Islamic. The theological orientation which stressed the basic equality of all Muslims most prominently were the Khawārij (those who left, or dissenters), who called themselves ahl al-istiqāma (people of uprightness). The Khārijī "cause" (Arab. daʿwa) and call for rebellion against the Umayyads reached the bilād al-maghrib by 719, and a majority of Imasighen rebellions which started in 739/740 were actually led by Khārijī emissaries. Their activities led to the emergence of two Khārijī dynasties based on tribal federations in the bilād al-maghrib: the (Ṣufrī) Banū Midrār dynasty as supported by the Miknāsa-Zanāta, who from 757 to 958 were able to control, from their center in Sijilmāsa, most of southern Morocco and the northern stretches of the trans-Saharan caravan routes; and the federation of the (Ibāḍī) Ḥawwāra, who supported the dynasty of the Rustamids in the central Maghrib as well as the Jabal Nafūsa region in Tripolitania with a political center in Tāhart (east of Tilimsān) (see map 9).

Both the Banū Midrār and the Rustamid dynasties were established and initially led by outsiders, as was Fes under Idrīs b. ʿAbdallāh. In the case of the Rustamid dynasty this outsider was a Persian, ʿAbd al-Raḥmān b. Rustam, who was entrusted with the position of imām of the Ḥawwāra federation, "as he had no tribe behind him which could protect him against punishment in case that he deviated from the right path" (Rebstock 1983: 70). The rulers of the states and dynasties which emerged from the rebellion against Umayyad rule were thus only nominal heads of tribal federations and not powerful kings or sulṭāns: they had to rely on the consensus of tribal leaders in order to exercise authority and to achieve their political aims. The important role of outsiders did not remain confined to the Idrīsid state in Fes as supported by the Awrāba federation, the Banu Midrār in Sijilmāsa, and the Rustamid dynasty in Tāhart, but they played an equally important role in the dynasties of the Fāṭimids, the Almoravids, and the Almohads and were a pervading feature of the historical development of Muslim societies in the bilād al-maghrib.

However, neutral outsiders were not the only ones to provide a model for the organization of states and dynasties in the bilād al-maghrib. There were two important exceptions: first, the Arab troops in Ifrīqiyya (Tunisia) did not join the Khārijī rebels in the south and west, but declared their loyalty to the new ʿAbbāsid dynasty in Baghdad. From 765 to 909, Tunisia was thus ruled by the Arab Aghlabid dynasty as an autonomous province of the ʿAbbāsid caliphate. The Aghlabid rulers not only created stability and wealth in Tunisia and contained Khārijī raids, but also started and completed the conquest of Sicily, which remained under Muslim domination until the eleventh century. Under Aghlabid rule, Tunisia also became the first region in the bilād al-maghrib where the Mālikī school of law could thrive under the influence of a major legal thinker, Saḥnūn, whose *mudawwana* continued the legal reasoning of Imām Mālik's *kitāb al-muwaṭṭā*.

The second exception to the rule was the federation of the Barghawāṭa on the Atlantic coast of western Morocco. This federation of more than a dozen tribes and sub-tribes, formed in the aftermath of the invasion of al-Andalus in the mid-eighth century, came under the influence of Khārijī-Ṣufrī thought in the eighth and ninth centuries. In the ninth century, however, the Barghawāṭa federation turned toward a new interpretation of the faith. The emergence of the Barghawāṭa as a federation of Imasighen tribes which cultivated their own interpretation of Islam seems to have taken place in fact under Ṣāliḥ b. Ṭarīf, the son of the founder of the federation (r. 748–93), and Ṣāliḥ seems to have passed on his teaching to his son Ilyās. Ṣāliḥ, then departed to the east and promised to return one day as the Mahdī under the rule of the seventh ruler of the dynasty. Ilyās b. Ṣāliḥ (r. 793–842) seems to have remained loyal to the Ṣufrite orientation of the Khārijiyya, however, and only his son, Yūnus b. Ilyās (r. 842–84), started to publicize his grandfather's secret message. Yūnus had been to Mecca and had acquired knowledge in a number of Islamic sciences, in particular astronomy. Despite his efforts to establish the new faith, only a part of the Barghawāṭa followed Yūnus. Still, the Barghawāṭa federation was able to defeat the Idrīsid dynasty in Fes in the late ninth century and to consolidate its power in western Morocco. For a number of reasons, the Barghawāṭa federation had to fight an almost constant war against neighbors and was finally eliminated by the nascent Almoravid movement of reform between 1059 and 1061.

Data on the religion of the Barghawāṭa are relatively scarce and probably biased except for two short accounts by Ibn Ḥawqal in the tenth and al-Bakrī in the eleventh century. Al-Bakrī's account was based on a report by the Ṣāḥib Ṣalātihim, "the venerable leader in prayer" of the Barghawāṭa, Abū Ṣāliḥ Zammūr, who had visited the court of the Umayyad Caliph in Cordoba, Abū Manṣūr 'Isā' (r. 953–79), in a diplomatic mission in 963. Essentially, the new religion may be seen as an effort by the Barghawāṭa to contextualize Islam in an Imasighen milieu. The Barghawāṭa, in fact, had their own Qur'ān, which consisted of eighty sūras. Although many of these sūras were translations from the Arabic Qur'ān, some of their names were different and referred to Prophets such as Ṣāliḥ and Yūnus, as well as Ayyūb (Hiob), or other names such as Fira'ūn (Pharaoh), Yagog and Magog, al-Dajjāl, and Nimrod. The first sūra of the Qur'ān of the Barghawāṭa allegedly started with these words:

> In the name of God: the one who has received his book in order to reveal it to mankind is the same as the one He has asked to bring the message. They say: Satan has knowledge over fate. God does not like this as Satan does not have the power to know what God alone may know. (quoted in al-Bakrī 1992, chapter 1380, 826f.)

In addition to a Qur'ān as transmitted by their own prophet in Imasighen language (but in Arabic script), the Barghawāṭa followed a number of additional ritual characteristics such as ten daily prayers and additional days of fasting. Also, the month of Rajab replaced the month of Ramaḍān as the month of fasting and Thursday replaced Friday as the day of communal prayer. Qur'ānic ḥudūd punishments were accepted and even increased. Thus, a slanderer could be expelled from his tribe. The Barghawāṭa religion, in particular, maintained that Berbers would now have their own War-iya-Wara (the prophet, after which no other prophet would come).

The Quest for Unity (909–1248)

The time between the tenth and the thirteenth centuries was characterized by the efforts of three major dynasties-cum-tribal federations to unite the lands of the Maghrib under a single political roof. Outsiders again played a major role in the foundation of these dynasties, and processes of religious opposition and political fragmentation again contributed to the eventual collapse of all three efforts of unification: neither the Fāṭimids, the Almoravids, or the Almohads were able to construct a political and religious platform which could overcome tribal and regional particularities.

The Fāṭimid dynasty (909–1049): The first attempt at unification was based on the Kutāma federation of present-day eastern Algeria and northwestern Tunisia. The Kutāma, a northern Ṣanhāja group, had been marginalized in the eighth and ninth centuries by both the Aghlabid dynasty in Tunisia and the Rustamid state in the south and west, and sought to break out of this marginal role. Eventually, an 'Irāqī Shī'ī

Today a majority of Shīʿīs in Iran, Syria, Lebanon, and the Gulf region follow the Ithnāʿashara orientation, which claims a series of eleven imāms, with a twelfth imām to one day (re-)appear as the last imām before the Day of Judgment. In the ninth and tenth centuries, the majority of Shīʿī Muslims adhered to a different interpretation of Shīʿī genealogy, which focused on the eldest son, Ismāʿīl, of the sixth imām, Jaʿfar al-Ṣādiq, as the seventh and last imām. Unfortunately, Ismāʿīl died before his father and a second (younger) son, Mūsā al-Kāẓim, eventually established the sequence of imāms leading to the Ithnāʿashara chain of imāms. In the ninth century, a majority of Shīʿī Muslims came to believe, however, that Ismāʿīl had not died but had been hidden (by God) in order to escape murder and would one day return, as the mahdī, or the rightly guided one, and last (seventh) imām. A growing number of Shīʿī dāʿiya set out to create favorable circumstances for the coming of the mahdī, trying to destabilize Abbasid rule. In later centuries, the Ismāʿīlī orientation of the Shīʿa split into several sub-groups. Disputes over dynastic succession in the Fāṭimid Empire in the late eleventh century led to the emergence of the Mustaʿlī and Nizārī groups, which gained a considerable number of followers in India, where these groups came to be known as Khōjas and Bohoras.

dāʿiya, Abū ʿAbdallāh, was accepted as imām of the federation and was able to lead the Kutāma to victory over the Aghlabid dynasty in Tunisia, and then to establish the first Shīʿī caliphate in the history of Islam. This Shīʿī caliphate eventually succeeded not only in uniting the whole of the bilād al-maghrib (until 958), but also in conquering Egypt (in 969), as well as Syria and Palestine, and even in threatening the ʿAbbāsid Caliphate in Baghdad. The rise of the Kutāma was thus based on the mediating role of an outsider who represented a legitimate concept of rule, namely the Shīʿī concept of the rightly guided imāms in direct descent from the family of the Prophet through ʿAlī, al-Ḥusayn, al-Ḥasan, ʿAlī Zayn al-ʿAbidīn, Muḥammad al-Bāqir, and Jaʿfar al-Ṣādiq.

In 910, due to the successful mission of Abū ʿAbdallāh, a Shīʿī caliphate was proclaimed in Tunisia. In order to legitimize its rule, the name of Fāṭima, the daughter of the Prophet who had married ʿAlī and had given birth to al-Ḥusayn and al-Ḥasan, was chosen as the dynastic name. The weakness of existing political structures and the weakening of ʿAbbāsid rule in Baghdad allowed Fāṭimid-Kutāma power to expand quickly in the bilād al-maghrib and later in the bilād al-mashriq. The Fāṭimid caliphate also developed a specific Shīʿī theology of redemption which triggered the opposition of Sunni-Mālikī scholars in the very heart of the Fāṭimid caliphate, in Ifrīqiyya. Fāṭimid theologians taught that mankind would go through a succession of seven eras of varying duration, each inaugurated by a spokesman (Arab. nāṭiq) who would reveal a divine message consisting of a law (sharī'a) and a hidden, esoteric truth (Arab. ḥaqīqa). The spokesmen of the first six eras of human history were Àdam, Nūḥ, Ibrāhīm, Mūsa, 'Isā, and Muḥammad. The final era would be initiated by the mahdī and seventh nāṭiq, Ismā'īl, who would also reveal the most hidden meaning, the da'wa al-ḥaqq of the Qur'ān. This message was difficult to digest for many Muslims, in particular the Sunni-Mālikī religious scholars. The oppressive rule of the Kutāma in the name of the Fāṭimid caliphs also triggered protest and rebellion, often under Khārijī leadership. At the end of the tenth century, the Fāṭimid caliphs transferred their capital from Tunisia to Egypt (al-Qāhira/Cairo) and delegated the administration of the western provinces to the Zīrīds, a Ṣanhāja sub-group, which, under the pressure of religious scholars and the Sunni-Mālikī population in Tunisia, eventually rejected their alliance with the Fāṭimid caliphs in Cairo and declared Tunisia an independent emirate. Zīrīd efforts to gain wider acceptance in the population started to gain momentum in the context of a popular rebellion in Qayrawān in 1016, which showed that the majority of the population was not willing to accept Shī'ī rule. Although the Zīrīds managed to suppress the rebellion, the new Zīrīd ruler, al-Mu'izz (r. 1016–1051), tried to reach an agreement with the religious scholars and eventually severed ties with the Fāṭimid caliphate in 1049. The Sunni-Mālikī opposition in Tunisia was represented most prominently by the major Sunni-Mālikī scholar of the time, Ibn Abī Zayd al-Qayrawānī (d. 996), the author of the *risāla,* which, together with the *mukhtaṣar* of Khalīl b. Iṣḥāq, came to be the most widely known text on Sunni-Mālikī law in North Africa, in the Sahara, and in the bilād al-sūdān.

The rebellion in the bilād al-maghrib cut the Fāṭimid empire off from its supply of Kutāma warriors. The Fāṭimid caliph was consequently not in a position, in the mid-eleventh century, to suppress the rebellions in the West in military terms. The Fāṭimid caliphate thus granted two Arab tribes in Upper Egypt, the Banū Hilāl and the Banū Sulaym, possession of the bilād al-maghrib. While the Banū Sulaym came to settle in the Cyrenaika, the Banū Hilāl invaded Tunisia and defeated the Zīrīd army in 1052. As a consequence, Tunisia disintegrated into a number of tribal principalities. Some coastal cities were even taken by the Normans, who also conquered Sicily. When the Almohad armies eventually took control of Tunisia in the twelfth century, they resettled the Banū Hilāl in the depopulated Barghawāṭa region in western Morocco, and thus laid the foundation for the emergence of a small but growing Arab tribal population in Morocco. Even before the Zīrīds declared their independence, other Ṣanhāja groups in the central bilād al-maghrib had rebelled in 1007 and established the Ḥammādid dynasty, based in Qal'at Banī Ḥammād and later in Bijāya. The Ḥammādids were not only able to stop the westward advance of the Banū Hilāl in the mid-eleventh century, but also opposed the eastward advance of the Almoravid empire. Only in 1163 was the Ḥammādid federation defeated by the Almohads and integrated into the Almohad empire, as was Tunisia (see map 10).

The Almoravid empire (1055–1144): Resistance and rebellion against the Fāṭimid empire was not confined to religious scholars and theological protest against Shīʿī cosmology, as in Ifrīqiyya, but was also expressed in terms of protest and opposition against Kutāma rule. The growing weakness of Fāṭimid rule in the western regions of the bilād al-maghrib led to the emergence of new tribal federations as political players in the early eleventh century. Notably the Maghrāwa, a Zanāta group, were able to gain control, in 970, over the most important northern entrepôts of the western trans-Saharan trade routes, in particular Sijilmāsa in the Tāfīlālt valley, the Darʿa valley, Aghmāt, and the Sūs valley.

The rise of the Maghrāwa threatened the Saharan Ṣanhāja, a group of several related but often competing Imasighen tribes in the western Sahara, including the Lamtūna, Masūfa, and Judāla, which had been allies of the Fāṭimids. Due to their disunity, the Ṣanhāja had already lost control over the most important southern Saharan trade center, Awdaghust, to the rising empire of Ghāna around 990. In the early eleventh century, they also lost control over Sijilmāsa and other entrepôts of the trans-Saharan trade in the north. As a result, the Saharan Ṣanhāja were deprived of two major sources of income, the fees of the caravan trade and the taxes of the major trading centers. In this situation of economic and political crisis, one Ṣanhāja leader, Yaḥyā b. Ibrāhīm, went on pilgrimage and sought the support of a well-known religious scholar in order to establish a regime of religious discipline among the Ṣanhāja. At this time, the Mālikī school of law had gained widespread support and respect due to its opposition to Fāṭimid rule, and its scholars were the obvious choice for Yaḥyā b. Ibrāhīm. Eventually, he was sent to a young scholar in southern Morocco, ʿAbdallāh b. Yāsīn, a Ṣanhāja of the Jazūla tribe, who agreed to follow Yaḥyā b. Ibrāhīm into the desert and to teach the Ṣanhāja the Sunni-Mālikī path of Islam. This scholarly endeavor, which started around 1039, soon turned into a full-scale campaign of reconversion to Islam, for ʿAbdallāh b. Yāsīn realized that Islam had been accepted by the Ṣanhāja only superficially. ʿAbdallāh b. Yāsīn started to teach the Ṣanhāja from scratch. This pedagogical exercise, related by al-Bakrī, assumed a rather harsh character. An important element of ʿAbdallāh b. Yāsīn's teachings was the ritual punishment of earlier misdeeds: anybody who wanted to join the movement of the al-murābiṭūn (those who fight from a ribāṭ to defend Islam) had to confess in public and was accordingly punished, following the norms of the Mālikī school of law. As soon as punishment had taken place, the community of the Almoravids had gained a new, ritually pure member. Al-Bakrī described these events as follows:

> When a man joins the daʿwa, they tell him: you have committed numerous misdeeds in your past, and thus it is necessary that you accept punishment and purification. They punish extra-marital intercourse with 100 lashes, slander with 80 lashes, equally the drinking of alcohol. Sometimes these punishments are even raised and they also deal in this way with those they have defeated. In case they know, however,

> that somebody has killed another person, they also kill him. Even his repentance does not change this verdict. Those who miss the Friday prayer get twenty lashes and those who forget a rakʿa get five lashes. Also, they say to a new member of their daʿwa: in your life you have missed many prayers, you have to make up for them and add additional rakaʿāt for them to the Friday prayer. (al-Bakrī, chapter 1442, 864; trans. in Levtzion 1981: 75)

This educational exercise led not only to the establishment of the Mālikī school of law as the one and only school of law in the western Sahara (and later, the bilād al-sūdān), but also to the emergence of a movement of Almoravid warriors who were united by firm religious discipline and an outstanding esprit de corps, a sense of belonging to a chosen elite, bound by a strong ʿaṣabiyya (group feeling) and a cause, namely to establish the Mālikī school of law as the one and only orientation of Islam in the bilād al-maghrib.

In the beginning, the daʿwa of the Almoravids suffered a number of setbacks, as some Ṣanhāja tribes refused to submit to the rigid discipline of the movement. Yet when the Almoravid warriors proved to be superior in fighting spirit, discipline, and resolution and reaped their first victories by regaining control, in 1055 and 1056, over both the southern and the northern entrepôts of the trans-Saharan trade, Awdaghust and Sijilmāsa, the success of the Almoravids knew no limits. Within a few years, the armies of the Almoravids not only established Almoravid control over the western and central Sahara, and, thus, complete control over the western trans-Saharan trade routes, but also crossed the passes of the Atlas Mountains and crushed the Barghawāṭa federation in the late 1050s, as well as the resistance of the northern Zanāta in 1069. After the conquest of the western and central bilād al-maghrib (the region of Algiers was taken in 1082), the Almoravids crossed the straits of Gibraltar in 1087, took control of the Muslim principalities in al-Andalus, and pushed the Christian Reconquista back to the Ebro.

In their new empire, governed from Marrākish (est. 1070), the Almoravids built an administration guided by the principles of Mālikī law as interpreted by Sunni-Mālikī fuqahāʾ (legal experts). As a result of these historical developments, the bilād al-magrib became staunchly Sunni-Mālikī. The increasingly rigid stress on Mālikī law as the guiding principle of the dynasty even led the Almoravid ruler ʿAlī b. Tashfīn (r. 1106–1143) to order the burning of the works of the Iranian Sufi philosopher and legal thinker, Abū Ḥāmid al-Ghazzālī (d. 1111). At the same time, the Almoravids cultivated a distinct identity as a Ṣanhāja elite. Their elite status was marked by the fact that only Ṣanhāja warriors had the right to wear in public the lithām, the facial veil of the men of Saharan tribes, which allowed the Ṣanhāja warriors to hide their identity and granted them freedom to execute punishment without being recognized. This prerogative of the Ṣanhāja-Almoravid warriors, in particular the Lamtūna elite, who were also called al-mulaththimūn (the veiled ones), led to transgressions and triggered opposition from other Imasighen tribal groups which were excluded from participation in government. In the early decades of the twelfth century, a formidable movement of opposition against Almoravid rule started to form among both Zanāta and Maṣmūda, which eventually succeeded in defeating the Almoravids and in establishing a new Maghribinian empire.

The Almohad empire (1144–1248): The emergence of opposition to Almoravid rule may be explained as a religious reaction against the legalistic regime of the Almoravid fuqahā', as well as a tribal reaction against the dominant and elitist position of the Ṣanhāja. As a consequence, the Almohad opposition movement was initially not confined to yet another Imasighen tribal federation but included a number of tribal groups from almost all the bilād al-maghrib, although Maṣmūda groups dominated. In terms of religious orientation, the Almohad movement did not reject the teachings of the Sunni-Mālikī scholars, but stressed a different aspect of Islamic theology, namely the doctrine of tawḥīd, belief in the unity of God. The followers of this doctrine, the al-muwaḥḥidūn, also gave their name to the new movement of protest. The doctrine of tawḥīd was viewed as a theological orientation deemed superior in religious terms to the legalism of the Almoravid fuqahā'. The Almoravid rulers consequently perceived Almohad opposition as a rebellion against their own claims to spiritual and religious superiority, and tried to suppress the Almohad movement as early as possible.

In 1129, the first charismatic leader of the Almohad movement, Muḥammad b. 'Abdallāh b. Tūmart (d. 1130), started the Almohad rebellion in the very heart of the Almoravid empire, in the capital city of Marrākish, and quickly withdrew with his followers into the Atlas Mountains when Almoravid repression started. When Ibn Tūmart, who had claimed to be the mahdī, died in 1130, a disciple of Ibn Tūmart, 'Abd al-Mu'min, took over the leadership and led the Almohad movement within a few years to complete victory over the Almoravid empire, a feat achieved by 1144. In 1146, the Almohad army invaded al-Andalus and established Almohad rule there as well. By 1160, Almohad forces had also conquered the eastern part of the bilād al-maghrib, including Ifrīqiyya/Tunisia, which had escaped Almoravid control. In contrast, the Almohad armies failed to gain control over the trans-Saharan trade routes which remained under the control of the Saharan Imasighen tribes. Although the Almohad empire managed to unite the bilād al-maghrib for the last time in history, their rule did again not remain without opposition. The motivation for rebellion was based on ethnic as well as religious grounds. First, Almohad rule increasingly turned out to be the rule of the Maṣmūda, to the detriment of other Imasighen groups. Second, Almohad rule established a system of supervision through a religious police, the so-called mizwār ("those who come to visit regularly"), which not only controlled market activities, collected taxes, and executed the law, but also supervised the religious life of the people and adherence to Almohad tenets of faith.

While Almoravid rule had been distinguished by a strong emphasis on the law (of Mālikī expression), Almohad rule was characterized by an emphasis on dogmatic unitarian theology. In the context of these rather one-sided interpretations of the faith, a new group of religious scholars emerged in the late twelfth and early thirteenth centuries who proposed to overcome the bias toward either fiqh or tawḥīd and to develop a synthesis of the religious teachings of Islam. These scholars may be ultimately linked to the first major Sufi scholars in the bilād al-maghrib, namely, Abū Madyan Shuʿayb (d. 1198) and his disciple Abū l-Ḥasan al-Shādhilī (d. 1258). The teachings of these Sufi scholars, who were again called al-murābiṭūn (or later, marabouts) sought to unite both fiqh and tawḥīd in a more comprehensive religious philosophy and to add a spiritual dimension, in particular the idea that Islam could not be reduced to the obvious, visible (Arab. ẓāhir) aspects of the faith, but had an inner, hidden (Arab. bāṭin) dimension, as manifested in personal faith and piety. The teachings of the early Sufi scholars quickly gained popular support, especially in the areas beyond the direct control of the Almohad authorities. Sufi scholars thus emerged as a new religious movement and managed to delegitimize Almohad rule without openly attacking the Almohad authorities. Opposition to Almohad rule and Maṣmūda domination, as well as a series of wars, in particular in al-Andalus, weakened the hegemony of the Almohad dynasty. In al-Anadalus, the Almohad empire suffered a crushing defeat in 1212 at Las Navas de Tolosa, which ended Muslim rule in al-Andalus except for the principality of Granada, which continued to lead a precarious existence until 1492.

Disintegration and Fragmentation

The political disintegration of the bilād al-maghrib may be attributed to the fact, amongst others, that the Imasighen tribes which led the rebellion against the Almohad dynasty were no longer able to form a federation which had broad popular support. Instead, the dynasties which ruled the bilād al-maghrib since the thirteenth century represented smaller tribal groups which did not manage to extend their influence beyond their own and often short-lived realm of power. This is particularly true for the history of Morocco under a series of dynasties from the Marīnids (thirteenth–fifteenth centuries) to the Waṭṭāsids (sixteenth century), the Ṣaʿdids (sixteenth–seventeenth centuries), and the ʿAlawids (from the seventeenth century). The central and eastern bilād al-maghrib, by contrast, came under Ottoman control in the mid-sixteenth century and developed into the Ottoman dominions of Algeria and Tunisia.

In the thirteenth century, the Almohad empire eventually disintegrated into three successor dynasties, the Ḥafsid dynasty in Ifrīqiyya/Tunisia (1226–1574), the Zayyānid dynasty in the central bilād al-maghrib (Algeria, 1230–1516), and the Marīnid-Waṭṭāsid dynasties in the western bilād al-maghrib (Morocco, 1269–1510). All three successor dynasties to the Almohad empire claimed to be legal heirs to the Almohad empire and tried to impose their own paramount rule over the bilād al-maghrib.

In Tunisia, the Ḥafsid dynasty, which traced its legacy to ʿAbd al-Wāḥid (d. 1221), a son of Abū Ḥafs ʿUmar, Ibn Tūmart's closest companion, who had been appointed governor of Ifrīqiyya in 1207, first claimed hegemony over the bilād al-maghrib. In contrast to earlier dynasties such as the Fāṭimids, Almoravids, and Almohads, as well as other dynasties such as the Zayyānids and the Marīnids, the Ḥafsid rulers of Tunisia, far removed from their tribal basis among the Maṣmūda of the Moroccan Atlas Mountains, no longer relied on the support of a single privileged tribal federation, but rather strove to form coalitions of local tribal groups of different origins, including a large number of Muslim refugees from al-Andalus. Despite (or because of) this structural difference, the Ḥafsid dynasty survived considerably longer than any other dynasty in the bilād al-maghrib, from 1207 to 1574, almost 370 years, and resisted not only two Marīnid invasions in 1347 and 1357 but also the crusade of King Louis IX of France in 1270. The Ḥafsids were initially able to unite the eastern and central bilād al-maghrib under Sulṭān Abū Zakariyyā Yaḥyā (r. 1229–1249) and his successor al-Mustanṣir (r. 1249–1277). Under their rule, Tunis became a major city in the bilād al-maghrib and even emerged, after the fall of Baghdad to the Mongols in 1258, as the paramount political center of the Islamic world until Cairo took this role under the Mamlūks in the late thirteenth century. After the death of Sulṭān al-Mustanṣir, Ḥafsid power collapsed and European states such as Aragon took control over the coasts of Tunisia. In the mid-fourteenth century, the Marīnid sulṭāns of Morocco conquered Tunisia twice for a short period of time, yet from the 1360s Tunisia recovered and the Ḥafsids repulsed both Marīnid and European encroachment. In the fifteenth century, the Ḥafsid rulers of Tunisia were able to regain control over Algeria, yet suffered another crisis in the late fifteenth century. In 1574, Tunis came under the control of the Ottoman empire which already controlled Algiers (from 1546), Egypt (from 1517), and Tripoli (from 1551), and thus all of the bilād al-maghrib except Morocco.

In the central Maghrib, the Zayyānid dynasty, supported by a number of Zanāta groups, in particular the Banū ʿAbd al-Wād and the Maghrāwa, established an independent state with a capital city in Tilimsān, later Algiers, yet had major difficulties in standing up against both the Marīnid dynasty and Ḥafsid territorial claims. Despite a short period of expansion between the 1260s and the 1330s, when the Zayyānid dynasty, supported by Aragon, managed to gain control over the central Saharan trade routes, the Zayyānid realm shrank vastly in size due to numerous Ḥafsid and Marīnid invasions. In the early fifteenth century, the Zayyānid dynasty eventually had to recognize the paramount position of the Ḥafsid rulers of Tunis. In 1516, a first Ottoman fleet landed in Algiers and established Ottoman rule, which was to last until 1830, when France invaded Algeria. The example of the Zayyānid dynasty shows most clearly that dynasties in the bilād al-maghrib were often unable to exert more than fluctuating control over the territories they claimed. Vast regions escaped central control for long periods of time (see map 11).

In Morocco, the Banū Marīn, another Zanāta group, was able to replace the Almohad dynasty and to establish their own power over major parts of the country, although this effort took from the 1240s to the 1270s. After defeating the Zayyānid state in Algeria (for the first time) in 1337 and occupying Tunis in 1347 (and again in 1357), Sulṭān Abū l-Ḥasan (r. 1331–1351) and his son Abū ʿInān (r. 1351–1358) were even able to establish Marīnid control over the central and eastern bilād al-maghrib for a short period of time. Marīnid control over the Maghrib quickly collapsed, however, after the death of Abū 'Inān in 1358. In the late fourteenth and early fifteenth centuries Marīnid rule over Morocco disintegrated completely and was eventually replaced, in 1420, by a new dynasty, related to the Marīnids, the Waṭṭāsids from the Rīf region in northern Morocco. The Waṭṭāsids were unable, however, to unite Morocco and to organize resistance against an increasing Portuguese presence on Morocco's coasts (Portugal had taken the port city of Sabta/Ceuta in 1415). Yet the Waṭṭāsids tried to increase their legitimacy as tribal rulers of Morocco by creating a trans-temporal link to the first Moroccan dynasty, the Idrīsids. These efforts were encouraged by the miraculous discovery of the tomb of Mawlay Idrīs, the founder of the Idrīsid dynasty, in Fes in 1437. Still, the Waṭṭāsids were not able to stop Portuguese encroachment and had to increasingly rely on the support of urban notables (Arab. a'yān) and the shurafā', the descendants of the Prophet. As a result, the autonomy of the urban centers was strengthened, and so was the position of the shurafā' and of the notables as social groups and political players. Political power was mediated by the shurafā' in the urban centers and by Sufi scholars in the rural regions. In the end, the task of rebuilding Morocco was assumed by a dynasty of Sufi scholars from the Sūs valley in southern Morocco, the Ṣa'dids, who took power in Morocco in 1510 and were able to defend Morocco, in the sixteenth century, against Ottoman expansion in the bilād al-maghrib and to revive the trans-Saharan trade.

Major factors affecting the crisis of the successor states of the Almohad empire, and their respective failure to unite the bilād al-maghrib, were not only their internal disputes and wars, but also a series of devastating plague pandemics which hit Egypt and the bilād al-maghrib (as well as Europe) from 1347. According to Dols, the fourteenth-century plague pandemics led to the death of at least one-quarter of the population (Dols 1977: 218) and triggered a serious economic crisis. Whole regions were depopulated and tax income was vastly reduced, as agricultural production dropped, hunger spread, and irrigation systems were neglected. The devastating effects of the plague epidemics in the fourteenth century were recorded by the famous Maghribinian historian Ibn Khaldūn (d. 1406) in his *muqaddima:*

> This was the situation until, in the middle of the eighth (fourteenth) century, civilization both in the East and the West was visited by a destructive plague (al-ṭā'ūn) which devastated nations and caused populations to vanish. It swallowed up many of the good things of civilization (al-'umrān) and wiped them out. It overtook dynasties at the time of their senility, when they had reached the limit of their duration. It lessened their power and curtailed their influence. It weakened their authority. Their situation approached the point of annihilation and dissolution. Civilization decreased with the decrease of mankind. Cities and buildings were laid waste, roads and way signs were obliterated, settlements and mansions became empty, dynasties and tribes grew weak and the whole world changed (. . . *Wa-ḍa'ufat al-duwal wa-l-qabā'il wa-tabaddala al-sākin;* Ibn Khaldūn, *muqaddima*, 33, trans. Rosenthal 1967: 30).

> After the demise of the Marīnid, Waṭṭāsid, Zayyānid, and Ḥafsid dynasties, major parts of the bilād al-maghrib came under Ottoman control (Tripoli in 1551, Tunis in 1574, Algiers first in 1516 and finally in 1546). Only Morocco escaped Ottoman control and managed to consolidate its hegemony over the western bilād al-maghrib under the Ṣaʿdid dynasty (in the sixteenth and early seventeenth centuries) and the ʿAlawid dynasty (from the mid-seventeenth century to the present day). Under Sulṭān Aḥmad al-Manṣūr (r. 1576–1603), Morocco gained control over Timbuktu and Jenné on the Niger. Under Sulṭān Mawlay Ismāʿīl (r. 1672–1727), Morocco achieved control over major parts of the Western Sahara and forced the Ottoman empire to finally recognize Morocco's independence. The Ottoman dominion in Algeria was governed by a dey and a number of subordinate beys in the provinces of Oran, Tittari, and Constantine. These Ottoman officials sought to consolidate Ottoman control over the vast hinterland regions of Algeria through the mediation of tribal authorities or Sufi leaders (until the French conquest in 1830). In Tunisia, Ottoman governors and army officers followed each other in quick succession until one family of deys, the Ḥusaynids, managed to gain control over Tunis in 1705. The Ḥusaynids ruled Tunisia until 1881, when Tunisia became a French Protectorate. In Tripoli, an Ottoman army officer, Aḥmad Qaramanlı, assumed supreme command in 1711 and established a family dynasty that ruled Tripolis until 1834, when the Ottoman empire resumed control (until 1911, when Italy invaded Tripolitania and forced the Ottoman empire to abandon its possessions in North Africa).

In Egypt alone, tax income dropped from 9.5 million dinār in 1347 to 1.8 million dinār in 1517. While the 1347/48 bubonic plague pandemic was a devastating but singular event for most parts of Europe, the bubonic plague remained endemic in North Africa and continued to haunt Egypt and the bilād al-maghrib until the nineteenth century. Between 1347 and 1517, Egypt alone saw twenty-eight further outbreaks of bubonic plague and the bilād al-maghrib suffered similar experiences: Tunisia, for instance, saw five plague epidemics in the seventeenth century, Morocco witnessed ten epidemics between 1500 and 1800, and five were recorded for Algeria and three for Tunisia in the eighteenth century. The last major plague pandemic devastated the bilād al-maghrib in 1818–1820. And while plague epidemics lost their devastating character in the nineteenth century, epidemics of cholera and smallpox led to major losses in population in the nineteenth century, even if these new pandemics had not the devastating character of the plague. Plague and other epidemics caused long-term stagnation in population development: only in the nineteenth century did the populations of Egypt and the bilād al-maghrib reach pre-1347 numbers again.

Bilād al-Makhzan and Bilād al-Sība

The collapse of the Fāṭimid, Almoravid, and Almohad empires and their successor states not only brought the history of large empires in the Maghrib to an end (the efforts of the Ottomans to gain control over the bilād al-maghrib in the sixteenth century misfired due to the successful resistance of the Ṣa'did dynasty in Morocco), but also showed that the political history of the bilād al-maghrib was characterized by yet another structural feature, namely the dynamics of center-periphery relations. The political history of both the large empires and of the later dynasties was characterized by the fact that central administrations, ruled by a sulṭān, a king (Arab. mālik) or an emir (Arab. amīr), not only tried to gain maximum control over the central lands of the respective dynasty, namely those lands which paid taxes into the treasury and were called the bilād al-makhzan ("the lands of the treasury"), but also to gain control over the peripheral regions which escaped efforts at taxation. Although these peripheral regions did not necessarily reject the sovereignty of a ruler, they were regarded as lands where cattle (and people) roamed freely, without a herdsman, as "bilād al-sība." In times of crisis, strong peripheries could exert pressure on the center and squeeze the imperial "sponge" to a small territorial core, perhaps even take control over the center and establish a new dynasty. In times of strength, by contrast, a dynasty could inflate the sponge and gain control over its peripheries. John Waterbury has described this process by looking at the example of Morocco:

> The bilād al-makhzan was never clearly delineated from the bilād al-sība, the one blended into the other according to relative degrees of submissiveness or defiance on the part of the tribes. It was not uncommon to find islands of submissiveness in seas of defiance and vice versa. This interminable process determined the very nature of the makhzan, which was never fixed in one place but wandered continuously along the perimeters of a triangle described by the major garrison cities of Fez, Meknes, Rabat, and Marrakesh. (Waterbury 1970: 20)

The bilād al-makhzan and the bilād al-sība should thus not be seen as lands loyal to a ruler and lands in rebellion, but rather as fluctuating spaces, sometimes under the control of a central authority, sometimes not, depending on the historical strength of the center or the success of the peripheral regions in escaping control while at the same time accepting the theoretical sovereignty of a ruler. But while the bilād al-sība escaped the control of the urban rulers, they were not devoid of order: tribal leaders and elders continued to rule their folk and herds and were accepted as supreme political leaders of their respective communities. Conflicts between families, clans, and tribal groups which could not be resolved by the elders had to be resolved by other means, though. In this context, the Sufi scholars mentioned above increasingly acquired the status of local and regional intermediaries. They gained acceptance as religious scholars, teachers, imāms, and healers, as well as judges and mediators in disputes that were eventually accepted by all, as feuds could lead to disaster and the death of many. As a consequence, religious scholars, often Sufi scholars and saints, acquired a major religious and political significance in the development of the bilād al-maghrib from the thirteenth century onward, and have retained their importance as "multi-functional" leaders of their communities well into the twentieth century.

The "model of the marabout" that gradually developed in the bilād al-maghrib was transmitted by traders, networks of students and teachers, and also regional shrine pilgrimages into the oases of the Sahara and eventually the bilād al-sūdān to the south. The importance of the bilād al-sība, the lands beyond the control of a sulṭān, for the history of the bilād al-maghrib led Ibn Khaldūn to develop a theoretical concept of the political history of the larger region. This concept was based on the assumption that rebellion and opposition often found initial support among the mountain and desert tribes, which eventually defeated the rulers of the cities, to establish a new dynasty, which rose and fell in a cycle of three generations to be replaced by a new movement of rebels. The concept of the bilād al-makhzan and the bilād al-sība has been so convincing that it was essentialized as a model to explain Maghribinian history. This is misleading, however, as it ignores the fact that center-periphery relations have informed the political histories of many regions of the world and have produced similar patterns of development.

3 The Sahara as Connective Space

Historical Themes and Patterns

In both North African history and the history of sub-Saharan Africa, the Sahara has been seen as a geographical, political, and economic periphery. As a result, the Sahara and its populations have been presented as forming merely an extension of either the bilād al-maghrib or the bilād al-sūdān. This perspective neglects the fact that the Sahara has been a major connective space and has been as such an intrinsic part of the economic systems of both the bilād al-maghrib and the bilād al-sūdān. Due to these entanglements, the Sahara cannot be seen as an isolated backwater of world history and economics. The economic importance of the Sahara and its trade routes in fact has been so important for the bilād al-maghrib and the bilād al-sūdān that the rulers in the north and the south have repeatedly tried to gain control over the Sahara and trans-Saharan trade routes. Consequently, knowledge of trade and trade routes, wells, oases, and terrain was of paramount importance and collected eagerly. At the same time, knowledge was withheld as far as possible from possible competitors, especially European nations and traders. Over a long history of more than a thousand years, trans-Saharan movement led to the emergence of major centers of trade such as Agadez in the Ahīr (Aïr) Mountains or Timbuktu on the Niger. In these centers of trade, Muslim scholars developed traditions of Islamic learning, which contributed to the development of Islamic learning in the bilād al-maghrib and the bilād al-sūdān. Rather than seeing the Sahara as a periphery, the Sahara and its various populations should thus be perceived as a major region in its own right that has survived and repeatedly denied efforts to impose outside control.

The Trans-Saharan Trade

The Sahara, the great desert, stretching from the Atlantic to the Red Sea and from the Atlas Mountains and Mediterranean coast to the edges of the bilād al-sūdān in the south, has often been depicted as a great divide, separating North Africa from sub-Saharan Africa. This has been far from the truth for most of the time. In reality, the Sahara has been one of the world's major connective spaces, crisscrossed by trading routes and dotted with numerous smaller or larger oases which made the crossing of the Sahara with an experienced guide a fairly uncomplicated undertaking. The major problem involved in crossing the Sahara was of a logistic nature: the central question was which route would sustain a caravan of which size in which season of the year. Not all oases would yield the water to supply a caravan of several thousand camels and a corresponding number of men (and women). Sometimes, caravans might choose a longer route when rainfall had produced good pastures in a specific region. The bigger the distances between watering places, the more water and fodder had to be transported by the caravan itself, to the detriment of trade goods. Supply of water and fodder, distances between watering places, and annual variations thus largely defined the size of caravans. In addition, there was the problem of recurrent feuding and raiding in the Sahara, often over the control of oases and caravan routes. Correspondingly, the knowledge as to which route would be best at which time of the year was crucial. Crossing the Sahara following one of the major routes was possible as soon as camels had been introduced into the Sahara and were raised by Saharan (often Imasighen/Tuareg, later also Arab) populations. There were a number of major routes and many smaller routes and their branches (see map 4).

The westernmost route collected the trade from southern Morocco, both the Sūs region and the Wādī Dar'a and their respective centers, Aghmāt and Sijilmāsa, as well as the Wādī Nūn region. It ran south at a distance of about 300–400 kilometers from the arid coasts of the Atlantic, until reaching the western Saharan Ādrār region and the oases of Shinqīṭ and Wadān. From here, trade either went west to the Atlantic, where the Portuguese created a trading post, Arguin, south of Cabo Blanco in 1455; or south, to reach the northern towns of Ghāna (later Mālī), namely Awdaghust, Tīshīt, and Walāta. According to the Arab geographer Ibn Ḥawqal, the journey on this route of approximately 1,400 kilometers took about two months. The long-distance trade on this westernmost route, though not the regional trade, collapsed in the late fifteenth century when European ships started to transport bulky goods on the Atlantic faster and cheaper than caravans: "Wherever the caravans competed directly with European shipping, they lost out and found their trading position considerably diminished" (Austen 1990: 313). Yet the logistic advantage that caravels and, later, the Iberian, Dutch, French, or British "galeones" had on the Atlantic did not extend to the central or eastern Mediterranean and the central or eastern Saharan trade routes: Tunis could already be reached faster by caravan from Timbuktu than by Portuguese caravels, which had to sail out into the mid-Atlantic to catch trade winds that brought them back to the Iberian peninsula, and then still had to make their way into the central Mediterranean.

From the southeastern Moroccan Tāfīlālt valley and its center of trade, Sijilmāsa, which collected the trade from central and northern Morocco, another important western route led to the oasis of Tuwāt, which constituted a link to the central Saharan trade routes and to the trade of the central bilād al-maghrib. The oases of Tuwāt stretched for a distance of 500 kilometers and provided an abundant supply of water and fodder. They consequently became a major hub of trans-Saharan trade. From Tuwāt, it was possible to fork out on a western route which led to the salt mines of Taghāzā (later, Tawdenni) and to continue west of the waterless Tanīzruft desert to the Azawād region and its center, Arawān, just north of the River Niger and its major

Sailing on the Atlantic changed character after the development of the caravel, in 1439/1440, by the Portuguese. The caravel was a comparatively small ship of about 100 tons which had a main mast with square sails as well as a foremast and a mizzen mast equipped with triangular lateen sails. The combination of Atlantic square sail rigging and Mediterranean lateen rigging gave caravels both speed and agility. Square sails could be moved quickly and horizontally on spars around the mast and allowed the crew to cruise easily, while lateen rigging allowed caravels to sail fast and hard against the wind. Lateen sails, in contrast, were difficult to handle due to their size, and the fact that the sail on its beam rested on one side of the mast only meant that lateen-rigged ships had "bad tack." In 1434, Portuguese ships reached Cape Bojador, southeast of the Canary Islands on the Saharan coast. Beyond Cape Bojador, prevalent northern winds as well as a strong southbound current made return on the Atlantic Coast impossible. With the caravel, the Portuguese could continue down the coast and then sail out into the mid-Atlantic until they caught trade winds that brought them back to the Iberian Peninsula via the Azores. In 1441, the Portuguese reached Cabo Blanco, about 500 kilometers north of the River Senegal and in 1444 Cap Vert. The introduction of the caravel enabled the Portuguese to sail around the Cape of Good Hope in 1498 and to quickly gain control over the Indian Ocean, where lateen-rigged dhows had no chance to compete with the highly maneuverable caravels.

entrepôts, Timbuktu and Gao (Kawkaw). An eastern branch would reach the Aïr Mountains and its centers, Agadez and Takedda, and then branch out again to either Gao on the Niger or the Hausa cities in the south. This route of 2,200–2,400 kilometers took between eighty and ninety days at an average traveling speed of about 35 kilometers a day for an average caravan, and was one of the most frequented routes.

The central Sahara was crossed by two major routes: central and eastern Algerian trade would go to the northern Saharan oasis of al-Aghwāt, then move south to the central trading place in the Mzab region, Ghardaia. From Ghardaia, one could either go west and reach Tuwāt and then proceed south to the Niger; or one could move on to Wārqala and then join a southeastern route which linked Wārqala with Ghadāmis. From Ghadāmis, caravans would follow a southern route to Ghāt, and subsequently pass through the Aïr Mountains to the urban centers of Hausaland, such as Katsina or Kano, a route of approximately 2,000 kilometers. Wārqala also collected the trade from eastern Algeria through Biskra and Tuqqurt, as well as southern Tunisia, through Nafta, and thus has to be considered as another major hub of the trans-Saharan trade.

Trade from southern Tunisia and Tripoli would go to Ghadāmis directly and then continue to Ghāt, which again provided a link with the oases of Fazzān in the east and was another important trade junction. This route had a length of about 1,800 kilometers.

Another major central trans-Saharan route was the network of routes linking Tripoli and Cyrenaika with the oases of the Fazzān and its center, Zawīla, from where caravans could either go to Ghāt and then continue south through the Hoggar (Ahaggar) mountains to Gao or Takedda/Agadez (and thus, ultimately, Hausaland), or go south directly across the Djado plateau and then on to the oases of Kawār and Bilma and from there to Kānim-Bornu and Lake Chad. This was a comparatively short and well-provided route of about 1,800 kilometers. According to al-Bakrī, the journey south from Zawīla could be done in forty days (stages) only (. . . *Wa-baina zawīla wa-balad kānim arba'ūna marḥala*, al-Bakrī 1992, 2: 658).

Further east, a route linked Benghasi and the Cyrenaika region in the north through Awjila (Jālū) with the oasis of Kufra and then continued south to Wadai. This route took sixty to seventy days and was developed in the nineteenth century only. It had a length of about 1,500 kilometers but it did not touch on any major oases, except Kufra in the north.

Probably the shortest route through the Sahara was the famous darb al-arba'īn, the "path of forty days" (about 1,400 kilometers) between northeastern Dārfūr and Asyūṭ in Upper Egypt, where goods would be reloaded onto boats cruising on the Nile.

All trans-Saharan routes were interconnected by east-west links and branched out to other harbor cities on the northern and southern shores (Arab. sāḥil) of the Sahara. The Fazzān, for instance, was linked by the oasis of Awjila and Sīwa with Egypt in the northeast and by the oases of Djado, Bilma, and Fashi with Kānim-Bornu in the south. It was equally possible to cross from the Fazzān to Ghāt and then to continue to Hausaland (via Agadez/Takedda) or, via the central Saharan Ādrār mountains and its commercial center, Tādmakka (Essuk) to the Niger in the south. However, these routes passed through stretches of desert without wells and oases, such as the Tanīzruft, which separated the western Ādrār from both the central Ādrār and the Hoggar mountains, or the Ténéré, which separated the Aïr region from the Tibesti mountains and the oasis of Bilma in the east.

The large trans-Saharan caravans, the so-called akābār ("biggest ones") which counted several thousand camels, left the northern sāḥil in the cool winter months (November or December) and arrived in the southern sāḥil after a trip of about two months. They then engaged in trade and started back north before the onset of the rainy season in the south (May), to arrive in the northern sāḥil by July or August, in time to recover before the next crossing. Smaller caravans (Arab. qawāfil, sing. qāfila) could be more flexible, but also sought to leave the southern sāḥil before the onset of the rains. In the northern and southern port cities of the Sahara, the goods that had been transported on the backs of camels had to be unloaded, not only for reasons of taxation and the payment of custom fees, but also due to the fact that camels could not go much beyond the great rivers of the south. Sleeping sickness would kill camels quickly. Equally, malaria was a problem for the Arab and Imasighen traders from the north. Also, riverboats were a cheaper and quicker way of transporting goods up and down the River Niger than camels. Again the boat proved to be more viable in economic terms than the camel in regions where boat and camel competed. Transport of goods on boats on the River Niger was in fact six times more effective and less costly than the transport of these goods in caravans: a single boat could transport 20–30 tons of freight as well as 16–18 people, and thus the same amount of goods as a caravan of 200 camels, assuming an average load of 100–150 kilograms per camel. Equally, camels were not competitive in the rugged and mountainous areas of the bilād al-maghrib in the north. Here, donkeys and horses were employed to transport goods from the northern Saharan market places to the port cities on the shores of the Mediterranean.

In the southern ports of the Mediterranean such as Algiers, Tunis, or Tripoli, ships from Spanish or Italian cities like Barcelona, Marseilles, Genoa, Pisa, Naples, Bari, or Venice loaded the goods which had come across the Sahara and the Atlas Mountains and shipped them to northern Mediterranean ports where goods had to be unloaded, taxed and reloaded again, this time onto horses, donkeys, and ox-carts, and, at least on the Rhone and Rhine, onto riverboats and barges. Goods which went even further north, from Venice via Passau, Linz, Regensburg, or Nuremberg to Prague and Görlitz, eventually reached the southern ports of the Baltic Sea, such as Lübeck, Rostock, or Wismar, where they were reloaded onto ships that crossed the Baltic to final destinations in Scandinavia. In contrast, goods that had been unloaded in Timbuktu in the south continued their journey on boats on the Niger and eventually reached destinations on the upper or lower Niger, where they had to be reloaded onto smaller boats or (mostly) donkey and oxen caravans, to be transported into the tropical forests of the Guinea coast, where goods from the north were exchanged for the major product of the south: gold.

The major driving force for trade on all these different legs of trans-Saharan trade was scarcity of specific products which had to be imported to serve regional needs and to cater to regional "sinks" of demand. The bilād al-sūdān had no major salt mines, and sea salt could be gained by solar evaporation on the coasts of the Atlantic south of the Gambia River to a limited extent only, as frequent rains and cloudy skies prevented sufficient evaporation. The bilād al-sūdān of sub-Saharan West Africa thus were a sink in terms of salt and had to import salt in exchange for other goods. The western and central bilād al-sūdān, in contrast, had access to gold and could exchange gold for salt from the Saharan oases: Regional complementarities were, thus, equally important to provide markets with goods. In addition to gold, the bilād al-sūdān exported ivory, slaves, hides, and tanned leather (which was important for the production of books), as well as gum Arabic (Arab. 'ilk), which came to be used as glue or as a basic substance for the production of perfumes, but which was also important for the production of a long-lasting ink. Regional sinks such as the bilād al-sūdān in terms of salt thus drove the dynamics of exchange that kept trans-Saharan trade alive for more than 1,000 years.

Other goods that were traded on the routes across the Sahara were weapons, guns, gunpowder, armory, different types of textiles, spices, books and paper, glass in different forms, iron and copperware, brass, horses, dates and grain (wheat; in small quantities for luxury use in the urban centers of the bilād al-sūdān), cowry shells, which were an important form of local currency in the bilād al-sūdān, probably from the eleventh century onward, and, from the early nineteenth century, green tea, which (in combination with respective imports of sugar) led to the creation of a "green tea (consumption) zone" (Lydon 2009: 397) stretching from the bilād al-maghrib across the Sahara to the western bilād al-sūdān. The trade in paper and books (manuscripts), which can be documented from a very early period, seems to have boomed from the fourteenth century onward, which not only attests to the growth of Islamic learning in the Sahara and sub-Saharan Africa, but also led to the development of private libraries, which came to constitute a major form of investment in cultural capital. Due to the prevailing dry climatic conditions in the Sahara and the southern sāḥil, manuscripts could be conserved over a long period of time, and numerous private libraries in places such as Timbuktu reflect long traditions of Islamic learning and writing. Due to the entangled nature of the different legs of the trade, all partners were interdependent, even if they had no direct knowledge of each other: trade routes and their logistics were kept confidential and not revealed to outsiders. Not many trading networks, trading houses, families, or companies were able to master more than one leg of the trade and its respective logistic demands: thus, in the Middle Ages, the Hanse cities in the north controlled a major part of the trade with Scandinavian countries, the Baltic Sea and northern Germany, but never managed to venture further south. Equally, some trading houses in the bilād al-maghrib managed to span the Sahara and had representatives on both the northern and the southern shores of the Sahara, but not beyond.

A famous example for trans-Saharan trade links was the Maqarrī family from Tilimsān in Algeria. In the thirteenth century, five brothers reorganized the trade from Sijilmāsa via the Taghāzā salt mines to Walāta in the south, by redeveloping wells which had been filled in by sand storms. They hired local guides and made sure that wells were maintained. Two brothers were in charge of the central trading house in Tilimsān, which was conveniently close to the shores of the Mediterranean, yet at a safe distance from the coast and possible raids of pirates or invaders. In Tilimsān, they bought goods from Jewish North African and European traders and sent them on the first leg of the trade route to the northern Saharan port of Sijilmāsa, where a third brother organized the southbound caravans. In Sijilmāsa, the third brother collected information on the development of prices and demand, as well as the situation in the bilād al-sūdān, and was able to dispatch caravans to destinations in the bilād al-sūdān correspondingly. Two other Maqarrī brothers were based in Walāta, an important city at the southern end of this route. They were in charge of the sale or reloading and transport of goods to other destinations. Equally, they organized the northbound caravans and cultivated contacts with the emperors of Mālī, who were the rulers of this region of the bilād al-sūdān at that period of time.

Trans-Saharan trade did not stop at the northern or southern shores of the Sahara, though. Both the bilād al-maghrib in the north and the bilād al-sūdān in the south were transmission belts for trade further north or south. By means of Mediterranean shipping, gold from the bilād al-sūdān reached the northern port cities of the Mediterranean and subsequently central and northern Europe, as well as the eastern port cities in Egypt and the Levant, in particular Byzantium, which acted as a transmission belt for the trade in (mostly eastern European) slaves, wood, and pelts. Goods from Europe or the Levant reached destinations in the bilād al-sūdān and further south by way of the trans-Saharan routes, probably from the ninth or tenth centuries onward. The trans-Saharan trade extended beyond the bilād al-sūdān to the lands on the Guinea coast further south. The major gold mining regions, Bambuk on the Upper Senegal and Falémé, Bure, on the Upper Niger and Tinkasso, Lobi, on the Upper Volta, and Asante in the hinterland of the Guinea Coast were in fact located in the southern zones of the bilād al-sūdān. Thus, they were not only beyond the control of the northern trade networks, but were also beyond the control of the empire of Ghāna, whereas Mālī and Songhay probably controlled Bambuk and Bure only.

While the trading empires in the western bilād al-sūdān (Ghāna, Mālī, Songhay) essentially relied on the export of gold and other trade goods to finance imports from the north, the central bilād al-sūdān (Kānim-Bornu, in particular) specialized in the export of slaves from an early period, due to the absence of gold fields in this part of sub-Saharan West Africa. The central bilād al-sūdān probably entered the trans-Saharan slave trade in the tenth century, while slaves became a major (but not the only) export item in the western bilād al-sūdān in the twelfth and thirteenth centuries. From the sixteenth century, raids into the southern slave-hunting peripheries provided Sudanese states from the Atlantic to the Red Sea (including Ethiopia and the empire of Sinnār-Funj on the Nile) with slaves which could be used as a commodity in the trade in the means of destruction (Roberts 1987: 9), namely guns and horses, that were necessary to maintain a court, an army, and an empire. Both the western and the central bilād al-sūdān knew peak periods in the trans-Saharan slave trade, such as the late sixteenth and early seventeenth centuries for the region of the middle Niger River, as well as slack periods, and in both regions the trans-Saharan slave trade ended later than the transatlantic slave trade, extending well into the late nineteenth century. Due to lack of sources, however, it is not possible to quantify the size of the trans-Saharan slave trade over the centuries. Existing calculations have to be regarded as highly speculative. Most slaves were walked north and ended, in fact, in Saharan and North African salt mines and oases. Others were recruited into the armies of North African rulers, such as Mawlay Ismāʿīl in Morocco (r. 1672–1727), while still others were sent east to Egypt and Syria, or ended as house slaves in the households of rich traders in North African cities, where they were employed as manual workers or were put into a ḥarām as concubines. Mawlay Ismāʿīl of Morocco became notorious for building an army of 150,000 black slaves in the late seventeenth century. These slaves came mostly from the pashālik of Timbuktu, which had been conquered by Morocco in 1591, and point to considerable slave trading from the middle Niger to Morocco at this time.

Slave raiding and the transport of slaves to the ocean as well as across the Sahara have to be considered as major factors for proper calculation of the true size and impact of the trans-Saharan and the transatlantic slave trade. According to Inikori (1982: 27), only two out of three slaves survived the transport and many people died in slave raids. Slave raiding also led to increasing insecurity in many regions of the bilād al-sūdān and tropical West Africa as well as the Nile Sudan from the sixteenth century. The increasing Islamization of the bilād al-sūdān and the fact that Islamic law prohibited the enslavement of Muslims (but not the institution of slavery as such) eventually motivated Muslim scholars, such as Aḥmad Bābā al-Tinbuktī (1555–1627), to write a number of legal opinions (Arab. fatāwa) on the legality of acquiring slaves from the bilād al-sūdān. In his treatise *Miʿrāj al-ṣuʿūd ilā nayl ḥukm mujallab al-sūd* (The ladder of ascent toward grasping the law concerning transported blacks), written in Moroccan exile, Aḥmad Bābā defined the territories of Islam in the bilād al-sūdān, where enslavement would be illegal, and the territories of non-Muslim rulers in the bilād al-sūdān where people could still be enslaved. His text which was based on a legal treatise of another scholar from Timbuktu, Makhlūf b. ʿAlī b. Ṣāliḥ al-Balbālī (d. 1533/1534), reflected the fact that many regions in the bilād al-sūdān, due to the fact that ruling dynasties claimed to be Muslim, had formally become Muslim by the sixteenth century.

The development of trans-Saharan trade across its different legs had repercussions on the economic, social, and political welfare of trading networks: when gold mines on the Guinea coast were cut off from markets further north by a political crisis in the bilād al-sūdān, the whole route was affected. Similar crises could occur when routes became unsafe due to raids by Saharan tribes, or when an economic crisis in Spain or Venice led to the collapse of demand on one of the European legs of the trade. Crises in the north and the south thus affected the trans-Saharan trade and could lead to a temporary or lasting demise of important centers of the trade. As control over trade promised large profit margins, the empires of both the bilād al-maghrib and bilād al-sūdān tried to control as many trading centers and trading routes as possible, and may consequently be called trading empires. The political, social, and economic stability of these trading empires was linked with the fate of the other legs of the respective trade route: when the raids of the Banū Hilāl in southern Tunisia, Tripolitania, and Fazzān ruined trade on the central Saharan routes from the mid-eleventh century, the Almoravid empire stabilized the trade routes in the western Sahara. The partners of the Almoravids and, later, the Almohads in the western bilād al-sūdān profited correspondingly. Both Takrūr and Ghāna, and later the empire of Mālī, were directly linked with west Saharan trade routes. In the mid-thirteenth century the trade from the bilād al-sūdān started to shift, however, from western routes to central routes, due to the collapse of the Almohad empire and subsequent political instability in the western bilād al-maghrib. At the same time, Egypt experienced a period of economic boom yet suffered from the fact that an important source of supply of gold for Egypt, namely the mines in Wadi ʿAllaqī in northern Nubia, had dried up. The gold from the Bambuk and Bure gold mines on the Upper Niger, as traded by the empire of Mālī across the Sahara from Timbuktu via Agadez and the Fazzān to Awjila and Sīwa, thus found a new sink in Egypt, and central Saharan trade routes profited correspondingly.

In the mid-fourteenth century, the crisis of the west Saharan trade routes was enhanced by the failure of the Marīnid dynasty to gain permanent control over the central and eastern bilād al-maghrib, and the realm of the Zayyānid dynasty in particular, which controlled access to the central Saharan trade routes. The fact that the Marīnid rulers Abū l-Ḥasan (r. 1331–1351) and Abū ʿInān (r. 1351–1358) entered into an intensive exchange of royal missions with the empire of Mālī reflect Marīnid geopolitical interests at this time:

> The interest which Abū l-Ḥasan and Abū ʿInān showed in the affairs of Mali at the time of their conquest of the central and eastern Maghrib suggests that their military expansion was related to the trans-Saharan trade. Through incorporating in their state the territories ruled by the Zayyānids and the Ḥafsids, they would not only become the rulers of a powerful Maghribi empire that could militarily withstand Christian threats; they would also take control of the extensive trade connections which these rulers had developed with the Sudan and Europe. In this way they could secure an important source of wealth and extensive means of exerting diplomatic pressure on the Christian states, especially Castile and Aragon. (Abun-Nasr 1987: 112)

The Marīnid failure to achieve these political aims not only contributed to the subsequent demise of the Marīnid dynasty and its successor, the Waṭṭāsid dynasty, in the fifteenth century, but also to the weakening of their Malian counterparts in the south and the subsequent rise of the Songhay empire in the mid-fifteenth century, which was located further east, at the southern termini of the central Saharan trade routes, in particular, Gao.

The rising importance of the central Saharan routes from the fifteenth century can be explained by a number of other factors: the Ḥafsid dynasty in Tunisia, which had emerged victorious from the confrontation with the Marīnids in Morocco, was forced, due to its own deficit regarding the production of grains, to import grain from Italy and the Ottoman empire. In 1455 alone, Tunisia imported 75,000 quintals of wheat from Sicily. These imports of grain as well as other European trade goods were financed with gold which Tunisia acquired in her trade with the Songhay empire in the bilād al-sūdān. Songhay imported gold from the Bambuk and Bure gold fields in the south by offering textiles and salt; Venice, at the other end of this trade route, used the Tunisian gold in order to finance its own deficit in the spice trade with Aleppo, Cairo, and Damascus. The size of this central and eastern Mediterranean trade, which linked the central Sahara and the central bilād al-sūdān with the Mediterranean, explains to some extent the stability of the Ḥafsid dynasty in Tunisia in the fifteenth century. The stability of Ḥafsid Tunisia was enhanced by the fact that the Ḥafsid dynasty was able to expand into the realm of the Zayyānid dynasty in the central bilād al-maghrib in this period of time and to consolidate its hold over this region and the respective trade networks.

At the same time, the Waṭṭāsid dynasty in Morocco suffered from a chronic economic crisis, triggered by the collapse of the western Saharan trade routes, which were unable to compete with the growing (European) trade on the Atlantic. Portuguese ships had reached the West African coast in 1441 and established their first trade post in Arguin in 1455, in São Joao da Mina (Elmina) in 1482. The decline of the Waṭṭāsid dynasty was enhanced by the fact that the Taghāzā salt mines in the northwestern Sahara became almost exhausted in the same period, while the mines of Tawdenni, which started to produce a major amount of Saharan salt in the sixteenth century, those of Ijīl in the western Sahara north of Wādān, as well as those of Tīshīt, twelve days northwest of Timbuktu, were beyond the reach of the Waṭṭāsids. The weakening of western Saharan trade contributed to the collapse of the Waṭṭāsid dynasty in Morocco in the mid-fifteenth century and to the rise of a new dynasty, the Ṣa'dids. In the late fifteenth century, under this dynasty, the cultivation of sugar cane as a new cash crop was developed in the region of Sūs in southern Morocco. This allowed Morocco to reenter international trade networks and to import modern arms from Europe. The Ṣa'did sulṭāns also used their increasing wealth to redevelop the western Saharan trade routes through Tuwāt to Timbuktu and to thereby reconnect with the gold exports from the bilād al-sūdān. The profits from this trade were used to finance the power politics of Sulṭān Aḥmad al-Manṣūr, to stop the westward advance of the Ottoman empire in the mid-sixteenth century, and to advance across the Sahara to the south.

The dynamics of economic interdependence were also valid for the southernmost leg of the trans-Saharan trade, namely the Guinea coast. As soon as European companies started to establish their trading houses on the Guinea coast and to attract the gold from the mines in the hinterland, offering goods from Mediterranean and western European markets (textiles, iron, weapons, glass, etc.), the flow of gold turned round in just a few years. Gold from the Bambuk and Bure gold mines, but also from Lobi (and later Asante), was redirected toward the European trade posts on the Guinea coast, instead of flowing, by mediation of the empire of Mālī and the west Saharan routes, to the western bilād al-maghrib. By 1447, the flow of gold from Guinea, which was soon labeled the Gold Coast, to Portugal had become so sizeable that Portugal was able to switch its currency, the Cruzado, to a gold standard. Between 1500 and 1520, Guinean gold exports attained an annual level of 700 kilograms of gold, and subsequently decreased in importance for European currencies only due to the increasing influx of gold and silver from American mines (Mexico, and later Peru) from the late 1520s. The redirection of gold exports from Guinea affected the fate of the major trading empire of the bilād al-sūdān, Mālī, which lost its mediating position almost completely in the mid-fifteenth century. Mālī's role as the major Sudanese trading empire was assumed by Songhay, which was situated in the central bilād al-sūdān and was not only untouched by the demise of the western trade routes but also controlled access to the central routes across the Sahara. Songhay's most important trading partner in the bilād al-maghrib was not the Waṭṭāsid dynasty in Morocco, though, but the Ḥafsid dynasty in Tunisia.

The history of the Sahara, as well as the history of the lands to the north and south of the Sahara, can thus be characterized as competition over control of the trans-Saharan trade routes, as well as the harbor cities of the north and south. At the same time, the fate of the trading empires was linked with the economic and political destiny of their respective trading partners in the next legs of the trade: a crisis in Venice affected the Venetian trade with Tunis and vice versa, and repercussions were felt by the partners of Tunis in the south (as well as those of Venice in the north). Traders and trading houses sought to escape the effects of crisis and usually tried to redirect their goods to other routes. Two major problems were associated with such endeavors: traders came into conflict with competing trade networks which controlled these other routes and wanted to keep control over and knowledge of them as exclusive as possible; in addition, both the prices of goods and the rent for transport camels rose due to growing distances and could reach levels at which trade was not profitable any more. Traders and trade networks were thus essentially interested in the long-term stability of trade routes and their port cities.

Knowledge Is Power: Arabic Sources on the Trans-Saharan Trade

Due to the importance of the trans-Saharan trade, and in particular the legendary amounts of gold that were exported from the western bilād al-sūdān, which helped to finance the budgets of entire empires, Arab geographers soon started to include chapters on these regions in their texts. Between the ninth and the seventeenth centuries, we can rely on at least seventy-five geographies-cum-itineraries of the bilād al-maghrib, the trans-Saharan trade routes and the bilād al-sūdān (as well as the Nile valley, Ethiopia, and East Africa), as documented by Cuoq, Hopkins/Levtzion, and Lewizki. A major feature of these descriptions of the world was detailed information on the exact position of trading centers and oases, the length of caravan routes and traveling times, that is, information on the logistics of the trade. The first Arab geographer who mentioned the bilād al-sūdān was al-Fazarī (fl. second half of the eighth century in Baghdad) in a text called *Kitāb al-zīj*. His report was adopted by a series of ninth-century geographers, like al-Khawārizmī (d. 846/7), Ibn ʿAbd al-Ḥakam (d. 871), and Abū l-Ḥasan ʿAlī al-Masʿūdī (d. 956), who mentioned for the first time Ghāna, "the land of gold dust," as well as the East African coast. The first account which gave a detailed presentation of the bilād al-sūdān was the *Kitāb al-buldān* by Aḥmad b. Abī Ya'qūb al-Ya'qūbī (d. 897), who mentioned the lands of Ghāna, Malal, Kawkaw (Gao), and Kānim (Zaghāwa). The more detailed nature of al-Ya'qūbī's text is due to the fact that the trans-Saharan trade had expanded quickly. Al-Ya'qūbī's text was followed by a number of further descriptions of the bilād al-sūdān which did not add much to existing knowledge. Only Abū l-Qāsim Muḥammad al-Nusaybī b. Ḥawqal (fl. late tenth century) added a detailed description of the bilād al-maghrib which he knew due to his own journeys. In his *Kitāb surāt al-arḍ* he provided a detailed description of the major north-Saharan port, Sijilmāsa. Ibn Ḥawqal estimated that the taxes paid by Sijilmāsa to the Fāṭimid caliph constituted half of the tax income of the bilād al-maghrib in the 970s, which were estimated to correspond to a sum of 800,000 dinār. Ibn Ḥawqal also mentioned that the journey across the Sahara to Awdaghust in the south, which he had accomplished personally in 951/952, took two months, and a further ten days to the capital city of Ghāna (Kumbi Saleh) for a light caravan.

The most detailed early description of the trans-Saharan trade as well as the bilād al-sūdān was compiled by the Arab geographer Abū 'Ubayd 'Abdallāh b. 'Abd al-'Azīz al-Bakrī (d. 1094 in Cordoba) in his *Kitāb al-masālik wa-l-mamālik* (publ. 1068). Al-Bakrī not only described the emergence of the Almoravid movement in the Sahara, but also mentioned the empire of Ghāna and other countries in the bilād al-sūdān, in particular Takrūr, an ally of the Almoravids against Ghāna. He wrote about Malal on the nīl ghāna (the Niger), whose king had converted to Islam under the influence of a Muslim scholar who had been able to end a terrible drought in his kingdom by praying for rain. With respect to Ghāna, al-Bakrī remarked that "Ghāna is unhealthy and scarcely populated and not good for health"; in particular during the rainy season (at the time of planting), "there are (many) deaths (epidemics) among foreigners" (*wa yaq'a al-mautān fī-ghurabā'hā 'aynda istiḥṣād al-zar'*, al-Bakrī 1992 2: 874), an early hint at the fact that sub-Saharan West Africa was highly insalubrious not only for Europeans but also for North African travelers. In 1154, Abū 'Abdallāh Muḥammad al-Idrīsī presented the next comprehensive account of the bilād al-sūdān in his book *Nuzhat al-mushtāq fi-ikhtirāq al-āfāq*, which essentially compiled all available information and updated these accounts. In his time, Ghāna still seems to have been a major political force in the bilād al-sūdān, and so was the Muslim kingdom of Takrūr on the Senegal. New information on the bilād al-sūdān was recorded by an Egyptian geographer, al-'Umarī (d. 1349), who, in his *Masālik al-abṣār fi-mamālik al-amṣār*, mentioned the downfall of Takrūr and Ghāna as well as the rise of Mālī, and in particular the pilgrimage of Mansā (king) Mūsa of Mālī.

The first North African Muslim geographer and scholar to actually visit the bilād al-sūdān was Shams al-Dīn Abū 'Abdallāh Muḥammad b. Baṭṭūṭa (d. 1368), who reached the bilād al-sūdān in 1352 in the context of a diplomatic mission for the Marīnid Sulṭān Abū 'Inān. The latter had tried to continue his father's efforts to unite the bilād al-maghrib under Marīnid rule and was keen to gain maximum control over the northern entrepôts of the trans-Saharan trade. Ibn Baṭṭūṭa's journey from Sijilmāsa to Walāta took fifty-five days, as recorded in his book *Tuḥfat al-nuẓẓār fī gharā'ib al-amṣār wa 'ajā'ib al-aṣfār,* or simply *Al-riḥla,* (The journey). Ibn Baṭṭūṭa's text was taken up later by the Maghribinian historian Ibn Khaldūn, as well as the last major traveler and chronicler before European times, al-Ḥasan b. Muḥammad al-Wazzānī al-Zayyātī al-Fāsī al-Gharnātī, alias Giovanni Leone alias Leo Africanus (d. 1552 in Tunis). Leo Africanus was taken prisoner in 1517 by Venetian pirates off the coast of Djerba and turned over, as a present, to Pope Leo X, but he was subsequently liberated by the pope under condition of his conversion to Christianity. In Italy, he composed a *Descrizione dell' Africa* which was published in 1550 on the basis of an earlier manuscript of 1526. According to Leo Africanus, who had visited Timbuktu and other places on the Niger in the context of two journeys between c. 1510 and 1514, Mālī had been replaced as the major trading empire in the bilād al-sūdān by Songhay (Gao), and the Askia (ruler) of Songhay had managed to conquer the trading cities of Hausaland, Kano, Katsina, Zaria, and Zamfara, while the eastern bilād al-sūdān were dominated by Bornu. In addition, Leo Africanus reported recurring epidemics of the plague, "every tenth, fifteenth or twentieth yeere" in the bilād al-maghrib, yet claims that the plague was rather scarce in "Numidia and in the land of Negros they know not the name of the disease." He also recorded the spread of a new disease, syphilis, the so-called Spanish (or French) pox from Spain into North Africa and Egypt, with devastating effects: "If any of Barbarie [i.e., Barbary, the colloquial European term for the bilād al-maghrib] be infected with the disease commonly called the French poxe, they die thereof for the most part, and are seldome cured" (Leo Africanus, trans. John Pory, 2010, vol. 1, 181–82).

From the seventeenth century, external (Arab) reports about the trans-Saharan trade and the bilād al-sūdān were increasingly replaced by local histories and chronicles, amongst others the two histories the *Ta'rīkh al-sūdān* (c. 1653, updated 1656) by 'Abd al-Raḥmān al-Sa'dī al-Tinbuktī and the *Ta'rīkh al-fattāsh* (c. 1664) by Maḥmūd Ka'ti, a scholar of Soninke origin based in Timbuktu, whose text was completed by his grandson Ibn al-Mukhtār. It has to be stressed, however, that these chronicles, written in Timbuktu's post-Moroccan pashālik period, represented the patrician outlook of the authors who were most probably rather ignorant regarding the earlier, pre-Moroccan history of the region and essentially tried to "write the Pashas into the history of the Niger bend" (Farias de Moraes 2003: lxxvii). In addition to the Timbuktu chronicles, there were a number of local chronicles such as the Kano chronicle which was probably composed, in a first version, in the late sixteenth century. Also, the history of Bornu was recorded in two texts by Aḥmad b. Furṭū in the late sixteenth century. From the eighteenth century, Muslim scholars recorded the history of kingdoms and of trading centers further south, such as, for instance, in the *Kitāb ghanja* (c. 1751/52) on the kingdom of Gonja, or the *Ta'rīkh ghanja* and the *Ta'rīkh wālā* in the nineteenth century. These texts are major sources for the precolonial history of the bilād al-sūdān and as such are indispensable for the reconstruction of social and religious dynamics which informed Muslim societies in the bilād al-sūdān at this time.

Trans-Saharan Empires

The long-term importance of the trans-Saharan trade motivated all states and dynasties on the southern and northern shores of the Sahara to gain control not only over a major port city, but also to control major parts of a trade route and even to conquer a southern or northern port, in order to eliminate intermediary trading networks and sources of possible disturbance in the guise of Saharan tribes. However, efforts to gain military and political control over a whole trade route were successful in only a few cases. The Almoravid empire could be regarded as the first venture in this sense, and the only one that was successful for some time. The Almoravid dynasty controlled the northern and southern harbors of the western Sahara for a century. The ʿAlawid dynasty in Morocco, which sent a military expedition to Timbuktu in 1590, also managed to hold a Moroccan garrison in Timbuktu for some years, until the garrison severed its links to Morocco and declared its independence by refusing to pay the annual tribute in gold and slaves. Attempts by the Qaramanlı rulers in Tripoli to establish Qaramanlı control over Bornu in the first decades of the nineteenth century failed, as did other Ottoman and Moroccan adventures in the late sixteenth and mid-eighteenth centuries. At the same time, rulers of the empires in the bilād al-sūdān tried to gain control over the northern reaches of the Saharan trade. In the thirteenth century, Kānim-Bornu controlled the oasis of Fazzān for some time at least; from the 1520s, the rulers of Songhay sent expeditions to the Taghāzā salt mines in the northern Sahara and to the outreaches of the Moroccan Atlas Mountains, but failed to establish a permanent basis in southern Morocco; and in the mid-seventeenth century, the rulers of Bornu again gained control over the Fazzān for some time. These enterprises were audacious yet bound to fail due to the immense costs for the maintenance of control over vast distances and the fact that Saharan populations were never willing to accept foreign control over their routes, which constituted a major form of income, whether in the form of custom duties, trade, fees for guides, or, in case of war, booty.

Kānim-Bornu's trans-Saharan venture: While the empires of Mālī and Songhay in the western bilād al-sūdān were oriented toward the River Niger as their major axis of communication and transport, and were focused on the western and central trans-Saharan trade routes, the empire of Kānim-Bornu, which had started to emerge, possibly as an entrepôt of trans-Saharan trade, in the sixth or seventh century, remained centered on Lake Chad and focused on the central and eastern trans-Saharan trade routes from Lake Chad to the oases of Kawār-Bilma and then north to Fazzān and Tripolitania as well as the Cyrenaika. In the eleventh century, a first ruler (mai) of Kānim-Bornu, Mai Arki (r. 1023–1067), may have converted to Islam, but his dynasty was replaced in the late eleventh century by a new ruling family, the Sayfuwa, who were to rule the empire until the early nineteenth century. Under Mai Dunāma I (r. 1086–1140), Kānim-Bornu became the paramount political power on Lake Chad as well as in the territories to the east, south, and west of Lake Chad. Under Mai Dunāma Dibalīmī II (r. 1210–1248), the empire not only consolidated its power around Lake Chad but also expanded into the lands of the Hausa in the west, as well as to the Fazzān in the northern Sahara. The empire of Kānim-Bornu was thus the first trading empire in the bilād al-sūdān, which was able to extend its influence almost to the shores of the Mediterranean in the north. In the fourteenth century, Kānim-Bornu's power in the Sahara declined considerably due to the interruption of trade on the eastern Saharan routes by Banū Sulaym attacks on caravans in the Fazzān and Teda attacks in the Tibesti. Under Mai ʿAlī Gajindeni (r. 1470–1503), Bornu was able to recover, however, and under his sons and successors Idrīs (r. until 1525), Muḥammad (r. until 1543/44), and Dunāma (r. until c. 1562/63), Bornu again became a major player in the central Sahara. Under Mai Idrīs Aloma (1569/70–1603), Bornu started a policy of military modernization, introduced firearms and a cavalry of camels, and established direct contacts across the Sahara with the Ottoman empire, which had taken control of Egypt, Tripolitania, Tunisia, and Algeria. Relations between Bornu and the Ottoman empire were rather tense, however, due to the fact that in 1577 the Ottoman empire occupied a number of oases in the Fazzān which were an important link in the trans-Saharan trade toward both Hausaland and Bornu. In order to protect herself against a possible trans-Saharan attack by Ottoman troops, Bornu sought support in Morocco, the only state in the bilād al-maghrib which continued to resist Ottoman expansion, and sent a mission to Morocco in 1583. When Moroccan troops conquered Timbuktu in 1591, Bornu abandoned this strategy, however. Eventually, neither a Moroccan nor an Ottoman attack materialized and Bornu was able to consolidate its reign over the Lake Chad region and the Bilma-Fazzān route in the seventeenth century. Mai ʿAlī (r. 1644–84) was even able to perform the pilgrimage three times, and in 1688 Bornu managed to decisively defeat the Kwararafa/Jukun coalition which had repeatedly threatened Bornu from the south. Only in the eighteenth century did the power of Bornu and its grip over the Bilma-Fazzān route wane.

Songhay's venture and the Moroccan counter-attack: In the sixteenth century, the empire of Songhay had become the most powerful Sudanic empire. Songhay was able to establish control over the western and central trans-Saharan trade routes, and to expand its domination far to the north. In 1539, Tuareg allies of the rulers of Songhay, the Askias, even attacked the Wadi Darʿa in southern Morocco and secured Songhay's control over the salt mines of Taghāza in the central Sahara. This triggered a Moroccan counterattack. In 1556, Moroccan troops reoccupied the salt mines of Taghāza, and when Sulṭān Aḥmad b. Manṣūr came to power in 1578, he ventured upon a much larger endeavor of conquest. In 1583, Moroccan troops occupied the oasis of Tuwāt, the most important trading place in the central northwestern Sahara. The Moroccan conquest of the oasis of Tuwāt stopped Ottoman expansion into the Sahara, which had started with the occupation of the oasis of Wārqala in 1552 and the Fazzān in 1577. Ottoman efforts to gain control over Tuwāt misfired in 1578 and 1582, however, and the Moroccan occupation of 1583 secured the Moroccan advance toward the south. In 1590, the Moroccan attack on Songhay began: on 22 December 1590, 4,600 Moroccan soldiers, mostly Spanish converts (Arab. ʿulūj, named after the Italian convert ʿUlūj ʿAlī Pāsha alias Giovanni Dionigi Galeni [d. 1587], a corsair who had risen to become an admiral of the Ottoman navy) and Andalusian Muslims under the leadership of Jūdār Pasha from Las Cuevas in Granada, started to cross the Sahara, armed with six large and several small cannons, as well as seventy musketeers. On 12 March 1591, the Moroccan expedition defeated the army of Songhay decisively at Tondibi and occupied Timbuktu on 30 May 1591. At this point of time, the Songhay empire had been weakened by a civil war and disputes over succession which had effectively split Songhay into two feuding fractions since 1583. In 1592 the Moroccan Arma (sharpshooters) also took Jenné and Gao. The Moroccan expedition was too small, however, to maintain control over vast stretches of the Songhay empire and thus concentrated on a stretch of the Niger between Gao and Jenné, which was administered as a Moroccan province (pashālik). A first rebellion by the inhabitants of Timbuktu against the Moroccan garrison was suppressed in October 1592, and a number of religious scholars from Timbuktu, amongst them the famous Aḥmad Bābā, were deported to Morocco. Aḥmad Bābā was allowed to return to Timbuktu only in 1608. Between 1591 and 1600 Sulṭān Aḥmad b. Manṣūr sent 23,000 Moroccan soldiers to the south, but many died on the Niger, while others married local women. As the Moroccan possessions on the Niger were too far removed from Morocco to be controlled effectively, the rule of the Moroccan governors assumed its own dynamics. In 1612, governor-pasha ʿAlī b. ʿAbdallāh al-Tilimsānī rose to the position of pāsha without an explicit authorization from the Moroccan sulṭān, and in 1657 the first pāsha refused the oath of loyalty (Arab. bayʿa) to the new ʿAlawid dynasty in Morocco. Since then, the name of the Moroccan sulṭān was not named anymore in the weekly khuṭba (Friday sermon), which symbolized the final break with Morocco.

The Qaramanlı venture: While Ottoman rule was established in the bilād al-maghrib in the course of the sixteenth century, administration of the Ottoman provinces (pashāliks) quickly passed to local governors (beys, deys and aghas). In 1711, Ottoman rule in Tripolitania collapsed completely in the context of a palace coup by an Ottoman officer, Aḥmad Qaramanlı, who subsequently established his own dynasty which stayed in power until 1835. Qaramanlı politics were focused on piracy in the central Mediterranean as well as control over the northern ports of the central Saharan trade routes. In order to achieve direct control over the central Saharan trade routes, the Qaramanlı rulers of Tripoli sent military expeditions to Fazzān in 1716, 1718, and 1731 and eventually consolidated their control over the Fazzān. Under Yūsuf Qaramanlı Pasha (r. 1795–1832), the dynasty saw its apex of power. The Qaramanlıs not only gained control over the Cyrenaika in the East, but also expanded their navy from three to twenty-four ships in 1805. The commander of this navy was a British citizen, Peter Leslie, alias Murad Rais. Subsequently, the Qaramanlı navy was able to enforce the payment of protection monies. The protection monies paid by European nations were used by Yūsuf Qaramanlı Pasha to finance an expedition to the south in order to complete the conquest of the central trans-Saharan trade route leading to Bornu. In 1807/08 Yūsuf Qaramanlı Pasha sent a first diplomatic mission to Bornu. Two military expeditions against the Teda in the Tibesti mountains and Borgu secured the route militarily in 1816. In 1821, Yūsuf Qaramanlı Pasha finally sent a military expedition to Lake Chad. This expedition of 450 cavalrymen and 1,300 soldiers was led by a Georgian convert to Islam, Muṣṭafa al-Ahmar (the Red). On Lake Chad, the Qaramanlı force joined the army of Bornu against the kingdom of Bagirmi to the southeast of Lake Chad, and was able to enslave 6,000 men and women. It thus seems as if the Qaramanlı endeavor to cross the Sahara was chiefly motivated by the profits of the slave trade and not by a plan to conquer and administer territories in the south. British opposition forced Yūsuf Qaramanlı Pasha to shelve a further expedition in 1824. A few years later, the Qaramanlı dynasty was deposed by an Ottoman expeditionary force and the Ottoman empire regained control over Tripolitania, the Cyrenaika, and the Fazzān.

Timbuktu: A Center of Trans-Saharan Trade

Like many urban centers in the bilād al-sūdān which had formed at the crossroads of trade routes, Timbuktu's development, boom, and decay were linked with the vagaries of trans-Saharan trade as well as the rise and fall of the major trading empires of the region, most prominently Mālī and Songhay. Besides Gao, Timbuktu was the northernmost port on the Niger, connecting the trans-Saharan trade to regions up and down the river. Timbuktu equally stood at the southern end of one of the shortest and commercially most attractive trade routes across the Sahara, from both southern Morocco and southwestern Algeria through the oases of Tuwāt to the Niger. This position at the intersection of the trans-Saharan trade with trade in the bilād al-sūdān stimulated the development of a trading entrepôt, possibly from the seventh or eighth century. From its very beginnings, Timbuktu also had the advantage of being beyond the control of the paramount trading empire in the region, Ghāna, and its Saharan harbor cities of Walāta, Tādmakka, Awdaghust, and Kumbi Saleh. In the course of time, a number of trading groups, artisans, and farmers, mostly Maghsharen (a Masūfa-Ṣanhāja group), Malinke, Soninke, Songhay, FulBe, Marka, and an array of Tuareg groups (Wulmdān/Iwillimiden, Kel Tadamakkat, Kel Tingeregif), later also Arabs (Barābīsh), settled in and around Timbuktu, which slowly turned into a veritable urban center since c. 1100.

When the empire of Ghāna eventually collapsed in the early thirteenth century due to an invasion by Sosso warriors, some of the trade from the western routes across the Sahara shifted east. Both Walāta and Timbuktu took over from Ghana and saw their trade expanding. However, Walāta and Timbuktu were quickly incorporated into the new paramount trading empire in the western bilād al-sūdān, Mālī, under Mansā Uli (r. 1260–1277). In the context of Mālī's rise as the supreme power in the bilād al-sūdān, Timbuktu experienced a first phase of prosperity, as manifested in the construction of a large Friday mosque, built by an architect from al-Andalus, Abū Isḥāq al-Sāḥilī, who died in Timbuktu in 1346. In this period, an intensive exchange of scholars between Timbuktu and Morocco started, as witnessed by Ibn Baṭṭūṭa in 1352/1353. This exchange continued more or less intensively until the late nineteenth century, although the links between Timbuktu and the bilād al-maghrib were interrupted again and again by political crises. One of these crises was an attack by Mossi warriors from the Volta region in the early fifteenth century. Although the Mossi were eventually defeated by Mālī, its power was weakened and Mālī withdrew its garrison from Timbuktu in 1433. For some years, regional tribal groups, in particular the Maghsharen, took control. Numerous families of Imasighen and Arab origin settled in Timbuktu at that time, among them the Aqīt family from Walāta, which was dominated by the Masūfa-Ṣanhāja federation. The most famous representative of the Aqīt family in the late sixteenth century was Aḥmad Bābā al-Tinbuktī, who compiled a famous text containing the biographies of Sunni-Mālikī religious scholars, including those in the bilād al-sūdān, entitled *Nayl al-ibtihāj* (The attainment of joy).

In the mid-sixteenth century, a new trading empire, Songhay, emerged on the Niger and rose to even greater prominence than Mālī before. On 18 January 1469, Songhay troops occupied Timbuktu and the Songhay emperor, Sonni ʿAlī, expelled the Maghsharen from Timbuktu. Most families of scholars subsequently chose to emigrate to Walāta or Tadmakka. In 1473, Sonni ʿAlī also expelled the rest of the population from Timbuktu, as the majority refused to accept Sonni ʿAlī's rule, possibly due to the fact that Sonni ʿAlī's status as a Muslim was not beyond doubt. The population of Timbuktu returned only when Sonni ʿAlī died in 1492 and a new dynasty, the Askias, rose to power. Askia Muḥammad (r. 1493–1528) invested in a number of building projects and particularly supported the development of the schools. The Tuareg tribes in the north submitted to the rule of the Askia, and in the early sixteenth century Songhay even occupied the salt mines of Taghāza and thus controlled the trans-Saharan trade far to the north.

The daily administration of the town was in the hands of a number of families of scholars and notables, most prominently of the Aqīt, Baghayughu, Gidado, and Maghia families, who shared the offices in the four major mosques, Sankore, (which was the major school), Jingerebir, Sidi Yaḥyā, and Jāmiʿat al-Sūq (the market mosque), as well as the office of the qāḍī. The scholars were led by the leading qāḍīs and imāms, who all had a thorough training as fuqahāʾ, followed by a larger group of highly respected ʿulamāʾ and an even larger group of teachers (Arab. muʿallimūn). The bottom of this scholarly hierarchy was formed by simple mosque functionaries and copyists (Arab. kuttāb, sing. kātib) as well as muddāḥ (praise singers who specialized in madḥ, panegyrics of the Prophet), who were often tailors by profession. In the sixteenth century, the group of fuqahāʾ-ʿulamāʾ comprised about 200–300 persons, although few occupied formal positions. Yet "becoming a learned colleague had immense status and influence ramifications" (Saad 1983: 159), and was, essentially, the precondition for acquiring recognition as a member of the patriciate that dominated Timbuktu throughout its history. However, the setup of the patriciate of wealthy families of traders, religious scholars, and administrators changed over time: while being dominated by traders, scholars, and notables in the fourteenth, fifteenth, and sixteenth centuries, the military aristocracy of the Arma came to dominate the patriciate in the seventeenth century, only to be replaced again by notables and scholars in the eighteenth and nineteenth centuries.

At its apex around 1580, Timbuktu counted about 150 qurʾānic schools visited by 15–50 students each, some by 200 students. This means that Timbuktu had become home to about 4,000–5,000 students while having a population of about 50,000. The metropolitan character of Timbuktu was expressed in the quality of its schools which not only taught Qurʾān and fiqh or ḥadīth, but also tafsīr (exegesis), manṭiq (logic), and naḥw (grammar). Equally, scholars from Timbuktu were prominent members of two royal pilgrimage caravans from Songhay in 1484 and 1496/97, which visited Cairo and met the most famous religious scholar of the time, Jalāl al-Dīn al-Suyūṭī (d. 1505), who was again willing to give ijazāt to a number of Sudanese scholars. This personal link with al-Suyūṭī explains the subsequent importance of al-Suyūṭī for the development of Islamic learning in the bilād al-sūdān and the so-called Suwaré-tradition, in particular. The meeting with al-Suyūṭī also signaled that scholarship in the bilād al-sūdān, as represented by Timbuktu, was now fully accepted as part of universal Muslim scholarship. In his Moroccan exile, Aḥmad Bābā al-Tinbuktī, who authored fifty-six texts himself, was eventually even able to claim that the *risāla* of Ibn Abī Zayd al-Qayrawānī had become the only text on Mālikī law that was studied in the bilād al-maghrib and that students from the bilād al-maghrib had started to come to Timbuktu in order to expand their knowledge.

After the occupation of Timbuktu early in 1591, the Moroccan army also conquered Jenné in 1592 and established a number of fortifications along the Niger, which became centers for Arab and Imasighen settlers from the north who started to arrive on the Niger in 1593, while others followed in 1595, 1604, and 1618. Among these settlers from the bilād al-maghrib were refugees from Spain, who had to leave Spain in the last wave of expulsion of Muslims and Jews in the early seventeenth century. The Spanish converts who had formed the bulk of the army of conquest by contrast returned north in 1599. In economic terms, the Moroccan conquest had started out as a profitable venture: in 1594 alone, a caravan shipped 3–3.5 tons of gold across the Sahara to the north, as well as a first delivery of 1,200 slaves. The death of Sulṭān al-Manṣūr led to a weakening of the trans-Saharan ties, however, and Moroccan governors in the pashālik of Timbuktu became increasingly independent. In 1612, the commander of the Arma, ʿAlī ʿAbdallāh al-Tilimsānī, deposed the Moroccan governor and proclaimed himself the new governor (pasha) of Timbuktu without seeking authorization from the Moroccan sulṭān. Moroccan efforts to regain control over Timbuktu misfired in 1618 and the Arma continued to nominate their own commanders, while formally recognizing Moroccan sovereignty (until 1657). Timbuktu and the Niger bend region had thus become a Moroccan bilād al-sība.

The rule of the Arma over Timbuktu lasted until 1737, but it was characterized by constant feuds and internal strife and the quick succession of pashas: from 1590 to 1833 Timbuktu saw 167 pashas, but only a few survived more than a year in power, among them Maḥmūd b. Zarqūn (1591–1595), Maḥmūd Longo (1604–1612), ʿAlī ʿAbdallāh al-Tilimsānī (1612–1617), and Masʿūd b. Manṣūr al-Zaʿrī (1637–1643). The position of the pasha in fact rotated among three paramount fractions of the Arma, namely the Fāsiyyīn, the Marrākishiyyīn, and the Shrāqa (from Tilimsān), while the Drāʿa (from the Wādī Darʿa) represented a weaker yet highly respected regional affiliation. Realizing their precarious position on the Niger, far removed from Morocco, the Arma soon started to integrate into local society and intermarried with the Songhay military aristocracy which had accepted Arma overrule. By the mid-seventeenth century, the paramount position of the Arma was weakened considerably, however, by a federation of Tuareg tribes, the Iwillimiden, who forced the Arma in Timbuktu to pay tribute in 1649. The Iwillimiden were replaced, in 1713, by the Kel Tadamakkat, another Tuareg federation, which came to dominate the Niger bend region between Gao and Timbuktu in the mid-eighteenth century and who defeated the Arma decisively in 1737. In 1787, they were again replaced by the Kel Tingeregif and finally, in the early nineteenth century, by the Kunta. In the eighteenth century, the ʿAlawid dynasty resumed Moroccan politics of expansion across the Sahara and established a Moroccan base in the southwestern Sahara. In 1738, a Moroccan expedition reached Ras al-Māʾ west of Timbuktu and four Moroccan royal missions visited Timbuktu between 1730 and 1745, yet failed to negotiate recognition of Moroccan sovereignty in Timbuktu. In the early nineteenth century, the Kunta scholars and their Iwillimiden allies became the paramount rulers of Timbuktu, although they had to accept the sovereignty of the imāmate of Masina in 1825. The demise of Timbuktu in the eighteenth century was aggravated by at least four plague epidemics. The year 1748/49 was even labeled a "year of calamity" (Arab. ʿām al-nāzila) (Lydon 2009: 97) due to a devastating outbreak of the plague, imported by a trans-Saharan caravan. Similar outbreaks of the plague, but also smallpox (in 1865/1866) and cholera (in 1869), hit a number of other Saharan oases and sub-Saharan trading centers in the late eighteenth and the nineteenth centuries and repeatedly decimated the populations of Timbuktu, Tīshīt, Shinqīṭ, Arawān, and Walāta. By the mid-nineteenth century, Timbuktu had not only lost its role as a major center of the trans-Saharan and trans-Sudanic trades, but had also suffered a significant decline of its population: Heinrich Barth, who visited Timbuktu in 1854, estimated its population to be no more than 13,000, possibly peaking at 23,000 at the height of the trading season.

The Sanūsiyya as a Trans-Saharan Sufi Order

The history of the Sahara was not only informed by efforts to establish control over the trans-Saharan trade, or the efforts of Saharan populations to fend off outsiders as well as local competitors. Religious scholars and Sufi saints also acquired a major role in the history and politics of the Sahara. This is particularly clear in the case of the Sanūsiyya Sufi order which even came to build and maintain, since the mid-nineteenth century, a trade route across the eastern Sahara which had not existed before. The Sanūsiyya was founded by an Algerian scholar, Muḥammad b. ʿAlī al-Sanūsī (1787–1859), who was a student of Aḥmad b. Idrīs (d. 1837), a Moroccan scholar who had settled in the Ḥijāz and had established a sober tradition of learning and ritual practice in Sufism which stressed the Sunna of the Prophet. His student, Muḥammad b. ʿAlī al-Sanūsī, was born in 1787 in al-Wāsiṭa near Mustaghanim in western Algeria. After completing his studies in Mustaghanim and Fes, he went on pilgrimage and settled in the Ḥijāz, where he became a student of Aḥmad b. Idrīs. After the death of his master, he returned to the Maghrib, but he was asked by local tribal groups and notables in the Cyrenaika to stay in Benghasi. He established a zāwiya in al-Bayḍāʾ, close to Benghasi, and started to teach and mediate in local conflicts. Al-Bayḍāʾ, as well as all later centers of the brotherhood, were characterized by the fact that they were positioned at the center of several, often overlapping pasture zones of competing tribes, as well as at the crossroads of trans-Saharan trade routes between Egypt and the bilād al-maghrib and between the Mediterranean coast and the bilād al-sūdān in the south. The zawāya of the Sanūsiyya thus came to form centers of communication, trade, and mediation.

By 1846, Muḥammad b. ʿAlī al-Sanūsī had built four additional zawāya in the Cyrenaika and, after his return from his last pilgrimage in 1854, he even shifted the center of the ṭarīqa from al-Bayḍāʾ to Jaghbūb in the middle of the Libyan desert, far removed from the Ottoman administration in the Cyrenaika. Jaghbūb was situated on an important trans-Saharan trade route linking Egypt with the Fazzān and offered the additional advantage of not forming part of the pasture land of any Saharan tribe. After the death of Muḥammad b. ʿAlī al-Sanūsī in 1859, his son Muḥammad al-Mahdī assumed leadership and immediately began to expand the influence of the Sanūsiyya further south. The move toward the south was marked by two further shifts of the spiritual and administrative center of the Sanūsiyya to Kufra in 1895 and to Qirū in 1899. This reflected not only an effort to remain independent from Ottoman influence in the north, but also to develop ties with the kingdom of Wadai which had started to emerge, in the early nineteenth century, as a new regional power in the Lake Chad/Dārfūr region. A new north-south connection from Cyrenaika via Kufra and Qirū to Wadai promised to replace the central trans-Saharan route from Fazzān to Bornu, which had become increasingly dangerous due to raids by Teda and Banū Sulaymān groups in the Tibesti and Fazzān in the 1830s. Contact between the Sanūsiyya and Wadai started in 1849 and was linked with pleas by the oasis of Waganqa for protection against Teda raids. The Sanūsiyya accepted this invitation and expanded south, building further zawāya in Wadai, Borku, Ennedi, on the Baḥr al-Ghazāl, in Bilma and the Tibesti, in the oasis of Fashi, and eventually on Lake Chad. Until then, these regions had been untouched by the activities of other Sufi orders and thus constituted a spiritual vacuum. The zawāya of the Sanūsiyya came to form, like stepping stones, the logistic structure of the new trade route to the south.

What were the specific characteristics of the Sanūsiyya as a religious, political, and economic enterprise? The ṭarīqa prohibited begging and cultivated a simple silent dhikr (Arab. Sufi meditation ritual) without music and chanting, while stressing the importance of physical work. All zawāya of the ṭarīqa were supposed to survive on their own and to produce essential subsistence goods themselves. The leaders of the zawāya were regularly swapped in order to prevent the emergence of local dynasties based on a single family of religious scholars. All zawāya of the Sanūsiyya were situated at the crossroads of trade routes as well as tribal groups and were secured by agreements with neighboring tribes. These agreements consisted of two parts: the tribal groups which bordered on the respective zāwiya had to bear the costs for the building of the zāwiya. In addition, the territory of the zāwiya was turned into a neutral zone where weapons were not allowed: it became a ḥarām, a place of asylum, and was regarded as a waqf (pious foundation) of the respective tribes. In exchange, the Sanūsiyya established a qur'ānic school. Travelers as well as caravans were accommodated without having to pay fees. The maintenance of a zāwiya was assured by donations, zakāt (the annual alms tax), inheritances, and the profit derived from its agricultural activities. All zawāya had multiple functions: they were the seat of the shaykh and his family, who administered the zāwiya and directed the students and simple followers, the ikhwān (brothers); they had a mosque, a caravanserai, a school, and rooms for accommodation. It provided provision for caravans and had a large well, storehouses, and a garden. Each zāwiya had a shaykh who was its religio-political leader, as well as a management board, directed by a wakīl. Each wakīl collected the fees from the caravans that passed through the zāwiya and organized the economic activities of the zāwiya. Ten percent of the income went to the shaykh, who had to provide for ten travelers or poor persons each day from that income. In the zāwiya, he directed the dhikr and acted as judge in disputes but did not act as imām or mu'adhdhin.

In the times of Muḥammad b. 'Alī al-Sanūsī, the leaders of all the zawāya converged once a year in Jaghbūb and reported on the activities in their region. Jaghbūb also had a collection of 8,000 manuscripts and a large mosque as well as an important madrasa. In the course of time, the zawāya of the Sanūsiyya developed into major hubs of local and regional trade and other economic activities. As the ṭarīqa took care of the maintenance of the wells, and dug new ones on new routes, the Sanūsiyya became, in the second half of the nineteenth century, a major religious, economic, and political power in the eastern Sahara between the Cyrenaika and Wadai as well as between the Fazzān in the west and the Nile: "To be a successful trader on the desert routes of eastern Libya and northern Wadai in the late nineteenth century, it was advisable to join the Sanūsiyya" (Cordell 1977: 33). The trade route developed by the Sanūsiyya was divided into three legs: a first leg from the Mediterranean port of Benghasi to the oasis of Awjila in the southern Cyrenaika, where the caravans were assembled, a second leg from Awjila to Kufra, which constituted the major provision base in the central leg, and a third leg to Arāda in northern Wadai, where the caravan would split into smaller groups. The crossing of the Sahara on this route took between sixty and seventy days. Virtually all tribal populations on the route profited from the trade, either as guides and caravan workers or as providers of food and camels, or even as traders. The Sanūsiyya not only organized and maintained the route, but also protected traders and caravans and thus assumed the role of a regional mediator and de facto ruling power in the eastern Sahara.

The case of the Sanūsiyya (and the corresponding example of the Kunta-Ineslemen group in the central Sahara, as well as the case of the Awlād Ibirrī in the southwestern Sahara) shows that states, trade networks, and tribes were not the only players in the Sahara. Trade could also be organized and protected by a Sufi order, and religious scholars played a major role in trans-Saharan networks of exchange. In structural terms, the emergence of the Sanūsiyya as a major player in the eastern Sahara in the nineteenth century can be compared with the emergence of religious scholars and Sufi saints as local and regional mediators in the bilād al-sība of North Africa from the thirteenth century.

4 Dynamics of Islamization in the Bilād al-Sūdān

Historical Themes and Patterns

As in the Sahara and the bilād al-maghrib, trade constituted a major factor for the development of Islam in the bilād al-sūdān, and economic and political development was consequently driven by the same dynamics as in the Sahara and in North Africa, namely, the effort to gain control over trade centers and trade routes. Often, the political centers of the trading empires of the bilād al-sūdān (see map 12) were identical with major emporia of trade, and Muslim trading communities came to coexist with the courts of local rulers. Regional economies and trade networks expanded and contracted, as will be shown in the case of Kano, in response to the capacity of Sudanese states to create and maintain favorable conditions for commercial activities and investment. In the late 1860s, the French explorer Réné Caillié thus observed that war between Masina and Segu had disrupted trade routes, and that trade had consequently shifted from Jenné to Nyamina, Sinsani, and Bamako to the southwest. What has been observed as a general pattern of trans-Saharan trade remained valid for the bilād al-sūdān until the nineteenth century: war and economic instability had negative effects for all parties and triggered the shift of trade routes to safer lands and port cities. Trade, economy, and politics in the bilād al-sūdān were not dominated, however, by Imasighen or Arab tribal populations, but by a multitude of Sudanese populations and Sudanese trade networks. Also, trade was not based on camels, but on riverboats and caravans of oxen and donkeys, as well as human porterage, and thus involved different logistics that were based on seasonal constraints.

The integration of the sub-Saharan empires into far-reaching trade networks stimulated processes of conversion and Islamization which continue to this day. Sudanic empires such as Takrūr, Ghāna, Mālī, Gao (Songhay), and Kānim-Bornu had their first contacts with Muslims more than 1,000 years ago, and processes of conversion and Islamization have led to the emergence of distinct traditions of Islamic learning in these regions. In the trading empires of the bilād al-sūdān, Islam did not replace African indigenous religious traditions, though, but coexisted for centuries with African religions and communal cults. Since most rulers of the empires of the bilād al-sūdān were Muslim since the eleventh or twelfth centuries, however, and honored Muslim traders and scholars, the polities of the bilād al-sūdān were increasingly regarded as Muslim by the religious scholars of the bilād al-maghrib and Egypt. Pilgrims, scholars,

> When the first Muslim traders reached the bilād al-sūdān in the late seventh century, sub-Saharan West Africa already had a flourishing regional trade, which had developed a distinct quality due to the spread of iron working technologies since the fifth century BC. The emergence of local and regional centers of trade has been documented most thoroughly by means of archaeology in the case of Jenné on the Niger, where a settlement existed from the third century CE. This settlement developed into a town of substantial size from approximately 400 CE. By 800, Jenné covered more than thirty hectares and was surrounded by a two-kilometer wall. Apart from Jenné, a number of smaller settlements have been excavated near Ja (Dia), Méma, and Timbuktu on the Niger, as well as in the Lake Chad region, attesting to the existence of African trading networks in sub-Saharan West Africa well before the advent of Islam. These centers of local and regional trade formed nuclei of pre-Islamic Sudanic kingdoms such as Takrūr, Ghāna, or Kano. The existence of pre-Islamic networks of trade not only had an important trans-regional economic dimension but may also explain the fact that major parts of sub-Saharan West Africa (and the Nile Sudan) such as Gao-Songhay, Kānim-Bornu, or Funj were familiar with the greater oriental (i.e., Egyptian, Arabian, Mesopotamian) master tale of epics, sagas, cultural heroes, dynasties, and religious traditions mediated most possibly by Nubia and/or Axum/Ethiopia.

and students from sub-Saharan West Africa were equally respected for their erudition. From the tenth and eleventh centuries, the bilād al-sūdān thus came to form an intrinsic part of a larger world of Islam. Only the movements of jihād in the eighteenth and nineteenth centuries led to the marginalization of African ritual practices in the new imāmates and confirmed the role of Islam as the sole source of political legitimacy.

The process of conversion to Islam, which had started on the Sahelian fringes of the bilād al-sūdān, continued along similar lines in the savannahs of sub-Saharan West Africa in the fourteenth, fifteenth, and sixteenth centuries, and in the tropical forests on the Guinea Coast from the seventeenth and eighteenth centuries. Traders, scholars, traveling students, pilgrims, and conquerors established outposts of Islam that turned into centers of learning. Eventually, Muslims came to constitute a majority of the population in most parts of sub-Saharan West Africa in the nineteenth and twentieth centuries, except the coastal regions and their immediate hinterlands. For better historical and geographical orientation in this chapter, I present short histories of the major trading empires and kingdoms of the bilād al-sūdān proceeding from west to east.

Numerous remarks in Arab descriptions of the kingdoms of the bilād al-sūdān, such as Qalanbū, Ghāna, and Mālī, point to traditions of divine kingdom in the bilād al-sūdān. These traditions were widespread in sub-Saharan Africa and in the Nile Valley: royal burials in tomb mounds, the sacred character of the king who was kept distant from his subjects, the royal umbrella and other insignia of royal power, his way of communicating with his subjects through a spokesman, large harems, the existence of sacred groves close to the courts, and the strong role of the queen (or queen mother) were repeatedly mentioned in Arab sources. These customs and traditions, as well as corresponding African indigenous religions and communal cults, coexisted with Islam at the courts of the various states in the bilād al-sūdān for a considerable time, and have also been reported for the empire of Sinnār-Funj in the early eighteenth century and the kingdom of Wadai in the mid-nineteenth century. The abolition of these traits of divine kingdom and of non-Islamic religious practices at the courts of the empires of the bilād al-sūdān were interpreted in the Arabic sources as a sign that an empire had become truly Muslim, as, for instance, in the case of Kānim-Bornu in the early thirteenth century under Mai Dunāma Dibalīmī II, Gao-Songhay in the late fifteenth century under Askia Muḥammad Turé, and Kaarta-Segu in 1860 under the influence of the imāmate of Masina.

The Trading Empires of the Bilād al-Sūdān

The westernmost Muslim trading empire, close to the Bānū Judāla on the nīl (the Senegal, in this case), was the kingdom of Ṣanghāna, which extended to the coasts of the Atlantic. Ṣanghāna, or Takrūr, as it came to be known due to the name of its major trading center on the Senegal, started to emerge, like most sub-Saharan players in the trans-Saharan trade, in the seventh or eighth century. In the eleventh century, Takrūr attained celebrity due to its alliance with the Almoravid movement against the competing trading empire of Ghāna. The first ruler of Takrūr to convert to Islam was Wārjābī b. Rābīs (d. 1040). Takrūr's alliance with the Almoravid movement influenced Arab perceptions of Muslims in the bilād al-sūdān to such an extent that for a long period of time all Muslims from the western bilād al-sūdān were called Takrūrī. In the alliance with the Almoravids, Takrūr gained control over the southwestern termini of the trans-Saharan trade and defeated Ghāna in 1076. Possibly as a reaction to this defeat, Ghāna's royal family converted to Islam or, another possible trajectory, from an Ibāḍī orientation to a Sunni-Mālikī orientation in Islam. Takrūr's eminent position on the Senegal was not to last long, however; after the demise of the Almoravid dynasty, Ghāna recovered, while Takrūr lost control over her eastern marches and was finally incorporated into the empire of Mālī in the fourteenth century. When Mālī's power declined in the mid-fifteenth century, the Senegal valley became tributary to the Wolof kingdom of Jolof until its conquest, in 1558, by an alliance of non-Muslim FulBe warriors, the Denianke, who were able to consolidate their hold over the region until the late eighteenth century. The rule of the Denianke possibly contributed to the emigration of local TorodBe Muslim scholars to the east, in particular Hausaland, where TorodBe scholars settled from the seventeenth century. Takrūr's neighbor in the east was the Muslim kingdom of Silā, which was characterized, like other Sudanic kingdoms such as Takrūr, Ghāna, Gao-Songhay, Wadai, Dārfūr, and Sinnār-Funj, by the fact that the capital city consisted of two towns, one dominated by the royal court, the other by the quarters of the North African Muslim traders. Twin towns consisting of royal courts and centers of trade can be described as a distinctive feature of Sudanese trading empires, and have also been identified in kingdoms of the West African tropical forest region, such as Asante. In the eleventh century, Silā and its province of Qalanbū (Galam) on the upper Senegal were still dominated by a largely non-Muslim population.

The empire of Ghāna (or Āwkār, according to al-Bakrī) further northeast seems to have been the paramount political player in the region in the tenth and eleventh centuries. Like Takrūr, Ghāna's emergence as a local power was connected with the trans-Saharan trade. However, Ghāna was not centered on a river, as Takrūr, Silā, Mālī, and Gao-Songhay were, but controlled the savannahs between the upper Senegal and the upper Niger and thus access to the routes leading to the Senegal and the upper Niger. Ghāna also controlled access to the gold mines of Bambuk and Bure and thus came to be regarded by Arab geographers as the first and most important trading empire in the western bilād al-sūdān. Although Ghāna suffered defeat in the confrontation with the Almoravids and Takrūr in the eleventh century, it continued to exist into the early thirteenth century. In the first extensive description of Ghāna and its capital city, Kumbi Saleh, al-Bakrī pointed out that this city was divided into two parts: the royal city, "al-ghāba" (the grove) and the quarter of the traders, which was large and had twelve mosques (*Wa-madīnat Ghāna madīnatan, iḥdāhumā al-madīna allatī yaskunuhā al-muslimūn wa-hiya madīna kabīra, fīhā ithnāʿashara masjidan*, al-Bakrī 1992 2: 869). Al-Bakrī also stressed that Ghāna's population was non-Muslim (Arab. majūs) and that people venerated idols (*Wa-diānatuhum al-majūsiyya wa-ʿibādat al-dakākīr*, al-Bakri 1992 2: 869). Al-Idrīsī, by contrast, reported in the twelfth century that the inhabitants of Kumbi Saleh had become Muslim and that the king of Ghāna claimed to be a descendant of the family of the Prophet. In the early thirteenth century, Ghāna had to make room for the rise of another trading empire, Mālī.

Mālī's rise was connected with the fact that Ghāna had suffered considerably from an attack by Sosso warriors from the south in the early thirteenth century, and was not able to recover from this attack. Even Ghāna's capital city had been destroyed and the survivors subsequently resettled further east, in the trading center of Walāta, which soon came to be dominated by Mālī. Mālī's power was based on its control of the upper Niger and the gold fields of Bambuk and Bure, as well as the central trade routes across the Sahara. A legendary first emperor of Mālī, Sundiata Keita, defeated the Sosso and established the rule of the Keita dynasty in the region, which soon stretched along most of the upper Niger. By 1240, Walāta was incorporated into the empire, by 1270 Timbuktu, and by the early fourteenth century Mālī had also gained control over Takrūr and reached the shores of the Atlantic as well as Gao on the Niger in the east. Mālī's most prominent and legendary emperor (Mansā) at this time was Mansā Mūsā (r. 1312–1337), who undertook the pilgrimage to Mecca. He left Mālī in 1324 in a caravan of eight to ten thousand people. During his stay in Cairo, he spent so much gold that the value of gold in Egypt remained below the pre-visit value of gold for a period of twelve years. Mansā Mūsā's fame even spread to Europe, where he appeared in 1339 as Rex Melli on the map of the world by the Catalan geographer Angelino Dulcer. According to the *Ta'rikh al-sūdān (TS)* (TS 1900: 7), Mansā Mūsā also conquered Gao, the political center of Songhay, on his way to Cairo, although this feat was most probably achieved by the first Malian royal pilgrim, Mansā Ulī (r. 1260–1277), a son of the founder of the dynasty, who gained control over Timbuktu and Gao before setting out on his own pilgrimage. Ibn Baṭṭūṭa in fact recorded for the early 1350s that Gao was firmly within the Malian empire, and failed to mention Songhay client rulers in Gao or a Malian conquest of Gao at the time of Mansā Mūsā. "Like a magnet, Mansā Mūsā seems to have attracted reports of great deeds from other reigns, which were ascribed to his own reign, such as the conquest of Gao" (Moraes Farias 2003: cviii). The Sudanic chronicles of the seventeenth century indeed reported a Malian conquest of Gao several times, although it was most probably conquered only once. In the context of their pilgrimages, Malian emperors would confirm, however, the submission of the eastern lands to the reign of Mālī by visiting Gao. The hagiographic character of the chronicles has been canonized since the times of Heinrich Barth by generations of (Western) historians, although the author of the *Ta'rīkh al-sūdān* only transferred the deeds of one famous Malian emperor to the reign of another cultural hero. The expansion of the empire of Mālī was linked with the expansion of networks of Mande traders, whose arrival in Kano, one of the Hausa cities in the east, was recorded for the mid-fourteenth century and, again, for the late fifteenth century. Under the emperors of Mālī, the Mālikī school of law was established as the dominant school of law in the western bilād al-sūdān, and also spread in the central and southern bilād al-sūdān. Students were sent for studies to Cairo, and a new style of imperial architecture was introduced by builders from the bilād al-maghrib and al-Andalus. A number of large mosques were constructed and libraries established. Muslim scholars from the bilād al-maghrib were invited to the court of the emperors of Mālī, among them Ibn Baṭṭūṭa, who visited Mālī in 1352 in the reign of Mansā Sulaymān (r. 1341–1360). In his account of his journey to Mali (*Ziyārat al-andalus wa-l-sūdān*), chapter 8, sections 4 (*Madīnat mālī wa-sulṭānuhā*) and 5 (*Madīnat Mālī wa-ʿādāt ahlihā*), Ibn Baṭṭūṭa extensively described the life and customs at the court of the emperor of Mālī, as well as religious practices in Mālī. Ibn Baṭṭūṭa stressed the religiosity of Mālī's population, although he also pointed out that non-Islamic customs were cultivated at the court. In particular, he stressed the eminent role of the first wife of the emperor, the qāsā, a daughter of the emperor's paternal uncle (Arab. bint ʿammihi) who was regarded as a queen (Arab. malika), who took part in the government according to the "customs of the blacks" (*ʿalā ʿādāt al-sūdān*), and whose name was even mentioned alongside the name of the emperor during the Friday prayers (*wa-yadhkaru ismihā maʿ ismihi ʿalā l-minbar;* Ibn Baṭṭūṭa 1985, 2: 788). He praised the "blacks" as "the most noble people" (*wa-l-sūdān aʿẓam al-nās,* Ibn Baṭṭūṭa 1985, 2: 784) and stressed the complete security of travelers in Mālī. He was impressed by the eagerness with which the Qurʾān was memorized and pointed out that there was a black qāḍī, ʿAbd al-Raḥmān Jāʾnī, numerous black fuqahāʾ, as well as many visitors (traders) from North Africa and Egypt (Ibn Baṭṭūṭa 1985 2: 781–791). In the late fourteenth and early fifteenth centuries, however, trans-Saharan trade started to shift further east, privileging other Saharan trading networks. In addition, Mālī was weakened by dynastic disputes over questions of succession. As a consequence, a new trading empire, Gao-Songhay, replaced Mālī in the mid-fifteenth century as the major trading empire in the bilād al-sūdān.

Gao-Songhay formed around a major center of trans-Saharan trade, namely Gao (or Kawkaw, in Arabic texts), on the middle Niger, east of Timbuktu. Like Kumbi-Saleh, Gao consisted of two towns, one accommodating the court, the other the quarters of the traders as well as the quarters of the local populations. Although Gao possibly had a Muslim ruler from the eleventh century onward, the majority of the population remained non-Muslim until the nineteenth century. Gao-Songhay was originally established by non-Muslim rulers (Arab. mulūk) of allegedly Yemeni origin (. . . *Ammā al-mālik al-awwal Zā al-Yaman aṣlī,* TS 1900: 4), namely, the Zā (Dia), who "all died in unbelief" (*mātū jamīʿan fī-l-jāhiliyyya*). The rather mystical character of these historical traditions is exemplified by the fact that the events allegedly "took place at the time of the pharaohs" (*Kāna fī-zamān firaʿūn,* TS 1900: 4). Later Zā rulers of Songhay may have turned Ibāḍī possibly in the eleventh century, although Ibāḍī influence cannot be substantiated, since Ibāḍīs did not leave funerary inscriptions as the later Sunni-Mālikī rulers of the region did. However, like other centers of trade in the bilād al-sūdān, Gao was in contact with Ibāḍī trade networks in the central and eastern bilād al-maghrib, and, as in Kānim-Bornu, Gao local traditions report a struggle for power among ruling groups which may have expressed disputes over the religious orientation of the ruling elite, namely early Ibāḍī influences and later Sunni-Mālikī influences. In the mid- to late thirteenth century, the Zā rulers of Gao-Songhay came under Mālian control and were possibly replaced by Mande-speaking vassals of Mālī, the Sonni. In the *Taʾrīkh al-sūdān,* Songhay's independence from Mālī is associated with the change of the dynasty from the Zā to the Sonni dynasty under Sonni ʿAlī Kolon in the late thirteenth century, but other sources, in particular Ibn Baṭṭūṭa, confirm ongoing Mālian control over Songhay-Gao until the mid-fourteenth century. However, Songhay may have achieved some form of autonomy for certain periods of time, until Mālī reasserted its control over Songhay. In the mid-fifteenth century, the Sonni, now based in Kūkiya, a center for both the trans-Saharan and the trans-Sudanic trade, some 150 kilometers downstream from Gao, finally achieved independence from Mālī. Like Mālī, Songhay's power relied on control of the middle Niger valley, as well as the central trans-Saharan trade routes. Based on a fleet of war pirogues on the Niger, the Sonni rulers of Songhay established their rule over the river and gained control over its internal delta under Sonni Sulaymān Dandi (d. 1464). Sulaymān Dandi's successor, Sonni ʿAlī Ber (r. 1464–1492), then consolidated Songhay's hold over the whole region, conquering Timbuktu in 1469 and Jenné in 1473. After Sonni ʿAlī's death, another dynastic change took place, symbolized by a shift of the political center from Kūkiya back to Gao. The new dynasty of the Askias, based in Gao, continued to expand Songhay's power. In particular, Askia Muḥammad Turé (r. 1493–1528) increased Songhay's influence in the east and established Songhay overlordship in Hausaland, while also expanding into the Sahara. In contrast to Sonni ʿAlī, who suppressed the most prominent center of Sunni-Mālikī learning, Timbuktu, and who was consequently labeled the "greatest kharijite tyrant" (*al-ẓālim al-akbar al-khārijī*) (TS 1900: 6), Askia Muḥammad Turé presented his new dynasty as a staunch Sunni regime and invited a well-known Maghribinian religious scholar, ʿAbd al-Karīm al-Maghīlī, to his court in order to boost the Islamic legitimacy of his rule. Askia Muḥammad Turé claimed in particular that the deposition of the Sonni dynasty had been legitimate, as Sonni ʿAlī had tolerated un-Islamic practices. Al-Maghīlī supported Askia Muḥammad Turé's position. For the first time in the recorded history of the bilād al-sūdān, a religious argument was thus introduced in order to legitimate a dynastic change. Al-Maghīlī's argumentation came to be quoted in the centuries to come to legitimize similar disputes between Muslim rebels and established (Muslim) rulers who were accused by the rebels of having violated basic teachings of Islam. Songhay's expansion continued under Askia Muḥammad Turé's successors, in particular his son Mūsā, as well as Askia Dawūd. Under his reign, Songhay was drawn into a conflict with Morocco, which eventually led to the Moroccan attack on Songhay in 1590/91 and Songhay's subsequent collapse. The only trading empire that continued to thrive in the bilād al-sūdān after the collapse of Songhay and its disintegration into a number of successor states was the empire of Kānim-Bornu.

In contrast to the other trading empires of the bilād al-sūdān which had been centered on a river, Kānim-Bornu was based around Lake Chad. Its original center lay to the east and northeast of the lake, in Kānim. Like Gao, Kānim could point to old trading links with the bilād al-maghrib, in particular Fazzān, Tripolitania, and Tunis. At the same time, Kānim never had any access to gold, unlike the trading empires of the western bilād al-sūdān, and specialized, from a fairly early period of time, in the export of slaves across the Sahara. Kānim-Bornu's slave raids into her southern periphery, in particular the regions of the Kirdi (heathen) populations south and southwest of Lake Chad, created "a boundary of terror and hostility, and slowed down state building and the expansion of Islam south of Lake Chad" (Levtzion 2003: 3), a process which also characterized the southern marches of the Sudanic kingdoms of Bagirmi, Wadai, and Dārfūr, the empire of Funj on the Nile, and Ethiopia. Due to the fact that all major centers of the trans-Saharan trade in the north, Sijilmāsa, the Jabal Nafūsa, the Fazzān and the Mzab, were dominated by Khārijī (Ṣufrī and Ibāḍī) trade networks until the eleventh century, Kānim's first ruling dynasty, the Zaghāwa, was probably under the influence of Khārijī trade networks, as were other sub-Saharan trading empires. In the mid-eleventh century, the last powerful Zaghāwa ruler, Mai Arki (r. 1023–1068), died during an expedition to the Fazzān, possibly in an effort to secure this major trade route against Banū Hilāl raids into the Fazzān. The first ruler of the next dynasty, the Sayfuwa, Mai Ḥummay (r. 1075–1086), has been depicted in Kānim's later historical traditions as the first Muslim ruler of the empire. This may be true, assuming that the Zaghāwa rulers did not convert to Islam. Mai Ḥummay's conversion to Islam, however, may also reflect a conversion to Sunni-Mālikī Islam, possibly under the influence of the Almoravid movement of reform in the western Sahara, and thus constituted a rejection of Ibāḍī influences which were increasingly marginalized in North Africa at this time. It has to be stressed, however, that the new dynasty chose a pre-Islamic Yemeni war hero, Sayf b. Dhī Yazan, who had defeated the Ethiopian army in the Yemen in the late sixth century, as its dynastic name giver and cultural hero, another parallel to the Zā rulers of Gao-Songhay. The Islamic character of the Sayfuwa dynasty was thus far from being entrenched. Arab sources in fact stress that the Islamization of Kānim only started under Mai Dunāma Dibalīmī II (Dunāma, the son of Dibalī, r. 1210–1248), who stopped non-Islamic cult practices at the court and destroyed a highly venerated sacral object, the munī (mune). However, this symbolic act must again not be taken as proof that Islam only started at the court of Kānim in the early thirteenth century: at many courts of the trading empires in the bilād al-sūdān, Islam and African ritual practices coexisted for a long time, often for centuries. In addition, traditions of conversion to Islam were often rewritten by local historians for multiple reasons.

As a powerful ruler, Mai Dunāma II was able to leave his realm for a number of years to go on pilgrimage as probably the first Muslim ruler from the bilād al-sūdān to undertake this arduous venture. In his time, Kānim donated a riwāq, a convent for students from Kānim at al-Azhar in Cairo and a madrasa in the Ḥammām al-Rīsh quarter of Fusṭāṭ (Old Cairo), which started to attract students and travelers from the bilād al-sūdān. After a climax of power under Mai Dunāma Dibīlāmī II, Kānim, still governed from its capital city Jīmī, experienced a serious crisis due to internal rivalries (from 1389 to 1459 Kānim was governed by twelve rulers from two different royal houses), as well as the rise of the Bulala on Lake Fitri in the east. During this period, the rulers of Kānim started to expand into the Sao and Kotoko regions south and southwest of Lake Chad (far removed from the Bulala), and to either integrate or submit the local Sao and Kotoko populations that were famous for their well-fortified settlements (sao or sawe). The Sao and Kotoko put up sustained resistance against Kānim and fought Kānim's rulers for almost two hundred years: in the fourteenth century, twelve out of fourteen rulers of Kānim died a violent death, mostly in wars against the Sao or the Bulala. Their resistance may be also viewed as a defensive reaction to Kānim slave-raiding expeditions, like the attacks of the Jukun against Kano in the seventeenth century, or the Mossi attacks against Mali in the early fifteenth century.

Due to the ongoing war with the Bulala, Mai 'Umar b. Idrīs (r. 1382–1387) was eventually forced to shift the political center of the empire to Bornu southwest of Lake Chad. From its new center, Birnin Gazargamo on the Yobe, the empire was able to recover and to finally defeat the Bulala (as well as the Sao and Kotoko) in the late sixteenth century. Mai 'Alī Gajindenī resumed Bornu's political expansion, and in the sixteenth and seventeenth centuries Bornu experienced a second period of bloom. Under Mai Idrīs Aloma (r. 1564–1596) Bornu saw the introduction of firearms on a large scale and their successful use in wars against Kano, Amsaka, and Ngizim, regional rivals of Bornu, but also rivalry with both the Ottoman empire and Morocco. Both Ottoman and Moroccan efforts to expand their influence across the Sahara, misfired, however, and Bornu was able to consolidate its realm in the seventeenth and eighteenth centuries and to even expand into the Sahara. In addition, Bornu forced the Jukun federation on the Gongola into submission and increased its pressure on Kano in the west as well as on the Kotoko states and Mandara in the south and southeast. In this period, Bornu also became known for its protection of Islamic learning and its Muslim scholars. The rulers of Bornu started to grant letters of protection (Arab. maḥram), a practice that also existed in other parts of the bilād al-sūdān, such as the empires of Songhay and Sinnār-Funj. These maḥrams were used by the rulers of Bornu to tie religious scholars to the court and to encourage the settlement of Muslim scholars in Bornu in general. Maḥrams were also issued to traders, and a number of protected settlements of scholars and traders started to develop in Bornu and contributed to its prospertity and stability. However, by the late seventeenth and early eighteenth century, Bornu increasingly suffered from a series of droughts and from Tuareg attacks on trade routes. Despite these adverse conditions, Bornu maintained its stability and control over the important salt mines of Bilma and Kawār until 1759. In the early nineteenth century, Bornu was drawn into the jihād in Hausaland and the Sayfuwa dynasty had to hand over power to a religious scholar, Muḥammad al-Kānimī, who had been asked to defend Bornu.

While Kānim-Bornu dominated the Lake Chad region proper, a number of smaller kingdoms such as Bulala, Bagirmi, and Wadai developed at Kānim-Bornu's fringes and eventually came to dominate the regions east and northeast of Lake Chad. As in the case of Kānim-Bornu, their history was linked with the development of the regional ecology that was characterized by the alternation of humid and dry periods. As a consequence, the water levels of Lake Chad and Lake Fitri would rise or sink, the Baḥr al-Ghazal, Shari, and Logone Rivers would flood or fall dry, and marshlands would expand or shrink. In the aftermath of the wars between Kānim-Bornu and the Bulala, a new paramount polity, Bagirmi, emerged in the early sixteenth century (possibly 1522) and established its own hegemony over the region southeast of Lake Chad and north of the Shari. Its ruler, the Mbang, resided in a large walled capital city, Massenya, and commanded a Muslim ruling elite, while a majority of the population seems to have remained attached to African religious traditions until well into the nineteenth century. Like other empires in the bilād al-sūdān, Bagirmi tried to gain control over regional trade routes as well as access to a trans-Saharan trade route, and thus access to means of destruction, in particular arms and horses. Arms and horses were needed in order to acquire slaves in the Kirdi slave-hunting peripheries of the south, who could be exchanged, often in the form of eunuchs, for new arms and horses in the trans-Saharan trade. In the seventeenth century, Bagirmi was able to gain supremacy over the Bulala on Lake Fitri, yet soon had to share this position of power with Wadai, another rising empire to the east. At the same time, Bagirmi increasingly came under the influence of Bornu, which had started to re-expand into the Kānim region east of Lake Chad. Whereas Bagirmi successfully exploited its own southern "predatorial zones" (Reyna 1990: 67), it became tributary to Bornu and later, from 1805, to Wadai, while Bornu maintained its pressure on Bagirmi.

The rise and fall from empire to tributary to predatory zone (and vice versa), as well as competition over tributaries and predatory zones, thus was a recurring feature of states in the bilād al-sūdān. This essentially meant making "war in order to accumulate (means of destruction), and to accumulate (means of destruction) in order to war" (Reyna 1990: 161). Access to trade routes which provided means of destruction was a decisive factor in this dynamic and consequently drove politics in the bilād al-sūdān to a considerable extent. The rise of Bagirmi's northeastern neighbor Wadai was likewise linked with efforts to gain access over regional trade routes, and to feed slaves (and other products of the bilād al-sūdān) into the trans-Saharan trade system. Like Bagirmi, Wadai started to develop into a Sudanese empire in the sixteenth century and was ruled by a Muslim elite from the early seventeenth century. The introduction of Islam at the court of Wadai is credited to a Muslim scholar, ʿAbd al-Karīm b. Jamʿ (r. 1635–1655), who seems to have come to Wadai (from the east) in 1610/11, and to have deposed an earlier, non-Muslim dynasty, the Tunjur. Like other empires in the bilād al-sūdān, Wadai was characterized, until the late nineteenth century, by the coexistence of Muslim and non-Muslim religious, social, and cultural practices. Thus, a German traveler, Eduard Vogel, was killed in 1856, just a few days after his arrival in Wara, the capital city of Wadai, when he dared to climb a holy hill at the edge of the town. Equally, Wadai, like Bagirmi and Funj, practiced the blinding of the brothers of a new ruler in order to disqualify them as rulers and to prevent struggles for power: only an intact person was thought to be fit to rule, a typical notion of divine kingship. While Wadai seems to have been tributary to both Bornu in the west and Dārfūr in the east until the eighteenth century, Wadai was able to exploit the decline of Bornu in the eighteenth century. At the same time, Dārfūr increasingly shifted its attention to the conquest of Kordofan in the east and neglected Wadai at its western periphery. In this political context, Wadai started to expand beyond its original core area and gained control over a number of tributaries and a predatory zone in the south, in particular Bagirmi, Dār Runga, Dār Sila, Dār Kuti, and Dār Tama, which were raided for slaves and ivory. These products were fed into the trans-Saharan trade, enabling Wadai to build an even more powerful army equipped with firearms. In the nineteenth century, Wadai tried to develop a new trade route through the Sahara that would not be controlled by traders from the Nile Sudan or Bornu. Under Sulṭān ʿAbd al-Karīm Sabun (r. 1805–1815), who had defeated Bagirmi in 1805, a trader from Awjila indeed found such a new route between Wara in the south and Benghazi in the north, and this route was constantly improved up to 1818, when Awlād Sulaymān raiders started to attack the caravans. Under Sulṭān Muḥammad al-Sharīf (r. 1834–1858), trade on this route resumed and from 1836 royal caravans were equipped to cross the Sahara in a two- to three-year cycle in order to provide Wadai with firearms. The trade between Wadai and the north eventually led to an alliance between Wadai and the Sanūsiyya. Sulṭān Muḥammad al-Sharīf (r. 1834–1858) defeated Bornu in 1846, sacking its capital city, Kukawa. His successor, Sulṭān ʿAlī b. al-Sharīf (r. 1858–1874), decisively defeated the Awlād Sulaymān, conquered Bagirmi, and sacked its capital city of Massenya in 1871. According to the German traveler Gustav Nachtigal, who visited Wadai in 1873/74, Sulṭān ʿAlī b. al-Sharīf also stopped the practice of blinding his brothers, a clear sign that the court of Wadai had become increasingly Muslim and was prepared to renounce non-Islamic cultural practices—perhaps prematurely, as Sulṭān ʿAlī b. al-Sharīf was subsequently deposed by his brother Muḥammad Yūsuf (r. 1874–1898). Muḥammad Yūsuf was able to defend Wadai against the Sudanese conquistador Rābiḥ b. Faḍl Allāh, who started to build his own Sudanic empire in 1884. Sulṭān Muḥammad Yūsuf even became a member of the Sanūsiyya which in exchange supported Wadai's opposition to the Mahdiyya in the Sudan in the 1880s and 1890s. By the 1890s, Wadai had become a major basis of the Sanūsiyya in the greater Lake Chad region and an important ally against the advance of the French in the Lake Chad region.

While the empires of Mālī, Songhay, and Kānim-Bornu were oriented toward either the Niger or Lake Chad, the kingdom of Dārfūr (the land of the Fūr) was located between the lands on the Nile and the kingdoms of the central bilād al-sūdān. At the same time, Dārfūr and its twin Wadai were linked with the trade routes leading toward Lake Chad and the easternmost trans-Saharan trade route, the dārb al-arbaʿīn, which connected Dārfūr with Asyūṭ in Upper Egypt. In contrast to Mālī, Songhay, and Kānim-Bornu, little is known about this country around the Jabal Marra mountain range: two dynasties, the Daju and the Tunjur, both influenced by Christian

Nubian traditions, seem to have dominated Dārfūr's development until the late sixteenth century, when a third dynasty, the Keira, rose to power. As in other kingdoms of the bilād al-sūdān, a wise stranger was seen as the mystical founder of dynasties in Dārfūr, establishing an 'Abbāsid-Arabo-Islamic legacy. The first Muslim ruler, Sulaymān Solongdungo (r. 1660–1680), established Islam as the dominant cult of the court, but non-Islamic traditions continued and millet beer was prohibited only in 1793 by Sulṭān 'Abd al-Raḥmān. At this time, Dārfūr also started to grant privileges to Muslim scholars in the form of letters of protection and tax exemption, and to stress its Islamic character. However, the kingdom of Dārfūr still knew the royal taboos and observances of a divine kingdom: the ruler had to wear a veil, spoke through an intermediary, had to eat alone, and visitors had to bare their chests, lie down, and cover their heads with dust.

In the seventeenth century, the Keira dynasty expanded and gained control over the trans-Sudanic trade route from the Nile to Lake Chad, as well as the darb al-arba'īn, although foreign traders, as in other kingdoms of the bilād al-sūdān, had to live in a separate town, Kobbei, a day's march north of al-Fāshir, which was Dārfūr's capital city from the late eighteenth century. As in the case of Sinnār-Funj on the Nile, long-distance trade in Dārfūr was controlled by the ruler, who dispatched a royal caravan under the direction of a royal caravan leader, the khābir. In many respects, Dārfūr (and Wadai) can be seen as a symbiosis of influences from the central bilād al-sūdān and the lands on the Nile in the east. Like many Sudanic and North African kingdoms, Dārfūr consisted of a center, a makhzan, surrounded by a periphery of semi-autonomous and tributary provinces, which could easily turn into bilād al-sība. And like a number of Sudanic kingdoms (as well as Ethiopia), Dārfūr coveted control over a southern slave-hunting zone, the Dār Fartit, the "land of the savages," where Dārfūr obtained her major export items, ivory and slaves. In the eighteenth century, Dārfūr continued to expand. Efforts to control Wadai failed, however, while Dārfūr managed to conquer the savannahs and steppes of Kordofan in the east in the second half of the eighteenth century. At the same time, Dārfūr tried to expand its hold over the Dār Fartit regions in the south, but eventually lost control over these regions to Arabic-speaking Baggāra tribes, in particular the Rizayqāt. In 1856, a Fūr army suffered a decisive defeat against the Rizayqāt. Dārfūr's efforts to control Kordofan also led to a conflict with Egypt, which invaded the Funj empire in 1820 and subsequently took control over Kordofan.

Although Dārfūr was defeated by an Egyptian army in 1821, the kingdom remained independent until the 1870s, when a northern Sudanese slave hunter, Zubayr Pasha, started to raid Dārfūr's southern marches for slaves. In 1874, Zubayr Pasha conquered al-Fāshir, Dārfūr's capital city, in the name of the Khedive of Egypt. Egyptian control remained nominal, however. In 1883, Dārfūr joined the rebellion of the Mahdī and regained some independence, until Dārfūr's Mahdist governor, Yūsuf Ibrāhīm, a son of the last Keira sulṭān, rebelled. His rebellion was defeated and Dārfūr remained a Mahdist province until 1898, when another Keira leader, 'Alī Dinār, reestablished

Dārfūr's independence. In the context of the European division of Africa, Dārfūr came under pressure, and after 'Alī Dinār declared a jihād on the British in the Sudan in 1915, Dārfūr was conquered by the British. With the death of 'Alī Dinār on 5 October 1916, Dārfūr became part of the Anglo-Egyptian Sudan.

After becoming firmly established in the Sahelian fringes of the bilād al-sūdān by the thirteenth, fourteenth, or at least fifteenth century, Islam continued to expand south into the savannah regions of sub-Saharan West Africa in the fifteenth, sixteenth, and seventeenth centuries and then moved even further south into the tropical forest regions on the Guinea coast in the eighteenth and nineteenth centuries. Between the thirteenth and the sixteenth centuries, the bilād al-sūdān experienced a series of devastating invasions by southern populations, Mossi in the middle and upper Niger region, Sao in the case of Kānim-Bornu, and Kwararafa in Hausaland, possibly as a reaction against northern slave raids into the savannah belt. In the middle and upper Niger region, Songhay was eventually able to defeat the Mossi in a number of counterattacks in 1483/84, 1489/99, 1549, and 1561/62, stimulating dynamics of state formation in the Volta region, which led to the formation of a number of (non-Muslim) Mossi kingdoms in the fifteenth and sixteenth centuries, most prominently Mamprussi, Dagomba, Nanumba, Wagadugu, and Yatenga, as well as Dagbon further south. In the sixteenth century, Mande raids and cavalry expeditions into the central and western Volta region led to the formation of the kingdom of Gonja, ruled by a Mande aristocracy, and to the settlement of Mande-speaking ruling clans (the Traoré, Cissé, Konaté, Kamagaté, Jabagaté, Watara, and Kulibali) in the subregion. These aristocratic Mande clans supported the establishment of Mande-speaking Muslim traders and scholars, the Juula and Jakhanke, who came to form a "second estate" (Goody 1967: 186) between the Mande aristocracy and the non-Muslim farming populations of the region. The rise of Gonja on the middle Volta in the mid-seventeenth century led to the destabilization of neighboring Dagbon, but by 1713 Dagbon was able to defeat Gonja and to stop its eastward advance. Dagbon, as well as other, smaller Mande states such as Wa and Buna, followed Gonja and integrated Muslim scholars and traders, often in twin settlements as in the political centers of the bilād al-sūdān. From the eighteenth century, some polities in the savannah and forest belt of the bilād al-sūdān, such as Kong under the leadership of the Watara family, started to stress their Islamic character, while Muslims achieved greater influence at courts in states such as Asante. At the same time, a new class of predatory warrior states emerged, such as Mamprussi in the Volta region or Zaberma on the lower Niger. The rulers of these predatory states were Muslim, but failed to develop an Islamic legitimatory basis for their military enterprises. In this respect these states resembled the early empire-building efforts of Samori Turé further west in the late nineteenth century. The advance of Muslim traders (Mande-speaking traders from the north, Hausa-speaking traders from the east) into the southern savannah and forest regions brought about the emergence of distinct trade routes and important trade centers which linked the savannah and forest belt of the bilād al-sūdān with the Sahelian trade routes and networks: from Jenné on the upper Niger, traders would move through Bobo, Bighu, and Buna to Asante in the south. Despite the growing influence of Muslim scholars and traders, the societies of the savannah and forest belt of sub-Saharan West Africa remained firmly anchored in African religious traditions until colonial times. At the same time, rituals such as the Hausa/Songhay/Nupe gani New Year festival were merged with Islamic festivals, most often the celebration of the mawlid al-nabī, the "birthday of the Prophet," and increasingly lost their African character and function. Such socioreligious processes could also be observed in North Africa with respect to the fusion of pre-Islamic Imasighen traditions with Islam, or in Ethiopia, with respect to the integration of pre-Christian/pre-Islamic ritual traditions into both Ethiopian Christianity and Islam. As in the Sahelian bilād al-sūdān, the expansion of Islam in the savannah and tropical forest regions of sub-Saharan West Africa was an expansion of Muslims, based on networks of traders and their diaspora, mostly Mande- and Hausa-speaking groups. As in the Sahelian bilād al-sūdān, local rulers in the savannahs and forests coveted Muslims as experts in new crafts and fields of knowledge, as interpreters and healers, as representatives of a world of prestigious goods and superior blessings, and sometimes even converted to Islam, although only a few rulers actually tried to Islamize their respective realm. As a result, Muslims remained a minority in most savannah and all forest regions of the bilād al-sūdān. Their position in society was similar in many ways to the position of Muslims in the Sahelian bilād al-sūdān in the thirteenth and fourteenth centuries.

A Trading Center in the Bilād al-Sūdān: Kano

In popular views, Africa has often been presented as a continent of villages, devoid of urban centers. This view ignores the fact that both sub-Saharan West Africa as well as the East African coast have a long tradition of urbanity. Urban centers emerged at the crossroads of trade routes, in particular when these crossroads were blessed by abundant water, natural protection, and rich soils which could sustain an agricultural surplus production sufficient to feed an urban population that was not primarily involved in food production. Such favored spots attracted traders and markets, as well as artisans and craftsmen of many different kinds. Sooner or later, such centers of population produced a government that evolved into local kingdoms and, in some cases, into trading empires. Some of these African urban centers, such as Gondär and Ḥarär in Ethiopia, Sinnār on the Nile, Kilwa and Mombasa on the East African coast, Jenné, Timbuktu, Katsina, Daura, Zaria or Segu in the bilād al-sūdān, or Agadez, Ghāt, and Ghadāmis in the Sahara, fired the imagination of both Arab and European travelers.

Apart from Timbuktu, no other urban agglomeration has attracted so much attention in the history of the bilād al-sūdān as Kano. In contrast to other important trading centers in the bilād al-sūdān, such as Gao, Kano's history is well documented in the Kano chronicle (KC), an account of Kano's history from its early and mystical beginnings to the nineteenth century, probably recorded for the first time in the sixteenth century. Updated and revised several times, it reflected the political dynamics of the times. Each new version of the chronicle mirrored the desire of new rulers to legitimize their own rule in an effort to reinterpret the past. The initial motivation to write a chronicle of Kano was thus possibly an effort by local rulers to create a legitimatory distance to the political overlord in the region, Bornu. Murray Last even characterized the KC as "a rather free compilation of local legends and traditions drafted in the mid-seventeenth century by a humorous Muslim rationalist who almost seems to have studied under Levi-Strauss" (Last 1983: 41). To a certain degree, it is possible, however, to give an account of Kano's history and the different dynasties on the basis of the chronicle, in particular when reading between the lines, by comparing the KC with the chronicles of neighboring countries such as Katsina and by adding additional evidence from archaeology.

An important topos in the Kano chronicle, as well as other local chronicles in the bilād al-sūdān, is the cultural hero who founded Kano and created a legitimatory link to a tradition of noble descent. Such cultural heroes may turn up several times in historical traditions and mirror specific changes and cultural, religious, and/or political reorientations. Thus, the leader of the first Wangarawa traders in the fourteenth century (who saw a second coming, in the time of Sarkin Kano Muḥammad Rumfa in the late fifteenth century) was depicted in the KC as the person who brought Islam to Kano, while the fifteenth-century religious scholar ʿAbd al-Karīm al-Maghīlī was described as the person who introduced both the Mālikī school of law as well as Sufism. The Sarkin (ruler) Kano Muḥammad Rumfa was depicted as the major statesman in Kano in the fifteenth and sixteenth centuries, credited with having introduced a plethora of useful innovations, while another religious scholar, ʿAbdallāh Sika, who had to flee Kano in the sixteenth century, was portrayed after the jihād in the early nineteenth century as a symbol of religious opposition to the rule of accommodationist kings. In truth, these cultural heroes represent developments which took place over a long period of time but were condensed into identifiable historical persons.

With respect to Kano's beginnings, the KC mentions that Barbushe had been the founder of the place, and that he had lived on top of Dala hill (Hau. Dutsen Dala), one of two inselbergs in the future birnin Kano (the walled city of Kano). Barbushe was the follower and priest of a local cult whose supreme deity was called Tsunburburai. This first "lord of the land" (Hau. sarkin noma) of Kano may be seen as representing the mystical origins of Kano and condensing a long period of non-recorded time. The first ruler (Hau. sarki) of Kano allegedly lived between 999 and 1063. He was called Bagauda and established a ruling dynasty which changed its residency several times, before a third Sarkin Kano, Gijimasu (r. 1095–1134, according to the chronicle), finally settled below Dutsen Dala and started to erect a first wall with eight gates. Thus, Kano ceased to be a gari (village, town) and became a birni (a walled city), a process which implied some form of administrative organization, as gates usually served to control and to tax people coming into a birni. The KC also mentions that Kano had a number of great leaders, implying that the Sarkin Kano was not yet a divine king but a "primus inter pares." Still, in this period Kano seems to have been able to defeat some important neighbors, such as Rano and Ringim, and to direct their trade into Kano. In its beginnings, Kano was thus one of many small centers in Hausaland which fought amongst each other for local hegemony.

Under Sarkin Kano Yusa (r. 1136–1194) the construction of the wall was completed. This wall was a form of fortification consisting of a ditch, a low wall, and thorn hedges as defense works; a proper wall came to be established much later. Only in the late fifteenth century did such a wall surround Kano, with a length of 12 kilometers, a height of up to 9 meters, a width of 7.5 meters at the foundations and 6 meters at the crown, and an internal runway to move cavalry around the town within the wall. The chronicle reports with regard to the next Sarkin Kano, Naguji (r. 1194–1247), that he was the first ruler to introduce a land tax in order to finance increased spending in his time. This could mean that Kano already had a basic administrative apparatus which had to be financed, as well as an executive force which imposed and collected taxes among the farmers of the region. The increasing differentiation of the administrative apparatus continued under the subsequent rulers of Kano. Under Sarkin Kano Tsamia (r. 1307–1343), Kano had nine men with distinct titles who were in charge of specific tasks. In the fourteenth century, under Sarkin Kano Yaji (r. 1349–1385), Kano managed to defeat Santolo, its major competitor, and to attract, as the major trading center in the region, the so-called Wangarawa, Muslim traders from Wangara (the Hausa term for Mālī) who were credited with having started Islam in Kano. The KC describes the arrival of the Wangarawa as follows:

> In the time of Yaji came the Wangarawa from Melle and brought Islam. The name of their leader was 'Abd al-Raḥmān Zagayte. . . . When they came, they asked the sarki to follow the daily prayers. He obeyed and appointed Gurdamus to be the first imām and Lawal to be the first mu'adhdhin. Auta slaughtered the cattle and Mandawali was the imām of the Wangarawa. Zayte became the alkali (al-qāḍī). The sarki commanded all towns in his realm of Kano to follow the times of prayer and they all followed his command. A mosque was established under the sacred tree and the prescribed prayers were performed there in the proper times. (quoted in Palmer 1967: 97ff.)

Despite the statement in the chronicle that Islam came to Kano with the Wangarawa from the west, and thus from the empire of Mālī, which was the major trading empire in the western bilād al-sūdān at that time, there are hints in the chronicle that Islamization may have started earlier and that Islamization was due to eastern influences, in particular the empire of Kānim-Bornu, which was Kano's overlord in the thirteenth century. Thus, the KC mentions the "two nights of idi" in the time of Sarkin Kano Bagauda, which probably refers to the two major Muslim holidays, 'Īd al-fiṭr, the breaking of the fast at the end of Ramaḍān, and 'Īd al-kabīr, the day of sacrifice in the month of pilgrimage. Assuming that Bagauda's rule was in the late eleventh century, an Islamic influence from Kānim-Bornu which already had a Muslim dynasty at this time is not improbable. Due to the fact that Kano, in its first centuries, tried to assert its independence from outside influences, in particular from Kānim-Bornu, Kānim-Bornu's historical legacy was thus probably written out of the chronicle, while the influence of the Wangarawa from distant Mālī was emphasized, even though they came to Kano in the fourteenth century only.

Other aspects of the KC strengthen the argument of an earlier and eastern origin of Islam in Kano. Thus, Sarkin Kano Usman (r. 1343–1349), who preceded Sarkin Kano Yaji, had a distinctive Muslim name. He is also credited with having expelled the Maguzawa, the heathen, from Kano. Kānim-Bornu's cultural influence on Kano is also reflected in many Hausa loanwords from Kanuri, such as karatu (from Arab. qarāʾ) "read" or rubutu (from Arab. rabaṭa) "write," as well as in numerous royal titles at the Kano court, and even birni (walled town) is of Kanuri origin. The advent of the Wangarawa may thus be viewed as reflecting Kano's successful reorientation toward the west (at a time of Kānim-Bornu's decline). In addition, the advent of the Wangarawa and their establishment at the court may be viewed as a sign that Islam had eventually prevailed against competing African religious traditions. Although a successor of Sarkin Kano Yaji, Sarkin Kano Kanajeji (r. 1390–1410), tried to reintroduce the old cult after some military defeats against heathen neighbors, Sarkin Kano Umaru (r. 1410–1421) seems to have been a pious Muslim ruler again.

The dynamics of Islamization are also reflected in other details in the KC. Kola nuts are mentioned as having come to Kano for the first time under Sarkin Kano Dauda (r. 1421–1438), pointing to the increasing integration of Kano into the trading networks of the southern bilād al-sūdān. The consumption of beer (alcohol) had obviously declined, while kola from Gonja came to be a new stimulant. Kola nuts were exchanged for textiles, and in the fifteenth century Kano slowly started to emerge as a major center of production of textiles in the central bilād al-sūdān. The decreasing consumption of millet in the form of millet beer enabled farmers to sell a larger part of their grain harvest to the court or caravans, for instance, while at the same time being able to exchange grain for salt, textiles, or other items offered in the Kano markets. Increasing Islamization led to an increasing demand for textiles (Hausa-speaking peoples had been referred to in Kānim-Bornu in rather pejorative terms as Afunu, "those who walk naked"), and stimulated the development of ever new patterns and fabrics, different techniques of dying and weaving, and the pounding of textiles into highly esteemed shiny fabrics, which stimulated the production of cotton and indigo, and consequently the further integration of Kano farmers into market production and trans-local exchange networks. Kano weavers soon produced not only for the local markets but also for the trans-Saharan and trans-Sudanic trade, and gained an increasing reputation for the high quality and low prices of their products in the fifteenth and sixteenth centuries. As a consequence, Kano textiles were traded to Gonja, and later Asante in the southwest, as well as across the Sahara to the bilād al-maghrib. Kano's increasing wealth attracted other traders and crafts and thus enlarged Kano's importance as a city of trade and production. Kano's wealth and subsequent economic and political rise was thus not based on the extraction of non-replaceable resources such as gold or slaves, as in other trade emporia of the bilād al-sūdān, but on the development of incentives for agricultural and manufacturing production, in particular the production of textiles. The increasing Islamization of Kano and the importance of textile production also affected the role of women, who were increasingly sought as home producers of textiles and consequently abandoned work in the fields. At the same time, the custom of seclusion (Hau./Ful. kulle) seems to have taken root in Kano.

In the early sixteenth century, Kano reached a peak of growth and economic wealth and started to attract traders from the bilād al-maghrib. One of these traders, the Venetian Vincenzo Matteo from Ragusa (Dubrovnik), which was under Ottoman sovereignty, was able to cross the Sahara with an Ottoman amān (letter of security). He described Kano as a large and wealthy trading center:

> Cheuno, a city which others call Cano is one of the three (major cities) of Africa. The two others are Fes and Cairo. About them, the Moors say that there is no product in this world which cannot be found there. Cano is equi-distant from both Fes and Cairo, a journey of about two months. The city (of Kano) is bigger than Ninive was, as described by the traders who come to Algiers. It is the only city of the Africans with a wall and this wall has been built with so many stones that none are to be found any more in the area. The wall has 18 gates and the city is the most civilized in these countries. People are living in great luxury. Also many white noblemen are living there, who have gone there a long time ago. Their way of life is of such a nature that many of them have their own horses on their own farms and that they have their own slaves. (quoted in Lange and Berthoud 1972: 338–41)

Kano's economic and political strength could develop under specific conditions only, however: low taxes and customs, low costs of production, security for farmers, traders, and craftsmen, longterm political stability, favorable regulations for all kinds of local, seasonal, periodic, rotating, or central long distance trade (Hau. fatauci) markets, safe trading routes and security for traders and producers in times of war. Whenever these conditions were met, Kano (and any other trading center in the bilād al-sūdān) would prosper and attract people, traders, craftsmen, producers. Equally, Kano would be able to extend its control over its periphery and to acquire a tributary zone. When Kano's rulers could not grant these conditions anymore, or even violated them in order to increase spending at court or by wasting surplus for wars with competing neighbors, Kano would enter a period of crisis, people would leave, and Kano's periphery (bilād al-sība) would shrink: power and prosperity in Kano and in the bilād al-sūdān in more general terms were not so much dependent on control over a territory (within well-defined boundaries) but indeed on the capability of a Sudanese state to attract and control people.

Kano's power reached its height under Sarkin Kano Muḥammad Rumfa (r. 1463–1499) and his successors in the sixteenth century. The city wall was extended in order to protect a growing population; a new central market, Kasuwar Kurmi, was built; and south of the market a new, large palace area was set up, which still exists today. The etiquette at court became increasingly refined, and for the first time offices and functions at the court were filled not with representatives of the nobility, the masu sarauta (the masters of nobility), but with slaves, often eunuchs, who were unable to form a hereditary elite. The Sarkin Kano ceased to be a primus inter pares and became a powerful ruler who could afford to marginalize noble families and to privilege others. The KC depicts Muḥammad Rumfa in the following terms:

> The 20th Sarki was Muḥamma Rimfa. . . . He was a good man, just and learned. No other Sarki equaled him in power, since the foundation of Kano until the very end. In his time, many shurafa (members of the family of the Prophet) came to Kano, such as ʿAbd al-Raḥmān (i.e. ʿAbd al-Raḥmān Zagayte, the leader of the fourteenth century Wangarawa mentioned above, who seems to serve here as a cultural hero a second time, RL) and his people. He brought many books and asked Rimfa to build a Friday mosque, to cut down the sacred tree and to build in its place a minaret. Rimfa was the source of twelve innovations in Kano: He built the new palace, and extended the walls in the next year. He established Kurmi market and was the first Sarki to employ horse knights in a war against Katsina. He also started the custom of seclusion of the women (Kulle) and introduced as first Sarki "Kakaki" (trumpets) as well as "Figinni" (ostrich feathers) as well as sandals ornamented with ostrich feathers. In his time, ʿīd was celebrated in Kano for the first time and he started to give positions at the court to eunuchs. (quoted in Palmer 1967: 111–12)

Thus the development of a new nobility started in Kano which was based on merit rather than descent, and which was loyal to the Sarki only. The gradual marginalization of the old nobility provoked resistence by the established noble families. In the decades to come, these families tried to win back lost privileges and power. After the death of Muḥammad Rumfa, due to this development, Kano entered a period of internal dispute and strife, which led to a structural crisis of the state in the seventeenth and eighteenth centuries. For the time being, however, under Sarkin Kano Muḥammad Rumfa's successors, Kano enjoyed a climax of its political power and was able to attack its most powerful neighbor, the kingdom of Katsina in the north, although Katsina had experienced a similar period of boom under Sarkin Katsina Ibrāhīm Sura (1493–1498) and Sarkin Katsina ʿAlī (1498–1524). Still, Kano was able to consolidate its leading role in the region until the time of Sarkin Kano Abubakar Kado (r. 1565–1573). The rise of Kano and its wealth also led to a confrontation with Kano's old overlord, the empire of Bornu, which tried to subjugate Kano in two wars. Sarkin Kano Abdullahi (r. 1499–1509) and Sarkin Kano Muḥammad Kisoki (r. 1509–1565) were able, however, to reject these attacks and to maintain Kano's independence. But constant war with Katsina and Bornu, the raids of the Kwararafa/Jukun from the south, and the costs of the court slowly undermined

Kano's economic foundations. Sarkin Kano Muḥamman Shashere (r. 1573–1582) was thus forced to impose new taxes and to raise fees, a policy which was continued by his successors. Due to this development, Kano's farmers had to suffer increasing burdens and withdrew into subsistence production. In addition, traders moved to other trading centers in the region such as Katsina, which offered better conditions and thus contributed to this downward development. The weakening of the Sarki offered the old nobility a chance to win back lost terrain, and their demands contributed to weakening Kano's power. Finally, Kano was so weak that the Jukun/Kwararafa invaded and devastated Kano twice in the mid- and late seventeenth century. Farmers stopped paying their taxes and Kano was increasingly dominated by Katsina.

Kano was not able to overcome its crisis in the eighteenth century and became easy prey to the troops of Usman dan Fodio in the context of the Sokoto jihād in the early nineteenth century. The last Sarkin Kano was deposed and replaced by an emir. He represented a new dynasty of Muslim rulers whose rule was based on the principles of Islam only. Forming part of the Sokoto caliphate, the emirate of Kano reemerged as a center of trade and production of textiles and eventually became the strongest emirate in the Sokoto caliphate, with a population of around 30,000–60,000 in the mid-nineteenth century. In 1851, Heinrich Barth witnessed Kano's integration into a trans-continental network of trade, which linked Kano not only to the other centers of trade in the western bilād al-sūdān and the bilād al-maghrib, but also to European markets north of the Mediterranean. He reported:

> The principal European goods brought to the market of Kano are bleached and unbleached calicoes, and cotton prints from Manchester; French silks and sugar; red cloth from Saxony and other parts ofd Europe; beads from Venice and Trieste; a very coarse kind of silk from Trieste; common paper with the sign of three moons, looking glasses, needles, and small ware from Nuremberg; sword blades from Solingen; razors from Styria. (Barth 1858, Vol. 2: 135)

Networks of Traders and Scholars

Networks of traders, as has been mentioned in several contexts, were the most important social groups to spread Islam in the bilād al-sūdān. Often these networks of traders were based on ethnic and linguistic affinity. Thus, Imasighen traders from the bilād al-maghrib dominated the trans-Saharan trade from the eighth century and came to establish trading outposts and traders' quarters in southern Saharan centers such as Timbuktu. Probably from the ninth and tenth centuries onward, Arab traders also started to frequent trans-Saharan routes, in particular the eastern and central routes leading to Wadai/Dārfūr, Kānim-Bornu, and Hausaland, and, from the fourteenth and fifteenth centuries, the routes in the western Sahara. In addition, Saharan populations, in particular (Imasighen) Tuareg, but also Kanuri (from Bornu) and Teda/Daza (from the Tibesti and Ennedi area), as well as Zaghāwa (from Wadai and northern Dārfūr), became active in the trans-Saharan trade. Imasighen traders, often of Ibāḍī or Ṣufrī orientation, dominated many important trading places in the northern sāḥil such as Sijilmāsa and the Mzab, and were still reported in the southern sāḥil in the mid-fourteenth century by Ibn Baṭṭūṭa, who mentioned in his account of his journey to Mālī that "a village called Zāgharī (today: Diarra), ten days from Walāta, was settled by black traders, the Wangārata, who lived in a community with white traders, Khārijites of Ibāḍī orientation, called Ṣaghnaghū" (*wa-yaskunuhā tujjār al-sūdān wa-yasmūna wanǧārata wa-yaskunu ma'hum jamā'a min al-bīḍān yadhhabūna madhhab al-Ibāḍiyya min al-Khawārij wa yasmūna Ṣaghnaghū;* Ibn Baṭṭūṭa, 1985, 2: 779). From the ninth century to the late fifteenth century, North African Jewish traders were active in a number of oases, such as Tuwāt and Wādān, as well as trading places in the

The markets of sub-Saharan Africa absorbed large numbers of European weapons, mostly guns, which had been phased out by European armies. As a consequence, African importers usually lagged one or two technological generations behind European military technological innovations. Still, some African rulers such as al-Ḥājj 'Umar Taal in mid-nineteenth-century upper Senegal were well and uniformly equipped with European guns, as was witnessed by French observers in 1878: "The troops do not have uniforms but they are uniformly armed with flintlock European rifles in unusually good condition, and armed with powder horns and leather sacks of balls. Officers have sabres and double-barreled piston-loaded firearms" (quoted in Roberts 1987: 92). Rivalries, competition, and war over, for instance, the control of trade routes equally stimulated African efforts to acquire ever new means of destruction. Apart from the introduction of firearms since the mid-sixteenth century, cavalries revolutionized warfare in the bilād al-sūdān since the seventeenth century. Cavalry troops were equipped with helmets, shields, and coats of chain and thus gained an advantage against archers. This revolution in warfare (and the respective arms race) in the bilād al-sūdān but also in Ethiopia shows that major parts of sub-Saharan Africa were well integrated into world markets. African polities which achieved parity in arms with European colonial powers were consequently able to put up sustained resistance against them. The tribal populations of the northwestern Sahara in the late nineteenth and early twentieth centuries, for example, were supplied by both Spain and Germany with modern rifles, and were only defeated by France in 1934, while Ethiopia was able to decisively defeat Italy in 1896 with guns and rifles supplied by Italy, Russia, and France.

southern sāḥil, such as Timbuktu, Gao, and Bornu, as is documented by letters found in the Cairo geniza (treasury, the deposit for old documents of the Jewish community). None of these groups, however, managed to make inroads into the trade systems of the bilād al-sūdān proper, where local trade networks prevailed.

Trade in the bilād al-sūdān was controlled in fact by Sudanese long-distance and regional trade networks, mostly Hausa-speaking traders in the central bilād al-sūdān, as well as a number of Mande-speaking trade networks in the central and western bilād al-sūdān. These trade networks were informed by the specific regional needs of the different ecological zones of sub-Saharan West Africa, which stimulated regional exchange patterns of salt, grain, weapons, horses, glass, and textiles from the northern, Sahelian, and Saharan regions, and kola, gold, guns, and other European trade goods from the forest belt and the Guinea Coast. Guns and horses as means of destruction were of major importance for regional wars over the control of trade routes as well as the acquisition of slaves. The latter were traded by different groups in exchange for more guns and horses, luxury products, and trade goods from other regions of the bilād al-sūdān, especially cotton for local textile production which blossomed in large parts of Hausaland and on the upper Niger. Sudanese traders organized transport and trade on the large rivers, the Niger and its confluences, the Senegal and the Gambia, the Volta and the Benue, and a plethora of smaller rivers flowing toward the Guinea coast, as well as the trade routes in the southern bilād al-sūdān. In addition, the Sudanese traders used overland routes which were well supplied by trade posts (Hau. zongo). These often developed into (Muslim) trading entrepôts and nuclei of Islamization. Both regional and long-distance traders in the bilād al-sūdān restricted their activities to the dry season, between October/November and April/May/June, not only because overland routes were not waterlogged during dry seasons, but also because many traders were farmers and needed to be on their farms during the rainy season. In addition, salt, which was susceptible to losses due to moisture, had to be transported in the dry season, in particular the loose Amersal salt from the Tīšīt salt ponds, which was important as cattle salt. The same applied to kola nuts, which perished quickly in the rainy season.

Usually, traders traveled by boat or caravan, often in convoy, and had to pay fees and taxes or protection monies to local rulers when passing through their territories. Consequently, they tried to bypass states where these fees were high. On arriving at their final destination, traders usually stayed with partner families. These relationships of exchange often turned into longstanding trading partnerships between specific Imasighen or Arab traders and their Kanuri, Hausa, or Mande trading partners. Equally, the traders from the bilād al-maghrib and the traders from the bilād al-sūdān entered into patronage relationships with local farmers: they bought their products preferentially, were allowed to graze their cattle and transport animals on their lands, and provided them with milk and meat. Many traders were thus not only traders, but entrepreneurs in many fields, as can be seen in the case of the Maraka traders on the Niger:

> Maraka merchants' decisions concerning destinations were contingent on market information but were finally determined by their desire to return home before the new agricultural cycle. The Maraka were not archetypical itinerant-traders who bought and sold continuously along the routes, maximizing small profits by shrewd deals. Instead, they were sophisticated managers of complex production-commercial firms who constantly balanced commercial profit against investment in production. They exported an assortment of goods that reflected the particular comparative advantages of the Middle Niger valley in the continental trade of West Africa. To the desert-side, the Maraka exported grain, cloth, slaves, and occasionally kola. To the south, Maraka traders carried salt, dried fish, slaves, and locally produced indigo-dyed cloth. After the early nineteenth century, slaves from the Middle Niger valley no longer moved southward; usually they moved westward and northward into the desert and sahel. (Roberts 1987: 61)

The conversion of an increasing number of people to Islam, and a consequent decline in the consumption of millet beer, as well as a corresponding rise in the consumption of kola nuts as a new stimulant, stimulated the expansion of regional trade networks in the bilād al-sūdān. Kola was harvested in the tropical regions of the Guinea coast and traded for weapons, textiles, salt, and luxury goods that had either been produced in the bilād al-sūdān, or imported via the trans-Saharan trade. In the context of this development, a new trade diaspora formed in the tropical forests, namely the zongos, the trading posts of the Hausa, which also came to form new centers of Islamic learning, such as Salaga, Kong, Buna, or Wa in the Volta region. In the nineteenth century, Salaga on the Volta River had become a major center of regional and long-distance (kola) trade and Islamic learning, with a population of 40,000 people. It had six mosques and numerous schools and was a well-known center for the production of amulets, which were keenly sought after by the rulers of the principalities and kingdoms of the south. While Hausa long-distance traders (Hau. farke, pl. fatake) were able to establish their zongos in all areas northeast of Asante, they had to fight against trading networks from Bornu. Bornu traders cultivated trade links with the kola-producing forests of the Guinea coast and could add natron to their array of trade goods. In the nineteenth century, the traders from Bornu were largely assimilated by the Hausa networks, while Hausa traders consolidated their hold over the lower Niger River, the Benue, and the eastern confluences of the Volta River. The spread of Islam in these regions, in particular in the Yoruba areas of the south, was consequently linked with the expansion of Hausa trade networks (see map 5).

The major network of traders in the bilād al-sūdān was controlled, however, by Mande-speaking groups, such as the Maraka, Juula (Juula), Yarsé, Malinke, Jakhanke (Diakhanke), and the Wangarawa. The expansion of Mande trade networks was possibly linked with the rise of the empire of Mālī and its efforts to gain control over the gold mines of the south. From the early fifteenth century, Mande traders linked the confluences of the Niger with the rivers of the south and eventually reached the Atlantic on the Guinea coast, probably around 1500. Even the collapse of Mālī had no negative effects on the Mande trading networks, especially that of the Juula, as they were much in demand in the south due to the fact that they had started to bring highly esteemed products of the trans-Saharan trade, in particular salt. The Mande/Juula trade in Saharan salt led to the establishment of first Mande/Juula trading enclaves in Worodugu, the land of kolanuts, in what is today southwestern Ivory Coast. Due to the fact that all Mande/Juula were Muslims, Islam came to be equated with trade and Mande/Juula identity:

> To be Juula, one had to be Muslim, and to be Muslim, one had to observe what were once only mory (scholarly) standards of piety. One could, however, be identified as "Juula," not only in Korhogo, but also in the new and fast-growing communities in the south of Côte d'Ivoire, where many Juula from Korhogo had emigrated during the first half of the twentieth century. In the south, all Manding-speaking Muslims were known as "Juula," whether they were from Côte d'Ivoire or from neighboring countries such as Guinea, Mali, or Upper Volta. In short, the Juula were a highly heterogeneous community of "outsiders" linked by a common language and a common religion. (Launay 1992: 65)

With a few exceptions, Mande/Juula trade did not lead to the emergence of Mande/Juula states, however: in the regions between the bilād al-sūdān and the Atlantic coast, local principalities and kingdoms continued to thrive, often on the basis of the slave trade with European trading posts on the coast, and tried to gain maximum control over the trade routes in their region. The most successful state in this respect was the kingdom of the Asante in present-day Ghana, as well as the Mossi kingdoms on the upper Volta and its confluences, in particular the kingdoms of Mamprussi, Dagomba, Wagadugu, Yatenga, and Fada N'Gurma. Muslims had started to live at the courts of Mossi kings in the early sixteenth century, but they did not exert real influence on their policies. The Mossi kings stressed their adherence to existing cults and followed restrictive policies with respect to Muslims, who were, for instance, not allowed to pray in public. Some Mossi rulers did convert to Islam, such as the king of Sakhabutenga. But at other courts, Muslims had to swear allegiance to the king and were represented at court by an imām who was exempt from non-Islamic court rituals.

In the territories between the Mossi kingdoms and Asante in the south, a series of smaller principalities formed in the eighteenth century, and some of these polities were foundations of Mande/Juula traders, such as Wa, Bono, Mamprussi, and Dagomba. These states attracted Mande/Juula scholarly families to settle in their territories, most particularly the Baghayogho family, which held the office of the imām of one of the great mosques in Timbuktu. The Baghayogho were an important family in Jenné as well. Jenné was another major trade emporium in the bilād al-sūdān, important for trade to the Guinea coast in the south and to Asante, where Mande/Juula traders and scholars started to gain positions at the court from the eighteenth century. The most powerful Mande/Juula state in this region, Kong, was formed in the early eighteenth century by Seku (Arab. shaykh) Keita Watara (d. 1740), and came to control the lands between the upper Comoé River and the upper Bandama, stretching in the north to the Bani, a southern tributary of the Niger, and to the Black Volta in the south. Based on a well-equipped army of Senufo warriors, Kong's aim was to develop a new trade route to the Atlantic, west of Asante. Due to the fact that it had risked war on two fronts, with Asante in the south and the Bambara of Kaarta in the north, Kong disintegrated into several smaller states after the death of Seku Keita Watara, and these states were eventually conquered, in the late nineteenth century, by Samori Turé. Yet, although Mande/Juula represented the ruling elite in Kong and its successor states, these states did not turn into imāmates ruled by religious scholars, as happened in the aftermath of the jihād movements in the bilād al-sūdān in the eighteenth and nineteenth centuries. The aim of Kong and its successors was not to convert the non-Muslim population in the region but to gain maximum control over long-distance trade routes.

Muslims in Asante

While Kano had a long history of Islamization, the kingdom of Asante in the hinterland of the Guinea coast came into contact with Islam much later, and never became a major center of Islam. To this day, Muslims in Asante and southern Ghana are a minority, and thus representative of a socioreligious situation that predominated in the northern bilād al-sūdān until the sixteenth through eighteenth centuries. However, from the sixteenth century, Asante traders acted as intermediaries between the European trading posts on the coast and the trade networks in the northern bilād al-sūdān. Asante may thus be described as another in a series of transmission belts that linked the Guinea coast with the bilād al-sūdān, the Sahara, and the bilād al-maghrib, as well as the Mediterranean. In addition, Asante was an important region for kola-nut production and it was a major exporter of gold and slaves. In contrast to the trading empires of the bilād al-sūdān, Asante was never a Muslim trading empire, although Muslims came to play an increasingly important role in Asante from the late eighteenth century. Asante history in the eighteenth and nineteenth centuries thus mirrors the dynamics of Islamization in the northern bilād al-sūdān some centuries earlier. This applies in particular to the gradual establishment and accommodation of Muslims and their integration into Asante society and politics.

Asante was probably founded in the sixteenth century, yet remained confined, for almost two centuries, to a small core area in the hinterland of the Gold Coast. From the early eighteenth century, Asante expanded and eventually became not only the most important trading empire on the Guinea coast, but also a formidable opponent of European, and especially British, colonialism in the second half of the nineteenth century. From the eighteenth century, the kings of Asante employed Muslim experts when developing their empire. First Muslims were reported at the court under Asantehene (king) Osei Kwadwo (r. 1764–1777). Under Osei Kwame (r. 1777–1798), they acquired a major role as advisors. Osei Kwame also sent Asante officials to the madrasa of ʿAbdallāh b. al-Ḥājj Muḥammad al-Watarawī in Buna on the

Upper Volta. Buna, a major center of Islamic learning about fourteen days north of Kumasi, Asante's capital city, and six days from Kong, thus played a major role for Asante as a center of learning. Buna was in fact a major center for itinerant Muslim scholars in the bilād al-sūdān and attracted Muslim scholars from Fuuta Tooro, Fuuta Jalon, and the whole upper Niger area. Buna also provided scholars for Asante. At the same time, Asante acquired first Islamic schools in Kumasi, and the Asantehene Osei Bonsu (r. 1800–1823) sent his children to these schools. The example of Asante shows that even those principalities and kingdoms of the southern bilād al-sūdān and the Guinea coast which were not ruled by Muslim rulers, and in which Islam was not the imperial cult, strove to integrate Muslims and their literary and linguistic skills into the administration of the state. Under Asantehene Osei Bonsu, Asante developed a chancery that relied on the expertise of Muslim scholars. In addition, the master of the treasury, the Gzaasewahene, had a number of Muslim advisors who were responsible for accounting, statistics, and the calendar. Even the history of the empire was recorded in Arabic from 1807.

In the early nineteenth century, Muslim advisors at the court had become so important that the British trading houses on the Gold Coast employed translators for Arabic in order to be able to negotiate with the court. When first treaties were concluded between Asante and the British in the 1820s, British diplomats had to swear an oath on the Qur'ān in the presence of the Muslim advisors to the Asantehene, confirming that they had come with good intentions. Bowdich, the British consul, confirmed the sacral role of the Qur'ān in Asante at this time: "The Ashantees without knowing the content of the Koran, are equally persuaded that it is a volume of divine creation, and consequently that it contains ordinances and prohibitions, which are most congenial to the happiness of mankind in general" (quoted in Wilks 1975b: 258). Both the king and his people had faith in the magical power of the Qur'ān, and incorporated into their own culture and daily life a number of magico-religious practices and customs as mediated by Muslims from the northern bilād al-sūdān. The Asantehene was said to have used Islamic invocations and had received a copy of the Qur'ān from a visiting scholar from Bornu, Sharīf Ibrāhīm al-Barnawī, who stayed at the court of Asante in Kumasi from 1815 to 1818. Muslim scholars acquired major importance in Asante, especially in the sphere of religio-therapeutic practices, and produced numerous amulets for the Asantehene and his court as well as for the army. Writing paper was consequently very valuable at Asante, and writing was a major source of income for Muslim scholars. The British consul Bowdich described the importance of amulets in 1817:

> The most surprising superstition of the Ashantees, is their confidence in the fetishes or saphies they purchase so extravagantly from the Moors, believing firmly that they make them invulnerable and invincible in war, paralyse the hand of the enemy, shiver their weapons, divert the course of balls, render both sexes prolific, and avert all evils but sickness, which they can only assuage, and natural death. (quoted in Wilks 1975b: 202)

Under Osei Bonsu, the community of Muslims in Asante grew considerably, even if Muslims continued to live in a quarter of their own, an established feature of Islamization in the bilād al-sūdān. Muslims also served in the Asante army and were able to mobilize around 7,000 warriors in 1818 in a war between Asante and the kingdom of Gyaman. The conflict with Gyaman posed a problem for Asante's Muslims, however, when Shaykh Bābā, the imām of the Muslim troops, realized that Muslims were also fighting on the side of Gyaman and that Muslims had come from Kong and Gonja in order to support Gyaman. The Muslim force thus withdrew from the campaign which subsequently triggered the ire of the Asantehene. Muslims lost their privileged position at the court of Asante for the time being.

In order to profit from trade, kingdoms and empires in the bilād al-sūdān tried to gain control over trade routes. Asante was no exception and started to expand along the routes to the north, as well as to the coast of Guinea in the south, in the eighteenth century. Due to this policy of expansion, Asante fought numerous wars with her neighbors, especially with Kong and its successor states in the north. In the nineteenth century, Asante was able to increase its control over the kola-nut trade, yet, due to the fact that Asante still controlled only one leg of this trade, traders were able to develop new routes which escaped Asante control. Due to their control over many of the trade routes, Mande/Juula trade networks, as well as Hausa traders from the northeast, remained independent of Asante's efforts to control them and were able to convince Asante to compromise. The superior position of Mande and Hausa traders thus granted Muslims an important role at the court of Asante, despite temporary setbacks and despite Asante restrictions on trade. However, when Muslim traders started to become increasingly powerful in the trade to the north, the Asantehene introduced restrictions here as well. In 1834, Muslim traders were banned from Kumasi. This prohibition was also valid for agents of the European trading houses on the Guinea coast, and must be seen as part of a larger policy aimed at retaining control over trade, at least within metropolitan Asante. Trade with Asante indeed attracted traders and travelers from many places. In the time of Asantehene Osei Bonsu, for instance, one Sharīf Aḥmad al-Baghdādī, who happened to have been to Iran and Khorasān, in Morocco and Tripoli, as well as numerous places in the bilād al-sūdān proper, stayed in Kumasi for some time. Some years later, in 1851, this Muslim traveler met Heinrich Barth in Kukawa, the capital city of Bornu, but was slain on the route from Yola to Kukawa in 1854. Despite being situated in the hinterland of the Guinea coast and on the southernmost leg of the trans-Saharan trade, Asante was linked with the wider world of Islam.

Traditions of Islamic Learning

In the context of the development of Muslim societies in the bilād al-sūdān, numerous local schools and traditions of learning started to emerge from an early point in time and were well established, at least in many northern regions of the bilād al-sūdān, by the fourteenth century. As in most parts of the Islamic world, traditions of Islamic learning in Africa were based on two essential steps: first, basic education in the qur'ānic school, where students would study the alphabet, the vocalization of all syllables, and reading, then start memorization (Arab. taḥfīẓ) of the Qur'ān with the sūrat al-fātiḥa and continue with the small sūras in the thirtieth juz' (part) of the Qur'ān, from sūra 114 to sūra 78. Having memorized this section, students would memorize the twenty-ninth juz', then the twenty-eighth, etc., until they had completed the taḥfīẓ of the Qur'ān as a whole. In addition, children would learn basic arithmetic (Arab. ḥisāb) and the fundamental prescriptions of the faith with its ritual obligations (Arab. 'ibādāt) in the form of a short catechism (Arab. 'aqīda), as well as the basic rules of proper behavior (Arab. adab, akhlāq). The primary task of the qur'ānic school was to train skills of memorization by constant repetition (Arab. takrīr) and incremental learning. Memorization and a firm discipline were regarded as preconditions for proper mastery of the Qur'ān. However, the major aim of memorizing the Qur'ān was not to inculcate rigid discipline but to provide skills and social knowledge that could be translated in meaningful ways into social competence. Knowledge was respected only when incorporated through memorization, not depending on the consultation of texts. When arguing, one had to have the mastery of a text without being constrained to consult a text. Basic knowledge of the Qur'ān, of the proper norms of the Islamic ritual and some knowledge of reading and writing the Arabic script, as well as faith in the magical and miraculous qualities of texts, came to form a mode of literacy that was widespread in Muslim societies in Africa and which has been described as restricted literacy (Goody 1975), a characteristic feature of originally non-literate societies which have started to see and appreciate the impact of literacy and its magic through the mediation of Muslim scholars.

After qur'ānic school, most students would stop their education and take up a profession, but some would continue to study with the most respected scholar known, learning specific texts such as the basic text in tafsīr studies, the *Tafsīr al-jalālayn* by al-Maḥallī and al-Suyūṭī, or the basic texts of Mālikī fiqh, such as the *Risāla* of Ibn Abī Zayd al-Qayrawānī (at least in the Sahara and the bilād al-sūdān; the Shāfi'ī school of law predominated in East Africa as well as some parts of Ethiopia and the Horn of Africa). Students would also study linguistic sciences, in particular naḥw (grammar), lugha, (linguistics), ṣarf (prosody), and 'arūḍ (metrics), and then delve into ḥadīth studies, read sīra and 'ilm al-falak (astronomy, astrology) and finally taṣawwuf (Sufism). In this quest for knowledge, students had to travel to the homes of the most respected scholars, a practice which was encouraged by a frequently quoted ḥadīth of the Prophet: *'uṭlub al-'ilm fa-lau fi l-ṣīn* (search for knowledge even if you have to go to China). The practice of ṭalab al-'ilm consequently contributed to the formation and cultivation of translocal scholarly entanglements which could at times acquire political and economic dimensions. As soon as students had completed their studies of tafsīr, they were entitled to wear a turban and were addressed as shaykh (scholar;

alternatively, malam in Hausa, alfa and/or fodio in FulFulde, karamoko in Mande languages). Part of the training in the esoteric disciplines, in particular ʿilm al-falak, was knowledge of specific prayers which were thought to have particular blessing, such as the prayer for rain, the ṣalat al-istisqāʾ, the prayer for protection, the ṣalat al-khawf, or the ṣalat al-istighfār and others against the evil eye, as well as prayers that were used for the production of amulets or the widespread practice of "drinking the writing," when a specific verse of the Qurʾān written with ink on a wooden board was washed off and drunk (Hau. sha rubutu; Swa. kikombe).

However, not all schools were equally important or had teachers who were recognized as experts for a specific text or discipline, so students would travel from scholar to scholar and establish, over time, a network of itinerant scholars. Some centers of Islamic learning were particularly well known, however, and attracted students from the whole of the bilād al-sūdān and beyond: Kalumbardo in Bornu, Kano and Katsina in Hausaland, Timbuktu, Jenné, and Kankan on the Niger, and Koki and Pir in Senegal, as well as the centers of learning in the central Ādrār and in Agadez (Air). Local centers of scholarship also produced eminent scholars, such as Aḥmad Bābā (d. 1627), whose library in Timbuktu was said to have contained 1,600 manuscripts. Local traditions of Islamic learning thus developed in many, even remote areas, of sub-saharan Africa, from the eleventh century. In regions where Islam was established only recently, the formation of a local tradition of learning is still identifiable today: thus, in the early twentieth century, the library of al-Ḥājj Ḥusayn in Savelugu (contemporary northern Ghana) contained forty-three titles, mostly on jurisprudence and grammar, which might be regarded as a representative selection. Apart from the Qurʾān and texts taken from ḥadīth collections, as well as a vast ʿaqīda literature, the *Risāla* of Ibn Abī Zayd al-Qayrawānī was the most widespread text, in particular when including commentaries, in particular the sixteen-volume work *Al-mudawwana al-kubrā* by the Tunisian scholar Saḥnūn, and the *Tuḥfa* of Ibn ʿAṣim, as the basic texts for the teaching of law. The *Muwaṭṭā* by Imām Mālik b. Anas could be found in only a few libraries, though, and likewise the (elsewhere very popular) *Mukhtaṣar* (*fī-l-fiqh ʿalā madhhab al-imām Mālik*) by the Egyptian scholar Khalīl b. Iṣḥāq, or works on the sīra of the Prophet. More widespread were Sufi manuals.

A major tradition of Islamic learning in the western bilād al-sūdān was represented by the Jakhanke ("those from Jakha"). The Jakhanke were not a distinct ethnic group, but formed part of the greater Mande language family. They were a group of scholars (and traders) who came to dominate scholarship on the upper Senegal, the upper Gambia, and in the Fuuta Jalon region, as well as on the upper Niger and in contemporary northern Ivory Coast. Jakhanke claims of origin refer to al-Ḥājj Sālim Suwaré (fl. late fifteenth century) who allegedly established a center and school in Ja (Dia) or Jakha (Diakha) on the Niger, which has been confirmed as a center of Islamic learning by the seventeenth-century *Taʾrīkh al-fattāsh*. Due to the Jakhanke reference to al-Ḥājj Sālim Suwaré, Western academia has introduced the term Suwarian or Suwarian tradition to describe a specific Jahkanke approach to Islamic learning. This approach was characterized by distinct methods of learning which focused on the teaching of tafsīr, as based on the *tafsīr al-jalālayn* of al-Maḥallī and al-Suyūṭī. The expansion of the Jakhanke may have been initially linked with the expansion of the Mālī empire, yet Jakhanke scholarship continued to flourish after the collapse of Mālī in the fifteenth century and spread into the south as well as the east. Thus, the legendary Wangarawa scholars and traders, who reached the trading center of Kano in the mid-fourteenth century under the leadership of ʿAbd al-Raḥmān Zagayte (Diakhite, Jakhite), could well have been early representatives of this type of scholars. At the same time, Jakhanke families migrated to the west and settled on the river Gambia and the upper Senegal.

A significant feature of the Jakhanke tradition was that Jakhanke scholarship developed beyond the influence of courts and refrained from taking political positions, stressing peaceful coexistence of Muslims and non-Muslims:

> Key to their beliefs was the rejection of active proselytization; true conversion occurs only in God's times. Jihad had therefore to be rejected as an instrument of change except, perhaps, in situations in which the very existence of the Muslim community was threatened. All unbelievers will, at various points in time, convert, but these times are preordained. Muslims who live among them have an obligation to keep pure the way of the prophet and, by providing their hosts with example (qudwa), will thereby make emulation (iqtidāʾ) possible. (Wilks 1995: 61)

The Jakhanke tradition eventually came to inform the myth of the peaceful Jakhanke scholar in European historiography. Curtin thus wrote: "The cultural features that set them off most decidedly from their neighbours are a combination of pacifism, avoidance of political power and worldy rule" (Curtin 1971: 229). The Jakhanke were probably innocent of such ideological constructions. The specific nature of their traditions of learning can rather be compared to a well-established model of division of tasks among Saharan tribal populations, where clans of warriors coexisted with clans of scholars and traders like the ineslemen or zawāya of the central and western Sahara. This model was developed in a particularly clear form by a scholar of the Kunta family of the Azawād region, north of Timbuktu, Sīdī al-Mukhtār al-Kuntī (1729–1811), who was famous not only for his widespread trading enterprises, but also for his role as a teacher and mediator, and the fact that he transformed his school and zāwiya into a center of the Qādiriyya Sufi order. From the late eighteenth century, his teaching and his model of combining trade, labor, and teaching in one center of learning radiated into other parts of the bilād al-sūdān and provided inspiration, not only for the leaders of the jihād in Hausaland and Masina, but also for the career of Shaykh Sidiyya Bābā (1776–1868) in Mauritania in the mid-nineteenth century, as well as for other scholars who rejected armed jihād as a means of transforming their respective societies. In the 1850s, the Jakhanke scholars of Fuuta Jalon, for instance, refused to support the jihād of al-Ḥājj 'Umar Taal, much to the chagrin of the latter, who had hoped to gain the support of the Jakhanke for his imperial plans. Jakhanke resistance to jihād was not linked to their dislike of war so much as to the fact that since the eighteenth century Jakhanke scholars had been affiliated with the Qādiriyya, while al-Ḥājj 'Umar represented a competing Sufi tradition and network, the Tijāniyya, which claimed spiritual superiority over all other Sufi ṭuruq, including the Qādiriyya.

At the same time, Muslim scholars were prepared, at least in some cases, to contribute to jihād, when the context seemed to favor such a position. Some Muslim scholars thus contributed to the formation of the imāmate of Wahabu on the Upper Volta, in the context of a jihād led by al-Ḥājj Maḥmud Karantaw ("the writer"). Al-Ḥājj Maḥmud Karantaw, the son of a Marka scholar from Sarro near Jennē, had studied with local Muslim scholars and had then gone on pilgrimage, together with 'Alī b. Ṣāliḥ Tarawiri from Wa, visiting Syria where he studied with a shaykh of the Qādiriyya and thus gained legitimacy, fed by a respected external source of blessing (Arab. baraka). After his return home, he initiated a movement of reform supported by some of the Muslim scholars of Wa. In a short period of time, his jihād gained control over the region of Wahabu. Due to the fact that most Mande communities in the larger region refused to submit to the authority of al-Ḥājj Karantaw, the imāmate remained confined to a small area. Al-Ḥājj Maḥmud's movement demonstrates, however,

> that peoples like the Juula belonging to the Suwarian tradition were aware of and not always impervious to the jihād movements that swept through much of West Africa (in this period). Second, like a number of other jihād leaders, al-Ḥājj Maḥmud sought legitimacy through a direct appeal to study in the Arabic-speaking world, effectively attempting to supersede the mediating role of local scholarly traditions. Finally, this attempt, though not entirely a failure, did not win the support of the vast majority of local Muslims, both scholars and ordinary believers, who continued to affirm their loyalty to the Suwarian tradition. (Launay 1992: 83)

5 Dynamics of Jihād in the Bilād al-Sūdān

Patterns of Jihād

In the eighteenth and nineteenth centuries, the bilād al-sūdān experienced a series of wars which led to the establishment of new states and empires that were ruled, for the first time in the history of these societies, by Muslim religious scholars. The wars which ended with the victory of these religious scholars were legitimated in religious terms and came to be regarded as jihāds, while the new states which arose from these movements of jihād came to be seen as imāmates. In major parts of the bilād al-sūdān, the jihāds of the eighteenth and nineteenth centuries brought to an end the rule of non-Muslim rulers and of those Muslim rulers who had tolerated the coexistence of Islam and local cults. They also set the stage for the European colonial conquest of Africa since the late nineteenth century which encountered a series of imāmates and Muslim empires, from the Atlantic to Lake Chad. When looking at the development of these Muslim states in the eighteenth and nineteenth centuries, we see that there was never a single model but a spectrum of expressions of jihād, and consequently not a single model of Islamic rule but a spectrum of expressions of rule: as each movement of jihād developed its own character, each imāmate developed its own style and structure of governance, from the almost ideal type of a Muslim state, Masina, to the empire of Samori Turé, which became Muslim only in the course of empire-building wars. In between were different models of Muslim states, such as the caliphates of Sokoto and Bornu and the Tukulóór empire of al-Ḥājj ʿUmar Taal. From a chronological perspective, these caliphates and imāmates may be seen as the result of a series of major jihāds which developed before the age of European conquest, and sometimes even came to an end, as in the case of Masina, before European conquest. In addition, there was a late series of lesser jihāds in the Senegambia region, which led to the formation of a number of short-lived imāmates, such as that of Ma Ba Jaxu (d. 1867), "Cheikhou" Amadou Ba (d. 1875), al-Ḥājj Mamadu Lamin Dramé (d. 1887), or Fode Kaba (d. 1901). Only these late movements of jihād were directly linked with the dynamics of European colonial conquest.

A significant feature of all movements of jihād was the fact that most leaders of the early jihāds, with the exception of al-Ḥājj ʿUmar Taal, were affiliated with the Qādiriyya, while most leaders of the late jihāds, with the exception of Samori Turé, who was supported by a network of Qādirī scholars, were linked to the Tijāniyya. Yet, although ṭarīqa affiliation came to be an important marker of religious identity for the scholarly elites of the jihād movements, and even came to be seen as a major element of their "corporate identity" (Brenner 1988: 47–50), ṭarīqa affiliation remained a characteristic feature of a scholarly elite only, and did not, as in late nineteenth-century East Africa, become a feature of popular adherence or of mass conversion to Islam. And despite the impression that the different movements of jihād seem to have evolved in a linear historical sequence, from Nāṣir al-Dīn's rebellion in the Senegal River valley in 1673/74 to Bundu from the 1680s; the jihāds in Fuuta Jalon from 1725, in Fuuta Tooro from 1775, in Hausaland from 1804, and in Masina in 1818; al-Ḥājj ʿUmar Taal's wars and jihāds from the 1850s, the Senegambian jihāds from the 1860s, and, finally, Samori Turé's policies of forceful Islamization from 1875, these jihāds did not form an

After the collapse of the great trading empires of the bilād al-sūdān, with the notable exception of Bornu, the bilād al-sūdān disintegrated into a large number of principalities and kingdoms which competed for access to resources, control over trade routes, and domination over taxable populations. Some of these principalities and kingdoms continued to cultivate the image of a Muslim state, while others, such as the Bambara states of Kaarta and Segu, emphasized pre-Islamic political and religious legacies. From east to west, the most important of these principalities and kingdoms in the bilād al-sūdān in the sixteenth, seventeenth, and eighteenth centuries were Wadai, the kingdom of Bagirmi southeast of Lake Chad, the Kotoko states and Mandara south of Lake Chad, the empire of Bornu west of Lake Chad, the Jukun federation (Kwararafa-Wukari, Pindiga, Jibu, Kam, Gwana) on the Gongola and middle Benue, and a series of Hausa states such as Kano, Katsina, Daura, Zaria, Zamfara, or Gobir between the Lake Chad basin and the middle Niger. To their west lay the pashālik of Timbuktu, controlled by the Arma; to their south, a plethora of Mossi states controlled the Upper Volta region. On the Upper Niger, the core region of the Mali Empire survived until around 1600 and was then incorporated into the Bambara kingdoms of Kaarta and Segu, which followed distinctively non-Islamic policies, although Muslims were tolerated. West of the Bambara kingdoms was a plethora of small principalities in the Senegal and Gambia regions, in particular, Fuuta Tooro and Waalo on the Lower Senegal; Gidimaxa and Gajaaga on the Upper Senegal; Jolof, Kajoor, Bawol, Siin, and Saloum north of the Gambia; Niumi and Kaabu on and south of the Gambia; and the numerous principalities of the Fuuta Jalon region.

interrelated chain of events, even if some of the religious scholars who led these movements knew each other or had studied under the same teacher (see map 13).

From a general perspective, the development of movements of jihād can be seen as evolving from the specific processes and dialectics of social, economic, and political change which characterized the history of the bilād al-sūdān from the sixteenth century. However, not all jihāds were successful: some failed, such as the very first jihād led by Nāṣir al-Dīn in the late seventeenth century, or the jihād in Bornu in the early nineteenth century. Other movements of jihād changed their character to become movements of conquest, such as the jihād of al-Ḥājj 'Umar Taal. As a consequence, the jihād movements were interpreted in different ways by local scholars, colonial historians, and western academia. The jihād of al-Ḥājj 'Umar Taal, for instance, was seen by some as a jihād of the Tijāniyya, while others regarded it as a movement of Tukulóór colonization on the Upper Niger. In colonial as well as postcolonial Senegal and Mali, al-Ḥājj 'Umar Taal was seen as a national hero and a conqueror. Similar variations in interpretation can be observed with respect to the imāmate of Fuuta Jalon in Guinea and the Sokoto caliphate in Hausaland, which not only had to fight constant wars against a multitude of enemies, but also had to come to terms with slave rebellions which were legitimated in Islamic terms as movements of resistance against oppressive (Muslim) rule. As a consequence, each movement of jihād developed its own myths and cultivated its own historiographic and hagiographic legacies, and these myths and legacies were again subject to interpretation. As David Robinson (2002: 107ff) has commented with respect to al-Ḥājj 'Umar Taal and the Tukulóór empire, his empire was neither an empire nor Tukulóór, even if Tukulóór, French, or postcolonial Senegalo-Malian constructions of history seem to support this idea.

In the literature, opposition to slave raiding has often been presented as the major explanation for the jihād movements in the bilād al-sūdān. In 1673, a religious scholar from southern Mauritania, Nāṣir al-Dīn (d. 1674), started a rebellion against the overlords of the region, the emirs of Brakna and Tagant, as well as the kings of Waalo and Jolof, and indeed legitimated his movement by saying that "God did not grant rulers the right to enslave, to rob or to kill their own populations. He rather commanded them to protect them, as rulers have been created to serve their peoples and not the other way round" (quoted in Barry 1988: 116). From the late sixteenth century, the development of the bilād al-sūdān was characterized by the disintegration of the great Sudanic empires, the emergence of numerous principalities fighting each other for resources and domination over trade routes, as well as the gradual integration of the Sudanic states into the economic sphere of the transatlantic slave trade, which added stress to sub-Saharan societies already affected by the trans-Saharan slave trade.

These political and economic developments brought about additional pressures on sub-Saharan populations when slave traders, in response to increasing prices for slaves on the West African coasts, started to raid the Sudanic interior. In some areas, such as the Senegambia, this shift to the Sudanic belt of sub-Saharan Africa came early, namely in the seventeenth century, while most parts of the Sudanic interior were affected by the transatlantic slave trade from the eighteenth century only. This explanation of the jihāds in the bilād al-sūdān as movements of protest against the trade in (Muslim) slaves, while convincing in hindsight, should not eclipse other, equally important motivations for jihād. Such explanations portray the jihāds as movements of protest against a large spectrum of social and economic grievances, including unjust rule and exploitation, that were reflected in a number of Sudanic chronicles such as the Kano chronicle or the chronicle of Aḥmad b. Furṭū in Bornu. These chronicles show that conditions of crisis were rampant in the bilād al-sūdān in the seventeenth and eighteenth centuries and thus conducive to jihād in large parts of the Sudanic subcontinent. In the Kano chronicle, the increasing destabilization of Kano under Sarkin Kano Muḥammad Sharefa (1703–1731) and Sarkin Kano Kumbari dan Sharefa (1731–1743) were described from a post-jihād perspective:

> The 37th Sarkin Kano was Muḥammad Sharefa, a powerful king. Yet, he introduced seven practices which constituted pure robbery, namely the taxes on Karo, Rinsua, Matafada, Yan Dawaki, Kuaru, the jizya tax on girls before marriage and the jizya on the Kurmi market. In addition, he found other ways of imposing taxes. Sharefa also sent the Wombai Debba into war against Kirru. The Wombai left Kano and came back with great bounty. He had captured many men. . . . In Sharefa's time, however, the war with the king of Zamfara, Yakubu Dan Mazura, started. In the battle of Yergana, the warriors of Zamfara defeated Kano. The 38th Sarkin Kano was Muhammad Kumbari dan Sharefa. He was a generous ruler but became angry very quickly. His advisors esteemed him, the people hated him. In his time there was a major war between Kano and Gobir, as well as with Bornu. Muhammad Kumbari really imposed the jizya tax on the Kurmi market and the market almost collapsed. In the following year, he even imposed the jizya tax on the religious scholars. This created so much protest that the Arabs left the town and went to Katsina and most of the poor people fled into the bush. (quoted in Palmer 1967: 124)

The history of the jihāds in the eighteenth and nineteenth century bilād al-sūdān can thus be best understood as resulting from a long historical evolution of Muslim societies in that region and their interaction with specific local social and political contexts.

External influences on the movements of jihād in the bilād al-sūdān can be largely ignored: only three jihād leaders, Muḥammad al-Kānimī, al-Ḥājj ʿUmar Taal, and Mamadu Lamin Dramé visited the holy places in Mecca and Medina, and Usman dan Fodio, the leader of the jihād in Hausaland, who had studied with a prominent Muslim scholar in the Aïr region, al-Ḥājj Jibrīl b. ʿUmar, came to reject the radical teachings of his mentor. Ideological links with movements of reform outside Africa, such as the Wahhābiyya, must be seen as historical constructions linked with French and British colonial policies which cultivated "Wahhābī" or "Mahdist" scenarios of revolt for legitimatory purposes. Only the fifteenth-century North African Muslim reformist scholar Muḥammad b. ʿAbd al-Karīm al-Maghīlī (d. 1503/04) had a major impact on theological discussions relating to the movements of jihād.

Al-Maghīlī was born in Tilimsān in the early fifteenth century, into an Imasighen family (the Maghīla). He studied in Tilimsān and Tunis, at a time when Jewish trade networks in North Africa were strengthened by Jewish refugees from Spain trying to make a living in the bilād al-maghrib. In 1477/78, al-Maghīlī settled in the oasis of Tuwāt, which had a large community of Jews, and composed a first text on the legal position of Jews and demanded that all Jews should be killed. Muslims who supported Jews should be regarded as unbelievers and should also be killed. These extremist positions were rejected by the Qāḍī of Tamantīt, Abū Muḥammad ʿAbdallāh b. Abī Bakr al-ʿAsnūnī, who granted the Jews the right to build synagogues in their quarters. As a consequence of this dispute, scholars from other parts of the bilād al-maghrib voiced their opinions and mostly supported al-ʿAsnūnī, except for Aḥmad b. Yaḥyā b. Muḥammad al-Wansharīsī (1430–1508), the Muftī of Fes, as well as two scholars from Tilimsān. Subsequently, al-Maghīlī placed a premium of seven mithqāl (gold coins) on the head of each Jew that was killed, triggering a pogrom in Tuwāt. Surviving Jews killed al-Maghīlī's son and fled from Tuwāt. After these events, al-Maghīlī traveled through the bilād al-maghrib and then across the Sahara to Kano (1492), where he wrote a text entitled *Tāj al-dīn fī mā yājib ʿalā l-mulūk* (The perfection of the faith regarding the duties of the kings), which became a key text on the basics of Islamic governance. Subsequently, he visited Katsina and Gao (1498), where he authored a second text on the principles of Islamic government for Askia Muḥammad Turé. This became a key text for Muslim reformers and leaders of jihād, often called *as'ilat asqiyya wa-ajwibāt al-Maghīlī* (The questions of the Askia and al-Maghīlī's responses). In it, al-Maghīlī accused the Askia's predecessor, Sonni ʿAlī, of having been a pagan despite having pronounced the shahāda. He also accused Sonni ʿAlī of having practiced two religions while neglecting his religious duties. In addition, he had killed Muslims, including religious scholars, and thus had to be regarded as an unbeliever. Regarding the legitimacy of a ruler, al-Maghīlī responded to the questions of the Askia in the following way:

> Your statement: if there is a land in which there are Muslims and their sultan is oppressive . . . should I or should I not drive away that oppressor from them. . . . Similarly, if there is a sultan who levies (unlawful) taxes and does not restrain wrongdoers, is it for me to curb him through fighting and killing or not? Also (there is the case of) the unjust sultan who opposes people and wherever he finds goods belonging to the Muslims seizes them. . . . Is such a sultan a wrongdoer (ẓālim) or an unbeliever (kāfir), on account of his declaring lawful that God has forbidden?
>
> 1. An ungoverned land (bilad al-sība) whose people have no amīr—indeed they are neglected. Allow such people to pay homage to you and enter into obedience to you. If they refuse that, then compel them to do so . . .

2. A land whose people have an amīr who looks after their worldly and religious interests so far as possible in this age: it is not lawful for anyone of these people to abandon their allegiance to him . . .
3. A land having an amīr from among those chiefs whom you described as levying (unlawful) taxes and being oppressive and evildoing and failing to set matters aright: if you can bring to an end his oppression of the Muslims without harm to them so that you set up among them a just amīr, then do so, even if that leads to killing and the killing of many of the oppressors and their supporters. (quoted in Hunwick 1985: 81)

Beyond the theological legacy of al-Maghīlī, the movements of jihād in the bilād al-sūdān were characterized by the fact that virtually all jihād leaders were affiliated with traditions of Islamic learning which had developed outside the royal courts. The leaders of the jihāds could thus be described in a terminology derived from the Senegambian context, as "sëriŋ fakk-taal" (Samb 1972: 25), religious scholars who make their own firewood, in order to be able to teach qur'ānic classes in the evening in the light of their own fire, thus depending on their own resources. At the same time, these independent scholars opposed those scholars who, again in the Senegambian context, were called "sëriŋ làmb," or scholars of the drum, as they were willing to sing praises and beat the drums for the rulers and to provide legitimization for those in power. From the late seventeenth century, Muslim religious scholars outside the courts became the spokesmen of the oppressed, as in the case of Nāṣir al-Dīn, but also in the cases of Usman dan Fodio, Muḥammad al-Kānimī, and Aḥmad Lobbo in Hausaland, Bornu, and Masina, respectively.

Even if Nāṣir al-Dīn's jihād was eventually suppressed by a coalition of local rulers and French slave-trading companies, in 1677/78, his movement established another pattern which was to reappear in subsequent movements of jihād: in their protest against arbitrary rule, Muslim religious scholars emulated a "prophetic model" (Robinson 2004: 199/209) of da'wa, hijra, and jihād. A Muslim religious scholar and his community (Arab. jamā'a) would interpret pre-jihād social contexts in the bilād al-sūdān as being analogous to the community of the Prophet while living in jāhilī (heathen) Mecca, and thus as being characterized by the rule of injustice (Arab. ḥukm al-ẓulm), often combined with chaos and strife (Arab. fitna); when appeals to change the policies that the religious scholars addressed to the unjust rulers failed, the unjust ruler (Arab. ẓālim) could, in the dialectic of takfīr (expiatio), be declared a non-Muslim who had tolerated un-Islamic practices. A Muslim ruler who was declared non-Muslim could then be fought in a jihād. Often, the rulers were not prepared to accept such critique and the community of the faithful would be forced to migrate to a safe place from where a jihād could be undertaken, like the Prophet and his community in their hijra to Medina. As in the Prophet's victory over the Meccans in the battle of Badr in 624, such a jihād would often (but not always) start with an initial,

Badr-like victory of a small jamāʿa of true believers against an overwhelming force of unbelievers. Eventually a jihād would lead to the overthrow of the unjust ruler and the subsequent establishment of an Islamic government of rightly guided scholars (Arab. ḥukm al-rāshidīn). These scholars would then have to face the problems of day-to-day government as well as opposition against their government, often coined in religious terms. The dialectic of opposition, rebellion, and jihād could thus start all over again, bringing about an increasing stress on religio-dogmatic and religio-political argumentation in the writings of the scholars.

From the late eighteenth century, Muslim religious scholars indeed became leaders of movements of social and political reform which were legitimized in the name of Islam for the first time in sub-Saharan West African history, if we disregard the Almoravid movement in the eleventh century. In these movements of reform, protest, and jihād, religious legitimization turned out to be a major element of dispute, since established pre-jihād rulers, despite the polemics of the jihād leaders, regarded themselves as Muslim rulers. If pre-jihād rulers were not willing to implement Islamic law, this was not because they rejected sharīʿa as such but because they were aware that they had to keep a precarious balance between established African and new (Islamic) foundations of religio-political legitimacy. Consequently, the leaders of the jihāds not only had to develop strategies of legitimization for their jihād but also to develop strategies of delegitimizing Muslim rulers in power. Corresponding patterns of religious argumentation thus became another major feature of the jihāds, particularly when the religious scholars who had come to power in the context of such movements started to fight each other, as in the case of Sokoto against Bornu, or al-Ḥajj ʿUmar Taal against Masina. Discourses of legitimization and delegitimization consequently dominated nineteenth-century Muslim historiography in the bilād al-sūdān, and Islam became both the most important foundation of political legitimacy and a major ideological source in a dialectic of events which led from rebellion against unjust rule to jihād, to the establishment of the rule of the faithful, and to resistance against the new Muslim rulers: Islam was translated into different local contexts as an ideology of liberation, an ideology of governance, and an ideology of protest. In these movements of jihād, various models of legitimization and delegitimization and a wide spectrum of realizations of Islamic governance were developed. After briefly presenting a series of early jihād movements between the late seventeenth and the late eighteenth century, I focus on four major jihād movements in the nineteenth century, namely the Sokoto jihād and the Bornu response, the jihād of al-Ḥājj ʿUmar Taal, the imāmate of Masina, and Samori Turé and his efforts to translate his conquests on the upper Niger into forms of Islamic legitimacy.

The importance of the local context for the emergence of movements of jihād, as well as these movements being situated in larger economic and political dynamics, such as the transatlantic slave trade, can be shown clearly in a series of early jihāds in the western bilād al-sūdān between the late seventeenth and the late eighteenth centuries.

Rivalries between a number of tribal groups over hegemony in the Qibla region north of the Senegal led to the escalation of conflict when claims to regional hegemony by the Awlād Daymān-Tashumasha federation, led by a religious scholar, Nāṣir al-Dīn, were rejected by other tribal groups. In 1673, the dynamics of alliance formation triggered the escalation of the tribal war into a movement of jihād which spilled into the Fuuta Tooro region and the lower Senegal valley, where local scholars supported Nāṣir al-Dīn's demands to stop the slave trade. These demands were directed against the economic interests of the established powers in the region, Wolof and Tukulóór principalities as well as European trading houses. Initially, the Tuubenaan movement of Nāṣir al-Dīn prevailed, but when Nāṣir al-Dīn died in 1674, the alliance of supporters of the slave trade defeated the jihād and reestablished the status quo ante by 1678.

From the late 1670s, another religious scholar, Mālik Sy (d. 1699), from Podor in Fuuta Tooro, managed to rally a number of Jakhanke villages as well as refugees from the Qibla and lower Senegal regions in the small kingdom of Gajaaga on the upper Senegal. He eventually formed a community which split off from Gajaaga and in 1699 became the imāmate of Bundu on the Falémé. Malik Sy had not taken part in the Tuubenaan movement of Nāṣir al-Dīn, but he had studied in the Qibla region in the 1650s and in 1667 had settled as an independent scholar in Gajaaga, where he worked for the local rulers. In 1672, the rulers of Gajaaga granted him land for his family, which became a center of Islamic learning in the region. After the split from Gajaaga, the imāmate of Bundu survived local rivalries until 1854, when the imāmate became part of the empire of al-Ḥājj 'Umar Taal.

A few decades after the formation of the imāmate of Bundu, local conflict between Jalonke principalities and FulBe pastoralists, as well as Muslim traders, led to a jihād in the Fuuta Jalon highlands, when Jam Jero, the most prominent Jalonke leader, tried to restrict religious freedom. The rebellion against the Jalonke lords started in 1725, yet, despite some initial success, the movement of jihād was not able to achieve stability until the 1750s under the leadership of Ibrāhīm Sori (d. 1791). After his death, the imāmate disintegrated into a federation of nine autonomous provinces which continued to quarrel over the question of succession to the position of imām, until the leading families, the Soriya and the Alfaya, agreed to alternate the imāmate among them. The imāmate of Fuuta Jalon soon developed a tradition of slave raids in the region. These slaves were not only sold to European trading houses on the coast, but also settled in special slave villages (Ful. runde) which provided a major part of the agricultural production of Fuuta Jalon. By the mid-nineteenth century, slaves (Ful. hubbu) already formed half of Fuuta Jalon's population. In 1850, a Muslim religious scholar, Mamadu Jahe, started to organize the resistance of the slaves and was even able to conquer Timbo, the political center of Fuuta Jalon. The imāmate was never able to defeat the Hubbu movement until Samori Turé crushed the Hubbu rebellion in 1883.

While the first jihād in the lower Senegal valley had failed in the late seventeenth century, a new rebellion against the non-Muslim Denianke rulers in the Fuuta Tooro

In his major programmatic texts, *Bayān wujūb al-hijra 'alā l-'ibād wa-bayān wujūb nasb al-imām wa-iqāmat al-jihād* (The exposition of the obligation of emigration upon the servants of God and the exposition of the obligation of appointing an Imām and undertaking of jihad), as well as in *Tamyīz al-muslimīn min al-kāfirīn,* Usman dan Fodio established the ideological (theological) case for the jihād. In *Bayān wujūb al-hijra,* he also elaborated on the different countries of the bilād al-sūdān and their status as Muslim or non-Muslim, following Aḥmad Bābā's classification. Among the non-Muslim countries, he counted Mossi, Gurma, Borgu, Yoruba, and Dagomba: "And all of them are lands of unbelief" (. . . *wa hadhihi kulluhā bilād kufr*). Lands where Islam predominated and unbelief was rare were Bornu, Kano, Katsina, Songhay, and Mālī. Yet these lands still had to be regarded as lands of unbelief, "as their rulers were unbelievers" (. . . *wa-ammā salaṭīnuhā fa-kuffār*). A third category of countries, where both rulers and the people followed Islam, did not yet exist in the bilād al-sūdān (dan Fodio 1978: 14; al-Misri 1978: 51).

region succeeded in 1775 under the leadership of Sulaymān Bal (d. 1776) and 'Abd al-Qādir Bokar Kan (d. 1806). The imāmate of Fuuta Tooro even managed to defeat the emir of Trarza in 1786 and to stop the export of slaves to St. Louis in 1785. Efforts to further expand the power of the imāmate into the lower Senegal valley misfired, however, in 1796, when the Wolof kingdom of Kajoor defeated 'Abd al-Qādir Bokar Kan. In 1806, the Bambara kingdom of Kaarta invaded Fuuta Tooro and devastated the region. The successors of 'Abd al-Qādir Bokar Kan managed to stabilize the imāmate, yet thousands of Tooranke left the region in the late 1850s to join the jihād of al-Ḥājj 'Umar Taal in Kaarta and Segu, and in 1891 the French colonial administration annexed the Senegal valley to the colony of Senegal.

Jihād in Hausaland and Bornu

Islam became established in Hausaland as a religion of the courts as well as among traders and parts of the population from at least the fourteenth century. By the late eighteenth century, Islam "was accepted by all, even by those who never practiced it, in the sense that they believed in its power and sought its blessing in such forms as amulets and charms" (Philipps 1985: 44). As in other parts of the bilād al-sūdān, jihād in Hausaland was thus not a jihād against unbelievers so much as "a reform movement reforming lax Muslims, not converting pagans. It was ideologically probably less concerned with the kufr (unbelief) of pagans than with the kufr of those Muslims who opposed the jihād" (Last 1967: 273). From 1804, the jihād in Hausaland led to the establishment of the largest Muslim state in the bilād al-sūdān, reaching from present-day western Niger to northern Cameroon, and from the fringes of the Sahara to the tropical forests of Yorubaland in the south. This empire came to be called a caliphate, as the leader of the jihād and his successors assumed the title of a caliph, amīr al-mu'minīn, "commander of the faithful." In addition, the Sokoto caliphate became a major point of reference for other movements of protest in the bilād al-sūdān, in particular neighboring Bornu, Masina, and the empire of al-Ḥājj 'Umar Taal, while the leader of the jihād, Usman dan Fodio, came to be regarded as the most important cultural hero of contemporary Northern Nigerian Muslim hagiographies.

Usman dan Fodio (1754–1817) was born in Maratta in the kingdom of Gobir, the paramount Hausa state of the region. Early in his life, he moved to Degel, a hamlet to the east of the Rima River, where he studied, first under his father, and then in the established tradition of ṭalab al-'ilm, by moving from teacher to teacher. From approximately 1774/75, Usman dan Fodio held his own classes, but from 1774 to 1791 he also visited most parts of Hausaland, such as Gobir, Zamfara, and Kebbi, as well as adjacent lands such as Aïr. From about 1794, he became the leader of a small but growing jamā'a in Degel/Gobir. Religious argumentation was an important issue for the preparation of the jihād, as well as the legitimization of political rule after jihād, as the rulers of Hausaland regarded themselves as Muslims and could not simply be discarded as unbelievers. A major precondition was thus to assess existing religious and social practices in Hausaland and to identify practices which could be considered as violating the prescriptions of the faith and thus be regarded as a basis for takfīr, the declaration of unbelief. In a number of texts partially inspired by the writings of Muḥammad b. 'Abd al-Karīm al-Maghīlī, such as *Iḥyā' al-sunna wa-ikhmād al-bida'* (The establishment of the sunna and the eradication of un-Islamic innovations) and the *Kitāb al-farq* (The book of differences), Usman dan Fodio elaborated on the un-Islamic practices of Hausa rulers.

Both in his *Kitāb al-farq* and in his *Tamyīz al-muslimīn min al-kāfirīn* (The differentiation between the Muslims and the unbelievers), which were based on the compendia of Mālikī law as well as the classical works of tawḥīd, fiqh, tafsīr, and taṣawwuf, Usman dan Fodio elaborated on the question as to who could be regarded as a true Muslim and who had to be regarded as an unbeliever. Among the true believers, Usman dan Fodio counted the 'ulamā', whose faith was steadfast, their students and those who followed the advice of the 'ulamā'. The group of unbelievers, by contrast, was defined as those who had never accepted Islam, those who mixed Islam with unbelief, and those who ridiculed Islam and the sharī'a. Of particular interest was a third group of people whose status was not quite clear. Usman dan Fodio defined them as those who introduced innovations into the faith while being steadfast in their personal beliefs. They committed sinful acts by praying without the proper ablutions, for instance, yet at the same time they did not claim that their (false) practices of the faith conformed to the prescriptions of the sharī'a. Usman dan Fodio thus referred to these people as "disobedient sinners" (Arab. ʿaṣī) and not as unbelievers, since their acts were based on ignorance and not on evil intention. Usman dan Fodio also viewed as "disobedient sinners" those jāhiliyyūn (ignorants) who accepted Islam without properly understanding the prescriptions of the faith. They had to be regarded as unbelievers as far as their personal relationship with God was concerned, yet true believers had to accept them as brothers in faith as long as they did not publicly practice acts of unbelief. The final judgment was God's only, and Muslims should accept the good intention (Arab. ḥusn al-niyya) of their acts (al-Misri 1978: 7). On the basis of his analysis of the "un-Islamic innovations" practiced in Hausaland, Usman dan Fodio came to the important conclusion that most of these practices did not constitute a basis for takfīr: Muslims who practiced these forms of bidaʿ could still be regarded as sinners. Takfīr would be legitimate only when a Muslim intentionally violated prescriptions of the faith and defended these practices in public. On the basis of such an inclusive definition of faith and unbelief, imān and kufr, Usman dan Fodio was able to identify the majority of Muslims in Hausaland as Muslim, and thus exempt from takfīr. Only those rulers who tolerated the bidaʿ of their populations and committed acts of unbelief had to be regarded as unbelievers against whom jihād was not only a legal but a religious obligation.

After a war of four years, from 1804 to 1808, Usman dan Fodio and his jamāʿa were able to defeat the Hausa kingdoms and to incorporate them into a new empire, administered from a new capital city, Sokoto, and organized in a series of semi-independent emirates. Although many companions of Usman dan Fodio had died in the jihād, the Sokoto empire turned out to be a federation of emirates ruled by religious scholars who now became political rulers, and who continued to legitimize their rule in religious terms. In the 1810s, Adamawa in the southeast was conquered and added to the realm of the jihād, while in the 1820s the emirate of Ilorin joined the caliphate in the south. In the north, the jihād met with major difficulties and eventually failed: a number of Hausa kingdoms which had been defeated in the jihād established successor states such as Gobir or Maradi on the northern fringes of the Sokoto caliphate and which continued to fight drawn-out wars with the caliphate, as a number of European travelers such as Hugh Clapperton or Heinrich Barth witnessed during their respective stay in this region. The Sokoto jihād equally failed in the east: when jihādist troops attacked Bornu in 1805, and in 1808 even managed to conquer Bornu's capital city, Birnin Gazargamu, the ruling king handed over power to his son, Mai Dunama, who turned for help to a well-known religious scholar, al-Ḥājj Muḥammad al-Amīn b. Muḥammad al-Kānimī (1775/76–1837/38). With the support of his own jamāʿa, Muḥammad al-Kānimī was able to defeat the attackers and to retake Birnin Gazargamu. In 1809, he defeated Sokoto forces again, and in 1813 he imposed his own rule over Bornu. Bornu thus escaped conquest but came to be ruled by a religious scholar who legitimized his rule, as in Sokoto, in Islamic terms. In his argumentation against the jihād, al-Kānimī could count on the fact that in 1805 Bornu had been not just another Hausa kingdom but an old and independent empire which had been ruled by a Muslim dynasty since the eleventh century and could thus refer to an undoubtedly Islamic legacy. The religio-dogmatic defense of Bornu was even more effective, as it was organized by a religious scholar who had established an independent jamā'a in Ngala south of Lake Chad, far away from the court of the rulers of Bornu. In addition, Muḥammad al-Kānimī had been raised and educated in Fazzān and Tripolitania, had gone on pilgrimage to Mecca and Medina in 1790, and had lived in the Ḥijāz for some years.

Muḥammad al-Kānimī's role in the conflict between Bornu and Sokoto is of particular interest for the development of movements of jihād in the bilād al-sūdān, as this religious scholar not only managed to defeat Sokoto in military terms, but also to delegitimize the jihād against Bornu in religious terms. Muḥammad al-Kānimī's major argument was that the mere occurrence of un-Islamic innovations did not automatically turn the rulers of Bornu into unbelievers. The only violation of Islam which could justify takfīr would be if a Muslim publicly declared things to be legal and acceptable which were prohibited by the Qur'ān, Sunna, and sharī'a. Rulers such as the rulers of Bornu, who unintentionally violated prescriptions of the faith but who did not command unbelief, should be regarded as sinning Muslims. Jihād against them would be illegal. In his argumentation, Muḥammad al-Kānimī thus adopted Usman dan Fodio's argumentation for jihād in Hausaland and his definition of kufr but turned it against Sokoto. Muḥammad Bello, Usman dan Fodio's son, who ruled the Sokoto empire from 1817 to 1837, was not able to refute this argumentation and consequently cultivated another argument to justify jihād, namely that in the context of the jihād in Hausaland, Bornu had supported unbelievers against Muslims and as a consequence had to be regarded as an ally of unbelievers. Although this argumentation was based on wrong assumptions, as Sokoto and not Bornu had started the war, and as pre-jihād Hausa rulers could be seen as Muslims as well, the strategy of delegitimizing a Muslim ruler on account of his association with unbelief was to serve in later movements of jihād as a justification for jihād among Muslims.

The Jihād of al-Ḥājj 'Umar Taal

While the jihād in Hausaland and the war between Sokoto and Bornu had led to the emergence of two different models of a Muslim empire, the jihād of al-Ḥājj 'Umar Taal al-Fūtī (1796–1864) may be seen as representing a third model. In comparison to Sokoto, Bornu, and Masina, the movement of jihād led by al-Ḥājj 'Umar Taal differed in two major respects: while the scholars in Sokoto, Bornu, and Masina, as well as in most other parts of the bilād al-sūdān, were affiliated to the Qādiriyya, al-Ḥājj 'Umar Taal came to stress his affiliation to the Tijāniyya, a ṭarīqa which claimed spiritual supremacy over all other Sufi orders. Second, the movement of al-Ḥājj 'Umar Taal turned into a movement of conquest which was increasingly dominated by a single group, the Tukulóór, a group of FulFulde-speaking populations (Halpulaaren) from Fuuta Tooro in Senegal. The jihāds in Hausaland and Bornu, but also those in Masina and Fuuta Jalon and the states resulting from these jihāds even if originally dominated by scholars of Halpulaaren origin, had a more inclusive character and could rely on the active or passive support of non-Halpulaaren groups, such as Hausa and Tuareg in Sokoto, Jakhanke in Fuuta Jalon, or Maraka in Masina. It is thus possible to present the jihād of al-Ḥājj ʿUmar Taal as a series of religiously legitimated wars of conquest by the Muslim Fuutanke of Fuuta Tooro against the allegedly pagan Bambara, Malinké, and Soninké populations of the upper Niger, even though parts of these populations could point to old traditions of Islamic learning.

After his return from an extended pilgrimage and journey to the holy places of Islam as well as most of the Sudanic imāmates between 1825 and 1840, al-Ḥājj ʿUmar Taal established a jamāʿa in Jegunko/Fuuta Jalon which attracted followers from all over Senegambia and Guinea, especially from the imāmates of Fuuta Tooro and Fuuta Jalon. His followers and students were initiated into the Tijāniyya and came to form the core of a Tijānī warrior-scholar elite, while affiliation to the Tijāniyya came to be the defining feature of this jamāʿa, especially when al-Ḥājj ʿUmar Taal's efforts to gain support among the scholars of the Jakhanke group of scholars in Fuuta Jalon and the Senegambia failed. These scholars were mostly affiliated to the Qādiriyya and as such were not willing to accept Tijānī claims of spiritual superiority or to submit to al-Ḥājj ʿUmar Taal's political authority. Bending to pressure to leave Fuuta Jalon, al-Ḥājj ʿUmar Taal organized a hijra to Dingiray in the neighboring principality of Tamba in 1849. In 1852, al-Ḥājj ʿUmar Taal deposed the ruler of Tamba and started to prepare a jihād against the kingdom of Kaarta, one of the two Bambara states in the upper Senegal and Niger valleys which controlled trade between the French colony of Senegal and the Niger River valley. In 1807/08, 1816–1818, 1831, and 1846, Kaarta had repeatedly attacked and devastated Fuuta Tooro, al-Ḥājj ʿUmar Taal's homeland. In order to improve his strategic position against Kaarta, al-Ḥājj ʿUmar Taal conquered a number of smaller dominions on the upper Senegal, such as Bundu, which had been established in the 1680s and 1690s as the first imāmate in the greater Senegambia region, and in 1855 he attacked Nioro, the capital of Kaarta. In the three subsequent years, al-Ḥājj ʿUmar Taal reorganized Kaarta, while Nioro became the new center of his jamāʿa. In 1856, the harsh rule of his army triggered a series of rebellions by the Bambara populations of Kaarta, which led to the devastation of the region. The wars of al-Ḥājj ʿUmar led to a downward cycle in the regional economy of the upper Senegal and upper Niger which induced long-distance traders to shift trade to more western or eastern routes. The rebellions in Kaarta (and later Segu), which al-Ḥājj ʿUmar and his successors were never able to defeat, also handicapped al-Ḥājj ʿUmar Taal's forces at a point of time when another war, this time with France, was impending: Kaarta and the upper Senegal region were seen by France as being part of a French sphere of interest in Senegambia, and al-Ḥājj ʿUmar Taal's expansion was regarded as a threat to French commercial and political interests. After a war of three years against French forces on the upper Senegal, al-Ḥājj ʿUmar Taal was forced to accept defeat and to give up hopes of gaining control over Fuuta Tooro. As a consequence, in 1858/59 al-Ḥājj ʿUmar Taal appealed to the population of Fuuta Tooro to leave home and move east to settle in Kaarta. This call for emigration (Ful. fergo) led to a movement of emigration of initially 40,000–50,000 people from Fuuta Tooro to the territories of al-Ḥājj ʿUmar Taal. The fergo continued until the late 1880s and brought tens of thousands of Fuutanke settlers, mostly young men, to the Fuutanke colonies in the east.

The end of war with France enabled al-Ḥājj ʿUmar Taal to start another jihād directed against Segu, the second Bambara state on the Niger, which was conquered in a military campaign from 1859 to 1861, a feat made possible by the fact that al-Ḥājj ʿUmar had gained possession of four small cannons and two grenade launchers with ammunition in his war against France in the upper Senegal. Facing defeat, the ruler of Segu, Bina ʿAlī, appealed to the neighboring imāmate of Masina for help and proclaimed Segu a protectorate of Masina. Masina accepted Segu's submission and sent religious scholars to Segu to destroy the icons of the local cults and to establish mosques, while Bina ʿAlī converted to Islam. The alliance between Segu and Masina came too late, however, to stop al-Ḥājj ʿUmar Taal's advance. An appeal by Aḥmadu b. Aḥmadu, the ruler of Masina, to stop the jihād, because Segu had become Muslim on account of the conversion of its king to Islam, was rejected by al-Ḥājj ʿUmar Taal. In February 1861, al-Ḥājj ʿUmar Taal's army defeated the united forces of Segu and Masina and marched into the capital city. The subsequent confrontation with Masina posed a serious problem for al-Ḥājj ʿUmar Taal, as Masina was beyond doubt an Islamic state. In a text entitled *Bayān mā waqʿ baynī wa-bayna Aḥmad* (Elucidation of the differences between me and Aḥmadu), al-Ḥājj ʿUmar Taal adopted Muḥammad Bello's argument against Bornu, claiming that a Muslim who joined forces with a non-Muslim in order to wage war against another Muslim became a legitimate target for a jihād, as such a Muslim had offered a public rejection (Arab. irtidād) of Islam by associating with a non-Muslim ruler. When Aḥmadu b. Aḥmadu was not able to convincingly refute this argument, as al-Ḥājj ʿUmar Taal's troops had found evidence of pre-Islamic religious practices in Segu even after Bina ʿAlī's conversion to Islam, al-Ḥājj ʿUmar Taal was free to continue the war against Masina. In 1862, al-Ḥājj ʿUmar Taal conquered Masina and, in 1863, even attacked Timbuktu, the major center of Qādirī traditions of learning on the River Niger. This attack overstretched the forces of his army. The humiliating treatment of Masina's ruling elite triggered a rebellion which forced him to retreat to Hamdallahi, Masina's capital, where he was trapped by the insurgents. In 1864, before an army of rescue under the command of his son, Aḥmad al-Kabīr, could reach Hamdallahi, al-Ḥājj ʿUmar Taal was killed in an effort to escape. In the end, al-Ḥājj ʿUmar Taal's jihād was not a single movement of jihād, but a series of jihāds and wars, against non-Muslim polities such as Tamba, Kaarta, Nioro, Segu, and the French, as well as against Muslim states such as Bundu, Goy, Kamera, Gidimaxa, Masina, and even Timbuktu. These different enterprises were not connected in legitimatory ways and enhanced the imperial character of al-Ḥājj ʿUmar Taal's conquests.

Masina

The different stages in the development of movements of jihād, and the evolution of an Muslim state based on jihād in the bilād al-sūdān, may be shown in an exemplary way in the case of Masina, although Masina's lifespan was rather short, from 1818 to 1864. In the beginning, the jihād in Masina had all the characteristics of a rebellion by the Masinanke-Halpulaaren groups against their Bambara overlords in Segu, yet the Masinanke rebellion soon acquired the features of a jihād. In 1818, the jamā'a of Aḥmad Lobbo (1773–1845), the future leader of the jihād in Masina, was able to defeat the vastly superior forces of the Bambara overlords of Masina, after a hijra from Jenné to Rundé Siru. This victory was immediately interpreted as another Badr and brought about a movement of political realignment within Masina which ended Bambara rule and confirmed Aḥmad Lobbo and his jamā'a as the new rulers in Masina. Within a few weeks, the jamā'a of Aḥmad Lobbo grew from about 1,000 fighters to more than 40,000 and gave Aḥmad Lobbo the military power to establish an independent imāmate. In 1819, Aḥmad Lobbo was able to extend Masina's sovereignty to neighboring Jenné, and, in 1825, to push the northern boundaries of the imāmate as far as Timbuktu. In the following years Masina successfully defeated the Kel Tadamakkat, subjugated the Dogon of Bandiagara, and, in 1843/44, invaded Kaarta.

After the consolidation of his victory, Aḥmad Lobbo concentrated on the organization of the new state, the Laamu Diina, the "state of religion," ruled by himself as the amīr al-mu'minīn. In a short period of time, the Diina became the most centralized imāmate in sub-Saharan West Africa, where Islamic concepts of governance were implemented in the most consistent manner. The imāmate was ruled by the amīr al-mu'minīn, Aḥmad Lobbo, who acted at the same time as imām of the grand mosque of the new capital city, Hamdallahi. The amīr al-mu'minīn consulted a great council (Ful. batu mawdo), which consisted of 100 members, 40 of them entitled to vote. These councilors, mostly religious scholars, the military commanders of the army, and the leaders (Ful. ardo'en) of the different tribal groups and Halpulaaren families of Masina, all beyond the age of forty, had to have studied the religious disciplines, in particular Islamic law. The batu mawdo met on a daily basis and discussed all political decisions. The stress on religious learning led over time to the exclusion of the military commanders from the batu mawdo. The territorial administration of the imāmate was based on five provinces (Ful. leydi) and 340 districts (Ful. lefol leydi), as well as the autonomous regions of Timbuktu in the north and Jelgooji in the south, all administered by an emir appointed by the batu mawdo. The districts and provinces collected the taxes, organized military service, supervised religious learning and discipline, and organized the annual migrations of the herds.

The capital city of the imāmate was Hamdallahi, which was built between 1820 and 1823, surrounded by a wall of six meters and accessible through four large gates. The center of Hamdallahi was dominated by the Friday mosque, the residence of the imām, the buildings of the batu mawdo and the library/archive of the imāmate, the court and prison, as well as a hostel for travelers. Mosques did not have minarets and houses had to remain one-story structures. All roads led to the central mosque, which could accommodate 3,000 people. Each of the eighteen quarters had its own market and its own schools which served a population of 30,000–40,000. In principle, the imāmate followed the prescriptions of Mālikī law, but also accepted, to some extent, the ethical code of the Halpulaaren populations, pulaaku, in particular as far as cases of corporal punishment for women were concerned. The schools of the Diina were initially supervised by Alfa Nūḥ Tayrū, and apart from the memorization of the Qur'ān, education stressed ḥadīth, tawḥīd, uṣūl al-fiqh, fiqh, taṣawwuf, naḥw, ṣarf, balāgha, and manṭiq. Girls had their own schools and were taught by female scholars. Everyday life in the Diina was ruled by religious laws: attendance at the Friday prayer was obligatory for all men and the consumption of tobacco was prohibited, as were games, music, and dance. Trade was supervised closely and the market police (Arab. muḥtasibūn) controlled weights and measures, which were standardized. The muḥtasibūn also acted as a religious police in the Diina. At the same time, the Diina maintained storage buildings for grain supplies in times of scarcity and organized the care of old people, the sick, and orphans, as well as pilgrims. The economy of the Diina relied on the cattle of the FulBe pastoralists. Each year, the batu mawdo discussed and distributed the pastures for each wuro (herd) and their ardo'en (commanders), the routes they had to take and their watering places. The central organization of the pastures led to the FulBe pastoralists gradually becoming sedentary and to the acceptance of transhumant pastoralism and its rules as defined by the batu mawdo. As a consequence, the Diina was able to provide considerable security, peace, and stability for its population.

The development of the Diina was not based, however, on general consensus. The traders in the two major centers of trade and commerce, Jenné and Timbuktu, were opposed to the strict regulation of commerce in Masina, for instance, with respect to the control of long-distance trade, and protested against the prohibition of the trade in tobacco which formed a major part of their trading activities. In addition, internal disputes became increasingly disruptive in Masina after the demise of the first imām, Aḥmad Lobbo, and that of his immediate successor, Aḥmadu Seku (1845–1853). When Aḥmadu Seku's twenty-year-old son, Aḥmadu b. Aḥmadu, claimed the position of imām, his claim was rejected by the military commanders as well as by a number of religious scholars in the batu mawdo. However, as these groups were unable to coordinate their opposition on account of their own competing claims to leadership, Aḥmadu b. Aḥmadu was able to prevail. The crisis of leadership was not resolved, however, as Aḥmadu b. Aḥmadu started to revise the religio-dogmatic foundations of the state. Thus, the age-group ceremonies of the Halpulaaren pasturalists, a central social tradition of Masina, condemned as un-Islamic by Aḥmad Lobbo, were tolerated again; Muslim holidays lost their status as state holidays and were simply regarded as family festivities, often connected with conspicuous consumption, and condemned by the religious scholars as an un-Islamic innovation; in addition, Aḥmadu b. Aḥmadu tried to break the political influence of the religious scholars by accusing them of collaborating with his enemies, and stopped discussing his decisions in the great council of the Diina. Aḥmadu b. Aḥmadu's isolation was increased by the fact that a number of religious scholars engaged in disputes over claims to spiritual superiority within the Qādiriyya, and even started to join the competing Tijāniyya. The corporate identity of the Diina, based on the affiliation of its scholars with the Qādiriyya, thus disintegrated as well.

When the attack of al-Ḥajj 'Umar Taal on the Diina started in 1862, Aḥmadu b. Aḥmadu was unable to organize an efficient resistance. Also, Ba Lobbo, Masina's most important military commander, joined al-Ḥājj 'Umar Taal at the very beginning of the war, and, after a defeat in the battle of Cayawal, the Masinanke forces disintegrated, enabling al-Ḥājj 'Umar Taal to occupy Masina's capital, while Aḥmadu b. Aḥmadu and his family were taken prisoner and executed. The subsequent rebellions by local commanders against the occupying forces were not aimed at restoration of the Diina, but opposed al-Ḥājj 'Umar Taal's regime and the loss of local autonomy. These rebellions were supported by the Kunta scholars in Timbuktu, the major representatives of Qādirī traditions of learning in sub-Saharan West Africa, who saw al-Ḥājj 'Umar Taal's conquest of Masina as a dangerous expansion of his empire. Having lost its independence, Masina became an object of rival claims within the greater region, and finally, until French occupation in 1893, a province in the empire of al-Ḥājj 'Umar Taal's sons and successors. The empire of al-Ḥājj 'Umar Taal was divided, in fact, into a number of autonomous polities: Segu under Aḥmad al-Kabir, Masina-Bandiagara under Aḥmad al-Tijānī, Konyakari under Mukhtar, Nioro under Mustafa, and Dingiray under Habibu. These dominions continued to function, in more or less open rivalry, until 1890–1893, when they were incorporated into the French colonial empire. Tens of thousands of Fuutanke, who had left the Senegal River valley in 1858, had to return to Fuuta Tooro after 1893, while the family of al-Ḥājj 'Umar Taal cultivated "paths of accommodation" (Robinson 2000b) with the French in both Mali and Senegal. For instance, in 1893, Agibu, a brother of Aḥmad al-Kabīr, was nominated "Roi du Macina" by the French colonial administration.

Samori Turé

While the movements of jihād presented so far were linked with movements of protest, rebellion, and reform directed by religious scholars, the movement of the military leader Samori Turé had a completely different character: it developed in the ethnic context of the Mande-speaking populations of the confluences of the upper Niger, and it started as a series of military conquests of Samori Turé and his efforts to establish a trading empire on the upper Niger. These wars of conquest were never legitimized as jihāds. Only after the consolidation of this empire was Islam cultivated as an ideological foundation of the state, and Islamic law was imposed from above and supervised by a religious police recruited among Mande/Juula scholars. In contrast to other leaders of jihād, Samori Turé did not justify his wars in religious terms, and although he became a staunch Muslim in his later years he did not become an author of religious texts. Finally, the empire of Samori Turé was not set in the "old" Muslim regions of the bilād al-sūdān but in the forests and savannahs of the upper Niger and upper Guinea Coast, where Islam was still a minority religion in the late nineteenth century, even though old centers of trade such as Kankan on the upper Niger, Odienne on the upper Bani, or Sikasso and Kong in the Comoé and the Upper Volta regions had existed for some centuries and were connected by the Milo, Bani, and Bago to the Niger.

Samori Turé was born around 1830 in the Konyan region. His father had been a trader but settled as a weaver and owner of cattle in Konyan. By 1845, Samori seems to have left home and started trading. He was introduced to a basic knowledge of Islam by a Mande/Juula scholar, Morifin Suwaré. In 1853, the Cissé warriors of Muri Weledugu abducted Samori Turé's mother; in order to liberate her, Samori joined the troops of a small kingdom in the region, Berété, only to raise his own troops in 1861 among his relatives, the Kamara of Konyan. In an alliance with the Cissé, he defeated the Berété in 1865 and then attacked and defeated the Cissé in 1866. He continued to expand his realm continuously and concluded an alliance with Kankan on the upper Niger in 1875. By 1878/79 he had reached the eastern boundaries of the imāmate of Fuuta Jaalon and in 1882/1883 the limits of French influence on the upper Senegal. He continued his expansion in the east and attacked Sikasso, though in vain. Eventually he defeated the French advance on the upper Niger, and in 1885 he forced the French governor of Senegal to respect his zone of influence south of the Tinkisso and east of the Niger. This victory gave him the strategic freedom to again attack Sikasso in 1888. The French used this opportunity to foster rebellion in his back and to move against Samori from two directions, forcing him to abandon his territories south of the Niger in 1889. He moved his troops east to the Comoé and Bandama as well as Kong, where he established a second empire from 1890, which was finally conquered by the French in 1898. Samori Turé died in exile in Gabon in 1900.

Despite almost constant war, Samori managed to establish an empire from 1861, Wasulu, which was strong enough not only to defeat the advancing French colonial power in the bilād al-sūdān (even if only for a short period of time) but also to conduct a war on a second front, Sikasso and (later) Kong. In this military empire, Islam did not originally play a major role. When Samori entered into an alliance with Kankan in 1875, the influence of Muslims in his empire gradually increased, however, and Samori realized that Islam could form a unifying force in his empire. In 1875, Samori started to gradually transform the character of his realm by initially recognizing the Islamic festivals and by introducing, in 1879, a tax labeled zakāt. In 1881, another tax was introduced, muddu, which served to pay the religious scholars. From 1881, religious scholars were indeed hired and employed, according to a respective decree, as religious teachers in the whole empire, and effectively formed the foundation for his administration as scribes and functionaries, advisors, and local governors. From 1881, Muslims represented a majority in the ruling council and decrees were increasingly supported by quotations from the Qur'ān in order to supply additional justification for Samori Turé's policies. Also, first efforts were made to apply sharī'a laws, possibly as an effort to present Wasulu as an Islamic empire to a powerful northern neighbor, the empire of al-Ḥājj 'Umar Taal and his successors.

In 1881, at the age of fifty, Samori Turé even became a student of a leading scholar of the Qādiriyya Sufi order in Kankan, Karamoko Ṣidīq Sharīf Haidara, in order to boost his credibility as a Muslim ruler. He memorized the Qur'ān and studied other Islamic disciplines, in particular jurisprudence. In December 1886, he was turbaned as a religious scholar and was entitled to carry the honorific title moriba and to lead the prayers. In July 1884, he started fasting in the month of Ramaḍān and announced that he should now be called "almami" (al-imām). All family members should convert to Islam. New mosques were built, qur'ānic schools were established, and the consumption of alcohol was prohibited. Juula scholars were employed to supervise these policies and to police the times of prayer. Children were sent to qur'ānic schools, while the practices of pre-Islamic secret societies were stopped. The application of sharī'a laws was increasingly enforced and religious scholars were obliged to suppress local, pre-Islamic customs and to command Islamic practices in the villages. In order to ensure the new policies and decrees, Juula scholars were employed as dugukunnasigi (those who know the paths in the village), religious police who acted as enforcers and informers in the villages. They even supervised local religious scholars who had to seek official recognition by going through an examination by a religious supervisory council directed by Amara Kandé. In addition, there were traveling inspectors who controlled the work of the religious teachers in the villages.

In February 1886, Samori Turé eventually proclaimed that all citizens of Wasulu had to be Muslim. When he learned that his own family was protesting against this decree, he went to his village, Sanankoro, and proclaimed after the Friday prayers that his family had to submit, to recognize Islam and sharī'a laws. When his father resisted and publicly sacrificed to the old cult, he was imprisoned by his son. This family conflict was resolved only some months later, when Samori was prepared to accept that established cults could be continued, but not in public, and under the condition that the practitioners of the old cults attend Friday prayers. Samori's policies of enforced Islamization were implemented against the resistance of a majority of the population and never became popular in Wasulu. When Samori was attacked in 1888 by the French in breach of a previous agreement, numerous villages used the opportunity to rebel and to reject Samori's policy of Islamization. Samori was able to suppress these rebellions, but he also realized that his politics had been too radical. He thus stopped forced conversion to Islam and revoked the application of sharī'a laws. Also, the old cults were tolerated again and the dugukunnasigi were disbanded. Personally, Samori remained steadfast and continued to support the qur'ānic schools, to build mosques, and to act as imām, although the wars for his second empire from 1889 never created a form of political stability which would have given him a chance to repeat the Wasulu experience. His attack on Kong and Buna in the east in 1895 was informed by the refusal of the Jakhanke scholars in these regions to condone his expansionist policies, and he was eventually even willing to ally himself with the pagan chief of Korhogo, Gbon Coulibaly, whose own conversion to Islam in about 1920 "is unlikely to have stemmed from deep moral convictions" (Launay 1992: 62).

The Legacy of the Jihāds

The caliphates, imāmates, and Muslim empires of the bilād al-sūdān tended to develop along two major lines of political organization. Some imāmates developed centralized political structures, such as Masina and the empire of Samori Turé. Yet Samori Turé had introduced Islam as a state ideology only after a formative period of state development from about 1875, and he abandoned Islam again as a paramount source of political legitimization after a devastating popular rebellion in 1888. Other imāmates, such as Fuuta Tooro, Fuuta Jalon, Sokoto, and the empire of al-Ḥājj ʿUmar Taal, were characterized by a history of fragmentation and disintegration. This tendency to disintegrate was contained in the Sokoto empire in a loose federation of emirates which acknowledged the supreme political and spiritual authority of the sulṭān of Sokoto until British conquest in 1903. The empire of al-Ḥājj ʿUmar Taal, in contrast, was torn by fratricidal rivalries until French conquest in 1890–1893. As these political developments were dominated by religious scholars who had turned into military and political leaders, text production for the sake of the legitimization and delegitimization of political agency became a major feature of Islamic scholarship. The jihāds in fact led to an explosion in text production in the bilād al-sūdān. An important feature of this text production was that religious scholars started to write increasingly in vernacular languages, in particular Hausa and FulFulde, in order to popularize their programs of reform as well as to advance Islamic education, including women's education.

However, the new imāmates eventually developed new and equally unjust structures of governance, such as slave-based economies. These slave-based economies may have been marginal in Masina, but acquired considerable size in al-Ḥājj ʿUmar Taal's realm, where French colonial officers estimated that slaves were 35 percent of the male and 44 percent of the female population in Bandiagara, 25 and 50 percent in Jenné, and 36.5 and 39 percent in Segu. Even larger were slave populations in Sokoto, as well as Fuuta Jalon, where in the second half of the nineteenth century slaves came to form more than 50 percent of the population. Large-scale agricultural production by slaves was an important feature of the economy of the Sokoto caliphate, where traders and members of the new religio-political elite had their own slave villages of 200–1,000 slaves working in their fields. In addition, 50,000 slaves were employed in the 15,000 indigo-dying pits in northern Zaria and southern Kano by the end of the nineteenth century. In Sokoto as well as Fuuta Jalon annual slave raids constituted a major pattern of political rule and came to decisively influence the history of the "slave hunting fringes" of each imāmate, in particular the so-called "middle belt" areas of Northern Nigeria, vast stretches of land on the Niger and Benue Rivers, and the Jos plateau. The slaves caught in these raids were not fed into the transatlantic or trans-Saharan slave trades anymore but set to work on state plantations, often cotton for the production of textiles. The residential slave populations in Sokoto and Fuuta Jalon consequently became foci for new movements of protest against oppressive rule and enslavement. Fuuta Jalon in particular was destabilized by a series of slave rebellions, the Hubbu, to such an extent that the imāmate was unable to oppose French conquest in 1890. Of particular importance was the fact that many slave rebellions in Fuuta Jalon but also in Sokoto, in particular the Ningi rebellion, were led by Muslim religious scholars such as Mamadou Jahe in Fuuta Jalon, and these religious scholars again legitimized their opposition to oppressive rule in Islamic terms.

After the conquest of the imāmates of the bilād al-sūdān by the French and the British, slaves were free to leave their masters. In Segu, the exodus of the slaves started in 1905, by late 1906 Bamako was almost completely devoid of slaves, and by 1910 the whole middle Niger valley had been evacuated. The governor general of French West Africa, William Ponty, could claim that 500,000 slaves had "liberated themselves" by 1911 (Roberts 1987: 197). Still, the imposition of colonial rule did not stop slavery immediately, as virtually all colonial powers were hesitant to destroy the institution of slavery which was seen as being central to the production of cash crops such as cotton on a large (and taxable) scale. At the same time, colonial powers such as France tried to reorganize former slaves in "villages de liberté" which continued to provide unpaid labor for colonial development purposes. The colonial powers, especially France, continued to tolerate domestic servitude as a means of stabilizing existing social structures and relied on forced labor and labor conscription in order to build roads and railway lines. In a number of West African societies, former slaves and their offspring also retained their social identity as slaves and are still seen today, in the social memory of their respective societies, as ex-slaves. Colonialism only meant a slow death for slavery, as Paul Lovejoy and Jan Hogendorn (1993) have emphasized.

The evolution and development of movements of jihād, the emergence of imāmates and the subsequent development of movements of opposition to the rule of religious scholars, were part of a dialectical development which, from the late eighteenth century, came to form a structural feature of the history of sub-Saharan Muslim societies. Traditions of coexistence of Islam and pre-Islamic communal cults became increasingly obsolete and pre-Islamic religious traditions were marginalized. Non-Muslim populations, while still representing a majority of sub-Saharan populations in the eighteenth and nineteenth centuries, became a minority in most parts of the bilād al-sūdān in the nineteenth and twentieth centuries. At the same time, the Muslim populations of these areas experienced a new phase in the development of Islam which could be characterized as a "second Islamization" or "second conversion" (Fisher 1985:

66) of their societies, as norms of Islamic law, for instance, became an accepted model for the organization of everyday life. Non-Muslim populations, by contrast, were able to achieve complete integration into the imāmates only by converting to Islam.

As a result of these political, religious, and social changes, conversion to Islam intensified in the Sudanic belt of sub-Saharan Africa and this development continued in colonial times, when Islam came to be seen as an ideology of resistance to colonial rule. The dialectics of legitimization and delegitimization continued to structure the religious and political development of Muslim societies in the bilād al-sūdān well into the twentieth century. Increasing public awareness of patterns of Islamic argumentation in political contexts can thus be regarded as one of the most important legacies of the jihād movements of the period. Yet, while movements of jihād have transformed the Sudanic belt of sub-Saharan Africa, the mostly non-Muslim societies of the tropical belt on the Guinea coast, which had been drawn into European spheres of influence and colonial conquest from the early nineteenth century, were largely untouched by these structural changes in Sudanese Muslim societies. In the context of the creation of the French, British, and German colonial empires, from the late nineteenth century, both Muslim minority areas in the forest belt and Muslim majority areas with an experience of jihād movements in the bilād al-sūdān were united in new colonial polities, such as Nigeria or Ivory Coast. Conflicts over political domination expressed in religious terms were consequently inscribed into the colonial and postcolonial histories of these West African states.

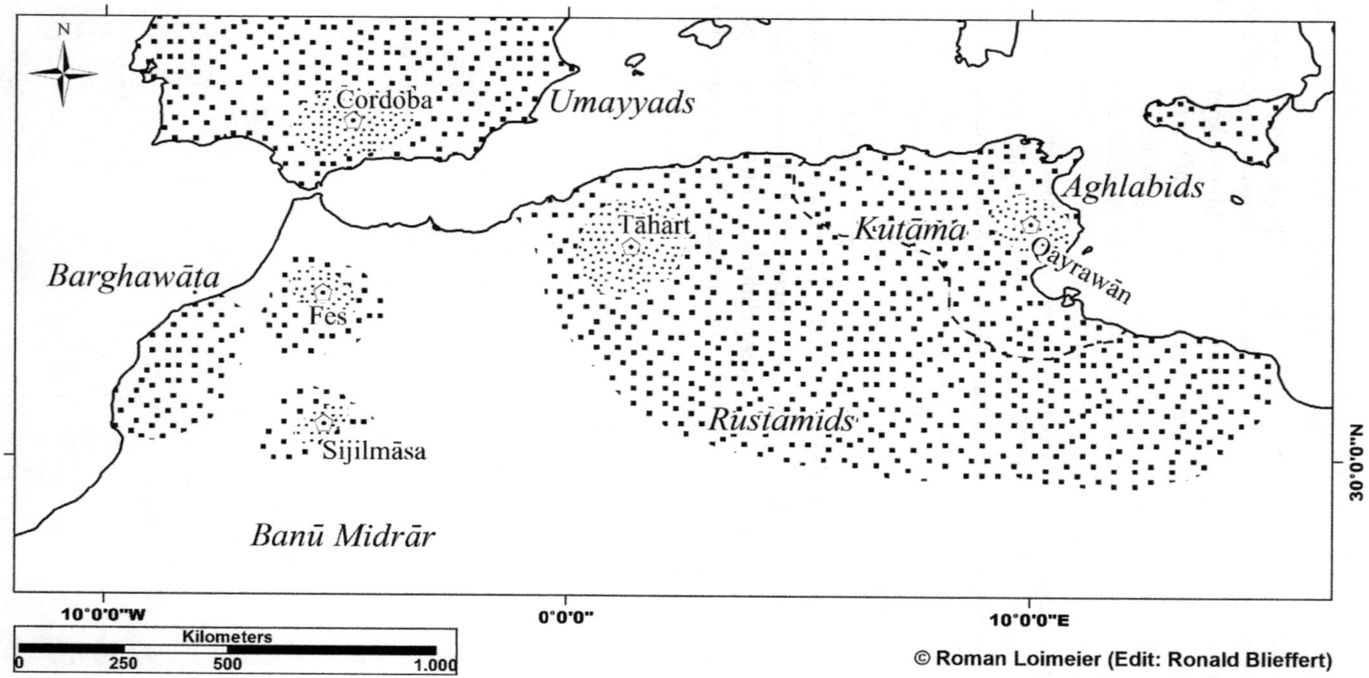

Map 9. The Bilād al-Maghrib in the ninth century

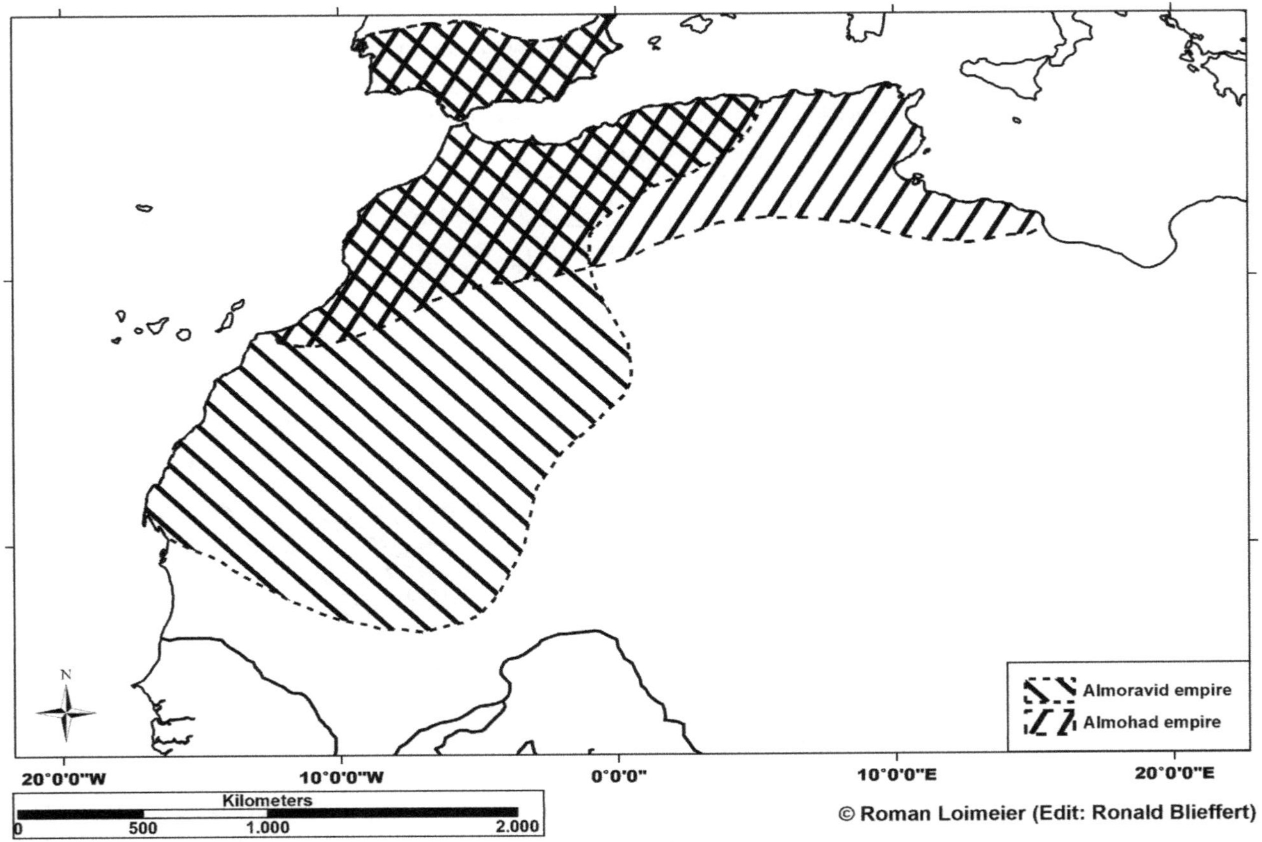

Map 10. The Almoravid and Almohad empires

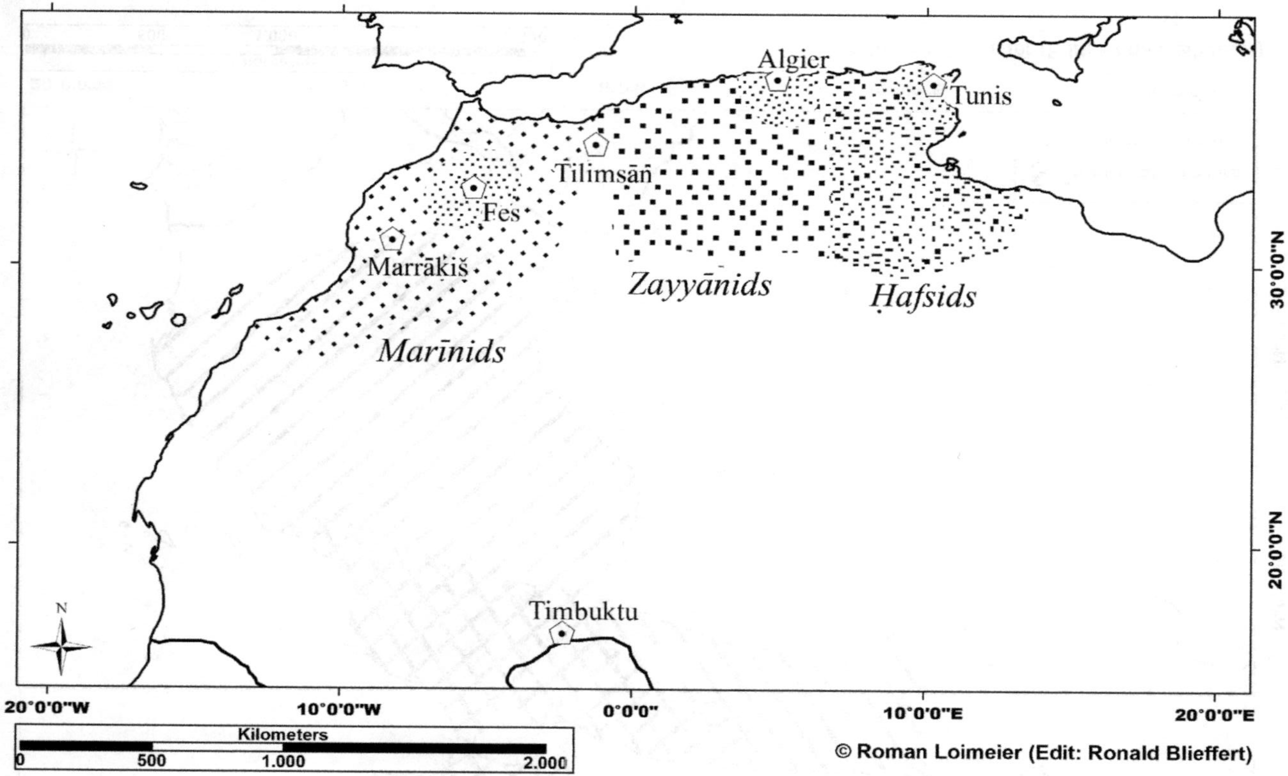

Map 11. The Bilād al-Maghrib in the early fifteenth century

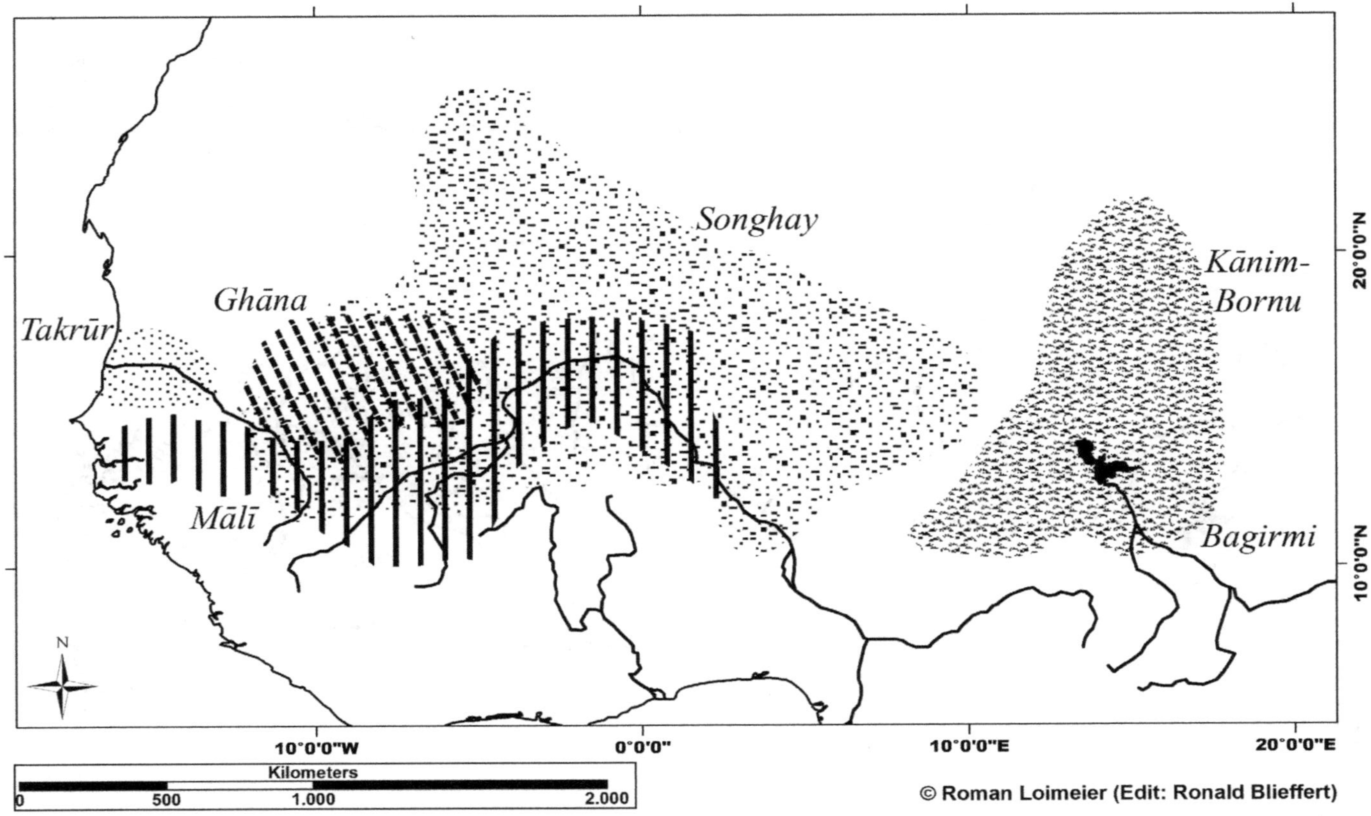

Map 12. The empires of the Bilād al-Sūdān

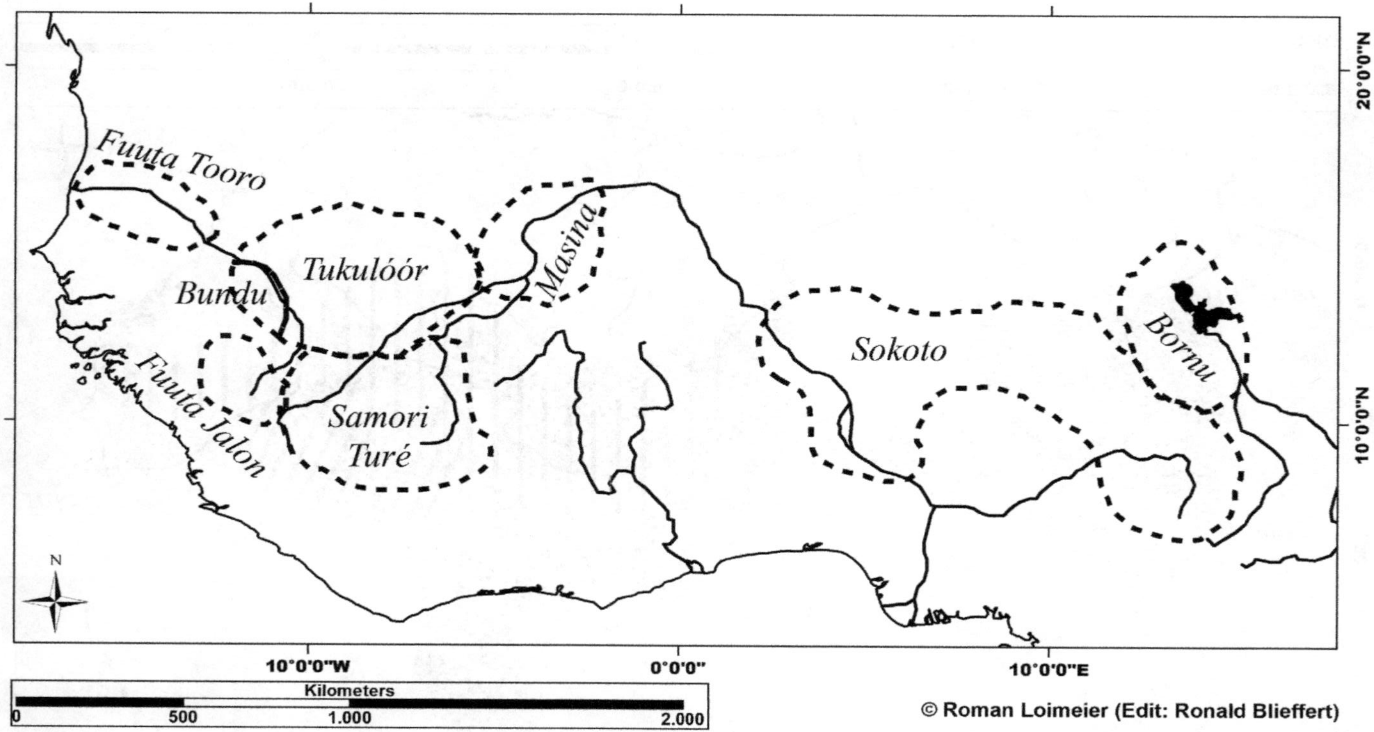

Map 13. The Muslim states of the Bilād al-Sūdān in the eighteenth and nineteenth centuries

6 Islam in Nubia and Funj

Historical Themes and Patterns

The focus on Egypt as the paramount power on the Nile since pharaonic times has preempted a similar strong focus on the history of the lands beyond the first cataract, south of Aswan. The lands between the first cataract in the north and the sixth cataract in the south and beyond, to the confines of Ethiopia, nevertheless saw the rise and fall of great empires, from Kush in pharaonic times to Meroe in Roman times, to Nubia in Byzantine, 'Abbasid, and Fāṭimid times and Sinnār-Funj in Ottoman times. These empires were informed in religious, political, and cultural terms by their closeness to Egypt and their entanglement with historical developments in the north. At the same time, the empires on the Upper Nile developed their own distinct identity and even met with Egypt on their own terms, as, for instance, in the context of military interventions in both pharaonic and Islamic times. The history of the populations on the Nile south of the first cataract can thus be described as being rooted in multiple cultural, social, political, and religious legacies, fusing pharaonic and post-pharaonic Egyptian, Roman, Greek, Arab, Ethiopian, and Iranian influences, as well as Islam and Christianity with ancient Nilotic and Sudanese traditions from the south. Sub-Saharan Nilotic and Sudanic traditions contributed to shaping the empires and populations on the Nile to such an extent that the lands on the upper Niles, the Blue Nile and the White Nile, cannot be seen as a simple extension of a pharaonic, Christian, or Muslim north. The strength of Sudanic influences became particularly clear in the sixteenth century, when the Funj federation stopped the southward advance of the Arab-Nubian 'Abdallāb tribal populations and delayed the process of Islamization on the Niles for more than 200 years. Even Funj was unable and unwilling, however, to isolate itself from her Muslim neighbors, in particular Egypt and Arabia, and eventually abandoned her foundations in pre-Islamic traditions. The shift to Islamic sources of political legitimacy in the early eighteenth century led to the demise of Funj as a major power on the Nile.

From Christian to Muslim Nubia

While Egypt may be seen as a gift of the Nile, depending on its annual floods, Nubia, the land of gold (nūb in Coptic) beyond the first cataract, may be seen, like the Sahara, as a transmission belt which linked the bilād al-sūdān on the Nile with Egypt in the north and vice versa. Like the Sahara, Nubia not only acted as a transmission belt but also as a filter, channeling and sieving influences in both directions. By contrast to the empires in sub-Saharan West Africa, Nubia reached far into the north and even influenced the history of Egypt in decisive ways. This was not only valid in pharaonic times, when Nubian kings came to rule Egypt in the twenty-fifth, Ethiopian dynasty (751–635 BC), but also for the Christian and Islamic periods of Nubian history. The rulers of Egypt, on the other hand, repeatedly tried to gain control over Nubia, which was not only a source of slaves and resources, but also, and most important, a major supplier of gold, in particular the mines of Wādī ʿAllaqī which came to supply most of Egypt's gold between the ninth and the thirteenth centuries CE. Political rule in Nubia was organized in many respects along Egyptian models, not only in terms of policies and administration but also in terms of religion. Again, this was true not only in pharaonic times but also in the Christian period of Nubian history, as well as during the spread of Islam since the ninth and tenth centuries. For most of the time, Nubia's kingdoms managed to preserve their independence, however, and to consolidate their rule between the first cataract (south of Aswan) and the sixth (north of contemporary al-Kharṭūm/Khartoum).

This was also true of the last pre-Christian kingdom of Nubia, Meroe, which resisted Roman advances to the south and managed to expand Nubian domination beyond the sixth cataract to the south into the fertile Jazīra region south of the confluence of the two Niles: the Blue Nile, which drains the annual floods from the highlands of Ethiopia, and the White Nile, linking Nubia with the region of the great lakes in the south. Meroe's expansion to the south, however, led to a confrontation with the empire of Axum (Ethiopia), and in around 350 CE an Axumite army defeated Meroe decisively. In the aftermath of Axum's victory over Meroe, Meroe disintegrated into a number of small principalities on the Nile, some of which kept some sort of local autonomy, while others, in particular those in the north, came under Roman influence and slowly came to accept Christianity. Due to the fact that Axum had turned toward the same orthodox (monophysite) orientation of Christianity which also dominated in Egypt, Nubian rulers seem to have been rather hesitant to follow the Egyptian (Coptic) Orthodox Patriarch in Alexandria and initially accepted the authority of the (anti-Axumite and anti-Egyptian) Byzantine (Greek) Orthodox Church. This was particularly true of the central Nubian kingdom, Maqurra, ruled from Dongola, which had united the Nubian principalities between the third and the sixth cataract since the sixth century. By contrast, both Nobatia in the north, which was ruled from Faras, and ʿAlwa, south of the sixth cataract, which was ruled from Sōba, accepted the authority of the Orthodox Patriarch in Alexandria in 543 and 580, respectively. Only when Nobatia and Maqurra formed one Nubian kingdom in the eighth century did all of Nubia join the Egyptian Orthodox Church. However, the Nubian church refused to adopt the Coptic language and retained Greek as the language of the liturgy until the end of the Nubian church in the late fourteenth century.

When Arab-Muslim armies conquered Egypt in the 640s and brought Byzantine rule to an end, they quickly advanced through the Nile valley to the south and in 646 met with Nubian troops, which were able to repulse the Arab raid. In 651, the Arabs came back with a larger army in order to conquer Dongola and to incorporate Nubia into the Arab-Muslim empire, but suffered a humiliating defeat at the hands of the Nubian army whose archers decimated the Arab cavalry. According to a tenth-century Shīʿī chronicler, Aḥmad al-Kūfī, "the Muslims never suffered a loss like the one they had suffered in Nubia" (*Kitāb al-futūḥāt,* quoted in Spaulding 1995: 582). In the aftermath of this defeat, the Arab governor of Egypt, ʿAbdallāh b. Ṣaʿd b. Abī Sarḥ, one of the generals of ʿAmr b. al-ʿĀṣ, the conqueror of Egypt, concluded a truce which came to be known as a baqṭ (pactus) with the ruler (Basileios) Zacharias of Nobatia. This baqṭ was to remain in force, with some interruptions, until 1276, and established the following rules: an agreement of mutual non-intervention; the mutual right of secure passage; an interdiction of settlement of Arab tribes in Nubia, and possibly a trade agreement which limited the slave trade to Egypt. Through the baqṭ Nubia became a dār al-ṣulḥ, a "territory of peaceful agreement," which preempted jihād against Nubia except in cases of a Nubian attack on Egypt. From a Nubian perspective, the baqṭ continued a tradition of diplomatic gift exchanges with the rulers of Egypt which had started in pre-Islamic times. And although its stipulations were often neglected, the baqṭ ensured the existence of Nubia as a Christian kingdom south of Egypt for more than 600 years and contributed to the emergence of a distinct Nubian identity, which continued to thrive after the collapse of the Nubian states in the thirteenth century. Numerous Nubian Orthodox monasteries and churches were built and Nubian pilgrims visited the holy places in Jerusalem and Egypt, as well as the seat of the Patriarch in Alexandria.

In 704, the two northern Nubian kingdoms of Nobatia and Maqurra were united under Basileios Mercurios (r. 697–710) and subsequently became so strong that in 750 Nubia was able to send an army down the Nile to al-Fusṭāṭ, the Muslim administrative center in Egypt, in order to enforce the liberation of the Orthodox Patriarch, Michael, who had been imprisoned for his protests against the increasing taxation of Christians in Egypt in the late Umayyad period. Further disputes were negotiated in peaceful terms, however, as for instance in the context of a Nubian embassy to Baghdad in the early ninth century. In Fāṭimid times, the baqṭ continued to be honored by the Muslim rulers in Egypt as well as the Nubian kings in Dongola, even though Nubia occupied Aswan in 989 in order to force the Fāṭimid ruler in Cairo to accept the regulations of the baqṭ. Due to the fact that the Fāṭimids were not interested in costly warfare in the south, they accepted the baqṭ until the end of their dynasty. In 1171, Fāṭimid rule was replaced by the Ayyubid dynasty which also accepted the regulations of the baqṭ. Only when the Mamlūks took power in Egypt in 1250 did this tradition of peaceful coexistence collapse.

The new political context was defined by the fact that since the early twelfth century Christian crusaders had repeatedly threatened Egypt as well as the trade routes in the northern parts of the Red Sea, and in 1182 even attacked the harbor of ʿAydhāb on

> Between the mid-thirteenth century and the Ottoman conquest of Egypt in 1517, Egypt was ruled by Mamlūk rulers of either Circassian or Turco-Kalmük descent. The Mamlūks replaced Ayyubid rule in 1250 and transformed Egypt into a feudal monarchy with an efficient army and administration. As a consequence, the Mamlūks were able to stop the advance of the Mongols into Syria in the thirteenth century and eventually controlled both Syria and the Ḥijāz. Mamlūk codes of honorable warfare prevented the modernization of the Mamlūk army, however, and Mamlūk Egypt came under Ottoman rule in 1517. The Ottomans retained Mamlūk institutions and administration and largely accepted Mamlūk autonomy under Ottoman sovereignty until 1798, when Ottoman–Mamlūk rule over Egypt came to an end in the context of Napoleon's invasion and the rise to power of the Albanian troops under Muḥammad ʿAlī.

the Egyptian coast of the Red Sea, which served as a major port for Egyptian pilgrims to Mecca. Due to the fact that the rulers of Egypt and Syria, first Ayyubids and then Mamlūks, were almost completely surrounded by Christian empires and kingdoms (Nubia, the crusader kingdoms in Palestine and Lebanon, Armenia in the north, the Byzantine empire in the eastern Mediterranean), the Muslim rulers of Egypt increasingly saw Nubia as a threat to Egypt's security. In 1266, the Mamlūk ruler Baybars (r. 1260–1277) thus occupied Suakin (Sawākin), an important port on the African shores of the Red Sea. This triggered an attack by Nubian troops on ʿAydhāb in 1272 and on Aswan in 1275, blocking not only pilgrimage routes from southern Egypt to the Red Sea, but also the supply of gold from Wādī ʿAllaqī to Egypt. In response, the Mamlūk army turned south and decisively defeated the Nubian army at Dongola in 1276.

After the death of King David of Nubia in 1277, the Mamlūk army imposed Prince Shakanda as the new ruler of Nubia and thus ended Nubia's independence. Prince Shakanda was regarded as a nāʾib (governor) of the Mamlūk sulṭān in Cairo. Also, Nubia was forced to pay an annual tribute to Egypt. Dongola was plundered by the Mamlūks, and Christian Nubians had to pay a jizyā of one dinār per head. Mamlūk rule over Nubia led to sustained resistance against Egyptian rule and to the gradual devastation of Nubia by Mamlūk troops. In 1315, the last rebellion was crushed by a Mamlūk army, and Karanbas, the last Christian ruler of Nubia, was followed in 1323/24 by a first Muslim Nubian governor, Sayf al-Dīn ʿAbdallāh of the Kanz al-Dawla tribal federation, which had dominated Upper Egypt since the late twelfth century, transforming Nubia into an Islamic polity. The Nubian Church continued to exist for some time, although many monks migrated to Egypt. In 1372, the last Orthodox bishop was installed in Faras, and the last Christian principality, Dotawo, in the baṭn al-ḥajar (belly of stones) region between the second and the third cataract ceased to exist in 1484.

While political relations between Nubia and the Muslim rulers of Egypt had evolved in largely peaceful terms for a long period of time, Nubia came to be threatened to a much larger extent by the gradual immigration of Arab tribal populations from the north, as well as by the expansion and the raids of the Bīja in the east, along the coast of the Red Sea. The Bīja, in particular, had started to raid Nubian settlements in the Nile valley and to disrupt trade routes as well as access to the gold mines in Wādī ʿAllaqī. When an ʿAbbasid adventurer eventually defeated the Bīja and their leader, ʿAlī Bābā, in 854, the Wādī ʿAllaqī became part of Egypt, depriving Nubia of an important source of income. In addition, the northern Bīja were forced to move south and started to interrupt the trade routes to the Red Sea, which particularly affected Nubian trade. The region of Nobatia, adjoining Egypt, increasingly passed into the hands of Muslim land owners, both traders and miners, and thus escaped Nubian domination.

The weakening of the Nubian state encouraged increasing immigration of Arab tribal populations, such as the Juhayna, and intermarriage between Arab-Muslim pastoralists and the Nubian-Christian population in the Nile valley. During a period of about 300 years, northern Nubia became largely Arabized. In addition, the Nubians, who did not know private ownership of land, as all land technically belonged to the ruler of Nubia, lost their land to Arabs who knew and accepted the concept of private ownership (Arab. milk, mulk) of land. Due to Nubian customs of matrilineal succession, lands increasingly passed into Arab hands when Nubian women married Arab men who followed laws of patrilineal succession and inheritance. Despite the resistance of Nubians against this gradual dispossession of their lands, Arab concepts of ownership prevailed, and by the fourteenth century had replaced preexisting Nubian concepts of land ownership. The historian Ibn Khaldūn, who witnessed these times, described the conversion of the Nubians to Islam as follows:

> Once they had converted to Islam, the Nubians stopped paying the jizyā. Also, the Juhayna started to spread in the whole country and settled and appropriated land and houses. The land was devastated by raids and the Nubian kings tried in vain to repel Arab (bedouin) attacks. Finally, they resigned and tried to pacify the intruders by giving them their daughters in marriage. But this was the end of their properties, as the children of these marriages between the Juhayna and Nubian women inherited the land of their mothers. . . . In this way, the lands of the Nubians slowly came into the possession of the Juhayna. (quoted in Cuoq 1986: 95, my translation)

The Arabization of Nubia continued under Mamlūk rule in Egypt, especially when the Mamlūks started to rely on an Arabized Nubian tribal group, the Kanz al-Dawla, in Upper Egypt. The political center of the Kanz al-Dawla was the town of Aswan. A major factor for their long-term success in the region was their control over the northern section of the darb al-arbaʿīn trade route, which ran through the region of Aswan down to Asyūṭ. In addition to these causes for the decline of Christian Nubia and the emergence of Muslim Nubia, some other factors need to be mentioned as well, such as Nubia's increasing isolation from the Mediterranean, the crisis of the Coptic Patriarchate in Alexandria in the thirteenth century, and the fact that the Nubian Church never developed a church language of her own, unlike Ethiopia, Armenia, or Egypt.

The disintegration of the Nubian kingdom in the fourteenth century and constant war and raids by Bīja and Arab tribes led to the rise of numerous feudal lords in the Nile valley, who stopped respecting the supreme authority of the Church and sought recognition by the Mamlūk overlords in the north. Starting probably in the eleventh century, the emergence of a Nubian feudal system based on a multitude of local principalities was not interrupted by the process of Islamization: rather, from the fourteenth century, Christian Nubian feudal lords converted and became Muslim Nubian feudal lords. Until the early nineteenth century, Muslim Nubian feudal lords, often called Danaqla, from the major city of Dongola, continued to rule over their respective realms and only the Egyptian invasion of 1820 disrupted this historical legacy.

However, even after the disintegration of Nubia, the southern Nubian kingdom of ʿAlwa continued to exist and was recognized as an independent state by the Mamlūks in Egypt. In the fourteenth century, ʿAlwa, which continued to accept the authority of the orthodox patriarch in Alexandria, also disintegrated into a number of smaller principalities, which eventually submitted in the fifteenth century to the authority of another Arab tribal federation, the ʿAbdallāb. Only the principality of Fāzūghlī on the Blue Nile remained Christian and independent, until it became part of Sinnār-Funj in the latter half of the seventeenth century. The ʿAbdallāb, by contrast, which represented the southern Arab tribal groups of the Juhayna in Nubia, came to form small tribe-based federations, mashāykhāt, from the fourteenth century. In the late fifteenth century, these mashāykhāt were united under the authority of a charismatic Juhayna leader, ʿAbdallāh Jammāʿ (the gatherer), who was an ally of the major Bīja tribal federation in the east, the Ḥaḍāriba, who controlled the trade routes from the Nile to the Red Sea. From the town of Qarrī on the sixth cataract, ʿAbdallāh Jammāʿ eventually succeeded in uniting all ʿAbdallāb and defeated the remaining principalities of ʿAlwa in the Jazīra, conquering the ʿAlwa capital city, Sōba, and killing the last king of ʿAlwa.

The Empire of Sinnār-Funj

The victory of the ʿAbdallāb over ʿAlwa in the late fifteenth century should have led to the emergence of an Arabo-Nubian confederation of Muslim mashāykhāt and feudal lords, or even a united Arabo-Nubian Muslim realm on the Nile, replacing Christian Nubia by a new Nubian empire, which could have acquired distinct Muslim features, such as the establishment of Muslim institutions of administration or Islamic institutions of learning. Yet this course of history did not occur, due to a twist in the fate of the peoples of Nubia that was connected with the invasion of a non-Muslim and non-Christian African tribal federation, the Funj, in the early sixteenth century. The history of the Funj empire shows that the history of the Nile Sudan has not only been defined by influences from the north, but also by interventions from the south. The establishment of the empire of Funj on the Nile preempted the further Islamization of Nubia and Nubian culture and strengthened African sacral traditions, such as the concept of divine kingdom, even if Islam was accepted in formal terms as the religion of the state. Conversion to Islam did not take place on a large scale until the eighteenth century, however, and only in the nineteenth century did the lands on the Upper Nile acquire their distinct Islamic character. In the Funj empire, pre-Islamic and pre-Christian customs and traditions prevailed and were cultivated both at court as well as in the villages, although ruling families often claimed Arab descent to document dynastic legitimacy. In reality, Funj was an African-Nubian empire with a Muslim façade, and only in the eighteenth century did Islam emerge as a competing source of legitimization, triggering a constitutional crisis and civil war as well as ongoing dynastic disputes which led to the downfall of Funj in the early nineteenth century.

The Funj were in fact a federation of small populations from the border region between the highlands of Ethiopia and the Blue Nile, which had been linked with both Christian Ethiopia and ʿAlwa without becoming Christian themselves. Traditions of the ʿAbdallāb maintain that the leader of the Funj, ʿAmāra Dūnqas (d. 1534), had been a Christian who had converted to Islam in 1523. Yet, although ʿAmāra Dūnqas converted to Islam, he probably was not a Christian before this. In fact, the empire of Funj had the character of a divine kingdom: not only did the ruler not appear in public but he also was not to be seen while eating. The court etiquette at Sinnār was similar to the ritual at the court of the rulers of the Shilluk on the upper Nile in the twentieth century, which combined African and ancient Egyptian traditions. Pre-Islamic and pre-Christian customs were also expressed in many other respects. Funj traditions thus demanded that commoner women walk bare-chested and commoner men bareheaded. The consumption of both beer and pork was accepted in Funj until at least the eighteenth century. Muslim scholars increasingly rejected these customs and attacked them as un-Islamic.

While the Funj managed to defeat the ʿAbdallāb federation at Arbajī on the White Nile in 1504 and consolidated their domination over the territories of ʿAlwa, the Funj were not able to conquer the Arabo-Nubian territories in northern Nubia. However, they concluded an agreement with the ʿAbdallāb which allowed the ʿAbdallāb to retain their autonomy in northern Nubia while their territories were regarded as forming part of the new empire of Funj, ruled from Sinnār on the Blue Nile. After gaining formal control over northern Nubia, including Dongola, the Funj also came to an agreement with the Bīja-Ḥaḍāriba in the east, who controlled the harbor of Suakin on the Red Sea. In this way, Sinnār-Funj managed to unite all lands on the Upper Nile politically and to establish lasting stability in this region between the early sixteenth and the mid-eighteenth centuries. As a result, pilgrimage routes from the western bilād al-sūdān which had passed across the Sahara to Cairo and then joined the Egyptian caravan to Mecca increasingly shifted to the shorter route across the eastern bilād al-sūdān and the empire of Sinnār-Funj to Suakin and then across the Red Sea to Jidda. The viability of this route was attested by the journey of Shaykh Aḥmad b. Muḥammad al-Nūbī al-Yamanī (1630–1712) from Ḥalfāya, who studied in Arbajī and then traveled through Dārfūr, Wadai, to Bornu and eventually reached Fes in Morocco in 1669. As a consequence of the reorientation of western pilgrimage routes toward the eastern bilād al-sūdān, the number of Muslim travelers, pilgrims, and traders from the western bilād al-sūdān who crossed and eventually settled in Sinnār-Funj grew over the years and led to the emergence of distinct colonies of "Westerners" in Sinnār-Funj in the eighteenth century. Due to the influence of the Muslims from the western bilād al-sūdān, the population of Sinnār-Funj slowly came to accept the Mālikī school of law and the traditions of Islamic learning as represented in the western bilād al-sūdān and in the bilād al-maghrib (see map 14).

The rise of Funj as a major power in the eastern bilād al-sūdān was closely monitored by her neighbors, in particular the Ottoman empire, which had taken control of Egypt and the Ḥijāz in the early sixteenth century. In order to keep the pilgrimage routes under Ottoman control, the Ottoman empire occupied Suakin in 1540/41 and established a permanent garrison in Say, south of the second cataract, in 1576. Despite these Ottoman advances, which were also driven by the Portuguese intrusion into the Red Sea in 1540, the relationship between the Ottoman empire and Funj seems to have been informed by a mutual will to cultivate peaceful trade links and to respect each other's spheres of influence. In the time of her greatest expansion under emperor Bādī II Abū Diqn (r. 1642–1677), Funj controlled the whole valley of the Nile from the third cataract in the north to Fāzūghlī in the south, and from the shores of the Red Sea in the east to the steppes of Kordofan (Kurdufān) and the outreaches of the mountains of Dārfūr in the west. The heartland and the bilād al-makhzan of the empire was the region of the Jazīra. Around the Jazīra were grouped a series of semi-autonomous provinces which accepted Sinnār's authority in formal terms and which turned, from time to time, into bilād al-sība. Among these provinces were the Arabo-Nubian provinces of the Buṭāna and the Bayūḍa in the north, Kordofan in the west, and the territories of the Bīja in the east. According to the Funj Chronicle, which confirms the dual Islamic and African sacral character of seventeenth century Funj, Bādī II Abū Diqn was a strong and generous ruler,

> honouring men of learning and religion. He used to send gifts to the 'ulamā' in Egypt and elsewhere with his caravan leaders. . . . It was this king who built the mosque in Sinnār, and likewise built the palace of the government. He made it of five storeys, one on the other, and he built numerous places for the deposit of government property, such as weapons and so forth, as well as houses for the womenfolk, and the office for his sessions. He had two offices, one outside the great palace, and one inside the palace wall. He made a great wall encircling everything. In that wall he made nine gates, and appointed each of the magnates of his state a gate whereby to enter and go out. Likewise he made for each of the magnates of his state an office of his own,

> in which to sit and look into what concerned him. If a magnate wished to enter the kings's office, he would enter alone. . . . All these gates opened in one wall in a straight line. In front of these gates was a roof supported by pillars. In it was a high bench known as "the bench of him who calls upon thee." (quoted in Holt 1999: 9–11)

The wealth of Sinnār-Funj soon attracted foreign visitors. Thus, a Jewish trader, David Reubeni, visited Sinnār in 1523 disguised as a sharīf, and even met ʿAmāra Dūnqas, the first ruler of Funj. He confirmed ʿAmāra Dūnqas's conversion to Islam, yet attributed it not to a demand made by ʿAbdallāh Jammāʿ in exchange for his submission, but to strategic and political reasons, namely the effort to unite the new empire in one faith. In 1672/73, Sinnār-Funj saw the visit of the Ottoman traveler Evliya Celebi, who reported that the ruler of Funj now had Muslim judges and that these judges followed the Mālikī school of law. Also, there was a naqīb al-ashrāf. The court of Sinnār knew an intricate etiquette ruled over by a master of ceremonies who was also the commander of the police and the market supervisors, and was correspondingly titled jundī al-sūq (soldier of the market). Sinnār was described by Evliya Celebi as a big city on the Blue Nile, surrounded by a wall of three kilometers, with three large gates, defended by fifty cannons, and surrounded by suburbs. Sinnār had a large mosque constructed of bricks and forty-seven mosques in the suburbs. Celebi counted 300 businesses (shops), as well as inns and coffeehouses: "Regarding the number of inhabitants, Sinnār is a great city, yet in contrast to Rūm, Arabia, Persia and Ḥalab (Syria), there are no hostels of stone, no ḥamāms, no kitchen for the poor, no fountains, no schools, no other buildings of stone, as there are no stones to be found in this region which are bigger than pebbles" (quoted in Prokosch 1994: 184, my translation). In 1700, the court of Sinnār was also described extensively by Theodor Krump, a Bavarian monk of the Franciscan order, who visited Funj on his way to Ethiopia:

> You should know that the town of Sinnār is the most prominent trading place in Africa, as far as the lands of the Moors are concerned. Caravans arrive all the time, from Cairo, Dongola, Nubia, from across the Red Sea, from India, Ethiopia, Fur, Bornu, Fazzān as well as other kingdoms. Sinnār is a free town where everybody may reside irrespective of his nation and faith. Also, it is, after Cairo, one of the most populous towns. A market takes place daily, where traders may sell their goods in public and in good order, here elephant tusks, there camels, horses and donkeys, in other places, wood, onions, dates, wheat and durra, but also straw, meat and chicken, each in its own place. Close to these goods, humans of both sexes and of all kinds of age are sold, 200 and more in one day, in particular, by Turkish traders, who then trade them to Egypt and India, making a good profit in this trade. . . . When a king dies in Sinnār, they elect a new one in this way: All shuyūkh and other nobles of the empire come together and vote for one of the royal princes and name him king. All the other (princes), who are still imprisoned in the palace, are killed with lances and if any of them is able to flee, the new king is obliged to pursue his brother and to kill him. This happens in order to prevent rebellion against the king or the division

> of the empire among a great number of princes and thus to secure peace. . . . On the fourth day, we were called into the royal palace to an audience with the king. He sat at a desk which was covered by a red carpet and asked us in Arabic where we came from, where we wanted to go and what we wanted to trade, and we responded that we were European Christians on our way to Ethiopia. (quoted in Streck 1989: 178–79, my translation)

At the times of Krump's visit to Sinnār, the language of communication at the court was Arabic and numerous court officials had Arabic titles such as the chief translator (sīd, i.e. sayyid, al-kalām, master of speech), the chief minister (amīn al-sulṭān), or the head of the emperor's council (sīd al-qūm), who was, as a rule, a brother of the emperor's mother, whose task was to maintain tradition and who also commanded the palace guard. The sīd al-qūm also was the only person in the empire entitled to spill royal blood. For that reason, he was excluded from all meetings of the court council which directly affected the emperor. Most other offices at the court were occupied by slaves, such as the office of the treasurer, the karalrau, and the master of the royal seal. In the case of the death of an emperor, the crown council met as presided by the sīd al-qūm and elected a successor among the sons of the former emperor. As soon as this task had been achieved, all other sons of the emperor were killed by the sīd al-qūm in order to prevent disputes over succession and government. Despite this efficient way of preventing internal disputes, royal princes managed to flee from the court into neighboring countries such as Dārfūr or Ethiopia in order to escape their fate, and subsequently led rebellions from their exiles. When one of the wives of the emperor had given birth to a son, she was banned from the bed of the emperor in order to prevent her giving birth to a second son and a full brother of the first. The daughters of the emperor were married to provincial rulers and dignitaries as well as high-ranking aristocrats, the arbāb. This policy led to the emergence of a network of dynastic links in Funj and provided for an additional element of stability and regional integration.

The administration of the central provinces was organized on several levels: at the top of the hierarchy was the governor of a province, the makk, often trained and raised in Sinnār, who commanded a stratum of local aristocrats and dignitaries, the mangil, often holders of land titles, who again commanded a lower level of local headmen, the kursī (chair). The provinces and regions beyond the central lands of the empire were administrated by autonomous provincial lords, the mekk, who continued to represent the legacy of the Nubian era well into the late eighteenth century. North of Sōba alone, more than a dozen mekks existed in the late seventeenth century in places such as Qarrī, Shandī, Berber, al-Dāmir, Merowe, and Dongola. The emperor could also create new land titles in order to change existing power structures or local alliances, and he alone was entitled to sentence a person to death. The central institution of the imperial administration was the treasury, which was under the command of a royal slave, the karalrau. The provinces had treasuries which were administered by a muqaddam al-quwwāriyya, who also commanded the local tax authorities, the jarai, under the supreme authority of the respective mangil. Of major importance were the royal messengers, the mursal, who brought news and commands. All villages in the empire were obliged to accommodate and feed the mursal and to supply them with horses. In each province the model of the central administration and of the court in Sinnār was reduplicated. Each province also had a representative of the imperial court who acted as sīd al-qūm and was entitled to carry out executions in the name of the emperor. All provincial lords were obliged, in addition, to visit Sinnār once a year, to see the emperor and to pay the annual tribute.

The Funj army consisted of a corps of imperial slaves as well as the slave soldier troops of the provincial lords who commanded their own troops, under the supreme command of the amīn al-jaysh (commander of the army) of the emperor. In addition, each lord was obliged to maintain a contingent of troops. Together with the troops of the provincial lords, these troops formed the army of Funj, mostly cavalry units that were protected by heavy armory. Finally, all provincial lords were obliged to send family members as hostages to the imperial court in Sinnār, where they were educated and eventually sent back to their provinces. Each year, an imperial expedition was organized to raid the periphery of Funj for slaves who became imperial property. These expeditions were mostly directed against the southern and southeastern marches of Sinnār-Funj and to the south of the kingdom of Dārfūr, which undertook similar slave-raiding expeditions, as did Wadai further west. These slave raids satisfied most of the demand for slaves within Funj, as well as a considerable part of the demand for slaves in Egypt. As in the western bilād al-sūdān, "each eastern Sudanic kingdom came to possess a bleeding southern frontier" (Spaulding 2000: 122).

Despite these mechanisms of control, Funj saw a number of rebellions and movements of secession over time. One of these rebellions was led by Prince ʿAjīb al-Kāfūta of Qarrī, who had been governor of this province. In 1576, Prince ʿAjīb defeated an Ottoman invasion and even marched north to Aswan to push Ottoman influence back to the first cataract. After this victory, he continued to expand his local basis. Supported by the ʿAbdallāb, he started a movement of secession of the north which led to a war with Funj. ʿAjīb was even able to cross the territory of Funj to the boundaries of Ethiopia and deposed the emperor of Funj, ʿAbd al-Qādir II Unsa, in 1606. However, the emperor managed to flee to Ethiopia and organized a counter-attack from there. ʿAjīb was defeated in two battles and was killed in 1611. His sons fled to Dongola, while the new emperor of Funj, ʿAdlān, was deposed by the sīd al-qūm, who proclaimed himself emperor and concluded a peace agreement with the family of prince ʿAjīb. This agreement divided the empire into two parts: the realm of the ʿAbdallāb north of the confluence of the two Niles, and the realm of the Funj proper, south of the confluence.

Despite the factual division of the empire into two halves, Funj experienced a period of cultural and economic prosperity, stability, and a blossoming of trade in the seventeenth century, which was characterized by long reigns of the emperors. At the same time, Funj was able to expand her influence to the west, where the steppes of Kordofan came under her dominion. Equally, Funj was able to defeat a number of Ethiopian attacks. The conflict with Ethiopia was induced, in particular, by the efforts of both empires to control the trade routes from the Jazīra to the Red Sea. When Funj was eventually able to submit a multitude of small tribes in the Ethiopian border region, Ethiopia had to abandon her plans of expansion into Funj. At the same time, Funj was able to expand her control into the southern marches and the territories of the Dinka on the White Nile, in an alliance with the Shilluk. The prosperity of Funj attracted numerous foreigners, Egyptians, Turks, Ethiopians, Jews as well as Portuguese, Greeks, and Armenians, who added to the trade in Funj by importing, for instance, firearms: in 1700, emperor Bādī III already had 200 musketeers.

In financial terms, the empire of Funj was based on the tax on harvests, the ushr (tenth). In the irrigated areas of the Jazīra, taxes were imposed on water wheels. In addition, peasant farmers had to do unpaid construction or maintenance work and to provide oxen or donkeys for work or transport when needed. The weavers had to deliver part of their produce as tax, and so did other craftsmen. In times of war, all inhabitants of Funj were obliged to contribute to the war effort. In theoretical terms, as in ancient and Christian Nubia, the ruler of Funj was the owner of all lands and all mineral resources, and thus entitled to take or donate land and property. In addition, the emperor of Funj was the master of all trade and regulated the export of gold. Like the economies of the western and central bilād al-sūdān, Funj knew various currencies of exchange such as cowries, textiles, or metal bars as well as the bartering of goods. In addition, the emperor of Funj controlled the export of slaves, which constituted a major source of income for the state, and he commanded the dispatch of royal trade caravans which were entitled to transport gold and slaves.

While trans-Saharan trade in the western bilād al-sūdān was mostly organized by individual traders and trading houses or families, trade in Funj (as well as Dārfūr and Wadai) was defined by a royal monopoly on trade, in particular as far as trade with the north was concerned. Part of the trade goods, in particular gold, ostrich feathers, ivory, slaves, and cattle, had to be paid to the court as a form of tribute and were then fed into the royal export trade. Royal control was also imposed on imported goods. Luxury products, specific textiles, and firearms were reserved for the imperial court. Often, trade was accomplished in terms of gifts and tribute. In this context, cheap gifts could trigger war, as they symbolized disrespect and rejection of authority: "Sending worthless presents was as serious an offence as sending none" (Kapteijns and Spaulding 1988b: 63). Different rules were valid for the long-distance trade, in particular to the Mediterranean. Funj organized royal caravans that were dispatched under the leadership of an imperial caravan leader, the khabīr, who "represented the state authority beyond its borders" (Kapteijns and Spaulding 1988a: 63f.). The emperor of Funj also had his own trading agents in Jidda, Ethiopia, and Egypt, and twice a year an imperial caravan was sent to both Egypt and the Red Sea.

Suakin, south of ʿAydhāb on the shores of the Red Sea, became the major outlet for trade for Funj from the sixteenth century and attracted the trade and pilgrim traffic from the western bilād al-sūdān. Suakin in particular sent cattle and corn to the Ḥijāz and received goods from India and Yemen such as spices, perfume, sugar, dates, coffee, and tea for further distribution in the bilād al-sūdān. Although imperial caravans primarily served the needs of conspicuous consumption at the court, they allowed individual traders to accompany the imperial caravan. Thus, traders would travel in a large caravan, protected by imperial troops and supported by letters of reference and licenses. When such an imperial caravan crossed the boundaries of Funj, a medical inspection was undertaken and often a period of quarantine was observed, to make sure that infectious diseases such as the plague would not be brought into Funj, although this preventive policy was not always effective. The Funj chronicle thus mentions an epidemic of smallpox in the reign of Unsa (r. 1677–1688), which was combined with a failure of the harvest and hunger so disastrous that people even ate dogs.

All members of a caravan and its goods were registered by imperial agents, and all traders were warned not to trade en route to Sinnār. Only then was passage granted, often in smaller groups. Before reaching Sinnār, the caravan reassembled, however, and then entered Sinnār under the protection of the emperor: "If a private trader was robbed, the king would make good his loss; if he killed a subject of the sulṭān, the king would pay blood money to save his life; if he died, the sulṭān would act as executor of his estate, gathering and registering his goods for safekeeping and notifying his heirs or business associates abroad" (Kapteijns and Spaulding 1988a: 66). Entry of a caravan into Sinnār was a major event: the khabīr went to the court and announced the arrival of the caravan to the emperor, and each trader was accommodated by a local counterpart who also represented his interests at the court. Then foreign traders would pay a market fee for the privilege of being allowed to trade in the local market. Often, they brought special gifts for the emperor. In addition, the emperor had the right of first choice and also made gifts to the traders in order to convince them to come back. When all goods were sold, traders received advance payment on goods to be imported with the next caravan. Access to the market was strictly regulated and could be prohibited any time. The emperor of Funj had final control over the markets and long-distance trade, which was confined to the bandar (harbor, market) of Sinnār.

Processes of Islamization in Sinnār-Funj

While ʿAmāra Dūnqas converted to Islam to unite the empire in one faith, the process of Islamization as such was stimulated by religious scholars and traders rather than the court. As all major trading partners of the empire, except Ethiopia, were Muslim, and as trade routes from the western bilād al-sūdān across Funj to the Red Sea became increasingly important, the number of those who converted to Islam and the number of Muslims who settled permanently in Funj grew gradually. In addition, Arabic was increasingly accepted as the lingua franca of the empire, due to the fact that neither the Funj federation nor the diverse populations of the empire had a common language. The acceptance of Arabic was linked with the slow adoption of Arab social and cultural customs, as well as an Arabo-Islamic identity: "Arab identity signified above all else, an Arab genealogy (nasb)" (McHugh 1994: 9). If not existent, such an identity was constructed. Thus, when religious scholars started to criticize court practices in religious terms, the emperors of Funj started to claim Umayyad ancestry.

The Islamization of Funj was a gradual and selective process. Only under emperor Bādī II Abū Diqn (r. 1642–1677) was a first mosque completed in Sinnār and first qāḍīs were appointed. The documents of the state were recorded in Arabic from the eighteenth century, but even in the eighteenth century Funj still had provincial governors who did not speak Arabic. Through trade, Nubian traders from Funj came into increasing contact with the neighboring Muslim countries; in particular, the provinces of the Ottoman empire learned Arabic and imported new fashions. Thus, a process of cultural reorientation toward the major (Muslim) power in the region was initiated. In addition, students from Sinnār started to study abroad, in particular at al-Azhar in Cairo, and became familiar with religious concepts and arguments which were instrumental to either confirming or criticizing existing social, cultural, and political structures in Funj. The "principles of the Arabs projected a potentially revolutionary image of a preferable culture very different from that of Sinnār, a world based upon antithetical concepts of personal status and community descent and inheritance, property and exchange, and source of legitimate authority" (Spaulding 1985b: 141). Their cultivation in Sinnār implied a constant and growing threat to the political establishment, and the more Islamic such critique became, the more precarious became the non-Islamic foundations of Funj power.

As in the western bilād al-sūdān, Islam started in small islands and enclaves which gradually grew both in number and size and eventually challenged the existing regime, for instance with respect to new concepts of ownership. For the time being, the emperor in Sinnār was the lord over all land and property in Funj, yet in the process of Islamization private ownership became more and more accepted and frequent, as expressed for instance in a shift from trade by exchange of goods to trade by bullion. While Funj still knew no (official) coins or currencies in the early seventeenth century beyond the market of Sinnār and the harbor of Suakin, with the exception of gold in form of gold dust or bracelets, (Spanish) silver coins (from American mines) increasingly entered the empire in the seventeenth century. This led to an accelerated export of gold and the establishment of silver coins in regional and even local markets in the eighteenth century, when silver replaced textiles and salt as currencies of exchange. This led to an even stronger import of small silver coins and the development of an imperial mint. In the late eighteenth century, the Spanish silver peso had become the major currency.

The development of Muslim enclaves in Funj was linked with the development of urban centers. In 1700, Funj knew only two major urban centers, Sinnār and Arbajī. In

1820, this number had increased to more than twenty (not counting the urban centers in Nubia, along the Nile). The development of urban centers was linked with the development of local centers of Islamic learning which often had an autonomous legal position. These centers were not only situated at the crossroads of trade routes, but also in centers of agricultural production. As patron of the Muslim population, the emperor granted Muslim scholars privileges such as small holdings of land which were exempt from taxation and beyond the control of imperial officials. Imperial decrees confirmed these privileges over time and expanded them, turning Muslim religious centers into places of asylum and refuge for the oppressed, ruled by their own (Islamic) laws. Religious scholars were also sought as neutral and knowledgeable intermediaries in local, regional, or imperial disputes, dynastic feuds and all kinds of conflict, and thus slowly became supreme legislators and mediators.

As legal experts or fuqahā' (in Sudanese Arabic: faki), the religious scholars enjoyed special protection: beating a religious scholar was punished twice as hard as beating a khawāja (a master, often a foreigner), and a faki's statement carried more weight at court than the statements of others. The fakis were not constrained to kneel before an aristocrat and did not have to pay taxes. These privileges were recorded in a charter and expanded over time. In particular, exemption from taxation was gradually extended to the community of a religious scholar, often even to their settlements. The inhabitants of these settlements only paid the canonical taxes. According to oral tradition, first charters granting special privileges to fakis were issued by Bādī II, but the earliest charter to have been conserved was issued in the time of Bādī IV Abū Shulūkh (r. 1724–1762) only. In the eighteenth century, charters were increasingly granted by subordinate governors; "even lowly arbābs made free to give away bits of the kingdom" (Spaulding 1985b: 159). Over time, these concessions were issued not only as a royal charter, a "wathīqa mulkiyya," to religious scholars, but also as charitable endowments, which supported the establishment of an Islamic legal order based on the Mālikī school of law. A charter by emperor Bādī IV thus granted freedom of taxation to a religious scholar, but this privilege was soon extended to his family and supporters, "whether sedentary or on journey, east or west" (Spaulding 1985b: 156).

The religious scholars were also free from restrictions on traveling and were thus in a position to trade. The privileges granted to religious scholars differed from those granted to aristocrats, due to the fact that these charters were not feudal fiefs but unrestricted in time. In the context of the collapse of the emperor's monopoly on trade, the provincial governors were increasingly able to acquire their own slaves and to raise their own slave troops which no longer served the emperor, but their own master. In addition, the land charters to religious scholars were granted on condition that they were managed under Islamic law. This implied the recognition of private property in the hands of the religious scholars. From the eighteenth century, an increasing number of transactions of land titles were no longer sanctioned by the emperor or one of his makks. This development brought about the emergence of multifunctional (Muslim) enclaves in the empire, which followed Islamic law and the command of religious scholars rather than the emperor of Funj.

Apart from the centers of Islamic learning, Muslim communities developed in the new trading centers, which were supported by the provincial and local lords who saw this as a way to increase their autonomy with respect to Sinnār. Local and regional lords appointed new qāḍīs for the new trading places, who then mediated the affairs of the foreigners and the traders, the khawāja and the jallāba. Thus, the emergence of new economic and political centers outside Sinnār was enhanced. And although local trading centers accepted the same rules for trade as the imperial bandar in Sinnār, local and provincial lords accepted and protected private trade. Due to the establishment of Islamic courts in the new regional centers, the number of persons who turned to the new courts grew, limiting the claims to hegemony of the Sinnār court. This led to conflicts between local qāḍīs and imperial lords. Islamic courts increasingly prevailed in these disputes, although both systems coexisted until the late eighteenth century. Only the Egyptian invasion in 1820 brought about the final victory of the Islamic judiciary in Sinnār.

For the development of Islam in Funj, holy men also were of major importance and came to settle on the Nile from the fifteenth and sixteenth centuries. These holy men, often representing the Mālikī school of law, were linked with Sufi orders, mostly the Qādiriyya, through scholars such as Tāj al-Dīn al-Baḥārī, Ghulām Allāh b. ʿAlī, and Idrīs b. Muḥammad al-ʿArabar, or the Shādhiliyya through scholars such as Ḥamad Abū Dunāna and Khogāli ʿAbd al-Raḥmān. As in the bilād al-maghrib and the western bilād al-sūdān, these Sufi scholars established their own centers of learning and taught a form of Sufism which was not yet linked with the formal structures of a ṭarīqa. The holy men stimulated practices of saint veneration and visits to their centers and tombs, which again led to the emergence of local cults. Muslims on the Nile thus developed a tradition "of mysticism personalized in the link between the ubiquitous holy man and his followers and institutionalized in Sufi doctrine and organization" (McHugh 1994: 10). The *Kitāb al-tabaqāt fi-khuṣūṣ al-awliyāʾ wa-l-ṣāliḥīn wa-l-ʿulamāʾ wa-l-shurafāʾ fī-l-sūdān* by Muḥammad al-Nūr Ḍayf Allāh (1729–1809), written in 1804, provides an overview of 281 biographies of shuyūkh, scholars, and fuqahāʾ since around 1500 and attests to the growth of literature in Funj from the late eighteenth century. Until the late seventeenth century, the *ṭabaqat* did not register affiliation with a particular Sufi order, and early Sufi saints such as those named above should possibly be seen as cultural heroes who were thought to show the early establishment of Islam in a specific region. Still, the abodes of the holy men became local centers of mediation, trade, teaching, and healing, and contributed to the process of Islamization on the Nile. Only in the nineteenth century did Sufi orders such as the Khatmiyya/Mirghāniyya, the Tijāniyya, the Majdhūbiyya, or the Sammāniyya emerge as organized bodies.

The Decline of Sinnār-Funj

The reasons for the decline of Funj may be summarized under three themes. First of all, revolts came to disrupt the development of Funj from the early eighteenth century. Under emperor Bādī III, a first major revolt erupted in 1705/06, when Bādī III tried to introduce firearms in the imperial army. This endeavor led to the protest of the provincial lords who were afraid of losing their military power, as they were not entitled to acquire firearms. Also, Dongola, the Shā'iqiyya, the Bīja groups, Kordofan, and the southern marches tried to increase their autonomy and to undermine the imperial monopoly on long-distance trade. In particular, the trade in slaves was increasingly dominated by private traders, which decreased the income of the emperor. The introduction of silver and other foreign coins equally undermined the monopoly of the emperor on the trade with bullion. Finally, Funj suffered from the erosion of her institutions in the context of increasing Islamization and the emergence of parallel Islamic institutions. The emerging networks of private trade often consisted of Muslim traders who rejected the non-Islamic customs and ritual practices at court. They established mosques and schools and supported literacy in Arabic. The traders also brought books, and the prestige of scholars rose. However, despite the crisis of the state in the eighteenth century, Funj did not experience a jihād movement, as did the western bilād al-sūdān in the eighteenth and nineteenth centuries. This may be attributed

> to the relentless dissolution of the old system during this entire period of time and the flow of concessions to the representatives of the new. In this way, mounting pressures were released. The deep divisions among the fuqara and their followers along the lines of family-tariqas . . . may have further inhibited their melding into a common cause. (McHugh 1994: 111)

In the eighteenth century, the court in Sinnār eventually lost her monopoly over the trade as well as customs and the privilege of minting. As a consequence, new currencies could be imported and undermined the monetary stability in Funj based on gold. Also, new trading groups of local traders, the ḥaḍāriba or ḥuḍūr (the locals), were able to form, in particular among the Bīja. They were increasingly able to organize their own caravans, and imperial caravans became obsolete. Due to decreasing income, the court and the aristocracy were forced to increase taxes and tributes. This increased the pressure on peasants and peasant farmer dissatisfaction grew. The traders initially profited from this economic crisis, as peasant farmers were forced to borrow money from them. In this system of sheil (shā'il) interdependency, peasant farmers borrowed grain from the trader's stock for a relatively high price and repaid these stocks after the next harvest at a relatively low price level, effectively paying an increasing share of their harvest to a trader in order to repay old (and growing) debts. In order to escape the accumulation of debt, peasant farmers either tried to become traders themselves or fled into the settlements of the Islamic religious scholars in order to escape taxation. This stimulated not only the Islamization of Funj, but also increased the political weight of the religious scholars, while at the same time challenging the authority of the emperor. The emperors of Funj were increasingly constrained by these dynamics of change to follow Islamic norms in order to retain some influence among their growing Muslim populations. Yet this could happen only by relinquishing pre-Islamic customs and features of divine kingdom: they stopped drinking alcohol, became increasingly visible to their people, and started to shave their hair and to pray in public. They abandoned their pre-Islamic titles, lost their god-like aloofness, and became increasingly human. The emperors of Funj thus abandoned their established foundation of power without really gaining a new source of legitimacy: the religious scholars continued to regard the emperors of Funj as not quite Muslim rulers and continued to criticize specific aspects of their rule.

The erosion of imperial power became particularly clear in 1718, when Funj's first dynasty, the Ūnsāb dynasty, was deposed by the sīd al-qūm, Nōl. Nōl happened to be a religious scholar, and established the Islamic Nōl dynasty of Funj, by handing over power in 1724 to his son Bādī IV, who ruled until 1762. In the context of this dynastic change, Islam was established as the one and only source of legitimization and the existing court ritual was abandoned. The new dynasty sought the support of the Islamic religious scholars who were subsequently able to increase their social and political influence. The new rulers of Funj granted privileges to the religious scholars, and new disciplines of Islamic learning were cultivated. Apart from memorization of the Qur'ān, this was fiqh, ḥadīth, sīra, and ta'rīkh. This development contributed to the Arabization of the empire. The new character of the empire was enhanced by the fact that under King Bādī IV, Funj stopped the custom of ritually killing the brothers of the new ruler. Equally, King Bādī IV switched from a tradition of matrilineal descent to patrilineal descent in dynastic succession. Until that time, the Ūnsāb dynasty of Funj had traced its origin back to a wise stranger, Bint 'Ayn al-Shams, and each ruler of the Ūnsāb dynasty had been obliged to marry among the descendants of the Bint 'Ayn al-Shams clan. Bādī IV also eliminated all representatives of the Ūnsāb dynasty, while keeping alive his own sons from different mothers. In each generation, the number of aspirants to the throne thus grew and added to the instability of the kingdom.

The power of the new dynasty was nevertheless demonstrated by a victory over an Ethiopian army in 1744, and Bādī IV was able to consolidate his power subsequently. Numerous positions were now filled with religious scholars, while opponents of the new dynasty were deposed. Bādī IV also expanded the court and increased the number of feudal lords, while appropriating many land titles of the old aristocracy. The struggle for power in Sinnār-Funj weakened imperial authority, however, and Funj suffered a first military defeat in 1747 when Dārfūr invaded Kordofan and defeated a Funj army under the command of Muḥammad Abū Likaylik, a Hamāj ally from the southern marches of Fāzūghlī. The Hamāj had become part of Funj in the seventeenth century only. They claimed to represent the legacy of ʿAlwa and remained Christian for some time after the end of ʿAlwa. Muḥammad Abū Likaylik managed to reverse this defeat, however, and reconquered Kordofan in 1755. As a result, he became the most powerful army commander and was able to organize the deposition of Bādī IV in 1762 and to replace the emperor with a son of Bādī IV, Nāṣir. He was followed, in 1769, by Ismāʿīl, who represented the old aristocracy. The real holder of power remained Muḥammad Abū Likaylik, however. The Funj chronicle described these events in the following terms:

> Then Shaykh Muḥammad (Abū Likaylik) appointed Makk Nāṣir, the son of Makk Bādī, as king. That was in the year 1175 (1761/62), and from that time the power of loosing and binding was in the hand of the Hamāj. They gained domination over the Funj; and Shaykh Muḥammad killed their magnates, and appointed and dismissed among them. Dating was according to the periods of the shaykhs of the Hamāj, disregarding their kings. (quoted in Holt 1999: 19)

Under Muḥammad Abū Likaylik, the Nōl dynasty was again removed from power, and the Likaylik-Hamāj came to rule Funj until the Egyptian conquest in 1820. This dynastic change led to the further fragmentation of Funj. The new dynasty was never able to reestablish Funj as an empire with more than nominal power over her provinces beyond the Jazīra. Only when Muḥammad Abū Likaylik died in 1776 were the rulers of Funj able to regain some authority for a short period of time. King ʿAdlān even regained control over Kordofan in 1782, which was soon conquered again, in 1785, by Dārfūr. In the southern marches, the empire also lost her power and the Shilluk were able to assert their independence. At the end of the eighteenth century, wars between feudal lords and imperial princes destabilized Funj more and more, and when a comparatively small but modern Egyptian army attacked Funj in 1820, the empire collapsed without major resistance.

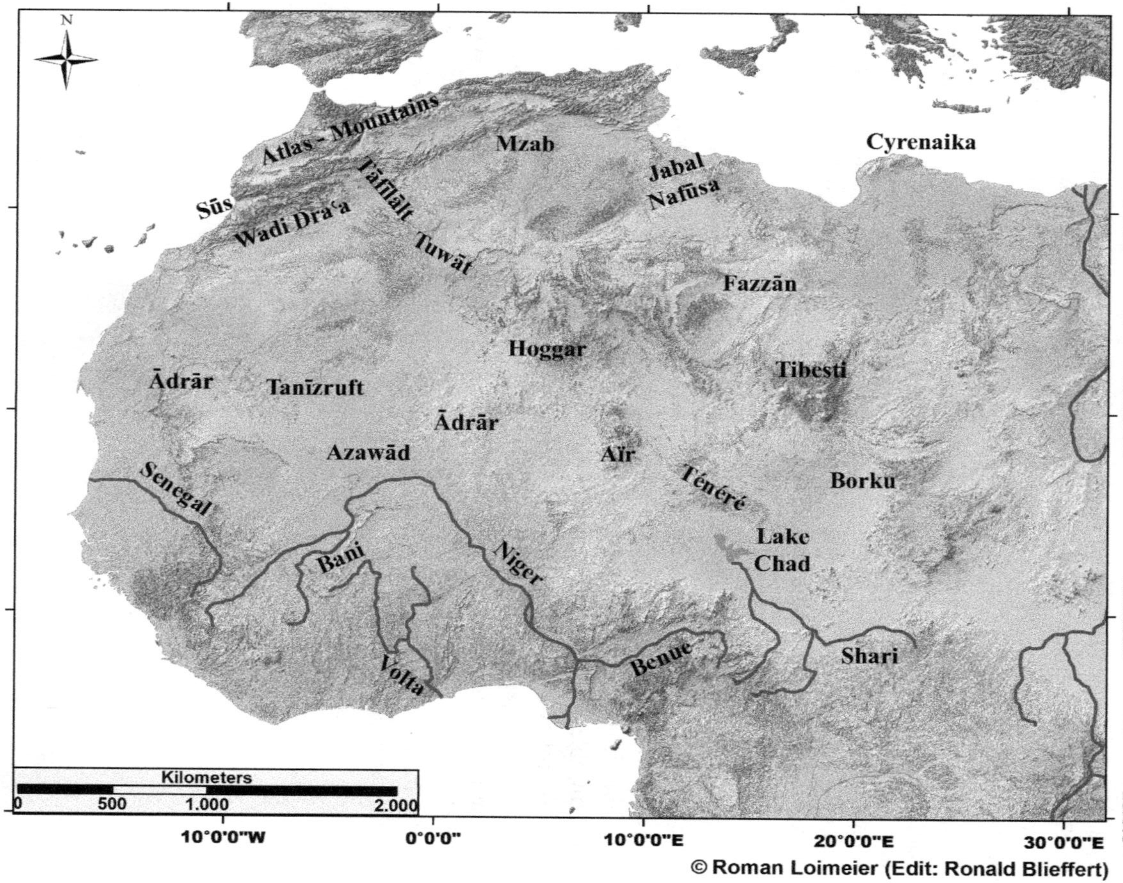

Map 1. North Africa, the Sahara, and sub-Saharan West Africa

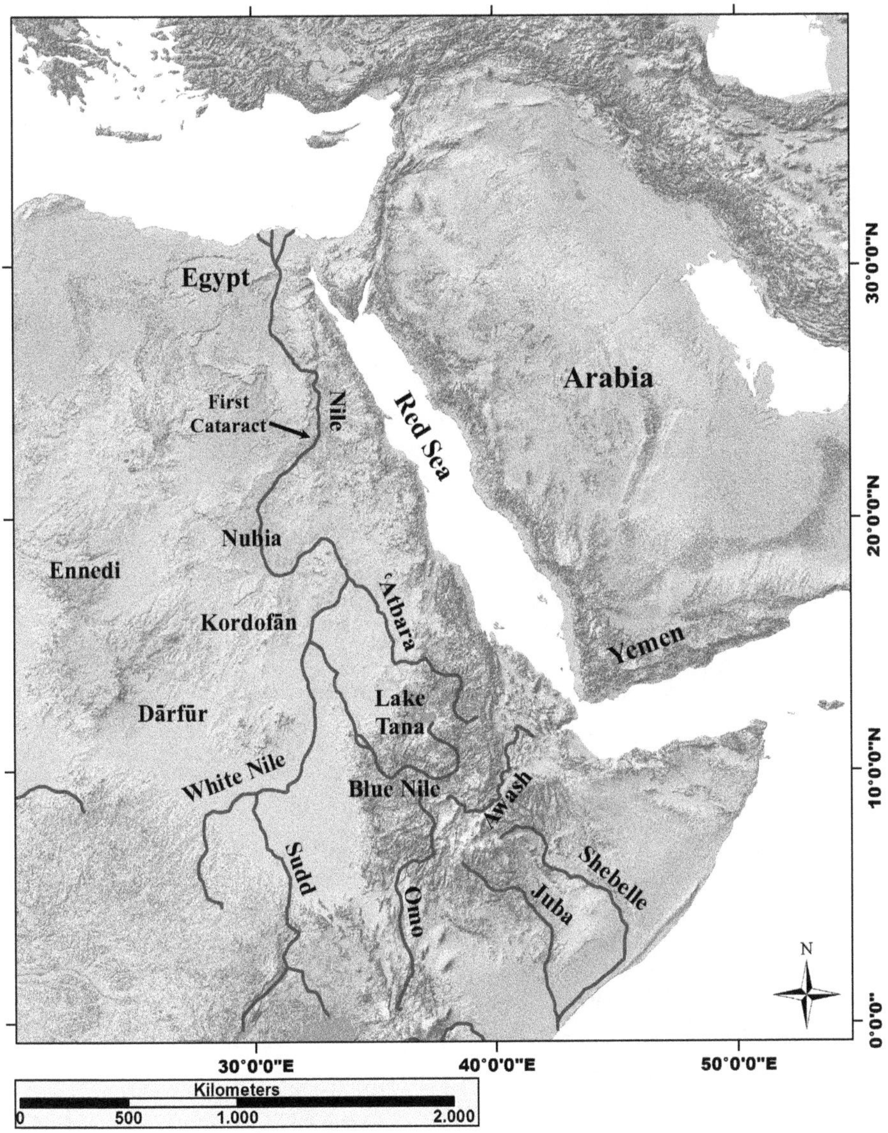

Map 2. The Nile valley and Ethiopia

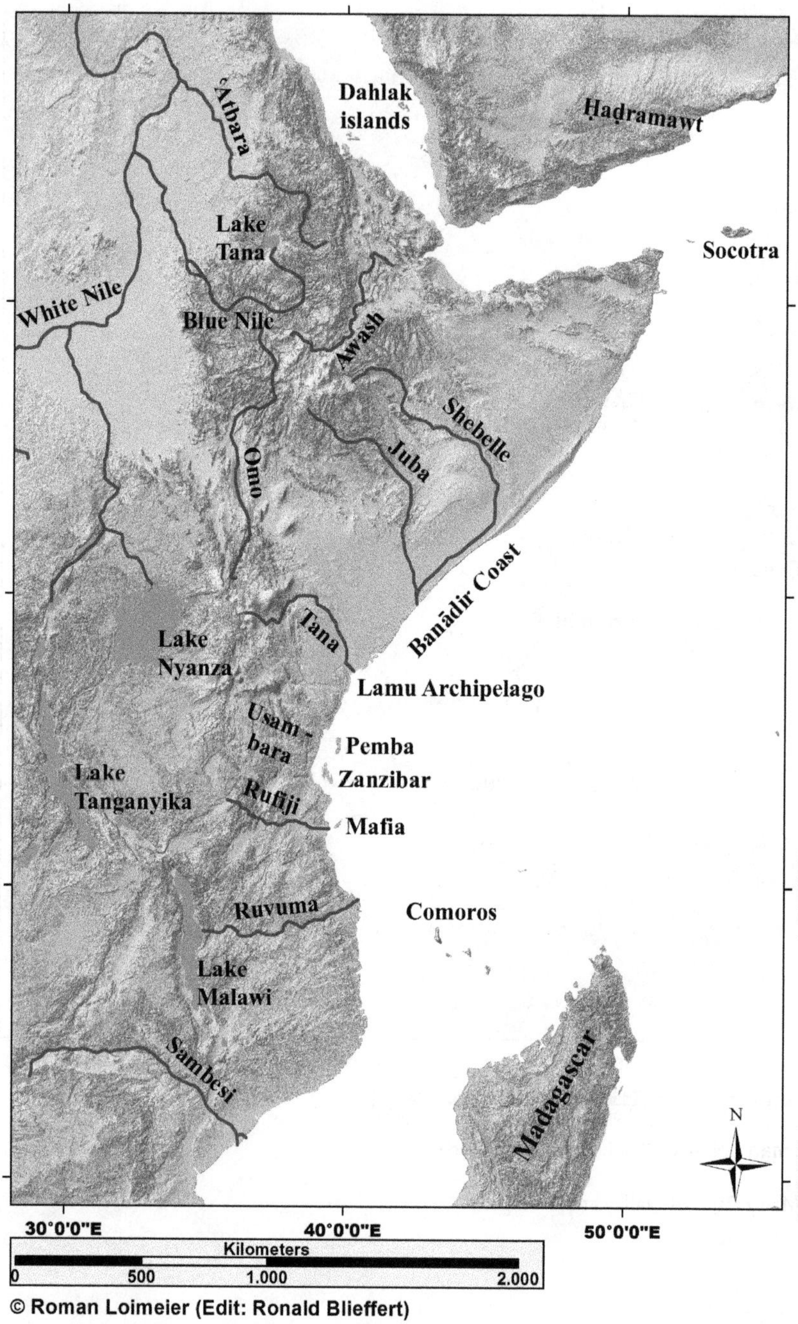

Map 3. The Horn of Africa and East Africa

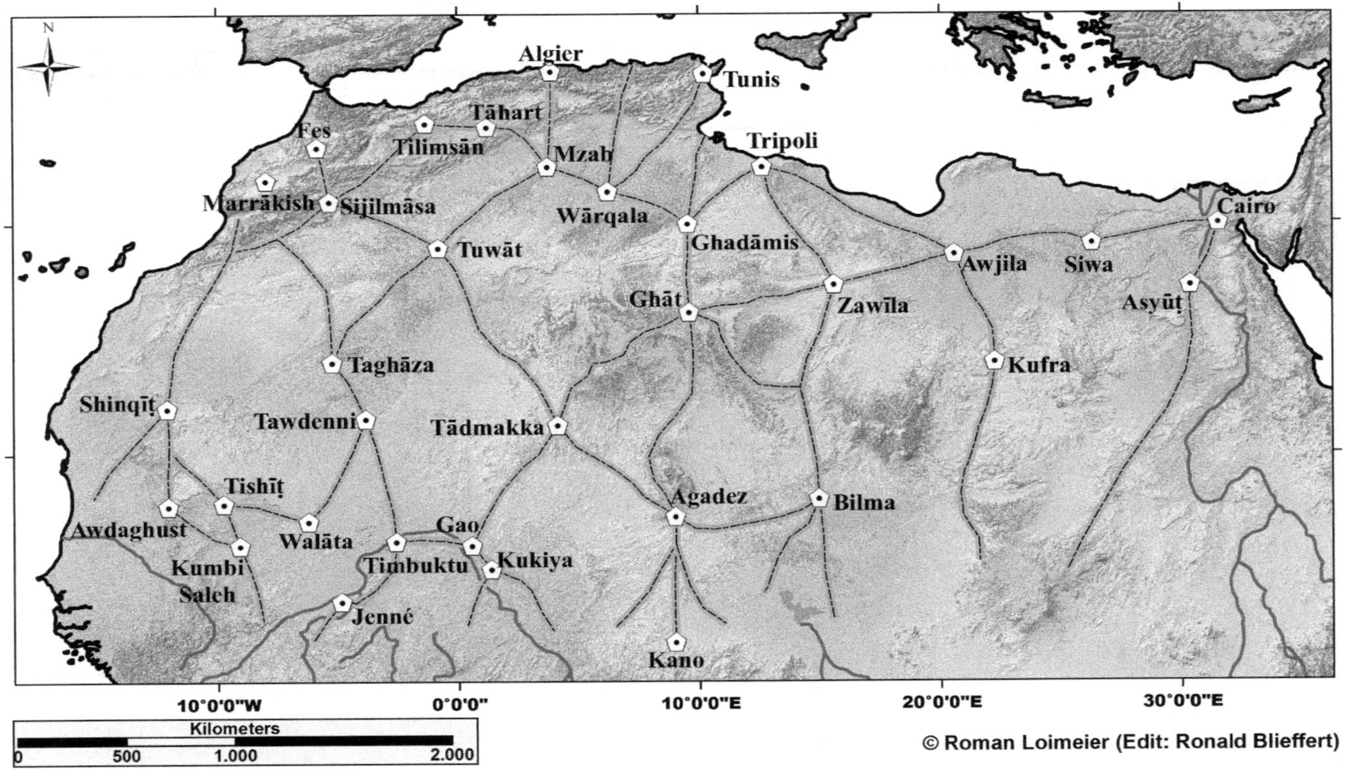

Map 4. The Trans-Saharan trade routes

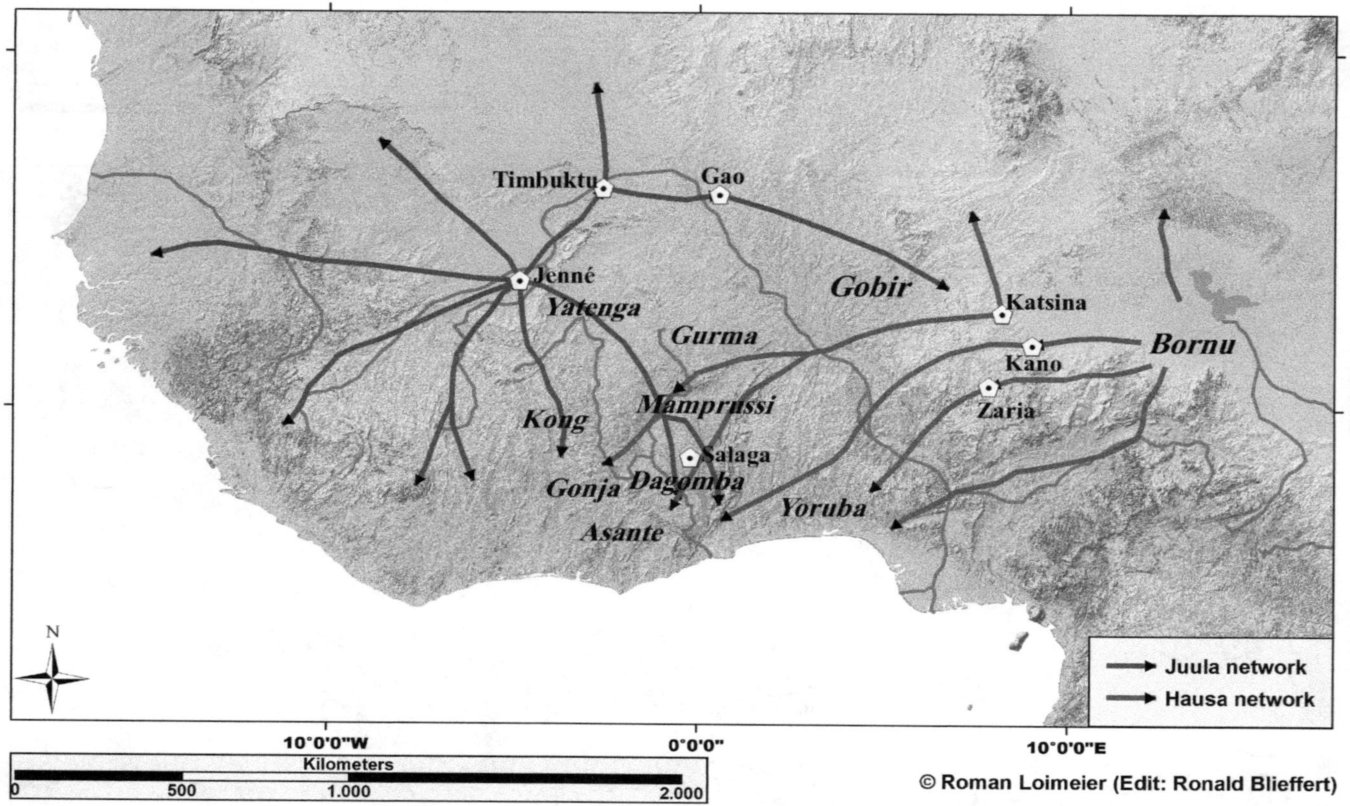

Map 5. The Juula and Hausa trade networks in the Bilād al-Sūdān

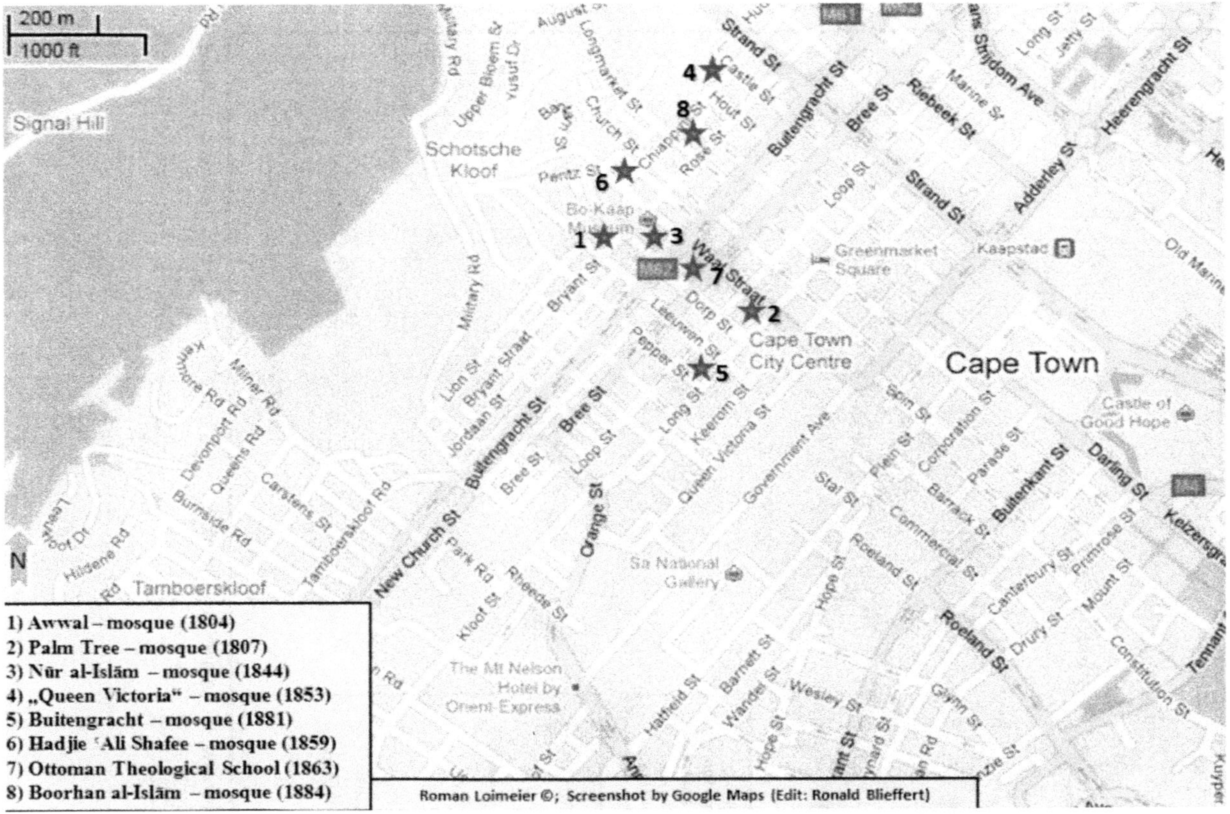

Map 6. The Cape Town mosques in the nineteenth century

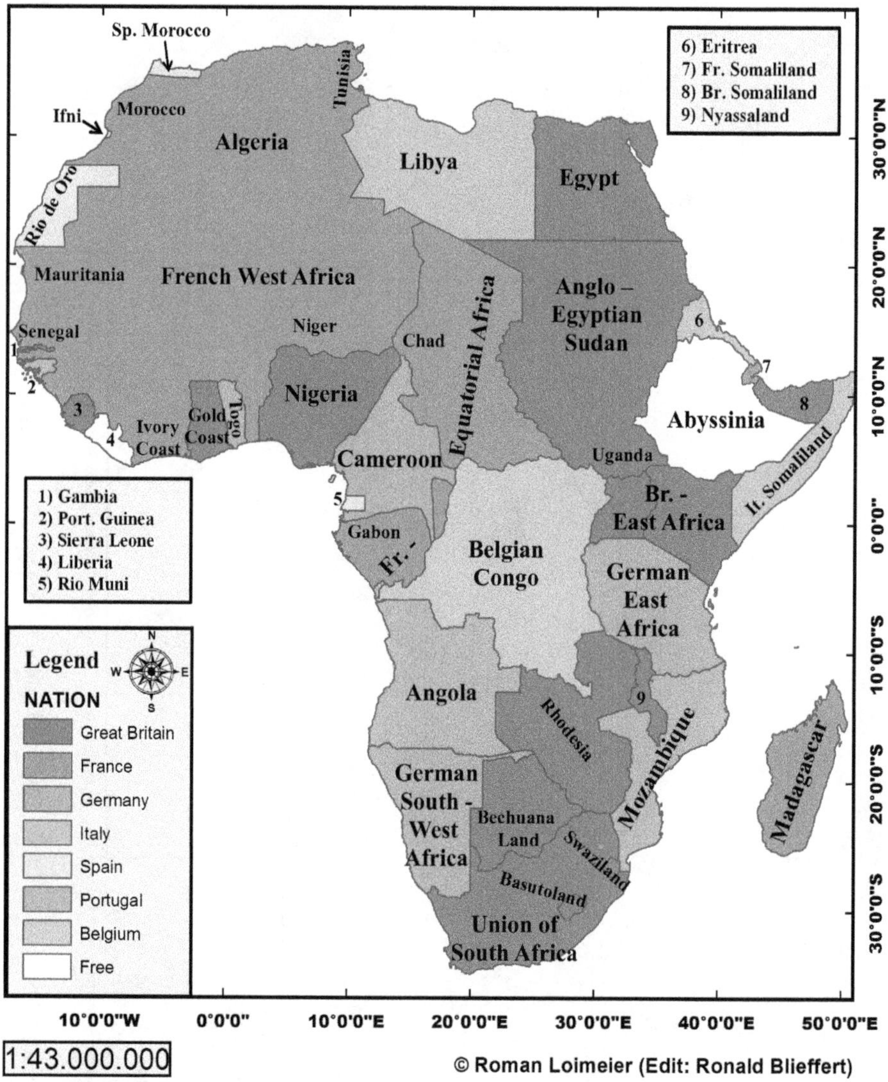

Map 7. The European colonial territories in Africa

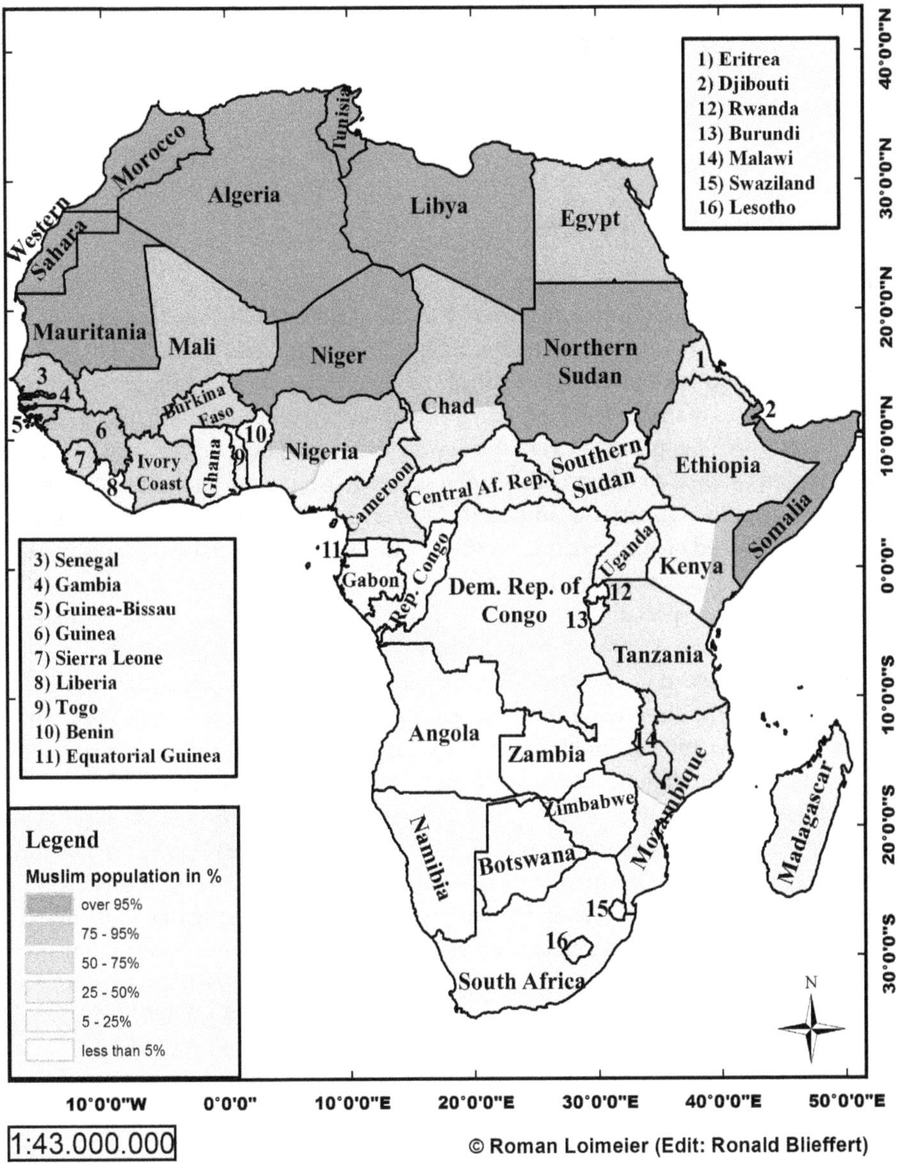

Map 8. The expansion of Islam in contemporary Africa

7 Egyptian Colonialism and the Mahdī in the Sudan

Historical Themes and Patterns

After the collapse of the Funj empire in the early nineteenth century, the lands on the two Niles became one of the few regions in Africa not colonized by a European colonial power but by an Arabo-African empire, Egypt. As in pharaonic times, Egypt sought to secure its southern marches, to control the Nile valley, and to gain access to the natural resources of the Sudan. Egyptian power politics were linked with a program of modernization in Egypt as well as in the new Egyptian provinces in the Sudan. While the Egyptian colonial conquest of the Sudan succeeded, Egyptian efforts to modernize the Sudan remained superficial and created unrest and instability. The new administration, often based on a bureaucracy staffed by Copts, turned social structures upside down, and marginalized established authorities while pampering new social and religious movements, especially among the Sufi orders and religious scholars. The extension of the Egyptian administration into the southern and western marches of the Sudan also threatened established trade networks, in particular when Egypt started to fight against the slave trade in the 1860s. As a result, opposition against the rule of the Turks grew and eventually led to the emergence of a millenarian movement of protest, led by the religious scholar Muḥammad Aḥmad, who proclaimed himself to be the Mahdi, the "rightly guided" redeemer from Egyptian oppression. In 1885, Egypt had to evacuate the Sudan and the movement of the Mahdi came to power, as possibly the first expression of a modern Sudanese nationalism. Yet the rule of the Mahdiyya proved to be disastrous for the Sudan and its populations, not only due to its inability to overcome ethnic and religious antagonisms, but also due to major failures in its social and economic policies. As a result, the Sudan suffered a devastating human catastrophe in the 1890s and was eventually reconquered by an Egyptian army under British command in 1898. The legacies of both the Egyptian colonization and the Mahdiyya continue to inform politics in the Sudan to this day.

Egypt's Conquest of Sinnār-Funj

When Napoleon landed in Egypt in 1798 and defeated the Ottoman-Mamlūk army, to take control over Cairo and much of Lower Egypt, the established system of the Mamlūk administration, which had governed Egypt since 1252, collapsed quickly. Although the French soon had to leave Egypt, the Mamlūks were not able to regain lost ground. Eventually an outsider, Muḥammad ʿAlī, the commander of the small Albanian garrison in Cairo, was able to claim and maintain power with the support of the local elite and religious scholars. Muḥammad ʿAlī, who was born in 1770 in Kavala (present-day northern Greece), soon outmaneuvered all competitors, not only among the last Mamlūks but also among the local elites, and established his own dynasty. His rule, as recognized by the Ottoman sulṭān in 1805, put Egypt on a course of modernization which eventually turned it into a major economic and military player in the eastern Mediterranean, the Arab peninsula, and northeastern Africa. His rule was linked with efforts to acquire territorial possessions in the form of an empire stretching from the upper Nile to the East African coast and across the Arabian peninsula. In the end, Egypt's imperial ambitions failed due to European intervention and the financial burden of overambitious projects such as the Suez Canal. Between 1820 and the early 1880s, however, Egypt largely defined the destiny of the Sudan.

The foundations of Egypt's path to modernity were based on a radical policy of reforms in Egypt, initiated by Muḥammad ʿAlī: the removal of old elites from positions of influence and power, including the religious scholars; the nationalization of the land fiefs of the Mamlūks as well as of all religious endowments in the guise of land titles, and, linked to that, a radical redistribution of land to the peasant farmers, who were constrained, however, to produce cash crops for the state, in particular cotton, which became the backbone of Egypt's exports and textile production; a number of social and institutional reforms, the establishment of a new system of state schools (Arab. kuttāb), as well as the recruitment of a new army, armed and trained along French models. Based on these instruments of power and fueled by rising income, Muḥammad ʿAlī was able, following an Ottoman plea, to conquer the Ḥijāz in 1812 and to oust the Wahhābī movement from Mecca and Medina. Up to 1819, Egyptian troops also conquered vast parts of the central and eastern Arabian peninsula and eventually crushed the Wahhābiyya in its central lands. In control of the eastern shores of the Red Sea, Muḥammad ʿAlī started to prepare the invasion of the Sudan. The motivations for the Egyptian conquest of the lands on the River Nile were manifold: control over the western shores of the Red Sea, control over the gold mines and suspected mineral resources of the Sudan, as well as ivory and other trade goods, direct control over the slave trade, recruitment of manpower for the Egyptian army, expansion of territory, elimination of the last Mamlūks who had fled to Sinnār, and control over the Nile valley to the sources of the river in Ethiopia and Central Africa. Egypt's conquest of the Nile valley in the early nineteenth century can thus be regarded as yet another effort to gain complete control over a trans-Saharan trade route and its port cities.

Before Egypt started with the conquest of the Sudan, Muḥammad ʿAlī sent a diplomatic mission (1812) and two geological expeditions (1816/17 and 1817/18) to Sinnār-Funj, in order to increase Egyptian knowledge on Funj. In October 1820, the invasion proper started, based on a comparatively small but well-equipped army of 6,000 soldiers (with twelve field guns) under the leadership of Muḥammad ʿAlī's son Ismāʿīl. In

March 1821, the Egyptian army took Berber and Shendi, the two major centers of the Ja'aliyyīn, the major Arab tribal federation in Nubia, and on 11 June 1821 the Egyptian army entered Sinnār. The last emperor of Funj, Bādī VI, was sent into exile in Cairo. In the same year, the Egyptian army secured control over the Jazīra, the fertile heart of Funj, and started to establish Egyptian rule and administration. Due to the fact that Egypt was formally still part of the Ottoman empire at this time, and that Ottoman-Turkish was the language of administration in Egypt, the period of Egyptian administration over the lands on the River Nile came to be known as Turkiyya. A majority of the Egyptian officials in the Sudan who administered the Egyptian possessions on the River Nile from 1820 to 1885 indeed came from the Ottoman empire and beyond: of twenty-three governors, there were eight Circassians, two Kurds, two Greeks, one Albanian, one Berber, one British, and five Turks, while only three were Egyptians. For the time being, Wad Madanī became the first administrative center, but in 1833 the capital moved to a new city on the confluence of the two Niles, al-Kharṭūm (Khartoum), which soon became the major urban center in the Sudan.

In 1821, a second Egyptian army conquered Kordofan in the west and defeated an army from Dārfūr without advancing into Dārfūr. Subsequently, four provinces were established, Dongola, Berber, Sinnār, and Kordofan. The Egyptian army also brought three religious scholars from al-Azhar who set up a judiciary and the administration of the religious endowments. While the Egyptian administration delegated the collection of the new taxes in Dongola and Berber to the established local lords, direct taxation in Sinnār led to a widespread rebellion of the population in 1822, which quickly spread to the north and found support among the Ja'aliyyīn. Due to the superior equipment and skills of the Egyptian army, this rebellion was crushed in 1824, but major parts of the Jazīra and Berber provinces were devastated. When new Egyptian troops under the command of 'Alī Khurshid Bey eventually arrived in 1826, the Egyptian administration restarted and began to rebuild a country which had been ruined by decades of warfare and exploitation. Under the administration of 'Alī Khurshid Bey (r. 1826–1838), the Egyptian administration thoroughly transformed the Sudan by reorganizing the judiciary, reorganizing the tax system, establishing Khartoum as the new administrative center, and establishing the first modern schools and a river transport system. Taxation was organized by Egyptian Copts who commanded allied tribes such as the Shā'iqiyya, which were exempt from taxation. Tribal leaders who refused to cooperate were replaced by accommodating headmen or by leaders of competing tribal fractions, a policy which often led to further tribal fragmentation.

'Alī Khurshid Bey also started to build a Sudanese army and to establish first factories in Khartoum for the production of soap and sugar, as well as a distillery. Trade was reorganized and expanded, ostrich feathers, ivory, indigo, gum Arabic, slaves, sugar cane, and cattle being the major items of trade. The slave trade, in particular, saw a rapid expansion from 1826, which was the year of the first state-organized slave raid in the southern marches. Year after year, the Egyptian administration pushed further south, penetrated the swamps on the upper White Nile in 1839, and reached Gondokoro, close to Sudan's present-day frontier with Uganda in 1841. The slave trade was organized mainly by the Jallāba, traders from northern Sudan, who expanded rapidly into the south under Egyptian protection and continued to expand, when the state trading monopoly collapsed, in 1840. Apart from the southern marches, the Nuba mountains were major slave-hunting grounds, but these areas desperately fought for their independence from Egyptian control and managed to resist conquest until 1884. Under Governor Aḥmad Abū Adhān (r. 1838–1843), the mineral resources of the Sudan were prospected and European companies and traders were allowed to enter and to do business in the Sudan. From 1843 to 1863, a period of stagnation under a series of powerless administrators followed, which saw the expansion of European commercial interests. The Ottoman empire, by contrast, relinquished its control over its possessions in the Red Sea, in particular the harbor cities of Suakin and Massawa that were taken over by Egypt. At the same time, the Sudan was ravaged by a number of Nile floods, droughts, and epidemics, in particular two yellow fever epidemics in 1836/37 and 1856, which were described in the Funj chronicle:

> As for the sickness which occurred in that year (1836/37), it was the Yellow Wind. . . . Its description (God protect us and the Muslims from it) is that a man would suffer from vomiting and diarrhea. His skin would become chilly and he would come out in a cold sweat. His eyes would change and his fingertips would be as if they were roasted in the fire. . . . Many died of it. . . . It was called "the Mother of Seven" because the majority of those who fell ill died on the seventh day and whoever survived it recovered. (quoted in Holt 1999: 106, 135, 143)

Despite these epidemics and calamities, Khartoum grew from 14,000 inhabitants in 1837 to 50,000 in 1883. Since 1850, a fleet of riverboats maintained postal, passenger, and transport services on the Nile between the sixth cataract in the north and the stations north of the sudd in the south. In 1856/57 the Egyptian ruler Saʿīd personally visited the Sudan and replaced Ottoman-Turkish as the language of administration with Arabic.

After the accession of Khedive Ismāʿīl (r. 1863–1879) to the throne, the Egyptian administration in the Sudan was revitalized. Numerous new projects were started, new mines were explored, the country was linked with Egypt by way of the telegraph, and a river police was established on the Nile. From 1862 to 1879, Khartoum was administered by the first Sudanese, Aḥmad Bey ʿAwad al-Karīm Abū Sinn, a Shukriyya from the Jazīra. Under Khedive Ismāʿīl, Egypt also started to fight against the slave trade, which was viewed as obsolete in the context of Egyptian policies of modernization and increasingly criticized by European powers, Britain in particular. These policies affected the Sudanese slave traders, the Jallāba, who started to shift their activities into the territories beyond Egyptian control in the west and the south: Muḥammad Aḥmad al-ʿAqqad on the Baḥr al-Ghazal and Zubayr Pasha in Dārfūr. The Egyptian ban on the slave trade not only hit the traders, but also the Baggāra and Kabābīsh tribes, which provided the logistics of the trade and protected the slave caravans. In addition, the large land owners on the Nile and in the Jazīra were affected as prices for slaves rose and farmers were increasingly unable to acquire slaves for the work on their farms. In order to end the slave trade, the Egyptian administration advanced into the territories frequented by the slave traders and started to employ Europeans in order to implement an effective policy of anti-slavery: thus, British army officers Baker Pasha and Gordon Pasha were hired as governors for Equatoria province, which had been Egyptian since 1871, the Italian Gessi became governor of Baḥr al-Ghazāl (Egyptian since 1873), the Swiss Munzinger became governor in Massawa in 1868, and the Austro-Hungarian Slatin Pasha became governor of Dārfūr in 1874. Having to face the advance of the Egyptian administration into the southern and western marches of the Sudan, the slave traders withdrew and started to establish their zarības (bases) in territories still further west and south.

At the same time, the Egyptian administration expanded along the coasts of the Red Sea: the harbors of Zaylaʿ and Berbera in northern Somalia were occupied by the Egyptian navy in 1870 and the Egyptian army occupied the hinterland of Massawa in 1872, preparing an attack on Ethiopia from different directions. This attack started in 1875 in the form of four military expeditions. The Scottish adventurer McKillop Pasha, commander of the Egyptian naval forces, quickly took the harbor cities on the Somali coast, even cities like Brawa and Kismayu which formed part of the possessions of the Sulṭānate of Zanzibar. The Swiss governor of Massawa, Munzinger, attacked through the Danakil desert but was ambushed by Dankali warriors and killed on 14 November 1875, while the Danish adventurer Ahrendrup Pasha, who had marched on Adwa from Massawa, was defeated by an Ethiopian army near Gundet on 16 November 1875. Only Raʾūf Pasha, the only Egyptian commander, marched from Zaylaʿ to the eastern highlands and took the Muslim city of Ḥarär, which had not yet been claimed by Ethiopia. Another attack on Ethiopia from Massawa, this time in the guise of an army of 20,000 Egyptian soldiers led by Mulay Ḥasan Pasha, was defeated in March 1876 near Guray by an Ethiopian army of 60,000. The Egyptian naval forces also had to evacuate the harbors on the East African coast and to return them to the sulṭān of Zanzibar. Egyptian plans to add Ethiopia to the Egyptian colonial empire thus misfired, and when Egypt was transformed into a British Protectorate in 1882, her possessions in Ethiopia and on the Horn were taken by Italy (Eritrea and Somalia), Britain (northern Somalia), France (Djibouti/Zaylaʿ), and Ethiopia (Ḥarär). The imperial policies of Khedive Ismāʿīl as well as his overambitious projects of modernization, in particular the construction of the Suez Canal, led to the financial collapse of Egypt in 1879. A rebellion of young nationalist officers under ʿUrabi Pasha against the international control of Egyptian finances led to British intervention in 1882 and the disintegration of the Egyptian empire. At the same time, Egypt lost control over the Sudan, where a religious scholar, who had proclaimed himself as the Mahdī, started a rebellion against Egyptian rule in 1881.

The Sufi Orders on the Nile

While holy men were present on the Nile from the early times of Sinnār-Funj, Sufi orders as organized bodies developed only in the nineteenth century, as in the western bilād al-sūdān, and then acquired a central role in society and politics. Often, pilgrims from Arabia or the western bilād al-sūdān settled on the Nile and established centers of Islamic learning and scholarship, and sometimes these centers of learning acquired particular fame, when a holy man proved to be particularly adept at healing or spiritual, social, political, and economic counseling. In such cases, a local saint cult and tradition of shrine visit (ziyāra) might emerge, yet, as mentioned above, in the eighteenth century these individual centers of holy men were not yet united by ties to a ṭarīqa. This situation changed completely in the context of the collapse of Funj in the early nineteenth century. Emissaries of Sufi orders based in the bilād al-maghrib and Egypt, such as the Shādhiliyya, the Sammāniyya-Khalwatiyya, and the Tijāniyya; in 'Iraq, such as the Qādiriyya; or in the Ḥijāz or Yemen, such as the Idrīsiyya, the Rashīdiyya, and Majdhūbiyya, found supporters in the Sudan and established local centers (zawāya) of their respective ṭarīqa.

While these Sufi orders managed to attract followers in some regions of the Sudan, they were not able to establish organizational networks that covered the whole territory. This role was eventually taken over by a new Sufi order, the Mirghāniyya, established by Muḥammad 'Uthmān al-Mirghānī, who, like Muḥammad al-Sanūsī, had been a student of Aḥmad b. Idrīs (d. 1837). Muḥammad 'Uthmān al-Mirghānī was born near al-Ṭā'if in the Ḥijāz and became a religious scholar, like his father and grandfather. After being accepted as a student of Aḥmad b. Idrīs, he was sent to the Sudan in order to propagate the teachings of his master. Muḥammad 'Uthmān al-Mirghānī was particularly successful in the north, in the lands of Nubia, but then returned to al-Ṭā'if in 1823 and continued to live with Aḥmad b. Idrīs. After his death, Muḥammad 'Uthmān al-Mirghānī was accepted by most families in Mecca and al-Ṭā'if as the successor of Aḥmad b. Idrīs, while Muḥammad al-Sanūsī eventually left the Ḥijāz. Muḥammad 'Uthmān al-Mirghānī subsequently sent his sons into other parts of the Islamic world in order to spread his path. Muḥammad 'Uthmān al-Mirghānī claimed that he had founded a ṭarīqa which would supersede all other Sufi orders, and which would unite sharī'a and ḥaqīqa; the new ṭarīqa would be the seal (Arab. khatm) of all Sufi orders. It was soon called the Khatmiyya.

Muḥammad 'Uthmān al-Mirghānī also sent one of his sons back to the Sudan to propagate the teachings of the Khatmiyya, namely Muḥammad Ḥasan al-Mirghānī, who had been born in the Sudan and who now started to propagate the Khatmiyya in Sinnār, on Kordofan, and among the Bīja in the Red Sea Hills. Building on the work of his father in Nubia, he became the true founder of the ṭarīqa in the Sudan and, after the death of his father in 1853, the leader of an independent branch of the Khatmiyya in the Sudan. He established the center of the ṭarīqa in Kassala, where he was buried in 1869, his tomb becoming the focus of a ziyāra tradition. His son and successor, Muḥammad 'Uthmān al-Aqrab Tāj al-Sirr (d. 1886), continued to expand the ṭarīqa in the Sudan and established zawāya in almost all parts of the country. Each zāwiya was led by a regional shaykh al-sajjāda (master of the prayer rug), as appointed by the supreme leader of the ṭarīqa, who commanded the local representatives (Arab. muqaddamūn) of the ṭarīqa. The shaykh al-sajjāda was the local administrator of the property of the ṭarīqa and organized its activities, such as the annual celebration of the birthday of the Prophet (Arab. mawlid al-nabī) and of the mawlid of Muḥammad 'Uthmān al-Mirghānī, as well as the weekly dhikr meetings. The Khatmiyyya was thus the first ṭarīqa in the Sudan to establish a hierarchical structure.

Due to its centralized hierarchy and firm organization, the Khatmiyya was soon coveted by the Egyptian administration as an ally in the administration of the Sudan, and services of the Khatmiyya were correspondingly remunerated. With Egyptian support, the Khatmiyya was able to establish a network of zawāya, schools, and mosques in vast parts of the Sudan, and to acquire a social and religious infrastructure which enabled the ṭarīqa to address major parts of the population of the Sudan. As the Egyptian administration followed a program of modernization which was accepted by the leaders of the Khatmiyya, the ṭarīqa was seen by the Egyptian administration as a transmission belt for its programs of reform in the Sudan and as an intermediary which could be used to approach local populations. The Khatmiyya thus became an important intermediary between the Egyptian administration and the local populations. It acquired considerable wealth in terms of, for instance, land holdings, and was able to translate this wealth into political influence. Social and political rise became easier when mediated by the Khatmiyya, and many local lords and notables turned to the Khatmiyya for support, thus strengthening the local roots of the ṭarīqa.

The rapid rise of the Khatmiyya as a Sudanese Sufi order must also be explained, however, in terms of its teachings: the Khatmiyya stressed that its members represented a spiritual elite united by the blessing power (Arab. baraka) of Muḥammad 'Uthmān al-Mirghānī and his sons, who were associated with numerous miracles (Arab. karāmāt). Thus, they were said to have provided for rain in the desert, to have punished unjust (local) rulers (by ways of an Egyptian military expedition), and to have traced stolen goods. The power of blessing of Muḥammad 'Uthmān al-Mirghānī was thought to be so strong that it was transmitted not only to all those who knew him when still alive, but also to all those who happened to meet those who had known him while alive, and so on, into the fifth rank: the fire of hell would not touch them. The baraka of Muḥammad 'Uthmān al-Mirghānī thus applied not only to his contemporaries but extended into the future. As a small child, Muḥammad 'Uthmān al-Mirghānī was credited with having special spiritual gifts. When visiting Sinnār in 1819, he prevented the visit of a religious scholar who had intended to ask him painful questions: this scholar had arrived in Sinnar on a Wednesday and wanted to see Muḥammad 'Uthmān al-Mirghānī the next day, but, unable to leave his house due to a thunderstorm, he became sick at noon and died on Friday morning, even before the communal prayer.

The success of the Khatmiyya as a Sudanese Sufi order can also be explained by the fact that many other Sufi orders in the Sudan with a strong local backing, such as the Majdhūbiyya, opposed Egyptian rule and were consequently punished by the Egyptian administration in as many different ways as those in which the Khatmiyya was rewarded. The leaders of the Majdhūbiyya had supported the rebellion against Egyptian rule in 1822, and their center in al-Dāmir was subsequently destroyed by the Egyptian army. The way in which the Majdhūbiyya was treated by the Egyptian administration after 1822 showed other religious leaders in the Sudan what they could expect from the Egyptian administration. Although the Egyptian administration removed some of the privileges that religious scholars had enjoyed in the time of Sinnār-Funj, such as exemption from taxation, and although the Egyptian administration put religious scholars and their schools under supervision, scholars who were willing to cooperate were privileged in many ways: their qur'ānic schools were supported, their children were sent to Egypt for further studies, and their cooperation was remunerated with financial privileges. The training of the sons of religious scholars at al-Azhar created a new class of 'ulamā' in the Sudan who advocated reforms "à l'égyptienne." They were not necessarily linked to a Sufi order any more, but formed a body of religious functionaries working for the Egyptian administration in schools and qāḍī courts. The alliance between the Khatmiyya and Egypt came to constitute a major disadvantage for the Khatmiyya, however, when the Mahdiyya movement, supported by many of the smaller Sufi orders, replaced the Egyptian administration in the Sudan in 1885. After the victory of the Mahdiyya, the leader of the Khatmiyya, Muḥammad 'Uthmān al-Aqrab Tāj al-Sirr, went into Egyptian exile, where he died in 1886. His sons and successors, 'Alī and Aḥmad, returned to the Sudan in 1898 and rebuilt the sociopolitical networks of the Khatmiyya, this time in cooperation with the new Anglo-Egyptian administration (see map 15).

The Movement of the Mahdī

On 29 June 1881, a religious scholar named Muḥammad Aḥmad declared himself the Mahdī and started a rebellion against Egyptian rule, which would eventually lead not only to its end in the Sudan, but also to one of the major defeats of the British empire, as well as the emergence of a Muslim empire on the Nile which in many ways resembled the imāmates of the western bilād al-sūdān. Although the Egyptian administration under Muḥammad Ra'ūf Pasha (r. 1880–1882) tried to contain the rebellion of the Mahdī by legitimizing the slave trade again, the Egyptian administration had become so unpopular that this measure was not enough to appease disgruntled traders and farmers. When the Egyptian administration came under British control in 1882, protests increased, and the fact that a quick succession of governors prevented coherent policies toward the Mahdī further enhanced the spread of the rebellion. Due to the fact that the Sudan, as part of the Egyptian empire, became part of the British empire, the conflict in the Sudan turned into a war between the Mahdī and the British.

Muḥammad Aḥmad was born on 12 August 1844 on the Nile island of Labab in the province of Dongola. His family claimed sharīfian descent and may thus be regarded as forming part of the religious establishment in the Sudan. Muḥammad Aḥmad studied with Shaykh al-Amīn al-Suwāyliḥ in the Jazīra and with Shaykh Muḥammad al-Dikayr 'Abdallāh Khōjalī in Berber, among others. In 1861, he continued his studies with Shaykh Muḥammad Sharīf Nūr al-Dīn al-Dā'im al-Bashīr, who also initiated him into the teachings of the Sammāniyya. In his seven years of studies with Shaykh Muḥammad Sharīf, Muḥammad Aḥmad became known as a scholar and was eventually asked to undertake some journeys to spread the teachings of the Sammāniyya. In the context of these journeys, he visited many parts of the Sudan and eventually settled, in 1870, on the island of Abā in the White Nile, about 300 kilometers south of Khartoum, just north of Kosti. His zāwiya quickly turned into a center of Islamic learning and attracted an increasing number of students. In 1878, the growing fame of Muḥammad Aḥmad led to a dispute with his teacher Muḥammad Sharīf, who subsequently excluded him from his branch of the Sammāniyya. Muḥammad Aḥmad had dared to criticize his teacher for celebrating the circumcision of his sons with dance and music, although these forms of festivity had been condemned by Muḥammad Sharīf himself. Subsequently, Muḥammad Aḥmad linked up with another shaykh of the Sammāniyya and was increasingly recognized as an independent religious authority. Shortly afterward, he undertook another journey through Kordofan where he managed to win a number of followers among the Baggāra tribes and the Jallāba who suffered from the decline of the slave trade. Muḥammad Aḥmad also gained support among the riverine farmers who depended on slave work, which had become increasingly expensive, as well as among numerous other Sufi scholars who felt threatened by the expansion of the Khatmiyya and who resented Egyptian rule. Equally, Muḥammad Aḥmad was able to gain sympathies among a number of tribal leaders who suffered under Egyptian Coptic tax collectors and their local allies among the Shā'iqiyya, 'Abābda, and Shukriyya tribes. Muḥammad Aḥmad finally won vital support among the Bīja in the Red Sea Hills, and a major Bīja leader, 'Uthmān Diqna, also gained the support of the Majdhūbiyya for the Mahdī.

In 1881, Muḥammad Aḥmad was visited by a Ta'āīshī-Baggāra, 'Abdallāh b. Muḥammad, who had settled in Dārfūr and who claimed that Muḥammad Aḥmad was the expected Mahdī who had come to end the tyranny of the Turkiyya. In a number of visions, this call was confirmed by Muḥammad Aḥmad, and on 29 June 1881 Muḥammad Aḥmed proclaimed himself as Mahdī. He took an oath of loyalty from his disciples, the Anṣār (helpers), and called upon them to end the tyrannical rule of the "Turks." In a number of letters to notables and religious scholars in the Sudan, he asked these persons to follow his example and to leave the territory of unbelief and unjust rule, as the Prophet had done. In a letter to his followers, the Mahdī justified this call to rebellion with the following arguments:

> It is obvious that the times have changed and that the Sunna has been abandoned. Nobody of faith and intelligence will accept this. Thus, it would be better if he left his home and his trade in order to revive religion and the Sunna. The hijra is obligatory for all those who are capable of fighting in the jihad which has been commanded by the Qur'ān by the following words: "Fight the unbelievers (mushrikūn) as they fight you" (9:36). Peace and wealth can be achieved only when one follows the religion and revives the Sunna of the Prophet and fights against the un-Islamic innovations which have been introduced recently. This has become of great importance today, as corruption and the decline of morals have spread over all countries. Facing the machinations of the unbelievers against the Muslims and regarding the errors they have established in the hearts of the faithful, religion has disappeared and the prescriptions of the Qur'ān and the Sunna are not obeyed any more. Injustice has spread and the un-Islamic innovations are everywhere. What has been forbidden by Islam is permissible now and the faithful are in great misery. (quoted in Peters 1979: 66–67)

In a further statement, the Mahdī responded to the polemical attacks of Yūsuf Ḥasan al-Salālī, the supreme commander of the Egyptian forces in the Sudan, who had asked the Mahdī to surrender and accused him of having killed Muslims:

> You claim that we have unlawfully killed a group of Muslims in this region. This claim is false as we have killed the people of Jabal al-Jaradah only when they had accused us of lying and had attacked us. The Prophet and the ahl al-kashf have informed me that all those who deny the coming of the Mahdī are unbelievers and may be killed. This is the reason why we have fought and killed them. On the other side, the Prophet has commanded us to fight the Turks and has told us that they were unbelievers as they have turned against the commands of the Prophet and want to extinguish the light of God. . . . The Turks have enchained our men, imprisoned our women and children and killed those whom God has said not to kill. They did all of this only to collect taxes which were not in accordance with the laws of God and follow the command of the messenger of God but execute slavishly the commands of the Turks, although they humiliated you and although they despise you? (quoted in Peters 1979: 68)

The proclamation of the Mahdī and his first calls for rebellion against Egyptian rule were answered by the Egyptian muftī of the court of appeal in Khartoum, Shākir al-Ghazzī, in another letter in which he condemned the Mahdī:

> Know, oh brothers, that God has arranged things for me and for you in such a manner that religion and authority have become two inseparable brothers. Religion is the fundament, while authority protects religion. Thus, religion exists only through the authority which protects her. God said: "Oh ye who believe, obey God and the Prophet and those in authority amongst you" (Quran 4:59). And the Prophet has said that to obey is an obligation even if an Ethiopian slave with brains like a raisin

> has command over you. And he has also said that you should obey even if your ruler beats you and takes your money. You know all of that and you also know that the Qur'ān and the Sunna say that it is obligatory to follow those who have the command and that it is illegal to rebel against the ruler. You will thus accept that somebody who withdraws from authority and obeyance rebels against God and will die as an unbeliever. Now, we have shown you the right path and have shown that Muḥammad Aḥmad is not the Mahdī. His followers are barbarians who dwell in the night of unbelief, driven by their longing for the wealth of their brothers in faith. They have sold their religion for the luxuries of the world. They are nothing but a bunch of stupid camel herders and foolish derwishes who only know plunder and murder. They are farther removed from religion than cattle and do not have knowledge or religion. God has prepared hell fire for them, as a punishment fot their rebellion against him and his prophet and those who are in command as they have killed human beings whom God has forbidden to kill: "Any one who kills a believer intentionally will be cast into hell to abide there forever" (Qur'ān 4:93). Know ye brothers that all schools of law agree that rebellion is one of the greatest sins, even if the Sultan is unjust. You should not revolt against him, while he may fight rebels. The Prophet has said: whoever leaves the community of the faithful has cut his links with Islam. In order to protect your religion and your goods, you thus have to fight these charlatans and kill them, wherever you find them. (quoted in Peters 1979: 71–73)

After the declaration of Muḥammad Aḥmad as the Mahdī, the conflict escalated quickly. The Egyptian governor in Khartoum, Ra'ūf Pasha, sent a military expedition against Abā, yet this detachment was defeated by the followers of the Mahdī in a battle on the island of Abā on 12 August 1881. The surprising victory of the Anṣār against an overwhelming and well-equipped force immediately boosted the prestige of the Mahdī, who compared his victory with the battle of Badr in 624, when the Prophet had defeated a superior force of heathen Meccans. As the Mahdī could not expect to defeat a second military expedition against Abā by surprise, he called for a hijra and moved to the Jabal Qādir mountains in southern Kordofan. The efforts of the Egyptian army to reach him in this remote region failed due to the onset of the rainy season. Only on 9 December 1881 did a second encounter take place between the Anṣār and Egyptian forces, near Fāshōda on the White Nile. The Anṣār again defeated the Egyptian troops, captured a large number of modern firearms, and increased their reputation as seemingly invincible warriors of the faith. The number of followers of the Mahdī continued to grow, and on 30 May 1882 the Anṣār were able to defeat a third Egyptian expedition at Jabal Qādir. This victory convinced a majority of tribes in Kordofan that the Egyptian administration was at an end and they joined the Mahdī in masses. While 8,000 Anṣār had faced an army of approximately 40,000 Egyptian soldiers in the Sudan in late 1881, these numbers now changed quickly. After the victory of Jabal Qādir, the Anṣār conquered the province of Kordofan and laid siege to its central city, al-Ubayyiḍ (al-Obeid), on 1 September 1882. After the conquest of al-Obeid in 1883, the Mahdī sought to expand his rule beyond the Sudan and sent letters to a number of religious scholars and political leaders, such as the ruler of Wadai, Muḥammad Yūsuf, the supreme leader of the Sanūsiyya, Muḥammad al-Mahdī al-Sanūsī, a leader of a major opposition movement in Sokoto, Ḥayāt b. Saʿīd, as well as the leader of a large slave-trader community in southern Dārfūr, Rābiḥ b. Faḍl Allāh, asking them to join his movement. Also, the emperor of Ethiopia, Yohannes IV, was ordered to convert and to submit to the command of the Mahdī, as was Muḥammad Tawfīq, the new Khedive in Egypt.

At this point of time, the administration of the Sudan shifted from Egyptian hands into British hands, and the British administration in Cairo quickly sent an army of 10,000 Egyptian soldiers against the Mahdī. Under the command of Colonel William Hicks, this army marched against the Mahdī in Kordofan, disregarding basic rules of warfare. In a battle over 3–5 November 1882, the Anglo-Egyptian army was massacred by the Anṣār, except for a German survivor, Gustav Klotz, one of the cooks of the expedition. The Egyptian forces in the Sudan were now crushed, and the Anṣār could collect thousands of modern firearms. Their troops were swelled by numerous new followers who expected further easy victories over the British and the Egyptians. In a short period of time, the provinces of Baḥr al-Ghazal in the south, as well as Dārfūr, fell to the Anṣār, while most Bīja tribes in the east, led by ʿUthmān Diqna, rose in open rebellion against Anglo-Egyptian rule, and made it impossible for the Anglo-Egyptian administration to retreat to the Red Sea. Facing a desperate situation, the British government decided to send General Gordon into the Sudan, to evacuate the remaining Anglo-Egyptian forces to the north. Gordon disregarded this command, however, and started to organize the defense of Khartoum. When the Anṣār took control of Berber, north of Khartoum, on 27 April 1884, there was no longer any possibility of relief through steamboats on the River Nile, and the siege of Khartoum began. The Mahdī reached Khartoum on 23 October and settled on the opposite shore of the Nile, in Umm Durmān (Omdurman). After a siege of three months, the Anṣār took Khartoum on 26 January 1885 and killed General Gordon. The Mahdī did not live long to enjoy his victory; he died on 22 June 1885, possibly of typhus.

The Rule of Khalīfa ʿAbdallāh

ʿAbdallāh b. Muḥammad, a Taʿāīshī Baggāra, became the successor (Arab. khalīfa) of the Mahdī. He was born in 1841 in Dārfūr. His father, Muḥammad Tor Shayn, was a scholar of the Sammāniyya who was linked through his own father, ʿAli al-Karār, and grandfather, al-Sayyid Mūsā, with a Tunisian religious scholar named Muḥammad al-Quṭbī al-Wāwī, who claimed sharifian descent. As told by his father, ʿAbdallāh b. Muḥammad left Dārfūr and went to the east to search for the Mahdī. In 1881, he met Muḥammad Aḥmad, became his student and follower, and helped him to establish his new zāwiya on Abā Island. In the context of the subsequent war against the Egyptian administration, ʿAbdallāh b. Muḥammad became the most trusted representative of the Mahdī and a successful leader in war. He was charged with the command of the black banner which united the mahdist troops from the western Sudan. The succession of ʿAbdallāh b. Muḥammad to the Mahdī was proclaimed in a public ceremony on 27 January 1883, when the Mahdī told his followers that he had received a prophetic vision telling him that ʿAbdallāh b. Muḥammad was the khalīfa al-khulafāʾ (the supreme successor) and the commander of the army. The Mahdī thus rewarded his closest companion and rejected the claims to leadership of his own family. ʿAbdallāh b. Muḥammad was subsequently seen and depicted by the family of the Mahdī as an ignorant imposter, who belonged to a marginal social group. This negative presentation of the Khalīfa by the family of the Mahdī was continued after the British conquest of the Sudan in 1898. The Khalīfa was linked with numerous atrocities, a strategy which might be interpreted as a clever ruse of the family of the Mahdī to put the blame for the Mahdiyya as an anti-British movement on the Khalīfa. In addition, his opponents accused the Khalīfa of being illiterate and incapable of speaking Arabic. This claim was false: although the Khalīfa was not a notable scholar and although he had secretaries to do his correspondence, he wrote texts in Arabic in his own warshī style, which was widespread in the bilād al-maghrib and the western bilād al-sūdān.

Like the movement of the Mahdī which had gone through a hijra and had called the followers of the Mahdī Anṣār, the new state was built on prophetic models. Before he died, the Mahdī himself had nominated four successors called Abū Bakr (ʿAbdallāh b. Muḥammad), ʿUmar (ʿAlī b. Muḥammad wad Ḥilū), ʿUthmān (Muḥammad al-Mahdī al-Sanūsī), and ʿAlī (Muḥammad Sharīf b. Ḥāmid). They again commanded the leaders of the individual army units, ʿAbd al-Raḥmān al-Najmī, ʿUthmān Diqna, Muḥammad Khayr ʿAbdallāh Khōjalī, and Ḥamdān Abū ʿAnga. Together, these men formed an inner circle of governance, led by the Khalīfa, who was the supreme commander of the army and who also commanded an elite force of 12,000 mulāẓimūn, mostly deserted soldiers of the Egyptian army who had modern firearms and good training. The Mahdiyya not only integrated these soldiers into the army, but also continued to work with the staff of the former Egyptian administration, such as the Coptic tax officers who were needed in the financial administration of the Mahdiyya. After the takeover of power by the Khalīfa, the administration of the provinces of the Mahdiyya was almost exclusively in the hands of the family of the Mahdī, the ashrāf. However, they either died in battle or were deposed by the Khalīfa when they dared to reject his authority, as did, for instance, Muḥammad Khālid, the mahdist governor of Dārfūr, who marched on Omdurman in 1886. The governor of Dongola, Muḥammad al-Khayr ʿAbdallāh Khōjālī, was deposed when he was defeated in 1889 by the Egyptian army after having tried to invade Upper Egypt. Facing increasing marginalization in the Mahdiyya, the ashrāf conspired against the Khalīfa in 1891 and tried to organize a rebellion; but their conspiracy was discovered and all rebel leaders were executed. The positions of the ashrāf were filled by persons appointed by the Khalīfa.

The financial administration of the Mahdiyya was organized by a general bayt al-māl al-ʿumūm (treasury), which got a fifth of all booty, while the rest was distributed within the army. The bayt al-māl al-ʿumūm was soon complemented by other treasuries such as the treasury of the household of the Khalīfa, the treasury of the mulāẓim troops, or a number of provincial treasuries. Apart from booty, the Mahdiyya raised zakāt and the ʿushr (tenth) as taxes, which could be paid in both money and goods. Each army unit, as well as each of the nine provinces, had its own bayt al-māl, while the central administration was in Omdurman. Apart from taxes, the finances of the Mahdiyya were based on a state monopoly on exports of gum arabic, slaves, ivory, ostrich feathers, and gold, fees taken from the Nile barges and ships, the income from land expropriated from Christians and Egyptians, as well as custom fees, market fees, and the fines that were imposed by the judiciary. The supreme administrator of finances was initially Aḥmad Sulaymān, who was deposed by the Khalīfa in 1885. He was replaced by Ibrāhīm ʿAdlān, one of the wealthiest men of Kordofan, who then served until 1890. Under the Khalīfa, the financial administration was considerably expanded and departments for the different forms of income were created, in addition to the household of the Khalīfa. The Khalīfa also fixed the level of taxation, while taxation as such was the task of the provincial governors. This system worked until 1889 when a severe drought and subsequent famine as well as a devastating rinderpest epidemic led to the collapse of the economy. In the last years of its reign, the Mahdiyya seems to have lived "hand to mouth" (Kramer 2010: 122).

In December 1884, the Mahdī himself had established new rates of exchange for the Sudanese currencies. When the Mahdiyya conquered the urban places and the trading centers of the Sudan, considerable stocks of Maria Theresien Thaler, the major currency in the Sudan, as well as in Ethiopia, the Arabian peninsula, and East Africa, fell into the hands of the Mahdiyya. These silver coins were melted down in 1885 and a new currency was created under the supervision of Ilyās ʿAbdallāh al-Kurdī, a watchmaker. In February 1885, the bayt al-māl started to issue the new currency which was based on a gold pound coin and a silver riyāl. Due to their high value, these coins quickly disappeared from circulation. As a consequence, the Mahdiyya was suffering from a shortage of silver and gold coins by 1886 and eventually stopped minting these coins. From late 1886, new coins of lesser gold and silver value were produced in order to finance the rising costs of the administration. These coins were so poor in value, however, that they were not accepted as currency. Still, the Mahdiyya continued to mint coins of lesser value until 1897, when only copper coins were made. A further problem was that the Khalīfa had started to build a private treasury, and thus withdrew further stocks of gold and silver from circulation. In addition, the annual raids carried out by the army increasingly ended in defeat, and booty stopped being a source of income. Another economic problem was that the Mahdiyya prohibited the import of foreign goods into the Sudan and raised the custom fees. As a consequence, trade suffered considerably.

In 1890, the economic crisis, drought, and famine were aggravated by a locust invasion in the most fertile area of the Sudan, the Jazīra, and the subsequent harvest proved to be a complete disaster. The Khalīfa thereupon commanded Ibrāhīm ʿAdlān to force farmers to hand over their remaining grain reserves to the financial administration and to move these grain stocks to Omdurman in order to feed the metropolitan population. Ibrāhīm ʿAdlān refused to obey and was executed. After the execution of Ibrāhīm ʿAdlān, the financial administration of the Mahdiyya was taken over by Muḥammad al-Zakī ʿUthman al-Taʿāīshī and ʿAwaḍ al-Marḍī, both former employees of the Egyptian administration. They reorganized the bayt al-māl in five departments, for the army, the ships, the market police, the mulāẓim troops, and the Khalīfa. The concentration of grain stocks helped to overcome hunger in Omdurman for some time, yet it meant that farmers did not have the seed grain stocks to plant the next harvest. As a consequence, the economic situation became even worse. This catastrophe was witnessed by Rudolph Slatin Pasha, the Austro-Hungarian former governor of Dārfūr, who had been taken prisoner in 1883:

> On both the Blue and White Nile corpses were sighted daily, a sign of the terrible condition in the whole country. In Omm Durman, most of those who died were of rural origin, while most of the urban people had hidden some corn despite the harsh commands of the Khalīfa. . . . The hunger crisis cost many more victims in other parts of the Sudan, and the Jaʿaliyyūn . . . suffered the most losses. Big and densely populated villages were extinguished to the last man. . . . The tribes of the Tabaniyya, Shukriyya, Agaliyyin, Hammada, and others were almost completely eliminated and the countryside became a wasteland. (Slatin 1922: 154–55, my translation)

Chronic famines in 1889 and 1890 also led to the outbreak of epidemics, in particular meningitis, cholera, typhus, and malaria, and contributed to a considerable decrease of the Sudanese population after 1890.

The judiciary of the Mahdiyya was based on the supreme authority of the Mahdī and the Khalīfa, who based their decisions on the Qurʾān and the Sunna of the Prophet. They presided over a judicial hierarchy consisting of the military commanders and the ashrāf. In addition, there was a supreme Qāḍī, Aḥmad Jubāra, who had studied at al-Azhar but who died in 1883. His successor was Aḥmad Wād Allāh, who was to stay in office until 1893. They commanded a group of provincial representatives, nuwwāb. In general terms, the Mahdiyya rejected the rulings of any single school of law, however, and tried to develop a new code of law based on the rulings of the Qurʾān, the Sunna of the Prophet, and the rulings of the Mahdī. A governor of Dārfūr, Muḥammad Khālid, was reprimanded when he dared to ask the ʿulamāʾ for advice, instead of trying to apply a qurʾānic ruling. Under the Mahdiyya, practices such as the production of amulets were shunned, and Sufi orders were prohibited. Women had to don the ḥijāb, and conspicuous spending for festivities such as marriages was criticized and limited to payment of the bride price.

The rule of the Khalīfa was characterized by the fact that he successively sought to eliminate all competing power groups, in particular those which had been linked with the Mahdī, and to favor, by contrast, his own tribal group, the Taʿāīshī-Baggāra.

In 1888, this Baggāra group had to move to Omdurman and thus provided the Khalīfa with the necessary armed support to eliminate other powerful groups. By 1891, the Khalīfa had eliminated the ashrāf as well as all other khulafā' and thus consolidated his power. His rule was still legitimized by reference to the Mahdī and his movement, but no longer had much in common with the original Mahdiyya. The Khalīfa's quest for absolute power also affected the Baggāra, in particular those groups that were not necessarily happy to submit to the rule of the Ta'āīshī fraction. In 1886, an influential leader of the Rizayqāt, Madibbu 'Alī, was executed for not being supportive enough. In 1887 a leader of the Kabābīsh, Ṣāliḥ Faḍl Allāh Sālim, suffered the same fate. In 1889, the Khalīfa even suppressed a revolt by the Ta'āīshī-Baggāra, and in 1890 executed their leader, al-Ghazzālī Aḥmad Khawwāf, who had dared to express the wishes of the Ta'āīshī to return to western Kordofan. However, the Khalīfa turned not only against some tribal groups or the networks of supporters and followers of the Mahdī, but also against individual religious scholars, such as the leader of the Majdhūbiyya, al-Ṭāhir al-Ṭayyib al-Majdhūb, who was deposed as leader of his ṭarīqa, and al-Mannā Ismā'īl, a shaykh of the Sammāniyya, who was executed in 1893. Also, tombs and zawāya of the Sufi orders were destroyed when the latter were suspected of voicing opposition to the Khalīfa. As a consequence, the Khalīfa lost support in the population and became increasingly isolated, limiting the military power of the state. Despite these internal policies, the Khalīfa tried to continue expanding the mahdist state: in 1885–1886 the lands of the Bīja were integrated into the empire, with the exception of Suakin, which remained under Anglo-Egyptian control, and in 1889 the Mahdiyya even tried to invade Upper Egypt, although this attack failed. In the south, the areas close to the Ethiopian border and the province of Equatoria were secured until 1889. In 1887, Abū 'Anga, one of the supreme army commanders, invaded Ethiopia and managed to briefly occupy Gondar, the Ethiopian capital city. In 1889, the troops of the Mahdiyya were able to repulse an Ethiopian counterattack in which the Ethiopian emperor, Yohannes, after an initially successful battle, was killed. In 1891, however, Britain started to prepare the reconquest of the Sudan. A military expedition started from Wādī Ḥalfā in Upper Egypt and was able to take Dongola in 1896. After a last-stand battle at Kararī near Omdurman, Omdurman was taken by British and Egyptian forces on 1 November 1898, and in November 1889 the Khalīfa was killed in a last skirmish. The Sudan came under an Anglo-Egyptian administration, the second Turkiyya, which was to last until independence in 1956.

A Sudanese Conquistador: Rābiḥ b. Faḍl Allāh

The development of Egyptian rule on the Nile in the nineteenth century was characterized for a considerable period of time by a flourishing slave trade. This trade was essentially organized by networks of Arab Sudanese traders, in particular those traders linked with the tribal federation of the Ja'aliyyīn, who cooperated with the Baggāra tribes in Kordofan. In the context of the expansion of the Egyptian administration, the restrictions on the slave trade extended south and westward. The slave-trading organizations were consequently forced to move onward into the marches of Equatoria in the south, the Baḥr al-Ghazal regions in the southeast, and beyond Dārfūr in the west, in order to remain outside Egyptian control. In 1856, the most important leader of a slave trading organization, Raḥma al-Manṣūr Zubayr Pasha (d. 1913), started to establish a chain of thirty-one zarības in the Baḥr al-Ghazal region. He also opened a new overland route to el-Obeid in Kordofan, which bypassed the Nile. By 1867, he felt so strong that he refused to pay taxes to the Egyptian administration. An Egyptian military expedition against him failed in 1872. In 1873, he managed to defeat the Rizayqāt, who blocked his path of expansion to the west, and in 1874 he attacked and defeated the kingdom of Dārfūr with an army of 6,400 slave soldiers and 9,000 Jallāba traders (as well as three field guns). The Egyptian administration eventually decided to recognize him as the Egyptian governor of Baḥr al-Ghazal province, but refused to recognize his claim to Dārfūr. When he tried to enforce this claim in Cairo in 1875, he was put under house arrest and was prohibited to return to the Sudan.

In the late 1870s and early 1880s, the slave trade in the Sudan almost collapsed, yet was revived after the victory of the Mahdiyya. The man who came to replace Zubayr Pasha and to continue his policies of expansion was Rābiḥ b. Faḍl Allāh, who was born in Omdurman in 1845. His father came from Sinnār and had joined the Egyptian army in the Sudan. Rābiḥ b. Faḍl Allāh also started to serve in the Egyptian army but then met Zubayr Pasha in 1864, joined his organization, and soon became one of his most loyal commanders. From the zarības of Zubayr Pasha in southern Dārfūr, Rābiḥ b. Faḍl Allāh started to undertake his own raids and in 1872–1873 took part in the conquest of the Zande region in southern Equatoria, then in the campaign against the Rizayqāt, and finally in the conquest of Dārfūr. After Zubayr Pasha's arrest, he served his son, Sulaymān, and in 1876–1877 explored the upper reaches of the Ubangi and Shari Rivers. When Sulaymān eventually rebelled against the Egyptian administration in 1878 and was killed by Gessi Pasha, the Italian governor of Baḥr al-Ghazal, Rābiḥ b. Faḍl Allāh escaped with a small army of 800 soldiers and nine chests of ammunition. He settled in the territory of the Kreish in southern Dārfūr, and his new zarība soon became a center for other displaced slave traders and their troops. As a consequence, Rābiḥ b. Faḍl Allāh was able to expand his realm and to move southwest, where he conquered a number of small tribal kingdoms, such as Dār Mara, Dār Kuti, and Dār Sila, and appointed local governors. In 1889, Rābiḥ b. Faḍl Allāh reached the Shari and opened the fight for control over the trade routes leading toward Lake Chad. The kingdom of Bagirmi, in contrast to Wadai, was not able to defeat his well-equipped and well-trained troops and was conquered in 1891. In 1893, Rābiḥ b. Faḍl Allāh even invaded and conquered the empire of Bornu on the western shores of Lake Chad.

Dikwa in Bornu now became his new center, which controlled access to the trans-Saharan trade route leading from Bilma to Fazzān and the Mediterranean, as well as access to the Benue in the south, which linked Lake Chad with the lower Niger and the

Atlantic. Rābiḥ b. Faḍl Allāh's position on Lake Chad was strengthened by the rebellion against Sokoto of Ḥayāt b. Sa'īd, who joined Rābiḥ b. Faḍl Allāh's forces and married one of his daughters, only to be killed by Rābiḥ b. Faḍl Allāh in 1894.

Rābiḥ b. Faḍl Allāh's empire was essentially based on his army, which had grown to twenty-three companies by 1895. Rābiḥ b. Faḍl Allāh was the supreme commander, yet had only little time to consolidate his realm, as he was soon confronted with the British, French, and German colonial conquest of Central Africa, which culminated in 1898 in an Anglo-Franco-German race to Lake Chad and the Nile. Although Rābiḥ b. Faḍl Allāh was able to defeat the first French expedition on 17 July 1899, all further confrontations with the French who had won Bagirmi as an ally were lost, and on 22 April 1900 he was killed in a skirmish near Kusri. His son, Faḍl Allāh, continued to fight for another year but was then killed on 23 August 1901 near Gujba on Lake Chad. This defeat signaled the end of the last effort to establish an African trading empire and marked the beginning of European colonial rule over Central Africa for a period of almost sixty years.

8 Ethiopia and Islam

Historical Themes and Patterns

In Ethiopia, interfaces between Islam, Christianity, African indigenous religions and perhaps even Judaism have been of particular intensity and longevity. However, in contrast to Egypt and Nubia, orthodox Christianity has remained the dominant faith, while Muslims have formed a powerful historical counterforce. In many respects, Christianity and Islam in Ethiopia have thus come to constitute each other's flipside and cannot be understood without regarding the respective other. A historical account of Christian Ethiopia consequently has to consider this important Muslim legacy. At the same time, the historical anthropology of Ethiopia has to explain why Christianity has prevailed and why Islam has remained marginal, at least in political terms, in Ethiopia to this day. The following account starts with an introduction into some features of Ethiopian historical development that have come to inform Ethiopia's Christian (and later Muslim) history in decisive ways.

Ethiopian political history from Axumite antiquity to contemporary times can best be seen as a succession of phases of expansion and fragmentation, even of collapse of states and empires, linked with processes of centralization and the (re-)emergence of strong peripheries. Ethiopia's history has equally been characterized by a series of geographical shifts of the greater region's political cores: the first major political center, Axum, was situated close to the shores of the Red Sea in the northern highlands, but moved, after a period of crises and fragmentation, to Roha/Lalibäla in the central highlands, in the tenth century. Due to the impact of the jihād of Imām Aḥmad in the sixteenth century, Christian Ethiopia's political center moved to Gondär on Lake Tana, and finally, in the nineteenth century, to Addis Abäba in the southern highlands. In the process of this move from the shores of the Red Sea to the fertile southern highlands, the Ethiopian empire incorporated numerous ethnic and linguistic groups on the way and, in alliance with the Ethiopian Orthodox Church (today, yä-ityop'ya ortodoks täwahdo beta krestyan) and its monastic orders, formed a vast Christian metropolitan population speaking several closely related languages such as Ge'ez, Tigre, Tigriña, and Amharic.

The move from the north to the south over time enhanced the development of specific doctrines of the Ethiopian Church, eliminating Ethiopian indigenous religious traditions as well as Jewish and dissident Christian concepts and ritual practices, while integrating both Muslims and adherents of Ethiopian indigenous religions in the newly conquered peripheries. The vanguard for the expansion of both the empire *expansion of Ethiopia*

and the Church were monks of the Ethiopian Orthodox Church who had to fight numerous obstacles, and were often killed as a result; yet they succeeded again and again in establishing the church in the conquered regions: "Over the longer term, the people became more conventionally Christians and the conquest zones were absorbed into the Solomonic heartland" (Marcus 2002: 22). Political disputes and crises of orientation in Ethiopian imperial history were reflected in theological quarrels within the Ethiopian Orthodox Church. At the same time, the struggle against external and internal enemies, in particular the Muslim emirates of the eastern highlands, dissident Jewish populations, and the Oromo, or, more recently, two wars against Italy, helped to forge Ethiopia's unique character. The integrative power of imperial Ethiopia may also explain why Ethiopia has not become a bilād al-Islām and why Christian Ethiopia has managed to retain her remarkable coherence, despite numerous crises in her history. *⮑ why Ethiopia is not majority Muslim*

Ethiopia from Axum to Lalibäla

Pre-Christian Ethiopian history and the history of the first Ethiopian empire and its capital city, Axum, were closely linked with the history of southern Arabia, and in many respects ancient Axum can be seen as an extension of the pre-Islamic culture of southern Arabia in northeastern Africa. Axum, in fact, was dominated by immigrant populations from southern Arabia and continued to maintain contacts across the Red Sea, not only in cultural but also in political terms. Thus, Axumite rulers intervened militarily at least twice in Yemen and seem to have controlled the Tihāma lowlands of Yemen on the Red Sea in the third century CE. In the fourth century, first Syrian Christian missionaries arrived and established Orthodox (monophysite) Christianity. However, conversion to Christianity did not affect the basic orientations of Axumite politics and Axum continued to expand in the region. Ellä Amida, the father of Ezana, who was the first Christian emperor of Axum, is credited with the conquest of Meroe on the Nile, which led to a period of Axumite domination over the lands of the Nile. Emperor Ezana is equally credited with military expeditions in both Nubia and southern Arabia. This expansion continued under the next emperors of Axum, in particular Ellä Aṣbeha (r. 493–535). When Axumite positions in Yemen were attacked in 518 by the Jewish-Yemenite kingdom of Himyar, Axum landed a fleet in Yemen in 524 and defeated the kingdom of Himyar, whose rulers became Axumite vassals and converted to Christianity. In 570, the Axumite governor of Himyar even undertook an expedition against Mecca, accompanied by elephants. Although this expedition failed, it became part of Muslim cultural memories, as the "year of the elephant" was allegedly the same year in which the Prophet Muḥammad was born. In 590, a (Persian) Sassanid army conquered Southern Arabia, however, and forced the Axumites to withdraw to the African shores of the Red Sea.

Although Sassanid influence was of short duration, Axum never tried to regain her positions on the Arabian shores of the Red Sea. Rather, Axum seems to have suffered from the decline of trade in the eastern Mediterranean and the Red Sea, due to the defeat of the Byzantine empire against the Umayyads, and the expansion into northern Axum of Bīja nomadic groups that started to destabilize the trade routes leading from the highlands to the sea, in particular the harbor of Adulis. Axum was increasingly cut off from direct access to the sea and seems to have become landlocked by the ninth century, although the center of the empire was still situated in the northern highlands. Contacts with the Patriarch of the Orthodox Church in Alexandria continued to be mediated by the Christian Nubian kingdoms on the Nile. The emergence of a strong monastic movement, as well as the subsequent establishment of numerous monasteries in Ethiopia, contributed to the consolidation of Christianity in Axum in this period of political decline. However, the increasing instability of the northern regions of the empire eventually forced Ethiopian rulers to abandon Axum as their capital city and to move south. Under the impression of an attack of Gwudit, a Jewish queen of the Agao populations on Lake Tana and in the central highlands, Emperor Anbäsa Weddem (r. 882–910) shifted his center of power to Ankobär (Ka'bar) in Shäwa, 500 kilometers south of Axum. For some centuries, Ethiopian emperors continued to move their centers of administration from one place to the next in the central (and later southern) highlands, establishing a system of palatinate courts which were in use as long as the resources of a specific region could support the court. As a consequence, the central highlands became the new center of the empire, while the north turned into a periphery.

The move to the central highlands also implied a move beyond the realm of the Tigre- and Tigriña-speaking regions in the north into the realm of Agao-speaking populations, who had already been mentioned as allies in Axumite texts in the sixth century CE. The shift from northern to the central highlands was last but not least linked with a dynastic change in which Mära Täklä Haymanot Zagwe, a son-in-law of the last Axumite emperor, took power and established Ethiopia's second Christian dynasty of Zagwe rulers. Their major court was Roha in Lasta, where the Zagwe emperors of Ethiopia started to build numerous churches and monasteries, in particular under Emperor Lalibäla (r. 1160–1207), who wanted to transform Roha, now renamed Lalibäla, into a second Jerusalem. The Zagwe emperors ruled Ethiopia for a period of about 350 years until the late thirteenth century. They were not only responsible for the establishment of Christianity in the central highlands, but also for the submission of Christian dissident and Jewish Agao populations in these regions and their conversion to Orthodox Christianity. The efforts of the Ethiopian emperors to subjugate the Jewish populations of the central highlands also led to the gradual marginalization of Jewish and Axumite "northern" Christian influences in Ethiopian Orthodox Christianity. In addition, the old religion of the Agao that knew a sky god named Zār was increasingly eliminated, a process in which Zār was incorporated as an evil spirit (Amh. genni) into Christian (as well as Muslim) religious practices, in particular the Zār spirit possession cult.

While the move from the northern to the central highlands between the tenth and the thirteenth centuries meant increasing distance from the Red Sea, it also opened access to new trade routes for the southern marches, in particular the kingdoms and principalities of Kaffa and Hadiyya which were rich in gold, slaves, and ivory. In the thirteenth century, the flourishing trade and corresponding wealth of the empire led to a new shift in power from the Agao-Zagwe to the Amharic-speaking populations of the southern highlands, Shäwa in particular, which profited most from the trade with the southern marches. In the context of internal disputes among the Zagwe, Shäwa lords supported Emperor Lalibäla and established their own paramount position in the empire. In 1270, Shäwa lords deposed the last Zagwe emperor and established Ethiopia's third dynasty.

The shift from the Zagwe dynasty to the new Amharic dynasty was engineered, according to Ethiopian traditions, by the leading monk Täklä Haymanot of the Däbrä Azbo monastery (later renamed Däbrä Libanos, about 110 kilometers north of Addis

> Slaves formed a major part of the Ethiopian trade, but numbers are difficult to establish. With regard to the Red Sea slave trade and the Indian Ocean slave trade, sources are extremely scanty and "tell us virtually nothing about the absolute quantity of slaves" (Sheriff 2010: 218). Lovejoy assumes that 2.4 million slaves were exported from both Ethiopia and East Africa across the Red Sea and the Indian Ocean between 800 and 1600, but these numbers are not based on consistent documentation and have to be regarded as highly speculative. In Arabia, on the Gulf, in Egypt, in Persia, and in India, male slaves from Ethiopia and East Africa often served as eunuchs and military slaves, female slaves as concubines. Many slaves were not exported across the seas, but they were kept within imperial Ethiopia and on the East African coast. They worked in grain production in southern Somalia and on clove plantations in Zanzibar in the nineteenth century, as well as on sugar cane plantations on Reunion and Mauritius in the eighteenth and nineteenth centuries. The number of slaves within imperial Ethiopia was estimated at 3–4 million in the late nineteenth century, and only in 1931 did Emperor Hailä Sellase end slavery in Ethiopia. The nineteenth century was a climax period for Ethiopian slaves, who mostly originated from the southern and western marches (Sidamo, Gurage, Wälläga, Ilubabor, Shankalla), Ethiopia's slave hunting periphery. They were sold across the Red Sea and up the River Nile. From 1821, Ethiopia exported 13,000–17,000 slaves annually to Egypt and 7,000–8,000 slaves across the Red Sea to Yemen and the Ḥijāz.

Abäba), who convinced the last Zagwe emperor, Yetbaräk, to retire and to hand over power to a descendant of the Axumite dynasty, Täsfa Iyässus, who ascended to the throne as Yekuno Amlak (r. 1270–1285). As emperor, he appointed Täklä Haymanot to the office of the Etchäge, the highest priest of the Ethiopian Church and head of all Ethiopian monasteries. Due to long-term absences of the Abunä, the supreme head of the Ethiopian Church, as appointed by the Patriarch of the Orthodox Church in Alexandria, the Etchäge was the de facto supreme leader of the Ethiopian Church. The appointment of Täklä Haymanot also led to the rise of the Däbrä Azbo monastery and the Täklä Haymanot order as the monastic order that represented the new dynasty. At the same time, the Täklä Haymanot order started to marginalize the established Ewosṭātewos order which was based in the monastery of Däbrä Bizän in the northern highlands near Asmara. The disputes among Ethiopian monastics not only reflected different orientations of the orders regarding questions of theology and ritual, but also informed issues of political and religious legitimacy.

Since the late thirteenth century, Ethiopian historiography was increasingly influenced by legitimatory constructions, in particular those that linked Ethiopia with Israel's legendary rulers, in particular King Solomon. As the kingdom of Axum had been connected with the Arabian Peninsula, the eastern Mediterranean, and Egypt since antiquity, Axum-Ethiopia was well acquainted with the master stories of Western Asian empires, kingdoms, and religious traditions, and was thus familiar with the major tropes of Judaic and early Christian, later Muslim, history and religious development. A close link between Axum and later Ethiopian dynasties with these historical and religious traditions served to legitimize the claims of Ethiopian emperors to be rulers chosen by God, privileged to rule Ethiopia in the name of a pure and sacred tradition which had started in the times of King Solomon. According to Ethiopian traditions, as fixed under Emperor ʿAmdä Ṣeyon (r. 1314–1344) in the *Kebrä nägäst* (Glory of the kings), the Axumite (first Solomonid) dynasty was founded by Menilek I, son of King Solomon and Queen Makeda of Ethiopia, who had visited King Solomon in order to learn the art of governance: "Ethiopians became the chosen people, an honour reinforced by their acceptance of Christianity" (Marcus 2002: 18). Yet, despite Ethiopian claims of an ancient link with Israel, these links must be seen as a historical construction which only developed from the early fourteenth century in the context of the efforts of Ethiopia's Amharic third dynasty to acquire dynastic legitimacy as the "second Solomonid" dynasty after the Zagwe era. This dynastic legitimacy was of major importance in the struggle against the populations of the central highlands who dared to oppose the holy, imperial, orthodox Church, and who were consequently branded, in the religious interpretation of these struggles, as either Christian dissidents or pagans or Jews (Fälasha, Beta Israel). The Jewish character of the Beta Israel/Agao populations of Ethiopia is hard to substantiate, however, as the Beta Israel never knew the Talmud or the Mishna and never celebrated characteristic Jewish festivals such as Purim that started after the Babylonian exile in the sixth century BC. The

Beta Israel did not speak Hebrew but Agao, a Cushitic language, and even their Torah was written in Ge'ez and was shared, in the form of the Pentateuch, with the Orthodox Christian populations. Also, the Beta Israel had no rabbis but knew a priest called "kahen" (pl. kahant), a word that points to the same semitic roots as "masgid" for the Beta Israel place of worship: In Arabic a masjid is a mosque, a kāhin a soothsayer. At the same time, the Beta Israel knew monks and nuns and had monasteries. Another unique tenet of faith was the Beta Israel concept of the Sabbath (on Saturday, as in the Orthodox Church, before Sunday was introduced as a second sabbath in the fourteenth century), which was not only seen as the weekly holiday but also as a (female) spiritual being, Sanbat. Like the Christian Agao and other Orthodox Christians, the Beta Israel accepted the biblical laws of purity and practiced the circumcision of both boys and girls. In addition, the Beta Israel knew the ritual sacrifice of animals which had been abandoned by Jews after the destruction of the temple in the sixth century BC, yet formed a tradition common to both Beta Israel and Orthodox Christians. Paul Henze has thus denied the very existence of Jews in Ethiopia: "There is no reference to Jews in Axumite inscriptions. There is no use of Hebrew in Ethiopia until modern times. No Falashas knew it until taught by Israelis in the 1950s. There is no mention of Beta Israel in Ethiopian chronicles before the fourteenth century. Beta Israel music and ritual have been shown to be derived from Ethiopian Christian tradition" (Henze 2001: 54). However, it is important to note here that opposition to Solomonid claims of hegemony was expressed in the same Judeo-Christian code that had become deeply entrenched in the thinking of the populations of the Ethiopian highlands. For this reason, references to Judaism have remained an important element of strategies of "othering" in the context of internal Ethiopian Christian disputes until at least the nineteenth century.

The very struggle against the Beta Israel and the establishment of the Ethiopian Orthodox Christian empire in the central highlands in the time of the Zagwe dynasty was based on an alliance between the emperors and the clergy, in particular the monasteries and monastic orders, which were rewarded for their efforts toward Christianization (and empire building) by generous donations of gult lands, lands which paid an annual rent to the Church. In addition, the monasteries maintained regular contact with the other centers of the Orthodox Church in Nubia, Egypt, and Palestine, as well as Armenia, and thus kept the emperors aware and informed of the political developments of their times. The tight link between the emperors of Ethiopia and the Church and its monastic orders explains to a certain extent why questions of dynastic legitimacy were negotiated in religious terms and based on conflicting interpretations of the Judeo-Christian heritage. The development of the Orthodox Christian ritual and theology in Ethiopia in this period, but also in later centuries, can thus be viewed as a development characterized by the effort to eliminate Jewish (and/or dissident Christian) influences, such as celebration of the Sabbath on Saturday, from a reformed Ethiopian Christianity, and to emphasize the links with mainstream orthodoxy as represented by Alexandria. This development was dominated, from the late thirteenth century, by the emergence of new yet competing monastic orders. Major opponents were the Ewosṭātewos order, based in the monastery of Däbra Bizän in the north, and the Täklä Haymanot order in Däbrä Libanos which dominated the southern and central highlands. While Ewosṭātewos monks claimed Saturday was the Sabbath, Täklä Haymanot monks supported Sunday as the Christian Sabbath. These ritual and theological disputes mirrored political conflicts: Ewosṭātewos represented the old dynastic and historical legacies of the northern highlands, while Täklä Haymanot represented the newly converted populations of the increasingly powerful central and southern highlands. And while the Ewosṭātewos order rejected the supremacy of Alexandria and advocated the independence of the Ethiopian church, Täklä Haymanot accepted Alexandria's supremacy in nominating the Abunä and thus represented translocal, Alexandrine orthodoxy against local Jewish and dissident Christian influences.

In the fourteenth century, the dispute between the Täklä Haymanot order and the Sabbatarians escalated. Sabbatarians were eventually refused ordination, were expulsed from monasteries and churches, and were driven from the court. Some retreated into remote regions, where they formed new communities which continued to prosper. A few settlements in Bägemdir around Lake Tana "might have 'purified' their Christianity to the point of returning to a form of Judaism. No other explanation accounts for the unique pre-talmudic faith of the Beta Israel, in which Ethiopian Christian borrowings abound" (Marcus 2002: 23). Despite persecution, the Ewosṭātewos order flourished, and in 1403 Emperor Dawit (r. 1380–1412) again permitted Sabbatarians to observe the Sabbath (on Saturday), in a move to unite the Ethiopian church. The disputes between the orders continued to bother the development of the Church in Ethiopia, and were only temporarily resolved in the council of Boru Meda in 1878. In the seventeenth century, the Ewosṭātewos order, for instance, claimed that Christ's human nature was subsumed in the divine only with his baptism (Amh. qibat) in the River Jordan and the subsequent epiphany of God in the guise of the Holy Spirit (as celebrated in Ethiopia in the timkat church festival), while Täklä Haymanot or täwahdo (unitarian) theologians stated that Christ's human nature was already subsumed in his divine nature at the time of his birth. These internal debates motivated Ethiopian emperors to seek conflict with external, often Muslim, enemies in order to bridge conflict within Ethiopian Christianity.

The first emperor of the second Solomonid dynasty, Yekuno Amlak, indeed opened a new period of imperial expansion and conquest, which was characterized by the consolidation of Ethiopian Christian power in the southern highlands, and by the struggle against the Muslim Emirates of the eastern highlands. Ethiopian expansion was characterized by the fact that newly conquered territories were secured by Amhara-Christian colonies as well as the establishment of monasteries, whereas Muslim territories were constrained to pay an annual tribute. Emperor 'Amdä Ṣeyon attacked the Muslim emirates in the eastern highlands, however, and was able to defeat them one by one.

> By contrast to the Ewosṭātewos order, whose founder emigrated and died in Armenia in 1352, the order of Abba Estifanos, established in the fifteenth century, did not survive the theological disputes. The Estifanos order opposed the cult of Mary which had reached Ethiopia in the fourteenth century under Emperor Dawit and which was propagated by the Täklä Haymanot order as a symbol of Ethiopia's connectedness with the wider world of Orthodox Christianity. Emperor Zära Ya'qob recognized the cult as a major and unifying element of Ethiopian Christianity and as part of the official credo of the empire. This was criticized by the Estifanos monks, who attacked the veneration of icons of Mary as an act of polytheism.

Yifat, the strongest emirate, was forced to pay tribute, and when Yifat formed a coalition with Däwaro, Hadiyya, and the Beta Israel on Lake Tana, 'Amdä Ṣeyon defeated even this alliance in 1331 and pushed the boundaries of the empire to the Awash River. Numerous Muslim principalities thus came under Ethiopian domination and had to pay tribute. At the same time, 'Amdä Ṣeyon was able to conquer the territories of the Beta Israel on Lake Tana in 1332 and to integrate these fertile regions into the empire. From 1413, Ethiopian emperors started to exert increasing pressure on the Beta Israel to convert to Christianity, which led to a number of rebellions in the fifteenth century. Since the sixteenth century, the Beta Israel ceased to be a major political force in Ethiopia and became an increasingly marginal minority.

The early fifteenth century saw a further expansion of the empire in military terms: in an audacious expedition, Emperor Yesḥaq (r. 1411–1429) managed to reach Zayla' on the shores of the Gulf of Aden in 1415, and also Adulis-Massawa in the north. In 1420, a Circassian governor of Mamlūk Upper Egypt, Altunbugha Mufarriq, fled to Ethiopia and entered the services of the imperial army. He helped to train the army, to build an arsenal, and to produce modern arms. Under Emperor Zära Ya'qob (r. 1434–1468), Ethiopia reached the climax of her power and in 1445 succeeded in defeating the emirate of Yifat. Yifat was eventually replaced by a new paramount Muslim emirate in the eastern highlands, Adal, with Ḥarär as its center. Ethiopia thus again acquired direct access to the shores of the Red Sea and reemerged as an international player in regional power politics. Equally, contacts with Europe were started and diplomatic missions took place, such as the visit of an Ethiopian mission to Avignon, Rome, and Genoa in 1310, and missions to Aragon in 1427, 1452, and 1453, as well as again to Rome in 1481. In 1430, a French mission reached Ethiopia, in 1482 a papal mission followed, as well as a first Portuguese mission in 1490, followed by a second in 1507. Ethiopia responded with missions to Portugal in 1509 and 1513–1517, while a Portuguese mission stayed in Ethiopia between 1520 and 1527. These diplomatic missions were set in the context of war between Ethiopia and the Muslim emirates of the eastern highlands. After the death of Emperor Zära Ya'qob, rivalries within the empire stimulated the emergence of competing regional forces which maintained unity only when faced with Muslim raids from the eastern highlands. Imperial Ethiopia was thus unable to prevent the emergence of Adal as a new Muslim regional power in the late fifteenth century (see map 16).

The Muslim Emirates in the Eastern Highlands

Surrounded by Muslims on the Nile, on the Horn and across the Red Sea in Yemen, Ethiopia perceived itself as an island of Orthodox Christianity in a sea of Islam, which was mirrored by a comparable self-perception of the Muslim emirates in the eastern highlands, in particular Ḥarär as a "bastion of Islam against Christianity" (Desplat 2008: 10). Ethiopia's imaginary as an island of Christianity in a sea of Islam was not only promoted by Emperor Menilek II in a letter to the European powers in 1891, but was also adopted by European historians and was presented prominently in the *Kebrä nägäst*. This imaginary found a mirror image in a major Muslim source for Ethiopian history, the *Futūḥ al-ḥabasha* (The conquest of Ethiopia), written in the late sixteenth century.

Muslims have in fact been present in Christian Ethiopia for a long period of time as traders and religious scholars. On the fringes of the Christian highlands, Muslim principalities developed from the eighth or ninth century, and entered into competition with the Christian emperors of Ethiopia from the twelfth century in a race for the control of the southern marches of Ethiopia. In this struggle, the emperors of Ethiopia were often able to defeat the smaller and disunited Muslim emirates of the eastern highlands, yet were decisively defeated themselves in a jihād led by Imām Aḥmad in the sixteenth century. The shock of this defeat was engraved into Christian Ethiopian history and strengthened the Ethiopian self-perception as a bastion of Christianity surrounded by militant Muslims. While the jihād of Imām Aḥmad shocked Ethiopian imperial historians, Ethiopian history also contained at least three episodes in which Ethiopian emperors initiated restrictive policies with respect to Muslims. These moments of repression of Islam in imperial Ethiopia were linked each time with crises in Ethiopian history and the threat of Muslim external intervention.

Under Emperor Yohannes I (r. 1667–1682), Muslims in imperial Ethiopia were forced to live like foreigners in quarters or villages of their own and were not allowed to own land. Christians would greet Muslims with their left hand only and refuse to share both meat and water with them. Emperor Yohannes I thus wanted to limit interaction between Muslims and Christians in the aftermath of the jihād of Imām Aḥmad and the ongoing threat of an Ottoman intervention. Also, he tried to confine Ethiopia's Muslim population which, according to Portuguese sources, had grown to about one third of the Ethiopian imperial population by 1630.

In the mid-nineteenth century, Emperor Tewodros II (r. 1855–1868) issued a decree which ordered all Muslims to convert to Christianity or to leave the country. At the same time, Tewodros II tried to reunite imperial Ethiopia after the era of Princes (Amh. zämana mäsafent), which had led to the fragmentation of imperial Ethiopia and the rise of Muslim provinces.

Two decades later, Emperor Yohannes IV (r. 1872–1889) issued a decree, at the council of Boru Meda in 1878, that Muslims should accept baptism or be banned from the country. Muslims who refused to convert were executed, and if they rebelled their villages were burned down. In order to escape these policies, many Muslims emigrated to Ḥarär, an old center of Islamic learning in the eastern highlands, only to be reintegrated again into imperial Ethiopia when Menilek II conquered Ḥarär in 1887. Yohannes IV also had to come to terms with a growing number of Muslim populations within imperial Ethiopia due to the recent conquest and incorporation of many Muslim territories, in particular Wällo and Ḥarär, and he had to fight off a Mahdist invasion in 1887. He was killed in a major battle against the Mahdiyya in 1889.

Emperor Menilek II (r. 1889–1909) stopped policies of forced conversion of Muslims and started a policy of integration by winning Muslims as allies, by building alliances, and by offering banquets where Muslims would eat together with Christians:

> In contrast to West Africa, the Red Sea and East African coasts are dotted with a multitude of off-shore islands and archipelagos, such as the Comoros, Zanzibar, and Lamu, the Dahlak islands or Socotra (Ṣuquṭra). The Dahlak islands (app. 900 sq. km.) off the coast of Ethiopia have been inhabited since ancient times by Ethiopian Tigre-speaking populations, who made their livings from pearl diving and fishing as well as piracy. A majority of the population of the Dahlak islands converted to Islam in the eighth century. The island of Socotra (app. 3600 sq. km.) off the Horn of Africa, by contrast, has been settled since ancient times by Southern Arabian populations which converted to Nestorian Christianity in the fifth century and then remained Christian until probably the fifteenth century, although contact with the Nestorian Patriarch in Baghdad collapsed in the early fourteenth century. The occupation of Socotra in 1480 by the Southern Arabian Mahra of al-Qishn started a slow movement of conversion to Islam, although populations in the mountainous interior of the island have retained pre-Islamic and pre-Christian religious practices to this day. Both the Dahlak islands and Socotra have been major stepping stones for the coastal and transoceanic trade from the Red Sea to India, as well from Oman to the East African coast.

"My predecessors dominated through massacres, I will triumph through banquets" (quoted in Ficquet 2006: 49). And he explained this policy to Christian critics:

> These people from Wollo, despite the fact that they are presently Muslims, in two or three years, they will become our brothers through baptism and communion. Here, they can rule with us this world given to us by God and by his Grace; they will be able to enter the Kingdom of Heaven with us. Do not hate them. . . . I want to attract the people of Wollo to me through humility and charity, and I want to teach them. (quoted in Ficquet 2006: 48–49)

Despite the negation of Muslim legacies in imperial Ethiopian history, Muslims lived side by side with Christians for a long period of time, possibly since 615, when the first hijra of Muslims from Mecca brought a group of about 100 Muslims to the court of Axum, where they remained until 628. While Christian sources claimed that those who did not return to Mecca converted to Christianity, such as the husband of Umm Ḥabība who later married the Prophet Muḥammad, Muslim traditions maintain by contrast, possibly for legitimatory reasons, that these first Muslims constituted the core of a small but growing Muslim community in the heart of Ethiopia.

After the first hijra of Muslims to Axum in 615, the first major encounter between Axum and Muslims was an attack by an Umayyad fleet on the harbor of Adulis in 702, which was answered by an attack by Axumite pirates on the harbor of Jidda in the same year. The increasing control over the coasts of the Red Sea, and the destruction of the Axumite fleet in 715 by an Umayyad fleet, led to increasing Muslim control over the coasts of Axum. In particular, Muslims controlled the Dahlak islands off the Axumite coast, which became a major entrepôt for trade with the Indian Ocean from the eighth century. Despite these early encounters, Muslims did not have a tangible impact on Ethiopian imperial history until probably the late thirteenth century, when conflict with the Muslim emirates of the eastern highlands started to escalate. Sizeable Muslim communities had developed by that time in the Danakil lowlands and the eastern highlands, often linked by trade routes to the harbor of Zaylaʿ. At the same time, Muslim traders and craftsmen, often weavers, settled in the northern and central highlands but were prohibited by imperial law from acquiring land. Due to this fact, Muslims in these regions were forced to concentrate on trade as their major source of income. Trade and Islam subsequently became synonymous terms in Ethiopian history: the Amharic words for trader (nägadde and jabarti) had the connotation of Muslim. Although Muslims had to live in villages or in a quarter of their own, such as Eslambet in Gondär, and despite recurring conflicts, Muslims mostly enjoyed toleration except for some specific episodes of Ethiopian history such as mentioned above.

Regarding the development of Islam outside imperial Christian Ethiopia, the harbor of Zaylaʿ on the Gulf of Aden developed as a major entrepôt for trade in the hinterlands of the Horn from the ninth century and became known as a Muslim trade emporium in the tenth century. Zaylaʿ acquired increasing importance from the tenth century, as Axumite trade increasingly came to use this harbor due to the insecurity

> The Muslim traders in imperial Ethiopia, the Jabarti, who came to dominate long-distance trade in the southern marches, the eastern highlands, and eventually also in the central and northern highlands, had a major advantage in their trading activities as compared to other trading networks: they were not only sons of the land and knew the routes, they were also Muslim and thus welcome in the markets beyond Ethiopia, which were often also Muslim. Jabarti traders thus came to establish communities in southern Arabia, Persia, and India, as well as Egypt and the Ottoman empire. A number of Jabarti traders studied at al-Azhar University. Al-Azhar even had a riwāq for the Muslim students from Ethiopia (al-Ḥabasha), and Egypt's famous historian of the early nineteenth century, ʿAbd al-Raḥmān al-Jabartī (d. 1835), had Ethiopian ancestors who had directed the riwāq of the Jabartīs at al-Azhar since the late fifteenth century. Due to their good contacts with Muslim countries, the Jabartī came to dominate trade within Ethiopia. The Jabartī also established three Islamic legal traditions in Ethiopia: the Mālikī school of law in the northwest and west, the Shāfiʿī school of law in the eastern highlands, and the Ḥanafī school of law on the Red Sea.

of the northern routes. From the tenth century, Axumite influence became smaller, however, and Zaylaʿ became a point of departure for the development of Muslim trade networks in the Afar-Danakil lowlands, as well as in the eastern highlands. By the fourteenth century, Zaylaʿ had become an important outlet for southern Ethiopian trade. Having control over trade in this region was important, due to the fact that the southern marches of Ethiopia promised rich profits from the trade in gold, ivory, musk, incense, slaves, and, later, coffee. At the same time, Ethiopia and the southern marches, like the bilād al-sūdān, had to import salt, which came from either the Arho salt plains at the foot of the Tigre escarpments close to the Red Sea, or from Lake Asal in the Danakil lowlands. Arho salt, in the form of amoleh salt bars, represented the most important currency in these areas until the eighteenth century, when the Maria Theresien Thaler gained increasing importance as a currency. In addition, the southern marches imported textiles and iron.

While Christianity consolidated her position in the northern and central highlands, Muslims came to increasingly dominate the Afar and Danakil lowlands, as well as the eastern highlands which opened access to the interior of the Horn, the territories of the Somaal and Oromo. In the context of the development of trade in this region, a number of small Muslim emirates developed which gained control over trade in the region, and which attempted to reach the fertile regions of southern Ethiopia. The most important of these Muslim emirates were Shäwa, Yifat, and Adal, as well as a number of smaller principalities such as Hadiyya, Wäj, Arabäbni, Gänz, Mora, Gedem, Däwaro, Fäṭägar, Sharka, Bale, Hubat, Gidayä, and Hargayä. These emirates fought constant wars against each other over regional hegemony. In 1288, the emirate of Mora came under control of Yifat, while others such as Wäj, Fäṭägar, Gänz, Hadiyya, Sharka, Arabäbni, and Däwaro came under Ethiopian control. Some of these emirates were able to establish a paramount position for some time, and then led the resistance against Ethiopian imperial raids, but none of these emirates survived more than one or two hundred years. The first major emirate, Shäwa, established possibly in the late ninth century (896) by the Makhzūmī family, was followed as a regional power from the late thirteenth century (1295) by Yifat, Shäwa's easternmost province, ruled by the Wäläshma dynasty. Under Ethiopian attacks, Yifat collapsed in a series of wars between 1414 and 1429 and eventually shifted its power base to Adal, but it was still ruled by the Wäläshma dynasty. Adal had to accept, however, Ethiopian control over the Hadiyya region in the south, and it experienced a period of Ethiopian colonization and Christianization. After a number of defeats by Ethiopia in the fifteenth century, Adal relocated its center of power from Dakar to Ḥarär, which had been founded in 1216, and which rose to prominence for a short period of time in the sixteenth century. Due to the fact that Ḥarär became the political center of Imām Aḥmad in the mid-sixteenth century, Ḥarär acquired fame beyond the confines of Ethiopia as the major city of Islam in Ethiopia. The rise of Yifat as the regional paramount power from the late thirteenth century signaled the beginning of a direct confrontation between the Muslim emirates of the eastern highlands and the Afar-Danakil lowlands, on the one hand, and Ethiopia, on the other. This struggle was to last for about 250 years and eventually led to the exhaustion of both sides. The major issue in this struggle was not religion, but control over the trade in the southern marches. Many Muslim emirates in fact fought on the side of the Ethiopian imperial forces. At the same time, Ethiopian victories did not lead to a lasting reversion of the balance of power in the region: while Muslims were unable to defeat Ethiopian troops decisively for more than 300 years, Christian Ethiopia, despite her military supremacy, equally failed to establish sustained domination over the Muslim emirates.

The Jihād of Imām Aḥmad

While Ethiopia's history was marked from the late thirteenth century by constant war between imperial Ethiopia and the Muslim emirates, the sixteenth century constituted a watershed in many ways: it marked the start of not only another era of fragmentation and the emergence of yet another set of important players, the Oromo, but also an era of external intervention in Ethiopian politics. In fact, both imperial Ethiopia and the Muslim emirates were drawn into a global conflict between the emerging maritime power of Portugal and the Ottoman empire, in the northern Indian Ocean and the Red Sea. Both sides sought to establish alliances with Ethiopian players in order to realize larger dreams of empire and the control of global trade routes. Muslim control over the trade routes to India had been a concern of European trading houses for a long time. Egyptian traders had been able to sell a load of Indian pepper, which brought a profit of only 50 dinars in Cairo, to European traders in Alexandria for 130 dinars. Both Mamlūk Egypt as well as the Ottoman empire wanted to retain this advantageous position and consequently restricted European trade contacts to the hinterlands of the Levant as far as possible. A major aim of both Spanish and Portuguese, and later Dutch, English, and French maritime endeavors, was to find new routes to India which would eclipse the Muslim monopoly over trade with the East.

Tension erupted into full-scale war in the Indian Ocean when Portugal found the sea route around the Cape of Good Hope in 1498, as well as the way up the East African coast and across the Indian Ocean. Only two years later, in 1500, the first Portuguese ships entered the Red Sea. Due to the naval superiority of Portuguese caravels, the Portuguese quickly gained control over maritime trade in the whole region, attacked ʿAden in 1508, conquered Hormuz in 1509 and Goa in 1510, and repeatedly entered the Red Sea to attack the Dahlak islands in 1515, Jidda in 1516, Suakin, Zaylaʿ, and Berbera in 1516, 1517, 1518, 1520, 1523, and 1524, until ʿAden accepted Portuguese domination. Portuguese control over the spice trade in the Indian Ocean and the Red Sea led to the collapse of the spice market in Cairo in 1505, and to first Mamlūk (and later Ottoman) efforts to develop a counter-strategy. A Mamlūk fleet, backed by Venice which resented Portuguese control over the spice trade, reached the Indian Ocean in 1508, but lost the decisive naval battle against the Portuguese off Diu in Gujarat in 1509. A second Mamlūk expedition suffered a similar fate off ʿAden in 1516. The Ottoman empire, which had gained control over Egypt in 1517, then started to organize an anti-Portuguese policy on a grander scale, built a new wharf in Suez, and established a position in Yemen in order to attack ʿAden, which controlled access to the Red Sea by land and sea. Yet a first Ottoman advance into the Indian Ocean in 1530 failed to achieve anything. Only in 1537 did the Ottoman empire gain control over ʿAden and strengthen its hold over Yemen, while sending a second fleet into the Indian Ocean which attacked Diu in 1539, without being able to conquer this Portuguese stronghold. The Portuguese reacted by sending a fleet of sixty-four ships into the Red Sea which reached Suez on 23 April 1541, bombarding the harbor. On its way back, the Portuguese fleet landed a troop of 500 soldiers in Massawa who joined Ethiopian imperial forces in their struggle against Imām Aḥmad.

Set in this global power game of the sixteenth century was the jihād of Imām Aḥmad al-Ghāzī (the Conqueror, b. 1506), who was also called Grāñ (the Left-handed) in Ethiopian Christian sources. As mentioned above, by the early sixteenth century imperial Ethiopia had been able to consolidate her paramount position over the Muslim emirates in southern Ethiopia and the eastern highlands. Then the situation changed completely and, for the first time in its history, imperial Ethiopia was about to lose a war against Muslims. This development was linked with the role of Imām Aḥmad, a Muslim scholar who in the 1520s was able to unite the quarreling Muslim emirates under his leadership, and to lead Muslim armies from one victory to the next. Imām Aḥmad originated from Ḥarär and seems to have taken over the rule of the emirate of Adal at a fairly early point in his career. He also managed to unite the different Somaal tribes in the region, and then turned his attention to imperial Ethiopia under the rule of Emperor Lebnä Dengel (r. 1508–1540). In 1527, he refused to pay Adal's annual tribute and thus triggered an Ethiopian attack. By this time, Imām Aḥmad had managed to acquire a sizeable number of firearms from the Ottoman empire, in addition to an Ottoman detachment of artillery. He also established a regular supply of these arms from the Yemeni harbor of Zabīd, through Zaylaʿ to Ḥarär. At the same time, the jihād of Imām Aḥmad brought soldiers from other parts of the world to Ethiopia. The *Futūḥ al-ḥabasha* records the presence of Indians, Omanis, Hadramis, and Maghribinians on the side of the imām, while Portuguese, Turks, Indians, and even Arabs were fighting on the side of the Christian emperors:

> The imām spent the night above the fort (on Amba Geshen, in April 1533). Now the Christians and the people of Tegre possessed (a) cannon and muskets that two Arabs would fire at the Muslims for them. One of them was called Ḥasan al-Baṣrī, and the other was ʿAbd Aṣfar Turkī. They used to recite the Qur'ān, but then they apostasised and became Christians. God curse them. They were part of the army. . . . The imām had sent Warajär Abūn to Zaylaʿ to buy cannons for him so that he could take this fort. He bought a large bronze cannon and two little ones made of iron and carried them by camel as far as the city of Gendebelo. . . . Accompanying the cannons were two skilled handlers, Indians, to whom the imam paid a hundred ounces of gold. (*Futūḥ al-ḥabasha*, 343–44)

Due to his initial technological advantage, Imām Aḥmad was able to defeat the Ethiopian imperial army and suddenly appeared to be the leader who could turn the tables in favor of the Muslims. Numerous warriors from the region, in particular Somaal, who hoped to achieve further victories, joined his forces. Based on the increasing strength of his army, Imām Aḥmad declared a jihād on imperial Ethiopia in 1529, defeated the Ethiopian army for a second time, and then conquered Ethiopia's important southern province of Shäwa. These first and easy victories of Imām Aḥmad were possible because imperial Ethiopia was divided by a number of internal rivalries, and some Ethiopian (Christian) provincial lords were willing to support Imām Aḥmad, hoping that his victories would weaken imperial power. In a number of surprise attacks, based on the collaboration of Ethiopian provincial lords, Imām Aḥmad defeated the Ethiopian army several times in 1530 and transformed his warrior forces into a regular army by eliminating the influence of the tribal leaders. With this army, Imām Aḥmad attacked the central highlands in 1531 and again defeated the imperial forces. Numerous monasteries were destroyed and Muslim garrisons were established. In 1533, major parts of the southern and central highlands were under Muslim control and Imām Aḥmad also started to conquer the north. This endeavor was so successful that the Ethiopian emperor had to abandon his residence and to flee from hideout to hideout. In 1535, when Imām Aḥmad concluded his conquest of the north, the emperor had become a refugee in his own realm. In this desperate situation, Lebnä Dengel sent a mission to Portugal, appealing for support, but before the Portuguese mission reached the Ethiopian highlands in 1541 Lebnä Dengel died, followed by Emperor Gälawdewos (r. 1540–1559). In 1540, following complete victory, the Ottoman artillery corps left Ethiopia, to be deployed to Yemen. In contrast to Emperor Lebnä Dengel, Emperor Gälawdewos managed to reunite a number of ambitious provincial lords who probably feared that a strong Muslim ruler would not be more favorably disposed toward their own political aspirations than a weak Christian emperor. At the same time, a Portuguese military expedition and artillery corps under the leadership of Christovão da Gama arrived and balanced Muslim military supremacy. From a number of mountain bastions, the Ethiopian army pushed back the exhausted Muslim troops and defeated the Muslim forces several times, although the Portuguese eventually lost a major battle near Wojarat against Imām Aḥmad, who had brought back the Ottoman artillery.

Imām Aḥmad now made the mistake, however, of sending the Ottoman artillery back again, possibly due to fear of an Ottoman intervention and supremacy, and withdrew to Lake Tana in late 1542 in order to recover from the hard fighting in the north. Emperor Gälawdewos used this chance to unite his forces and to march against Imām Aḥmad, together with the remaining Portuguese troops. In a decisive confrontation on 22 February 1543, Imām Aḥmad was killed. The death of the imām symbolized the end of the jihād. The defeated Muslim troops dissolved and returned to the eastern highlands. In less than one year, Emperor Gälawdewos reconquered all of imperial Ethiopia and many Ethiopians who had converted to Islam, now reverted to Christianity. The regional lords who had allied with Imām Aḥmad rejoined the emperor, and thus gave Emperor Gälawdewos the power to reverse the fates of war and to attack the eastern highlands again in 1546. In a series of devastating wars, the Ethiopian troops defeated the Muslim emirates one by one and in 1559 even marched on Ḥarär, where Emperor Gälawdewos was killed in battle. The death of the emperor stopped the war and the imperial troops left the eastern highlands. The successor of Imām Aḥmad in Ḥarär, Amīr Nūr b. al-Mujāhid (d. 1567), tried to reorganize Muslim forces but failed to achieve this aim, although he was able to fortify Ḥarär with a wall. Adal in fact attacked imperial Ethiopia one last time in 1576, but Emperor Särṣä Dengel (r. 1563–1597) answered with a devastating attack on Ḥarär in the same year. Muslim resistance collapsed, and in 1577 the rulers of Adal decided to move to the Danakil desert oasis of Awssa, where they reestablished the emirate, far removed from imperial Ethiopia, while Ḥarär eventually claimed her independence from Adal-Awssa. The eastern highlands were now without protection and disintegrated quickly, while imperial troops withdrew across the Awash.

The territorial situation in 1570 resembled the situation in 1330: imperial Ethiopia was too strong to be defeated by even a coalition of Muslim emirates, yet too weak to defeat the Muslim emirates decisively and to integrate them into the empire. However, there was a major difference with respect to the situation in 1330: major parts of Ethiopia were devastated by war; disputes among Muslim leaders in the eastern highlands aggravated the condition of the population; in addition, several epidemics of plague had devastated many parts of Ethiopia in the mid-sixteenth century and led to a further loss of population in the highlands, intensified by a famine in 1567–1568. By 1570, whole areas in the southern and eastern highlands had become depopulated, in particular Däwaro, Fäṭägar, and Wäj, where more than 80 percent of the population may have died. This situation was exploited by southern Oromo groups which entered the vacuum and occupied major parts of the eastern highlands and, later, of the southern and central highlands as far as Lake Tana.

The invasion by the Oromo (sons of Orma, in Ethiopian Christian sources pejoratively known as Galla, "landless perons, vagabonds") was essentially an expansion of pastoral Oromo groups, which had escaped pestilence and starvation due to their marginal geographical position in the south and southeast. From the 1530s, these Oromo moved into the empty territories of old Oromo groups in northwestern Bale, Sidamo, Däwaro, Hadiyya, and Wäj, who had suffered from war, pestilence, and hunger. By taking over and integrating the remaining Oromo settlements, the new Oromo groups were able to gain control over major parts of the eastern highlands from the late 1530s. By the early 1570s, first Oromo settlers reached Wäj and the central highlands. At the same time, pastoral Oromo groups occupied the pastures of the western Somaal groups who had also suffered from war, epidemic, and famine. Imperial Ethiopia under Emperor Särṣä Dengel, by contrast, tried to push back the Oromo and repeatedly defeated small detachments of Oromo warriors in Hadiyya, which even became part of imperial Ethiopia again in 1577. The ongoing immigration and small-scale raiding by Oromo troops exhausted the Ethiopian forces, however, and, in a number of further campaigns against Emperor Susneyos (r. 1603–1632), the Oromo were able to defeat a major Ethiopian ally, Maya, to enter the central highlands and push into Wällo and Shäwa. The intrusion of the "barbaric Galla" in imperial Ethiopia was represented in rather negative terms in Ethiopian imperial history. The Oromo were depicted as anathema to the civilizing mission of imperial Ethiopia. Abba Bahrey thus wrote in his *Ye galla tarik* (History of the Galla) of 1593: "I have started to record the history of the Galla in order to make known the number of their tribes, and their disposition to kill human beings as well as the brutality of their traditions" (quoted in Hassen 1990: 2).

In the seventeenth and eighteenth centuries, the Oromo consolidated their territorial gains and reached the western highlands and even Lake Tana. Different Oromo groups eventually settled in major parts of the western, southern, and central highlands of imperial Ethiopia and started to form, in the eighteenth and nineteenth centuries, a series of small states in Ethiopia's western and southern peripheries which were integrated into the Ethiopian empire in the late nineteenth century. In contrast to the

> In contrast to the Oromo settlements in Bale and Sidamo, which had been in contact with Islam and Christianity since at least the fourteenth century, the pastoral Oromo followed the old Oromo religion which knew a supreme God, Waaqa, whose laws were represented by a high priest, the Qallu Abbaa Muuda. An Oromo pilgrimage to the seat of the Abbaa Muuda in Dello Guddo in the Medda Welabu district of Bale took place every eight years. This visit to the shrine started in the early seventeenth century but was replaced in the nineteenth century by the Muslim visit to the sanctuary of Shaykh Ḥusayn in Anajina. Oromo society knew an age group organization, the gada), with a maximum of ten gada of eight years each. Each gada had its own leader, the Abba Gada and a legislative assembly, the seylan, directed by an Abba Sera, a father of the law, who supervised gada regulations and Oromo laws. Integration into Oromo society was thus defined by affiliation with a gada, not through ethnic, linguistic, or religious criteria. When a change from one gada to the next occurred, the age group of the warriors engaged in ritual raids. Oromo expansion followed the temporal pattern of gada generations and expanded into ever new regions: from Sidamo and Bale in the southeast, along the ridges of the eastern highlands to the northeast, as well as down the slopes of the eastern highlands into Somaal territories. At the same time, the Oromo expanded northwest and in the nineteenth century reached their contemporary boundaries, which extend from Tigre in the north and Hargeisa in the northeast, to the Omo in the south, and from Wälläga in the west to the upper reaches of the Shebelle in the east. In the course of their migrations, the Oromo split into two major federations, namely, the western Barentu and the eastern Baretuma that were divided into sub-groups such as the Wällo, Macca, Tulama, Arsi, Gugi, Gabra, and Orma.

eastern highlands, where an Oromo majority gradually produced a largely Oromoized society which followed Oromo religion and converted or reverted to Islam from the late eighteenth century, the Oromo of imperial Ethiopia became either Muslim or Christian and were gradually integrated into an Amharic-speaking imperial Ethiopia. The Oromo never acted in fact as a united force, and from the 1590s Oromo units within the imperial army even fought intruding Oromo bands. From the seventeenth century, Oromo acquired leading positions in the army and at the court, and thus came to share the history of imperial Ethiopia. At the same time, loyal Oromo settlers were employed by imperial Ethiopia as military settlers in Damot, Bägemdir, and Gojam.

Fragmentation and Unification

The expansion of the Oromo and the conquest of the last Muslim emirates by the Oromo in the late sixteenth century ended the history of Muslim emirates in Ethiopia. Although Islam continued to exist on a local level among traders and religious scholars in a few centers of learning, Muslims have not played any major political role in Ethiopia since this period of time. In fact, Islam almost disappeared from the eastern highlands and southern marches due to the effects of war, pestilence, and hunger, but also due to the integration of Muslims into Oromo society. Only in a few centers, such as the holy city of Ḥarär, were Muslim scholars able to survive. In some of these centers, Sufi scholars settled and their schools became centers of local shrine pilgrimage. As in the bilād al-maghrib or the bilād al-sūdān, Islam accommodated non-Islamic traditions instead of eradicating them completely: "Several of the pre-Islamic rituals were fused with new ones, modified and given new meaning. Rather than destroying existing places of worship, the propagators of Islam (in Bale), often started their activities at or in the vicinity of such places, transforming them into sites for the veneration of Muslim holy men" (Østebø 2008: 76).

The most important of the new centers of saint veneration was the sanctuary of Shaykh Nūr Ḥusayn, Dirre Shaykh Ḥusayn (the field of Shaykh Ḥusayn) in Anajina in northern Bale. Shaykh Nūr Ḥusayn seems to have been a rather enigmatic figure, though, a typical wise stranger who lived, according to different sources, in the nineteenth, fifteenth, or tenth centuries. According to local traditions in Anajina, he was born around 1150. His grandfather allegedly emigrated from Arabia to Marka on the East African coast, but he then moved inland and eventually settled in Bale. From the thirteenth century, Bale had been disputed territory between imperial Ethiopia and the Muslim emirates of Yifat and Adal, and then became a major center of the jihād of Imām Aḥmad. From 1560, Bale and the sanctuary of Shaykh Nūr Ḥusayn came under Oromo domination. From the sixteenth century onward, the influence of the sanctuary of Shaykh Nūr Ḥusayn in Anajina spread into the remoter regions of the Horn, mediated by Shaykh Abūbakar b. ʿAbdallāh al-Aydarūs, a Ḥaḍramī scholar. In the eighteenth century, Ḥarär and the sanctuary of Shaykh Nūr Ḥusayn in Anajina in Bale in the eastern Ethiopian highlands became the center of a supra-regional tradition of shrine-pilgrimage. The land around the sanctuary of Shaykh Nūr Ḥusayn in Anajina was called Biyo Shaykh Ḥusayn, the land of Shaykh Ḥusayn. In this sanctuary, weapons were prohibited and all visitors shared the same food and were clad in the same type of dress. Also, differences in status were suspended. In a temporal sequence of eight years, a large shrine pilgrimage to the tomb of Shaykh Nūr Ḥusayn took place and attested the integration of this Islamic cult into the gada age-group system of the Oromo who dominated the region of Bale.

In addition to the sanctuary of Shaykh Nūr Ḥusayn, a number of other centers of Islamic learning and saint veneration developed along the major trade routes in

> Despite its failures against the Portuguese, the Ottoman Empire continued to strengthen its position in the Red Sea and the northern Indian Ocean throughout the sixteenth century. Thus, for its acquisitions in the Red Sea, which were called pashālik Ḥabesh, the Ottoman empire established administrative headquarters in Suakin. In the late sixteenth century, after the collapse of the Portuguese seaborne empire, this foothold in the Red Sea enabled the Ottoman Empire to gain control over the trade with coffee from Ethiopia, which brought considerable wealth to the Red Sea trade and to markets in Cairo. The importance of the trade in coffee also explains why the Ottoman empire maintained its position in the Red Sea and in Yemen, and its major harbor in the Red Sea, Mokha, after the decline of Portuguese sea power. The Ottoman Empire continued to intervene in the affairs of both Yemen and Ethiopia in the sixteenth and seventeenth centuries, although these interventions usually ended in failure, such as the expedition of the Beylerbey of Yemen, Özdemir, into the northern Ethiopian highlands in 1557, which was defeated by the ruler of the sea, the Baḥer Nägash of imperial Ethiopia, Yesḥaq. From this period of time, the pashālik Ḥabesh remained confined to the Dahlak islands and Massawa, although further (futile) interventions followed in 1562, 1576, 1589, and 1592. The threat of Ottoman invasion continued to bother imperial Ethiopia in the sixteenth and seventeenth centuries, which explains why Ethiopia looked for regional allies, even unlikely ones, such as the Imāms of Yemen, who also sought independence from Ottoman rule and were willing to cooperate with Ethiopia.

Ethiopia, in particular on the northern routes, which also saw some pilgrim traffic. In the nineteenth century, for instance, Ya'a in Wälläga came to see the development of a sanctuary that was linked with a Muslim scholar from Bornu, Shaykh al-Fakkī (al-Faqīh) al-Barnawī. Islam equally survived in Wällo and grew to considerable strength in the nineteenth century, when Sufi scholars such as Muḥammad Shāfī b. ʿAskarī Muḥammad established a center of Islamic learning in Qallu. The nineteenth century also saw the conversion of a majority of the eastern Oromo to Islam, and when these regions were eventually integrated into Ethiopia in the context of its political expansion after 1855, the proportion of Muslims within imperial Ethiopia grew considerably.

In southern Ethiopia, and in particular in Hadiyya, Sidamo, and Kaffa, Islam collapsed completely, although some Oromo converted to Islam after the sixteenth century. In most regions, local populations joined the gada system of the Oromo and abandoned both Christian and Muslim religious practices. In some regions, local religious traditions merged with remnants of Christianity and Islam and formed new cults, such as the Fandano cult in Hadiyya, which knew a taboo on eating pork (as in both Ethiopian Christianity and Islam), a ritual prayer (sagidda), a form of fasting (somu) for fifteen days, and burial of the dead according to the Muslim ritual, whereas other elements of Islam were abandoned. While the Fandano cult in Hadiyya took some Muslim forms, other regions of the southern marches of Ethiopia, such as Kaffa, developed new local cults which incorporated Christian influences. Due to the collapse of the Church in these regions after the jihād of Imām Aḥmad, Christianity disappeared as an organized church and was revived in the late nineteenth century only, when Ethiopia expanded again and organized the agrarian colonization of the south. The expansion of Ethiopia into its southern periphery since the late nineteenth century in fact brought about the reversion of former Christian sedentary populations to Christianity, while the pastoral populations of the southeast rather converted or reverted to Islam. As Islam had been the dominant religion in these areas prior to Oromo expansion, "the Islamization of the Oromo (in these regions) contained two parallel processes of Oromo elements being Islamized and pre-Oromo Islamic elements undergoing a similar process of Oromization" (Østebø 2008: 90).

While Islam in an organized political form disappeared from Ethiopia in the late sixteenth century, imperial Ethiopia survived the jihād of Imām Aḥmad and slowly came to terms with the Oromo. At the same time, the emperors of Ethiopia were unable to reestablish the empire in its old grandeur. Rather, provincial lords increasingly claimed influence over local, regional, and imperial politics. As a result, from the late sixteenth century Ethiopia witnessed another period of fragmentation of the central state. This crisis became acute in the mid-eighteenth century and lasted until the mid-nineteenth century. For the time being, however, the emperors of Ethiopia managed to consolidate imperial rule in the northern, western, central, and southern highlands and established a new permanent court in Gondär, on Lake Tana. Gondär had the advantage of being situated in one of Ethiopia's most fertile regions, far removed from the war- and pestilence-ridden southern and central highlands, and equally far removed from the major concentrations of the Oromo.

After the victory over Imām Aḥmad, Portugal achieved major influence at the court and an increasing number of Catholic missionaries tried to persuade the emperors to convert. Emperor Susneyos (r. 1607–1632) eventually complied in 1612, proclaiming the diophysite dogma (of the two natures of Christ as taught by the Catholic Church) in 1616. This conversion and its theological repercussions triggered the protest not only of the Ethiopian Church but also of many feudal lords, and Susneyos finally resigned in 1632. His son, Fasilädäs (r. 1632–1667), revoked all religious pronouncements made by his father, forced the Portuguese to leave the country, and discontinued diplomatic relations with European countries in order to prevent further intervention in Ethiopian affairs. At the same time, Fasilädäs sought new allies and found them in the guise of the imāms of neighboring Yemen. Yemen had opposed Ottoman rule since the late sixteenth century and in 1636 achieved the evacuation of the Ottoman troops from Yemen. Both imperial Ethiopia and Yemen profited from the fact that they had access to two harbors which escaped both Portuguese and Ottoman control: Baylul, north of Assab, for Ethiopia, and Mokha for Yemen. In 1642, Fasilädäs sent a first diplomatic mission to the court of Imām al-Mu'ayyad bi-llāh (r. until 1644). The Ethiopian mission was answered by a Yemeni mission in 1643, and in 1647 Ethiopia sent a second mission to Yemen in order to intensify these contacts. Again, Yemen reacted positively and sent a mission to Ethiopia under al-Qāḍī Sharaf al-Dīn al-Hasan b. Aḥmad al-Ḥaymī (d. 1660), who wrote an extensive report entitled *Sīrat al-Ḥabasha* (The story of Ethiopia), an extensive account of life in Ethiopia in this period. However, the exchange of missions between Ethiopia and Yemen did not develop into a political alliance. Due to centrifugal forces in Ethiopia, the power of the emperors became smaller and smaller in the late seventeenth and early eighteenth centuries, and a number of strong regional players developed: Tigre in the north, Gondär on Lake Tana, Lasta in the center, and Shäwa in the south. In all these regional centers, Oromo soldiers and administrators gained in power, and between 1769 and 1855, the time of the princes (Amh. zämana mäsafent), the emperors of Ethiopia became virtually puppets of regional lords (Amh. ras). This development came to an end only in 1853 when one regional lord, Ras Kassa, managed to break Oromo domination in his region and to gain power in Gojam, Bägemdir, Tigre, and Shäwa. In 1855, he proclaimed himself the new emperor, Tewodros II (r. 1855–1868), and started another era of centralization and expansion of imperial Ethiopia.

The expansionist policies of Tewodros II and later Yohannes IV (r. 1868–1889) sought to regain control over the southern marches and the eastern highlands, which had been beyond Ethiopian control since the late sixteenth century. At the same time, Ethiopia became conscious of a number of new powers in the larger region, such as Egypt, which was advancing on the Nile, as well as Britain, France, and Italy, which also sought to establish positions in the region. Ethiopia managed to defeat a first Egyptian advance in 1846, and although Egypt gained control over Massawa's hinterland in 1872, an Egyptian invasion of Ethiopia was defeated in 1875 and a second in 1876. Egyptian troops only managed to march on Ḥarär and to occupy this major city in the eastern highlands, which were still beyond the reach of Ethiopia. However, when Britain declared a protectorate over Egypt in 1882, Egyptian rule on the Nile and in East Africa collapsed and in 1884 Egyptian troops evacuated Ḥarär, which was then taken on 7 January 1887 by Ethiopian troops under the command of the future emperor Menilek. Other Egyptian positions were occupied by Italy (Massawa), France (Djibouti), and Britain (Zayla' and Berbera).

In the same period, Ethiopia's expansion in the southern marches was stopped by the expansion of the Mahdiyya on the Nile, and only Emperor Menilek II (r. 1889–1909) was eventually able to continue Ethiopia's expansionist policies. Supplied generously with modern firearms by Italy, but also France and Russia, he conquered the southern marches and completed the conquest of the eastern highlands as well as of the Ogaden region from 1878 to 1894. In addition, he occupied the oasis of Awssa in the Danakil lowlands in 1896, and thus ended the existence of the last Muslim emirate in this region. In order to have better access to these rich new territories, Menilek established yet another Ethiopian imperial court city, Addis Abäba, in 1883. In the new territories, imperial Ethiopia founded military settlements (Amh. kätämā) and resettled farmers as soldier-settlers (Amh. näfṭänna; lit. rifle-men) from the highlands in the southern marches. The resistance of the Oromo and Sidamo populations of the south was quickly broken, as Ethiopian imperial forces were not only superior in military technology and organization—after 1890, Ethiopia even had Hotchkiss rapid fire guns—but the populations of the south also suffered from an epidemic of rinderpest in 1888 and 1889, leading to the almost complete collapse of Ethiopia's cattle populations. Epidemics of cholera, typhoid fever, and smallpox from 1889 to 1892, as well as widespread invasions of locusts, aggravated the crisis and caused hunger on a scale that engraved these years as *anni horribili* into Ethiopian historical memories. The decimated populations of the southern marches were integrated as serfs (Amh. gäbbar, pl. gäbbaroch) into the Ethiopian colonial settlement system, and their lands were handed over as land titles to soldiers of the imperial army, who came to form a stratum of local land holders (Amh. melkenyawoch). Depopulated areas were distributed among settlers from the north, and churches were established in the agrarian settlements, which became the foci for conversion to Christianity for the gäbbar from the 1930s. Only the pastoral populations, which could not accept the extensive prescriptions of the Ethiopian Church regarding the rules of fasting (no meat, milk products, or eggs on at least 140 days of the year), turned to Islam. Conversion to Islam also came to be seen as a symbol of opposition to Ethiopian rule.

Despite Italy's initial support for Menilek's policies of expansion in the southern marches, Italy constituted the major threat to Ethiopia at this time. However, Italy's military expansion into Ethiopia's northern highlands suffered a first defeat at Dogali in January 1887. After the treaty of Wechale of 1889, in which Ethiopia recognized Italian control over Massawa, Italy continued to expand into the northern highlands despite its military defeat and even claimed Ethiopia as a protectorate. In 1893, Ethiopia rejected Italian claims and Italy subsequently started to prepare a full-scale invasion of Ethiopia. The Italian invasion of Ethiopia was combined with an Italian advance from Massawa into the Sudan as part of the war against the Mahdiyya. In 1894, Italian troops occupied Kassala. This policy led to an exchange of letters between Emperor Menilek II and the Khalīfa 'Abdallāh in which they agreed upon a counter-strategy. When Italy attacked Ethiopia in 1896, the troops of the Khalīfa attacked Italian positions in Kassala and stopped the Italian advance in the Sudan. In Ethiopia, an Italian army of 17,500 was decisively defeated near Adua. Italy lost 5,000 troops in battle as well as 1,900 prisoners to an Ethiopian army which Italy had provided with modern rifles at a time when Italy still wanted to gain Ethiopia as an ally in northeast Africa. The defeat of the Italian army near Adua was the most consequential defeat of a European army in a colonial war in Africa, as it led to the full international recognition of Ethiopia's sovereignty. Ethiopia thus remained the only region in Africa free of colonial rule and was even able to consolidate her own colonial rule over the southern marches as well as the Ogaden region in the years to come. When Italy invaded Ethiopia again, in 1935, it attacked a consolidated empire which fought Italian occupation. After six years of guerrilla warfare, the Italian army in Ethiopia had to capitulate to Ethiopian and British forces and to accept the return of the emperor, Ras Tafari Makonnen "Hailä Sellase" (the power of the trinity), to the throne in Addis Abäba. Also, the Italian colony of Eritrea, which had been annexed from Ethiopia in 1889, was returned to Ethiopia.

9 Muslims on the Horn of Africa

Historical and Thematic Patterns

The Horn of Africa forms one of the smallest regions of Islam in Africa. The arid lowlands of the Horn are characterized by fairly homogeneous ethnic, linguistic, and religious structures dominated by Somaal tribal groups. The history of the Horn has been characterized by competition over scarce resources, as well as tribal feuds. At the same time, the region has been marked by the absence of a central government until the early twentieth century. As such, the Horn can be seen as a huge bilād al-sība, where tribal self-governance has historically prevailed over processes of state formation.

While Ethiopia was linked with the lands on the Nile and those on the Red Sea, the Horn of Africa formed links with southern Arabia in the north and the East African coast in the south. Islam in the Horn originated in three regions: the ports of Zaylaʿ and Berbera in the north; Ḥarär and other centers of Islamic learning in the eastern Ethiopian highlands; and the ports of the Banādir coast, namely Mogadishu, Brawa, Marka, and Kismayu. From at least the thirteenth century, these market places, harbors, and trading places had sizeable settlements of traders and scholars from Ḥaḍramawt in Yemen, often of sharīfian descent. Ḥaḍramī scholars introduced Sufi teachings, and, probably in the early nineteenth century, the Qādiriyya and the Shādhiliyya orders established a foothold in some centers of learning. Until the nineteenth century, the Sufi orders remained confined, however, to the circles of scholars and traders in the major port cities and market places. This chapter focuses on the movements of reform in the nineteenth century and the jihād of Muḥammad ʿAbdille Ḥasan in particular, as his movement of reform and resistance against European colonialism informed the history of Somalia in the twentieth century in decisive ways.

Processes of Islamization

The development of Islam on the Horn, as in many other parts of Africa, was linked with trade. Ibn Baṭṭūṭa, in the context of his report on the East African coast, mentioned his visit to Zaylaʿ in 1331 and noted that Zaylaʿ was a city of black Berbers (the Arabic term for the Somaal), who followed the Shāfiʿī school of law (. . . *Wa-hiya madīna al-barābira wa-hum ṭāʾifa min al-sūdān shāfiʿiyya al-madhhab,* Ibn Baṭṭūṭa 1985 1: 279). Zaylaʿ was described as a major trading place, but also as one of the dirtiest cities on earth (Ibn Baṭṭūṭa 1985 1: 279). Due to the stench of the carcasses of slaughtered camels and dried fish, which were exported to the Arabian peninsula, Ibn Baṭṭūṭa decided to

From approximately the fifth century, the Somaal expanded from their original pastures at the headsprings of the Juba and Shebelle in a northeasterly direction and became the dominant population in the eastern highlands of Ethiopia and the northern Horn by the tenth century. Despite their clear Cushitic linguistic and ethnic identity, Somaal oral traditions claim Arab origin through two mystical clan ancestors, Shaykh Darood and Shaykh Isaaq, who allegedly arrived in the northern Horn in the tenth and thirteenth centuries, respectively, where they married local women. Shaykh Darood and Shaykh Isaaq are presented as being of noble Qurayshī origin and thus related to the tribe of the Prophet. Somaal tribal groups constituted the major basis of support for the jihād of Imām Aḥmad, and suffered accordingly when the jihād collapsed. The weakened Somaal subsequently had to move into the more desert-like regions of the northern and central Horn as well as the region of Ogaden, where they forced smaller Somaal groups to move south toward the Juba and Shebelle. In the nineteenth century, the northern and central Somaal resumed their movement toward the south and disrupted established economic structures on the Lower Juba and Shebelle, a dynamic that was accelerated by Ethiopian expansion into the Ogaden in the late nineteenth century. By 1840, the southernmost Somaal had reached the lower Shebelle, and in 1909 they crossed the Tana in Kenya. To this day, the expansion of the Somaal has continued into northern Kenya, as well as back into southeastern Ethiopia, where Somaal groups encounter southern Oromo groups.

spend the night on board his ship. Mogadishu was also an important Somaal harbor, where many traders lived. When Ibn Baṭṭūṭa's ship entered the harbor of Mogadishu, he discovered that smaller boats came out, each containing a group of young men who carried dishes of food. They offered this food to individual traders on the ship and then proclaimed, "This is my guest" (hadhā nazīlī). When the trader left the ship, he would go nowhere except to the house of his host who would take care of him and his trade. This custom points to an important tradition in Somaal society, namely the role of the patron (Som. abbaan), who provided protection for his respective guest. As Ibn Baṭṭūṭa was recognized as a faqīh, a legal scholar, he was not claimed by a trader but adopted by the Qāḍī of Mogadishu, one Ibn al-Burhān al-Miṣrī. Like Zaylaʿ, Mogadishu was governed by a pious "Berber" sulṭān, Abū Bakr b. al-Shaykh ʿUmar, who spoke Arabic. Ibn Baṭṭūṭa also recorded a large number of ashrāf at the court of the sulṭān of Mogadishu (Ibn Baṭṭūṭa 1985 1: 279–83).

The centers of trade on the coast cultivated trade links with the interior of the Horn and the eastern highlands of Ethiopia. These trade routes also constituted routes for the expansion of Islam. Trade goods were luxury goods as well as grains from the southern floodplains of the Juba and Shebelle, while the interior generated livestock (mostly camels), frankincense, ivory, and slaves. For the transportation of these goods, camels were used, as in the Sahara, and over time a number of trade routes developed. At the same time, impulses for trade and the development of Islam came from Ḥarär, which came to be seen as the major Somaal center of Islamic learning in the late fifteenth and early sixteenth centuries, although most Ḥarär scholars in this period originated from Ḥaḍramawt and had settled in Ḥarär since 1490 only. Ḥarär scholars supported the jihād of Imām Aḥmad, as did a majority of the Somaal in this region. The jihād, epidemics, and famine hit the Somaal particularly hard. As a result, their pastures in the eastern highlands of Ethiopia were occupied by the expanding Oromo, Ḥarär lost its paramount importance as a center of Islamic learning for the Horn, and Ḥaḍramī emigration turned toward coastal centers from the sixteenth century. Also, many scholars and their families left Ḥarär after the 1570s and resettled on the coast. They became known among the Somaal by the nickname of "gibilaad" (white-skinned people).

In the segmentary society of the Somaal, as in the bilād al-sība of the bilād al-maghrib, the religious scholars (Som. wadaad) had a central role as neutral outsiders and carriers of knowledge. Their centers of settlement and learning, often situated at watering places, were regarded as sacrosanct, as neutral zones where conflict was resolved in peaceful ways. After the death of a respected wadaad, these centers of religious learning, watering places, and markets developed into centers of local shrine pilgrimage and whole regions were called after such a shrine. Apart from the sanctuary of Shaykh Nūr Ḥusayn, the Horn had a number of smaller shrine-sanctuaries, such as Qulunqūl in the Ogaden region, which were often affiliated with a specific Somaal clan or sub-clan. The wadaad of these minor centers mediated in conflicts and disputes and provided a basic education for children in their qur'ānic schools. As leaders of their communities, these wadaad also acquired importance as therapeutic experts and healers, although their almost hegemonic role in these fields came to be challenged, from the early nineteenth century, by the rise of religious scholars linked with the Sufi orders, in particular the Qādiriyya and the Aḥmadiyya. These new religious scholars seem to have taken possession of some established shrine-sanctuaries, such as Qulunqūl, in the nineteenth century, transforming them into centers of Sufi learning.

Movements of Reform in the Nineteenth Century

In the nineteenth and early twentieth centuries, the Horn of Africa was characterized by the growth of Sufi orders and the emergence of movements of reform such as the Ṣāliḥiyya. The development of these movements of reform may be viewed from different perspectives: as forming part of a movement of resistance of the Somaal against colonial encroachment and domination; as a struggle against the religious establishment as represented, most prominently, by the scholars of the Qādiriyya, or as an expression of conflict among warring Somaal tribes and clans. In the latter half of the nineteenth century, the Horn of Africa indeed came under external control: first Egypt (from 1872), later Britain (from 1888), France (1881), and Italy, as well as Ethiopia in the interior (from 1893), started to divide the region. The most important player in this period was Italy, which from 1889 claimed major parts of the coast, from Cape Guardafui in the north down to the southern Banādir coast, including Mogadishu, Brawa, and Marka. Like other European colonial powers, Italy took some time to secure control over the hinterland, however, and only by 1925 were major parts of Italian East Africa under effective Italian administration.

A closer look at Muslim movements of reform in nineteenth-century Somalia shows that the first two or three generations of Muslim reformers did not so much react against a not yet present European (or Ethiopian) presence as they tried to bring about changes in the established setup of Somaal society. These early reform endeavors have to be understood as a reaction to internal social dynamics. Early and mid-nineteenth-century reform movements were particularly inspired by the teachings of the North African Muslim Sufi scholar Aḥmad b. Idrīs, who had settled in Mecca and later in the ʿAṣīr region of southwestern Arabia, and whose teachings and career were set in contexts not yet influenced by colonial expansion or European conquest. The character of the early movements of reform may be illustrated by looking at the case of the community of Baardhere (Bardera) on the Juba River. This jamāʿa was founded around 1819 by a religious scholar called Shaykh Ibrāhīm Ḥasan Jeberow and initially consisted of a few dozen persons in a dār al-hijra. In the early 1830s, the jamāʿa seems to have been led by ʿAbd al-Wāḥid al-Abqālī (al-Abgalī), a student of Aḥmad b. Idrīs, and focused largely on Islamic education. In the mid-1830s, however, under the leadership of Shaykh ʿAlī Duure (d. 1836) and Shaykh Abiker Aden Dhurow (d. 1838/1839), the jamāʿa acquired an increasingly militant character. It managed to establish an alliance with Darood tribal groups from the northwest, which had settled on the Juba and taken control over the agricultural settlements there, including the major center of trade, Luuq, which happened to be the most important trading place between Lamu on the East African coast and Ḥarär in Ethiopia's eastern highlands. Under the leadership of Shaykh Abiker Aden Dhurow, the jamāʿa turned against un-Islamic practices. The jamāʿa sought in particular to prohibit the consumption of tobacco, dancing, and the mixing of men and women in public. The women of the jamāʿa wore the ḥijāb and the jamāʿa prohibited the trade in ivory, as the "teeth" of the elephants were considered impure and so therefore was the profit from the ivory trade.

In the late 1830s, the jamāʿa had grown to almost 20,000 persons, and from 1836 armed detachments of the jamāʿa started to raid villages in the region and force the people to perform the daily prayers. This policy of religious coercion was directed specifically against the established wadaad, who had to suffer the prohibition of established magico-religious practices. By 1840, the jamā'a of Baardhere had become so strong that it could gain control over the coastal town of Brawa, and both Marka and Mogadishu were within its reach. The quick expansion of the jamā'a triggered the formation of a coalition of opponents in the region. The opponents of Baardhere resented the embargo imposed by the jamā'a on long-distance trade through Luuq, as well as the destabilization of agricultural activities on the Lower Juba and Shebelle Rivers. In 1843, a coalition of opponents of the jamā'a, mostly Digil tribal warriors under the leadership of the sulṭān of Geledi, Yūsuf Muḥammad, defeated the forces of the jamā'a, mostly Darood warriors led by Shaykh 'Abd al-Raḥmān and Shaykh Ibrāhīm, and destroyed Baardhere completely. The leaders of the jamā'a were killed and trade through Luuq was reopened. The policies of the jamā'a of Baardhere had shocked Somaal society on the Lower Juba and Shebelle Rivers, as they offered a new model of political, religious, and social organization which was not accepted by the established political and religious leaders in the region. In particular, the sulṭān of Geledi was not willing to accept a competing center of power. After his victory over the jamā'a of Baardhere, Sulṭān Yūsuf Muḥammad became the paramount political leader in the region. He was killed in 1848, however, in a battle with Bimaal tribal groups which controlled Marka and its hinterland and resented Geledi expansion. In the decades to come, the lower Juba and Shebelle region was characterized by rivalry between the Geledi federation and the Bimaal, which was finally resolved in 1878 by another victory of the Bimaal over the sons of Sulṭān Yūsuf Muḥammad, leaving the Bimaal, for the time being, as the strongest power in the region. The legacy of Islamic reforms as represented by Baardhere continued to live on in this region, however, and was revived in the movement of Muḥammad 'Abdille Ḥasan in the early twentieth century.

The confrontation between the community of Baardhere and the Geledi federation was informed by the economic dynamics of the larger region rather than religious reform: while long-distance trade was largely organized in the coastal cities of Mogadishu, Brawa, and Marka, as well as Lamu, the nineteenth century saw a massive expansion of trade between the coast and the southern Ethiopian marches through Somaal lands. It has to be stressed, however, that the size of the trade through the southern regions of the Horn was still rather small by comparison to trade in other parts of East Africa. External traders, Arabs, Indians, or Europeans were thus scarcely interested in establishing their own trade networks in this area. For the Somaal trading communities in the banādir coastal cities as well as on the Lower Juba and Shebelle, this trade was again too important to accept permanent interruption as represented by the policies of the community of Baardhere. A major object of the trade between the coast and the interior was ivory, as in other parts of East Africa, as well as slaves. In the course of the nineteenth century, the ivory frontier, which was situated on the lower Juba and Shebelle in the early 1800s, moved to the southern Ethiopian marches in the 1890s. In that context, Luuq developed as the major trading place. In the context of the expansion of trade, Somaal traders from the coastal regions started to penetrate into the interior and to compete with caravan leaders and traders, fighting for control over the different stages of the trade from the coast to the Ethiopian highlands. During the nineteenth century, not a single group was able to establish control or dominance over the whole route. Rather, traders had to pay tribute to a local patron (Som. abbaan) and were at the same time protected by such an abbaan against competing traders:

> Generally a man of prestige and respected lineage in a specific locale, the abbaan oversaw the transactions performed by a trader passing through that locale. The abbaan negotiated the customs duties and presents expected by clan elders; he saw to the accommodation of the travelers; and he procured guides and camels for the ongoing journey. His also was the responsibility for securing reparations for goods stolen from or injuries inflicted upon his clients. (Cassanelli 1982: 157)

Often the abbaan provided credit and acted as an intermediary trader. Through the abbaan, the traders were integrated into respective clan structures (and rights), as well as obligations, and acquired protection for the duration of their stay in a specific community. This system of patronage kept bandits at bay, yet when trade routes became too insecure, traders would search for alternate routes and alternate sources of protection:

> Thus from Dulbahante country there were formerly two main caravan routes to the port of Berbera. . . . Caravans of sometimes as many as several hundred camels carrying gum, ye'eb nuts, ostrich feathers and ghee, and driving sheep and goats, and horses and camels for sale, made their way to the coast. At Bohotle they came under the protection of the Habar Tol Ja'lo (sub-clan); at Burao the Habar Tol Ja'lo handed over to the Habar Yuunis, at Sheikh they came under the protection of the Habar Awal 'Iise Muuse, and at Berbera they were protected by the Habar Awal Sa'ad Muuse, Reer Aḥmad. Another route lay through the Sarar plain where the Habar Tol Ja'lo conducted the caravans as far as Berbera. Here the patronage of the Habar Tol Ja'lo Reer Daahir was exchanged for the patronage of the Habar Awal, Reer Aḥmad. In this interlineage caravan trade, a protector was selected for his own good character and for the strength of his lineage and was paid a fee or given presents for his work. (Lewis 1961/1999: 187)

On the basis of this system of patronage and exchange, traders and Somaal clans developed long-term alliances of trade and protection which also provided security for the wadaad, the religious scholars and their educational activities. At the same time, the wadaad gave both traders and abbaan their spiritual protection, as in the case of the family of Shaykh Mu'min which dominated the route between Luuq and Mogadishu: "They were widely respected and feared for their purported ability to cast the evil eye" (Cassanelli 1982: 159). As religious scholars, they were respected and accepted as intermediaries in cases of conflict: "In return for fees they adjudicated commercial disputes or invoked supernatural protection for caravans" (Cassanelli 1982: 159). Due to this structure of long-distance trade, the Somaal and their coastal trading partners in Mogadishu, Brawa, and Marka, as well as Berbera in the north, largely managed to keep out external competitors from their trade routes, although this system of alliances between traders, abbaan, and wadaad seems to have weakened considerably in the course of the nineteenth century (see map 17).

The Jihād of Muḥammad ʿAbdille Ḥasan

Whereas the Muslim movements of reform in the early and mid-nineteenth century were not affected by schemes for colonial occupation, the movement initiated by Muḥammad ʿAbdille Ḥasan in the late nineteenth and early twentieth centuries developed very much in the context of Ethiopian, British, and Italian occupation of Somaal lands. Muḥammad ʿAbdille Ḥasan, who was addressed with the honorific title Sayyid by his followers, although his family could not claim sharīfian descent, was born in 1856 (1864 according to other sources) into the Dulbahante tribal group of the Nogal region of the northeastern Horn. His grandfather, Shaykh Ḥasan Nūr, was a religious scholar from the Ogaden region, and Muḥammad ʿAbdille Ḥasan also started out on a path of religious learning by memorizing the Qurʾān. After completing this task within a period of three years, he became an assistant to his teacher, and by the age of twenty he had acquired the reputation of a well-read scholar. In 1883, he left home and, in his ṭalab al-ʿilm, first visited Ḥarär, then the Sudan, where he witnessed the rise of the Mahdī, and then Mogadishu. In 1891 he settled in his home region and married, but left again in 1894 in order to undertake the pilgrimage. In Mecca, he was introduced by Shaykh Muḥammad b. Ṣāliḥ al-Rāshidī into the teachings of Aḥmad b. Idrīs and became a member of the Ṣāliḥiyya Sufi order, which was known for its sober teachings.

After his return to the Horn in 1896, he settled in the harbor city of Berbera, where he started to teach and preach his notions of reform. He attacked the consumption of alcohol, the use of tobacco and the chewing of qāt during the dhikr; he criticized the practice of tawassul (intercession) of the Sufi scholars, and quickly came to be known as an opponent of the local religious establishment, which consisted chiefly of scholars of the Qādiriyya. In addition, he was seen as a critic of the local traders, who were often linked with the scholars of the Qādiriyya, and who profited from the trade with the British in Berbera. In 1897, a consultation took place between the religious scholars of Berbera, in the presence of representatives of the most respected center of Islamic learning in the Ogaden region, the zāwiya of Shaykh ʿAbd al-Raḥmān al-Zaylaʿī (d. 1882) in Qulunqūl. In the course of this meeting, Muḥammad ʿAbdille Ḥasan told the religious scholars present that he was a member of the Ṣāliḥiyya Sufi order, and that the founder of this ṭarīqa would be the quṭb al-zamān (the pole, the supreme Sufi saint of the time). The scholars of the Qādiriyya responded to the claims of Muḥammad ʿAbdille Ḥasan by retaliating with their own polemics. Thus, Shaykh ʿAbdallāh b. Muʿallim Yūsuf al-Quṭubī al-Qulunqūlī (1881–1952), a scholar of the Qādiriyya, a follower of Shaykh ʿAbd al-Raḥmān al-Zaylaʿī in Qulunqūl, and a student of Shaykh Uways b. Muḥammad al-Barawī (see below), wrote a number of texts in the early twentieth century entitled *Al-sikkīn al-dabīḥa ʿalā l-kilāb al-nabīḥa* (The butcher's knife for the barking dogs) or

> The qāt tree or bush grows in highland Yemen, highland Ethiopia, and the higher regions of the northern Horn. The leaves of the qāt tree should preferably be chewed on the day of harvest. The chewing of qāt together with a group of friends is an integral part of the Yemeni siesta and has become the major event structuring the afternoon in the Muslim societies of Yemen, Ethiopia, and the Horn. In recent times, qāt has been adopted by Christian Ethiopians and has spread through Kenya. Religious scholars have long held theological discussions regarding the consumption of qāt, the intoxicating effects of which have been declared un-Islamic, similar to alcohol. However, while alcoholic drinks result from a process of fermentation, qāt, like coffee, tea, or tobacco, belongs to a category of drugs which have often been accepted by Muslims, due to their having both stimulating and soothing effects. In fact, Muḥammad ʿAbdille Ḥasan attacked the consumption of qāt only during religious ceremonies. It was this context, and not the consumption of qāt as such, that was the major bone of contention.

Naṣr al-mu'minūn ʿalā l-marāḍa al-mulḥidīn (The victory of the faithful over the rebellious heretics). In these polemical texts, the Ṣāliḥiyya was equated with the Khārijites, the Muʿtazilites, the Shīʿītes, and the Murjiʾites, as well as the Wahhābiyya, and accused of having taken its evil and obnoxious teachings from these groups. Also, Muḥammad ʿAbdille Ḥasan's teachings were said to be erroneous, "pharaonic," and "satanic," and the idea of killing one of his disciples was as recommended as the killing of one hundred unbelievers (quoted in Martin 1976: 200).

As Muḥammad ʿAbdille Ḥasan was unable to achieve anything in Berbera, he returned in 1898 to his home region, where he was respected as a religious scholar, and quickly acquired a reputation as a mediator in disputes and tribal feuds. Also, he started to prepare for the confrontation with his enemies and to assemble both arms and followers. In particular, he branded the British colonial power as the major enemy, for the British had started to extend their influence from Berbera into the hinterland; in addition, he targeted a Catholic mission in the region, the Franciscans, who had established a foothold in the northern Horn in 1891. The aim of the British at that time was simply to secure control of the coasts opposite ʿAden, the major British base on the way from the Mediterranean to India through the Suez Canal, and to prevent other colonial powers from gaining access to this strategic region. Muḥammad ʿAbdille Ḥasan had an early confrontation with the British, when he landed in Berbera on his way back from the pilgrimage and was asked by a British officer whether he had paid his custom fees and who had given him permission to land in Berbera at all. Muḥammad 'Abdille Ḥasan allegedly responded by asking the British officer whether he himself had paid any custom fees and who had given him permission to enter his country. When this response was translated, the Somaal translator added to his translation that this man was "the crazy shaykh" (Arab. al-shaykh al-majnūn) or "mad mullah"' (Martin 1976: 181), a nickname which stuck to Muḥammad 'Abdille Ḥasan in British colonial reports.

Only one year after Muḥammad 'Abdille Ḥasan's return to the Horn, an incident occurred which triggered a military conflict between him and his enemies: a detachment of tribal militia, armed by the British, visited Muḥammad 'Abdille Ḥasan and allegedly sold him a gun, while claiming after their return to Berbera that he had stolen the gun. The British consul in Berbera sent Muḥammad 'Abdille Ḥasan a letter asking him to return this weapon. The Sayyid refused to do this, convened a meeting of his followers, and asked them to join him in a jihād against the British:

> Unbelievers from foreign countries have attacked our country. They want to corrupt our religion and want to force us to become Christians, supported by the power of their government, their guns, their great numbers. You have only your faith in God, your guns and your courage. Don't be afraid of their soldiers and armies, as God is more powerful than them. Be patient and steadfast in this crisis. When you see people who help the unbelievers by showing them watering places or guide them on paths, they are spies and agents, attack them, as the Prophet has said: "Whoever turns his arms against us, is none of us." Our aim is to liberate the land from the unbelievers. (quoted in Martin 1976: 182)

The Dulbahante sub-clans of the region largely accepted this call to jihād and donned the white turban of the derwishes, as the followers of the "mad mullah" were called, probably as an echo of the British war against the Khalīfa 'Abdallāh and the Mahdiyya in the Sudan at the same time. The Dulbahante had a number of good reasons to put their energies into a jihād: first, the British had not concluded a trade agreement or treaty with them and favored competing clans; second, the Dulbahante felt threatened by the Ethiopian advance into the Ogaden, which formed part of Dulbahante pastures. The Ethiopians had actually started to raid their cattle and steal their camels. In 1899, more than 3000 Dulbahante warriors joined the jihād, and after a successful mission of mediation between two feuding Isaaq clans, the Habar Yunis and the Habar Tol Ja'lo, the Sayyid also gained the support of these groups which dominated the northwestern Horn. On 1 September 1899, Muḥammad 'Abdille Ḥasan formally opened the jihād against the British: on that day, the British consul in Berbera received a letter from the Sayyid in which Muḥammad 'Abdille Ḥasan accused the British of suppressing Islam. Subsequently, the British declared the Sayyid a rebel and started to organize military action against the "mad mullah."

Although Muḥammad 'Abdille Ḥasan had initially been successful in uniting a number of Somaal clans under this leadership, he did not manage to win the support of other clans which opposed his movement of reform. Thus, the jihād soon turned into a conflict between feuding Somaal clans. The British and later the Italians used these rivalries, and armed the enemies of the Sayyid in order to defeat the derwishes. One of the first actions of Muḥammad ʿAbdille Ḥasan was directed against the Sulṭān of the Habar Yunis, who refused to join the jihād. In this case, the Sayyid was able to convince the clan to depose their leader and join him. Two other religious communities in the region which refused to join the Sayyid were raided and destroyed. However, even among the Dulbahante not all were willing to join the jihād. When Muḥammad ʿAbdille Ḥasan sent out a commando to kill these dissidents, other Dulbahante came to their support. The Sayyid was forced to leave the Dulbahante region and to join the clan of his grandfather in the Ogaden.

One of the first military successes of the Sayyid was a raid on the Ethiopian garrison of Jigjiga. Although the Ethiopian army succeeded in repulsing this attack, the warriors of Muḥammad ʿAbdille Ḥasan recuperated all cattle which had been stolen by the Ethiopians. In a further raid against an Isaaq clan allied with the British, the Sayyid was able to take 2,000 camels and to gain control over some valuable pastures which had been disputed for some time. While Muḥammad ʿAbdille Ḥasan cultivated these guerrilla tactics in the following years with variegated success, the British organized four major military expeditions against the Sayyid, the last in 1904. These expeditions brought no result, however, and in one case even led to a major British defeat: in a skirmish in the Gumburu hills, the British lost nine officers and 189 soldiers, as well as ten maxim guns. As both sides were exhausted by this time, Muḥammad ʿAbdille Ḥasan and the British entered into negotiations and eventually concluded a treaty on 5 March 1905 which granted Muḥammad ʿAbdille Ḥasan sovereignty over his followers, religious freedom, and free trade. The Italian administration granted Muḥammad ʿAbdille Ḥasan a territory of his own in the north of the Italian colonial realm, which had not yet come under direct Italian control, and Muḥammad ʿAbdille Ḥasan subsequently started to establish his own state in this region.

The foundations of Muḥammad ʿAbdille Ḥasan's state were the Qurʾān and the sharīʿa, based on the teachings of the Shāfiʿī school of law. The tribal laws of the Somaal were prohibited. Women were granted a greater role in the community and even formed their own cavalry units, but had to wear the ḥijāb. The armed forces of the community were not organized according to clan loyalties but transgressed tribal boundaries. Islamic rituals were strictly enforced. However, even before this community could consolidate into a state, the British were able to score a remarkable propagandistic coup against the Sayyid: one of his old allies, ʿAbdallāh Sheheri of the Habar Tol Jaʾlo, who was angry because a number of his relatives had been imprisoned by the Sayyid, was persuaded by the British in 1908 to go on a mission to Mecca, where he met the leader of the Ṣāliḥiyya Sufi order, Muḥammad b. Ṣāliḥ. Responding to the account of ʿAbdallāh Sheheri, Muḥammad b. Ṣāliḥ wrote a letter to the Sayyid in which he condemned his actions and threatened to exclude him from the Ṣāliḥiyya. Both the British and the Italians instrumentalized this letter and circulated it in their territories, with the result that many followers of the Sayyid left him in 1909, while others, like the qāḍī of Illig, ʿAbdallāh Koryo, who stayed despite their critique, were executed.

Even before this crisis hit the community of the Sayyid, war resumed in 1908. Muḥammad ʿAbdille Ḥasan had used the time since 1905 to win allies in the south, where the collapse of the slave trade from the 1870s and Ethiopian advances along the Juba and Shebelle had led to economic disruption. In addition, an epidemic of rinderpest in 1890 and 1891 had decimated the cattle of the Somaal clans on the lower Shebelle and Juba, as in many other parts of Africa at this time. This catastrophe had been aggravated by a serious drought in the late 1890s. In 1891, an Italian administrator, Ugo Ferrandi, reported that the cattle of the Somaal in the lower Juba and Shebelle region had been virtually wiped out, and that the hinterland of Mogadishu was "whitened by bones" (Reese 2008: 106). As a consequence, many indigenous Somaal traders who had entrusted their merchandise to people in the interior received no return on their investment and were squeezed out of business in the years to come by Indian and Arab traders from Zanzibar. The hegemony of local traders under the abbaan system thus collapsed due to the ecological catastrophe and epidemics of the 1890s. The establishment of Italian control over the coastal cities of Mogadishu, Brawa, and Marka in the 1890s, and a first Italian expedition to Luuq in 1895, added to insecurity and led to the religious reorientation of sizeable parts of the population in these regions. The people either joined movements of reform within the Qādiriyya, led by Shaykh Uways al-Barawī, or started to listen to the emissaries of Muḥammad ʿAbdille Ḥasan, who was able to win new followers among the Bimaal on the lower Shebelle and Juba Rivers.

While Muḥammad ʿAbdille Ḥasan was successful among the Bimaal, other Somaal in the region tended to follow Shaykh Uways b. Muḥammad al-Barawī, who was probably the first religious scholar from Brawa not only to visit the holy places in the Ḥijāz, but also to study at the center of the Qādiriyya in Baghdad, and to acquire a direct and thus powerful spiritual link to the oldest Sufi order in Islam. His teacher in Baghdad was Shaykh Muṣṭafā b. al-Sayyid Salmān al-Jīlānī, who also initiated Shaykh Uways al-Barawī into the teachings of the Qādiriyya. After his pilgrimage and further years of study in Baghdad, Shaykh Uways al-Barawī returned in 1883 to Brawa, where he tried to claim leadership of the local Qādiriyya, a claim disputed by other local Qādirī scholars. Still, he was very successful in other parts of the East African coast, in particular Zanzibar, and eventually gained respect in Brawa. This development seems to have been linked with the expansion of Muḥammad ʿAbdille Ḥasan's movement of reform in southern Somalia. The spread of his movement of reform convinced leading scholars of the Qādiriyya in Brawa to shelve their personal disputes and to unite in the struggle against Muḥammad ʿAbdille Ḥasan, who was known to have attacked the Qādiriyya in northern Somalia. In one of his poems, Shaykh Uways al-Barawī attacked

Muḥammad 'Abdille Ḥasan and the derwishes in a rather rude way, reflecting the style of scholarly confrontation at the time:

> Blessed are the Prophet and his family: turn to him in disaster. He who is guided by the law of the Prophet will not follow Satan. He who approves of the killing of the scholars; and those who steal money and women: they are outlaws. They oppose the sciences, like law and grammar; any shaykh like al-Jilani, they dispute their link to God. Do not follow the men with long hair: they are characterized by this haircut of the Wahhabis. In public, they sell the paradise for money. In our lands they are a sect of dogs: they have illicit sexual intercourse with all women, even their own mothers. They follow their own subjective opinions and not a book, as we do. Their light comes from Satan, they reject God in their dhikr: they are unbelievers in words and deeds. (quoted in Martin 1976: 161–62)

In their endeavors to oppose Muḥammad 'Abdille Ḥasan, the leaders of the Qādiriyya were supported by the recently established Italian colonial administration which desperately sought local allies for its efforts to expand into the hinterland, in particular the Bimaal region on the lower Shebelle and Juba Rivers. Due to the fact that the Italian administration supported the scholars of the Qādiriyya, the latter were soon accused of collaborating with the colonial power and of having abandoned Islam. This argument was taken up by Muḥammad 'Abdille Ḥasan in his polemics against the scholars of the Qādiriyya dating from 1904, in particular in his *Risālat al-bimāl* (The Bimaal epistle), written in 1905 in the context of a first Bimaal war against the Italians. In 1907, the followers of Muḥammad 'Abdille Ḥasan among the Bimaal, led by Abdi Abiker Gafle, again took up the jihād against the Italians in the south, and attacked the allies of the Italians, in particular the communities of Shaykh Uways, in southern Somalia. On 14 April 1909, in one of these attacks on Biyole, a community of his disciples 150 kilometers north of Brawa, Shaykh Uways was killed by followers of Muḥammad 'Abdille Ḥasan. His tomb soon became a center of local shrine pilgrimage. The Italian administration, on the other hand, managed to suppress the resistance of the Bimaal by 1910. In January 1908, followers of the Sayyid also attacked a British position in the north, triggering a complete British withdrawal to Berbera from all inland positions, following a mission of enquiry led by Sir Reginald Wingate, the British governor of the Sudan, as well as Rudolph Slatin Pasha, the Austro-Hungarian advisor on Islamic affairs to the British government in the Sudan. At the same time, the British started to arm the major opponents of the Sayyid in the north, the Isaaq, who now became the major enemies of the Sayyid in this region. In the following three years, the northern Horn saw a bloody civil war between the Isaaq and the forces of the Sayyid, a period which came to be called by Somaal elders the "time of eating dirt" (Lewis 1988: 77).

As war and famine led to the complete collapse of the meat supply for the British garrisons in Berbera and 'Aden, the British decided to explore the interior again in 1912. They realized that one-third of the population had died by that time. With their new camel corps, however, the British were able to regain control over their old sphere of influence and to push the troops of the Sayyid into the Ogaden. When they tried to gain control over the Ogaden, in 1913, they suffered a humiliating military defeat, in which the commander of the British forces, Corfield, was killed. At the same time, the Sayyid gained a surprising new ally: the Ethiopian emperor Lij (Prince) Iyassu (r. 1913–1916) established contact with Muḥammad ʿAbdille Ḥasan in 1915 and supplied him with arms. He also sent a German engineer, Emil Kirsch, who was forced to help the Sayyid to transform the major basis of the jihād, Taleh, into a system of modern fortifications. Emil Kirsch later tried to flee from Taleh but died of thirst on his way to the coast. The fortifications in Taleh, constructed by Yemeni builders, enabled the troops of the Sayyid to hold out against the British until 1920. In 1914, the derwishes even conquered Hargeisa and Burao and attacked Berbera. These victories were spectacular yet easy due to the fact that the British had almost completely evacuated Somaliland during World War I. In 1917, Muḥammad ʿAbdille Ḥasan again wrote a polemical letter to the British Commissioner in Berbera:

> You insinuate that we have been in contact with Lij Iyassu and that we had relations with the Germans and with the Turkish Sultan, because we were weak and needed support. You insinuate that if we had been strong, we would not have been in need of such friendship. These are the most characteristic arguments of your letter, and here is my response: I tell you, what stupidity! . . . You know, and I know what the Turks have achieved and what the Germans have achieved against you. Your assumption was that I was weak and that I would have to look for friends. Yet, even if this had been true and if I had been forced to look for allies, then this was only due to you, the British and the problems you have created for me. You have been the ones to have allied with the peoples of the world, with whores and do-no-goods, with slaves even, as you are so weak. If you would have been strong, you would have been able to stand for yourself, independently and free, as we do. However, you have concluded alliances with the Somaal, those lakays, and the Arabs, the Sudanese and the Kafirs, those perverted ones, the Yemenites and the Nubians, Indians, Balutch, French and Russians, Americans, Italians, Serbs, Portuguese and Japanese, Greek and cannibals, Sikhs and Banyans, Moors, Afghans and Egyptians. They are strong and they are strong because you are weak, so that you have to ask them for help like prostitutes. (quoted in Lewis 1988: 79 and del Boca 1992: 856)

As the British were not able to fight Muḥammad ʿAbdille Ḥasan properly during World War I, they imposed an embargo on the coast and tried to cut off his supply of arms. In 1920, they finally started a major military operation against Taleh and bombed this stronghold from airplanes, as they had done in their war against Sulṭān ʿAlī Dinār in Dārfūr in 1916. The troops of the Sayyid tried to escape into the Ogaden but were machine-gunned from the air. On Ethiopian territory, Muḥammad ʿAbdille Ḥasan was able to reorganize his forces yet had to move further south due to attacks by his old enemies, the Isaaq. In late 1920, he reached the community of Shaykh Muḥammad Gulayd on the Shebelle. In southern Somalia, Shaykh Muḥammad

Gulayd (d. 1918) had introduced the same reformist teachings of Shaykh Muḥammad Ṣāliḥ that Muḥammad ʿAbdille Ḥasan had taught in the north, and that linked the Ṣāliḥiyya through Ibrāhīm al-Rashīd (d. 1874) to Aḥmad b. Idrīs. Soon after his arrival, Muḥammad ʿAbdille Ḥasan died on 21 December 1920 (on 23 November 1920, according to other sources), possibly a victim of the global influenza pandemic which had started to ravage the world in 1918 and which did not stop at the coasts of Somalia or in the deserts of the Horn.

10 The East African Coast

Historical and Thematic Patterns

Whereas seas of sand connect the northern and southern shores of the Sahara, the Indian Ocean and annual monsoon winds connect the East African coast with the shores of India and Arabia. The regional orientation toward India and southern Arabia also informed the development of East Africa's Muslim societies. The Shāfiʿī school of law came to predominate in eastern Africa, whereas the Muslims in sub-Saharan West Africa joined the Mālikī school of law. In contrast to the bilād al-maghrib, the Sahara and the bilād al-sūdān, as well as the Nile Sudan and even Ethiopia, Islam in East Africa remained confined for almost one thousand years to the littoral zones, the sawāḥil, where a Muslim culture developed, characterized by a common language (Kiswahili) and a culture of seafaring and long-distance trade. In the East African interior, Islam started to spread, again through Muslim traders, in the nineteenth century only. The possible emergence of Muslim states, as in Buganda, was stopped by encroaching colonial rule. We have to understand thus the historical development of Muslim East Africa as two separate histories: the long history of the Muslim societies on the coast which were oriented toward the Indian Ocean; and the short history of the Muslim populations of the East African interior, upcountry Kenya, Uganda, mainland Tanzania, and also eastern Congo, where small Muslim communities started to develop from the late nineteenth century. While the history of Islam in the East African hinterland is a comparatively recent development, Muslim societies on the coast could look back, in the nineteenth century, on a history of more than one thousand years.

Despite their linguistic, cultural, religious, and economic homogeneity, Muslim coastal societies have been characterized by a history of competition (Swa. mashindano) between different coastal towns such as Brawa, Lamu, Pate, Malindi, Mombasa, or Kilwa, most of which are situated like a string of pearls on peninsulas or islands off the coast. The trading centers and towns of the East African coast never came to form empires in the Sudanic style, and at those times when the East African coast was united in political terms it was united by external powers, namely the Portuguese in the sixteenth and seventeenth centuries, and the Sulṭānate of Oman in the nineteenth century. The history of the western Indian Ocean was equally characterized by the fact that the west and south Asian continental empires, such as the Sulṭānate of Delhi, the Moghuls, and the Safawids in Iran, never attempted to establish and sustain political hegemony over the ocean by building and maintaining a navy, unlike the Mediterranean and Atlantic, where littoral powers such as Venice, Genoa, France, Spain, and the Ottoman empire tried to gain hegemonic control over the seas. The Mediterranean concept of naval domination and armed trade was imported by the Portuguese into the western Indian Ocean in the sixteenth century, defeating the efforts of the Ottoman empire to gain a foothold there. In the seventeenth century, other European powers, as well as Oman, eventually joined the competition for hegemonic control over the western Indian Ocean.

As mentioned above, East Africa's coastal ("Swahili") settlements never achieved political unity, although trading centers such as Mombasa and Kilwa tried to control large stretches of the coast. Coastal settlements can thus be seen as a series of independent and competing centers of trade, each ruled by a patriciate of aristocrats, nobles, religious scholars, and rich traders. These elites cultivated trade interests across the western Indian Ocean and often invested in ships or plantations, yet were not really interested in establishing (costly) political domination over the hinterland, the bush (Swa. nyika). Equally, coastal settlements competed among each other and were prepared to conclude alliances with external powers, which promised to damage the interests of local competitors. At the same time, coastal settlements developed symbiotic links with their immediate neighbors, the "bush people" (Swa. wanyika). These included the Pokomo on the Lower Tana, who came to supply the islands of the Lamu archipelago with grains; the Digo, the Mijikenda, and other groups in the neighborhood of Mombasa; the Segeju of Vanga; or the Zaramo on the mainland opposite Zanzibar. These wanyika populations supplied the settlements and towns of the Swahili on the coast and on the islands off the coast with specific foods and raw materials, such as mangrove poles, which were then traded across the Indian Ocean. The East African coastal strip between the Juba in the north and the Rufiji in the south can thus be understood as a narrow stretch of more or less fertile land along the coast, which did not extend more than ten to fifteen kilometers inland, perhaps more along rivers such as the Juba/Shebelle, the Tana, and the Pangani, and acted, at least until the nineteenth century, as a transmission belt for trade further inland.

Although the wanyika populations on the coastal strip developed symbiotic relationships with the Swahili proper, they remained anchored in African religious traditions until the nineteenth century, when a movement of conversion to Islam began. The Pokomo, Segeju, Mijikenda, Digo, and Zaramo on the East African coast thus cannot be regarded as being an intrinsic part of Swahili history and society until the nineteenth century. Rather, the wanyika villages of the coastal strip formed a node between the Swahili settlements on and off the coast as well as the trading groups from the hinterland, linking the coastal strip with the upcountries of East Africa. At the same time, the Swahili settlements on the coast or on the islands off the coast constituted the node for the trade across the ocean. The Swahili settlements focused on their gardens, their crafts, and the sea and saw no need to establish direct contact with the inland trade. Only in the nineteenth century, with the increasing integration of the wanyika

> It should be mentioned in this context that the term Swahili (Arab. sawāḥila) became current only in the nineteenth century, and originally was a derogatory Arabic term for "de-tribalized" Africans living on the coast, often of slave descent. This term was accepted, however, in the late nineteenth and early twentieth centuries by an increasing number of coastal Africans, who used the term to identify themselves with an esteemed coastal culture and to create a distance between themselves and more recent migrants to the coast from the East African hinterlands. European visitors equally adopted the term as an umbrella label for coastal Africans, who were seen as having corrupted pure Arabic Islam while having abandoned at the same time their authentic and rustic African village traditions.

populations into Swahili society, and the expansion of Indian and Omani traders on the coast, did coastal traders start to go beyond the coastal strip, establishing direct contacts with the hinterland while hinterland trading groups started to bring their goods directly into the settlements and towns of the Swahili.

In the greater trade network of the western Indian Ocean, the East African coast seems to have provided iron ore, at least in an early stage of commercial development up to the eleventh century, which was eventually replaced by a much more valuable product, gold. Gold came to dominate the exports of the coast from at least the thirteenth century. In addition, the harbors of the coast exported ivory, mangrove poles, and grains, as well as slaves. Slaves from the East African harbors were identified in Arabic and Persian ports as Zanj (Pers. black) and were exported from East Africa at least from the seventh century onward. Major destinations were India, the oases of southern Persia, the Gulf, and Oman, as well as the large irrigation-fed plantations of southern Mesopotamia, where Zanj slaves became notorious for their repeated rebellions in 695, 751, and 869, recorded by Arab historians such as al-Ṭabarī. The major rebellion of the Zanj in 869 led to the establishment of an independent state of former slaves in southern Iraq. In 869, Zanj armies not only destroyed the major city in southern Iraq, Baṣra, but also held out against ʿAbbasid repression until 883. In general, the history of the East African slave trade may be divided into two boom periods, which are difficult to assess in terms of numbers, due to lack of sources: an early period from the seventh to the tenth centuries, and a later period from the seventeenth to the nineteenth centuries. In the second peak period, slaves were still brought from the East African hinterlands to southern Arabia, Persia, and India, but an increasing number went to the European sugar plantations on Mauritius and Reunion, or to plantations established on the East African coast proper, in particular on the islands of Unguja and Pemba, as well as the hinterlands of the northern coastal towns of Lamu, Malindi,

> At least from the eleventh century, Zanj slaves from East Africa, as well as Ḥabshi slaves from Ethiopia, were brought to India, in particular to Sindh, Gujarat, and Karnataka. From the harbor cities on India's western coast, slaves were traded to the Sulṭānate of Delhi, to Bengal, and to the principalities of the Dekkan, where they were employed as military slaves (Arab. mamlūk). In Bengal, African military slaves eventually became so powerful that they were able to take over the government in 1483 and to rule over Bengal until 1493. In the Bahmani kingdom of Dekkan, which had split from the Sulṭānate of Delhi in the late fourteenth century, Ḥabshi slaves took power in 1481 for a short period of time. Not all Ethiopians in Arabia or India were slaves, however. In the context of his maritime journey down the Indian Malabar coast in the early fourteenth century, Ibn Baṭṭūṭa reports that transport security and protection against pirates was ensured by archers from Ethiopia: "wa-kāna fīhī khamsūn rāmiyan wa-khamsūn min al-muqātila al-ḥabasha wa-hum zu'amā' hadha al-baḥr wa-idhan kāna bi-l-markab aḥad minhum tuḥāmāha luṣūṣ al-hunūd wa-kuffārihim" (". . . and on it [the ship] were fifty archers and fifty Ethiopian warriors. They are the guarantors [of peace] of this ocean and if only one of them happens to be on the ship, he protects it against the Indian pirates and unbelievers") (Ibn Baṭṭūṭa 1985 2: 632).

and Mombasa. In the Gulf, in southern Persia, in Arabia, and in Oman, East African slaves were employed in crafts, such as pearl diving, the maintenance of irrigation channels, or work in the date palm groves and plantations. In the nineteenth century, the fight against the slave trade from East Africa served as a legitimization for European intervention on the East African coast, and the trade was eventually suppressed in the late nineteenth century.

In contrast to the neighboring wanyika of the coastal strip, or the "washenzi" (savages) from the hinterlands, the inhabitants of the coastal settlements saw themselves as waungwana (civilized, free). In addition, they conceived of themselves as citizens of Lamu, Pate, Malindi, Mombasa, or Zanzibar, and thus not as a single people or even a nation, but rather as a plethora of coastal populations, united by a common culture yet divided by a multitude of parochialities. Within the coastal settlements, the citizens of Lamu or Mombasa made internal distinctions between families of Arabic (Omani, Ḥaḍrami, Yemeni, Ḥijāzi), Persian, or Indian origin, or by identifying themselves as coming from other coastal cities such as Brawa or Malindi. A major identifying factor for life in the Swahili settlements was that they combined a multitude of occupations: traders, fishermen, farmers, gardeners, craftsmen, and scholars lived side by side in coastal settlements which were semi-urban and semi-rural, stone houses mixed with huts and gardens. Swahili settlements consisted of village-like quarters (Swa. mikao); the inhabitants of a quarter were bound by alliances of mutual help, cooperation, and exchange, and in cases of a serious external threat they would form a greater alliance with the other quarters of the respective town (Swa. mji). Only some settlements, such as Kilwa, Malindi, Pate, Mogadishu, Brawa, Lamu, and Mombasa, as well as Zanzibar from the nineteenth century, acquired a more urban character; here, gardens and plantations gradually disappeared from the towns, and were replaced by an increasing number of two- or three-storey stone houses. Within such an old town (Swa. mji mkongwe), communities remained stratified, however, with established waungwana populations forming ruling elites, which relegated slaves and immigrants in both spatial and social terms to the lower and outer spheres of the settlement. For these marginal populations, conversion to Islam came to mean a way into the town and into social acceptance. This dynamic also applied to slaves. Within a few generations, they could aspire to rise from their status as plantation slaves to the status of (Muslim) house slaves, and thence to the status of former slaves, employed as educated servants, and eventually to the status of independent craftsmen, tenant farmers, fishermen, and sailors, in other words non-propertied but free people who could even start their own trade in slaves with the hinterland. The spread of coastal culture can thus be understood as the expansion of a way of life rather than the spread of a political model. This way of life was characterized by the blending of different economic activities, with a distinct coastal architecture, religion, and language. And although Kiswahili eventually came to comprise about twenty local dialects from Kiamu (Lamu) in the north to Kingajiza on the Comoros in the south, and later also Kingwana on the Upper Congo, it became a language of communication that was understood not only on the coast but also in the African hinterlands, as well as in other port cities of the Indian Ocean, particularly in Southern Arabia.

The history of the East African coast has been interpreted and reinterpreted over time. Colonial discourses, for instance, stressed external sources of inspiration as being paramount for the development of the coastal culture, and saw East African coastal history as being informed by a series of immigrants from southern Arabia, Iran, and India; by contrast, postcolonial historians have stressed the Africanité of East African coastal history and deemphasized external influences, interpreting coastal culture as Bantu. In recent years, a readjustment of these paradigms of explanation has taken place, and East African coastal history is increasingly viewed as a result of both African and Indian Ocean influences, remixed in many different ways in different coastal microhistories. Having said this, it has to be stressed that both colonial and postcolonial paradigms of interpretation rely on the formulation of precolonial histories and myths. Depending on the time and the respective cultural orientation, local histories were presented as being formed by immigrants from Oman, Ḥaḍramawt, or Shiraz, or as a history of symbiotic relationships between the populations of a specific coastal region, such as Mombasa and its immediate hinterland. The development of Islamic traditions of learning on the coast has indeed been influenced by the migration of Muslims to the East African coast from across the Indian Ocean. East African coastal history has consequently been presented as a history of immigration of Muslims from Arabia, India, and Persia. Due to the development of local centers of Islamic learning in coastal settlements such as Mogadishu, Brawa, Lamu, Pate, Mombasa, Malindi, or Kilwa, historical sources on the East African coast are fairly comprehensive, as in the bilād al-sūdān, and give a good impression of the development of the coast from the early sixteenth century.

The first instances of Arab (Muslim) immigration may have occurred in the seventh century, bringing Muslim dissident groups from Oman as recorded in the chronicle of Pate. In the eighth century, other dissident groups may have come from Syria (Shām), coming to be known in Kilwa and Pate as Wa-Shami, although the Nabahānī family in Pate which claimed Syrian origin in fact came from Oman. The thirteenth century saw the first large wave of migrants from Ḥaḍramawt to the East African coast, and from this time onward Ḥaḍramī migrants came to represent a major immigrant group in many settlements. In particular, families of sharīfian descent from Tarīm and Shibām established trade interests and even took power in Kilwa around 1300.

The Comoro islands (Arab. juzur al-qamr) may be regarded as the remotest point of Muslim expansion on the East African coast except for Madagascar. Four major islands, Ngajiza, Nzawani, Mayuta, and Mwali, form a continuation of the East African coast toward the south. At the same time, the Comoros have acquired a distinct character due to their closeness to Madagascar and strong historical links to the Ḥaḍramawt. The Comoros have been a major place of Islamic learning and produced a number of eminent scholars in the nineteenth and twentieth centuries. Since the sixteenth century, the Comoros have been split into small Sultanates, each ruling over a few valleys only. From the late eighteenth century, the Comoros, like parts of the East African coast, suffered under Betsimisaraka and Sakalava slave raids. These raids increased between 1795 and 1816; only in 1817 did Betsimisaraka and Sakalava raids come to an end, when the Omani navy destroyed a large fleet of Sakalava outrigger war-canoes in the Ruvuma delta. In the 1820s, both the Sakalava in western Madagascar and the Betsimisaraka in northeastern Madagascar were defeated by the Imerina kingdom of central Madagascar, while the Comoros came under the influence of the sultanate of Zanzibar and remained formally part of Zanzibar until 1886, when France took control of Ngajiza.

A further but very small group of immigrants were Khātimī Arabs from al-Andalus, who reached the East African coast in the early sixteenth century, looking for a new home and eventually settling in Brawa and Pate. In the sixteenth century, a second wave of settlers from Ḥaḍramawt came to the East African coast and reached the Comoros. These immigrants strengthened local centers of Islamic learning and helped coastal settlements to fight Portuguese hegemony and Christian mission endeavors in this period. In the nineteenth century, a third wave of immigrants from Ḥaḍramawt reached the East African coast, as did a considerable number of families from Oman. In 1850, about 85 percent of all religious scholars on the East African coast were affiliated with Ḥaḍramī families. It has to be stressed, however, that these migrations were never sizeable enough to dominate coastal society. The migrants blended into the local societies and were seen as local by the next generation of immigrants. In addition, migrants from either the African interior or the immediate coastal hinterlands equally settled on the coast and on the islands, and formed a majority of the population in the Swahili settlements. As a result, each coastal settlement developed a unique history of immigration and interaction with migrants of different origins. These different historical legacies were recorded in local chronicles, often serving to support efforts at legitimization in respect of political change in specific places and at specific times.

As in the bilād al-sūdān of sub-Saharan West Africa, the East African coast saw a veritable explosion of local literatures in the nineteenth century, when existing disciplines of Islamic learning, as well as historical records and poetry, were complemented by new literary genres, such as biographies and travel accounts. A literary genre which developed in the nineteenth century in the context of the emergence of the celebration of the mawlid al-nabī was madḥ (praise) poetry. Mawlid celebrations were initially based on the solemn recitation of the mawlid barzanjī, which seems to have been translated into Kiswahili relatively early, and which was then transformed into a rather ecstatic "mawlidi ya Kiswahili." The popularity of new rituals in the nineteenth century, and their contextualization in Kiswahili, was closely linked with the influx of non-Muslim migrants and slaves to the coast from the African interior in this period of time. These newcomers saw conversion to Islam and participation in Islamic ritual as a way of achieving integration in coastal society and gaining the acceptance of local Muslims. In the context of their social rise, migrants and slaves adopted Islamic rituals and practices but often transformed the Arabic versions of these rituals into local versions, which were eventually condemned by established religious scholars as un-Islamic innovations.

Conversion to Islam and the adopting of Islamic lifestyles was thus an important factor in the development of an East African coastal identity. A major obstacle for converts, however, was the fact that control over Islamic institutions, mosques, schools, and religious foundations, as well as the administration of Islamic law, lay in the hands of the Waungwana elites who refused to accept conversion and the social integration of converts. Due to the exclusion of slaves and immigrants from the sphere of established religion and social institutions, converts started to organize their own Islamic ritual life. Islamization was also expressed in patterns of dress, in the spread of Islamic amulets, in the acceptance of male circumcision, and in rituals of healing. Even if problematic from a short-term perspective, integration into established coastal society was viable from a long-term perspective, and while conversion to Islam was an important step, the acquisition of symbols of status such as a house of stone, ownership over a shamba (farm), education, and dress were important as well.

The development of Islam on the coast was thus influenced by three major factors. In the course of time, Muslims in the coastal settlements formed local traditions of learning which continued to evolve over time in the context of local dynamics of development. At the same time, local traditions of learning and Muslim modes of daily life received inspiration from other parts of the Muslim world, mostly other regions of the Indian Ocean, often in the form of a movement of reform. These traditions of learning and Muslim modes of life finally had to come to terms with the immigration of non-Muslims from the African hinterlands, often slaves and workers, a fact which has often been neglected in the history of the East African coast. The development of Islamic traditions of learning and the emergence of Muslim modes of life on the coast can thus be understood best as a process of cumulative adoption of Islam, and as the gradual intensification of an Islamic coastal identity from Mogadishu in the north to Sofala in the south (see map 18).

From Shungwaya to Kilwa

The center of origin of a distinct coastal culture was probably a region called Shungwaya, where first settlements developed, such as Lamu, Pate, Shanga, Faza, and Siyu. These settlements were set in a maze of islands north of the delta of the Tana River, protected by inlets, sandbanks, and reefs against enemies from both the hinterland and the ocean. The name of the region, Shungwaya, also came to connote the early phase of the history of the coast from the seventh to the eleventh centuries. This period of time can be regarded as the formative period of a distinct coastal culture and as the period in which Islam became the dominant religion on the coast, although the origins of Swahili culture are still obscure and not documented by local sources. Chronicles provide hard data for the history of places like Kilwa and Pate from the sixteenth century only, while Arabic sources are silent about the historical roots of Swahili society. From Shungwaya in the north, Swahili culture spread to other places in the north such as Mogadishu, Brawa, Marka, and Kismayo, as well as down the coast, and eventually reached the region of Kilwa, south of the Rufiji in the eleventh century.

In the twelfth century, Swahili culture already reached so far south that Arab geographers started to use three terms for the different sections of the coast: Shungwaya in the north, often also called Berber, then Zanj in the center, dominated by Malindi, and finally Sofala, the land of gold, in the south. The first proper description of the East African coast by the Arab geographer al-Masʿūdī (d. 956) mentions that a king of the Zanj was called mfalme (chief, pl.: wafalme). The Zanj regarded their rulers as sacred, and the island of Qanbalu (possibly a location on Pemba) had a Muslim population speaking a Zanj language (al-Masʿūdī 1982: 185). More detailed information was offered by al-Idrīsī, who named a number of places such as Malindi, Mombasa, Sofala, and Angatija (Ngazija). Al-Idrīsī also mentioned that the Muslim population of the East African coast knew healers (maqanqa; Swa. mganga, pl. waganga). A number of other Arab geographers added to this knowledge of the coast in the twelfth and thirteenth centuries, pointing out that Mogadishu in the north had a black population and that there was a whole series of settlements down the coast, apart from Lamu, such as Qanbalu on Pemba, Gedi between Mombasa and Malindi, or Manda, as well as Pate, Kilwa, and Unguja Ukuu. In the twelfth and thirteenth centuries, further settlements emerged, such as Marka and Brawa in the north, Faza in the Lamu archipelago, or Vumba and Kilwa further south. These all rose to regional prominence, although many experienced a period of decline later, often due to the fact that harbors silted up and had to be refounded on other stretches of the coast or on islands off the coast.

A second and better documented period of East African coastal history started in the eleventh century and saw the emergence of a number of Shirazi ruling families, first in Mogadishu and later in coastal settlements further south. Due to the major historical importance of the Shirazi, the period of cultural and economic blooming from the eleventh to the early sixteenth century has been labeled the Shirazi period. At the same time, the Shirazi period marks a regional shift of the center of Swahili culture from the north to the south, and saw the emergence of Kilwa as the paramount urban center on the coast. The Shirazi period was a period of cultural and economic boom on the East African coast: numerous new settlements were founded, trade with the African hinterland developed, more and more houses were built in stone, larger mosques were constructed, and Islam became the established religion on the coast. Also, Swahili developed as the language of communication on the coast and the Shāfiʿī school of law became the accepted school of Islamic law. Still, coastal settlements and towns kept their independence and tried to gain maximum control over the coastal trade, in competition with other settlements. In this competition, Kilwa achieved a paramount role since it controlled the sea routes down the coast to Sofala. The history of the coast thus was characterized by a shift from one major city to another, each trying to control as much of the coast as possible, while smaller settlements would be keen to guard their independence.

Whereas Mogadishu seems to have been paramount in the north until the thirteenth century, Kilwa rose to prominence in the south in the early thirteenth century. At the same time, Mogadishu's role in the north was eclipsed by Pate. Under the reign of Muḥammad II b. Aḥmad (1291–1331), Pate gained hegemony within the Lamu archipelago and was eventually able to extend its influence over the Bajuni islands in the north, then Brawa and finally even Mogadishu. Muḥammad II b. Aḥmad's son ʿUmar (r. 1331–1347) expanded Pate's influence south to Manda, and perhaps even Mombasa.

> From the eleventh century, a number of migrant groups on the East African coast became known as Shirazi, credited with having established a number of ruling families. In a chronicle of the Comoros, the advent of the Shirazi was described as follows: "Seven sons of the king of Shiraz, each one with his own ship, came to the East African coast: one to Qumr (Comoros), one to Swahili, one to Zanzibar, one to Kilwa, one to Nguji (Angoche, on the African coast opposite the Comoro islands), one to Nzuwani (Anjouan, another island of the Comoros) and the last to Bukini (Madagascar). In each place, the Shirazi took power and became the kings" (quoted in Rotter 1976: 25). Trade and seafaring in the Indian ocean have indeed been informed by Iranian influences, as expressed in Persian loanwords in Kiswahili or the celebration of the Iranian new year festival Nauroz on the East African coast. Also, Siraf, a major harbor on the Iranian coast of the Gulf between the eighth and the tenth centuries, could have constituted a link between Shiraz and the East African coast. Followers of the Shīʿī Buyid dynasty, who ruled both Shiraz and Baghdad from 945 but were defeated by the Sunni Saljuks in 1055, could have fled from Shiraz through Siraf to the East African coast in the eleventh century and were seen there as noble outsiders and cultural heroes: Shirazi descent thus provided a tale of dynastic legitimacy for a number of new ruling families on the East African coast and served to demonstrate the connectedness of the new rulers with a prestigious center of the Islamic world. Shirazi Iranian descent could be claimed particularly by southern coastal settlements in their endeavors to distinguish themselves from competing sharīfian Arab legacies on the northern coast. Shirazi descent could equally express the wish of Shungwaya populations to show their newly acquired rootedness in an increasingly metropolitan Muslim identity, similar to the way in which dynastic changes in Kānim or Gao expressed reorientation toward Sunni Islam in the eleventh century.

Only when the Portuguese established control over the East African coast was Pate's paramount position broken and taken over by both Mombasa and Malindi. Until the late fifteenth century, Kilwa was the most important center of the southern coast, however. The Kilwa chronicle, a sixteenth-century record of the city of Kilwa, documented Kilwa's development. Being situated, like most coastal settlements, on a small island off the coast, south of the delta of the Rufiji, Kilwa was probably founded in the tenth century and was integrated fairly early into the transoceanic network of trade, probably by the early eleventh century. Before the early thirteenth century, however, Kilwa was less important than Manda, Qanbalu, Malindi, or Mombasa. In the eleventh century, Kilwa had come under the control of a new ruling family which claimed Shirazi descent. In the Kilwa chronicle, this episode acknowledged Hanzawān (Anjouan, Comoros) as the place of immediate origin of the new rulers:

> The first man to come to Kilwa came in the following way: There arrived a ship in which there were people who claimed to have come from Shiraz in the lands of the Persians. It is said there were seven ships. . . . They say all the masters of these six ships were brothers, and that the one who went to the town of Hanzuan was their father. God alone knows all the truth. (quoted in Freeman-Grenville 1962: 75)

Under the rule of its first Shirazi kings, ʿAlī b. al-Ḥasan and his sons, Kilwa saw a quick rise to prominence on the southern coast. This rise was linked with the building of townhouses of stone, as well as a large mosque. Due to its strategic position, south of all other major Swahili settlements, and the fact that the monsoon winds enabled ships to make the journey from Arabia and India to Kilwa but not further south and back in one monsoon season, Kilwa was able to control the sea routes beyond Cape Delgado to Sofala. Control over the southern stretches of the coast was important, because this meant control over access to the Zambezi and thus access to the empire of the Mwene Motapa, the major source of gold in East Africa for a number of centuries. In the late thirteenth century, Kilwa's Shirazi rulers were deposed, however, and replaced by the Mahdalī, a family of sharīfian descent from Ḥaḍramawt which also settled in Brawa on the northern coast. Under Mahdalī rule, Kilwa's paramount role and wealth increased. This wealth was expressed in representative buildings in Kilwa, such as a large palace, a market, and an even larger mosque. The Mahdalī rulers introduced a new architectural technique in Kilwa, namely the cupola which enabled Kilwa builders to expand the roofs of their buildings. The new palace of Kilwa, in particular, seems to have caught the attention of Muslim travelers at this time, as it had a huge court for receptions, illuminated by hundreds of lamps in the night. The palace was surrounded by numerous shops of the various trading families which attested to the size of Kilwa's commercial enterprise. Kilwa's wealth was attested by Ibn Baṭṭūṭa, who visited Kilwa in 1331:

> We sailed to Mombasa, a big city . . . and then continued our journey to Kilwa, an outstanding city on the coast whose inhabitants are Zanj and black. Their faces are tattooed. . . . A trader told me that Kilwa is situated half a month of travelling from Sufāla, and Sufāla again a month of traveling from Yūfī in the bilād al-līmīyīn and that the gold of Yūfī was brought to Sufāla. Kilwa is one of the most beautiful and best built cities of this world. The roofs of the houses are built with mangrove poles. . . . The most important characteristics of its inhabitants are their faith and their religious devotion. They follow the Shāfiʿī school of law. When I arrived in Kilwa, Abū l-Muẓaffar Ḥasan was the sulṭān. . . . He often organizes raids into the lands of the Zanj, attacks them and makes booty (wa-ya'akhadha al-ghanā'im), keeping one-fifth,

The empire of the Mwene Motapa (in Kiswahili, "mwinyi mtapo" can mean either the master of fear or the master of ore) was formed in the early fifteenth century by Rozwi migrants from the Katanga region who had crossed the Zambezi and managed to submit most Karanga (today Shona) populations south of the Zambezi. The first Muslim traders reached the royal residence (zimbabwe) of the Rozwi ruler Nyatsimba Mutota in the mid-fifteenth century. Under his successors, the Rozwi state continued to expand and was divided into a number of semi-autonomous provinces ruled by paramount chiefs (mambo). By the late fifteenth century, some of these paramount chiefs, in particular Changa, the mambo of Gurushwa claimed independence. He was recognized by Muslim traders as the amīr (ruler) of his fiefdom, which came to be known as Changamire in Portuguese sources. By the late fifteenth century, thousands of Muslim traders were living on the Zambezi and at the court of the Mwene Motapa and linked this region of Africa with the Indian Ocean. When the Portuguese arrived on the Sofala coast, internal rivalries multiplied and Muslim traders as well as Portuguese traders tried to evict the respective other from the trade with the Mwene Motapa. A Portuguese mission to the court of the Mwene Motapa failed in 1561, however, due to the opposition of the Muslim party at the court of the Mwene Motapa. In retaliation, the Portuguese destroyed the Muslim settlements in the Zambezi valley in 1568 and established their own rule over the Zambezi. Despite their control over the lower Zambezi valley, the Portuguese were never able to occupy the Zimbabwe of the Mwene Mutapa. In the seventeenth century, the Changamire kingdom confined the Portuguese to some few fortifications on the Zambezi. Traces of the Muslim presence at the court of the Mwene Motapa can be found in Zimbabwe until today: the Waremba populations of the region claim Arab ancestry, as shown in names such as Ali, Sharifi, Bakari, or Mustafa. Also, they place a taboo on pork and practice the ḥalāl slaughter of animals.

as prescribed by the Qur'ān. The part which is due to the shurafā' is stored separately in the treasury and when shurafā' visit Kilwa, they get their share of the booty. The shurafā' are coming from 'Irāq, Ḥijāz, and many other countries. I have seen shurafā' from all parts of the Ḥijāz. . . . The sulṭān himself is very modest, he eats and sits with the poor, respects the holy men and the shurafā'. (Ibn Baṭṭūṭa 1985 2: 283–84)

In the sixteenth century, the East African coast experienced a major crisis, however, and old settlements declined while new settlements were able to develop. This crisis was linked with two disruptive forces which threatened the very survival of coastal societies: the invasion of the Zimba as well as the establishment of Portuguese control over much of the Indian Ocean and major parts of the East African coast. Even when Portuguese control eventually collapsed in the mid-seventeenth century, most coastal settlements were not able to regain their former autonomy, but came under the control of the Sulṭānate of Oman, which dominated the East African coast until the late nineteenth century. These developments also informed the history of Kilwa. Destroyed three times by the Portuguese, Kilwa experienced a revival in the seventeenth century which was linked with the fact that the Yao populations of the African interior developed a new trade route to the coast near Kilwa, thus linking Kilwa with a very profitable item of export, ivory. However, Kilwa remained under Portuguese domination until 1698 and was only then able to achieve independence with Omani support, although the Portuguese retook Kilwa in 1726 for a short period of time. When Oman established control over Kilwa again in 1744, the Yao shifted their trade route to Mozambique, which subsequently became the most important center for the southern trade on the East African coast. When trade on the central Coast revived in the late eighteenth century, the Yao moved north and brought their trade back to Kilwa which had a permanent Omani garrison from 1786. At the same time, Mozambique suffered from attacks by Sakalava fleets from Madagascar. The Sakalava threat was stopped in 1817 only, when an Omani fleet defeated the Sakalava in the Ruvuma delta. This provided much needed security for the southern trade route and granted Kilwa a new lease of activity. In 1850, Kilwa already had a population of 10,000–12,000 and was

The Zimba were Marawi (Malawi) warriors from the lower Zambezi valley. Until the early sixteenth century, Marawi lords had controlled the trade up and down the Zambezi. When the Portuguese blocked the Zambezi delta, took Sofala in 1506, and even sailed up the Zambezi in order to gain control over the trade themselves, reaching Tete in 1531, the up-river Marawi had to find a new route to the coast in order to bypass the Portuguese forts on the lower Zambezi. After a series of disputes among the Marawi, one group, the Phiri, tried to break the paramount position of the Lundu on the lower Zambezi in the 1570s, yet failed due to Portuguese support for the Lundu. As a reaction, the Phiri took a more northern route to the coast, attacked Kilwa in 1588, and massacred the population. In 1589, they attacked Mombasa and Malindi but were eventually defeated off Malindi by a coalition of Portuguese and Malindi forces. In order to eliminate the Phiri threat in the south, the Portuguese again allied with the Lundu in 1608 and, after a war of more than fourteen years, Phiri power collapsed in 1622.

the most important coastal settlement south of Zanzibar. The history of Kilwa shows that rise and decline of power and wealth were closely linked and were intrinsically connected with control over the sea trade in the Indian Ocean, as well as access to trade routes into the African interior.

The Portuguese Interlude

The establishment of Portuguese control over the East African coast was linked with the fact that since the early fifteenth century Portugal had sought to circumnavigate Africa in order to establish an independent link to the spice markets of Asia. While the attacks of the Zimba in the late sixteenth century had a devastating short-term effect on a number of coastal settlements, Portuguese trade policies in the Indian Ocean defined the development of the East African coast for almost 200 years. In 1498, the first Portuguese expedition under Vasco da Gama had reached the Indian Ocean and sailed from Malindi to India, guided by an Indian pilot, "Malemo Canaqua" (Sheriff 2010: 110). Thus, the sea route to India via the Cape of Good Hope had been explored and became a major oceanic highway under Portuguese control. In a series of naval raids, the Portuguese attacked and destroyed a number of harbor cities in the Indian Ocean, including Mogadishu in 1499, Kilwa and Mombasa in 1505, Brawa in 1507, Malakka in 1511, Hormuz in 1515, Diu in 1538, and Daman in 1559. As Portuguese caravels were larger than most dhows in the Indian Ocean, the Portuguese soon became the unrivaled naval power in the Indian Ocean. Caravels could also carry more bulk as well as heavy artillery, and they had a flexible rigging technology. Thus, the Portuguese were able to outmaneuver and outshoot any other ship in the Indian Ocean and to block every harbor. The Portuguese were too weak numerically, however, to establish permanent settlements on all coasts of the Indian Ocean. They thus built a few coastal fortifications only, such as Mozambique, Fort Jesus in Mombasa, Masqaṭ in Oman, and Diu and Goa in India, and were otherwise happy to control the seas and the coasts from their ships: any ship that was not registered by the Portuguese and did not pay tribute was plundered and sunk, and coastal settlements which refused to pay tribute were bombarded by the Portuguese ships until they eventually gave in. Kilwa was destroyed three times until it accepted Portuguese dominion. Portuguese control over the East African coast relied on a system of commandantes who leased their positions from the Crown and then tried to make good their expenses by exploiting their respective territories. Thus, the Portuguese raised a tax of 100 mithqāl (gold coins) annually on Zanzibar, 1,500 mithqāl on Mombasa, and 2,000 mithqāl on Kilwa. In addition, the Portuguese commandantes prevented all non-licensed naval activity, and thus maintained Portuguese naval hegemony in the Indian Ocean. Less important settlements such as Malindi exploited the decline of places like Mombasa to rise to prominence as allies of Portugal.

In their endeavors to control the coast, the Portuguese relied on a policy of violence against those places which refused to pay tribute, such as Mombasa, Kilwa, and

In a curious twist of world history, Portugal lost its only male heir to the throne in a war with Morocco in 1580. As a consequence, the house of Habsburg, which ruled Spain, inherited the Portuguese crown. Spain thus acquired the Portuguese colonial empire without firing a shot. Due to the fact that Spain had lucrative possessions in Mexico, Peru, and Colombia, as well as in the Caribbean, it was not interested in maintaining costly possessions in Africa, the Indian Ocean, and South East Asia. Portuguese domination in the Indian Ocean consequently collapsed, and other European powers, in particular the Netherlands, France, and Britain, established a foothold in the India trade. On the East African coast, the united Iberian empire retained only three major bases: Mozambique, Malindi, and Mombasa. In 1640, when Portugal regained its independence, it tried hard to recapture its lost territories. But by this time, other European powers were solidly entrenched, and Portugal lost control not only over the trade with India but also over its possessions in the Indian Ocean, with the exception of the colony of Goa in India and the colony of Mozambique in southeastern Africa.

Brawa, and alliances with otherwise secondary coastal settlements, such as Malindi and Lamu, which hoped to gain political influence by allying with the Portuguese. However, the northernmost Swahili town, Mogadishu, escaped Portuguese control and consequently became a major center of local resistance to Portuguese domination on the coast. The only real threat to Portuguese domination of the East African coast, apart from the Zimba attack on Mombasa and Malindi in 1589, materialized in 1585, when an Ottoman fleet sailed down the coast and occupied Mogadishu, Brawa, and Mombasa, as well as Pate and Lamu. In Faza, a small settlement in the Lamu archipelago, the Ottoman naval commander, Amīr ʿAlī Bey, established an Ottoman dynasty which survived into the late nineteenth century. Only Malindi rejected Ottoman over-rule and was eventually relieved by a Spanish-Portuguese fleet which reestablished Iberian control over the coast. Amīr ʿAlī Bey was taken prisoner and deported to Spain. As a consequence of both Zimba raids and Portuguese control over the seas, East African coastal identity became even more accentuated in the sixteenth and seventeenth centuries as an exclusive coastal culture defined by simultaneous rejection of the nyika, the bush, as well as intruders from the sea. Following the collapse of the trade with the African interior, due to the Zimba raids in the south, as well as a series of Oromo raids in the north between 1600 and 1650, the coastal settlements suffered an economic crisis which was overcome in the eighteenth century only, when trade with the hinterland resumed.

In the mid-seventeenth century, Oman became Portugal's most dangerous enemy in the western Indian Ocean. Between 1643 and 1650, Oman managed to gain control over the Portuguese strongholds on the Omani coast, in particular Masqaṭ, and in 1652 an Omani fleet attacked Portuguese positions in Zanzibar. Although the Portuguese managed to regain control over the coast, they had to abandon Pate in 1679 and were trapped in Fort Jesus in Mombasa. After a siege of three years, the Portuguese garrison in Fort Jesus capitulated on 12 December 1698, and Portuguese control over the northern and central East African coast came to an end. At the same time, Oman was not yet capable of replacing Portuguese domination. The coastal towns consequently regained their independence and, as in the case of Mombasa, rose to regional prominence. The end of Portuguese domination also signaled the end of Malindi's brief rise to power: Malindi declined in a short period of time, was destroyed in an Oromo raid in the early seventeenth century, and was even reported deserted in 1846. Some years later, Malindi achieved a modest recovery under Omani control, when it became a major exporter of grain from the East African hinterland.

While Malindi was able to rise to regional prominence on the coast for a brief period only, Mombasa was one of those coastal settlements which tried particularly hard to gain not only local but also regional hegemony over a stretch of the coast for a longer period of time. In this endeavor, Mombasa had to compete with Pate, later Malindi, and still later Lamu in the north, as well as Zanzibar in the south. Mombasa historical tradition ascribes original settlement of the island to an alliance of twelve settlements (Swa. miji kumi na mbili), ruled by the taifa tatu (three clans), namely Changamwe, Kilindini, and Tangana. In the early fourteenth century, local power shifted to the Shirazi who controlled the town until 1592, when the Portuguese took control of Mombasa and started to build Fort Jesus. Until that time, Mombasa had suffered Portuguese attacks in 1500, 1505, and 1528. Although accepting Portuguese overlordship, Mombasa was quick to recognize Ottoman control when the Ottoman navy appeared on the East African coast in 1585 and again in 1588, establishing a garrison in Mombasa commanded by Amīr ʿAlī Bey. Consequently, the Portuguese encouraged the marauding Zimba warriors to attack Mombasa and the Ottoman troops. The Zimba massacred the population of Mombasa, while an Iberian fleet under Mateus Mendes de Vasconcelhos bombarded the Ottoman troops from the sea. The Ottoman garrison capitulated on 16 March 1588, and when the Zimba moved on to Malindi they were defeated off Malindi by united Iberian, Malindi, and Segeju forces. In reaction, the Iberian crown decided to build Fort Jesus in 1593, a task completed by 1599. The establishment of Fort Jesus also brought about the establishment of an Augustine mission. At the same time, control over the population, which had suffered considerably under the Zimba attack, was taken over by the ruling family of Malindi, in alliance with the Portuguese. In order to entrench their position on the coast, the Portuguese sent the heir to the throne of Mombasa, Yūsuf b. Ḥasan, to Goa in India for an education in a Portuguese school managed by the Augustine order. In Goa, Yūsuf b. Ḥasan converted to Christianity, took the new name Dom Jeronimo Chingulia, married a woman from an aristocratic Portuguese family, and was eventually knighted. After his return to Mombasa in 1626, he rejected Portuguese rule in 1631, possibly due to a dispute with the Portuguese governor. Yūsuf b. Ḥasan organized a massacre of the Portuguese garrison as well as the Augustine mission and was able to hold out in Fort Jesus against a siege by the Portuguese fleet for a period of four months. In 1632, he fled and eventually reached Jidda in the Red Sea, where he died in 1638.

The return of the Portuguese to Mombasa convinced the population of the town to seek outside support, and in 1649 they sent a mission to Oman. Three years later, an Omani fleet attacked the Portuguese in Zanzibar, starting a series of raids across the ocean which eventually led to the collapse of Portuguese control over the northern and central coast. Most important, the Omani fleet defeated the Portuguese garrison in Fort Jesus in 1698, taking the major fortification on the East African coast into their own possession. The new ruler and governor of Mombasa was Nāṣir ʿAbdallāh al-Mazrūʿī. In the following decades, the Mazrūʿī governors of Mombasa not only had to fight against the efforts of the Portuguese to regain control over the town, but also to struggle against the interests of local families which resented Omani overlordship just as they had resented Portuguese control. In 1735, in the context of disputes over succession to power in Oman, in which the Bū Saʿīdī family prevailed over the ruling Yaʿrūbī family, the Mazrūʿī themselves declared their independence from Oman. As a consequence, the Mazrūʿī gained greater acceptance in Mombasa and consolidated their rule over Mombasa until 1837, when they had to accept Omani rule again.

Although the Mazrūʿī rulers of Mombasa tried to extend their control over other parts of the coast in this period, they eventually failed. In 1812, Mombasa forces suffered a humiliating defeat off Lamu, which had the support of Oman, and in 1822 Mombasa forces were also defeated off Pate and lost Pemba to the Bū Saʿīdī dynasty. By accepting British overlordship, Mombasa was able to ward off Omani efforts to take control over the city in 1829 and 1833, but in 1837 the British abandoned Mombasa to the sulṭān of Oman, who was regarded as a more important ally in the western Indian Ocean. The last Mazrūʿī ruler of Mombasa, Rashīd Sālim al-Mazrūʿī, was deposed and exiled to Bandar ʿAbbās in the Gulf. Oman imposed a new ruling family, the Mbaruk, which subsequently administrated Mombasa in the name of the sulṭān of Oman. In order to escape Mbaruk-Omani control, part of the Mazrūʿī family established a new stronghold in Gazi near Lamu. In cooperation with the Digo population in Mombasa's hinterland, the Mazrūʿī of Gazi started to destabilize Mbaruk rule over Mombasa. These politics allowed smaller settlements such as Vumba and Wasini to escape Mbaruk control in the late nineteenth century. Gazi-Mazrūʿī efforts to expand its influence over Vumba misfired, however, and in 1882 Zanzibari forces defeated the Mazrūʿī of Gazi, although they were unable to eliminate Gazi completely. This was achieved by a British military expedition in 1896. The history of competition between Mombasa, Kilwa, Malindi, Pate, Lamu, Gazi, and Vumba since the seventeenth century shows that coastal towns and their patriciate families jealously tried to guard their independence and used every chance to reject outside control, even if such policies enabled powerful outside players such as Portugal and Oman in the sixteenth–nineteenth centuries, as well as European colonial powers such as Britain and Germany in the late nineteenth century, to impose their domination over large stretches of the coast.

Oman and the Rise of Zanzibar

The rise of Oman as a naval power in the Indian Ocean was linked with the fact that Oman had achieved political unity in 1624 under the leadership of the Yaʿrūbī family, and was subsequently able to evict the Portuguese from their positions on the Omani coast. In 1650, the sulṭān and imām of the Ibāḍiyya in Oman, Sulṭān b. Sayf, conquered Masqaṭ, the last Portuguese stronghold in Oman. In 1652, an Omani fleet sailed to the East African coast in response to an appeal by the citizens of Mombasa, Pate, and Pemba, and attacked Portuguese positions in Zanzibar. In 1660, the Omani fleet attacked Pate, Mombasa, and Faza, and in 1669 even Mozambique. In 1698, Fort Jesus was taken and Oman was able to repulse a last Portuguese effort to regain control over the central coast in 1728/29. Pax Omanica enabled many coastal settlements to recover from Portuguese domination. Also, Omani presence in East Africa remained, for the time being, weak, and was based on agreements of cooperation and alliance rather than occupation. Only in some places such as Mombasa in 1698 or Zanzibar in 1709 did Oman establish permanent bases. When Oman saw a change of dynasties in 1741, a number of allies such as Mombasa used this chance to cut their ties with the new rulers of Oman, the Bū Saʿīdī family.

Under the Yaʿrūbī dynasty, Oman had expanded its commercial activities considerably and established Omani positions in India, Iran, the Gulf, southern Arabia, and the Red Sea. Omani wealth was based on its exports of dates to India from date palm plantations in Oman's interior. These plantations were worked by African slaves. Oman thus had an intrinsic interest in protecting its trade links with East Africa as the major supplier of slaves. The success of the Omani naval expeditions to East Africa stimulated the emergence of an Omani commercial aristocracy, which soon marginalized the religio-political influence of the imāms of Oman. The change of dynasty in 1741 can thus be explained as a shift from religio-political leadership to a new political elite that was informed by commercial interests. In order to realize their entrepreneurial policies, the sulṭāns transformed Oman's armed forces of tribal warriors united by family alliances into a more conventional army and navy, which consisted of slaves from Africa and mercenaries from Baluchistan. The new army enabled Sulṭān Saʿīd b. Sulṭān (r. 1804–1856) to build a commercial empire which covered the whole of the western Indian Ocean. In this empire, the East African coast turned out to be the most profitable shore, due to its exports of slaves and ivory, and later cloves; Oman consequently started to establish a more permanent presence on the East African coast.

Oman's paramount position in the western Indian Ocean was based on its control over three maritime trade routes: the one to the East African coast, which provided slaves for Omani plantations and ivory for the Indian market, the one into the Gulf, which provided, like Oman, dates and pearls for the Indian market, and the third to Gujarat, which assured access to the Indian market. From 1798, these Omani trade interests were secured by an Anglo-Omani trade agreement which acknowledged Oman as a British ally in this region, while at the same time excluding other trade interests, in particular France. During the Napoleonic wars (up to 1815), Britain put her commercial navy in the Indian Ocean under Omani flag and thus protected her ships against French naval attacks in the Indian Ocean. At the same time, the British navy put French prize ships under Omani flag in order to provide neutral status for them. Due to this agreement, Omani tonnage expanded considerably, and by 1804 Oman had a commercial navy of fifty-five sailing ships with a tonnage of 40,000. Oman was regarded as neutral by all warring parties, and transport on safe Omani ships increased considerably. As Oman also granted comparatively low freight rates, it emerged from the Napoleonic wars with the largest commercial navy in the Indian Ocean. This situation changed slowly after 1815, due to the increasing age of the Omani commercial navy, as well as the emergence of new competitors in the Indian Ocean trade, in particular a number of emirates in the Gulf, which were able to marginalize the Omani position in the Gulf from the 1820s. As a consequence, Oman came to focus even more on the trade with India and the East African coast, and to intensify its presence in East Africa. These efforts were supported by Britain, which hoped to frustrate French efforts to gain a foothold in East Africa. As a consequence, Oman was able to establish hegemony over most East African harbor cities between the 1810s and the 1830s: in 1812 Lamu, in 1821 Pate and Brawa, in 1823 Pemba, in 1824 the rest of the Lamu archipelago, and in 1837 Mombasa. In the 1820s, Oman's supreme rule was acknowledged by most Comoro islands and even extended, for a short period of time, to Nosi-Bé, an island off Madagascar's northwestern coast.

With the end of Portuguese domination on the East African coast in the early eighteenth century, a period of Omani overrule started that lasted until the end of the nineteenth century. With its fleet of originally seventy to eighty ships, the Sulṭānate was not only able to effectively protect its trading connections in the Indian Ocean but also to exert effective control over the East African coast north of Mozambique. As a consequence, Oman, like Portugal in the sixteenth century, was never actually forced to occupy the coastal strip and to maintain costly fortresses and bases: the Sulṭānate could cut off all seaborne communication and the trade of any coastal settlement at any time. The territorial forces of the Sulṭānate, by contrast, remained rather small: in the 1840s, they comprised about 400 soldiers, 200 of them based in Mombasa, and mostly recruited in Baluchistan or Ḥaḍramawt. Only in the 1880s was the army expanded to a force of 1,200 soldiers, which were used for military expeditions on the mainland against rebellious local rulers such as Gazi. Yet Oman's military backbone for most

Islam in Madagascar was linked with the development of a few small Muslim communities on the northern and eastern coasts of the island. The Muslim communities in Mahajanga in the northwest, and those around Antseranana (Diego Suarez) in the north, managed to remain in contact with the wider world of Islam, and the Comoros, as well as the East African coast. Portuguese naval hegemony in the Indian Ocean, however, led to the isolation of two smaller Muslim communities on the eastern coast, the Antaimoro of Manankara and the Antambahoaka of Manajary. In the late nineteenth century, these Muslim communities had became part of local society and had lost their Islamic identity, except for a few relics such as words like sorabe (writing; from sūra), a taboo on pork, and the cultivation of ʿilm al-falak, actually an array of sciences such as astrology, astronomy, and numerology, as a discipline of learning. Antaimoro were described by Muslim travelers of the time as mutawaḥḥishūn, "those who have turned wild." Despite the fact that the Antaimoro had abandoned Islam, they had conserved the Arabic script and had developed an Arabic transcription for their dialect of Malagasy. This explains why the emerging Imerina kingdom in central Madagascar started to employ Antaimoro scribes in the late eighteenth century for the administration of their kingdom. By the 1820s, a part of the Imerina elite was able to write Malagasy in the Arabic script, which was eventually replaced by a Latin transcription. The art of sorabe constituted a major legacy of the Antaimoro, although the link with Islam as a religion had been lost by this time.

of the nineteenth century was its navy. In the nineteenth century, a major part of the income of the Sulṭānate was spent in fact on the navy, the maintenance of the court, and the alimentation of numerous clients and allied families on the coast.

In the context of this development, Oman became the paramount political power on the East African coast, a development reinforced by the shift of Oman's seat of government from Masqaṭ to Zanzibar in 1840. Sulṭān Saʿīd had already come to Zanzibar in 1829 for the first time. He first stayed at Mtoni, north of Zanzibar Town, and later, from 1832, at the Bait al-Sāḥil in what was to become the Old Town. Before he died in 1856, Sulṭān Saʿīd b. Sulṭān split his empire among his sons, Mājid and Thwaynī, who now effectively ruled two separate states, the Sulṭānates of Masqaṭ and Zanzibar. Sulṭān Mājid (r. 1856–1870), the first ruler of the Sulṭānate of Zanzibar, continued the policy of expansion started by his father, although he had to overcome a number of problems such as a rebellion by his brother Barghash in Zanzibar, as well as Thwaynī's attempt to invade Zanzibar from Masqaṭ in 1859. With British support, he was able to master these difficulties and start a program of modernization inspired by Egypt which came to be seen as a model for Zanzibar's development. Among Mājid's specific achievements was the consolidation of Zanzibar's rule over the mainland, a development that was underlined by his decision to construct a new harbor, Dar es Salaam, south of Bagamoyo, which was intended to become the sulṭān's new capital city. Mājid's successor, Barghash (r. 1870–1888), continued his policy of modernization. In 1871/72, Barghash went on pilgrimage and in 1875 he visited Syria, Jerusalem, and Egypt just before Egyptian army and naval forces started their attack on Ethiopia and the Banādir coast. From Syria, he imported Zanzibar's first printing press, which was put to work in 1879. In Egypt, he met Khedive Ismāʿīl and had a chance to acquaint himself with the processes of reform that had been implemented in Egypt. In 1872, Barghash's policies of modernization also led to the establishment of a regular postal service between Zanzibar and Aden, and in 1879 a telegraph cable was installed between Zanzibar and Aden. Zanzibar was thus directly connected with the world's emerging communication network.

Mājid's and Barghash's reforms had immediate repercussions on life on the East African coast: whereas numerous travel accounts from the mid-nineteenth century reported that the palace of the sulṭān contained only three rows of chairs, the Zanzibari court in the 1880s rather resembled the court of an Indian maharaja. A bayt al-ʿajāʾib (house of wonders) exhibited numerous mirrors, clocks, European furniture, and curiosities that Mājid and Barghash had acquired, and also had East Africa's first electric elevator. In front of the palace, a lighthouse-cum-clock tower was built in 1879, and, with the earnings from clove production, toll fees, and ivory exports, Zanzibar was able to finance a fresh water supply, street lighting with gas lamps, a fleet of six steam ships, and an army that was trained and equipped according to European models. The huts and gardens of the Old Town were increasingly replaced by stone houses; storage houses and barracks were constructed; and in the vicinity of the sulṭān's palace other representative buildings came to house consulates, hotels, trading factories, trading houses, an ice factory, new market buildings, and the rich city houses and villas of the plantation owners, notables, and aristocrats. These changes exerted strong attraction. Zanzibar and the lifestyle of the Arab-Omani elite became a new cultural model, and the ideal of coastal civilization, ungwana, was replaced by the wish to live like an Arab (Swa. ustaarabu). This cultural change was expressed in the adoption of Arab ways of dressing and Arab fashions, but also by the adoption of Arab names. Zanzibar's economic boom was expressed in the growth of Zanzibar town, which from 1838 spread across the creek, an arm of the sea that separated the Old Town "from the other side" (Swa. ng'ambo) and the rural areas. At the same time, Zanzibar's urban population grew from around 5,000 inhabitants in 1819 to around 80,000 in 1885. This population was a mix of many nations: Swahili, Somaal, Arabs, and Indians, as well as Africans from different hinterland regions. All these groups were subdivided into social, religious, and regional identities: different Muslim Indian orientations, as well as Banian (Hindu Indians), Ḥaḍramis, Omanis, Comorians, people from Madagascar, Europeans, Baluchis, and Persians, again split into different families such as the ruling Bū Saʿīdīs, but also the Riyāmīs and Mughayrīs, Lamkīs and Barwānīs from Oman, the ʿAlawī families from Yemen, Ḥaḍramawt and the Comoros, and Indian families such as the Topans and the Sewjis.

While iron ore, gold, and slaves had been major items of export from the East African coast, the nineteenth century saw the emergence of an array of new trade goods, in particular cloves, ivory, and cocopalm-nuts as well as copra (the fibers of the coconut), but also sugar cane, oil palms, sesame, gum copal, and rice. The cultivation of clove trees started in Zanzibar in 1815, and the export of cloves soon became the major source of income for the Sulṭānate and established Zanzibar's wealth in the mid-nineteenth century. In 1823, Zanzibar sold its first clove harvest and exports to India, later also to Europe and the United States. In 1846, Zanzibar exported 99,000 frasila of cloves (one frasila corresponds to about thirty-five pounds), and by 1856 this quantity had grown to 143,000 frasila. In this year, Zanzibar was the biggest producer of cloves in the world. Due to Zanzibar's importance as a trading partner, European and North American companies concluded treaties of cooperation with Zanzibar, the United States starting in 1833, Britain following in 1841, France in 1844, and the German Hanse Cities of Hamburg, Bremen, and Lübeck in 1859. Due to the fact that the sulṭān imposed high import taxes on luxury goods, the income of the Sulṭānate grew even further and enabled investment in public works in the 1860s. In 1856, Zanzibar had become the undisputed hub of trade on the East African coast: about 300 commercial ships were recorded to have anchored alone in this year in the harbor of Zanzibar.

Trade was not only in the hands of European or North American companies, however. Zanzibar also initiated independent commercial activities: in 1839, the Sulṭāna reached New York with a cargo of carpets, dates, coffee, cloves, ivory, and copra, and returned with firearms, textiles, and gunpowder. In 1845, the Caroline reached London. Apart from slaves and cloves, as well as various other agricultural products, Zanzibar also became a major exporter of ivory in the nineteenth century. Until the eighteenth century, ivory had come mostly from Mozambique and the Zambezi, but in the nineteenth century the territories between the coast and Lake Malawi as well as Lake Tanganyika became the major sources of East African ivory, which was exported mainly to India. By the mid-nineteenth century, elephants had became increasingly rare in the hinterlands of the coast, and Zanzibari traders consequently pushed the ivory frontier further inland to the upper reaches of the Congo, as well as into the interior of the Horn. In the second half of the nineteenth century, other agricultural products also became important items of export, however, and brought increasing income for Zanzibar's trade: coffee, cotton, sisal, coconuts and copra, indigo, sugar cane, pepper, and other spices were added to the list of export items. Still, ivory kept its leading role in Zanzibar's export trade for some time: in 1859, ivory exports from

Zanzibar amounted to $733,000, while slaves came second ($400,000), followed by cloves ($278,000), cowries ($257,000), gum copal ($186,000), hides ($128,000), sesame seed ($104,000), copra ($67,000), and coconut oil ($20,000) (Martin and Martin 1978/2007: 29). Slaves thus accounted for less than 20 percent of the export value of more than 2.1 million dollars. Due to falling prices for imported goods, Zanzibar achieved a growing surplus in its balance of trade. This was invested in public works and representative buildings in Zanzibar, as well as other coastal towns, adding to Zanzibar's prestige. A peculiarity of the trading empire of Zanzibar was that the rulers of Zanzibar did not establish an administration to collect customs fees, but sold the right to collect such fees to wealthy Indian entrepreneurs for a limited period of time: in 1865, the Sewji family bought this right for a period of five years for 310,000 pounds sterling annually. In 1876, the Topan family managed to outbid the Sewji family and bought Zanzibar's customs income for 450,000 pounds, only to be outbid again by the Sewjis in 1880 with 500,000 pounds. These sums of money attest to the economic boom on the coast, which experienced a further boost after the opening of the Suez Canal in 1869, when Zanzibar's sea routes to Europe and North America became dramatically shorter and cheaper.

In political terms, the Sulṭānate of Zanzibar came under the growing influence of Britain, in particular in 1859 when Britain blocked an Omani fleet which tried to reunite both parts of the empire on its way to Zanzibar. As a consequence, Britain was able to impose first restrictions on the slave trade and to stop the transoceanic slave trade in a number of agreements with Zanzibar between 1867 and 1873. The trade on the East African coast and to the islands remained legal for the time being, though. This brought about a boom of plantations, in particular cloves (Pemba), coconuts (Unguja), sugar cane, sesame, and grains on the coast between Mombasa and Brawa, and a corresponding growth of the coastal settlements: Mombasa grew to a population of 12,000 in 1870, Lamu and Siyu to populations of about 10,000. From 1870, Mājid's successor, Barghash, was able to partly reestablish Zanzibar's freedom to act, in particular on the coast and in the African hinterland. After a devastating hurricane in 1872 which destroyed most clove-tree plantations on Unguja, Zanzibar's southern island, as well as Zanzibar's commercial navy, Barghash shifted the focus of plantation crops in Unguja from clove trees to cocopalms, and rebuilt Zanzibar's navy, this time in the guise of six steam ships. Also, the administration and the army were modernized, the possessions of the Sulṭānate were organized in provinces administered by governors (liwalis and mudirs), and all provinces got qāḍī courts. The existing rights of autonomy of the coastal settlements were curtailed.

Despite these measures, the influence of the sulṭān in Zanzibar on the quotidian administration of places like Malindi or Mombasa remained small, and the power of the sulṭān was even smaller in the hinterland regions. Zanzibar remained a trading empire without fixed boundaries, and the authority of the sulṭān was often only nominal, for instance when local rulers flew the red flag of the Sulṭānate. Yet, although

> The cyclone of 1872 led to a political crisis in the Sulṭānate, which had already been hit by an epidemic of cholera in 1868/1870. The epidemic was part of the fourth cholera pandemic which reached Zanzibar from India in the nineteenth century. The first started in 1818 and arrived in Zanzibar in 1821; the second started in 1826 and hit Zanzibar in 1836; while the third started in 1842 and hit Zanzibar in 1858. The fourth cholera pandemic started in India in 1865 and hit Zanzibar in 1869. By that time, the supply of slaves to the islands had almost collapsed, due to wars between 1860 and 1865 in Unyamwesi, on the central trade route.

the sulṭān of Zanzibar had little or no power to impose his will on African hinterland territories, the very fact that the Sulṭānate controlled the coast and access to the sea, and thus access to the wider world, was reason enough to convince local rulers in the hinterland regions to comply with the wishes of the sulṭān. When a German explorer, Albrecht Roscher, was murdered on the shores of Lake Malawi in 1860, the local ruler not only caught the murderers but also handed them over to the Sulṭānate's authorities in Zanzibar, where they were subsequently executed. This episode supported the Sulṭan of Zanzibar's claim that "his writ ran far inland" (Beachey 1996: 85).

The erroneous views of representatives of Europe's colonial powers regarding the alleged weakness of Zanzibar's position on the coast was based on a misconception of Zanzibari policies, which did not rely on a military apparatus and an omnipresent administration, but on the voluntary acceptance of Zanzibar's rule: the sulṭān was not regarded as an autocratic or even absolute king, but as a supreme mediator and patron of multiple local activities and interests. He was the protector of a plethora of clienteles, which were instrumental to his policy of ruling his realm by consensus and through the workings of an intricate network of family ties and commercial interests. The sulṭān cultivated links with other commercial entrepreneurs and influential families, and marginalized opponents by intrigue if he could not win their support. Only in rare cases did he resort to armed intervention. Formal symbols of sovereignty were useless in this concept of governance, although they were increasingly displayed from the 1870s, in order to counter European claims to territory. European powers did not understand these workings of local politics, assuming that the sulṭān had no power whatsoever and that the coast was in effect without a master. In 1884, the British Consul in Zanzibar, Kirk, thus described Sulṭān Barghash's policies with respect to the coast as "utter apathy to what takes place away from Zanzibar so long as he receives his revenue" (Bennett 1978: 110). However, this statement was made at a time when the British had started to show their own interest in what took place on the East African coast.

In order to counter European territorial claims, the Sulṭānate in fact started to increase its symbolic and military presence on the East African coast: in 1869, Zanzibar established a new fort in Kismayo on the southern Banādir coast, in order to protect the trade routes from the interior to the coast against Oromo attacks, as well as the coastal trade routes up and down the Banādir coast, linking Kismayo with Lamu and Malindi. In 1880, Zanzibar established garrisons in Mamboya and Usagara, about 100 kilometers inland, west of Dar es Salaam, as well as positions in Tabora and Ujiji on Lake Tanganyika. Existing fortifications and garrisons in Brawa, Mogadishu, Marka, Mombasa, Malindi, and Lamu were strengthened, and new forts were built in Vanga, Takaunga, and Gasi. By this time, Zanzibar also controlled about 100 customs stations on the coast, representing the sulṭān and administered by an akida (toll master). Even European diplomats were eventually forced to accept these new realities. Still, European arrangements regarding the division of Africa prevailed over African realities: in 1886, Zanzibar was forced to abandon her mainland territories, except for a ten-mile coastal strip, to Britain, Germany, and Italy, a fact which was eventually translated into a boundary agreement between Britain and Germany in 1890. In 1888, Zanzibar was forced by a German naval expedition to renounce the remainder of her mainland territories, and was then incorporated into the British colonial empire as a protectorate in 1890. Zanzibar's territories on the Kenyan part of the coast retained a measure of their Zanzibari identity, though, and formed an autonomous Sayyidiyye province. Zanzibar's possessions on the Banādir coast came under Italian colonial rule.

Crisis and Religious Reform on the East African Coast

In the nineteenth century, the societies of the East African coast came to experience a series of crises which were linked, in political terms, with the rise and demise of the Sulṭānate of Zanzibar and the subsequent colonial partition of East Africa between Great Britain and Germany. This was symbolized in the bombardment of Zanzibar in 1896 by British naval forces, which sealed Zanzibar's transformation into a British protectorate. In economic terms, these transformations were linked with the development of a plantation economy based on slave work on an unprecedented scale in East Africa, while in religious terms, East Africa saw the emergence of a number of movements of reform dominated by Sufi orders, in particular the Qādiriyya, the ʿAlawiyya, and the Shādhiliyya. Sufism in ṭarīqa form came to be established on the East African coast, as in the bilād al-sūdān of sub-Saharan Africa in the nineteenth century only. Yet, by contrast to Sudanic West Africa, religious scholars linked with Sufi orders did not rise to become leaders of jihād movements; rather, they supported movements of reform in the spheres of ritual practice and education. These movements of reform can be interpreted as a response to popular dissatisfaction with the economic, political, and social development of the East African coast in the nineteenth century.

The processes of social change on the East African coast were expressed in the shifting of labels: while old inhabitants of the coastal settlements had proudly called themselves waungwana (free, civilized people), in contrast to the washenzi (savages) of the hinterland regions, the migrants to the coast soon also started claiming to be waungwana in order to express their own aspirations. Established town populations subsequently switched to the term Shirazi to point out their noble descent regarding the migrant hamali (carriers) or vibarua (porter-slaves). Slave hierarchies expressed social differentiation as well: the major categories were watumwa, the lower servants and plantation slaves, as well as wazalia, house slaves, who were often born on the coast. Watumwa who worked on the plantations of their masters had the chance to become sharecroppers over time, while wazalia had the chance to rise to wafundi (craftsmen). Social differentiation was even practiced with respect to newcomers from across the ocean: thus, Waarabu (Arabs) from Oman called all strata of coastal population indiscriminately sawāḥil' (coastals). At the same time, poor Arab immigrants who had come to the East African coast looking for work were referred to (on the East African coast) as Shihiri (Ḥaḍramis from Shiḥr) or Manga (Omanis), a term derived from the Arabic naqaʿa (to soak), denoting those poor Omanis who had to sail on often overcrowded dhows, and were consequently "soaked in water" when arriving in Zanzibar (Glassman 2011: 195).

The dissatisfaction of the Muslim populations on the East African coast was due to many causes: first of all, the imposition of Omani rule produced increasing pressure on the established families on the coast, as these families were marginalized, in political and economic terms, by the new Omani elites and their Indian partners in commerce and finance. In order to differentiate themselves from the new political elites, the prominent families of Mombasa, Lamu, and Malindi stressed their cultural identity as families of noble Shirazi origin. The prominent families in the coastal towns, however, were not the only ones to be excluded from political affairs and economic development: commoners were also affected because the rapid growth in size and number of clove and sugar cane plantations on the coast led to considerable migration from the East African interior to the coast. On the coast, these non-Muslim migrants competed with local populations for work, employment, and income. Threatened from more than one side, the communities on the coast reacted by emphasizing their social position as Shirazi citizens of Lamu or Mombasa, and refused to accept the social and religious integration of non-Muslim migrants and slaves, even if these newcomers to the coast converted to

Islam. Refusal of conversion and exclusion of converts from existing social and religious structures were connected with claims to cultural superiority: while the coastal populations regarded themselves as the harbingers of civilization, as waungwana, they saw outsiders, in particular those from the East African hinterlands, as washenzi (savages), devoid of cultural and religious roots. The washenzi were perceived as an additional threat to the established social order when they started to convert to Islam, which was regarded by the waungwana as a major feature of their own culture.

From the second half of the nineteenth century, Shirazi elites came to experience pressure in the sphere of religion as well, when another series of migrants started to question their role as religious elites. This time, the migrants came not from the African interior or from Oman, but from Ḥaḍramawt, the Banādir coast of contemporary southern Somalia as well as the Comoro islands. Many migrants from Ḥaḍramawt and the Comoros were connected with the ʿAlawiyya or Shādhiliyya Sufi orders and could claim descent from the family of the Prophet, while the migrants from Banādir coastal towns were often connected with the Qādiriyya. On the coast, the immigrant scholars from Ḥaḍramawt, the Banādir coast, and the Comoros started to compete with local scholars for influence and social positions and, suffering from similar strategies of exclusion, cultivated support among the marginalized groups of the coast. Thus, a coalition of the marginalized and excluded formed, which promised slaves and migrants social emancipation through conversion while providing the new scholars with a social base. Islam consequently became an arena of dispute where matters of inclusion and exclusion were negotiated. These processes of religious reorientation gave rise to a number of problems, as African slaves and migrants adopted not only features of local and allegedly authentic Islam, but continued to practice African rituals such as ngoma (drum) dances and to mix African with Islamic ritual practices.

The development of Islamic ritual was expressed in the dichotomy between established and new forms of the celebration of the birthday of the Prophet, the mawlid al-nabī, or the different forms of Sufi rituals, especially the dhikr. From the late nineteenth century, the dhikr of the Qādiriyya, in particular, saw important ritual innovations such as the zikri ya dufu, a dhikr implying the playing of dufu drums, and the zikri ya kukohoa, a dhikr implying rhythmic inhaling and exhaling (Arab. anfās; lit. breath). With respect to mawlid celebrations, the coastal Shirazi elites tended to cultivate the mawlid Barzanjī, recited in Arabic, whereas converts tended to follow the mawlidi ya Kiswahili as practiced, for instance, by Ḥabīb Ṣāliḥ Jamal al-Layl (1853–1935) from Lamu, a form of the mawlid characterized by performance in Kiswahili and ecstatic ritual. While the new rituals, in particular the different new forms of the dhikr and the mawlidi ya Kiswahili, were perceived by converts as being part of their new Islamic identity, the Shirazi elites resented these processes of innovation and reinterpretation of coastal Islamic culture as well as their transformation into convert concepts of Islam. Consequently, they attacked the new customs as un-Islamic innovations and condemned the egalitarianism of the new rituals.

Their critique was specifically directed at the dhikr ceremonies, as female spirit possession cults had some affinities to the dhikr and women often developed dhikr groups of their own. To Muslims with little formal learning, the dhikr seemed to offer a way to spiritual fulfillment that did not depend on literary accomplishment. Sufi ritual had an inherently egalitarian appeal to newcomers to Islam, and to townspeople who had been relegated to the margins of established religious institutions. The Sufi orders were of enormous importance in bringing newcomers to Islam; their egalitarian flavor posed a great appeal to the recent migrants, upcountry converts, slaves, and ex-slaves who had been routinely excluded from power "in patrician religious institutions" (Glassman 1995: 138). By the mid-1880s, some Qādirī versions of the dhikr became a popular form of worship on the coast, especially among slaves, and by 1883 Qādirī scholars were instrumental in gaining new converts for Islam on the coast. And although many Shirazi patricians rejected the new rituals, they sooner or later resigned and even started to support them in order to maintain their influence on the commoners. The adoption of these rituals by converts acquired such momentum that even some Qādirī scholars started to criticize them: they were not prepared to accept all forms of localization of Islamic rituals. Still, the efforts of tajdīd (reform) connected with the spread of the Qādiriyya led to an opening of the Islamic ritual, in particular the mawlidi ya Kiswahili and the dhikr of the Qādiriyya. The popularization of Sufi teachings by new scholars enabled uneducated Muslims and converts to acquire access to Sufi ritual. For some converts, access to Islam was even limited to Sufi ritual. This popularization of the ritual was later repeated with respect to the reform of Islamic education, in the context of the emergence of a new generation of ʿAlawī scholars who stressed the need to open access to Islamic education to all Muslims.

The scholars from Ḥaḍramawt and the Banādir coast were thus willing to defend convert practices of Islam and to provide a certain degree of religious legitimacy. For marginal groups in the coastal areas, as well as the migrant populations, affiliation with the new scholars, and participation in their religious and social activities, came to be an important avenue for social mobility, as these ritual practices were legitimized by the new scholars in Islamic terms against the critique of the local establishment. In these local disputes over the Islamic character of ritual innovations, legitimatory references to external centers of spiritual authority in the Ḥaḍramawt, ʿIrāq, the Ḥijāz, and Egypt were activated in order to gain external support for respective claims to religious authority. Actual contact with other parts of the Muslim ecumene, such as Egypt and the Ḥijāz, remained confined, however, to a minority of religious scholars and became more widespread, as in sub-Saharan West Africa, in the context of colonial rule only and the subsequent intensification of long-distance transport, trade, and state-organized pilgrimages, as well as the introduction of new media and new means of transport from the 1920s.

The critique of the established scholars was particularly directed against the new dhikr ceremonies of the Qādiriyya, as propagated by scholars such as Shaykh Uways

b. Muḥammad al-Barawī (1847–1909). Shaykh Uways was one of the few East African Muslim scholars who had studied in Baghdad, the spiritual center of the Qādiriyya, for a fairly long period of time in the 1870s and 1880s, returning to Brawa in 1883. After his return to Brawa, he claimed to be entitled to lead the local scholarly establishment on account of his scholarship and his direct connections with the center of the Qādiriyya. Although it was rejected in Brawa, his claim found considerable recognition in other parts of East Africa, in particular in Zanzibar, which after 1884 became a major center of his activities. In addition, Shaykh Uways cultivated good contacts with a number of sulṭāns of Zanzibar, in particular Barghash, Khalīfa b. Saʿīd (r. 1888–1890), and Ḥāmid b. Thwaynī (r. 1893–1896), and was able to transform his branch of the Qādiriyya into a religious mass movement. From the late 1880s, his interpretation of the teachings of the Qādiriyya, connected with a number of new and distinctive religious practices, especially the zikri ya kukohoa, became popular among converts to Islam. The new dhikr practices were attacked as an un-Islamic innovation and polemically described as a "dhikr of coughing" by other scholars, even scholars of the Qādiriyya who had become part of the local religious establishment, such as Shaykh ʿAbd al-Azīz b. ʿAbd al-Ghanī b. Ṭāhir b. Nūr al-Amawī (1838–1896). Since the 1860s, Shaykh al-Amawī had propagated another form of the dhikr, namely the zikri ya dufu, and probably felt threatened, in his position as paramount scholar of the Qādiriyya in Zanzibar, by the rapid spread of the new dhikr movement of Shaykh Uways. The perception of the zikri ya kukohoa as an un-Islamic innovation must thus be seen as a function of local disputes: while the established Amawī branch of the Qādiriyya depicted the zikri ya kukohoa in the context of competition with Shaykh Uways as a bidʿa, the zikri ya kukohoa was perceived by the scholars of the Uways branch of the Qādiriyya as a religious practice which could be regarded as even more authentic than the local practices of the Qādiriyya, since it was practiced in the very center of the Qādiriyya in Baghdad. The new form of the dhikr, as defended and propagated by Shaykh Uways, eventually became a major feature of convert practices of Islam, as many converts sought affiliation with the Uways branch of the Qādiriyya which, in contrast to Shaykh al-Amawī's branch, was not associated with established Islam.

The rapid spread of the dhikr movement was not confined, however, to Zanzibar and the East African coast, but seems to have been a major force in the conversion of non-Muslims to Islam in the East African hinterlands in the late nineteenth and early twentieth centuries. Both Glassman and Nimtz correlate the movement of conversion to Islam in Tanganyika, from the late nineteenth century, with the activities of Qādirī dāʿiya and the ritual attraction of the dhikr. The expansion of the Qādiriyya and its ritual practices led to a massive spread of new Muslim rituals, in particular the different forms of dhikr. On the basis of these new rituals, new concepts of community came to be cultivated. These concepts were no longer characterized by competition but by the communal dhikr. At the same time, the new Sufi scholars became foci for social and religious reorientation and were able to challenge existing social and religious structures which had been characterized by their exclusivity.

While the efforts of reform of the Qādiriyya had focused on ritual, a second reform movement on the East African coast concentrated on the propagation of the mawlid al-nabī and the reform of Islamic education. This movement was represented by scholars of the ʿAlawiyya, a network of families of sharīfian descent from Ḥaḍramawt. For many years, ʿAlawī families had formed networks of scholarship and trade all over the Indian Ocean. In East Africa, Lamu, and the Comoros, ʿAlawī families such as the Jamal al-Layl and Abū Bakr b. Sālim had been established since the early sixteenth century, while other ʿAlawī families had settled in Zanzibar more recently and were represented, in the late nineteenth century, by the families of Aḥmad b. Sumayṭ (d. 1925) and ʿAbdallāh Bā Kathīr al-Kindī (d. 1925). As a religious movement, the ʿAlawiyya, like the related Shādhiliyya, traced its origin to the Andalusian scholar and saint Shuʿayb Abū Madyan (d. 1198), and stressed, as did the Shādhiliyya, the importance of Islamic law and veneration of the Prophet as the major source of knowledge and inspiration. Veneration of the Prophet was emphasized through celebration of the Prophet's birthday, and in East Africa the celebration of the mawlid al-nabī came to be known as the major ʿAlawī ritual. At the same time, the scholars of the ʿAlawiyya adopted a critical position not only toward the Shirazi religious and political establishment, but also toward the scholars of the Qādiriyya and their concepts of the Islamic ritual which allowed for ecstatic practices. ʿAlawī scholars, in particular, tried to marginalize the growing social influence of Qādirī scholars by advancing new approaches to Islamic education. These efforts at education were expressed in the foundation of new schools, such as the ribāṭ al-riyādha in Lamu, established by Ḥabīb Ṣāliḥ Jamal al-Layl, or the madrasat Bā Kathīr in Zanzibar, established by ʿAbdallāh Bā Kathīr. These new schools taught Qurʾān and fiqh as well as a wide spectrum of the Islamic canon of disciplines. At the same time, scholars of the ʿAlawiyya started to make Islamic education available to all Muslims, even slaves. The popularization of the ritual brought about by scholars of the Qādiriyya was thus repeated, in structural terms, with regard to the reform of Islamic education by ʿAlawī scholars. Yet while the Qādiriyya and, to a certain extent, the Shādhiliyya under the influence of Muḥammad Maʿrūf (d. 1905) became religious mass movements in major parts of East Africa, including rural areas, from the late nineteenth century, the efforts of reform of the ʿAlawiyya in the late nineteenth and early twentieth centuries remained largely confined to a comparatively small group of Muslims in the coastal areas, and mainly in the urban centers.

Muslims in Upcountry East Africa

As mentioned, Islam did not start becoming established in the upcountries of the East African coast before the mid-nineteenth century. By contrast to the bilād al-sūdān in sub-Saharan West Africa, which formed a broad belt of Muslim cultures and countries, expanding gradually from the Saharan sāḥil toward the tropical forest belt of the Guinea coast, Muslim societies on the East African coast remained confined to a chain of settlements on the shores of the Indian Ocean and the islands off the coast until the early nineteenth century. The historical division into a Muslim coast and non-Muslim upcountries is amazing and can be explained, in part, by the deep-rooted refusal of coastal Muslims to turn their attention from benign seas to forbidding nyika hinterlands, while trade connections between upcountry regions and the coast, as far as they existed at all, were maintained by upcountry populations that saw little reason to convert to Islam when coming down to the coast to do some trade. After all, they were integrated into old networks of exchange which reached far beyond the East African coast to the great lakes and beyond, to the upper Congo and its confluences.

In historical terms, and in contrast to sub-Saharan West Africa, the East African coastal hinterland has also been characterized by fairly low population densities between the southern Ethiopian highlands and the Ruvuma, which today constitutes the boundary between Tanzania and Mozambique. Only the interlacustrine region, which was far removed from the coast, had higher populations, as well as dense trade networks. At the same time, East African upcountry populations, in particular those in the interlacustrine region, were able to cover a major part of their needs by regional trade networks. Also, the interlacustrine region did not constitute a salt sink like sub-Saharan West Africa: salt deposits such as Kibiro on Lake Albert were available and formed part of local and regional exchange networks. As in West Africa, salt and copper deposits formed the basis for indigenous long-distance trade routes at fairly early periods; but these resources were also located in the interior zones, thus providing no incentive for penetration of the nyika and "very little linkage with coastal trade until the nineteenth century" (Austen 1987: 58). Last but not least, slaves from the hinterlands could be exported to the coast only as long as they were non-Muslim. Local rulers in the hinterland regions of the central East African coast, who traded with the coast, were not keen thus on encouraging conversion to Islam in their respective realms. Widespread Muslim allegiance would have interfered with their assertion of privileged contact with the coast. Moreover, ignorance of Islam was part of what marked out slaves on the coast: the big men's customers had "no enthusiasm for Muslim slaves" (Becker 2008: 37). People who wanted to become Muslim had to go down to the coast.

The division between the coast and the upcountry regions was to change only in the eighteenth and nineteenth centuries, when coastal settlements developed an increasing demand for both workers (carriers, slaves) and trade goods such as ivory, and were willing and able to pay for these imports with new technologies, in particular guns and ammunition. It has to be stressed again, however, that most of the immediate hinterlands of the northern and central coasts were barely settled, except for some pastoralists and hunter gatherers; the way to the fertile and more densely settled regions on Lake Victoria, and to the other Great Lakes, was arduous and long. Thus, in pre-Portuguese times the most profitable trade routes from the coast into the East

African hinterlands were in the south, in particular the route up the Zambezi to the gold mines of the Mwene Motapa, which led to the prosperity of Kilwa and the southern coast between the thirteenth and the fifteenth centuries. After the disruptions by the Portuguese and the Zimba, southern routes were also the first to be revived in the eighteenth century, in particular those controlled by the Yao, connecting Mozambique and Kilwa with Lake Malawi.

Over time, three networks of routes from the coast to the interlacustrine regions of East Africa developed: first, the southern routes from Kilwa to the Ruvuma and

First Muslims reached Buganda in the 1840s under Kabaka (king) Suna (r. 1832–1856) in the guise of a trader called Aḥmad b. Ibrāhīm. Islam gained a major position at the court, when Kabaka Mutesa I (r. 1856–84) allowed a Muslim trader, ʿAlī Nakatukula, to instruct him in the new religion. His work was continued by another trader, Khamīs b. ʿAbdallāh, from 1867. Eventually, the Kabaka himself taught Islam to the lords of his kingdom and introduced public recitation of the Qur'ān at court. In 1867, Ramaḍān was practiced for the first time, a mosque was built, and ritual ablution was introduced, not only at the court but in all provincial centers. The growing group of Muslims was opposed by a party of tradition, which, however, suffered a massacre in 1875, resulting in mass conversion to Islam. By 1874, the Kabaka seems to have spoken both Kiswahili and Arabic, and by 1875 Arabic was established as the language of correspondence at the court. The court cultivated relations with Zanzibar. Indeed, Zanzibari fashion set the standards in Buganda. In the late 1870s, Egyptian imperial expansion up the Nile was perceived as an increasing threat to Buganda, however: in 1872, an Egyptian basis was established in Fatiko, south of Gondokoro, close to Buganda's northern borders, and in 1876 an Egyptian expedition reached Lake Victoria. This led to a revision of Buganda's politics: the Kabaka rehabilitated the party of tradition and allowed Christian missionaries to come to Buganda. Muslim critique was silenced in a massacre of prominent Muslims in late 1876. The arrival of Christian missionaries in 1877 started a period of competition between Muslims, Christians, and the party of tradition, in which the Kabaka changed sides several times. This situation did not change under Mutesa's successors, Muwanga (r. 1884–88) and Kalema (r. 1888–90). In 1890, under the impression of the advance of the Mahdiyya, the Christian party organized a revolt and defeated the last Muslim strongholds in northern Buganda in 1891.

thence to Lake Malawi. Transport on these routes was organized largely by Yao traders from the seventeenth century. Second, there were the central routes from Zanzibar and Bagamoyo via Tabora to Ujiji on Lake Tanganyika and beyond. These routes were dominated by the Nyamwesi and were extended to the Upper Congo in the second half of the nineteenth century. And finally, there were the northern routes from Mombasa and Pangani to either the north or the south of the Usambara and Pare mountains into the highlands beyond Mount Kilimanjaro and Mount Kenya, as well as, eventually, to Lake Victoria (Nyanza) and Buganda on the northern shores of Lake Victoria. Only from the early nineteenth century onward were traders from the central and northern coasts able, however, to establish those long-distance trade routes through the arid wastelands of the Maasai Mara toward Lake Victoria, which eventually connected these areas of trade with the coast. These routes, in particular the northern branches, were dominated by the Kamba and were fully developed by the mid-nineteenth century, although the Kamba lost control over this route by the 1860s. In addition, there were the even more northern routes, from Lamu, Brawa, Marka, and Mogadishu, up the Tana and Juba/Shebelle to the southern highlands of Ethiopia. On each route, African peoples of the interior were the first to establish domination over each route and controlled the trade as well as the logistics of the trade. Over time, traders from the coast, Arabs, Indians, and Swahili, established their own trade networks and concluded agreements of cooperation with local rulers, expanding gradually toward the interior.

While Muslim traders from the coast and Nyamwesi networks controlled trade on the central routes, the southern routes were dominated by Yao traders, who had established contact with Kilwa and other coastal centers of trade since the seventeenth century. Despite their long history of contacts with Muslims on the coast, the first Yao seem to have converted to Islam only in the 1870s, but conversion to Islam accelerated in the last decades of the nineteenth century, possibly under the impression of Portuguese colonialism and the increasing presence of Europeans in East African trade. At the same time, the Yao, who were not united in political terms, suffered from the political expansion of the Makua in the south. In order to escape Makua pressure, many Yao resettled in the late nineteenth century on the northern shores of Lake Malawi and established new centers of trade in this region. Lake Malawi had already been reached by a Muslim trader from the coast, Sālim b. ʿAbdallāh, in 1840, and the center of trade established by him, Kota Kota, soon became the most important center for long-distance trade on the southern routes in the interior. Sālim b. ʿAbdallāh even built a fleet of dhows on Lake Malawi and thus consolidated his paramount role in the region. Sālim b. ʿAbdallāh flew the flag of the sulṭān of Zanzibar, encouraged local chiefs to send their sons for studies to Zanzibar, and seems to have been the local ruler who handed over the assassins of Albrecht Roscher to the sulṭān of Zanzibar in 1860. During his first visit to Kota Kota in 1866, the British explorer Livingstone remarked that "indeed most of the houses here are square for the Arabs are imitated in everything" (quoted in Shepperson 1966: 254).

When Kota Kota came under British control in 1895, a majority of the population had become Muslim and Kota Kota was a major center of Islam in the region. By way of caravan trade, Muslims also reached new destinations in the East African interior and beyond: in 1841, a first coastal expedition, led by Nāṣir b. Sālim al-Ḥarthy and ʿAbd al-ʿĀl, reached the Kasai in the Western Congo, and in 1852 the first three traders from Zanzibar crossed Central Africa and reached the Portuguese harbor of Benguela on the Atlantic. In 1853, the British explorer Livingston also met a group of Swahili traders led by Saʿīd b. Ḥabīb al-ʿAfīfī in Linyati, in contemporary northern Namibia, yet, as sea routes around the Cape proved to be faster than the trade across the land, the development of a Muslim East African trade network between the Indian Ocean and the Atlantic never materialized. Still, these new trade routes contributed massively to a new flourishing of the East African coast from the early nineteenth century, based on two major items of export: ivory and slaves.

East African trade, like trans-Saharan trade, was organized in the form of caravans. Due to the fact that parts of the East African interior were infested with tsetse flies which transmitted sleeping sickness, East Africa did not have a tradition of animal-based caravans but had to rely on humans. The logistics of a caravan were complex. Caravans were organized by a majumbe or akida, a master of the caravan: they supervised the recruitment of the carriers (Swa. hamali) and were responsible for discipline in the caravan. For a number of East African societies, to work as a carrier came to mean a form of social advancement that would eventually lead to the position of a majumbe. Often a majumbe would also act as imām or as a healer (Swa. mganga) and lead the religious ceremonies during a caravan. The return of the caravan to the coast was linked with a feast, as young men saw their return as porters from a caravan as a form of initiation into the community of adult men. From the early nineteenth century, the Nyamwesi specialized as carriers and tried to earn the funds needed for proper marriage. In order to be accepted as a man, one had to have been in Zanzibar.

Due to the fact that caravans provided valuable work and income, the transport of goods never became the work of slaves: slaves were needed as unpaid workers on the plantations on the islands and on the coast, but not as hamali in caravans. A caravan thus had to recruit a sufficient number of porters for the loads carried inland, as well as back to the coast. These loads included necessities for the survival of the caravan itself and goods that were needed as toll fees in order to be granted passage (Swa. hongo) through the territories of local rulers on the way to the different markets. A caravan usually had hundreds of carriers, in addition to armed guards, the employees of the traders, their families, and numerous craftsmen, in particular smiths, carpenters, and constructors who were in charge of repairs, the manufacture of spare parts, and the construction of camps. Finally, a caravan took on a number of elephant hunters. All carriers and participants in a caravan concluded a contract with the trader or entrepreneur who organized it. The carriers, in particular, were hired for a specific period of time and often got an advance payment for their services. Still, carriers deserted repeatedly, an experience that European caravans frequently had in the second half of the nineteenth century. Each carrier was given a load of about 25–30 kilograms, and each group of carriers had its own leader. To cover the distance from Bagamoyo to Tabora, the major center of the Nyamwesi, a caravan would need about 45–50 days, and to Ujiji another 20–25 days. Often, the caravan had to be reconstituted in Tabora, as many carriers did not want to go further and preferred to return to the coast. Also, many caravans split in Tabora and continued in different directions. The Nyamwesi had managed to establish contact with Kazembe, south of Lake Mweru, and thus with Yao trade networks leading to Lake Malawi in the south, as well as with the much larger trade networks that ran from Kazembe into Katanga, beyond Lake Tanganyika and Lake Malawi. At the same time, the Nyamwesi developed a trade route from Tabora to the north, which eventually reached Lake Victoria from the south.

The major item of export on all routes was ivory, which was a highly esteemed material for the production of jewelry in India, and which came to be highly valued for the production of piano keys and billiard balls in nineteenth-century Europe and America. In 1859, Zanzibar alone exported more than 221,000 kilograms of ivory, and this seems to have remained the annual average until the 1890s. One kilogram of ivory fetched 120–180 dollars on the market in the 1890s. The ivory craze in India, Europe, and North America led to the quick extinction of elephants on the East African coast and pushed the ivory frontier farther and farther into the East African interior. In the 1840s, on the northern and central routes, the coastal trade had reached the old trade networks in the interlacustrine regions and subsequently linked up with the trade networks which connected the interlacustrine regions with the territories on the upper Congo. The major products of trade for the interlacustrine region were textiles, palm oil, and guns from the coast, and ivory, slaves, and copper from the interior. The major center of this trade on the central route was Ujiji on Lake Tanganyika, whose ruler, Mwinyi Kheri, was eventually acknowledged as master of Ujiji by Sulṭān Barghash in the 1870s. From the 1870s, Ujiji also became the transmission belt for further expansion of the coastal trade into the Congo region, an expansion which was linked with the endeavors of two Muslim traders, ʿAbd al-Ḥamīd Muḥammad Jumaʿ al-Murjibī and Muḥammad b. Khalfān alias Rumaliza, originally a major ally of ʿAbd al-Ḥamīd Muḥammad Jumaʿ al-Murjibī, who later appropriated his properties on Lake Tanganyika.

ʿAbd al-Ḥamīd b. Muḥammad b. Jumaʿ al-Murjibī (d. 1905) was better known among European travelers as Tippu Tip (the one who flickers with his eyelids). The German consul in Zanzibar, Heinrich Brode, wrote and published his biography in 1903 under the title *Autobiographie des Arabers Schech Hamed bin Muhammed el Murjebi, genannt Tippu Tip.* Tippu Tips's great-grandfather originated from Masqaṭ in Oman, but married on the East African coast and started a trading business, which was subsequently expanded by his son, Muḥammad b. Jumaʿ, and his grandson, ʿAbd al-Ḥamīd. Muḥammad b. Jumaʿ settled permanently in Tabora, which, as the center of the Unyamwesi region, came to form the major crossroads for trade with the African interior. The ruler of Tabora, Fundi Kira, privileged traders from the coast by exempting them from taxes, and married one of his daughters to Muḥammad b. Juma'. In 1858, Tippu Tip undertook the first of many journeys with his father, traveling via Ujiji to Urua, west of Lake Tanganyika. They brought back large loads of ivory which earned a good profit in Zanzibar and helped Tippu Tip to equip his own caravan. With this caravan, he ventured into the regions south of Lake Tanganyika, to Urungu, where he again acquired a great amount of ivory. Also, he proved himself as a capable caravan leader and was thus deemed worthy of credit by the Indian bankers on the coast. On his third caravan trip, he reached the northern shores of Lake Malawi and made good gains there, then explored the Bamba region south of Lake Tanganyika, and eventually reached Itowa, southwest of Lake Tanganyika, which was ruled by Nsama, a local ruler who was known to have robbed traders from the coast. However, Tippu Tip succeeded in taking Nsama's stronghold and seizing his rich stores of ivory. In this local conflict, Tippu Tip could rely on firearms and the efficient use of them for rapid fire. This superior fire power gave Tippu Tip military supremacy over local rulers, comparable to that of the Sudanese conquistador Rābiḥ b. Faḍl Allāh, or of European military expeditions, and this is reflected correspondingly in his biography. After a first victorious encounter with the "washenzi" of Itahua, Tippu Tip describes the next attack of the shensis (i.e., washenzi, "savages"):

> The next morning, about a quarter to seven, our men went out, and saw that about 600 Shensis had fallen, and the weapons—spears, arrows, bows, drums and axes—which they had thrown away were not to be counted. They had stood in groups, you see. We waited a short time. When it was two o'clock, the Shensis advanced on us in great crowds. However, they were already frightened. We let them come close to the *boma,* then our people charged; and not seven minutes had passed when they took to flight, and 150 men had fallen, while we had been lucky—only two men fell. (Tippu Tip as recorded by Brode 1903/2000: 17)

In 1869, Tippu Tip was back in Dar es Salaam, the new harbor on the coast, and asked the Indian banker Tharia Topan to finance a new, larger caravan. He equipped his fourth caravan with a great number of firearms, and left in 1870 for the southern reaches of Lake Tanganyika, where he established a major base for his excursions into Itawa, Katanga, and Kazembe, as well as Urua and Manyema to the west of Lake Tanganyika. Equally, he aimed at the Lualaba, a tributary of the Congo River, which had been reached so far by only one trader from the coast, Juma' b. Sayf Merikani, who had become famous for introducing American cotton textiles (Merikani) on the Upper Congo. On the Lualaba, Tippu Tip learned about rich ivory stocks on the upper Lomami and subsequently pushed with his troops into the tropical forests of the Upper Lomami. After defeating the Utetela, Songye, and Kasa, he reached Nyangwe, west of Lake Tanganyika, on his way back in 1874. From Nyangwe, he sent to the coast the ivory stocks he had acquired so far and continued his forays into the Upper Congo, now from a second base in Kasongo, in western Manyema, where he also came to meet the Anglo-American traveler Henry Morton Stanley. He accompanied Stanley down the Congo to the mouth of the Ulindi and then turned west to the Lomami, where he was able to acquire further stocks of ivory. After arriving back in Kasongo, he put together a huge caravan of more than 3,000 carriers to transport his ivory to the coast. The profit he made on this caravan enabled him not only to pay all his debts, but also to finance his own caravan, and to build a stock of capital for further expeditions. These expeditions took him far west into the tropical forests of the Congo and its confluences. Here he met European travelers and explorers, who saw in him a major problem for the expansion of European trade in this region and who were not at all amused when they realized that they had to rely on Tippu Tip's logistics for the transport of their own goods from one trading center to the next. In the Congo, agents of King Leopold of Belgium, who had started to explore this vast region as his own private empire, tried to strike a deal with Tippu Tip, yet failed as he presented himself as a representative of the sulṭān of Zanzibar. In 1883, Tippu Tip in fact went to the Upper Congo in order to establish the authority and the flag of the sulṭān of Zanzibar in this region, and established a base in Kisangani, on the upper Congo, in 1884, thus disputing the claims of King Leopold (as represented by Stanley). As Kisangani was situated below the last cataracts of the upper Congo, the way downstream to the Atlantic seemed to be free for Tippu Tip and the sulṭān of Zanzibar. In a series of small expeditions, Tippu Tip secured control over the Lower Lomami and the Aruwimi in the north, which linked the Congo River system with the territories of the Zande on the upper Nile and its confluences. The Sulṭānate of Zanzibar was not able to defend these territorial claims internationally, however, and eventually lost all its mainland territories to disputing European powers in the aftermath of the Berlin Congo Conference in 1885. And although the European powers were not physically present in most of these areas, they had the naval power to force Zanzibar into submission.

Tippu Tip eventually left the territories conquered by him in the Congo to the authority of his younger brother, Bwana Nzige, who was subsequently able to stop the Belgian advance toward Kisangani, and returned to Zanzibar in 1886. In Zanzibar, Tippu Tip found that the Sulṭānate had been forced to abandon most of its mainland territories to Britain and Germany, as well as King Leopold, in an agreement reached on 7 December 1886. He still assisted Stanley in his endeavors to trace Emin Pasha alias Eduard Schnitzler, the German governor of Equatoria, a province of the Anglo-Egyptian Sudan. Unknown to Stanley, Emin Pasha had established a base in Upper Equatoria. Tippu Tip eventually returned to Zanzibar when he realized that the Belgian advance in the Congo could not be stopped. He retired in Zanzibar and was able to win a number of legal cases against his banker, Tharia Topan, against Rumaliza, who had tried to appropriate his possessions on Lake Tanganyika and the Congo, as well as against Stanley, who had falsely accused him of being responsible for the disaster of the Emin Pasha rescue operation. He died in 1905. By the time of his death, he was the second biggest owner of plantations in Zanzibar, worked by 10,000 slaves, as well as being the owner of numerous houses.

Muslim traders in the upper Congo resented the Belgian advance and organized armed resistance, defeating two Belgian expeditions in 1892 and attacking Belgian positions on the Lomami. In 1893, Belgium was forced to equip a major military force to win this war, eventually occupying all Muslim positions on the upper Congo, including Kasongo. In 1894, the Belgians defeated a military expedition commanded by a former ally of Tippu Tip, Rumaliza, thus ending Zanzibar's political influence in the region. Still, Muslim presence on the upper Congo could no longer be denied, and was particularly prominent in Kasongo, the major base of Tippu Tip: in 1889, Kasongo had a population of about 20,000 inhabitants, consisting of Muslims from the coast, as well as a mix of peoples from the upper Congo and Manyema regions. The town had a qur'ānic school and a mosque, Swahili fashion had been established, and new crops had been introduced from the coast. Kasongo thus came to be a center for the establishment and spread of Islam in the upper Congo, and for the spread of Kiswahili as the language of communication in this region.

11 Muslims on the Cape

Community and Dispute

Historical Themes and Patterns

In the academic discussion of the history of Muslim societies in Africa, Muslim communities in South Africa are often ignored. They are usually seen as being not old and not African enough. Such a perspective omits the fact that Muslims have formed an integral part of society on the Cape since the mid-seventeenth century and came to be a decisive social force in Cape Town in the nineteenth century. In contrast to other regions of Africa, Cape Muslim history was always intrinsically linked with the colonial history of the Cape. From the very beginnings of the community in the 1660s, the community of Cape Muslims had to come to terms with religious, political, legal, and social structures dictated by a Christian majority population, the Afrikaaner settlers, organized by the Vereenigde Oostindische Compagnie (VOC) and the Nederduitse Gereformeerde Kerk (NGK). Despite the restrictions imposed by the VOC and the NGK, the Cape Muslim community developed into a growing and thriving community in the eighteenth century. In the nineteenth century, when the restrictions imposed by VOC and NGK were abolished, the Cape Muslim communities became a major player in Cape Town politics, although internal struggles over leadership prevented the emergence of a politically united Cape Muslim community. Due to its old links with India and Indonesia, the community of Muslims on the Cape has been cosmopolitan from an early point of time, and became even more so in the nineteenth century, in particular when first Cape Muslims went on pilgrimage and were awarded their own place in Mecca. This chapter focuses on the development of the Cape Muslim community since the seventeenth century and show how this small Muslim community has survived more than 300 years of European hegemonic domination.

The Origins of the Cape Muslim Community

For most other regions in Africa, contacts to either the bilād al-maghrib, Egypt, the Ḥijāz, or southern Arabia were important for the development of local traditions of learning and the question of which school of law would be adopted, The emergence of the Cape Muslim community, however, was dominated by contacts with India and Indonesia. The establishment of a Muslim community in Cape Town was initially linked with the needs of the VOC to build up a reliable workforce: the indigenous Khoikhoi and San populations were pasturalists or hunter-gatherers. They were not regarded as reliable and were soon reduced to a tiny minority, due to massacres and diseases. Jan van Riebeeck, the first governor of the VOC on the Cape, thus asked for slaves in 1653 in order to solve the workforce problem, and in 1658 the first (non-Muslim) slaves from Dahomey and Angola were sent to the Cape. The first Muslims to come to the Cape, also in 1658, were Mardycker (Ind. merdeka, free) from Ambon, an island in the Moluccas, who had been working for the VOC and decided to stay with their masters on the Cape. Yet until 1700, the majority of Muslims on the Cape did not come from Indonesia but from other parts of Africa and Madagascar, as well as Sri Lanka and Bengal, regions which had come under Dutch control in 1638, after the demise of the Portuguese sea-borne empire in the Indian Ocean. In total, between one and two hundred Muslim and non-Muslim slaves reached the Cape annually between 1658 and 1795, but this population was often hit by epidemics, such as a smallpox epidemic in 1713, when the servant and slave community on the Cape was reduced from 570 to 370 persons.

As a result of this epidemic, the servant and slave community on the Cape lost its African and Indo-Bengal character and became increasingly Malay and even came to be labeled as Cape Malays in the literature. The Malay character of the Cape Muslim population increased after a number of deportations from South East Asia to the Cape in 1725, 1737, and 1749. Eventually, the importation of Muslim slaves from Southeast Asia was prohibited, as their numbers had become too large. Still, free Muslims from this region continued to come to the Cape, in particular workers from Amboina, as well as some Buginese from Sulawesi. In addition, a smaller number of Muslims, often deportees, from India, as well as slaves from India, Madagascar, and other parts of

> Small pox epidemics were a recurrent event in Cape Town. Outbreaks occurred in 1755, 1767, 1807, 1812, 1440, 1858, and 1882, and led to vaccination campaigns and the development of policies of sanitation in respect of the overcrowded and poor Malay and African quarters in the nineteenth century. They also led to social revolt among Cape Muslims, when policies of sanitation acquired an anti-Muslim connotation. In 1882, vaccination, quarantine, and hospitalization campaigns, as well as denial of burial rites, led to protest, when Cape Muslim spokesmen such as Abdol Burns realized that these sanitation measures were connected with plans to relocate Muslim urban cemeteries. Sanitation arguments were also used to resettle complete residential areas, but these plans were stopped by Cape Muslim protests in 1882 and were implemented in 1901 only, in the context of an outbreak of bubonic plague in Cape Town. As a consequence, the "kaffirs" of Woodstock and the "Malays" of Bloem Street were relocated to Uitvlugt.

Africa, added to the kaleidoscope of the Cape Muslim population. Among the political prisoners who were sent to the Cape, deportees from Southeast Asia dominated by a ratio of 2.5:1 throughout the eighteenth century when compared to those deported from India. Among the Indian deportees, people from Bengal dominated, while the Javanese dominated among the Southeast Asians.

The slave and servant population on the Cape was increased by slaves from the Cape region, mostly Khoikhoi and San, some of whom converted to Islam. In the nineteenth century, the Cape slave and servant population expanded further due to the incorporation of freed slaves from the East African coast. These had been liberated by the British in the course of their anti-slavery campaign in the western Indian Ocean and brought to South Africa, mostly to Durban (Natal), as "Zanzibaris." Many of these former African slaves converted to Islam on the Cape. The movement of conversion of Africans was stimulated by the policy of the NGK, which had decided in 1618 that Christians could not be slaves. Slaves who converted to Christianity and were baptized achieved their freedom automatically and became vrije zwarten (free blacks) who could inherit, earn money, own property, and even carry arms. As a consequence, the Dutch-Afrikaaner slave owners on the Cape were not interested in the conversion of their slaves to Christianity. In 1770, the Raad van Indie in Batavia also decided that slaves who had been baptized were protected and could not be sold any more: they would be granted freedom after the death of their owners. As a consequence of this policy, some Dutch slave owners encouraged their slaves to convert to Islam. At the same time, the NGK supported the restrictive position of the Afrikaaner slave owners and did not recognize baptisms, marriages, and other rites which had been conducted without the consent of the NGK. Most slaves were thus denied the chance to become Christians, and conversion to Islam became the only path open to slaves for improving their personal situation:

> Conversion to Islam was encouraged by the slaves' virtual exclusion from Christianity, but was also apparently due to the ministry of the Muslim imāms who, unlike the Christian clergy, identified with the black population and performed marriages and funerals which the slaves could not obtain in Christian churches (Elphick and Giliomee 1989: 192).

Due to the conversion of African slaves to Islam, the British colonial administration which took control of the Cape during the Napoleonic wars decreed in 1812 that conversion to Christianity should not affect the personal status of the converted; thus a slave would remain a slave. Despite this regulation, which remained in force until 1833, when slavery was abolished, conversion to Islam continued among the African populations of the Cape. The growth of the Cape Muslim population was also stimulated by the fact that Muslims were willing to adopt orphans and to marry non-Muslim women, in particular European women, who had come to the Cape in the nineteenth century and were excluded from white society by the rigid moral code of the NGK, due to the fact that they were divorced or single, widows, or women who had left or had been left by their husbands. Often, these women married Muslims, as Muslims "did not know billiards and brandy—the two diseases of Capetown," as remarked Lady Duff Gordon in the 1860s (quoted in Shell 1983: 5). The openness of the Cape Muslim population to integrate virtually everybody thus granted the continued existence, as well as the growth, of the Muslim population on the Cape: in 1822, there were 3,000 Muslims in Cape Town and 6,435 in 1842, representing a third of the total population. By 1891, their number had reached 11,300 in Cape Town and 3,800 in the Cape Province. In economic terms, Muslims made their living as fruit sellers, teachers, fishermen, craftsmen, candle makers, laborers, and tailors, and were often able to build considerable capital, which was invested in houses, property, and even slaves.

The community of Cape Muslims was characterized not only by its growth and its willingness to integrate marginalized populations on the Cape, but also by the fact that it developed a culture of resistance against the domination of the VOC and the NGK, which was important for the survival of the servant and slave community on the Cape as a distinct group: Islam became the language of the oppressed and the language of resistance. Muslim rites as well as communitarian solidarity provided for a secret code which allowed Muslims to create zones of freedom in a realm of legal, political, and social oppression. Due to this fact, Muslims were regarded as increasingly unreliable workers, and a number of decrees in 1767, 1784, and 1792 eventually prohibited the importation of Muslim slaves, in particular from Southeast Asia. Although the VOC formally prohibited Muslims from practicing their faith, as the NGK was recognized as the one and only official church on the Cape, Muslims still cultivated their traditions and Muslim religiosity became more and more pronounced in the eighteenth century. In 1772, the mawlid al-nabī was celebrated publicly for the first time, and Muslims started organizing secret places of prayer (Ind. langar), or prayer rooms, in their houses. The first langar was the Palm Tree mosque in a house in Long Street, which was established by Jan van Bougis in 1777. Other data indicate, however, that a first langar was established in 1712, eight years after the building of the first church in Cape Town. By 1811, Cape Town had twelve langars.

Muslim political prisoners played a major role in the establishment of Islam on the Cape. One of the first political prisoners on the Cape was Shaykh Yūsuf al-Tāj al-Khalwatī al-Maqassarī (d. 1699), who was born in Goa (Sulawesi) and was related to Sultan ʿAlā al-Dīn of Goa. In 1644, he visited Mecca, where he was initiated into the Khalwatiyya. He also studied the Qur'ān, tafsīr, ḥadīth, and fiqh, and possibly met ʿAbd al-Ra'ūf al-Singkilī, who was one of the most famous Muslim scholars in Southeast Asia in the seventeenth century. After his return to Southeast Asia, he settled in Banten (Java) where he became advisor to Sultan ʿAbd al-Fātiḥ Ajung and married his daughter. He supported the sultan in his fight against the Dutch and was finally taken prisoner by the Dutch in 1683. In 1694, he was deported to the Cape in a group of forty-nine persons, among them twelve other Muslim scholars. He died on 23 May 1699. His tomb, on the Zandvliet farm near Faure, soon became a center of local shrine pilgrimage and the first of several tombs of saints (Afr. kramat, from Arab. karāma) in and around Cape Town. Shaykh Yūsuf was later credited with having started proper Islamic learning on the Cape. He also authored fifteen texts on the principles of Islam as well as on the teachings of the Khalwatiyya, such as *Zubdat al-asrār* (The essence of the secrets).

After Shaykh Yūsuf, a series of other political prisoners came to the Cape, such as the Raja of Tambura on Java, ʿAbd al-Bāriʾ, in 1697, and Chakra Denigrat, the Raja of Madura, who was sent to Robben Island in 1742. Another important scholar was Tuan (Sir) Saʿīd ʿAlawī, who came to Robben Island in 1744 but was released in 1755 and stayed on the Cape. As a guard in the service of the VOC, he had access to the slave quarters, and slaves received some teaching from him. He was also credited with numerous miracles, such as transforming a load of potatoes belonging to a Dutch farmer into a load of stones and back into potatoes. His kramat was built in the Tana Baru cemetery in Longmarket Street in the Bokaap quarter of Cape Town. Last but not least, ʿAbdallāh Qāḍī ʿAbd al-Salām, alias Tuan Guru, a religious scholar from Tidore in the Moluccas (d. 1807), must be mentioned. He was deported to the Cape in 1780 and released from Robben Island in 1793. While in prison, he wrote a six-hundred-page text on the basics of Islam, Ashʿārī kalām, and Shāfiʿī law, entitled *Maʿrifat al-imān wa-l-Islām* (The knowledge of the faith and Islam), in Arabic with comments in Melayu and Buginese. His text also contained a translation into Melayu of the *ʿAqīdat ahl al-tawḥīd* of Abū Muḥammad b. Yūsuf al-Sanūsī from Tilimsān, a basic text on Ashʿārī theology. Finally, the text had ten pages on magico-religious practices such as the production of amulets and medicine. This work by Tuan Guru remained the major text for teaching in the qurʾānic schools and madāris on the Cape until the 1950s and 1960s and was repeatedly used as a work of reference in scholarly disputes on the Cape. Due to its importance, the text was translated into Afrikaans in the late nineteenth century. The latest edition of *Maʿrifat al-imān wa-l-Islām* was published in 1983 by M. A. Fakier, under the title *Akidatoel Muslim: n kietaab oor Tougied in afrikaanser taal.* After his release from prison, Tuan Guru settled on Dorp Street in Cape Town, where in 1793 he received permission to open the first Islamic school on the Cape and a langar in 1794. Until his death in 1807, he was the imām of the first official mosque of Cape Town, the Awwal mosque, built on Dorp Street in 1804. His tomb in the Tana Baru cemetery became a kramat for the Cape Muslim population. The emergence of an increasing number of kramats in and around Cape Town points to the development of a sacred geography of Islam there: from the early eighteenth century, seven (today forty-nine) kramats came to form a circle around Cape Town, becoming centers of local religiosity and shrine visits.

The influx of religious scholars from India and Southeast Asia also brought about the establishment of Sufi orders on the Cape. The foundation of the Khalwatiyya was linked with the name of Shaykh Yūsuf al-Tāj al-Khalwatī al-Maqassārī, and the Khalwatiyya seems to have been the dominant Sufi order in the eighteenth century on the Cape. However, other Sufi influences also arrived comparatively early, in particular the Rifāʿiyya, established in Baṣra by Aḥmad b. ʿAlī al-ʿAbbās al-Rifāʿī (d. 1182), known for its ecstatic practices and well established on the Malabar coast of India, as well as in Sri Lanka. In the nineteenth century, other Sufi orders followed, in particular the Qādiriyya, the Naqshbandiyya, the Sammāniyya, the Shādhiliyya, and finally in the 1880s the 'Alawiyya. The development of these Sufi orders was linked with the establishment of corresponding Sufi centers, zawāya, which came to be new centers of scholarly authority in Cape Town in the nineteenth century.

The Cape Muslim Community in the Nineteenth Century

During VOC rule, Muslims were restricted in both religious and political activities, even when they were not slaves. They were not accepted as burghers (free citizens) and thus had no say in the communal administration of the Cape which was in the hands of the burgher-raad, and they remained deprived of free citizens' rights until the very end of VOC rule. Their marriages were not legally accepted, they needed a special residence permit, and they could be deported at any time. Also, they had to take their passes with them everywhere, could not move freely outside Cape Town, and had to provide unpaid work services. This situation of discrimination ended in the context of the French Revolution: in 1795, the Netherlands was occupied by French troops and was transformed into the Republic of Batavia. In order to prevent a French takeover of the Cape, British troops landed in September 1795 and ended VOC rule. In the context of the peace treaty of Amiens, concluded in 1802 between France and Britain, the Cape was put under the administration of the Republic of Batavia, but with changed political conditions: in order to achieve the support of the Cape Muslim population in any future confrontation with the British, the Batavian General Commissioner for the Cape, J. A. de Mist, granted religious freedom to the Cape Muslims on 25 July 1804.

In 1803, a spokesman of the Cape Muslim community, Frans van Bengalen, had already negotiated the establishment of the first official Muslim cemetery and the construction of the first official mosque, Awwal mosque on Dorp Street, which had been demanded in a number of petitions since 1795. In exchange for these concessions, the Cape Muslim community supported the Republic of Batavia against imminent British invasion. They mobilized a Muslim military unit, the Javaanse Artillerie, commanded by the Muslim field priest, Frans van Bengalen, and in 1806 the Javaanse Artillerie fought against the British when they landed near Blouberg. British troops nevertheless occupied the Cape for a second time in 1806, and in 1814 the Cape became part of the British empire. Under British domination, the restrictions on religious and social life were gradually lifted. A right to vote was introduced for all Freiburgher, linked to property and European standards of education, a condition which could not be met, however, by most Cape Muslims and many (white) Afrikaaners. But in 1839, the criteria of qualification for electors were changed, and an increasing number of Cape Muslims acquired the right to vote for the communal bodies, namely wards and the Board of Commissioners which dominated Cape Town's politics in the nineteenth century. In 1842, Cape Muslims already had a voting power of 830 votes, which amounted to almost

50 percent of the electorate in Cape Town. In 1853, Cape Muslim voters with a minimum annual income of at least fifty pounds also acquired the right to elect members into the House of Assembly, the newly established parliament of the Cape Province.

As the external pressure on the Cape Muslim community slowly decreased in the nineteenth century, internal disputes among the Cape Muslims surfaced, which led to a number of splits within the Cape Muslim community and to the emergence of different mosque communities. In the context of these disputes, established scholars slowly lost their communitarian power, while a new brand of religious scholars gained influence. Disputes over the leadership of mosques became a central issue of communitarian disputes, and imāms played an important and instrumental role in negotiating and solving these disputes. Consequently, leadership of a mosque became a contentious issue. As a result, the number of imāms in Cape Town grew from three in 1811 to seven in 1825 and thirty in 1834. By 1860, their number had decreased again to fifteen, and then remained on this comparatively high level in view of the total number of Cape Muslims. The position of the imām of a mosque (or a langar) was not the only position that became a matter of dispute, however. Rather, Cape Town mosques developed a hierarchy of positions, which were all highly sought after. Apart from an imām, each mosque had an assistant imām, a senior gatiep (Arab. khaṭīb), a junior gatiep, and a billal (Arab. mu'adhdhin). In Cape Town religious terminology, these positions were transcribed into Christian terms, an imām thus often being called a mohammedan priest, while the khaṭīb was a deacon, and the mu'adhdhin an elder. At the same time, the imāms conducted naming ceremonies, burials, and marriages and were the teachers of their community. Still, the position of imām remained an honorific title for most of the early nineteenth century. Only from the mid-nineteenth century was the title linked with a formal position. The title of imām implied recognition as a notable of the community and was "much sought after" (Jeppie 1996: 150). It was even possible that men who led the prayers in one of Cape Town's mosques only from time to time, or who taught a small class of students, would claim this title. Their efforts to assert their claims informed the development of the Cape Muslim community in general, and communitarian conflict in particular, in the nineteenth century.

The imām of Cape Town's first official mosque was Tuan Guru, who established a langar on Dorp Street in 1794, which became Cape Town's first mosque in 1804. His successor, in 1807, was Frans van Bengalen, and when Frans van Bengalen died in 1822, Imām Achmat (Aḥmad) from Chinsura in Bengal followed him as the imām of the Awwal mosque. Imām Achmat stayed in office until 1843. Due to a family conflict, Muḥammad 'Abd al-Bāri', the senior khaṭīb of the Awwal mosque, became the next imām of this mosque until his death in 1851, to be followed by Mogamed (Muḥammad) (b.) Achmat, the eldest son of Imām Achmat. He held this position until his own death in 1872 and was then followed by his brother Achmat Sadiek (Ṣadīq) Achmat (see below), who was imām until he died in 1879. He was replaced by Gamya Mogamed Achmat, who was imām until 1912.

The death of Tuan Guru in 1807 had led to a first dispute over succession to the position of imām, and in the context of this dispute Cape Town's second mosque, the Palm Tree mosque, was founded on Long Street in 1807. This mosque was identical with the langar which had existed there since 1777, established and led by Jan van Bougis, who built it together with Frans van Bengalen. They had both been Mohammedan field-priests in the Javaanse Artillerie, and when Frans van Bengalen became imām of the Awwal mosque in 1807, Jan van Bougis assumed the imāmate at the Palm Tree mosque, a title he held for the rest of his life. In 1811, he became the solitary owner of the property. After his death in 1846, the property was administered by his wife, Samida, and a caretaker committee, led by Imām Abdul Logies (until 1851), and then by Imām Mahmat (Maḥmūd, until 1866). When Samida died in 1861, she gave the property to the mosque community, as represented by her son Mahmat. The new group of caretakers was not able to agree over the distribution of competences, however, and split into two communities: the family of Jan van Bougis, led by Imām Mahmat, kept control over the mosque, while a second group followed the senior khaṭīb, al-Ḥājj Danie, who had returned from Mecca in 1862 (see map 6).

The Awwal and Palm Tree mosques were the only mosques in Cape Town before 1844, when a number of new mosques began to be established. The foundation of these mosques was linked with communitarian disputes, mostly over questions of succession, proper religious practice, or questions of scholarship. Mosques became places for the negotiation of conflict, in particular after the death of an imām: "Although madrasah classes provided the venue for acquiring knowledge, thus empowering the student for a position in the mosque, the mosque was the institution which displayed that acquired power" (Tayob 1995: 47). Between 1866 and 1900, at least twenty cases of succession disputes over the position of an imām or other mosque positions were fought among Cape Muslims and brought to court, in some cases even to the Supreme Court in Cape Town.

The foundation of Cape Town's third mosque in 1844, the Nūr al-Islām mosque in the Buitengracht, was linked with such a conflict of authority: just before he died, Tuan Guru had appointed Frans and then Achmat van Bengalen to become the next imāms of the Awwal mosque. The sons of Tuan Guru were still under age and respected this wish of their father, but they eventually rebelled against Imām Achmat, and in 1834 they established an association within the community, namely the Muhammedan Shafee Congregation, which was led, for a short period of time, by Tuan Guru's eldest son, 'Abd al-Raqīb (d. 1834), followed by his younger brother 'Abd al-Ra'ūf (d. 1869). The foundation of the Muhammedan Shafee Congregation triggered the scorn of Imām Achmat, who, in 1843, just before he died, nominated his senior khaṭīb, Muḥammad 'Abd al-Bāri', to become his successor.

At this point of time, the sons of Tuan Guru and Imām Achmat established the Nūr al-Islām mosque, led by Imām 'Abd al-Ra'ūf b. Tuan Guru, to be followed after his death in 1869 by his eldest son Abdol Rakiep ('Abd al-Raqīb), who soon triggered another dispute among Cape Muslims and subsequently established the Buitengracht Hanafee mosque on Long Street in 1881. Further conflicts of authority led to the establishment of the Queen Victoria Jāmiʿ-mosque on Lower Chiappini Street in 1850 by Achmat Sadiek Achmat, a younger brother of Muḥammad Achmat. In 1859, Imām Hadjie ʿAlī (d. 1869) established the Shafee mosque in Upper Chiappini Street, which eventually managed to unite two separate communities in 1876. In 1881, the small Ḥanafī Muslim community, led by Abdol Rakiep, Mohammed Dollie, and Jongie Siers, established the Buitengracht Hanafee mosque and thus separated from the (Shāfiʿī) Nūr al-Islām mosque in the Buitengracht. Further foundations in the context of communitarian disputes were the establishment of the Boorhanol Islam mosque in 1884 on Longmarket Street, in the context of a split in the Queen Victoria Jāmiʿ mosque community, the foundation of the Quwatul Islam mosque on Loop Street in 1892, which served the needs of a growing Indian (Ḥanafī) population in Cape Town, and the establishment of the Masjid Nurul Muhammadiyyah in 1899.

Mosques were not the only important institution for the development of the Cape Muslim community. Another institution was the madrasa. The first madrasa had been established in 1793 by Tuan Guru in Dorp Street. It focused on the memorization of the Qurʾān and tajwīd, the rules of proper recitation of the Qurʾān. In 1807, this school had 372 students, expanding to 491 in 1825. In the first half of the nineteenth century, two large madāris emerged which eventually had more students than all other schools in the Cape Colony. In 1832, Cape Town had twelve madāris of different sizes, as well as eighty Muslim private teachers who taught children in their own houses. Until 1854, the madāris did not have a uniform syllabus, but in 1854 the imām moota (deputy imām), Achmat Sadiek Achmat, introduced a uniform syllabus for all madāris.

Achmat Sadiek Achmat (d. 1879), the youngest son of Imām Achmat van Bengalen and Saartje van de Kaap, was indeed of central importance for the development of Islamic education in Cape Town. In the 1830s, he started out as a madrasa teacher on Dorp Street, a school which had by then grown to more than 1,000 students. Subsequently, he rose to become the imām moota of Cape Town and was responsible for all Islamic schools in Cape Town. He also supervised a number of madāris which had been established by white converts to Islam. Their madāris offered English and Dutch, as well as accountancy. This system of education was further expanded in 1863 when Abūbakar Effendi established the Ottoman Theological School at the intersection of Bree and Wale Streets. Although Effendi translated the school's textbooks into Afrikaans and had them printed in Istanbul, a new dispute arose between Abūbakar Effendi and Achmat Sadiek Achmat. Disputes over community leadership and religious guidance thus started to include issues involving true and authentic Islamic education.

In 1834, Achmat Sadiek Achmat became a founding member of the Muhammedan Shafee Congregation, and in 1846 he asked permission to establish his own mosque. This was granted in 1853 and led to the establishment of the Jāmiʿ mosque on Lower Chiappini Street. This mosque became known as the Queen Victoria Jāmiʿ mosque, as the land on which it was built had been donated by the British crown in order to thank the Cape Muslim population and the Cape Malay Corps for its support in the war against the Xhosa in 1846. Achmat Sadiek Achmat protested against Christian missionary efforts, and in the 1870s he condemned a small booklet entitled *Abdullah ben Yussuf or the Story of a Malay as Told by Himself,* distributed by the Anglican Church on the Cape in Melayu, English, and Dutch—but not in Afrikaans, the language of communication of the Cape Muslim population. This text raised the scorn of the Muslim population in Cape Town, as Islam was presented as a sectarian error and the Qur'ān as a fabrication, while Cape Town's imāms were attacked as being ignorant. This attack was not only polemical but thoroughly unfair. In the course of the development of the madāris in Cape Town, the Cape Town Muslim community had developed considerable literary activity and contributed to forming a new language of communication, Afrikaans. Until the late eighteenth century, Melayu had been the major code of communication among Cape Muslims. Yet when immigration from Southeast Asia stopped in the late eighteenth century, the servant and slave populations of the Cape increasingly switched to a new language, formed from a Dutch basis with a large input of Melayu, Arab, and African (Bantu) words. This "kitchen-Dutch" was soon spoken not only by the servant and slave populations of the Cape, but also by their Dutch-Afrikaaner masters, even if both Afrikaaner and English settlers despised Afrikaans as the language of the slaves and the blacks, as the British journalist C. E. Boniface remarked in 1830. Cape Muslim scholars continued to develop Afrikaans, however, and since the 1830s developed an Arabic script for Afrikaans: "While white society still considered this language not worthy of print, the imāms began writing religious texts in it by using a modified Arabic alphabet" (Tayob 1995: 44).

Thus, a new literature started to be produced on the Cape in Afrikaans, in an Arabic script. The first book ever to be printed in Afrikaans was the *Kitāb al-qawl al-matīn fī bayān umūr al-dīn* by Shaykh Aḥmad al-Ishmūnī, written for teaching children and printed in Cape Town in 1856. Also, classes at the Ottoman Theological School, established in 1863, were taught in Afrikaans, while the first school to teach Afrikaans to Afrikaaner children, the Daljosafatskool of the Afrikaanerbund, did not open until 1882. The first tafsīr of the Qur'ān in Afrikaans was published in 1915, about twenty years before the first Afrikaans Bible was published. Between 1845 and 1957, at least seventy-four texts in Arabo-Afrikaans were written and an unknown number still exist as fragments. Afrikaans thus started out as the language of the Cape Muslim population before it became the accepted language of the Afrikaaner population. At the same time, Arabic maintained its role as the language of ritual: in the second half of the nineteenth century, the khuṭba at Cape Town mosques was given in Arabic. The mastery of Arabic was so important as a marker of identity for the Capetonian Muslim community that a leading religious scholar even welcomed the new British governor on the Cape, Sir Philip Wodehouse, in 1862, with a speech in Arabic.

In the context of the increasing integration of the Cape into the world economy and world trade, the community of Muslims in Cape Town intensified its contacts with other parts of the Islamic ecumene. By 1854, only four Muslims from the Cape had undertaken the pilgrimage, the first probably being al-Ḥājj Gassonnodien (or Gezenodien) Carel Pilgrim, a tailor and imām of a mosque on Keerom Street, who had traveled to Mecca in 1834. In the second half of the nineteenth century, however, the number of pilgrims from the Cape multiplied. The ḥajj was regarded as a sort of grand tour and bolstered the prestige of the pilgrims. In the 1880s, due to their growing number, the Ahl Kāf (people from the Cape) were given their own section in Mecca, close to the Jāwāh. In 1877 alone, around seventy Muslims from the Cape performed the pilgrimage, despite the high cost of about one hundred pounds. The pilgrims not only contributed to the further improvement of local schools and expansion of teaching traditions, they also stimulated local conflicts, as many pilgrims established new mosques or schools after their return from the holy places. These sjegs (Arab. shuyūkh), as they were called in Cape Town, also introduced textbook standards on the Cape, which followed the traditions of learning on the Arabian peninsula and in Egypt. In the course of time, the sjegs came to form a second pillar of authority beside the imāms. In the framework of Cape Town religious authority, the term sjeg denoted a religious scholar who had earned his recognition as a scholar abroad, while the title imām remained confined to those religious scholars who had earned their recognition as scholars at home.

Religious Disputes and Forms of Negotiation

The constant disputes among the Muslims of Cape Town, and in particular the disputes over the question of the imāmate in the Palm Tree mosque, eventually motivated a member of the Cape Parliament, P. E. de Roubaix, who happened to be the General Consul of the Ottoman sulṭān for the Cape, to send a letter to Sulṭān ʿAbd al-Majīd in 1862, asking for support. De Roubaix's petition was supported by Queen Victoria and expedited to the Ottoman sulṭān, who complied by sending the Ḥanafī legal scholar Abūbakar Effendi (d. 1880) to Cape Town. Abūbakar Effendi al-Khashnāwī was born in 1835 in the Lake Urmia region of Persia, of Kurdish origin. After studying the Islamic sciences in Shahrizar, he went to Istanbul for further studies. In 1862, he was asked by the sulṭān to go on this mission to the Cape, where he traveled via Britain, arriving the same year. He married twice: in 1863 Rukea (Ruqaya) Maker, the daughter of an immigrant from Britain and a saddle maker, al-Ḥājj Harun, on Keerom Street; and in 1866, Tahara Cook, one of his students in the Ottoman Theological School and daughter of Jeremiah Cook, a shipbuilder from Yorkshire. He had several children from both marriages. One of these was Aḥmad ʿAṭāʾullāh Effendi (Achmat Effendi), who in 1893 was the candidate of the Cape Muslim community for the Constituent Assembly of Cape Province.

After his arrival in Cape Town, Abūbakar Effendi established the Ottoman Theological School, as well as the first Muslim girls school in the 1870s. He also initiated

Abūbakar Effendi was not the only qāḍī the Ottoman sulṭān sent on missions of mediation by request of Queen Victoria, but one in a series of diplomatic missions. In the early 1860s, another Ottoman qāḍī, ʿAbd al-Raḥmān b. al-Baghdādī al-Dimashqī (d. 1881), was dispatched to mediate in a legal dispute in British India, but his ship was blown off course and eventually landed in Rio de Janeiro, where he was approached by members of a Muslim underground community. He was asked to teach these Muslims the prescriptions and rituals of Islam, which had been prohibited since the last Muslim slave rebellion in Brazil in 1835. ʿAbd al-Raḥmān Effendi consented and stayed for a period of two years, living mostly in Rio de Janeiro and San Salvador de Bahia. He documented his experiences in a text entitled *Musalliyāt al-gharīb* (Strange and entertaining occurrences).

other Islamic schools in Kimberley and Port Elizabeth, as well as in Laurenço Marques (today's Maputo) in Mozambique. Abūbakar Effendi wrote a text book entitled *Bayān al-dīn* (Clarifications of the religion), which circulated in Cape Town from 1869 and was printed in Istanbul in 1877. This text was in fact a copy of a major textbook of the Ḥanafī school of law, *Multaqā al-abhur* (The meeting of the oceans), by Burhān al-Dīn Ibrāhīm b. Muḥammad b. Ibrāhīm al-Ḥalabī (d. 1549), which was widely used in the Ottoman empire from the late sixteenth century. The *Bayān al-dīn* focused largely on the ʿibadāt (religious and ritual obligations) and some muʿāmalāt (the legal norms defining relations among humans). It consisted of an Arabic text with Abūbakar Effendi's commentary (Arab. sharḥ) in Arabo-Afrikaans.

In Cape Town, Abūbakar Effendi was sought after as a mediator in legal disputes. He composed fatāwa on legal and ritual issues and also tried to impose the rulings of the Ḥanafī school of law, which had few followers on the Cape, where the majoritarian school of law was Shāfiʿī. The work of Abūbakar Effendi and his Ḥanafī partisanship quickly led to disputes and to a further split in the Cape Muslim community. A first bone of contention seems to have been his divorce from his first wife. Rukea Maker belonged to a respected Cape Town Muslim family, and the lawsuit showed that he had not only mistreated his wife but also refused to pay alimony for his son from this marriage. The Cape Town Supreme Court of Law eventually ruled that he had to pay alimony, but his image as a religious scholar was tainted. This image continued to suffer when he tried to impose regulations from the Ḥanafī school of law which contradicted local traditions as well as the regulations of the Shāfiʿī school of law. In 1869, for instance, he issued a fatwā which prohibited the consumption of snoek (a local fish) and crayfish which were accepted by the rules of the Shāfiʿī school of law and were, in addition, part of the daily diet of the Cape Town Muslim community. Also, Abūbakar Effendi attacked

Imām Shāfiʿī, in the *Bayān al-dīn*, in polemical ways, especially with regard to the ritual slaughtering of animals: "The laws of religion have remained as they were under the Prophet of God, for about 200 years. But then al-Shāfiʿī has broken the rules of law and he has fabricated fatāwa which contradicted the verses of the Qurʾān and the Sunna of the Prophet and his followers. Al-Shāfʿī has to be regarded thus like the Jews and Christians who have also altered the book of God" (quoted in Kähler 1960: 108–109).

In 1866, this anti-Shāfiʿī polemic led to a motion of deposition, organized by Abdol Burns in the name of the Cape Muslim community, which remained ineffective, as Abūbakar Effendi received his salary not from the British Crown but from the Ottoman sulṭān. However, in 1869, the seafood fatwā motivated the Cape Muslim community to send a delegation of scholars to Mecca and Istanbul, in order to obtain clarification. This delegation consisted of two scholars, al-Ḥājj ʿAbdallāh and Gafieldien (Khafīʾ al-Dīn) Muntingh. Unfortunately, Gafieldien Muntingh spoke Afrikaans, Melayu, and English, but not Arabic or Turkish, and he did not understand much of the conversations in Mecca and Istanbul, while al-Ḥājj ʿAbdallāh, as it turned out later, was a friend of Abūbakar Effendi. Their trip thus failed to bring the desired results. In a later lawsuit at the Supreme Court, al-Ḥājj ʿAbdallāh even declared that neither in Mecca nor in Istanbul had he addressed the controversial fatwā.

The ongoing dispute with Abūbakar Effendi eventually led to a further split of the Cape Muslim community and the emergence of an Ḥanafī mosque community. In 1869, Abdol Rakiep b. ʿAbd al-Raʾūf b. Tuan Guru had taken over the imāmate of the Nūr al-Islām-mosque in the Buitengracht, as has been mentioned above. Shortly after having been invested as imām, he introduced the Ḥanafī ritual in this mosque. This led to the protest of the Shāfiʿī majority of the mosque community, which complained that he did not insist on the Shāfiʿī rule which requested at least forty community members to be present for the Friday prayers, a rule which was not followed by the Ḥanafī school of law. Although Achmat Sadiek Achmat, one of the founders of the mosque, tried to mediate, he was rejected by Abdol Rakiep with these words: "Now I am imām in my mosque and can do what I want" (Da Costa and Davids 1994: 99). This claim led to further escalation and the dispute was eventually presented to the Supreme Court of Cape Town in 1873. The major issue was whether Abdol Rakiep should be allowed to use the Nūr al-Islām mosque, as this mosque had been allocated to the Shāfiʿī community of Achmat Sadiek Achmat, and was thus open to members of the Shāfiʿī community only. This argument was refuted by Abūbakar Effendi, who had been invited to participate in the procedures as a neutral observer. He mentioned that the respective mosque was a waqf and thus exempt from any regulations in respect of admission or non-admission. The Supreme Court followed Abūbakar Effendi, who had misleadingly presented himself at court as a member of the Shāfiʿī school of law. The Supreme Court completely ignored the fact that waqf statutes could imply all kinds of regulations, including admission. It is possible, though, that Achmat Sadiek Achmat did not object to this verdict, as the document which declared the Nūr al-Islām mosque as a waqf did not contain such a regulation. After the death of Abūbakar Effendi in 1880, the small Ḥanafī community under the leadership of Abdol Rakiep, Muḥammad Dollie, and Jongie Siers left the Nūr al-Islām mosque in the Buitengracht and established a new mosque on Long Street, the Buitengracht Hanafee mosque, in 1881.

Religious disputes thus defined the development of the Cape Muslim community and blocked its emergence as a strong and united political force in the late nineteenth century. From time to time, a public council, a bechara, was organized to mediate in a mosque, yet these councils did not lead to results. The establishment of the Ḥanafī ritual in the Buitengracht Hanafee mosque triggered a general debate about the conditions of Friday prayers in Cape Town, and the permissibility of several juma' mosques. The Shāfi'ī school of law ruled that juma' prayers could be held only when a community of forty Muslims had assembled, which would have excluded most mosques in Cape Town from juma' status. In addition, the Shāfi'ī school of law also provided that each community of Muslims should have only one juma' mosque. However, in the context of several splits of mosque communities, Cape Town had seen the emergence of a number of juma' mosques. In 1874, a pilgrim from the Cape, Imām Shahibo (Shu'aib), sought a fatwā on this issue while in Mecca. Meccan religious scholars responded and asked the Muslims in Cape Town to return to one juma' prayer in one juma' mosque only. After the return of Imām Shahibo, another bechara was organized and the fatwā was generally accepted. Only khaṭīb Jakoof, the speaker of Achmat Sadiek Achmat, refused to agree, and the Cape Muslim community remained split: the followers of Achmat Sadiek Achmat stuck to Awwal mosque, while all other Muslims alternated between the Palm Tree Mosque and the Nūr al-Islām mosque for Friday prayers.

The dispute over the issue of Friday prayers eventually moved the religious scholars of Cape Town to undertake another effort to resolve this question. In 1912, Muḥammad Ṣāliḥ Hendricks, a convert from Swellendam who in 1888 had studied in Mecca under 'Umar b. Abī Bakr Bā Junayd (1853/54–1915/16), a leading scholar of the 'Alawiyya, wrote a letter to his teacher in 1912, asking for advice. 'Umar b. Abī Bakr Bā Junayd sent this petition to his students in Zanzibar, Aḥmad b. Sumayṭ and 'Abdallāh Bā Kathīr al-Kindī. 'Abdallāh Bā Kathīr, who knew Hendricks from his own studies in Mecca in 1888, traveled to Cape Town in 1913 and managed to negotiate a compromise, the Juma-a Onderrichten (juma' agreement), signed on 24 January 1914, which provided that juma' prayers should be held in one juma' mosque in Cape Town only, but that the khuṭabā' should rotate in giving the khuṭba. Despite its constructive intentions, the juma' agreement of 1914 misfired due to the ongoing internal disputes in the Cape Muslim population. The examples of Abūbakar Effendi and the "Ba Kathier delegation" (Bang 2003: 115) thus show that mediation by outsiders does not necessarily lead to an end of local conflicts.

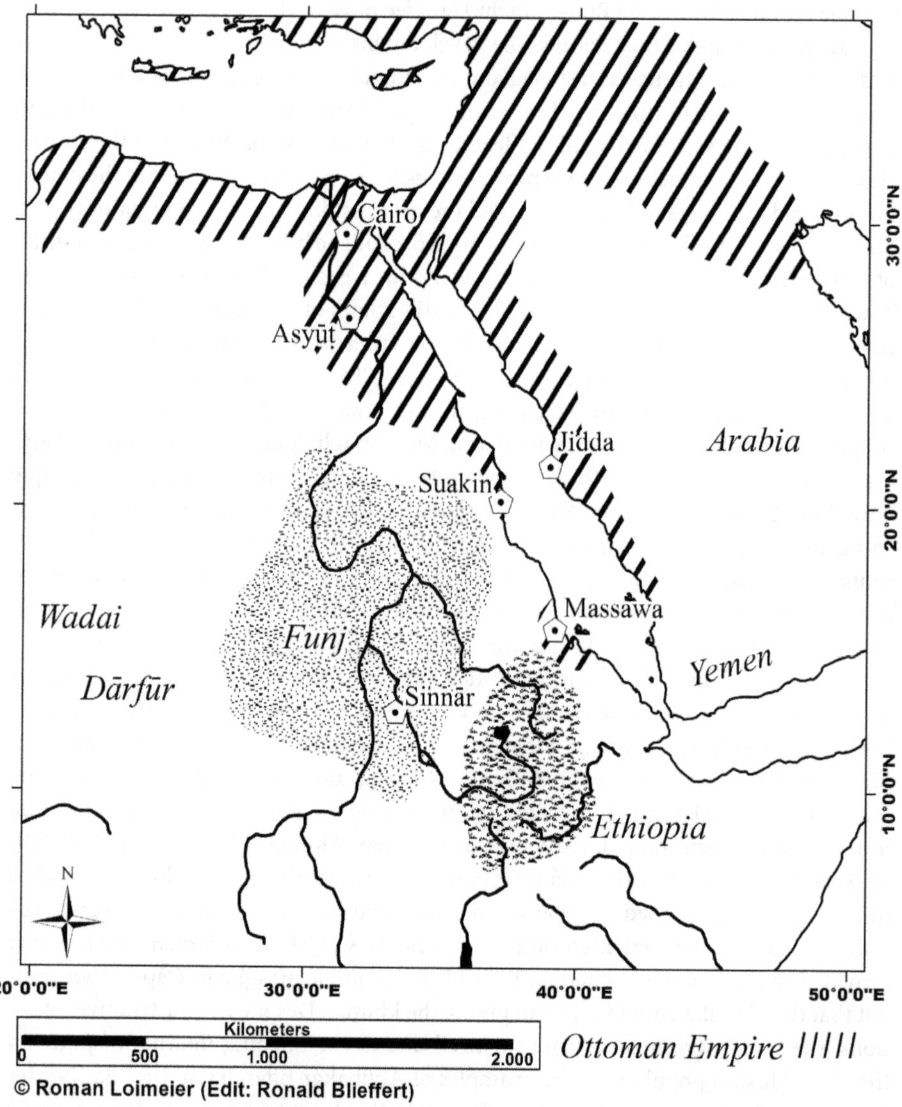

Map 14. The Nile valley and Sinnār-Funj in the mid-seventeenth century

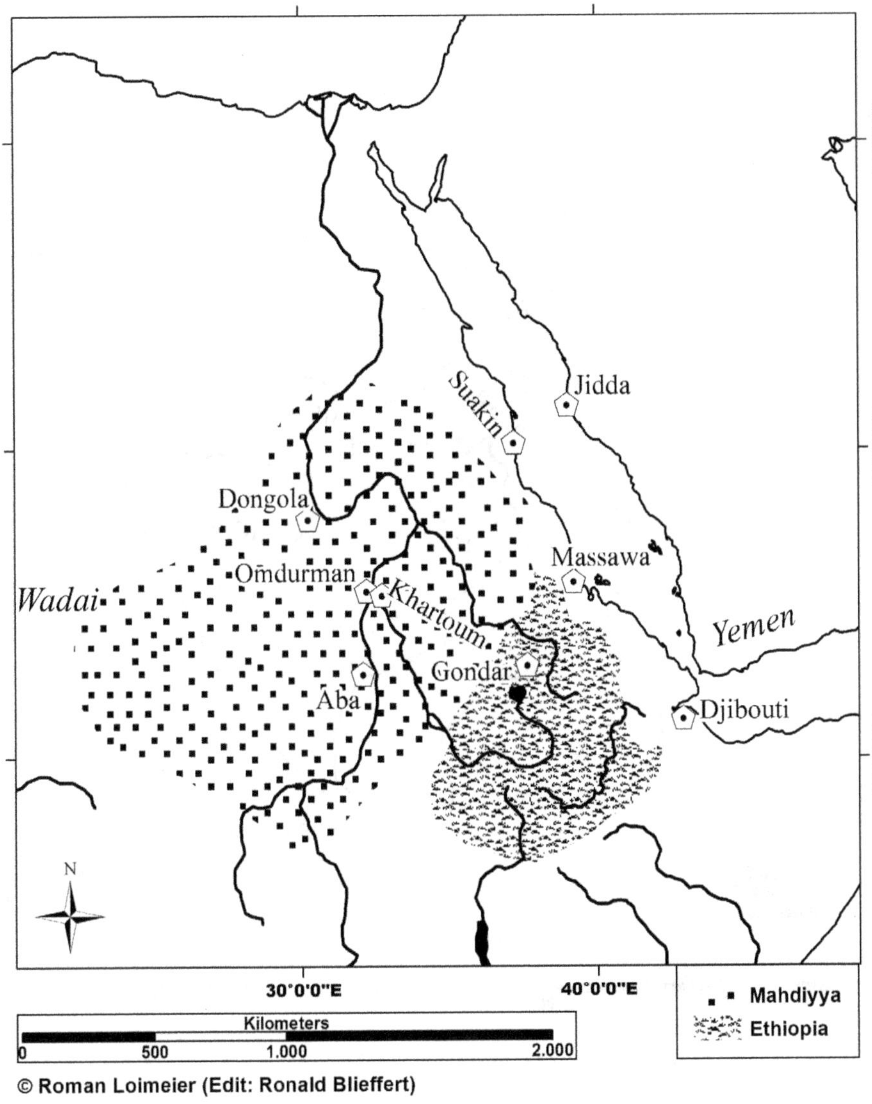

Map 15. The Nile Sudan in the late nineteenth century

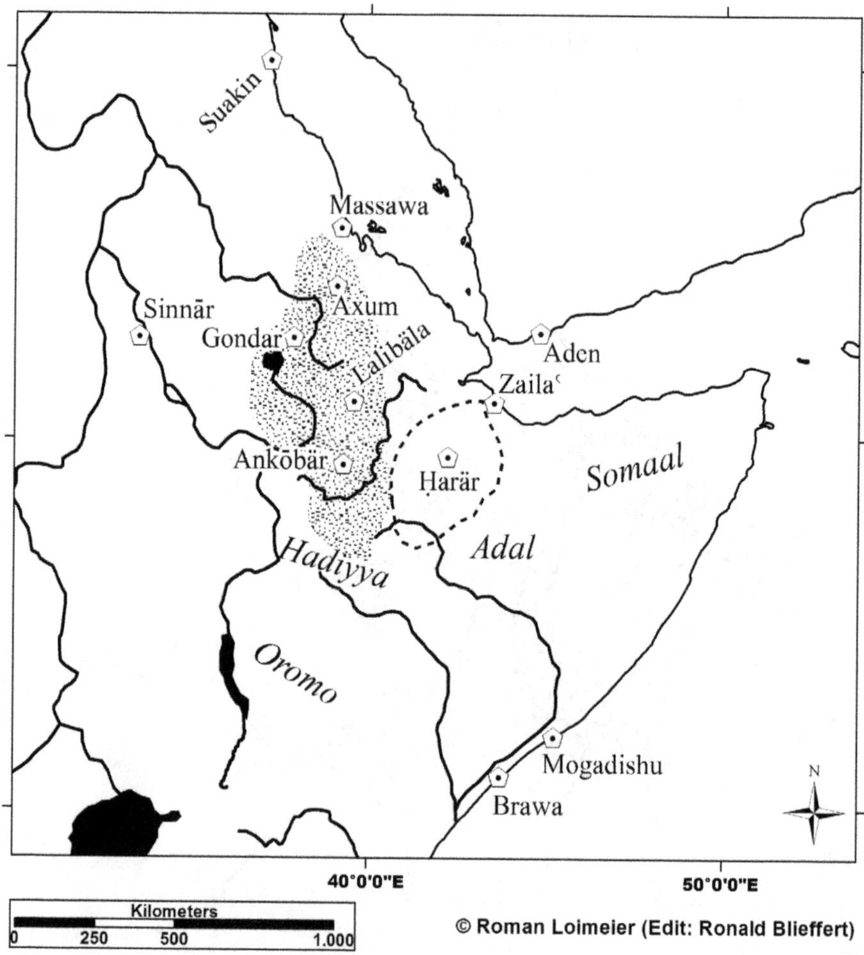

Map 16. Ethiopia in the sixteenth century

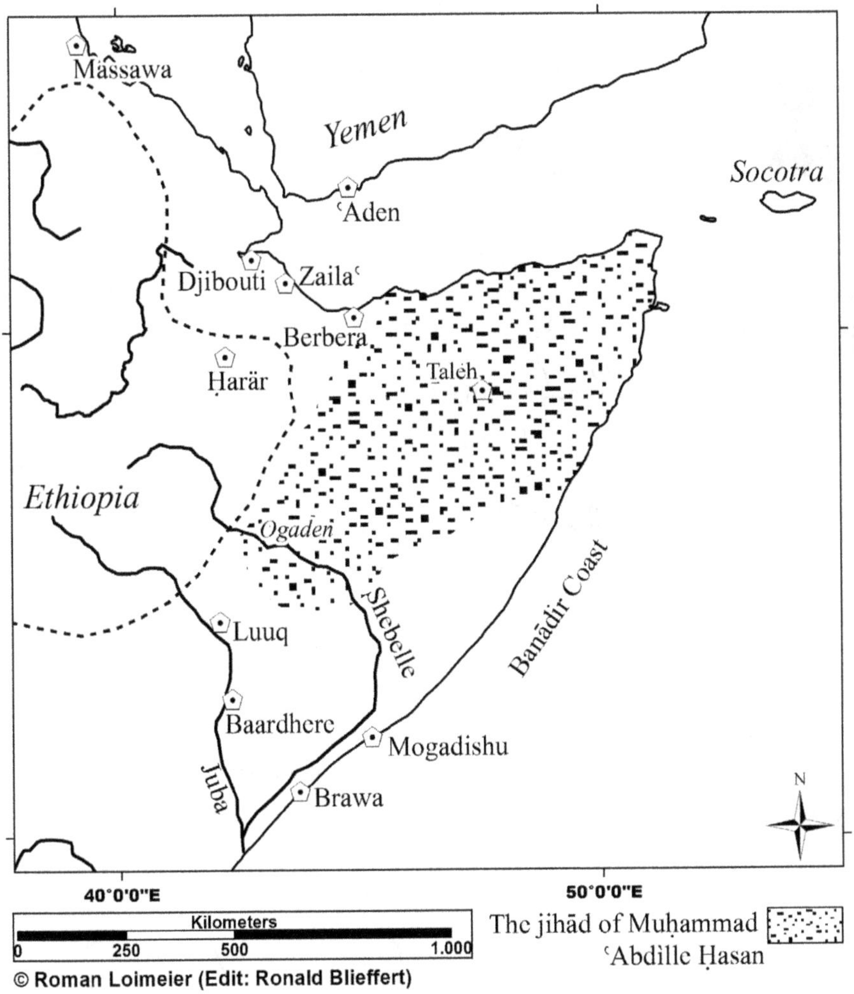

Map 17. The Horn of Africa in the nineteenth century

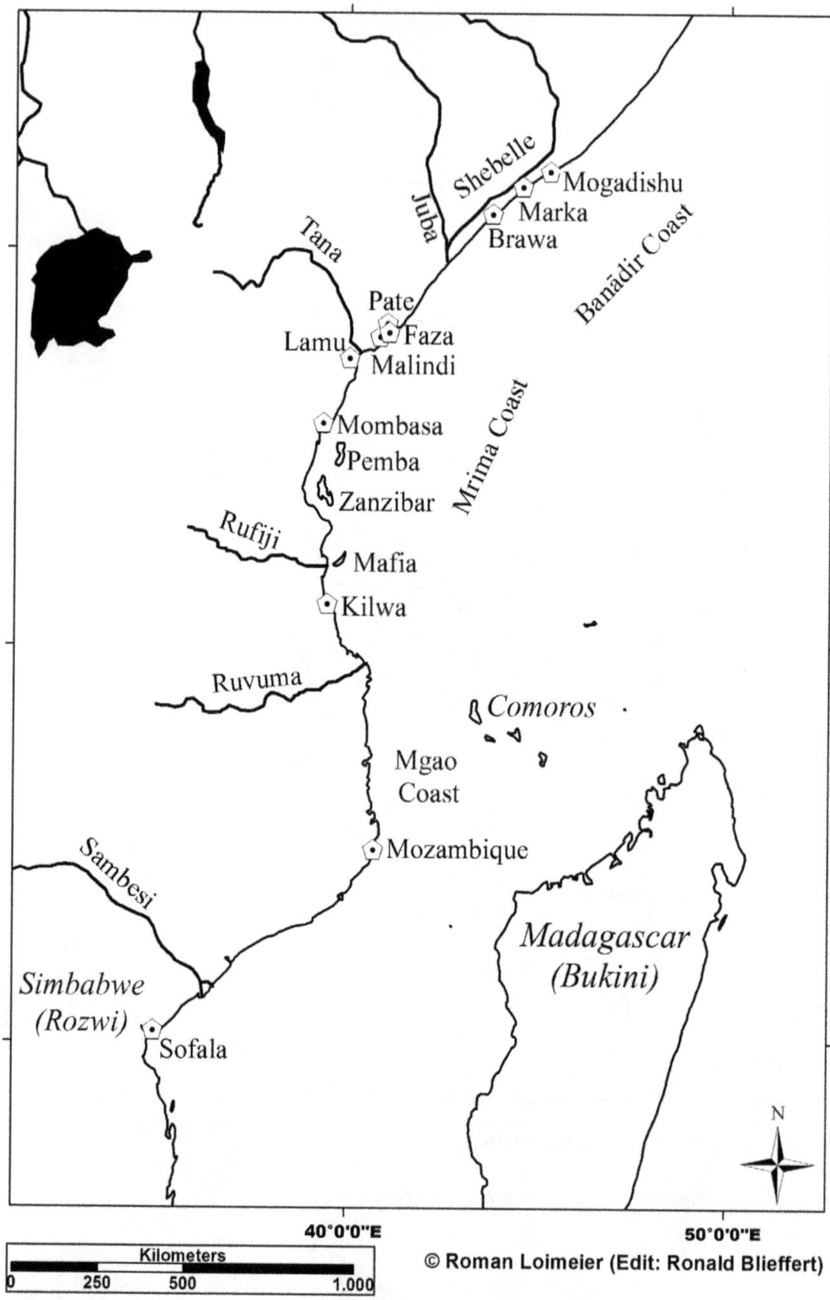

Map 18. The East African coast in the early sixteenth century

12 Muslims under Colonial Rule

Comparative Perspectives on Colonial Modernity in Africa

European encounters with Africa had been confined for a long time to trading stations on the coast. In North Africa before the mid-nineteenth century, Europeans were mostly unable to travel beyond the coastal towns and their immediate hinterlands, mainly due to fears of espionage or policies of economic blockade. In sub-Saharan Africa, European endeavors to penetrate the coastal hinterlands inevitably failed, due to the toll that tropical diseases such as malaria, sleeping sickness, and yellow fever took among the European sailors, soldiers, and traders. These conditions changed only in the second half of the nineteenth century, with medical research into tropical diseases, the development of superior firepower, and the disintegration of African polities which were unable to overcome the crisis triggered by the end of the slave trade in the early and mid-nineteenth century. In the last two decades of the nineteenth century, European colonial conquest of Africa became an increasingly realistic enterprise. Colonial conquest had in fact begun in 1830, in the context of the French intervention in and the subsequent conquest of Algeria. This conquest was completed in the 1870s, against the resistance of major parts of the Algerian population, but with the support of other groups which saw in the French intervention a welcome relief from Ottoman domination.

The Algerian experience provided France with a testing ground for further conquests in both North and West Africa, while the British had already acquired such testing grounds in India in the eighteenth century. The scramble for Africa from 1885, and the ultimate conquest and division of the continent by the early 1900s, was started by King Leopold II of Belgium, who aspired to the acquisition of a private colonial empire in the Congo, and the efforts of the European nations to confine these aspirations and to define terms of colonial occupation. The key to acceptance of claims to a specific territory was the effective presence of the respective colonial power in the territory, and thus effective control in situ. This requirement started a mad race through the continent, which lasted for approximately fifteen years and resulted in the military occupation of the continent and the definition of colonial boundaries in an impressive number of colonial boundary agreements. The only territories which remained free of European control were Liberia, which had acquired U.S. protection as a settlement of freed slaves from America, and Ethiopia, which had decisively defeated an Italian army in 1896 and had forced Italy to accept Ethiopian independence.

By 1900, most of Africa had come under European colonial domination, although in some regions, such as Mauritania or Somalia, the establishment of a proper administration took until the late 1920s or mid-1930s. In most cases, European colonial rule came to an end by the early 1960s. In this comparatively short period of time, Muslims developed a number of strategies for coming to terms with European colonialism, which included armed resistance in the form of a jihād, but also withdrawal and hijra to distant lands and numerous "paths of accommodation" (Robinson 2000). Seen from a longue durée perspective of more than 1,300 years of Muslim history in Africa, the question can be asked as to why such a short period of time, sixty or seventy years for most colonial territories, deserves our attention at all. The answer, of course, is that the colonial period not only created new boundaries in Africa and redefined the role of Africans, but also gave birth to political and religious legacies that continue to haunt both Muslims and non-Muslims until today.

This chapter focuses on the role of Muslims in those European colonial possessions in Africa which had sizeable Muslim populations, namely, the British, the French, the German, and the Italian colonial empires. As the Cape Muslim community has been discussed in the last chapter, this chapter does not address the role of Muslims in twentieth-century South Africa, nor does it discuss the colonial policies of Spain, Portugal, and Belgium, the other European colonial powers. Muslim populations in their colonial realms were relatively small, with the exception of the Muslim minorities in eastern Congo as well as the Muslim populations of northern Mozambique. Also, Spain, Portugal, and Belgium did not strive to present themselves as Muslim powers and protectors of Islam, as did Britain, France, Germany, and Italy. In my analysis I do not differentiate between the various legal statuses of the different European possessions, such as protectorates (Egypt since 1882, Morocco since 1912), condominiums (the Anglo-Egyptian Sudan since 1898), mandate territories (the German colonies after 1919), overseas departments (French Algeria since the 1830s), or colonies, as all these territories, despite different legal constructions, were characterized by one basic fact, namely that African and Muslim populations did not have the same rights as the European colonial masters and were usually treated as subjects, sujets (French), Unterthanen (German), or sudditi (Italian), deprived of those civil rights which the metropolitan populations enjoyed. In some colonial territories such as Senegal, Northern Nigeria, or German East Africa, colonial powers nevertheless privileged Muslim rulers, notables, and scholars as allies in administrative matters. In European evolutionist worldviews, Islam was seen as a religion almost as developed as Christianity, and Muslims were consequently viewed as welcome partners in development schemes that aimed at the colonial modernization of sub-Saharan Africa. Processes of modernization had started in many parts of Africa in precolonial times, and some polities such as Egypt, Ethiopia, and Zanzibar had gone quite far on their own paths toward modernity and managed to define the process of modernization to some degree in their own terms. In the colonial period, Africans lost their power to define modernity to Europeans, even if this loss of power varied from colony to colony and throughout time, and even if Africans never lost complete agency to Europeans.

A major feature of colonial and postcolonial rule in all parts of Africa was that lands of dissidence (bilād al-sība), the peripheries where resistance and withdrawal from central administrations were possible, gradually disappeared. By the mid-1930s, the colonial powers had subdued all niches of resistance and had established a more or less densely woven net of administrative control which enabled, for instance, relatively reliable population censuses in the 1950s, registration of taxpayers and recruitment for labor services, colonial armies, and development campaigns. Another important aspect of colonial rule was technical modernization, especially in the realm of transport and communication, but also with respect to health and education. Combined with increasing security, this led to a growing traffic of pilgrims, students, and traders, and to increasing awareness among African Muslims of contemporary political development outside Africa, such as, for instance, the independence of India in 1947 or the Suez Canal crisis in 1956. The colonial period also witnessed the astounding numerical growth of Muslim communities in many parts of Africa, where colonial territories such as Soudan (contemporary Mali) acquired Muslim majority populations, although French colonial administrators such as Maurice Delafosse tried their best to develop policies of containment. Equally, German East Africa (later Tanganyika) saw a massive movement of conversion to Islam that was accelerated in the context of the disruptions in World War I: while 3 percent of the population had been Muslim in 1914, the strength of the Muslim population had grown to 25 percent by 1924. August Nimtz explains this movement of conversion to Islam as being due "to the desire to bring order into a chaotic situation after the disruptions of the Maji-Maji war (1904/05) and World War I" (Nimtz 1980: 15).

However, the expansion of Islam in Tanganyika was not only due to the fact that many people saw conversion to Islam as a form of resistance against colonial rule, but may also be explained by the fact that Islam had been known as a religion before the colonial period, through the mediation of traders and scholars. In addition, the German colonial administration largely relied on local cadres, the so-called jumbes, akidas, and liwalis, who were mostly Swahili-speaking Muslims. Swahili culture, as well as Islam, thus acquired the nimbus of a superior culture. Still, the colonial period was a time of hardship and crisis for Tanganyika's Muslims: referring to the 1930s, Richard Reusch (1931: 335) stresses, for instance, that "the Weltgebäude des Islam (the global house of Islam) was seemingly about to crumble: the caliphate had come to an end, movements for the emancipation of Muslim women had started to spread, and Muslim reform movements had started to challenge the established authorities." In addition, Muslims were subject to an increasing western influence that would, in their eyes, bring about atheism and unbelief. In the course of their integration into the new political structures of Tanganyika, the Muslim populations in the coastal areas had also become a minority in a country dominated by Christian elites, both colonial administrators and missionaries. The interference of the colonial administration in Muslim affairs, in particular the far-reaching bureaucratization of Islamic jurisdiction and the administration of the awqāf (the religious foundations), severely disrupted coastal society.

While Muslims in most parts of Africa, until the late nineteenth century, had lived in their own local communities, sometimes under the rule of an imām, an amīr, or a sulṭān, in the twentieth century they had to adapt to the challenge of the modern colonial state. Under colonial rule, Muslim concepts of law, either in terms of the sharīʿa or in terms of locally accepted norms of ʿurf, and Muslim institutions were thoroughly modified and redefined by European colonial concepts of sharīʿa and usually confined to the sphere of Islamic personal law. In theory, the British accepted local customs (and Islamic law) "insofar as they were not repugnant to natural justice" or not judged (by the respective British colonial officer) as being "repugnant to British notions of justice, equity and good conscience," as the famous phrase ran (Whitaker 1970: 41, Umar 2006: 42). The majority of Muslims in sub-Saharan Africa found multiple paths of accommodation with colonial rule and even identified with aspects of the modern state, in particular as far as education and new modes of administration were concerned. As soon as initial conquest had been achieved, Muslim opposition to colonial rule or even armed resistance was thus rather exceptional. Opposition remained mostly confined to an anti-colonial, anti-modern rhetoric, which deplored the new times, the alleged decay of public morality, and un-Islamic innovations, as in the following poem written in Hausa by an anonymous author in the 1930s (quoted in Hiskett 1973: 164):

> Today unbelief is established, and also innovation; well, as for us, we have no use for this in our time; this that I am about to say, there is no jesting in it; . . . whatever article of their clothing, if you wear it; . . . if you pray a thousand times you will not be vindicated; and the same applies to the maker of hurricane lamp globes; your short trousers together with your tight fitting trousers; whoever puts them on, his unbelief is wide; whoever wears suits with buttons, he has apostatized; he has no religion at all, only pride; . . . one should not wear shirts with collars; whoever wears them, his unbelief is wide; khaki and pyjamas, whoever it is; who wears them and prays in them, he has committed a crime; here they are, three things, do not use them; all of them, avoid them, you have seen them; . . . towel and washing blue and powder, whoever uses them, certainly on the Last Day, the fire is his dwelling.

The colonial division of Africa among the European colonial powers also brought together many different and historically diverse African regions in a few colonial realms which transcended historical, regional, and even continental divisions. British colonial administrations trained local staff in the Sudan for British government schools in Nigeria or Zanzibar, while the French built similar schools in Senegal. Equally, colonial armies became arenas of promotion for a plethora of peoples from different colonial backgrounds. Participation in both world wars, either in the colonies, in Europe, or in Asia, contributed to expanding horizons and knowledge about the (Islamic) world among African Muslims. To the chagrin of colonial administrations, improved communications and transport technologies also helped to spread newspapers, books, and information and thus supported, for instance, pan-Islamic propaganda. New venues of trade introduced new styles of clothing, new modes of consumption, and new approaches to ritual, which often triggered ambivalent local responses. Muslims found themselves in new political contexts where hegemony had passed to new, non-Muslim masters (see map 7).

While Britain and France had acquired some experience of administrating Muslims, Germany and Italy were rather inexperienced in this respect. In their experiments in colonial administration, they oscillated between the adoption of the British philosophy of indirect rule (as expounded by Lord Lugard in *The Dual Mandate in Tropical*

Three German colonies, Togo, Kamerun (The Cameroons), and Deutsch-Ostafrika (German East Africa), had Muslim minority populations, probably numbering not more than one million in a total population of thirteen million. German politics with regard to Islam were informed by a number of German Africanists and Orientalists, such as Carl Heinrich Becker (1876–1933). In 1911, Becker published a study entitled *Materialien zur Kenntnis des Islam in Deutsch-Ostafrika,* which today still constitutes a major work of reference for Islam in East Africa. This text was written in a specific context: in the first years of the twentieth century, missionary organizations had started to claim that Islam would constitute a growing danger in the colonies. A series of anticolonial risings, such as the Maji-Maji war in German East Africa in 1904/05, the Mecca Letter affair in Togo in 1905 and later in German East Africa in 1908, and a series of local Mahdist risings in Kamerun in 1907, seemed to confirm these anxieties. As a consequence, Islam became a central theme of the German Colonial Congress in Berlin in 1905, which discussed colonial politics. In 1908, the German government financed three studies on Islam in the colonies. Becker's study showed that Islam had acquired considerable influence in the colony. Still, to the annoyance of the missionaries, Becker declared that Islam would not constitute a threat to the German colonial administration. Rather, the German colonial administration should see Islam as a way to promote the civilization of the Africans. Becker proposed to strengthen existing indigenous authorities and to set up a system of indirect rule in predominantly Muslim territories. Also, he stressed the necessity for the administration to keep out of religious questions and disputes. At the same time, Muslims should be granted autonomy in specific spheres of the law, in particular personal law, and in the administration of the awqāf.

Africa), which sought to identify local rulers and theoretically recognized their autonomy in legal and political terms, and the French direct administration system, which sought to implement France's "mission civilisatrice." In truth, neither Britain, France, Germany, or Italy followed pure doctrine in the administration of their respective colonial empires; their colonial policies were shaped by local experience, pragmatism, and, most often, lack of funds. The British concept of indirect rule actually "passed through three stages, the first as a useful administrative device, then that of a political doctrine, and finally that of a religious dogma" (Lord Hailey 1939, quoted in Collins 2008: 38). However, the British were also prepared, at least in the early period of their rule in Northern Nigeria between 1903 and 1910, and passed despite the subsequent fetish they made of indirect rule, to interfere directly in administrative situations which seemed to individual officers very unworkable" (Fika: 1978: 107). In the end, improvisation ruled supreme and granted local administrators a disproportionate amount of power. Thus, the British were forced to set up direct administrative structures in southern Nigeria, where a sulṭān of Sokoto failed to materialize, while France accepted local rulers and religious scholars as partners in administration in some West African territories. Equally, Germany ruled vast parts of inland Kamerun, Togo, and German East Africa by means of a few residents, while establishing direct control over the coastal regions of these countries. Italy, in a way, was an exception, as the conquest and colonial occupation of Libya and Somalia was completed in the late 1920s and early 1930s only, and came to an end in the early 1940s in the context of World War II. Furthermore, the Italian conquest of Libya, and later Ethiopia (1935–1941), can be characterized as an effort to establish colonial rule by way of massacre. This does not imply that the imposition of British, French, or German colonial rule was achieved by peaceful negotiation. All colonial powers had recourse to the force of arms, often in the guise of machine guns, sometimes airplanes, at various points of time: in the case of Germany, this was true in the context of the Bushiri rising in 1889 and the Maji-Maji war in German East Africa in 1904–1905; in the case of France, it applies to the conquest of Algeria and a number of massacres during the conquest of the French West African colonial realm; in the case of Britain, it happened in the invasion of the Sudan, as well as in the conquest of the Sokoto empire between 1900 and 1903:

> Indirect rule was not meant to let the old Sokoto caliphate march on unscathed. Lugard was quite explicit to the new Sarkin Musulmi (amīr al-mu'minīn) and his entourage in Sokoto that he had conquered Sokoto; he was not making a treaty with anyone. . . . When attempts were made to get rid of the new order at Satiru near Sokoto and at Hadejia [both in 1906] the risings were both put down with exemplary violence. This was standard practice: force was rarely used but when it was it had to be ruthless and meant to shock. (Last 1997: 81)

Despite the atrocities of colonial conquest, Italy, Germany, France, and Britain tried to present themselves as protectors of Islam and to win their respective Muslim colonial subjects as allies in two world wars. This was partially successful, as the

European colonial powers were never confronted with a united response in their colonial conquests. The Muslim populations from the Indian Ocean to the Atlantic, and from the Mediterranean to the Zambezi, were characterized by multiple fragmentations and numerous local frictions. As a consequence, it was often easy for the colonial powers to establish colonial rule by the principle of "divide and rule" and to install those local leaders as brokers who were willing to cooperate with the colonial power. As a consequence, the imposition and practice of colonial rule produced multiple paths of accommodation: from jihād to withdrawal and dissimulation (Arab. taqiyya), from emigration (hijra) to partial cooperation and outright submission, collaboration, and alliance (in Islamic terms, muwālāt, friendship). These paths of accommodation were never static but continued to be negotiated throughout the colonial period and in post-colonial times: some religious scholars were willing to cooperate with the colonial state, while others continued to resist state encroachment or withdrew into political non-activity, indifference, or conscious isolation. The political role of Muslim religious movements has always been negotiated, and thus has ranged from being in power or being close to power, to accommodation and cooperation, political withdrawal, and quietism, and finally political resistance to the colonial state. At the same time, colonial administrations were too weak to establish control over all aspects of everyday life, especially in the distant regions of the different colonial empires, which gave Muslims some freedom and allowed collaborators to manipulate the colonial masters.

How the Arch-Enemy Became an Ally: The Anglo-Egyptian Sudan

In 1885, Britain experienced one of her most bitter defeats in a colonial war when the Sudanese Mahdī Muḥammad Aḥmad conquered Khartoum, the capital city of the Sudan, and established the rule of the Mahdiyya. Khartoum was defended by General Charles Gordon, who did not survive this encounter with the Mahdiyya. In 1898, a British army, consisting mostly of Egyptian soldiers under British command, reconquered the Sudan and inflicted a decisive defeat on the Mahdiyya in the battle of Kararī, just outside Omdurman. In the aftermath of their triumph, the British destroyed the tomb of the Mahdī and threw his remains into the Nile, in order to eliminate all chances of a possible cult of the Mahdī centered on his tomb. Also, the rātib of the Mahdī, a set of prayers in memory of the Mahdī, was prohibited. Soon, British colonial rule had overcome the last vestiges of the Mahdiyya in the Sudan, and a new Anglo-Egyptian administration was established in the old capital city of Khartoum. Here, Gordon College started to train an elite of indigenous Sudanese administrators who were commissioned to service in other British colonies, in particular Northern Nigeria. In 1908, the British eventually allowed a surviving son of the Mahdī, Sayyid ʿAbd al-Raḥmān al-Mahdī (1885–1959), to return to Omdurman, recognizing him in 1914 as the official leader of his followers, the Anṣār. The British also legalized the rātib again and allowed donations of land to his family in 1915. How was this remarkable change possible, and how could a religious movement that had been depicted for decades as the arch-enemy of the British empire become an ally of the British colonial administration in the Sudan in such a short period of time?

When the British started to build the new colonial administration of the Sudan, they soon realized that they needed allies to control and develop this huge territory. Of utmost importance was the Egyptian army (13,000 in 1924), which initially provided the military backbone for British rule in the Sudan, as well as a group of Egyptian experts, administrators, qāḍīs, and teachers who came to staff the lower and medium echelons of power, serving in the fields of jurisdiction, education, and other areas of the colonial administration, such as public works and health services. Only from 1914 were first Sudanese administrators appointed to positions in the colonial administration, after training at Gordon College. However, the majority of early colonial development projects, such as the construction of a new harbor in Port Sudan (from 1906), the Jazira Cotton Scheme (from 1900), and the construction of railway lines (from 1899), were realized by British engineers and Egyptian technicians, craftsmen, and workers. The vast areas of Kordofan and Dārfūr became laboratories of indirect rule for the Sudan, as well as for Northern Nigeria and other British colonies. The British native administration in the Sudan often suffered, however, from the fact that the British were unable to identify social and political units that could be organized in administrative terms. Such administrative units had to be created first:

> An elaborate veneer of academic respectability was lent to the policy by reference to anthropological texts, bogus genealogies and biblical tribalism, and empirical studies of India and, especially, Northern Nigeria. Well-known tribal entities that had survived the cataclysms of the last hundred years saw their already considerable autonomy recognized and extended, under hereditary rule; some ironically—and tellingly—suffered new limits to independence that had, in practice, already exceeded anything the government was willing to recognize. Budgets were drawn up, tribal headquarters established, with staffs. . . . But what of the many small tribes or people who did not seem to belong to tribes at all? These were now in theory to be consolidated or amalgamated, assigned, reassigned—in short to be made into tribes, with notable individuals recognized or appointed as shaykhs. Such individuals could not always be discerned, and some areas and populations became permanent problems. . . . In a few cases whim was indulged from an early date, as may be seen in the "Emirate of Dar Masalit." (Daly and Hogan 2005: 30–31)

While the administration of the huge but peripheral lands in the Sudan (Kordofan, Dārfūr, the South) challenged the administrative imagination of the British, the central lands on the Nile could point to an old tradition of indirect rule through local mediators, in particular the Sufi orders. The demise of the Mahdiyya enabled the return of the major competing religious movement in the Sudan, the Khatmiyya, led by Sayyid ʿAlī al-Mirghānī (1878–1968). The Khatmiyya soon reestablished its old networks in Khartoum, Kassala, the northern Nile valley and the east, and revived a tradition of cooperation with the Anglo-Egyptian administration, serving as intermediary between the colonial administration and the population of the Sudan. For his services to the British colonial empire, Sayyid ʿAlī al-Mirghānī was knighted in 1916 and eventually had the honor of leading a Sudanese delegation to London in 1919, to assure Britain of Sudanese loyalty, at a period of time when Egyptian politicians were already proposing independence and had sent a delegation (Arab. wafd) to London to claim independence.

The threat to the empire in World War I and the impending loss of Egypt, as well as Egyptian demands for the unity of the Nile valley (under Egyptian rule), sent shock waves through the Anglo-Egyptian Sudan and fired British endeavors to find new allies. The movement of the Mahdī, the Anṣār, as led by Sayyid ʿAbd al-Raḥmān al-Mahdī, was more than willing to become a new partner of the British, thereby not only escaping isolation but also eclipsing the competing Khatmiyya in terms of pro-British declarations. As a consequence, Sayyid ʿAbd al-Raḥmān al-Mahdī proclaimed himself an ally of the British already in 1914 and supported British (and anti-Ottoman) propaganda in the Sudan. When Egyptian demands for independence increased after World War I, Sayyid ʿAbd al-Raḥmān al-Mahdī became an outspoken opponent of Egyptian overrule and proclaimed himself in support of the formula "Sudan for the Sudanese." As a consequence, the rātib of the Mahdiyya was printed by the British colonial administration, and British support for land transactions of the Mahdiyya was increased. By 1933, Sayyid ʿAbd al-Raḥmān al-Mahdī was the wealthiest man in the Sudan.

Anglo-Egyptian rivalries eventually escalated in the context of the emergence of a first Sudanese political party, the White Flag League, supported by the Khatmiyya, which wanted political union with Egypt. In 1924, the crisis in Anglo-Egyptian relations culminated in a rebellion of Sudanese junior army officers in Khartoum and Egyptian army officers in ʿAtbara. In reaction, the British evacuated the Egyptian army from the Sudan, started to build an indigenous Sudan Defense Force, and terminated the condominium agreement with Egypt regarding the administration of the Sudan. This led to the withdrawal of Egyptian staff and the Sudanization of the colonial administration from 1924. In this crisis, the Anṣār movement of Sayyid ʿAbd al-Raḥmān al-Mahdī proved to be a reliable ally of the British, while the Khatmiyya stuck to a pro-Egyptian political position and was hence regarded by the British as increasingly unreliable. From a situation of virtual powerlessness in 1899, the Mahdiyya had thus become a major political ally by the mid-1920s and continued to develop these ties of cooperation in the years to come, working effectively and successfully for the eventual independence of the Sudan against the plans of the Khatmiyya to form a federation with Egypt.

British support for Sayyid ʿAbd al-Raḥmān al-Mahdī and the Mahdiyya was expressed in numerous land concessions, making Sayyid ʿAbd al-Raḥmān al-Mahdī the biggest land owner in the Sudan in the 1930s, with an annual income of £15,000–40,000. Sayyid ʿAbd al-Raḥmān al-Mahdī used this wealth and his influence to transform the movement of the Anṣār into a political party and a well-organized religious brotherhood, although the Anṣār never managed to make major inroads into Khatmiyya heartland, namely, Kassala province, the Nile valley, and Khartoum. The Khatmiyya responded to the Mahdist challenge by also developing new religio-political structures, which eventually led to the formation, in 1938, of a political movement allied with the Khatmiyya, the (Gordon College) Graduates General Congress. This movement came to form the nucleus of the National Unionist Front (NUP), which expressed the political program of the Khatmiyya. In reaction to the political efforts of the Khatmiyya and other pro-Egyptian groups, the British were willing to support a moderate political party, Umma, which expressed the political program of the Anṣār and supported Sudanese independence. The administrative framework of British colonialism thus stimulated the transformation of the two major religious movements of the Sudan, the Anṣār and the Khatmiyya, into religio-political movements which influenced pre-independence politics in the Sudan to a considerable extent. The history of the Sudan in the 1940s and 1950s was characterized by the efforts of these two religio-political movements not only to expand their paramount religious and political role in the Sudan, but also to exclude each other from participation in politics. The stalemate of Sudanese politics in the embrace of these two religio-political blocks was to have tragic consequences for the political development of the Sudan after independence.

An Ornamental Sulṭānate: Zanzibar

In the mid-nineteenth century, the East African coast was dominated by the Sulṭānate of Zanzibar, which also exerted considerable control over vast territories as far as Lake Tanganyika and even the Congo. Zanzibar's political decline started in the 1870s, when British pressure forced the Sulṭānate to stop the overseas slave trade in 1873. Also, a great part of the clove production on the island of Unguja, and the Zanzibari commercial navy, were destroyed in 1872 by a devastating hurricane. And finally, Zanzibari companies had to fight against the competition of European trading companies, as well as the political intervention of the European powers. As a result, the sulṭān increasingly lost control over Zanzibar's possessions and markets on the mainland to the Germans; control over the northern coast was lost to the British. Zanzibar suffered a further setback when Mombasa in British controlled Kenya became the new and major harbor in East Africa after the construction of the Uganda railway in the early twentieth century. Zanzibar did not have any real chance to assert its claims on the mainland after Britain and Germany had come to a mutual agreement concerning the division of the territories of the Sulṭānate in 1888.

When Zanzibar finally became a British Protectorate on 7 November 1890, its last scraps of independence were gradually cut down to size as well. The Foreign Office, responsible for Zanzibar's administration until 1913, initially started to support the existing administrative structures, as was common practice in other British dominions, such as India or, later, Northern Nigeria, where indirect rule came to be the administrative norm. From the very beginning, however, the British started to interfere in Zanzibar's internal affairs: on 1 August 1890, Sulṭān ʿAlī b. Saʿīd (r. 1890–1893) was already forced to sign an anti-slavery decree that prohibited all sales or exchanges of slaves. In addition, he had to close the slave markets and grant slaves the right to purchase their freedom. Only total abolition of slavery was rejected by the sulṭān. The arrival of Sir Gerald Portal as the first Consul General in 1891 produced other radical changes in Zanzibar's political setup, as Portal was committed to the idea of establishing direct control over Zanzibar's internal affairs. To him, "Arab administration was an embodiment of all the worst and most barbaric characteristics of primitive Arab despotism" (Flint 1965: 642). Only two months after his arrival, Portal undertook what Flint called a coup d'état by seizing control of the sulṭān's finances and administration, and by appointing Europeans, removable only with British consent, to take control of the treasury, army, police, customs, post office, and public works. The sulṭān lost control over the public revenue and was eventually granted a civil list fixed at 250,000 rupees per annum for personal expenses and his court.

Although the sulṭān and the court were shocked by these measures, and although even Lord Salisbury urged Portal to be cautious, the British continued to undermine the sulṭān's sovereignty, not only under Portal's administration but also under that of his successor, Rennell Rodd. Rodd, in particular, used the opportunity of Sulṭān ʿAlī b. Saʿīd's death in 1893 to intensify the British grip on Zanzibar's administration by more or less enforcing the succession of Ḥāmid b. Thwaynī (r. 1893–1896). Rodd also forced the new sulṭān to renounce further rights of sovereignty by naming all heads of departments himself, reducing the sulṭān's authority to mere ceremonial functions. This policy had repercussions on the position of the sulṭān, who suffered additional humiliation in the context of the dissolution of the British East Africa Company (BEAC) in 1895 and the subsequent establishment of the British East Africa Protectorate. In the context of these developments, the British Government appropriated a fund of £200,000 that the sulṭān had received from Germany as compensation for the loss of his mainland territories. This fund was taken to cover most of the £250,000 debt of the bankrupt BEAC.

As a consequence of these policies, the sulṭān started to support the anti-British party at the court and replaced Muḥammad b. Sayf as muftī of Zanzibar by Hilāl b. ʿAmūr, who was known for his critical views of the British. In addition, the sulṭān started to build a private bodyguard that reached a strength of one thousand soldiers in October 1895. He was forced to disband these troops in December 1895, when the British Consul, General Hardinge, brought in naval forces. When Sulṭān Ḥāmid b. Thwaynī died on 25 August 1896, Khālid b. Barghash, who had been pushed aside by the British as successor to the throne in 1893, seized the opportunity to take over control of the palace and proclaim himself the new sulṭān. The British naval forces off Zanzibar's coast reacted quickly and on 27 August 1896 shelled the sulṭān's Palace, forcing Khālid b. Barghash to flee into the German consulate and ending the shortest war in history, according to the Guinness Book of Records. The new sulṭān selected by the British, Ḥamad b. Muḥammad (r. 1896–1902), was an admirer of European ways of life and sent his son and successor Sulṭān ʿAlī b. Ḥamūd (r. 1902–1911) to Harrow School in Britain. In order to ensure his son's succession, he made further concessions to the British: "From this time forward, the sultan's sovereignty was to be no more than a legal fiction" (Flint 1965: 646). In April 1897, the sulṭān was compelled to abolish slavery for good, and in 1911 Sulṭān ʿAlī b. Ḥamūd was convinced by the Foreign Office to abdicate. Thereafter he led a life of luxury in Europe. His successor, Khalīfa b. Ḥārub (r. 1911–1960), was a fervent admirer of British rule.

Existing structures of power and administration were thus completely transformed between 1890 and 1913 to fit British ideas of administration: after the first administrative measures taken in 1890 and 1891, a new wave of reforms started in the early twentieth century. In 1906, French and other European jurisdictions were surrendered to British jurisdiction. In the context of these reforms, the First Minister's position was reduced in its functions while the Consul General became a quasi-governor controlling the local administration. Also, the sulṭān's courts, which had been comparatively independent so far, came under British control in 1908, and the Departments of Public Works, Finance and Trade, Public Health, and Education were set up in 1907. In 1905, a waqf commission was created which became responsible for the administration of the awqāf. In 1897, under Sulṭān Ḥamad b. Muḥammad, British courts of law were installed parallel to the existing courts of law, while the administration of Islamic law remained divided into Shāfiʿī and Ibāḍī sections. Also, Indian legal codes were introduced to replace existing sharīʿa regulations on personal matters. From 1897, the qāḍīs were appointed by the British, while the sulṭān had the right to confirm these appointments. From 1908, the qāḍīs were placed under the direct control of a British judge and lost their right to judge criminal cases. In addition, the British colonial administration introduced examinations for qāḍīs, relying on consultants from al-Azhar. Also, the British introduced a dual system, with a British High Court, responsible for all British and foreign subjects as well as mixed cases, and a Qāḍī Court, subordinate to the High Court that was to deal with the subjects of the sulṭān only. The sulṭān thus retained his position as the highest institution of jurisdiction in a formal sense only, while the Chief Native Court (with a supreme Shāfiʿī qāḍī and a supreme Ibāḍī qāḍī, as well as four deputy qāḍīs) in Unguja and Pemba constituted the higher echelon of jurisdiction. Following the Zanzibar courts decree issued in 1908, the jurisdiction of the qāḍīs was limited to civil matters in 1923. Ultimate control over the sulṭān's courts passed to a British magistrate with two qāḍīs as assessors, while local qāḍīs lost any formal say in the decisions of the court. In addition, Europeans were appointed to supervise the liwalis, the local representatives of the sulṭān, in the rural areas, "since the Arab allegedly had no idea of time or punctuality" (quoted in Pouwels 1987: 176).

In 1913, Zanzibar was transferred from the auspices of the Foreign Office to the Colonial Office. A new position of British Resident was created, combining the functions of the Consul General and the First Minister. The Resident was no longer subordinate to the administration of British India in Bombay, but to the Governor of the British East Africa Protectorate. Due to the sulṭān's protests concerning this administrative reorientation, the Colonial Office created new institutions of Protectorate government that were designed to stress Zanzibar's formal autonomy. The new Protectorate Government consisted of the Protectorate Council, presided over by the sulṭān, and the Resident as Vice-President. Other members were the Chief Secretary, the Treasurer, the Attorney General, two representatives for Zanzibar's Arab and Indian populations, and later a representative for the Africans. The functions of the council were vague, neither properly executive nor properly legislative, and in practice only consultative, while the real power lay with the Resident. In a further series of administrative reforms after 1925, the Governor of Kenya lost his position as High Commissioner for Zanzibar. The British Resident in Zanzibar now reported to the Colonial Office in London only. Also, in 1926 the Protectorate Council was abolished and replaced by an Executive Council, consisting of the Chief Secretary, the Attorney General, and the Treasurer, directed formally by a President, namely the sulṭān, but governed effectively by a Vice-President, the British Resident, as well as a Legislative Council (LegCo). As a result, the sulṭān of Zanzibar had merely ceremonial functions by 1926, while the British colonial administrators came to enjoy their role in a truly ornamental Sulṭānate.

Indirect Rule and Muslim Modernizers

The cases of Anglo-Egyptian Sudan and the Sulṭānate of Zanzibar have shown that the British were quite willing to intervene in local affairs and to interpret the concept of indirect rule rather liberally in accordance with local circumstances and political whims. This also applied to other British colonies such as Northern Nigeria, even if in different degrees. The vast territories of the Sokoto empire and its emirates, which had become a British colony by 1903, were left mostly intact after the ruling elite had submitted to British rule. In Northern Nigeria, the British had fewer than 100 political officers, in the early years of their administration, for a territory of more than 500,000 square kilometers, and a population of around 9 million; in the huge emirate of Kano, the British staff "never exceeded about half a dozen at any one time" (Fika 1978: 161). As a consequence, the British had to rely on local personnel as organized in the so-called native administration under the command of the respective local ruler (emir), who had to follow the advice of a British resident and his staff of political officers (district commissioners). However, British colonial intervention in the daily affairs of the Northern Nigerian emirates evolved over the years, as it did in the case of the Sudan and Zanzibar, and was no less direct than in many French colonies. The British also started to redefine local institutions in Northern Nigeria, especially in the sphere of jurisdiction and local administration, for instance by abolishing slavery in

1901 and 1904 and by establishing native (sharīʿa) courts in 1906 and the native administration (in a series of ordinances up to 1933). They deposed any emir who dared to oppose British ideas of proper administration, as happened in the case of the Shehu of Dikwa (Bornu), Muṣṭafā III, who was removed from office in 1954 under the pretext of "autocratic bearing, reliance on personal favorites, and failure to consult the council" (quoted in Loimeier 1997: 116). Recalcitrant local rulers were subsequently replaced by more willing individuals.

In general terms, the British had managed to impose direct control of local affairs in all of their Muslim territories by the 1920s. In contrast to the French colonial system, however, the British strove to train and to employ local staff in the lower and medium echelons of local administration at a comparatively early point of time, and, in addition, were also keen to train an elite of indigenous administrators in colonial schools in the Sudan (Gordon College and Bakht al-Rūḍa College) and Northern Nigeria (Kano Native Administration Law School). These were allowed (and supposed) to climb to comparatively high levels of colonial administration by the 1930s. These British-educated Muslim administrators were quite willing to implement British ideas of colonial modernity. In case of conflict, British-trained local administrators usually sided with the "infidel" British against Muslim local authorities to impose their own ideas of colonial modernity. It is no surprise that these indigenous colonial administrators were also willing to support Muslim reformers in their own struggle against established religious authorities. As a consequence, coalitions of colonial Muslim modernizers and Muslim reformist scholars developed, which used British colonial structures in order to smash seemingly obsolete social and political structures and to impose their own political and religious hegemony. As a result of British colonial policies (and policies of modernization), established Muslim political authorities, such as the sulṭān of Sokoto, the amīr of Kano, or the sulṭān of Zanzibar, became mere puppets in a system of administration which was increasingly defined by a new elite of Muslim colonial technocrats.

A famous case of conflict between an established political authority and a Muslim modernizer was the conflict between Ahmadu Bello and the sulṭān of Sokoto in the 1930s: Bello, himself an heir to the throne of the sulṭān of Sokoto, had been sidelined in 1938 at the time of the death of Sulṭān Ḥasan. The succession was decided in favor of the Sardauna of Sokoto, Abubakar, who subsequently acted as sulṭān of Sokoto until his own death in 1988. Bello had been educated, as one of the first representatives of his generation, at a British school, the Sokoto Provincial school, which had been established as the first high school in Northern Nigeria in 1922, in order to train indigenous administrators. In 1931, Bello was appointed as a teacher at the Sokoto Middle School and then rose quickly in colonial institutions to become the head of Rabah district in 1934, as well as Sardauna, head of the sulṭān's guard, in 1938. In order to keep his competitor away from the court, the new sulṭān sent Ahmadu Bello to the provincial town of Gusau, where Bello became responsible for the administration of fourteen rural districts. In Gusau, Bello was able to demonstrate his abilities as an administrator and modernizer, in particular when Gusau was connected with the Nigerian railway grid and became a major center for the cultivation of groundnuts. In 1943, some FulBe herdsmen falsely accused Bello of having collected the cattle tax (Hau. jangali) from them and of failing to pay their taxes into the public treasury. This accusation of embezzlement led to a charge of misappropriation of funds against Bello by the court of the sulṭān. Bello faced not only punishment, if found guilty of a criminal offense, but also deposition, a popular strategy in those times to get rid of troublesome officials or emirs. The sulṭān's court in fact declared Bello guilty and condemned him to one year of imprisonment, which would have meant the end of his career. Bello lodged an appeal against this verdict, however, and made a request for revision at a British court of appeal: "At that time, it was unheard of for a Sokoto subject to appeal to the secular British magistrate against a decision of the Sarkin Musulmai [the commander of the Faithful] . . . but the Sardauna did so successfully" (Whitaker 1970: 350). After his acquittal and rehabilitation, Bello was not only able to return to Sokoto and take over the direction of the Sokoto Native Administration Office, practically under the nose of the sulṭān, but had also shown that the power of the sultan had limits, defined by the colonial administration. In the years to come, Bello became the leader of a young generation of administrators, technocrats, and bureaucrats, as well as Muslim reformers, who were willing to follow him on a path of modernization that was not defined by established political authorities any more.

In their colonial policies, the British (as well as all other colonial powers) also often gained the support of religious scholars against established (Muslim) political authorities such as the sulṭān of Zanzibar. Thus, in the first decade of the twentieth century Zanzibar saw a conflict between a respected religious scholar, Aḥmad b. Sumayṭ, and the sulṭān of Zanzibar, which was instrumentalized by the British colonial administration as well as Aḥmad b. Sumayṭ in their efforts to curtail the power of the sulṭān. Around 1903, Aḥmad b. Sumayṭ had published a fatwā against the dhikr practices of the Qādiriyya Sufi order, which constituted a major social and religious force in Zanzibar. In 1903/04, Burhān b. ʿAbd al-ʿAzīz al-Amawī, the Chief Qāḍī of Zanzibar, a leading scholar of the Qādiriyya and one of the advisors of Sulṭān ʿAlī b. Ḥamūd (r. 1902–11), managed to get Aḥmad b. Sumayṭ dismissed as qāḍī of Zanzibar Town and his responsibilities restricted to the rural areas. As a result of this intrigue, Aḥmad b. Sumayṭ seems to have been willing to cooperate with the British against Sulṭān ʿAlī b. Ḥamūd and his ally, Burhān b. ʿAbd al-ʿAzīz al-Amawī, when the British decided to remove the right to decide appeal cases from the sulṭān, in the context of the 1908 jurisdictional reforms. Sulṭān ʿAlī b. Ḥamūd, in contrast to his predecessors, was not knowledgeable in fiqh and had been educated in Britain. In the course of the 1908 legal reforms, which further weakened the position of the sulṭān, Aḥmad b. Sumayṭ was restored to his position as town qāḍī in 1908, and "was even acknowledged as muftī in the context of the reorganization of the jurisdiction" (Bang 2003: 123). In this position,

Aḥmad b. Sumayṭ was able, with British support, to overrule any legal decision based on Islamic law and the jurisdiction of the sulṭān, thus effectively eclipsing the legal authority of both the sulṭān and his Chief Qāḍī, Burhān b. ʿAbd al-ʿAzīz al-Amawī. This case shows that religious scholars were not necessarily allies of Muslim rulers, and that conflict in a country such as Zanzibar was not informed by membership of a Sufi order (or religious affiliation) so much as by family politics and other motivations.

French Muslim Policies: Islam Arabe and Islam Noir

French colonial policies with respect to Islam were informed to a large extent by France's colonial experiences in Algeria, where French colonial rule went through four major stages of development:

I. Conquest, and confrontation with Muslim opposition, often in the form of a jihād against the infidel intruders, and usually crushed by military campaigns and massacres.
II. Establishment of colonial control and administration.
III. The development of paths of accommodation and the identification of allies and enemies.
IV. Decolonization.

This pattern of development of Franco-Muslim relations can also be identified in different degrees and temporal sequences in British, German, and Italian colonial territories. However, in contrast to the British, German, and Italian colonial experiences, the French colonial administration produced a series of political studies, starting from a very early period, based on research in a particular colonial territory, most often Algeria, later also Senegal, Mauritania, Soudan (Mali), and Ivory Coast. These studies tried to analyze the situation as found in situ and to develop a cohesive "politique musulmane." Such policies acquired dogma-like status in the French colonial administration, until revised by the next generation of colonial scholars. The first study of French Islamic policies, based on the Algerian experience, was made by a member of the scientific commission of Algeria, Captain de Neveu, and titled *Les Khouans: ordres religieux chez les musulmans d'Algérie* (1845). It set a distinct pattern, identifying the Sufi orders in Algeria as the major enemies of the French colonial project. This work reflects the first stage of colonial conquest and anti-colonial resistance, which was organized by Sufi leaders, such as ʿAbd al-Qādir al-Jazāʾirī for the Qādiriyya, and other Sufi orders, such as the Raḥmaniyya, and later the Sanūsiyya.

The second stage of French colonialism in Algeria and France's efforts to gain administrative control over Muslim populations after their submission to French rule were mirrored in a study by Louis Rinn entitled *Marabouts et khouans* (1885). This study referred to information collected by the bureaux arabes, established in 1844, which had started to collect data on Algerian religious leaders. On the basis of these data, Rinn proposed to create a corps of loyal Muslim notables and functionaries, a sort of Muslim clergy, and to use them to combat inimical Sufi orders, which were still seen as the major source of political and religious unrest in Algeria. This political program had already been applied in Senegal in the 1850s by General Louis Faidherbe after the victory over al-Ḥājj ʿUmar Taal, when Faidherbe had actually claimed: "In Algeria as well as in Senegal, the goal is the same: to rule the country with minimal costs while drawing maximum advantage from commercial activities; also, the difficulties are the same and so are the means to overcome these problems" (quoted in Cohen 1973: 24, my translation). From the mid-1850s, Faidherbe and subsequent colonial administrators at the école des ôtages (school of hostages) in St. Louis sought to raise an elite of loyal Muslim clerks, notables, and qāḍīs which could be used for the effective administration of a growing number of Muslim sujets.

In a third stage of development, French colonial officers, first in Algeria, then in Senegal, came to see that the leaders of the Sufi orders were potential allies. This realization was based on the field work of two colonial officers in Algeria, Olivier Depont and Xavier Coppolani, and their text *Les confréries religieuses musulmanes* (1897), in which they presented Sufi orders in Algeria as important religious movements which should be cultivated as allies and not be seen as enemies any more. This political conclusion was soon applied to Senegal by a friend of Coppolani, Robert Arnaud, and accepted as French political doctrine by the French governor general of French West Africa, Ernest Roume, as well as his successor, William Ponty. Robert Arnaud's study was entitled *Précis de politique musulmane* (1906). His study, as well as the subsequent study by Alain Quellien, *La politique musulmane dans l'Afrique Occidentale Française* (1910), and again Arnaud (*L'Islam et la politique musulmane française en Afrique Occidentale Française* [1912]), proposed that one could work with Muslims, but that prudence with respect to the Sufi orders was still a good line to follow. In particular, Sufi orders should be reduced, by respective politics, into controllable units.

The third stage of French colonial writing about Islam and French efforts to argue theoretically in favor of a policy of accommodation were represented most prominently by Paul Marty, who had first served in Algeria and later became the director of the Services des Affaires Musulmanes in Dakar from 1913 to 1930. His work came to define French colonial policies with respect to Islam up to the time of World War II and was based on an impressive number of studies of Islam in local contexts, in particular Senegal, Mauritania, and Soudan (Mali). Marty, as well as other French colonial administrators in French sub-Saharan colonies, realized that Islam and local practices of Islam in many territories (including North Africa) were still influenced by pre-Islamic customs. Although pre-Islamic legacies were also identified in North Africa and used to construct the idea of an "Islam Berbère," Islam in sub-Saharan Africa was conceived in more political terms as a specific Islam Noir, a bastardized form of Islam, which was not yet influenced by radical, militant and orthodox Arab Islam. It was thus thought possible to establish ties of cooperation with tolerant African Muslims and to support them as a bulwark against dangerous Near Eastern and pan-Islamic (later,

Wahhābī) influences. This new political paradigm eventually served to rationalize the system of échange de services (exchange of services) which had come to inform Senegalese colonial policies since the late 1890s, and which granted religious movements in Senegal, in particular the religious leaders of the Murīdiyya and the Tijāniyya, some degree of local political and religious (not legal) autonomy, thus establishing a form of French indirect rule in some parts of the French colonial empire.

The fourth stage of French Muslim policies, informed by the dynamics of decolonization, did not bring about any change in the established policies of exchange of services, but produced a series of French orientalist studies, in particular Vincent Monteil's *L'Islam Noir,* as well as texts by Alphonse Gouilly and J.-C. Froelich on the political structure and history of Muslim societies in sub-Saharan Africa. This last generation of French colonial studies on Islam reflected a certain disentanglement from colonial administrative issues and transferred the study of Islam and its historical development in Africa into academic contexts. This was expressed in the transformation of the Centre des Hautes Études d'Administration Musulmane (CHEAM, est. 1936) as the major think tank for colonial Islam into the (academic) Centre des Hautes Études sur l'Afrique et l'Asie Modernes (CHEAAM) in 1959.

A "System of Exchange of Services": Senegal

In the nineteenth century, Senegal's political and social development was characterized by far-reaching processes of change connected with the rise of groundnut cultivation, the end of the slave trade, and the corresponding fragmentation of political authority, along with increased instability and resistance to the rule of the established aristocracies. This situation stimulated the development of local jihād movements directed against established forms of rule labeled as pagan by Muslim scholars. Most leaders of Senegalo-Gambian jihād movements were linked with the Tijāniyya, a Sufi order that claimed spiritual superiority over all other Sufi orders. The best-known Tijāni figure in the Senegalo-Gambian region was al-Ḥājj 'Umar Taal (c. 1796–1864) from the Fuuta Tooro region, who established his empire further east, in Kaarta and Segou, in contemporary Mali. Al-Ḥājj 'Umar was still able, however, to recruit followers in Senegal who either followed him east or supported his reform policies (and anti-colonial resistance) in Senegal proper. Shaykh Ma Ba Jaxu (1809–1867) was thus able to establish, from 1860, a small imāmate on the Gambia and Saloum, capable of withstanding French military advances, while Cheikhou Amadou Ba or Amadou Seku (d. 1875), another Tijāni jihād leader, established an imāmate in the Jolof region of central Senegal in 1869.

The long wars against these imāmates disturbed French colonial policies considerably and informed French views of seemingly rebellious religious scholars, such as Aḥmad Bamba (1850–1927), who refused to acknowledge French colonial authority by withdrawing into the wilderness of Bawol in the 1890s. To prevent escalation, Aḥmad Bamba was imprisoned in 1895 and exiled to distant Gabon. His followers, the Murīds, tried to rescue their spiritual leader, eventually discovering a way to do so in the very setup of the French colonial system itself: in 1848, France had granted French community status to its major coastal settlements, first St. Louis, later Gorée, Dakar, and Rufisque. This status implied equal political rights as French citizens for all inhabitants of the Quatre Communes, including the Muslim population. Muslim-born French citizens subsequently came to play a vital role in the political dynamics of the Quatre Communes, which each sent one deputy to the French parliament. The candidates for this seat campaigned in the local electorate, a process which in the nineteenth century usually implied an exchange of services between candidates and prospective voters. This arrangement encouraged Murīd leaders such as Cheikh Ibra Fall, one of Aḥmad Bamba's first disciples, to use the money earned by Murīd farmers from groundnut cultivation to finance the campaign of François Carpot, a méti (colored) candidate for the National Assembly, in exchange for Carpot's promise to do something, if elected, for Aḥmad Bamba's release from exile.

Carpot indeed won the 1902 elections with Muslim support and kept his promise, enabling Bamba's return, first to Mauritania in 1902 and then to Senegal in 1907. His return was celebrated by the Murīds as a manifestation of Bamba's powers as a saint, even over non-Muslim France. Bamba realized, however, that times had changed and in 1912 accepted French rule over Muslims, asking his followers in a letter to tolerate French rule, which had brought peace, stability, and equality to Senegal. Bamba's return from exile not only calmed relations between his supporters and the French, but also established a pattern of understanding that proved to be profitable for both sides: Murīd farmers continued to produce Senegal's major cash crop, groundnuts, and supported the colonial system (i.e., paid taxes and supported French war efforts in World War I and World War II), while France (and later the Senegalese state) granted Murīd marabouts a certain degree of internal autonomy, particularly with respect to religious affairs, a privilege that found expression in French material support for Murīd development projects such as the construction of a railway line from Dakar to the seat of the Murīd supreme leader, the Khalifa Général, in Touba.

This perspective on Franco-Murīd cooperation largely holds true for the Tijāniyya and the smaller Sufi orders in Senegal, the Qādiriyya and the Layènes: although linked by spiritual chains (Arab. salāsil, sg. silsila) with the founder of the ṭarīqa, Aḥmad at-Tijānī (1737/8–1815), in the twentieth century the Tijāniyya disintegrated in Senegal into a number of competing branches and family networks which cultivated internal rivalries. Essentially, the Tijāniyya was represented by the Taal, Sy, and Niass family branches, as well as the Dème family in Sokone established by al-Ḥājj Ceerno Aḥmad Dème (1885–1973), and a number of smaller families, such as the community of al-Ḥājj Mamadou Ceerno Seydou Bā (c. 1900–1980) in Madina Gounasse (Casamance), or the community of Cheikh Hamallāh and his disciple Yacouba Sylla in Soudan (Mali), Mauritania, and Côte d'Ivoire, which represented, for some time at least, a walkout option on the colonial state. In contrast to the role played by Tijāni scholars in the jihād movements of the nineteenth century, most Tijānī families became collaborators of the colonial government in the twentieth century. This was particularly true for the family of al-Ḥājj ʿUmar Taal, and his grandson Seydou Nourou Taal, who was regarded by the French colonial administration as an "africain sûr" (reliable, loyal African) (Johnson 1991: 183) and who, in the context of his journeys through French West Africa, contributed to the acceptance of French colonial rule.

A second major Tijāni family was represented by al-Ḥājj Malik Sy (1855–1922) in Tivaouane, the first prominent shaykh to support French colonial rule publicly, in 1912, in a statement similar to that of Aḥmad Bamba, proclaiming France a government blessed by God (Robinson 1993: 189). In contrast to the Murīds and the Niass family, Sy economic activities did not focus on groundnut cultivation so much as on commerce. Traders, entrepreneurs, and notables subsequently became the major clientele of the Sy network. This legacy was continued by al-Ḥājj Malik Sy's successors, especially Abubakar Sy (1890–1957) and ʿAbd al-ʿAzīz Sy (1905–1997), who managed to transform the Sy branch of the Tijāniyya into the most prominent urban Sufi movement in Dakar and the greater Cap Vert region.

The Niass branch of the Tijāniyya, based in Kaolack, developed a different approach to colonial rule that was characterized by greater caution, although never going so far as to advocate active opposition to French rule. ʿAbdallāh Niass (1845–1922), the founder of this branch of the Tijāniyya, developed groundnut production in the Saloum area on a scale comparable to Murīd cultivation projects in Bawol, which earned him the respect of the French colonial administration. His successors, Muḥammad Niass (1881–1959) and Ibrāhīm Niass (1900–1975), continued along these lines, contributing to the transformation of the Saloum region into a major zone of groundnut cultivation. Ibrāhīm Niass, who had provoked a first split within the family in 1930 by refusing to accept the authority of his elder brother, became an opponent of colonial rule for a short period, and even joined a group of dissident Murīd sheikhs and Muslim reformers who demanded immediate independence in 1958, only to return to moderate positions when their endeavors misfired.

In the colonial period, Senegal thus saw the emergence of a system of exchange of services between the French colonial administration and the marabouts of the Sufi orders. This system of exchange of services not only cemented the paramount role of religious leaders in the politics and the economy of the country, but was also an important factor for the sustained stability of the Senegalese colonial (and postcolonial) state, where important social and political changes such as independence were negotiated, and not achieved by armed struggle as, for instance, in Algeria. Due to the paramount role of marabouts in Senegalese politics and social life, reformist scholars such as Cheikh Touré (d. 2005) and movements such as the Union Culturelle Musulmane (UCM), which Touré founded and which criticized the collaboration of the marabouts with the colonial system, never had a real chance to advance their own positions and to acquire popular support on the scale of the Sufi brotherhoods. As such, the "contrât social sénégalais" (Senegalese social contract) (Cruise O'Brien 1992: 9) has to be seen as a rather unique development within the French colonial realm. Although relationships based on the exchange of services developed in other French colonial territories, such as Soudan (Mali), Niger, Ivory Coast, and Guinea, marabouts and Sufi orders never acquired the same paramount religious, political, social, and economic role as in Senegal, and were even completely eclipsed in Guinea by Sekou Touré in 1959 and 1960 in a nationwide campaign of demystification against maraboutage, fétichisme and superstition. In Soudan (Mali) and Ivory Coast, reformist Muslims, often polemically yet misleadingly labeled "Wahhābis" by the colonial authorities, were able to gain a first foothold in society from the mid-1940s and played a major role in the struggle for independence in these countries, even if they did not manage to acquire a dominant position in post-independence politics, which were informed, as in many African post-independence nations, by different concepts of African socialism.

Italy as a Defender of Islam

Like the German colonial realm, the Italian colonial empire was a rather recent creation and also fairly small in size when compared to the British and French colonial territories in Africa. In contrast to the British, French, and German colonies, the Italian colonies, namely, Libya (divided into the regions of Tripolitania, Cyrenaika, and Fazzān), Eritrea, and Somalia, had a small, but largely Muslim population (with the exception of Eritrea, where Muslims formed 50 percent or less of the population), amounting to possibly two million in 1935 (but approximately nine million after the conquest of Ethiopia). Italy's conquest of Libya, which was completed only in the early 1930s, was marked by a clear decrease of population, not only due to Italian massacres but also due to the fact that Italy had put the majority of the population of the Cyrenaika region (more than 100,000 people) into fifteen concentration camps in order to break Libyan resistance.

During the colonial era, the Italian state attained notoriety in military aggressions: the world's first military use of airpower and aerial bombardments (during the 1911–1912 Italo-Turkish war); the first country to widely use gases in violation of the 1925 Gas Protocol (in Libya and Eritrea in the 1920s, in Ethiopia since 1935, formally and officially admitted by Italy in 1996 only); the first European country to wage a large-scale war after World War I (the Ethiopian invasion which actually was the largest European colonial war of all times); and the first European country in the twentieth century to employ genocidal tactics outside of the context of world war (in the late 1920s and early 1930s, in the Cyrenaika region of Libya, through a combination of mass population transfers, forced marches, and mass detention in concentration camps).

Like German colonialism, Italian colonialism could not build on historical administrative experience and developed rather late: in 1869, Italy claimed Assab on the Danakil coast of the Red Sea, close to Djibouti, but effectively occupied this small harbor only in 1882. In early 1885, Italian marine troops occupied the harbor of Massawa and subsequently tried to acquire a foothold in the northern Ethiopian highlands, which were occupied by Italy after the treaty of Wechale in 1889, and came to constitute the colony of Eritrea on 1 January 1890. The conquest of Ethiopia as such, attempted in an Italian invasion in 1896, failed, however, and forced Italy to abandon its dreams of an East African empire for the time being. In 1886, Italy started to claim a zone of influence on the Banādir coast of Somalia and in 1888 declared an Italian protectorate over the coastal areas. From 1888 to 1905, these regions were administrated by a private company (Filonardi), and Italy assumed direct control over the coastal areas in 1905. Effective control over major parts of the vast hinterland of the Banādir coast was realized in the late 1920s only, after the collapse of the resistance of Muḥammad ʿAbdille Ḥasan in 1920.

In 1912, Italy also invaded the Ottoman provinces of Tripolitania and Cyrenaika and occupied the coastal cities, which subsequently formed the colony of Libya. Due to local resistance, most prominently organized by the Sanūsiyya Sufi order, as well as due to the distractions of World War I, Italy was not able to effectively control its North African territories. Only after the ascent to power of the Fascist regime in 1922 did Mussolini advance Italian claims in Libya and in 1929/30 occupy the oases of Fazzān and Kufra in the south. In 1931, the Italian army, commanded by General Badoglio (who also commanded the Italian invasion of Ethiopia in 1935/36), broke the resistance of ʿUmar al-Mukhtār in the Cyrenaika after a war of eight years. This military success was achieved mainly by means of constant air raids and the deportation and subsequent imprisonment of 80 percent of the tribal populations of the Jabal Akhḍar and Marmarica regions of the Cyrenaika in fifteen Italian concentration camps in the Sirte region. As such, the war in Libya became a laboratory for Italy's wars to come, not only in Ethiopia but also in Europe, in terms of both the sheer size of Italian involvement and the means of destruction that came to be employed. As a result of twenty years of colonial warfare, conquest, disruption, and massacre, the Libyan population had shrunk in 1934 to a total number of 655,000 (from 723,000 in 1911 and 775,000 in 1928). More than 40,000 had died in the concentration camps alone. The population in Cyrenaika had suffered most and was reduced from 225,000 in 1928 to 142,000 in April 1931. A 1979 film about the life and struggle of ʿUmar al-Mukhtār, entitled *The Lion of the Desert,* starring Anthony Quinn and directed by the Syro-American director Muṣṭafā Akkad, was still banned in Italy in 2005.

Despite its inclinations to break resistance by way of massacres and relocating populations in concentration camps (as in Cyrenaika, and later Ethiopia), Italy, like other European colonial powers, tried to portray itself as a protector of Islam, in particular after the rise to power of the Fascist government of Mussolini. The apex of Mussolini's efforts to present himself as the defender of Islam against other European colonial powers, in particular France and Britain, was a highly advertised ceremony that took place in Tripoli on 18 March 1937, when he received a sword of Islam and subsequently proclaimed Italy's sympathy toward Muslims in Libya and Ethiopia, and toward Islam and toward Muslims in the whole world. His Islam policy was turned into a political strategy in the context of the war against Ethiopia in 1935–1936. In the context of Fascist Italian efforts to create a colonial empire in East Africa, the Muslim regions of Ethiopia were united with Italian Somalia or granted province status in Africa Orientale Italiana (Ḥarär and Galla-Sidamo). The person in charge of this policy was General Rodolfo Graziani, who had commanded Italian military actions in the Cyrenaika up to 1932 and organized the concentration camps in the Sirte and Cyrenaika regions of Libya. One of his major advisors was the "sottosegretario all'Africa italiana," Enrico Cerulli, "one of the most respected Italian Ethiopianists" (Dominioni 2008: 71), who became a vice-governor of Ethiopia. In Ethiopia, Italy supported Muslim interests in order to weaken Ethiopian resistance. As a consequence, the Italian occupying forces recruited a Muslim Ethiopian army of 35,000, which subsequently fought on the Italian side against Ethiopian troops. Equally, Italy relied heavily on Muslim auxiliary staff and militias in its efforts to establish colonial administration in Ethiopia and effectively tried to expand the old center of Islam, Ḥarär, into a major center of Islamic learning in Italian East Africa. Muslims were granted full religious freedom and freedom of proselytization in Christian areas, Ethiopian judges were replaced by qāḍīs, and Arabic became the official language in Ḥarär and was taught in Muslim schools. Italy also embarked on a program of drilling wells in the semi-arid Ogaden region, and built or rebuilt mosques and Islamic schools, while Muslims were sent on pilgrimage at the expense of the Italian government: in 1939 alone, 3,585 Ethiopian pilgrims went to Saudi Arabia. As a consequence, Muslims, as well as Muslim leaders such as Abba Jobir of Jimma, Shaykh ʿIsāʾ b. Hamza al-Qatbārī of Gurage, the sulṭān of Awssa, Imām Shaykh Ḥusayn, Muḥammad Saʿīd of Bale, and Imām Raḥitu Nūh Dādī of Arussi cooperated with the Italian administration and believed that Italy would make Ethiopia Muslim. Italian attempts to rule vast stretches of Ethiopian territory by building ties of collaboration with Muslim populations not only antagonized the majority of Christian Ethiopians, however, they were also short-lived, as Italian control over Ethiopia collapsed in 1941 in a matter of months.

Legacies of Colonialism

By and large, Muslims came to terms with the colonial state quite well, and often rose to leading positions in colonial administrations, which allowed them to define modernity in their own terms, at least to a certain degree. The emergence of Muslim technocratic and bureaucratic elites in colonial times, however, often led to a struggle against the established religious and political authorities. Yet not a single Muslim politician in the late colonial era advocated the establishment of an Islamic state after independence. Rather, politicians of all religious denominations (Mamadou Dia, Leopold Sédar Senghor, Kwame Nkrumah, Jamāl ʿAbd al-Nāṣir, Julius Nyerere, Jomo Kenyatta, Modibo Keita, among others) advocated almost unanimously the ideal of African socialism. The question was whether Africa's new leaders would be able to fulfill the promise of creating a bright future for a majority of the citizens in their respective countries, and develop modern institutions which would support the development of secular national cultures. Such development was again informed by the fact that postcolonial governments in most cases had to deal with rather diverse national populations and their often vastly different historical experiences. Colonial partition and territorial reorganization have thus come to form a major legacy for Africa's development in the postcolony. Although some colonial boundaries such as the one between Niger and (Northern) Nigeria reflected precolonial political divisions, others, such as the boundary between Senegal and The Gambia, were completely arbitrary. At the same time, the new boundaries united regions and populations that could not look back on a common heritage or history. This was particularly true for most of the colonial territories and states in West Africa that included not only the populations of the tropical forest regions on the Guinea coast but also those of the Sudanic interior. While the coastal regions had come under the influence of European trading houses and, later, Christian missions and churches since the fifteenth century, the bilād al-sūdān in the interior had developed a distinct Islamic legacy that became dominant in the context of the movements of jihād since the eighteenth century. In the context of British, French, and German colonialism in West Africa, both coastal and Sudanic regions were united in colonial territories such as Ivory Coast (Côte d'Ivoire), Togo, Dahomey (Benin), Nigeria, or Cameroon. However, the long-term effects of colonial boundary making can not only be identified in sub-Saharan West Africa, but also in other regions in Africa such as the Anglo-Egyptian Sudan (Republic of Sudan) or the East African countries (Tanganyika/ Tanzania, Uganda, and Kenya), where populations with different historical traditions were equally united in new colonial and postcolonial administrative units.

Colonial partition and territorial reorganization indeed seem to inform the postcolonial development of conflicts between Muslim and non-Muslim populations in countries such as Senegal, Nigeria, and Sudan to a major extent. In Senegal, for instance, a rebel movement in Lower Casamance has been fighting for independence from Senegal since the early 1980s, and this struggle has been presented, nationally as well as internationally, as a struggle of the largely non-Muslim (partly Christian) Diola-speaking populations of the Lower Casamance against the increasing dominance of mostly Wolof-speaking Muslim cadres and migrants from the north. Nigeria has been destabilized since the mid-1980s by bloody skirmishes and local civil wars in Nigeria's so-called middle belt region. In these middle belt areas, Muslim areas interlock with non-Muslim tribal areas, where Christian missions, in particular Pentecostal churches, have been highly active since the early 1980s. In Sudan, a fifty-year war of liberation waged by the Christian South since 1954 against the Muslim North has only recently been shelved in a peace agreement between the two parties and the independence of Southern Sudan in 2011. These conflicts are set on and across historical fault lines between the realm of Islam and non-Muslim territories, and thus seem to confirm Huntington's dictum of "Islam's bloody borders" (Huntington 1996: 254ff.). In fact, these fault lines are the result of long, yet diverging historical development processes: Senegambia can look back on a long tradition of Islamization from the eleventh century and a series of jihād movements from the late seventeenth century, while Lower Casamance came into the realm of influence of a small Muslim emirate, Fuladu, only by the end of the nineteenth century. In the region between Niger and Lake Chad, the Sokoto empire developed in the early nineteenth century to become sub-Saharan Africa's largest Muslim empire, stretching from the middle Niger to Adamawa in present-day Cameroon, while large areas, even within the Sokoto empire, remained rooted in African religions. On the Nile, Egyptian colonial rule disintegrated in 1884–1885, to be replaced by the empire of the Mahdī and his successor, Khalīfa ʿAbdallāh, who continued Egyptian endeavors to conquer the non-Muslim southern regions.

Even if short-lived, Muslim empires, imāmates, and emirates resulting from jihād movements in the eighteenth and nineteenth centuries constituted an important political experience for these regions of sub-Saharan Africa, not only because Islam has been a formative element of local traditions for centuries, but also because Islam became, for the first time in sub-Saharan history, the only source of political legitimacy. Also for the first time, Muslim scholars took political power in these Muslim emirates and empires. Muslim scholars in power not only legitimized their rule in exclusively Islamic terms, but also accepted the enslavement of all those who were or could be declared as non-Muslims. This development points to a new quality in the evolution of Muslim societies in sub-Saharan Africa from the eighteenth and nineteenth centuries: the Muslim emirates and empires of the nineteenth century created a historical legacy that is still remembered today by contemporary sub-Saharan Muslims, in particular those in contemporary Northern Nigeria, as a marker of their own, proper (Muslim) identity as against imposed, colonial, western, secular identities, and this legacy is quoted as a source of inspiration and orientation. The same applies, even if in different terms, to East Africa, where Muslims dominated cultural and political development along the coast for centuries. In the nineteenth century, East Africa's coastal Muslim communities were united by the sulṭān of Zanzibar, who established a grid of Islamic institutions, in particular qāḍī courts, which allowed Muslims to see themselves as citizens of a larger Muslim realm.

In the context of colonial conquest in the late nineteenth and early twentieth centuries, the Muslim emirates and empires, such as Fuladu, Sokoto, the realm of the Mahdī, and the sulṭānate of Zanzibar, as well as all other Muslim states in sub-Saharan Africa, were dismantled and integrated by the colonial powers into new territorial constructions. These new polities were characterized by the fact that they brought together countries and regions with distinct and diverging historical experiences: the non-Muslim population of the Lower Casamance became a minority group in largely Muslim Senegal; the Sokoto caliphate was subdivided by a number of colonial powers, the largest chunk becoming Northern Nigeria, a part of British colonial Nigeria. In the colonial period, Nigeria was dominated by predominantly non-Muslim groups from the south and east (mostly well-educated Christian Yoruba and Igbo elites); the East African coast was also split up among several colonial powers (Portugal, France, Germany, Britain, and Italy), with Muslims remaining majoritarian in the Comoros and in Somalia only. In German East Africa/Tanganyika, Muslims formed the largest religious denomination yet not an absolute majority, while in Kenya and Mozambique Muslims came to form regional (coastal/northern) majorities. The non-Muslim populations of the upper Nile were finally integrated, even if with a semi-autonomous status, into a Sudan dominated by the Arab and Arabo-Nubian Muslim elites of the north.

Relations of power which had evolved in the colonial period were retained and even consolidated in the postcolonial era: Lower Casamance thus continued to be administered by largely Muslim cadres from the north; in Sudan, postcolonial (Muslim) military and civilian governments in Khartoum imposed northern hegemony in the south and tried to secure control over the resources of the south. In Kenya, by contrast, the Muslim coastal region was integrated as Sayyidiyye province into a largely Christian-dominated nation state; the non-Muslim populations of the Nigerian Middle Belt used a plethora of postcolonial crises, such as the Biafra war, to achieve emancipation from Northern Nigerian Muslim elite domination, often through army channels.

Although colonial legacies thus seem to provide a convincing explanation for a plethora of colonial and postcolonial conflicts, we still have to ask whether all these conflicts are truly rooted in the colonial past and can be explained as religious conflicts between Muslims and non-Muslims. When taking a closer look at the conflicts mentioned above, it is indeed possible to isolate a considerable number of non-religious motivations and constellations of conflict that may be seen as the hidden agendas of religious conflicts. It would indeed be much better to describe the causes of conflict in the cases mentioned above as a cocktail containing many ingredients, religion being only one of them and many of them rooted in postcolonial development. In these cocktails, economic and financial, social and political, ethnic and regionalistic issues may all be identified as vectors of conflict, each having varying importance in varying contexts at different times. In addition, political, economic, social, and/or ethnic affiliations have often been markers of identity as strong as religion in many religious conflicts. In Lower Casamance, for instance, the Christian rebel movement at various times included a Muslim element. The southern war of independence in the Sudan was equally characterized by the fact that Christian rebel leaders repeatedly chose to take sides with the Muslim north, just as ethnic antagonisms in the south, such as the conflict between the Nuer and the Dinka, had become a more important driving force of dispute than religious affiliation. Taking a closer look at Northern Nigeria, it can be seen that access to land, disputes between local and migrating groups, distribution of oil income, and disputes between old and new (political) elites have been paramount motivating forces for conflict. However, when presented on a national level, local conflicts in Nigeria are easily interpreted as religious conflicts and are instrumentalized in order to delegitimize Muslim northerner or Christian southerner political opponents. At the same time, international media coverage has fallen back on well-established yet simplistic patterns of explanation of conflict in Africa, as there is usually not the time or space to go into the deeper causes of a conflict. Thus, disputes in Northern Nigeria are customarily presented as Muslims against Christians.

As these conflicts and their underlying dynamics are grounded in complicated local structures and complex histories of conflict, and as such are unique, they can easily be marketed and engineered, on both national and international levels, as religious conflicts rather than as having a plethora of different causes. The Lower Casamance conflict, for instance, which probably started from the forceful interruption of an initiation ceremony in a Diola shrine, has gone through a number of stages. Rebel groups have united and split so often since the early 1980s that the conflict has adopted characteristics of a struggle for autonomy, independence, and/or civil rights. It could be presented as a jihād as well as pure banditry. The Lower Casamance conflict has even acquired features of a trans-border conflict with both The Gambia and Guinea Bissau, and as such has become tied to another set of issues, such as smuggling, military intervention, access to natural resources, conflict over land, and ethnic disputes.

Second, and perhaps more important, Africa has seen a number of conflicts that were effectively conflicts among Muslims. The conflict in Dārfūr is such a case, where (Muslim) rebel groups have tried to justify their demands for autonomy or independence by referring to an old tradition of independent Muslim polities in Dārfūr. Equally, the rebellions by (Muslim) Tuareg in Niger and Mali in the 1990s and most recently, in Mali in 2012, were directed against Muslim governments and Muslim majority populations in these countries. Ongoing tensions in Mauritania are an expression of a legacy of discrimination of sedentary "black" (Muslim) populations on the River Senegal by "white" (Muslim) Arabs. Equally, the civil war in Somalia from the early 1990s has been a war among Muslim warlords and was, in addition, linked with the postcolonial development of Somalia, in particular the authoritarian rule of President Siad Barre (r. 1969–1991). Here, religion was activated as an political instrument in 2005, when the Union of Islamic Courts (Arab. ittiḥād al-maḥākim al-islāmiyya) started to use religious arguments to delegitimize the plethora of (Muslim) warlords who had been unable to create convincing conditions for the consolidation of Somalia after the civil war of the 1990s.

An even stronger argument against a simplistic presentation of conflict in Africa as rooted in the colonial past and in purely religious dichotomies is, however, the fact that there are states in Africa that are, like Nigeria, Senegal, and the Sudan, situated on or across historical fault lines. Yet, at the same time, such states have managed to come to terms with diverging historical legacies, to overcome colonial imbalances to a certain extent, and to develop a policy of national integration that implies, at least to a certain degree, access to power (even if only for a limited time) and to resources, for comparably large sections of the population. These states have mostly escaped situations of crisis or civil war, as well as global media attention. In these states, religion has rarely been a major vector of diverging local and/or national identities. In West Africa, Ghana is such an example, and Cameroon could also be named here, although the development of these two countries in the postcolonial era has been very different, and they have had to face a series of other problems since independence. In East Africa, Tanzania could be named as a paramount case of peaceful development, where strategies of othering on the basis of religion have failed to gain currency. Even though considerable Muslim populations in these countries can identify with precolonial traditions of Islamic rule, religion has not constituted a primary model of oppositional identification or led to the construction of divergent models of nation building. To a certain extent, this argument could also be applied to those parts of Senegal north of the Gambia, where subsequent postcolonial governments have successfully managed to integrate a number of different ethnic and religious local traditions, such as the Christian Sereer populations of the Fatick/Siin region. All this shows that religion can be instrumentalized for the management of conflicts in certain historical constellations, and that religion can indeed become a vector of mobilization in political, economic, or social conflicts. It is also clear, however, that recourse to religion is never an automatism: it is a deliberate choice.

Conclusion

When considering more than 1,300 years of historical development of Muslim societies in Africa, it is tempting to look through the lens of politics and to see Muslim societies in a longue durée perspective as primarily political bodies: after all, Muslims have built powerful empires and have inscribed Islam in African history in a way which cannot be disputed, in particular considering the emergence of the imāmates of sub-Saharan West Africa in the context of the movements of jihād in the eighteenth and nineteenth centuries. I would contend, however, that the true dimensions of the impact of Islam cannot be grasped by looking at political development only. Islam has become the religion of more than 450 million Africans today (see map 8), because Muslims have offered multiple solutions in periods of crisis as well as in contexts in which Africans were looking for new orientations. In addition, Muslims have advanced an agenda of societal development that was and is attractive beyond purely political considerations, such as stability and protection, as well as economic prosperity through trade, new modes of production, and integration in translocal networks of exchange. In this agenda, economic, educational, and social dynamics were paramount across time and in different cultural contexts: Muslims have become famous as successful traders in all of Africa and beyond, they have been important interpreters and mediators, they have attained respect and prestige as holders and interpreters of knowledge, as educators and healers, and they have defended and propagated, in many different contexts, the rights of those who were marginalized while criticizing those in power. The key texts of Islam could be quoted easily, if need arose, to attack unlawful rulers and to legitimize action for a better and a more Islamic mode of life.

However, it is also misleading to privilege a positive perspective which views Muslims solely as successful traders, pious scholars, educators, and social liberators. Muslims have also contributed to the tragedies of African history as slavers and as autocratic rulers, as conquerors and destroyers: Muslims have simply been players in African realpolitik and have not been better or worse than other Africans. What Muslims could offer, however, was access to a larger world of knowledge and expertise, to prosperity through trade and trans-local networks, to social advancement and equality within the framework of Islamic jurisdiction. It is clear that many ideals of Islam which have fired Muslims across the ages have never been fully implemented in social realities, due to the fact that those (men) who interpret often represent the social establishment, but periods of rebellion and social readjustment have given marginal groups, women, slaves, and minorities a chance to gain greater freedom and emancipation or at least some sort of economic improvement. Islam has thus repeatedly been imagined as a religion promising a better life, providing access to a larger world, even if the hopes and promises have often come to little or nothing. The revolutionary potential of Islam has survived all crises, however, and continues to inspire the aspirations of many. This explains why Islam has gradually, and over a long period of time, become Africa's biggest religion, even if Christian denominations have had considerable success in the more recent past.

All this should not hide the fact that Muslims in Africa are not a single body. They have quarreled and are still quarreling over many issues, such as the interpretation of key texts and their translation into societal realities. They continue to challenge, if need arises, established political, social, and religious authorities, and they are divided into numerous local communities characterized by their vastly different historical experiences and their different cultural orientations. Thus, Muslims in Senegal have much more in common with Muslims in Morocco than with Muslims in Cape Town or in Somalia, and vice versa; and they may have better links nowadays to parts of the African Muslim diaspora in the United States of America than to Muslims in Eritrea, although Muslim emigrants from Senegal and Eritrea may discover astonishing commonalities when meeting in the American diaspora, as students, refugees, or migrant workers. This reflects historical experiences, when Muslims from various parts of Africa would meet in Arabia in the context of the pilgrimage, or at al-Azhar University in the context of their studies of the Islamic sciences. In attempting to assess the longue durée of Muslim history in Africa, we need to remember indeed that the history of Muslim societies in Africa (and beyond) is characterized not only by their different historical trajectories, including war, but also by a history of multiple entanglements across the continent and beyond: Muslims have been avid travelers, and networks of exchange informed the worldview of African Muslims to a considerable extent long before the times of European journeys of discovery.

Muslims in Africa were, however, not only integrated in horizontal terms into a larger world of Islam and Muslim societies worldwide, but also rooted in vertical terms across time with different historical traditions of Islam. These vertical roots were cultivated by "chains of memory," in Hervieu-Leger's (2000) phrase: the memory of scholars and students, the memory of traders, the memory of families and of Muslim institutions. A central expression and a key element of these chains of memory are the texts that Muslims have written at different times. These have come to form the basis of larger cultural memories that in turn rely on key texts (and their interpretation). The central role of texts for societal development and the development of a "cultural memory" may thus be seen as a major feature that distinguishes Muslim societies in Africa from non-Muslim societies. Texts indeed have the potential not only to transmit memories but also to create and to feed particular identities, as well as to establish claims to specific legacies. Such claims can be presented as issuing from a deeper history than competing claims based on oral transmission, although texts are as open to debate and interpretation as oral sources. Their basic interpretability has to be taken into account when using them as historical sources. Yet a record of (possibly contradictory) written sources at least provides an additional pillar for the study of history. And if we accept that historical texts are written with an intention, we can possibly also peel off the different layers of history telling in a text and identify what has been hidden or rewritten. Texts and their different agendas thus open up multiple avenues of interpretation and broaden access to historical dynamics. This is well known to Muslim scholars who have been trained in a scholarly tradition of interpretation and of balancing views of texts and authors, as for instance in the discipline of tafsīr or in the interpretation of the law. The importance of texts again explains why traditions of Islamic learning have been so central to the development of (different) Muslim communities and societies, and their respective social and historical development: traditions of learning are the physical expression of virtual chains of memory and provide the kind of interpretation of texts that each society needs in its own respective time.

In this book I have consciously spoken about Muslims in Africa as Muslims. Efforts at categorization of Muslims as orthodox or less orthodox or even unorthodox, as lax, superficial, formal, nominal, true, or false, are not only highly biased and often influenced by particularistic interests, but also omit the fact that Muslims worldwide are always rooted in local traditions of Islam. Such traditions of Islam are, as mentioned in the first chapter of this book, the result of multiple historical dynamics. Interaction with local Christianities or with African (Indian, Southeast Asian) indigenous religions has further contributed to generating specific local practices of Islam, for instance in the fields of saint veneration and regional shrine pilgrimage, or medicine and healing. As a result, any tradition of Islam may appear to be particularly orthodox or unorthodox from the perspective of another tradition of Islam, or from the perspective of another age. This is not only true of Muslim societies in Africa, but also applies to those in Arabia, Turkey, Central Asia, Europe, India, and Southeast Asia. And it is also valid for another favorite mode of categorizing Muslims as Sufis and reformers. Such categories are relational and situational in respect of a specific context. They may make sense for a certain period of time, yet become obsolete in the following generation. Efforts at categorization may of course be used by Muslims themselves, for instance in contexts of conflict, as a way of delegitimizing the respective other as a less orthodox Muslim or even as a kāfir. Yet Muslims have realized again and again that they have to accept the "good intention" (Arab. ḥusn al-niyya) of sinning or mixing Muslims, as long as these brothers and sisters in Islam profess to be Muslims: the final judgment is God's only. I would thus like to conclude by quoting from Mervyn Hiskett, who has warned against the efforts of outsiders to define who may be seen as a proper Muslim on the basis of pre-Islamic survivals in local practices of Islam in Africa:

The point of view of those who make much of a *bori* spirit called Alhaji, or who see ancestor-worship in a women's visit to the tomb of a *wālī*, while at the same time ignoring that she dresses as a Muslim, was married as a Muslim and will be buried as a Muslim, seems to me equally unrealistic. It is not that statements about the survival of pre-Islamic practices in West African Islam are untrue; they are simply inconclusive as evidence in the matter of deciding whether individuals and societies are Muslim or something else. They have to be balanced against such evidence as how people dress, how they marry, how they inherit, how they conduct funerals and so on. They also have to be weighed against the evidence of political institutions, literature, folklore and so on—are these wholly Islamic or partly Islamic or not Islamic at all? If such evidence points, in the main, toward Islam, then it seems reasonable to argue that for all practical purposes the society is a Muslim one, despite the fact that it retains some of its old beliefs. (Hiskett 1984: 309)

Appendix

In Europe and North America, sub-Saharan Africa has been presented until at least the mid-twentieth century as a continent devoid of pre-modern literatures. This perspective on sub-Saharan Africa has been widely shared by orientalists and is reflected in the fact that Carl Brockelmann's monumental *Geschichte der Arabischen Literatur*, published between 1937 and 1942 (five volumes), had very few entries on scholars from sub-Saharan Africa. In recent decades, however, research has shown that Muslim societies in sub-Saharan Africa have not only produced a large number of chronicles and local histories (see chapter 4), but a tremendous number of texts on a large array of themes, as documented, for instance, in the current four (soon six) volumes of the *Arabic Literature of Africa* series, edited by John Hunwick and Sean Rex O'Fahey or in Ulrich Rebstock's *Maurische Literaturgeschichte*. As of today, we know that the corpus of Arabic writings composed in the central bilād al-sūdān comprised more than 2,200 texts, not considering king lists, diplomatic notes, and business or private letters, as well as amulets or recipes. Yet this number, though impressive, is still defective. Many texts have been lost or are still hidden, as Muslim scholars chose to hide their libraries when colonial administrations as well as postcolonial national and international bodies, such as museums or universities, appeared too keen on appropriating private libraries for their own purposes. Only recently (since 1996), twenty-one private libraries have been made accessible in Timbuktu alone, among them the Mamma Haidara collection (9,000 manuscripts), the Fondo Kati (7,026 manuscripts), and the Wangari collection (3,000 manuscripts). A similar situation prevails in the western bilād al-sūdān, in Ethiopia, and on the Horn, as well as on the East African coast: it is possible that we know even now only a small portion of the literature written by African Muslim scholars.

When looking at the historical development of the corpus of Arabic writings in the central bilād al-sūdān, it becomes clear, however, that only a few texts were written by sub-Saharan Muslim scholars before the nineteenth century (see the tables below). Yet, from the late eighteenth and early nineteenth centuries, local writing of texts exploded in the central bilād al-sūdān, as well as in the rest of sub-Saharan Africa. This impression has been confirmed by Amar Samb for the Senegambian Sudan: his analysis of Arabic texts compiled in Senegambia shows that local scholars may have written texts in a number of disciplines of Islamic learning before the nineteenth century, but the explosion of local writing took place in the mid-nineteenth century. Khadim Mbacke and Thierno Ka have further developed Amar Samb's analysis by compiling a list of 555 texts from Senegal written by local scholars in the nineteenth and twentieth centuries. These texts are mostly identifiable as religio-dogmatic texts, poetry, biographies, and texts on Islamic law and Sufism. The work of Osswald and Massignon on the western Sahara, by contrast, shows a clear focus on Islamic law. Thus, the library of Shaykh Sidiyya (fl. nineteenth century) in Boutlimit, southern Mauritania, contained 1,195 manuscripts from many parts of the Islamic world: 33 percent of them focused on religio-dogmatic issues (in the central bilād al-sūdān, or CBS, 12 percent), 20 percent on fiqh (CBS, 10 percent), 10 percent on Sufism (CBS, 16 percent), and 14 percent on language-related disciplines (CBS, 3 percent). Other disciplines that were strongly represented in the central bilād al-sūdān, such as religio-political texts (CBS, 11 percent) or poetry (CBS, 16 percent), were not as strong in Mauritania. The development of new Muslim empires in the bilād al-sūdān in the eighteenth and nineteenth centuries led to the incorporation of disciplines of Islamic learning such as ḥadīth or sīra, which had until then been cultivated by local scholars in marginal ways only. These disciplines became increasingly important, however, as they were needed as legitimatory disciplines, providing examples from the life of the Prophet for the development of a new mode of Islamic daily life in the bilād al-sūdān after the jihād movements had come to power. At the same time, many jihād leaders were highly respected Sufi scholars, and as a consequence the study of Sufi texts and the teaching traditions of the Qādiriyya, and later the Tijāniyya, also increased considerably in the nineteenth century.

These preliminary remarks show that a proper analysis of the historical development of Arabic literature in sub-Saharan Africa needs to look at the various regions of Africa, as the development of literatures took different paths in the central bilād al-sūdān (Hausaland, Bornu, etc.), in the western bilād al-sūdān (Mālī, Songhay, Senegambia, Guinea, and the greater Volta region, including contemporary Ghana), in the Nile Sudan, in Ethiopia and on the Horn, as well as on the East African coast. In order to get an approximate idea regarding the development of Arabic literatures in these regions, I have gone through five (four published and one unpublished) volumes of the *Arabic Literature in Africa* series and organized the data along two major lines, namely themes and chronological order. In terms of themes, I have identified eighteen major categories:

1. religio-dogmatic texts (ʿaqīda, tawḥīd, kalām; including poetry and prayers, duʿāʾ)
2. ḥadīth (tradition of the Prophet and related disciplines)
3. tafsīr (exegesis of the Qurʾān)
4. religio-political texts (polemics, waʿẓ, advice, nasīḥa, etc., including poetry)
5. fiqh (Islamic jurisdiction; often fatāwa, legal opinions)
6. language-related disciplines (lugha, naḥw, ṣarf, ʿarūḍ, etc.)
7. taṣawwuf (Sufism; including poetry)
8. sīra (biography of the Prophet, but also of other historical personalities, autobiographies, and family histories)
9. taʾrīkh (history of regions, not family histories)
10. magico-therapeutical texts and practices (ʿilm al-falak, incl. numerology and ḥisāb)
11. ṭibb (medicine)
12. travel accounts (riḥla, often of the pilgrimage), geography
13. adab, akhlāq, tarbiya, taʿlīm (good manners, education, belles lettres)
14. falsafa (philosophy)
15. madḥ al-nabī, panegyrics of the Prophet Muḥammad, often in the form of qaṣīda (poetry)
16. madḥ: other praise poems
17. other disciplines
18. secular/modern themes

In the tables below, only those texts which could be assigned clearly to a specific theme and/or a specific author are registered. This means that a considerable number of existing texts of unknown authors or unassigned themes have not been entered in the tables. Also not included are texts in African languages such as FulFulde, Wolof, Hausa, Amharic, Somaal, or Kiswahili. Literatures in these languages have grown, at first slowly, since the eighteenth century, often in the context of movements of reform that stressed the need for education. In the eighteenth and nineteenth centuries, texts in African languages (apart from local histories, dynastic histories, or praise poetry) thus often had a pedagogic character. Finally, both the Arabic literature from the Sahara, in particular Mauritania (historically Shinqīṭ), and the literary production in the Nile Sudan during the Mahdiyya have not been considered here.

When looking at the following tables, the lack of texts written by local scholars in the respective regions earlier than the fifteenth century is obvious. Yet this lack of written sources will probably have to be revised with ongoing research and the discovery of still-hidden libraries which might contain earlier texts. Second, it is significant that there was a virtual explosion in the number of texts written in the western and central bilād al-sūdān, as well as on the Nile, from the eighteenth century; on the East African coast from the nineteenth century; and in Ethiopia and on the Horn in the twentieth century. In the case of the western and central bilād al-sūdān, this is certainly linked with the early emergence of traditions of learning in some outstanding centers of Islamic learning, such as Timbuktu, Jenné, Katsina, or Kano; second, with the movements of jihād in the eighteenth and nineteenth centuries and the need to legitimize or discredit certain political and religious ideas and objectives. This also explains why a major part of text production happened in a few fields of knowledge only, namely Islamic jurisdiction (no. 5 in the tables), religio-dogmatic texts (no. 1), and religio-political texts (no. 4), as well as Sufism (no. 7). The increasing number of texts on Sufism in the eighteenth and nineteenth centuries can be explained by the fact that all leaders of jihād and the new scholarly elites were linked to either the Qādiriyya or the Tijāniyya. The ongoing production of texts on Sufism, as well as religio-political polemics and advice (nasīḥa) in the twentieth century in the western and central bilād al-sūdān, can be explained by the fact that religious disputes between leading representatives of the Sufi orders continued, and were complemented by the increasing number of conflicts with Muslim reformers, such as Abubakar Gumi in Northern Nigeria, or Cheikh Touré in Senegal, who attacked the activities of the Sufi orders. These texts may add up to several thousand and need to be added eventually. Interesting is the fairly late development of interest in non-religious and non-scientific themes in the central bilād al-sūdān. This was a phenomenon of the nineteenth and twentieth centuries.

In the case of the lands on the Nile, the nineteenth-century explosion of texts was linked with Egyptian colonial rule and reactions to Egyptian colonialism, as expressed in a growth of religio-dogmatic texts (no. 1) that sought to either justify or criticize the new order. Also, the establishment of organized Sufism in the guise of the Mirghāniyya, as well as smaller Sufi orders, is expressed in the table in a significant rise in the number of texts written on Sufi-related issues (no. 7). In the case of the lands on the Nile, the table is rather misleading in one important respect: the huge number of texts (of mostly administrative nature) produced by the Mahdī and the administration of the Mahdiyya between 1881 and 1898 has been omitted.

The comparative lack of literary production in Arabic in Ethiopia and on the Horn until the early twentieth century may be explained by the fact that many authors are anonymous (and have therefore not been registered in the tables), and that an even greater number of texts are rooted in the oral traditions of Somalia and have not (yet) been printed. On the other side, Ethiopia and the Horn can point to a considerable literature on local history (in Arabic) in the twentieth century. This development may be linked with the efforts of a number of nationalities in the region to claim their own history (as in the case of Eritrea).

Equally, Sufism (no. 7), religio-dogmatic issues (no. 1), and (praise) poetry (no. 16) have seen a significant growth in the nineteenth and twentieth centuries, a development linked with the emergence of a number of movements of reform in the region. In both Somalia and Ethiopia, an increasing number of texts were written in English and French from the mid-twentieth century.

The development of Arabic literature on the East African coast is characterized by the fact that Kiswahili became a written language at a fairly early period of time, at least from the eighteenth century, and possibly even from the twelfth century. In the nineteenth century, an increasing number of texts, mostly epic poetry (Swa. utenzi) and/or poems (Swa. ushairi), were written in Kiswahili in Arabic script. In the twentieth century, Kiswahili marginalized Arabic almost completely, and the publication of texts in Arabic has stagnated. At the same time, the number of texts written in Kiswahili exploded, yet this development is not reflected in the table below, which indicates texts in Arabic only. When looking at the development of Arabic literature on the East African coast, we notice a remarkable focus on ta'rīkh (no. 9), that is, local history and chronicles. To a certain extent, this focus reflects the fragmented character of East African coastal societies and their political history. At the same time, the number of texts on fiqh (no. 5) and religio-dogmatic issues (no. 1) has increased considerably in the nineteenth and twentieth centuries.

If we examine the literary production of Muslim sub-Saharan Africa since the fifteenth century in more general terms, some significant patterns emerge: first, the explosion of text production in all regions from the nineteenth century, as well as a remarkable co-temporal expansion of themes. Second, the increasing number of texts written in African languages (not registered here) from the nineteenth century has to be stressed: the number of texts registered in the different tables (5632) thus represents only a portion of the total number of texts produced by Muslim scholars and intellectuals. When looking at the themes of literary production, the general trends observed for the different regions have to be mentioned: religio-dogmatic texts (no. 1), religio-political texts (no. 2), texts on jurisdiction (no. 5), Sufism (no. 7), and (praise) poetry (nos. 15 and 16) are most prominent, while texts on language-related issues (no. 6) come second in all regions. There are, however, a number of significant particularities: on the East African coast, for instance, the large number of local histories and chronicles (ta'rīkh, no. 9) has to be pointed out, and the same is valid for Ethiopia and the Horn; also, the central and western bilād al-sūdān have seen a significant growth of travelogues (riḥla, no. 12) in the twentieth century, a development linked with the increasing number of pilgrims; finally, we can observe another significant growth of literature (in Arabic) on non-religious issues in the central bilād al-sūdān in the twentieth century. This growth of the number of texts on non-religious issues can also be observed, however, in the western bilād al-sūdān, in the Horn of Africa, and on the East African coast, yet in these regions Arabic has been replaced in this field of literary production by either French or English (western bilād al-sūdān), Somaal (Horn of Africa), or Kiswahili (East Africa).

Table 1. The Development of (Arabic) Literature in the Western Bilād al-Sūdān

Themes	before 1400	15th c.	16th c.	17th c.	18th c.	19th c.	20th c.	Total
1	—	1	6	15	81	20	210	333
2	—	—	2	5	4	4	7	22
3	—	—	—	—	—	1	16	17
4	—	—	—	2	9	143	155	309
5	—	2	6	43	36	65	109	261
6	—	—	6	7	—	10	48	71
7	—	1	2	4	36	52	229	324
8	—	—	—	3	1	2	30	36
9	—	—	—	2	4	24	68	98
10	—	—	—	—	—	1	10	11
11	—	—	—	—	—	—	2	2
12	—	—	—	—	—	2	15	17
13	—	—	—	—	—	—	19	19
14	—	—	—	—	—	—	5	5
15	—	—	—	—	4	27	109	140
16	6	1	—	—	3	78	210	298
17	—	—	—	—	—	1	—	1
18	—	—	—	—	—	—	34	34
Total	6	5	22	81	178	430	1276	1998

Table 2. The Development of (Arabic) Literature in the Central Bilād al-Sūdān

Themes	before 1400	15th c.	16th c.	17th c.	18th c.	19th c.	20th c.	Total
1	—	5	2	7	8	101	122	245
2	—	—	—	—	1	13	20	34
3	—	1	1	1	1	8	11	23
4	—	5	4	2	4	150	137	302
5	—	7	5	5	9	67	105	198
6	—	3	—	3	6	19	41	72
7	—	1	—	1	—	95	245	342
8	—	—	—	1	1	21	48	71
9	—	—	2	2	4	15	55	78
10	—	—	—	1	4	9	19	33
11	—	—	—	—	1	15	4	20
12	—	—	—	—	1	2	32	35
13	—	—	—	—	—	—	6	6
14	—	—	—	—	—	1	—	1
15	—	1	1	3	1	10	36	52
16	—	—	—	2	6	59	199	266
17	—	—	—	1	2	18	33	54
18	—	1	—	1	1	149	285	437
Total	—	23	13	29	48	721	1367	2201

Table 3. The Development of (Arabic) Literature in the Nile Sudan

Themes	before 1400	15th c.	16th c.	17th c.	18th c.	19th c.	20th c.	Total
1	—	—	1	11	27	48	22	109
2	—	—	—	—	—	7	2	9
3	—	—	—	—	—	4	1	5
4	—	—	—	—	—	14	4	18
5	—	—	2	14	11	13	13	53
6	—	—	—	—	2	7	2	11
7	—	—	1	2	1	253	157	414
8	—	—	—	—	2	26	20	48
9	—	—	—	—	4	26	29	59
10	—	—	—	—	—	4	—	4
11	—	—	—	—	—	7	—	7
12	—	—	—	—	—	9	1	10
13	—	—	—	—	—	—	—	—
14	—	—	—	—	—	—	—	—
15	—	—	—	6	7	149	59	221
16	—	—	—	—	—	22	3	25
17	—	—	—	—	—	—	—	—
18	—	—	—	—	—	—	—	—
Total	—	—	4	33	54	556	307	954

Table 4. The Development of (Arabic) Literature in Ethiopia and on the Horn

Themes	before 1400	15th c.	16th c.	17th c.	18th c.	19th c.	20th c.	Total
1	6	—	—	—	1	6	18	31
2	—	—	—	—	—	—	—	—
3	—	—	—	—	—	—	2	2
4	—	—	—	—	—	1	9	10
5	4	—	—	—	—	—	11	15
6	—	—	—	—	—	1	5	6
7	1	—	1	—	7	16	7	32
8	—	—	—	—	—	—	15	15
9	—	—	1	2	1	—	41	45
10	—	—	—	—	—	—	3	3
11	—	—	—	—	—	—	—	—
12	—	—	—	—	—	—	2	2
13	—	—	—	—	—	—	—	—
14	—	—	—	—	—	—	—	—
15	1	—	1	1	—	2	3	3
16	—	—	—	2	—	3	18	23
17	—	—	—	—	—	—	26	26
18	—	—	—	—	—	—	8	8
Total	12	—	3	5	9	29	168	226

Table 5. The Development of (Arabic) Literature in East Africa

Themes	before 1400	15th c.	16th c.	17th c.	18th c.	19th c.	20th c.	Total
1	—	—	—	—	1	18	25	44
2	—	—	—	—	—	3	6	9
3	—	—	—	—	—	1	4	5
4	—	—	—	—	—	—	—	—
5	—	—	—	—	—	28	23	51
6	—	—	—	—	—	8	10	18
7	—	—	—	—	—	9	9	18
8	—	—	—	—	1	3	12	16
9	—	1	1	1	—	24	22	49
10	—	—	—	—	—	—	—	—
11	—	—	—	—	—	2	3	5
12	—	—	—	—	—	3	4	7
13	—	—	—	—	—	3	5	8
14	—	—	—	—	—	—	—	—
15	—	—	—	—	—	15	8	23
16	—	—	—	—	—	—	—	—
17	—	—	—	—	—	—	—	—
18	—	—	—	—	—	—	—	—
Total	—	1	1	1	2	117	131	253

Table 6. The Development of (Arabic) Literature in Sub-Saharan Africa (total)

Themes	before 1400	15th c.	16th c.	17th c.	18th c.	19th c.	20th c.	Total
1	6	6	9	33	118	193	397	762
2	—	—	2	5	5	27	35	74
3	—	1	1	1	1	14	34	52
4	—	5	4	4	13	308	305	639
5	4	9	13	62	56	173	261	577
6	—	3	6	10	8	45	106	178
7	1	2	4	7	44	425	647	1130
8	—	—	—	4	4	52	125	185
9	—	1	4	7	13	89	215	329
10	—	—	—	1	4	14	32	51
11	—	—	—	—	1	24	9	34
12	—	—	—	—	1	16	54	71
13	—	—	—	—	—	3	31	34
14	—	—	—	—	—	1	5	6
15	1	1	2	10	12	203	215	444
16	6	1	—	4	9	162	430	612
17	—	—	—	1	2	19	59	81
18	—	—	—	1	1	149	327	479
Total	18	29	43	149	291	1853	3249	5632

Glossary of Arabic Terms

ʿāda	customary law, tradition
adab, pl. ādāb	good manners, refinement; literature
adhān (muʾadhdhin)	call to prayer (Muezzin)
akhlāq (ʿilm al-)	morals, ethics
ʿālim, pl. ʿulamāʾ	religious scholar
ʿaqīda	confession (of the faith); catechetic theology
ʿarūḍ	prosody, metrics
ʿaṣr	afternoon prayer
aʿyān	Notables, people of distinction
(ʿilm al-) balāgha	rhetoric, good style
baraka	blessing power
bāṭin	hidden, inner meaning
bayʿa	oath, agreement of loyalty
(ʿilm al-)bayān	rhetoric
bidʿa, pl. bidaʿ	(un-Islamic) innovation
darsa	class
daʿwa	call; cause; message (dāʿiya, a person who represents a cause)
dhikr	Sufi meditation exercises, ceremony, ritual
diya	blood money
duʿāʾ	supplication, supererogatory prayer
fahm	understanding, comprehension
fajr (ṣubḥ)	morning (prayers)
(ʿilm al-)falak	(knowledge of the) stars, astrology, astronomy
falsafa	philosophy
faqīh, pl. fuqahāʾ	jurist, legal expert
fatwā, pl. fatāwā	formal (yet, not binding) legal opinion
fiqh	law, jurisprudence
(uṣūl al-)fiqh	Islamic legal theory

fitna	chaos, disorder, disunity
ḥadd, pl. ḥudūd	Qur'ānic (iron) regulations and punishments
ḥadīth, pl. aḥādīth	the (discipline of) Prophetic traditions
ḥajj (ḥājj)	pilgrimage (pilgrim)
ḥalqa, pl. ḥalaqāt	circle (of students around their teacher); class, lecture
ḥaqīqa	truth
ḥaraka	speed (of recitation)
ḥāshiya, pl. ḥawāshin	super-commentary
ḥijāb	amulet; protection
hijra	(e)migration
ḥisāb	calculation, arithmetic
ḥizb, aḥzāb	group; part (one of sixty recitational sections of the Qur'ān)
ʿibādāt (pl.)	acts of devotion; religious obligations
ʿīd, pl. aʿyād	festival day (such as ʿīd al-kabīr/al-aḍḥā and ʿīd al-fiṭr, the feast of immolation and the feast of breaking the Ramadan fast)
ijāza	authorization (to represent and/or to teach a text)
ʿilm, pl. ʿulūm	discipline (of learning), science
ʿilm al-falak	astrology, numerology, astronomy
īmām	leader (of prayers)
īmān	faith
irshād	right, correct, proper guidance
ʿishā'	night prayer
iṣlāḥ	reform, purification
iṣṭilāḥ	usage, term; technical term
jāhiliyya	(time of) ignorance, heathendom
jamāʿa	community
jihād	exertion
jizyā	head tax for Christians, Jews, ahl al-kitāb (people of the book)
juz', pl. ajzā'	part, portion (thirtieth part of the Qur'ān)
kalām	theological disputation
karāma	miracle

khalīfa	successor; deputy
khaṭīb, pl. khuṭabā'	preacher (of the Friday sermon: khuṭba)
khaṭṭ	(hand)writing, script
kuttāb, pl. katātīb	qur'ānic school
lawḥ	slate (Kiswahili: ubao; Hausa: allo)
lugha	language (discipline)
('ilm al-)ma'ānī	rhetoric
madḥ (al-nabī)	praise (poem for the Prophet)
madhhab, pl. madhāhib	school of Islamic jurisdiction and legal thinking
madrasa, pl. madāris	school
maghrib	evening prayer; west; sunset
ma'had, pl. ma'āhid	institute
mahdī	the rightly guided one
manṭiq	logic (discipline), phonetics
ma'rifa	knowledge, insight
masjid, pl. masājid	mosque
mawlid (al-nabī)	(the celebration of the) Prophet's birthday
mīrāth (pl. mawārīth)	inheritance (laws of division of inheritance)
mu'adhdhin	Muezzin (see adhān)
mu'āmalāt	obligations regarding human mutual relations (Islamic law)
mukhtaṣarāt (pl.)	comprehensive presentations, concise versions (of larger texts)
muftī	legal expert; official expounder of Islam law
muqri'	reciter (of the Qur'ān)
naḥw	grammar
qāḍī, pl. quḍāh	judge
qarāba	closeness
qaṣīda, pl. qaṣā'id	poem
qirā'a	reading; recitation; punctuation and vocalization of the Qur'ān
rātib	litany of prayers, prayers in honor of someone
riwāq, pl. arwiqa	student convent, hostel
riyāḍa, riyāḍāt	exercises

riyāḍiyyāt	mathematics
ṣaḥāba	companions (of the Prophet)
ṣalāt	prayer
ṣarf	morphology, inflection
shahāda	confession of the faith
sharḥ, pl. shurūḥ	commentary
sharīʿa	(the principles of) Islamic law
sharīf, pl. ashrāf, shurafāʾ	noble (person); descendant of the Prophet
sharṭ, pl. shurūṭ	conditions, clauses
shaykh, pl. shuyūkh	honorific title
sīra	biography (of the life of the Prophet)
ṣubḥ (fajr)	morning prayer
sūra, pl. suwar	chapter of the Qurʾān
taʿālīq (pl.)	glosses, glossaries, comments
tafsīr	exegesis (translation and interpretation) of the Qurʾān
taḥfīẓ	memorization (of the Qurʾān)
tajdīd	reform, rejuvenation
tajwīd	the rules of recitation (of the Qurʾān)
takbīr	the invocation "Allāhu akbar" (God is great)
takrīr	repetition
ṭalab al-ʿilm	the quest for knowledge
ṭālib, pl. ṭullāb	student
talqīn	catechism
tarbiya	education, formation
taʾrīkh	history
ṭarīqa, pl. ṭuruq	Sufi order
taqārīr (pl.)	summarizing accounts
taṣawwuf	Sufism
tawassul	plea, intercession
tawḥīd	dogmatic theology
ṭibb	medicine
ummuhāt	"mothers": central texts of a canon

ʿurf	customary law, tradition
ustādh, pl. asātidha	professor
uṣūl (al-fiqh)	foundations, principles (of the law)
waqf, pl. awqāf	charitable foundation
ẓāhir	outward, visible
zakāt	alms tax
zāwiya, pl. zawāya	Sufi convent, center
ziyāra, pl. ziyārāt	local pilgrimage, shrine pilgrimage
zuhr	noon prayer

Sources for Further Reading

Introduction

For a general overview of the history of Africa as well as interfaces with nature, ecology, and epidemics, see John Iliffe, *Africans: The History of a Continent,* Cambridge, 1995.

Highly recommendable for both ecological and economic history are Ralph A. Austen, *African Economic History,* Oxford, 1987; Stephen Baier, *An Economic History of the Central Sudan,* Oxford, 1980; E. W. Bovill, *The Golden Trade of the Moors,* London, 1958; George E. Brooks, *Landlords & Strangers: Ecology, Society, and Trade in Western Africa 1000–1639,* Boulder, 1993; Richard W. Bulliet, *The Camel and the Wheel,* Cambridge, Mass., 1975; Anthony G. Hopkins, *An Economic History of West Africa,* London, 1980; Timothy Insoll, *The Archaeology of Islam in Sub-Saharan Africa,* Cambridge, 2003; Robin Law, *The Horse in West African History,* Oxford, 1980; Paul Lovejoy, *Caravans of Kola: The Hausa Kola Trade 1700–1900,* Zaria, 1980; Leif O. Manger (ed.), *Trade and Traders in the Sudan,* Bergen, 1984; E. A. McDougall, "Salts of the Western Sahara: Myths, Mysteries, and Historical Significance," IJAHS 23.2 (1990): 231–57; Paul Oliver, *Shelter in Africa,* London, 1971; Abdul Sheriff, *Dhow Cultures of the Indian Ocean: Cosmopolitanism, Commerce and Islam,* London, 2010; James A. Webb, *Desert Frontier: Ecological and Economic Change along the Western Sahel 1600–1850,* Madison, 1995.

For a discussion of the concept of segmentary societies, see L. V. Cassanelli, *The Shaping of Somaali Society: Reconstructing the History of a Pastoral People 1600–1900,* Philadelphia, 1982; Steven Caton, "Power, Persuasion, and Language: A Critique of the Segmentary Model in the Middle East," IJMES 19 (1987): 77–192; E. E. Evans-Pritchard, *The Sanusi of Cyrenaika,* Cambridge, 1949; Raymond Jamous, *Honneur et Baraka. Les structures sociales traditionnelles dans le Rif,* Cambridge, 1981; Ioan M. Lewis, *A Modern History of Somalia: Nation and State in the Horn of Africa,* London, 1988; and E. L. Peters, "Some Structural Aspects of the Feud among the Camel-Herding Bedouin of Cyrenaika," *Africa* 37.3 (1967): 261–82.

For a history of Jewish communities in North Africa, see, amongst others, André Chouraqui, *Histoire des Juifs en Afrique du Nord,* Paris, 1985; Maurice Lombard, *Blütezeit des Islam—Eine Wirtschafts—und Kulturgeschichte 8.–11. Jahrhundert,* Frankfurt, 1992.

For the rinderpest (and other aspects of ecological and epidemic history), see Ralph Austen, *African Economic History,* Oxford, 1987; John Ford, *The Role of Trypanosomiasis in African Ecology,* Oxford, 1971; James Giblin, "Trypanosomiasis Control in African History: An Evaded Theme," JAH 31 (1990): 59–80; John Iliffe, *Africans: The History of a Continent,* Cambridge, 1995; Helge Kjekshus, *Ecology Control and Economic Development in East African History: The Case of Tanganyika, 1850–1950,* London, 1996; Juhani Koponen, *Development for Exploitation: German Colonial Policies in Mainland Tanzania, 1884–1914,* Helsinki, 1994; Roman Loimeier, "Die Rinderpest in Afrika 1887–1898," *Periplus: Jahrbuch für außereuropäische Geschichte,* 2011, 68–92; Holger Weiss, *Banga-Banga: Streß und Krisen im Hausaland (Nord-Nigeria) im 19. Jahrhundert,* Hamburg, 1995; and Bahru Zewde, *A History of Ethiopia 1855–1991,* Oxford, 1991.

1. Is There an "African" Islam?

Major studies for the regions mentioned in this chapter are Jamil M. Abun-Nasr, A History of the Maghrib in the Islamic Period, London, 1987; R. A. Adeleye, *Power and Diplomacy in Northern*

Nigeria, 1804–1906, London, 1977; Hussein Ahmed, "Trends and Issues in the History of Islam in Ethiopia," in M. Nur Alkali (ed.), *Islam in Africa: Proceedings of the Islam in Africa Conference,* Ibadan, 1993, 205–20; Hussein Ahmed, *Islam in Nineteenth Century Wallo, Ethiopia,* Leiden, 2001; Amadou Hampaté Bã, *L'empire peul du Macina,* Paris, 1955; F. R. Bradlow and M. Cairns, *The Early Cape Muslims: A Study of Their Mosques, Genealogy and Origins,* Cape Town, 1978; Louis Brenner, *West African Sufi: The Religious Heritage and Spiritual Search of Cerno Bokar Saalif Taal,* London, 1984; Louis Brenner, *Controlling Knowledge: Religion, Power and Schooling in a West African Muslim Society,* Bloomington, 2001; Eva Evers-Rosander and David Westerlund, *African Islam and Islam in Africa,* London, 1997; Paul Henze, *Layers of Time: A History of Ethiopia,* London, 2005; John Hunwick, "Secular Power and Religious Authority in Muslim Society: The Case of Songhay," JAH 37 (1996): 175–94; Timothy Insoll, *The Archaeology of Islam in Sub-Saharan Africa,* Cambridge, 2003; Steven Kaplan, *The Monastic Holy Man and the Christianization of Early Solomonic Ethiopia,* Wiesbaden, 1984; Steven Kaplan, *The Beta Israel (Falasha) in Ethiopia—From Earliest Times to the Twentieth Century,* New York, 1992; Nehemia Levtzion, *Conversion to Islam,* New York, 1979; Nehemia Levtzion and Randall Pouwels, *The History of Islam in Africa,* London, 2000; Ioan M. Lewis, *A Pastoral Democracy,* London, 1961/1999; Roman Loimeier, *Islamic Reform and Political Change in Northern Nigeria,* Evanston, 1997; Roman Loimeier, "From the Cape to Istanbul: Transnational Networks and Communal Conflicts," *Yearbook of the Sociology of Islam* 2 (1999): 85–98; Roman Loimeier, "Die islamischen Revolutionen in Westafrika," in I. Grau, Chr. Mährdel, and W. Schicho (eds.), *Afrika. Geschichte und Gesellschaft im 19. und 20. Jahrhundert,* Wien, 2000, 53–74; Roman Loimeier, *Säkularer Staat und islamische Gesellschaft: Die Beziehungen zwischen Staat, Sufi-Bruderschaften und islamischer Reformbewegung in Senegal im 20. Jahrhundert,* Hamburg, 2001; Roman Loimeier, "Patterns and Peculiarities of Islamic Reform in Africa," JRA 33.3 (2003): 237–62; Roman Loimeier, *Between Social Skills and Marketable Skills: The Politics of Islamic Education in Zanzibar in the Twentieth Century,* Leiden, 2009; Maurice Lombard, *Die Blütezeit des Islam,* Frankfurt, 1971/1992; Neil McHugh, *Holy Men of the Blue Nile,* Evanston, 1994; Hamza M. Njozi, *Mwembechai Killings and the Political Future of Tanzania,* Ottawa, 2000; H. T. Norris, *The Tuaregs: Their Islamic Legacy and Its Diffusion in the Sahel,* Warminster, 1975; Randall Pouwels, *Horn and Crescent: Cultural Change and Traditional Islam on the East African Coast, 800–1900,* Cambridge, 1987; Charlotte A. Quinn and Frederick Quinn, *Pride, Faith, and Fear: Islam in Sub-Saharan Africa,* Oxford, 2003; David Robinson, *Paths of Accommodation: Muslim Societies and French Colonial Authorities in Senegal and Mauritania, 1880–1920,* London, 2000; David Robinson, *Muslim Societies in African History,* Cambridge, 2004; Robert Shell, "Rites and Rebellion: Islamic Conversion at the Cape, 1908–1915," in Chr. Saunders, H. Philips, E. van Heyningen, and V. Bickford-Smith (eds.), *Studies in the History of Cape Town,* 5 (1983): 1–45; Bernhard Streck, *Sudan: Steinerne Gräber und lebendige Kulturen am Nil,* Köln, 1989; Leonardo A. Villalón, *Islamic Society and State Power in Senegal: Disciples and Citizens in Fatick,* Cambridge, 1995; David Westerlund, "Ahmad Deedat's Theology of Religion: Apologetics through Polemics," JRA, 33.3 (2003): 263–78; and Ivor Wilks, *Asante in the XIXth Century,* Cambridge, 1975.

On Egypt see for example David Ayalon, *Studies on the Mamluks of Egypt (1250–1517),* London, 1977; Heinz Halm, *Die Kalifen von Kairo. Die Fatimiden in Ägypten 973–1074,* München, 2004; Michael Winter, *Egyptian Society under Ottoman Rule, 1517–1798,* London, 1992.

For theoretical debates see Talal Asad, "The Idea of an Anthropology of Islam," *Occasional Papers of the Center for Contemporary Arab Studies,* Georgetown, 1986; Julian Baldick, *Imaginary Muslims: The Uwaysi Sufis of Central Asia,* London, 1993; Miriam Cooke and Bruce Lawrence, *Muslim Networks from Hajj to Hiphop,* Chapel Hill, 2005; Donal B. Cruise O'Brien and Christian Coulon (eds.), *Charisma and Brotherhood in African Islam,* Oxford, 1988; Dale Eickelman, "The Study of Islam in Local Contexts," *Contributions to Asian Studies* 17 (1982): 1–16; Dale Eickelman and James

Piscatori (eds.), *Muslim Travellers: Pilgrimage, Migration and the Religious Imagination*, London, 1990; Patrick Gaffney, *The Prophet's Pulpit: Preaching in Contemporary Egypt*, Berkeley, 1994; Gerrie ter Haar, "World Religions and Community Religions: Where Does Africa Fit In?" in *Occasional Papers*, Center of African Studies, University of Copenhagen, Copenhagen, 2000; Ulrich Haarmann, *Geschichte der arabischen Welt*, München, 1987; Marshall G.S. Hodgson, *The Venture of Islam*, vol. 1, Chicago, 1974; Filippo Osella and Benjamin Soares, *Islam, Politics, Anthropology*, Milton Keynes, 2010; Robert Redfield, *Peasant Society and Culture*, Chicago, 1956; Abd al-Hamid el-Zein, "Beyond Ideology and Theology: The Search for the Anthropology of Islam," *Annual Review of Anthropology* 6 (1977): 227–54.

For a radical Muslim perspective on reform see Sayyid Qutb, *Maʿālim fi l-ṭarīq*, Kairo, 1981.

On processes of conversion to Islam see Abū ʿUbayd ʿAbdallāh b. ʿAbd al-ʿAzīz al-Bakrī, *Kitāb al-masālik wa-l-mamālik*, 2 vols., Tunis, 1992, Felicitas Becker, *Becoming Muslim in Mainland Tanzania, 1890–2000*, Oxford, 2008; Richard W. Bulliet, *Conversion to Islam in the Medieval Period: An Essay in Quantitative History*, Cambridge, Mass., 1979; Robert L. Bunger, *Islamization among the Upper Pokomo*, Syracuse, 1979; Mamadou Diouf and Mara Leichtman, "Introduction," in *New Perspectives on Islam in Senegal: Conversion, Migration, Wealth, Power, and Femininity*, New York, 2008, 1–20; Mark R.J. Faulkner, *Overtly Muslim, Covertly Boni: Competing Calls of Religious Allegiance on the Kenyan Coast*, Leiden, 2006; Humphrey J. Fisher, "Conversion Reconsidered: Some Historical Aspects of Religious Conversion in Black Africa," *Africa* 43.1 (1973): 27–40; Humphrey J. Fisher, "The Juggernaut's Apologia: Conversion to Islam in Black Africa," *Africa*, 55.2 (1985): 153–73; Humphrey J. Fisher, "Many Deep Baptisms: Reflection on Religious, Chiefly Muslim, Conversion in Black Africa," BSOAS 57 (1994): 68–81; Humphrey J. Fisher and Charlotte Blum, "Love for Three Oranges, or the Askiya's Dilemma: The Askia, al-Maghili and Timbuktu, c. 1500 AD," JAH 34 (1993): 65–91; Jonathon Glassman, *Feasts and Riot: Revelry, Rebellion, and Popular Consciousness on the Swahili Coast, 1856–1888*, London, 1995; Robin Horton, "African Conversion," *Africa* 41.2 (1971): 85–108; Robin Horton, "On the Rationality of Conversion, Part I: Africa," *Journal of the International Africa Institute* 45.3 (1975): 219–346; John O. Hunwick, "Sub-Saharan Africa and the Wider World of Islam: Historical and Contemporary Perspectives," JRA 26.2 (1996): 230–57; Timothy Insoll, *The Archaeology of Islam in Sub-Saharan Africa*, Cambridge, 2003; Murray Last, "Some Economic Aspects of Conversion in Hausaland," in N. Levtzion (ed.), *Conversion to Islam*, New York, 1979, 236–46; M. Last and M. A. al-Hajj, "Attempts at Defining a Muslim in Nineteenth Century Hausaland and Bornu," JHSN 3.2 (1965): 231–40; Nehemia Levtzion, *Conversion to Islam*, New York, 1979; Nehemia Levtzion, "Islam and State Formation in West Africa," in S. N. Eisenstadt, M. Abitbol, and N. Chazan (eds.), *The Early State in African Perspective*, Leiden, 1988, 98–108; Brian J. Peterson, *Islamization from Below: The Making of Muslim Communities in Rural French Sudan, 1880–1960*, New Haven, 2011; John E. Philips, "The Islamization of Kano before the Jihad," *Kano Studies, New Series*, 2.3 (1985): 32–52; David Robinson, *Muslim Societies in African History*, Cambridge, 2004; and James Searing, "The Time of Conversion: Christians and Muslims among the Sereer-Safen of Senegal, 1914–1950s," in Benjamin F. Soares (ed.), *Muslim-Christian Encounters in Africa*, Leiden, 2006, 115–41.

On spirit possession cults in general as well as the question of pre-Islamic "survivals" see Janice Boddy, *Wombs and Alien Spirits: Women, Men and the Zar Cult in Northern Sudan*, Bloomington, 1989; Ioan M. Lewis, "The Past and the Present in Islam: The Case of African 'Survivals,'" *Temenos* 19 (1983): 55–67; Ioan M. Lewis, *Women and Islamic Revival in a West African Town*, Bloomington, 2009; Ioan M. Lewis, Ahmed al-Sari, and Sayyid Hurreiz (eds.), *Women's Medicine: The Zar-Bori Cult in Africa and Beyond*, Edinburgh, 1991; Adeline Masquelier, *Prayer Has Spoiled Everything: Possession, Power and Identity in an Islamic Town of Niger*, Durham, 2001; and Tapio Nisula, *Everyday Spirits and Medical Interventions: Ethnographic and Historical Notes on Therapeutic Conventions in a Zanzibar Town*, Saarijärvi, 1999.

2. The Bilād al-Maghrib

Major sources for the history of the bilād al-maghrib are Abū ʿUbayd ʿAbdallāh b. ʿAbd al-ʿAzīz al-Bakrī, *Kitāb al-masālik wa-l-mamālik*, 2 vols., Tunis, 1992 (c. 1064); and (Ibn Khaldūn) ʿAbd al-Raḥmān Abī Zayd b. Muḥammad b. Khaldūn, *The Muqaddimah—an Introduction to History*, Princeton, 1967 (trans. Franz Rosenthal).

A general overview of the history of the Maghrib is provided by Jamil M. Abun-Nasr, *A History of the Maghrib in the Islamic Period*, Cambridge, 1987; Ulrich Haarmann (ed.), *Geschichte der arabischen Welt*, München, 1987; Ira M. Lapidus, *A History of Islamic Societies*, Cambridge, 1988; and Maurice Lombard, *Blütezeit des Islam—Eine Wirtschafts—und Kulturgeschichte 8.-11. Jahrhundert*, Frankfurt, 1992.

The history of epidemics in Egypt and North Africa is presented in Michael W. Dols, *The Black Death in the Middle East*, Princeton, 1977; and John Iliffe, *Africans: The History of a Continent*, Cambridge, 1995.

On the question of conversion to Islam, see Richard W. Bulliet, *Conversion to Islam in the Medieval Period: An Essay in Quantitative History*, Cambridge, Mass., 1979; Nehemia Levtzion, *Conversion to Islam*, New York, 1979.

On the development of the early "Khārijī" movements and dynasties, see Ulrich Rebstock, *Die Ibaditen im Maghrib (2./8.-4./10. Jahrhundert): Die Geschichte einer Berberbewegung im Gewand des Islam*, Berlin, 1983.

On the Fāṭimid dynasty, see Heinz Halm, *Das Reich des Mahdi: Der Aufstieg der Fatimiden*, München, 1991; on the development of the Ismāʿīlī movement, see Farhad Daftary and Zulfiqar Hirji, *The Ismailis: An Illustrated History*, London, 2008.

The Barghawāṭa federation has been examined by Mohamed Talbi, "Hérésie, acculturation et nationalisme des Berbères Bargawata," in M. Galley and D. R. Marshall (eds.), *Proceedings of the First Congress of Mediterranean Studies of Arabo-Berber Influence*, Algiers, 1973; as well as al-Bakrī 1992 (see above).

For the Almoravid and Almohad dynasties see, in addition to the sources quoted above, Nehemia Levtzion, *Ancient Ghana and Mali*, New York, 1973; N. Levtzion and J.F.P. Hopkins, *Corpus of Early Arabic Sources for West African History*, Cambridge, 1981; and Roger Le Tourneau, *The Almohad Movement in North Africa in the Twelfth and Thirteenth Centuries*, Princeton, 1969.

For discussions of the bilād al-makhzan and bilād al-sība see Germain Ayache, "La Fonction d'Arbitrage du Makhzen," in G. Ayache (ed.), *Études d'Histoire Marocaine*, Rabat, 1983, 159–76; Raymond Jamous, *Honneur et Baraka: Les structures sociales traditionnelles dans le Rif*, Cambridge, 1981; C. R. Pennell, "Makhzan and Siba in Morocco: An Examination of Early Modern Attitudes," in E.G.H. Joffe and C. R. Pennell (ed.), *Tribe and State—Essays in Honour of David Montgomery Hart*, The Cottons, 1993, 158–81; Richard Roberts, *Warriors, Merchants and Slaves: The State and the Economy in the Middle Niger Valley, 1700–1914*, Stanford, 1987; and John Waterbury, *The Commander of the Faithful—The Moroccan Political Elite—A Study in Segmented Politics*, London, 1970.

3. The Sahara as Connective Space

The early history of the trans-Saharan trade and the emergence of trading empires in the bilād al-sūdān has been presented in Nehemia Levtzion, *Ancient Ghana and Mali*, New York, 1973.

Nehemia Levtzion and J.F.P. Hopkins also give an excellent overview of Arabic sources on the Sahara in their *Corpus of Early Arabic Sources for West African History*, Cambridge, 1981; the same is true for Joseph Cuoq, *Recueil des sources arabes concernant l'Afrique occidentale du VIIIè au XVIè siècle (Bilād al-Sūdān),* Paris, 1975; see also Tadeusz Lewicki, *Arabic External Sources for the History of Africa to the South of the Sahara,* London, 1969, and Paulo F. de Moraes Farias, *Arabic Medieval Inscriptions from the Republic of Mali, Epigraphy, Chronicles and Songhay-Tuareg History,* Oxford, 2003; on more recent aspects of the trans-Saharan trade, see Ulrich Haarmann, "The Dead Ostrich: Life and Trade in Ghadames (Libya) in the Early Nineteenth Century," *Die Welt des Islams* 36 (1998): 9–94; apart from the Arabic sources mentioned in this chapter, in particular al-Bakrī (*Kitāb al-masālik wa-l-mamālik,* 2 vols., Tunis, 1992), Ibn Baṭṭūṭa (*Tuḥfat al-nuẓẓār fī gharā'ib al-amṣār wa 'ajā'ib al-aṣfār, 'al-riḥla',* 2 vols., Beirut, 1985), and 'Abd al-Raḥmān al-Sa'dī (*Ta'rīkh al-sūdān,* Paris, 1900), an important Arab source written in Italian (Eng. trans. John Pory, 1600) is Leo Africanus, *The History and Description of Africa,* Cambridge, 3 vols., 2010 (based on the new edition by Robert Brown, London, 1896). For an English translation of Ibn Baṭṭūṭa's travels to the East African coast and to the bilād al-sūdān, see Said Hamdun and Noël King, *Ibn Battuta in Black Africa,* Princeton, 1994; for a critical perspective on the (eastern) journeys of Ibn Baṭṭūṭa see Ralf Elger, "Lying, Forging, Plagiarism: Some Narrative Techniques in Ibn Baṭṭūṭa's Travelogue," in Ralf Elger and Yavuz Köse (eds.), *Many Ways of Speaking about the Self: Middle Eastern Ego-Documents in Arabic, Persian and Turkish (14th–20th Century),* Wiesbaden, 2010, 71–87.

The trans-Saharan trade is discussed in Ralph A. Austen, "Marginalization, Stagnation and Growth: The Trans-Saharan Caravan Trade in the Era of European Expansion, 1500–1900," in J. Tracy (ed.), *The Rise of Merchant Empires,* Cambridge, 1990, 311–50; A. Adu Boahen, "The Caravan Trade in the Nineteenth Century," JAH 3.2 (1962): 349–59; E. W. Bovill, *The Golden Trade of the Moors,* London, 1958; Dennis C. Cordell, "Eastern Libya, Wadai and the Sanusiya: A Tariqa and a Trade Route," JAH 18 (1977): 21–36; basic texts are Julia A. Clancy-Smith, *Rebel and Saint: Muslim Notables, Populist Protest, Colonial Encounters (Algeria and Tunisia, 1800–1904),* Berkeley, 1994, for the northern Sahara and the nineteenth century, and Ghislaine Lydon, *On Trans-Saharan Trails: Islamic Law, Trade Networks, and Cross-Cultural Exchange in Nineteenth Century Western Africa,* Cambridge, 2009; for the different European sections of the trade, see Fernand Braudel, *Das Mittelmeer und die mediterrane Welt in der Epoche Philipps II.,* 3 vols., Frankfurt, 1990, and Erich Landsteiner, *Kein Zeitalter der Fugger: Zentraleuropa im langen 16. Jahrhundert,* in Friedrich Edelmayer, Peter Feldbauer, and Marija Wakounig (eds.), *Globalgeschichte 1450–1620,* Wien, 2002.

Trans-Saharan relations are a focus for Jamil M. Abun-Nasr, *A History of the Maghrib in the Islamic Period,* Cambridge, 1987; John Hunwick, "Ahmad Baba and the Moroccan Invasion of the Sudan (1591)," JHSN 2.3 (1962): 311–28; Nehemia Levtzion, "Ibn Hawqal, the Cheque, and Awdaghost," JAH 9.2 (1968): 223–33; and E. A. McDougall, "The View from Awdaghust: War, Trade and Social Change in the Southwestern Sahara, from the Eighth to the Fifteenth Century," JAH 26.1 (1985): 1–3.

Transport in the bilād al-sūdān is discussed by Richard Roberts, *Warriors, Merchants and Slaves: The State and the Economy in the Middle Niger Valley,* Stanford, 1987.

The role of Saharan populations, in particular the Tuareg, is discussed by H. T. Norris, *The Tuaregs: Their Islamic Legacy and Its Diffusion in the Sahel,* Warminster, 1975; and Rainer Osswald, *Die Handelsstädte der Westsahara: Die Entwicklung der arabisch-maurischen Kultur von Šinqīṭ, Wadān, Tīšīt and Walāta,* Berlin, 1986.

Ecological change and history as well as the importance of the salt trade are a major focus in James L.A. Webb, *Desert Frontier: Ecological and Economic Change along the Western Sahel 1600–1850,* Madison, 1995; George E. Brooks, *Landlords & Strangers: Ecology, Society and Trade in Western Africa 1000–1639,* Boulder, 1993; E. A. McDougall, "The Ijil Salt Industry: Its Role in the Precolonial Economy of the Western Sudan," Ph.D. diss., University of Birmingham, 1980, and E. A. McDougall, "Salts of the Western Sahara: Myths, Mysteries, and Historical Significance," IJAHS 23.2 (1990): 231–57.

On slavery and the slave trade in Africa see Ralph A. Austen, "The Trans-Saharan Slave Trade: A Tentative Census," in H. A. Gemery and J. Hogendorn (eds.), *The Uncommon Market,* New York,

1979, 23–76; Philip D. Curtin, *The Atlantic Slave Trade,* Madison, 1969; J. E. Inikori, *Forced Migration: The Impact of the Export Slave Trade on African Societies,* London, 1982; Paul Lovejoy, *The Ideology of Slavery in Africa,* Beverly Hills, 1981; Paul Lovejoy, *Transformations in Slavery: A History of Slavery in Africa,* Cambridge, 1983; Patrick Manning, *Slavery and African Life: Occidental, Oriental and African Slave Trades,* Cambridge, 1990; S. Miers and I. Kopytoff, *Slavery in Africa: Historical and Anthropological Perspectives,* Madison, 1977; Abdul M.H. Sheriff, *Slaves, Spices and Ivory in Zanzibar: Integration of an East African Commercial Empire into the World Economy, 1770–1873,* London, 1987; and J. R. Willis, *Slaves and Slavery in Muslim Africa,* 2 vols., London, 1985.

On Kānim-Bornu see Dierk Lange, *Chronologie et Histoire d'un Royaume Africain,* Wiesbaden, 1977; Dierk Lange, *A Sudanic Chronicle: The Bornu Expeditions of Idrīs Alauma (1564–1576),* Wiesbaden, 1987; as well as Dierk Lange, "Progrès de l'Islam et changements politiques au Kanem du XIe au XIIe siècle: un essai d'interpretation," JAH 19 (1978): 495–513; and Jean Claude Zeltner, *Pages d' Histoire du Kanem: Pays Tchadien,* Paris, 1980.

Timbuktu, the Songhay-Moroccan encounter, and the reign of the Arma are discussed by Michel Abitbol, *Tombouctou et les Arma: De la conquête marocaine du Soudan nigérien en 1591 à l'hégémonie de l'empire Peul du Macina en 1833,* Paris, 1979; Heinrich Barth, *Travels and Discoveries in North and Central Africa,* 5 vols., Cambridge, 2011 (1858); John O. Hunwick, "Ahmad Baba and the Moroccan Invasion of the Sudan (1591)," JHSN 2.3 (1962): 311–28, as well as John O. Hunwick, *Timbuktu and the Songhay Empire: Al-Sa'dī's Ta'rīkh al-sūdān Down to 1613 and Other Contemporary Sources,* Leiden, 1999, and Elias Saad, *A Social History of Timbuktu: The Role of Muslim Scholars and Notables 1400–1900,* Cambridge, 1983.

On the Qaramanlı venture, see Kola Folayan, "Tripoli-Bornu Political Relations 1817–1825," JHSN 5.4 (1971): 463–76; and Kola Folayan, *Tripoli during the Reign of Yusuf Pasha Qaramanli,* Ile Ife, 1979.

The movement of the Sanūsiyya has been discussed by D. Cordell (see above, 1977); Helmut Klopfer, *Aspekte der Bewegung des Muhammad ben Ali as-Sanusi,* Kairo/Wiesbaden, 1967; Jean-Louis Triaud, *La Légende Noire de la Sanusiyya: Une Confrérie Musulmane Saharienne sous le Regard Français (1840–1930),* 2 vols., Paris, 1995; Knut Vikör, *Sufi and Scholar of the Desert Edge: Muhammad b. Ali al-Sanusi and His Brotherhood,* London, 1995; and Nicola Ziadeh, *Sanusiyah: A Study of a Revivalist Movement in Islam,* Leiden, 1958.

Apart from the Sanūsiyya, scholars of the Qādiriyya Sufi order played a major role in the establishment of Islamic learning in the central Sahara from the sixteenth century. For their legacy and the history of the Kunta family in particular, see Norris (above, 1975) and A. A. Batran, "Sidi al-Mukhtar al-Kunti and the Recrudescence of Islam in the Western Sahara and the Middle Niger," Ph.D. diss., University of Birmingham, 1971; and A. A. Batran, "The Kunta, Sidi al-Mukhtar al-Kunti, and the Office of Shaykh al-ṭarīqa al-Qādiriyya," in J. R. Willis (ed.), *The Cultivators of Islam,* London, 1979, 113–46; on Shaykh Sidiyya and the Qādiriyya in Mauritania in the early nineteenth century, see Charles C. Stewart, *Islam and Social Order in Mauritania,* Oxford, 1973.

4. Dynamics of Islamization in the Bilād al-Sūdān

On the history of the trading empires in the bilād al-sūdān, see, amongst others: al-Bakrī, *Kitāb al-masālik wa-l-mamālik,* 2 vols., Tunis, 1992; A. A. Batran, *A Contribution to the Biography of Shaykh Muhammad ibn 'Abd al-Karīm ibn Muhammad al-Maghīlī al-Tilimsānī,* JAH 14.3 (1973): 381–94; Ibn Baṭṭūṭa, *Tuḥfat al-nuẓẓār fī gharā'ib al-amṣār wa 'ajā'ib al-aṣfār, 'al-riḥla',* 2 vols., Beirut, 1985; Paulo F. de Moraes Farias, *Arabic Medieval Inscriptions from the Republic of Mali, Epigraphy, Chronicles and Songhay-Tuareg History,* Oxford, 2003; Djibo Hamani, *L'Islam au Soudan Central: Histoire de l'Islam au Niger du VIIè au XIXè siècle,* Paris, 2007; John O. Hunwick, "Al-Maghili's Replies to the Questions of Askia al-Hajj Muhammad," Ph.D. diss., University of London, 1974; John O. Hunwick,

Sharīʿa in Songhay: The Replies of al-Maghili to the Questions of Askia al-Ḥājj Muḥammad, Oxford, 1985; Timothy Insoll, *The Archaeology of Islam in Sub-Saharan Africa,* Cambridge, 2003; Nehemia Levtzion, *Ancient Ghana and Mali,* New York, 1973; ʿAbd al-Raḥmān al-Saʿdī al-Tinbuktī, *Taʾrīkh al-sūdān* (c. 1653, updated 1656, trans. Octave Houdas), Paris, 1900; for Aḥmad b. Furṭū, see D. Lange, *A Sudanic Chronicle: The Bornu Expeditions of Idris Alauma (1564–1576),* Wiesbaden, 1987, and D. Lange, "Progrès de l'Islam et changements politiques au Kanem du XIe au XIIe siècle: un essai d'interpretation," JAH 19 (1978): 495–513; see equally Nehemia Levtzion and J.F.P. Hopkins, *Corpus of Early Arabic Sources for West African History,* Cambridge, 1981, as well as N. Levtzion, "Slavery and the Slave Trade in the Early States of the Bilād al-Sūdān," conference paper (2003), published in his *Islam in Africa and the Middle East: Studies on Conversion and Renewal,* Aldershot, 2007.

For the Lake Chad region, the Sao, Kotoko, Mandara, the Jukun-federation, Bagirmi, Wadai, and Dārfūr, see Hamadou Adama, *L'Islam au Cameroun: Entre tradition et modernité,* Paris, 2004; Anders Bjørkelo, *State and Society in Three Central Sudanic Kingdoms: Kanem-Bornu, Bagirmi and Wadai,* Bergen, 1976; Dennis C. Cordell, "Eastern Libya, Wadai and the Sanusiya: A Tariqa and a Trade Route," JAH 18 (1977): 21–36; Hermann Forkl, *Die Beziehungen der zentralsudanischen Reiche Bornu, Mandara und Bagirmi sowie der Kotoko-Staaten zu ihren südlichen Nachbarn unter besonderer Berücksichtigung des Sao-Problems,* München, 1983; Lidwien Kapteijns and Jay Spaulding, *After the Millennium: Diplomatic Correspondence from Wadai and Dar Fur on the Eve of Colonial Conquest 1885–1916,* East Lansing, 1988; Dierk Lange, "L'éviction des Séfuwa du Kanem et l'origine des Bulāla," JAH 23 (1982): 315–31; Dierk Lange, "Préliminaires à une histoire des Sao," JAH 30 (1989): 189–210; R. Sean O'Fahey, *The Darfur Sultanate: A History,* New York, 2008; Stephen P. Reyna, *Wars without End: The Political Economy of a Precolonial African State,* Hanover, 1990; Jean Claude Zeltner, *Pages d'Histoire du Kanem: pays tchadien,* Paris, 1980.

On the history of pre-Islamic sub-Saharan Africa, see J.F.A. Ajayi and Michael Crowder (eds.), *History of West Africa,* vol. 1, Burnt Mill, 1971; John Iliffe, *Africans: The History of a Continent,* Cambridge, 1995; as well as Roland Oliver and Brian M. Fagan, *Africa in the Iron Age c. 500 BC to AD 1400,* Cambridge, 1975.

On the development of cities in sub-Saharan Africa, see Catherine Coquery-Vidrovitch, *Histoire des villes d'Afrique Noire: des origins à la colonisation,* Paris, 1993.

On the history of Kano, see Heinrich Barth, *Travels and Discoveries in North and Central Africa,* 5 vols., Cambridge, 2011 (1858); Polly Hill, *Population, Prosperity and Poverty: Rural Kano 1900 and 1970,* Cambridge, 1977; Dierk Lange and Silvio Berthoud, *L'interieur de l'Afrique occidentale d'après Giovanni Lorenzo Anania (XVI siècle), Cahiers d'Histoire Mondiale* 14.2 (1972): 299–351; Murray Last, *From Sultanate to Caliphate: Kano ca. 1450–1800,* in B. Barkindo (ed.), *Studies in the History of Kano,* Ibadan, 1983, 67–92; H. R. Palmer, *The Kano Chronicle,* in *Sudanese Memoirs,* London, 1967, 92–141.

On networks of trade and scholarship in the bilād al-sūdān, as well as the emergence of Muslim communities in the lands on the Guinea coast and the Jakhanke tradition, see Victor Azarya, *Traders and the Center in Massina, Kong and Samori's State,* in IJAHS 13 (1980): 420–56; A. A. Batran, "The Kunta, Sīdī al-Mukhtār al-Kuntī and the Office of Shaykh al-Ṭarīq al-Qādiriyya," in J. R. Willis (ed.), *The Cultivators of Islam,* London, 1979, 113–46; Philip D. Curtin, *Pre-Colonial Trading Networks and Traders: The Diakhanké,* in C. Meillassoux and D. Forde (eds.), *The Development of Indigenous Trade and Markets in West Africa,* Oxford, 1971; T.G.O. Gbadamosi, *The Growth of Islam among the Yoruba, 1841–1908,* London, 1978; Jack Goody (ed.), *Literacy in Traditional Societies,* Cambridge, 1975; Jack Goody, "The Over-Kingdom of Gonja," in Daryll Forde and P. M. Kaberry (eds.), *West African Kingdoms in the Nineteenth Century,* Oxford, 1967, 179–205; Sean Hanretta, *Islam and Social Change in French West Africa: History of an Emancipatory Community,* Cambridge, 2009; Mervyn Hiskett, *The Development of Islam in West Africa,* London, 1984; John O. Hunwick, *A Contribution to the Study of Islamic Teaching Traditions in West Africa: The Career of Muhammad Baghayogho,* ISSS 4 (1990): 149–66; Robert Launay, *Beyond the Stream: Islam and Society in a West African Town,* Berkeley, 1992;

Robert Launay, *Pedigrees and Paradigms: Scholarly Credentials among the Juula of the Northern Ivory Coast,* in D. Eickelman and J. Piscatori (eds.), *Muslim Travellers. Pilgrimage, Migration, and the Religious Imagination,* London, 1994, 175–99; Nehemia Levtzion, *Muslims and Chiefs in West Africa: A Study of Islam in the Middle Volta Basin in the Precolonial Period,* Oxford, 1968; Stefan Reichmuth, *Islamische Bildung und soziale Integration in Ilorin (Nigeria) seit ca. 1800,* Bayreuth, 1998; Richard Roberts, *Warriors, Merchants and Slaves: The State and the Economy in the Middle Niger Valley,* Stanford, 1987; Elias Saad, *A Social History of Timbuktu: The Role of Muslim Scholars and Notables 1400–1900,* Cambridge, 1983; Lamin Sanneh, *The Jakhanke: The History of an Islamic Clerical People of the Senegambia,* London, 1979; Charles C. Stewart, *Islam and Social Order in Mauritania: A Case Study from the Nineteenth Century,* Oxford, 1973; Holger Weiss, *Between Accommodation and Revivalism: Muslims, the State and Society in Ghana from the Precolonial to the Postcolonial Era,* Helsinki, 2008; as well as the work of Ivor Wilks, in particular, "The Juula and the Expansion of Islam into the Forest," in N. Levtzion and R. Pouwels (eds.), *The History of Islam in Africa,* Oxford, 2000, 93–116; Ivor Wilks, "The Transmission of Islamic Learning in the Western Sudan," in J. Goody (ed.), *Literacy in Traditional Societies,* Cambridge, 1975, 161–97; Ivor Wilks, *Asante in the Nineteenth Century,* Cambridge, 1975b; Ivor Wilks, "Consul Dupuis and Wangara: A Window on Islam in Early Nineteenth Century Asante," SA 6 (1995): 55–72; Ivor Wilks, *Wa and the Wala: Islam and Polity in Northwestern Ghana,* Cambridge, 1989.

On paper and the production of books in the western and central bilād al-sūdān, see Jonathan M. Bloom, "Paper in Sudanic Africa," and Murray Last, "The Book in the Sokoto Caliphate," both in Shamil Jeppie and Souleymane Bachir Diagne (eds.), *The Meanings of Timbuktu,* Cape Town, 2008, 45–58 and 135–164, respectively.

On the development of warfare and the introduction of firearms, see Humphrey J. Fisher and Virginia Rowland, "Firearms in the Central Sudan," JAH 12.2 (1971): 215–39.

5. Dynamics of Jihād in the Bilād al-Sūdān

The movements of jihād in the bilād al-sūdān have been analyzed extensively, although regional foci can be detected. In particular the jihād in Hausaland and the jihād of al-Ḥājj ʿUmar Taal have been described in detail, while other movements of jihād, such as Masina, have been neglected, often due to a lack of primary sources. Major sources are Boubakar Barry, *La Sénégambie du XVème siècle. Traité négrière, Islam et conquête coloniale,* Paris, 1988; A. F. Clark, "Imperialism, Independence and Islam in Senegal and Mali," *Africa Today,* 46 (1999): 3–4; Philipp D. Curtin, "Africa North of the Forest (1500–1880)," in P. D. Curtin, S. Feierman, L. Thompson, and J. Vansina (eds.), *African History from Earliest Times to Independence,* London, 1995; John Hanson, *Migration, Jihad and Muslim Authority in West Africa: The Futanke Colonies in Kaarta,* Bloomington, 1996; B. G. Martin, *Muslim Brotherhoods in Nineteenth Century Africa,* Cambridge, 1976; Charlotte A. Quinn, *Mandingo Kingdoms of the Senegambia,* London, 1972; David Robinson, "Revolutions in the Western Sudan," in N. Levtzion and R. Pouwels (eds.), *The History of Islam in Africa,* London, 2000a; David Robinson, "D'empire en empire: l'empire toucouleur dans la stratégie et la mémoire de l'empire français," ISSS 16 (2002): 107–20; Yusuf Bala Usman, *Studies in the History of the Sokoto Caliphate,* New York, 1995.

For al-Maghīlī see John O. Hunwick, *Sharīʿa in Songhay: The Replies of Al-Maghīlī to the Questions of Askia al-Ḥājj Muḥammad,* Oxford, 1985.

For the links between movements of jihād and the Atlantic slave trade, see P. D. Curtin, *The Atlantic Slave Trade,* Madison, 1969; P. D. Curtin, "Jihad in West Africa: Early Phases and Inter-Relations in Mauritania and Senegal," JAH 12 (1971): 1; P. D. Curtin, "The West African Coast in the Era of the Slave Trade," in P. D. Curtin, S. Feierman, L. Thompson, and J. Vansina (eds.), *African*

History from Earliest Times to Independence, London, 1995; and Paul E. Lovejoy, *Transformations in Slavery: A History of Slavery in Africa*, Cambridge, 1983.

For the movements of jihād in the Senegambian region, see M. A. Gomez, *Pragmatism in the Age of Jihad: The Precolonial State of Bundu*, Cambridge, 1992; David Robinson, *Paths of Accommodation: Muslim Societies and French Colonial Authorities in Senegal and Mauritania, 1880–1920*, Oxford, 2000b; Amar Samb, *Essai sur la contribution du Sénégal à la littérature d'expression arabe*, Dakar, 1972.

For the Bambara states of Kaarta and Segu, see Nehemia Levtzion, "Islam in the Bilad al-Sudan to 1800," in N. Levtzion and R. Pouwels (eds.), *The History of Islam in Africa*, Oxford, 2000, 63–92, as well as Richard L. Roberts, *Warriors, Merchants and Slaves: The State and the Economy in the Middle Niger Valley, 1700–1914*, Stanford, 1987.

For the jihād in Hausaland and Bornu, and the development of the Sokoto caliphate and Bornu, see R. A. Adeleye, *Power and Diplomacy in Northern Nigeria 1804–1906*, London, 1971; Heinrich Barth, *Travels and Discoveries in North and Central Africa*, 5 vols., Cambridge, 2011 (1858); Louis Brenner, *The Shehus of Kukawa*, Oxford, 1973; Louis Brenner, "The Jihād Debate between Sokoto and Bornu: An Historical Analysis of Islamic Political Discourse in Nigeria," in J.F.A. Ajayi and J.D.Y. Peel (eds.), *Peoples and Empires in African History: Essays in Memory of Michael Crowder*, London, 1992; Louis Brenner, "Concepts of Ṭarīqa in West Africa: The Case of the Qādiriyya," in Donal B. Cruise O'Brien and Christian Coulon (eds.), *Charisma and Brotherhood in African Islam*,, Oxford, 1988, 33–53; Usman dan Fodio, *Bayān wujūb al-hijra 'alā l-'ibād* (ed. and trans. F. H. el-Masri), Khartoum, 1978; Mervyn Hiskett, *The Sword of Truth: The Life and Times of the Shehu Usuman dan Fodio*, Oxford, 1973; Murray Last, *The Sokoto Caliphate*, London 1967; Beverly Mack and Jean Boyd, *One Woman's Jihad: Nana Asma'u: Scholar and Scribe*, Bloomington, 2000; H. R. Palmer, *The Kano Chronicle*, in *Sudanese Memoirs*, London, 1967, 92–141; John E. Philipps, "The Islamization of Kano before the Jihad," in *Kano Studies (New Series)* 2.3, 1985.

For Fuuta Tooro, see D. Robinson, *Chiefs and Clerics: Abdul Bokar Kane and Fuuta Tooro 1853–1891*, Oxford, 1975.

For al-Ḥājj 'Umar Taal and his empire as well as the confrontation with Masina, see John Hanson, *Migration, Jihad and Muslim Authority in West Africa: The Futanke Colonies in Kaarta*, Bloomington, 1996; John Hanson and David Robinson, *After the Jihad: The Reign of Ahmad al-Kabir in the Western Sudan*, East Lansing, 1991; Sidi Mohamed Mahibou and Jean-Louis Triaud, *Voilà ce qui est arrivé. Bayān ma waqa'a d'al-Ḥāǧǧ 'Umar al-Fūtī: Plaidoyer pour une guerrre sainte en Afrique de l'Ouest au XIX siècle*, Paris, 1983; B. G. Martin, *Muslim Brotherhoods in Nineteenth Century Africa*, Cambridge, 1976; D. Robinson, *La guerre sainte d'al-Hajj Umar. Le Soudan occidental au milieu de XIXème siècle*, Paris, 1988; David Robinson, "Revolutions in the Western Sudan," in N. Levtzion and R. Pouwels (eds.), *The History of Islam in Africa*, London, 2000a; as well as David Robinson, "D'empire en empire: l'empire toucouleur dans la stratégie et la mémoire de l'empire français," ISSS 16 (2002): 107–20.

For the non-Halpulaaren groups in the movements of jihād, see Robert Launay, *Beyond the Stream: Islam and Society in a West African Town*, Berkeley, 1992; B. G. Martin, *Muslim Brotherhoods in Nineteenth Century Africa*, Cambridge, 1976; D. Robinson, *Muslim Societies in African History*, Cambridge, 2004; Lamin Sanneh, *The Jakhanke: The History of an Islamic Clerical People of the Senegambia*, London, 1979; I. Wilks, "The Transmission of Islamic Learning in the Western Sudan," in J. Goody (ed.), *Literacy in Traditional Societies*, Cambridge, 1975, 161–97.

For the terms Halpulaaren and Tukulóór, as well as the Halpulaaren ethnogenesis, see Louis Brenner, "Histories of Religion in Africa," JRA 30.2 (2000): 143–67; P. D. Curtin, "Africa North of the Forest (1500–1880)," in P. Curtin, S. Feierman, L. Thompson, and J. Vansina (eds.), *African History from Earliest Times to Independence*, London, 1995, 152–81; M. A. Gomez, *Pragmatism in the Age of*

Jihad: The Precolonial State of Bundu, Cambridge, 1992; C. Hilliard, "Al-Majmu an-Nafis: Perspectives on the Origins of the Muslim TorodBe of Senegal from the Writings of Shaykh Musa Kamara," *ISSS* 11 (1997): 175–88; B. G. Martin, *Muslim Brotherhoods in Nineteenth Century Africa,* Cambridge, 1976; D. Robinson, *La guerre sainte d'al-Hajj Umar. Le Soudan occidental au milieu de XIXème siècle,* Paris, 1988; J. R. Willis, *Studies in the History of West African Islamic History I: The Cultivators of Islam,* London, 1979.

For Masina, see A.-H. Ba and J. Daget, *L'empire peul du Macina (1818–1853),* Paris, 1955; W. A. Brown, "The Caliphate of Hamdullahi, ca. 1816–1864: A Study in African History and Tradition," Ph.D. diss., University of Wisconsin, Madison, 1968; Bintou Sanankoua, *Un empire peul au XIXème siècle: La Diina du Maasina,* Paris, 1990.

For Samori Turé and the legacy of his wars see Mervyn Hiskett, *The Development of Islam in West Africa,* London, 1984; Robert Launay, *Beyond the Stream: Islam & Society in a West African Town,* Long Grove, Ill., 1992; Yves Person, "Samori and Islam," in J. R. Willis (ed.), *The Cultivators of Islam,* London, 1979, 259–277; Brian J. Peterson, *Islamization from Below: The Making of Muslim Communities in Rural French Sudan, 1880–1960,* New Haven, 2011; and Ivor Wilks, *Wa and the Wala: Islam and polity in Northwestern Ghana,* Cambridge, 1989.

For the sub-Saharan slave economies and the Hubbu movement as well as the Ningi rebellion, and twentieth century abolition of slavery, see Boubakar Barry, *La Sénégambie du XVème siècle. Traité négrière, Islam et conquête coloniale,* Paris, 1988; P. D. Curtin, "The Commercial and Religious Revolutions in West Africa," in P. Curtin, S. Feierman, L. Thompson, and J. Vansina (eds.), *African History from Earliest Times to Independence,* London, 1995, 325–51; Paul Lovejoy, *Transformations in Slavery: A History of Slavery in Africa,* Cambridge, 1983; Paul Lovejoy and Jan Hogendorn, *Slow Death for Slavery: The Course of Abolition in Northern Nigeria, 1897–1936,* Cambridge, 1993; Adell Patton, "An Islamic Frontier Polity: The Ningi Mountains of Northern Nigeria, 1846–1902," in I. Kopytoff (ed.), *The African Frontier,* Bloomington, 1987, 193–213; and Brian J. Peterson, *Islamization from Below: The Making of Muslim Communities in Rural French Sudan, 1880–1960,* New Haven, 2011.

For the movements of jihād as a second conversion to Islam, see Humphrey J. Fisher, "The Juggernaut's Apologia: Conversion to Islam in Black Africa," *Africa* 55.2 (1985) 153–73.

6. Islam in Nubia and Funj

For the early history of Nubia and Nubia in the Christian period, see William Adams, *Nubia: Corridor to Africa,* London, 1977; Joseph Cuoq, *Islamisation de la Nubie Chrétienne,* Paris, 1986; David N. Edwards, "Meroe and the Sudanic Kingdoms," JAH 39.2 (1998): 175–93; H. A. MacMichael, *A History of the Arabs in the Sudan,* London, 1922/1967; Jay Spaulding, "Medieval Christian Nubia and The Islamic World: A Reconsideration of the Baqt Treaty," IJAHS 28.3 (1995): 577–94; Bernhard Streck, *Sudan, Steinerne Gräber und lebendige Kulturen am Nil,* Köln, 1989.

For the history of Sinnār-Funj, see, amongst others, Janet J. Ewald, *Soldiers, Traders and Slaves: State Formation and Economic Transformation in the Greater Nile Valley, 1700–1885,* Madison, 1990; Yūsuf Faḍl Ḥasan, *Malāmiḥ min al-ʿalāqāt al-thaqāfiyya baina al-Maghrib wa-l-Sūdān mundhu al-qarn al-khāmis ʿashara wa-ḥatta al-qarn al-tāsiʿ ʿashara,* Rabat, 2009; Albrecht Hofheinz, "Internalising Islam: Shaykh Muḥammad Majdhūb—Scriptural Islam and Local Context in the Early Nineteenth Century Sudan," 2 vols., Ph.D. diss., Bergen, 1996; P. M. Holt, "Egypt, the Funj and Darfur," CHA 4 (1975): 14–57; P. M. Holt, *The Sudan of the Three Niles: The Funj Chronicle 910–1288/1504–1871,* Leiden, 1999; Lidwien Kapteijns, "The Organization of Exchange in Precolonial Western Sudan," in Leif O. Manger (ed.), *Trade and Traders in the Sudan,* Bergen, 1984, 49–80; Lidwien Kapteijns and Jay Spaulding, "Precolonial Trade between States in the Eastern Sudan, c. 1700-c.1900," in Norman O'Neill and Jay O'Brien (eds.), *Economy and Class in Sudan,* Aldershot, 1988a, 60–89; Lidwien

Kapteijns and Jay Spaulding, *After the Millennium: Diplomatic Correspondence from Wadai and Dār Fūr on the Eve of Colonial Conquest, 1885–1916*, Ann Arbor, 1988b; Manfred Kropp, "Äthiopisch-Sudanische Kriege im 18. Jahrhundert," in Rolf Gundlach, Manfred Kropp, and Annalis Leibundgut (eds.), *Der Sudan in Vergangenheit und Gegenwart*, Wiesbaden, 1995, 111–31; Neil McHugh, *Holymen of the Blue Nile: The Making of an Arab-Islamic Community in the Nilotic Sudan, 1500–1800*, Evanston, 1994; Sean O'Fahey and Jay Spaulding, *Kingdoms of the Sudan*, London, 1974; Sean O'Fahey (ed.), *Arabic Literature of Africa I: The Writings of Eastern Sudanic Africa to c. 1900*, Leiden, 1994; Erich Prokosch, *Ins Land der Geheimnisvollen Func. Des türkischen Weltenbummlers Evliya Celebi Reise durch Oberägypten und den Sudan nebst der osmanischen Provinz Habes in den Jahren 1672/73*, Graz, 1994; Jay Spaulding, "The Evolution of the Islamic Judiciary in Sinnar," IJAHS 10.3 (1977): 408–26; Jay Spaulding, "The End of Nubian Kingship in the Sudan, 1720–1762," in M. W. Daly (ed.), *Modernization in the Sudan*, New York, 1985a, 17–28; Jay Spaulding, "The Management of Exchange in Sinnar, c. 1700," in Leif O. Manger (ed.), *Trade and Traders in the Sudan*, Bergen, 1984, 25–48; Jay Spaulding, *The Heroic Age in Sinnār*, East Lansing, 1985b; Jay Spaulding, "The Historiography of the Northern Sudan from 1500 to the Establishment of British Colonial Rule: A Critical Overview," IJAHS 22.2 (1989): 251–66; Jay Spaulding, "Precolonial Islam in the Eastern Sudan," in Nehemia Levtzion and Randall Pouwels (eds.), *The History of Islam in Africa*, Oxford, 2000, 117–30.

7. Egyptian Colonialism and the Mahdī in the Sudan

The history of the lands on the River Nile including Dārfūr in the nineteenth century has been the focus of numerous publications, the most eminent of which are Anders Björkelo, *Prelude to the Mahdiyya: Peasants and Traders in the Shendi Region, 1821–1885*, Cambridge, 1989; Anders Björkelo, "Turco-Jallāba Relations 1821–1885," in Leif O. Manger (ed.), *Trade and Traders in the Sudan*, Bergen, 1984, 81–107; M. W. Daly (ed.), *Al-Majdhubiyya and al-Mikashfiyya: Two Tariqas in the Sudan*, London, 1985; Colette Dubois, "Morphologies de Khartoum: Conflits d'identité (1820-début de XXe siècle)," in Hervé Bleuchot, Christian Delmet, and Derek Hopwood, eds., *Sūdān, History, Identity, Ideology*, Oxford, 1991, 13–33; Nicole Grandin, "Sayyid Muhammad Uthman al-Mirghani (1793–1853): Une double lecture de ses hagiographies," in F. Constantin (ed.), *Les Voies de l'Islam en Afrique Orientale*, Paris, 1987, 35–58; Richard Hill, *Egypt in the Sudan 1820–1881*, Westport, 1959; Albrecht Hofheinz, "Internalising Islam: Shaykh Muḥammad Majdhūb—Scriptural Islam and Local Context in the Early Nineteenth Century Sudan," 2 vols., Ph.D. diss., Bergen University, 1996; P. M. Holt, "Egypt and the Nile Valley," CHA 5 (1976): 13–50; P. M. Holt, *The Sudan of the Three Niles: The Funj Chronicle 910–1288/1504–1871*, Leiden, 1999; Ali Salih Karrar, *The Sufi-Brotherhoods in the Sudan*, London, 1992; Awad al-Sid al-Karsani, "The Tijaniyya Order in the Western Sudan: A Case Study of Three Centers, Al-Fasher, An-Nahud and Khursi," Ph.D. diss., University of Khartoum, 1985; Neil McHugh, *Holymen of the Blue Nile: The Making of an Arab-Islamic Coomunity in the Nilotic Sudan, 1500–1800*, Evanston, 1994; R. Sean O'Fahey and Jay Spaulding, *Kingdoms of the Sudan*, London, 1974; Sven Rubenson, "Ethiopia and the Horn," CHA 5 (1976): 51–98; Jay Spaulding, "Precolonial Islam in the Eastern Sudan," in Nehemia Levtzion and Randall Pouwels (eds.), *The History of Islam in Africa*, Oxford, 2000, 117–30; John O. Voll, "A History of the Khatmiyya Tariqah in the Sudan," 2 vols., Ph.D. diss., Harvard University, 1969; Gabriel Warburg, *Islam, Nationalism and Communism in a Traditional Society*, London, 1978.

For the period of the Mahdiyya (including Dārfūr), see P. M. Holt, *The Mahdist State in the Sudan, 1881–1898*, Oxford, 1958; Lidwien Kapteijns, "The Emergence of a Sudanic State: Dar Masalit, 1874–1905," IJAHS 16.4 (1983): 601–13; Lidwien Kapteijns, *Mahdist Faith and Sudanic Tradition: The History of the Masalit Sultanate 1870–1930*, London, 1985; Lidwien Kapteijns and Jay Spaulding, *After the Millennium: Diplomatic Correspondence from Wadai and Dar Fur on the Eve of Colonial Conquest 1885–1916*, East

Lansing, 1988; Robert S. Kramer, *Holy City on the Nile: Omdurman during the Mahdiyya 1885–1898*, Princeton, 2010; Aharon Layish, "The Legal Methodology of the Mahdi of Sudan, 1881–1885: Issues in Marriage and Divorce," SA 8 (1997): 37–66; Yitzhak Nakash, "Fiscal and Monetary Systems in the Mahdist Sudan, 1881–1898," IJMES 20 (1988): 365–85; R. Sean O'Fahey, *The Darfur Sultanate: A History*, New York, 2008; Rudolph Peters, *Islam and Colonialism: The Doctrine of Jihad in Modern History*, Den Haag, 1979; Heinrich Pleticha, *Der Mahdiaufstand in Augenzeugenberichten*, München, 1981; Haim Shaked, *The Life of the Sudanese Mahdi*, New Brunswick, 1978; Rudolph Slatin, *Feuer and Schwert im Sudan*, Leipzig, 1922; Alan B. Theobald, *Ali Dinar: Last Sultan of Darfur 1898–1916*, London, 1965; John O. Voll, "The Sudanese Mahdi: Frontier Fundamentalist," IJMES 10 (1979): 145–66; John O. Voll, "Abu Jummayza: The Mahdi's Musaylima," in Edmund Burke III and I. M. Lapidus (eds.), *Islam, Politics and Social Movements*, London, 1988, 97–111; Viviane Amina Yagi, "Le phénomène mahdiste et le Khalifa Abdullahi, sa vie et sa politique," Ph.D. diss., Université de Montpellier III, 1990.

For Rābiḥ b. Faḍl Allāh see Jean-Claude Zeltner, *Les Pays du Tchad dans la Tourmente 1880–1903*, Paris, 1988.

For an account of the British reconquest of the Sudan, see Winston S. Churchill, *The River War: A Historical Account of the Reconquest of the Soudan*, London, 1899.

For the Wahhābiyya see the entry by Esther Peskes and Werner Ende in the *Encyclopaedia of Islam*, as well as Richard B. Winder, *Saudi Arabia in the Nineteenth Century*, London, 1965.

8. Ethiopia and Islam

For the history of imperial Ethiopia see Mordechai Abir, *Ethiopia and the Red Sea: The Rise and Decline of the Solomonic Dynasty in Muslim-European Rivalry in the Region*, London, 1980; Andrzej Bartnicki and Joanna Mantel-Niecko, *Geschichte Äthiopiens* (vol. 1), Berlin, 1978; Joseph Chelhod, *L'Arabie du Sud: Histoire et Civilisation*, Paris, 1984; Marilyn E. Heldman, "The Role of the Devotional Image in Emperor Zar'a Yā'eqob's Cult of Mary," in Sven Rubenson (ed.), *Proceedings of the 7th International Conference of Ethiopian Studies*, Addis Ababa, 1984, 131–35; Paul Henze, *Layers of Time: A History of Ethiopia*, London, 2005; Steven Kaplan, *The Monastic Holy Man and the Christianization of Early Solomonic Ethiopia*, Wiesbaden, 1984; Harold Marcus, *A History of Ethiopia*, Berkeley, 2002; Richard Pankhurst, *The Ethiopians: A History*, Oxford, 2001; Christian Robin, "La premiere intervention abyssine en Arabie meridionale," in Tadesse Beyene (ed.), *Proceedings of the 8th International Conference of Ethiopian Studies*, Addis Ababa, 1989, 147–62; Sergew Hable Selassie, *Ancient and Medieval Ethiopian History to 1270*, Addis Ababa, 1972; P.-P. Shinnie, "The Nilotic Sudan and Ethiopia c. 660 BC to c. 600 AD," CHA 2 (1984): 210–71; and Tadesse Tamrat, *Church and State in Ethiopia 1270–1527*, Oxford, 1972.

On the Kebrä Nägäst see E. A. Wallis Budge, *The Kebra Nagast*, New York, 2004.

On the question of the Beta Israel, see Paul Henze, *Layers of Time: A History of Ethiopia*, London, 2001; Steven Kaplan, *The Beta Israel (Falasha) in Ethiopia—From Earliest Times to the Twentieth Century*, New York, 1992; Harold Marcus, *A History of Ethiopia*, Berkeley, 2002; James Quirin, *The Evolution of the Ethiopian Jews: A History of the Beta Israel (Falasha) to 1920*, Philadelphia, 1992.

On the slave trade in Ethiopia and East Africa, see for instance Mordechai Abir, "The Ethiopian Slave Trade and Its Relation to the Islamic World," in J. R.Willis (ed.), *Slaves and Slavery in Africa*, vol. 2, London, 1985, 123–36; Paul Lovejoy, *Transformations in Slavery: A History of Slavery in Africa*, Cambridge, 1983; François Renault and S. Daget, *Les traites négrières en Afrique*, Paris, 1985; Abdul Sheriff, *Slaves, Spices & Ivory in Zanzibar*, Oxford, 1987; and Abdul Sheriff, *Dhow Cultures of the Indian Ocean: Cosmopolitanism, Commerce, and Islam*, London, 2010.

On Socotra, see Zoltan Biedermann, *Soqotra: Geschichte einer christlichen Insel im Indischen Ozean vom Altertum bis zur frühen Neuzeit*, Wiesbaden, 2006.

On the history of Islam in Ethiopia, see Hajj Abbas, "Le role du culte de chaikh Hussein dans l'islam des Arssi (Éthiopie)," ISSS 5 (1991): 21–42; Shihāb al-Dīn Aḥmad b. 'Abd al-Qādir, *Futūḥ al-Ḥabasha* (The conquest of Abyssinia), trans. P. L. Stenhouse, Hollywood, 2003; Mordechai Abir, "Ethiopia and the Horn of Africa," CHA 4 (1975): 537–77; Hussein Ahmed, *Islam in Nineteenth Century Wallo, Ethiopia: Revival, Reform and Reaction,* Leiden, 2001; Hussein Ahmed, "Introducing an Arabic Hagiography from Wallo," in Tadesse Beyene (ed.), *Proceedings of the 8th International Conference of Ethiopian Studies,* Frankfurt, 1988, 185–97; Hussein Ahmed, "Trends and Issues in the History of Islam in Ethiopia," in M. Nur Alkali (ed.), *Islam in Africa: Proceedings of the Islam in Africa Conference,* Ibadan, 1993, 205–20; Ulrich Braukämper, "On Food Avoidances in Southern Ethiopia: Religious Manifestation and Socio-Economic Relevance," in Sven Rubenson (ed.), *Proceedings of the 7th International Conference of Ethiopian Studies,* Addis Ababa, 1984b, 429–45; Ulrich Braukämper, "Vestiges médiévaux et renouveau musulman sur les hauts-plateaux éthiopiens," in F. Constantin (ed.), *Les Voies de l'Islam en Afrique Orientale,* Paris, 1987a, 19–34; Ulrich Braukämper, "Medieval Survivals as a Stimulating Factor in the Re-islamization of Southeastern Ethiopia," *Zeitschrift der Deutschen Morgenländischen Gesellschaft* 137 (1987b): 20–33; Ulrich Braukämper, "Aspects of Religious Syncretism in Southern Ethiopia," JRA 22.3 (1992): 194–207; R. A. Caulk, "Harär Town and Its Neighbours in the Nineteenth Century," JAH 18.3 (1977): 369–86; Enrico Cerulli, *Studi Etiopici, I: La Lingua e la storia du Harar,* Roma, 1936; Enrico Cerulli, "L'Islam en Etiopie: sa signification historique et ses methodes," in *Correspondance d'Orient, V: Colloque sur la sociologie musulmane,* Bruxelles, 1961, 317–29; Joseph Cuoq, *L'Islam en Ethiopie des origines au XVIème siècle,* Paris, 1981; Patrick Desplat, "Heilige Stadt—Stadt der Heiligen: Manifestationen, Ambivalenzen und Kontroversen des islamischen Heiligen in Harar/Äthiopien," Ph.D. diss., University of Mainz, 2008; Éloi Ficquet, "Flesh Soaked in Faith: Meat as a Marker of the Boundary between Christians and Muslims in Ethiopia," in Benjamin Soares (ed.), *Muslim-Christian Encounters in Africa,* Leiden, 2006, 39–56; Camilla T. Gibb, "Baraka without Borders: Integrating Communities in the City of the Saints," JRA 29.1 (1999): 88–108; Lidwien Kapteijns, "Ethiopia and the Horn of Africa," in N. Levtzion and R. Pouwels (eds.), *The History of Islam in Africa,* Oxford, 2000, 227–50; Jonathan Miran, *Red Sea Citizens: Cosmopolitan Society and Cultural Change in Massawa,* Bloomington, 2009; Rashid Moten, "Islam in Ethiopia: An Analytical Survey," in M. Nur Alkali (ed.), *Islam in Africa: Proceedings of the Islam in Africa Conference,* Ibadan, 1993, 221–31; Terje Østebø, *Localising Salafism: Religious Change among Oromo Muslims in Bale, Ethiopia,* Stockholm, 2008; Carl E. Petry, "From Slaves to Benefactors: The Habashis of Mamluk Cairo," SA 5 (1994): 57–66; John S. Trimingham, *Islam in Ethiopia,* London, 1952/2008.

On the Oromo see Ulrich Braukämper, "Islamic History and Culture in Southern Ethiopia," Hamburg, 2004; Ulrich Braukämper, *Geschichte der Hadiya Süd-Äthiopiens,* Wiesbaden, 1980a; Ulrich Braukämper, "La conquête et l'administration éthiopiennes du Kambata au temps de Menelik II," in Joseph Tubiana (ed.), *Modern Ethiopia: From the Accession of Menelik II to the Present,* Rotterdam, 1980b, 159–76; Muhammed Hassen, *The Oromo of Ethiopia: A History 1570 to 1860,* Cambridge, 1990; Sven Rubenson, "Oromo Country of Origin: A Reconsideration of Hypotheses," in Gideon Goldenberg (ed.), *Ethiopian Studies: Proceedings of the 6th International Conference,* Rotterdam, 1986, 25–40; A. W. Schleicher (ed.), *Geschichte der Galla: Bericht eines abessinischen Mönches über die Invasion der Galla im 16. Jahrhundert,* Berlin, 1893 (a translation of Abba Bahrey's *Ye galla tarik*); Alessandro Triulzi, *Salt, Gold and Legitimacy: Prelude to the History of a No-Mans Land, Bela Shangul, Ethiopia,* Naples, 1981; Thomas Zitelmann, *Nation der Oromo: Kollektive Identitäten, nationale Konflikte, Wir-Gruppenbildungen,* Berlin, 1994.

On Ethiopian relations with Yemen see Emeri Johannes Van Donzel, "Fasiladas et l'Islam," in Joseph Tubiana (ed.), *Modern Ethiopia: From the Accession of Menelik II to the Present,* Rotterdam, 1980, 387–97; Emeri Johannes Van Donzel, *A Yemenite Embassy to Ethiopia 1647–1649,* Wiesbaden, 1986a; Emeri Johannes Van Donzel, "Correspondence between Fasiladas and the Imams of Yemen," in Gideon Goldenberg (ed.), *Ethiopian Studies: Proceedings of the Sixth International Conference*, Rotterdam, 1986b, 91–100.

On Ethiopia and Italy in the 1890s see Angelo del Boca, *Gli italiani nell'Africa Orientale, Vol. 1: Dall'unità alla Marcia su Roma*, Milano, 1992.

9. Muslims on the Horn of Africa

The literature on Somalia and the Horn of Africa is still rather small in comparison to other regions of Islam in Africa. Important introductory texts and sources for this chapter are Ibn Baṭṭūṭa, *Al-riḥla*, vol. 1, Beirut, 1985; R. Beachey, *The Warrior Mullah: The Horn Aflame 1892–1920*, London, 1990; Mark Bradbury, *Becoming Somaliland*, Oxford, 2008; L. V. Cassanelli, *The Benadir Past: Essays in Southern Somaali History*, Madison, 1973; L. V. Cassanelli, *The Shaping of Somaali Society: Reconstructing the History of a Pastoral People 1600–1900*, Philadelphia, 1982; Ioan M. Lewis, *A Pastoral Democracy*, London, 1961/1999; Ioan M. Lewis, "Literacy in a Nomadic Society: The Somaali Case," in J. Goody (ed.), *Literacy in Traditional Societies*, Cambridge, 1975, 265–76; Ioan M. Lewis, *A Modern History of Somalia: Nation and State in the Horn of Africa*, London, 1988.

On Islamic scholarship, and the "mad mullah" in particular, see Angelo del Boca, *Gli italiani in Africa Orientale, Vol. 1: Dall'unità alla marcia su Roma*, Milano, 1992; Aleme Eshete, "A Page in the History of the Ogaden: Contact and Correspondence between Emperor Menelik of Ethiopia and the Somaali Mahdi, Muhammad Abdallah Hassan (1907–1908)," in Sven Rubenson (ed.), *Proceedings of the 7th International Conference of Ethiopian Studies*, Addis Ababa, 1984, 301–14; Vinigi L. Grottanelli, "The Peopling of the Horn of Africa," in H. N. Chittick and R. I. Rotberg (ed.), *East Africa and the Orient*, New York, 1975, 44–75; Ali Abd al-Rahman Hersy, "The Arab Factor in Somaali History: The Origin and Development of Arab Enterprise and Cultural Influences in the Somaali Peninsula," Ph.D. diss., University of California, Los Angeles, 1977; D. J. Jardine, *The Mad Mullah of Somaliland*, London, 1923; Lidwien Kapteijns, "Ethiopia and the Horn of Africa," in N. Levtzion and R. Pouwels (eds.), *The History of Islam in Africa*, Oxford, 2000, 227–50; B. G. Martin, "Muslim Politics and Resistance to Colonial Rule: Shaykh Uways b. Muhammad al-Barawi and the Qadiriyya Brotherhood in East Africa," JAH 10.3 (1969): 471–86; B. G. Martin, *Muslim Brotherhoods in Nineteenth-Century Africa*, Cambridge, 1976; Scott Reese, *Renewers of the Age: Holy Men and Social Discourse in Colonial Benadir*, Leiden, 2008; Said S. Samatar, *In the Shadow of Conquest: Islam in Colonial Northeast Africa*, Trenton, 1992; Abdi Sheik-Abdi, *Divine Madness: Muhammad Abdulle Hassan (1856–1920)*, London, 1993.

10. The East African Coast

Basic sources are H. N. Chittick, "Kilwa and the Arab Settlement of the East African Coast," JAH 4 (1963): 179–90; H. N. Chittick, "The Shirazi Colonization of East Africa," JAH 6 (1965): 275–94; H. N. Chittick, *Kilwa: An Islamic Trading City on the East African Coast*, 2 vols., Nairobi, 1974; H. N. Chittick, "The East Coast, Madagascar and the Indian Ocean," CHA 3 (1977): 183–231; 'Abdallāh Ṣāliḥ al-Farsy, *Baadhi ya Wanavyuoni wa Kishafi wa Mashariki ya Afrika*, Mombasa, 1972; G.S.P. Freeman-Grenville, *The Medieval History of the Coast of Tanganyika*, Berlin, 1962; G.S.P. Freeman-Grenville, "The Coast 1498–1840," in R. Oliver and G. Mathew (eds.), *History of East Africa*, Oxford, 1971, 129–68; G.S.P. Freeman-Grenville, *The Mombasa Rising against the Portuguese, 1631*, London, 1980; G.S.P. Freeman-Grenville, *The East African Coast, 2nd to 19th Centuries*, London, 1988; Ali Mbarak al-Hinawi, *Al Akida: The Life Story of Muhammad b. 'Abdallah b. Mbarak Bakashweini*, London, 1950; Ibn Baṭṭūṭa, *Riḥla Ibn Baṭṭūṭa*, 2 vols., Beirut, 1985; Jan Knappert, *Swahili Islamic Poetry*,

3 vols., Leiden, 1971; Tadeusz Lewicki, *Arabic External Sources for the History of Africa*, London, 1969; B. G. Martin, "Notes on Some Members of the Learned Classes of Zanzibar and East Africa in the Nineteenth Century," IJAHS 4.3 (1971a): 525–45; B. G. Martin, "Migrations from the Hadramaut to East Africa and Indonesia c. 1200 to 1900," *Center of Arabic Documentation Research Bulletin Ibadan* 1–2 (1971b): 1–18; B. G. Martin, "Arab Migrations to East Africa in Medieval Times," IJAHS 7.3 (1975): 367–90; Abū l-Ḥasan al-Mas'ūdī, *Bis zu den Grenzen der Erde*, trans. G. Rotter, Stuttgart, 1982; Gervase Mathew, "The East African Coast until the Coming of the Portuguese," in R. Oliver and G. Mathew (eds.), *History of East Africa*, Oxford, 1971, 94–128; Al-Amīn b. 'Alī al-Mazrū'ī, *The History of the Mazru'i Dynasty of Mombasa*, Oxford, 1995; Jack D. Rollins, *A History of Swahili Prose: From the Earliest Times to the End of the Nineteenth Century*, Leiden, 1983; Gernot Rotter, *Muslimische Inseln vor Ostafrika—Eine arabische Komoren-Chronik des 19. Jahrhunderts*, Beirut, 1976; Justus Strandes, *Die Portugiesenzeit von Deutsch- und Englisch-Ostafrika*, Berlin, 1899; John Sutton, *Kilwa: A History of the Ancient Swahili Town with a Guide to the Monuments of Kilwa Kisiwani and Adjacent Islands*, Nairobi, 2000; Marina Tolmacheva, "'They Came from Damascus in Syria': A Note on Traditional Lamu Historiography," IJAHS 12 (1979): 259–69; Marina Tolmacheva, *The Pate Chronicle*, East Lansing, 1993.

The literature on the history and anthropology of the East African coast is abundant; important texts include James de Vere Allen, *Swahili Origins: Swahili Culture and the Shungwaya Phenomenon*, London, 1993; E. A. Alpers, *Ivory and Slaves: Changing Patterns of International Trade in East Central Africa to the Late Nineteenth Century*, Berkeley, 1975; Anne K. Bang, *Sufis and Scholars of the Sea: The Sufi and Family Networks of Ahmad ibn Sumayt and the Tariqa Alawiyya in East Africa, c. 1860–1925*, London, 2003; R. Beachey, *A History of East Africa 1592–1902*, London, 1996; N. R. Bennett, *A History of the Arab State of Zanzibar*, London, 1978; Klaus Hock, *Gott und Magie im Swahili-Islam. Zur Transformation religiöser Inhalte am Beispiel von Gottesvorstellung und magischen Praktiken*, Köln, 1987; John Middleton, *The World of the Swahili: An African Mercantile Civilization*, New Haven, 1992; C. S. Nicholls, *The Swahili Coast: Politics, Diplomacy and Trade on the East African Littoral 1798–1856*, London, 1971; Derek Nurse and Thomas Spear, *The Swahili: Reconstructing the History and Language of an African Society 800–1500*, Philadelphia, 1985; Roland Oliver and G. Mathew (eds.), *History of East Africa: Vol. I*, Oxford, 1971; Randall L. Pouwels, *Horn and Crescent: Cultural Change and Traditional Islam on the East African Coast, 800–1900*, Cambridge, 1987; Ahmad I. Salim, *The Swahili-Speaking Peoples of Kenya's Coast 1895–1965*, Nairobi, 1973; J. S. Trimingham, *Islam in East Africa*, Oxford, 1964.

On the Indian Ocean specifically see E. A. Alpers, "Gujarat and the Trade of East Africa, c. 1500–1800," IJAHS 9.1 (1976): 22–44; E. A. Alpers, *East Africa and the Indian Ocean*, Princeton, 2009; K. N. Chaudhuri, *Trade and Civilisation in the Indian Ocean: An Economic History from the Rise of Islam to 1750*, Cambridge, 1985; G. F. Hourani, *Arab Seafaring in the Indian Ocean in Medieval Times*, New York, 1975; Maurice Lombard, *Blütezeit des Islam—Eine Wirtschafts—und Kulturgeschichte 8.–11. Jahrhundert*, Frankfurt, 1992; Michael Pearson, "The Indian Ocean and the Red Sea," in N. Levtzion and R. Pouwels (eds.), *The History of Islam in Africa*, Oxford, 2000, 21–36; Dietmar Rothermund, *Das 'Schießpulverreich' der Großmoguln und die europäischen Seemächte*, in F. Edelmayer, P. Feldbauer, and M. Wakounig (eds.), *Globalgeschichte 1450–1620*, Wien, 2002, 249–60; Abdul Sheriff, *Dhow Cultures of the Indian Ocean: Cosmopolitanism, Commerce and Islam*, London, 2010.

Studies of specific aspects of the history of the East African coast, as well as the hinterland, include Ed Alpers, "The Mutapa and Malawi Political Systems," in T. O. Ranger (ed.), *Aspects of Central African History*, London, 1980, 1–28; F. Becker, *Becoming Muslim in Mainland Tanzania, 1890–2000*, Oxford, 2008; F. Berg, "The Swahili Community of Mombasa 1500–1900," JAH 9.1 (1968): 35–56; F. Berg, "Mombasa under the Busaidi Sultanate," Ph.D. diss., University of Wisconsin, 1971; D. Bone, "Islam in Malawi," JRA 13 (1982): 126–38; Alan W. Boyd, "To Praise the Prophet: A Processual Symbolic Analysis of 'Maulidi,' a Muslim Ritual in Lamu, Kenya," Ph.D. diss., Indiana University, 1980;

Ann P. Caplan, *Choice and Constraint in a Swahili Community,* London, 1975; Lena Eile, *Jando: The Rite of Circumcision and Initiation in East African Islam,* Lund, 1990; Stephen Feierman, "The Shambaa Kingdom: A History," Ph.D. diss., University of Wisconsin, 1974; John Iliffe, *Africans—The History of a Continent,* Cambridge, 1995; Ephraim C. Mandivenga, *Islam in Zimbabwe,* Gweru, 1983; T. Price, "The 'Arabs' of the Zambezi," *Muslim World* 44 (1954): 31–37; H. J. Prins, *Sailing from Lamu,* Assen, 1965; Thomas Spear, *The Kaya Complex: A History of the Mijikenda People of the Kenya Coast to 1900,* Nairobi, 1979; David C. Sperling, "Islamization in the Coastal Region of Kenya to the End of the Nineteenth Century," in B. A. Ogot (ed.), *Kenya in the Nineteenth Century,* in *Hadith* 8 (Nairobi), 33–82, 1985; David C. Sperling, "Rural Madrasas of the Southern Kenyan Coast, 1971–92," in L. Brenner (ed.), *Muslim Identity and Social Change in Sub-Saharan Africa,*London, 1993, 198–209; Justin Willis, *Mombasa, the Swahili and the Making of the Mijikenda,* Oxford, 1993; Marcia Wright, "East Africa, 1870–1905," CHA 6 (1985): 539–91; Marguerite Ylvisaker, *Lamu in the Nineteenth Century: Land, Trade and Politics,* Boston, 1979; Abd al-Hamid el-Zein, *The Sacred Meadows: A Structural Analysis of Religious Symbolism in an East African Town,* Evanston, 1974.

On the Shirazi myth, see for instance James de Vere Allen, *Swahili Origins: Swahili Culture and the Shungwaya Phenomenon,* London, 1993; H. N. Chittick, "The Shirazi Colonization of East Africa," JAH 6 (1965): 275–94; Lena Eile, *Jando: The Rite of Circumcision and Initiation in East African Islam,* Lund, 1990; John Middleton, *The World of the Swahili: An African Mercantile Civilization,* New Haven, 1992.

On Buganda, see Arya Oded, *Islam in Uganda,* New York, 1974; David Robinson, "Buganda: Religious Competition for the Kingdom," in *Muslim Societies in African History,* Cambridge, 2004, 153–68.

For a more recent historical account of the coast and its hinterlands, see Ralph Austen, *African Economic History,* Oxford, 1987; Jonathon Glassman, *Feasts and Riots: Revelry, Rebellion and Popular Consciousness on the East African Coast, 1856–1888,* Portsmouth, N.H., 1995; Jonathon Glassman, *War of Words, War of Stones: Racial Thought and Violence in Colonial Zanzibar,* Bloomington, 2001; John M. Gray, *History of Zanzibar from the Middle Ages to 1856,* London, 1962; John M. Gray, "Zanzibar and the Coastal Belt 1840–1884," in R. Oliver and G. Mathew (eds.), *History of East Africa,* Oxford, 212–51, 1971; John Iliffe, *Tanganyika under German Rule 1905–12,* Cambridge, 1969; George Shepperson, "The Jumbe of Kota Kota and Some Aspects of the History of Islam in Malawi," in Ioan M. Lewis (ed.), *Islam in Tropical Africa,* London, 1966, 253–64; D. Sperling, "The Coastal Hinterland and the Interior of East Africa," in N. Levtzion and R. Pouwels (eds.), *The History of Islam in Africa,* Oxford, 2000, 273–302.

On Tippu Tip, see F. Bontinck, *L'autobiographie de Hamed ben Mohammed el-Murjebi, Tippo Tip (ca. 1840–1905),* Brussels, 1974; Heinrich Brode, *Tippu Tip: The Story of His Career in Zanzibar & Central Africa,* trans. C. Elliot, Zanzibar, 1903/2000; Iris Hahner-Herzog, *Tippu Tip und der Elfenbeinhandel in Ost- und Zentralafrika im 19. Jahrhundert,* München, 1990; François Renault, *Tippo Tip: un Potentat arabe en Afrique Centrale au XIXème siècle,* Paris, 1987.

On Madagascar and the Comoros, see Ed Alpers, *East Africa and the Indian Ocean,* Princeton, 2009 (esp. chaps 7–8); Maurice Bloch, "Astrology and Writing in Madagascar," in J. Goody (ed.), *Literacy in Traditional Societies,* Cambridge, 1975, 277–97; Gwyn Campbell, *An Economic History of Imperial Madagascar, 1750–1895: The Rise and Fall of an Island Empire,* Cambridge, 2005; N. J. Gueunier, *Les chemins de l'Islam à Madacascar,* Paris, 1994; Jean Martin, *Comores: Quatre îles entre pirates et planteurs,* 2 vols., Paris, 1983.

On the East African slave trade, see, amongst others, J. L. Bacharach, "African Military Slaves in the Medieval Middle East: The Cases of Iraq (869–955) and Egypt (868–1171)," IJMES 13 (1981): 471–95; Paul Lovejoy, *Transformations in Slavery: A History of Slavery in Africa,* Cambridge, 1983; E. B. Martin and C. P. Martin, *Cargoes of the East: The Ports, Trade and Culture of the Arabian Seas and Western Indian Ocean,* London/Zanzibar, 1978/2007; Francois Renault and S. Daget, *Les traites négrières en Afrique,* Paris, 1985; Abdul Sheriff, *Slaves, Spices and Ivory in Zanzibar: Integration of an East African Commerical Empire into the World Economy, 1770–1873*, London, 1987; Abdul Sheriff, *Dhow Cultures of the Indian Ocean: Cosmopolitanism, Commerce and Islam*, London, 2010.

11. Muslims on the Cape

The literature on Islam in South Africa and the history of the Cape Muslim community has acquired an impressive volume, due to a vibrant tradition of historical research in South Africa. Major sources are E. Adam, "The History of Islam in South Africa," in *The Muslim Digest*, 8 (1958): 27–32; Shouket Allie, "A Legal and Historical Excursus of Muslim Personal Law in the Colonial Cape, South Africa, Eighteenth to Twentieth Century," in Shamil Jeppie, Ebrahim Moosa, and Richard Roberts (eds.), *Muslim Family Law in Sub-Saharan Africa: Colonial Legacies and Post-Colonial Challenges*, Amsterdam, 2009, 63–84; W. J. Argyle, "Muslims in South Africa: Origins, Development and Present Economic Situation," JIMMA 3.2 (1981): 222–55; Vivian Bickford-Smith, *Ethnic Pride and Racial Prejudice in Victorian Cape Town*, Johannesburg, 1995; A. J. Böeseken, *Slaves and Free Blacks at the Cape 1658–1700*, Cape Town, 1977; Frank R. Bradlow, "Islam at the Cape of Good Hope," *South African Historical Journal* 13 (1981): 12–19; Frank R. Bradlow and M. Cairns, *The Early Cape Muslims: A Study of Their Mosques, Genealogy and Origins*, Cape Town, 1978; Mia Brandel-Syrier, *The Religious Duties of Islam as Thought and Explained by Abu Bakr Effendi*, Leiden, 1971; Yusuf Da Costa and Achmat Davids, *Pages from Cape Muslim History*, Cape Town, 1994; Suleman Dangor, "The Expression of Islam in South Africa," JIMMA 17.1 (1997): 141–51; Achmat Davids, *The Mosques of Bo-Kaap*, Athlone, 1980; Achmat Davids, *The Afrikaans of the Cape Muslims*, Cape Town, 2011; Achmat Davids, "Politics and the Muslims of Cape Town: A Historical Survey," in Christopher Saunders (ed.), *Studies in the History of Cape Town*, 4 (1981): 174–220; Achmat Davids, "The Revolt of the Malays—A Study of the Reactions of the Cape Muslims to the Smallpox Epidemics of Nineteenth Century Cape Town," in Chr. Saunders, H. Philips, E. van Heyningen, and V. Bickford-Smith (eds.), *Studies in the History of Cape Town*, 5 (1983): 46–78; Achmat Davids, "My Religion Is Superior to the Law: The Survival of Islam at the Cape of Good Hope," *Kronos* 12 (1987): 57–71; M.A.G. Davies, "Elections in Cape Town in the Nineteenth Century," *Historia* (Pretoria) 7 (1962): 257–66; I. D. Du Plessis, *The Cape Malays: History, Religion, Traditions, Folk Tales: The Malay Quarter*, Cape Town, 1972; L. T. Du Plessis, "Die Maleier-Afrikaanse Taalbeweging," in L. T. Du Plessis (ed.), *Afrikaans in Beweging*, Bloemfontein, 1986; Mogamat Hoosain Ebrahim, *The Cape Hajj Tradition: Past & Present*, Cape Town, 2009; Richard Elphick and Hermann Giliomee, *The Shaping of South African Society, 1652–1840*, Cape Town, 1989; F. J. Hagel, "Der Islam in Südafrika," ZMR 36 (1952): 28–36; A. R. Hampson, "The Mission to Moslems in Cape Town," *Moslem World* 24 (1934): 271–77; Shamil Jeppie, "Leadership and Loyalties: The Imams of Nineteenth Century Colonial Cape Town, South Africa," JRA 26.2 (1996): 139–62; Hans Kähler, "Studien zur arabisch-afrikaansen Literatur," *Der Islam* 36.1–2 (1960): 101–21; Hans Kähler, "Die Kultur der Kapmalaien," in H. Gottschalk, B. Spuler, and H. Kähler (eds.), *Die Kultur des Islams*, Frankfurt, 1971, 439–60; Timothy Keegan, *Colonial South Africa and the Origins of the Racial Order*, London, 1996; Gerrie Lubbe, "Robben Island: The Early Years of Muslim Resistance," *Kronos* 12, 1987, 49–55; Ebrahim Mahomed Mahida, *History of Muslims in South Africa: A Chronology*, Durban, 1993; John Schofiled Mayson, *The Malays of Capetown*, Manchester, 1861; Jacobus A. Naudé, "Islam in South Africa: A General Survey," JIMMA 6.1 (1985): 21–33; Jacobus A. Naudé, "Aspects of Sufism in South Africa," unpublished conference paper, Utrecht, 1995; Samuel A. Rochlin, "Aspects of Islam in Nineteenth Century South Africa," BSOAS 10 (1939): 213–21; Robert Shell, "Rites and Rebellion: Islamic Conversion at the Cape, 1808 to 1915," in Chr. Saunders, H. Philips, E. van Heyningen, and V. Bickford-Smith (eds.), *Studies in the History of Cape Town* 5 (1983): 1–45; Abdulkader Tayob, *Islamic Resurgence in South Africa: The Muslim Youth Movement*, Cape Town,

1995; Abdulkader Tayob, *Islam in South Africa: Mosques, Imams, and Sermons,* Gainesville, 1999; Lesley and Stephen Townsend, *Bokaap . . . Faces and Facades,* Cape Town, 1977; S. M. Zwemer, "Islam at Cape Town," Moslem World 15 (1925): 327–31.

On the Ottoman diplomatic missions in the nineteenth century, see Rosemarie Quiring-Zoche, "Glaubenskampf oder Machtkampf? Der Aufstand der Malé in Bahia nach einer islamischen Quelle," SA 6 (1995): 115–24.

On the Ba Kathier delegation, see Anne Bang, *Sufis and Scholars of the Sea: Family Networks in East Africa, 1860–1925,* London, 2003.

12. Muslims under Colonial Rule

On colonial Islam policies in general, see Jamil M. Abun-Nasr, *A History of the Maghrib in the Islamic period,* Cambridge, 1987; Jamil M. Abun-Nasr and Roman Loimeier, "Die unabhängigen Staaten Schwarzafrikas," in W. Ende and U. Steinbach (eds.), *Der Islam in der Gegenwart,* München, 2005, 430–47; Michael Crowder, *West Africa under Colonial Rule,* London, 1968.

On the difficulties of European conquest see Philip D. Curtin, *Disease and Empire: The Health of European Troops in the Conquest of Africa,* Cambridge 1998.

On British Islam policies and Muslims in the British colonial territories, see Charles Allen, *Tales from the Dark Continent: Images of British Colonial Africa in the Twentieth Century,* London, 1979; Anne Bang, *Sufis and Scholars of the Sea: Family Networks in East Africa, 1860–1925,* London, 2003; Robert O. Collins, *A History of Modern Sudan,* Cambridge, 2008; M. W. Daly, *Empire on the Nile: The Anglo-Egyptian Sudan 1898–1934,* Cambridge, 1986; M. W. Daly and Jane R. Hogan, *Images of Empire: Photographic Sources for the British in the Sudan,* Leiden, 2005; J. E. Flint, "Zanzibar 1890–1950," in Vincent Harlow, E. M. Chilver, and Alison Smith (eds.), *History of East Africa, Vol. II,* Oxford, 1965, 641–71; Adamu M. Fika, *The Kano Civil War and British Over-rule, 1882–1940,* Ibadan, 1978; L. H. Gann and Peter Duignan, *The Rulers of British Africa 1870–1914,* Stanford, 1978; Mervyn Hiskett, *The Sword of Truth,* New York, 1973; Hassan Ahmed Ibrahim, *Sayyid Abd ar-Rahman al-Mahdi: A Study of Neo-Mahdism in the Sudan, 1899–1956,* Leiden, 2004; Anthony Kirk-Greene, "The Thin White Line: The Size of the British Colonial Service in Africa," *African Affairs* 79.314 (1980): 25–44; Murray Last, "The Colonial Caliphate," in David Robinson and Jean Louis Triaud (eds.), *Le Temps des Marabouts. Itineraires et stratégies islamiques en Afrique Occidentale Française v. 1880–1960,* Paris, 1997, 67–84; Marc Lavergne (ed.), *Le Soudan Contemporain. De l'invasion turco-égyptienne à la rebellion africaine (1821–1989),* Paris, 1989; G. J. Lethem and G.J.F. Tomlinson, *History of Islamic Political Propaganda in Nigeria,* London, 1927; Roman Loimeier, *Islamic Reform and Political Change in Northern Nigeria,* Evanston, 1997; Tim Niblock, *Class and Power in Sudan: The Dynamics of Sudanese Politics 1898–1985,* New York, 1987; Rex S. O'Fahey, "Islamic Hegemonies in the Sudan: Sufism, Mahdism and Islamism," in L. Brenner (ed.), *Muslim Identity and Social Change in Sub-Saharan Africa,* London, 1992, 21–35; Randall L. Pouwels, *Horn and Crescent: Cultural Change and Traditional Islam on the East African Coast, 800–1900,* Cambridge, 1987; Gerard Prunier, "Le mouvement des Ansars au Soudan depuis la fin de l'État mahdiste (1898–1987)," ISSS 2 (1988): 61–79; Abdul Sheriff and Ed Ferguson (eds.), *Zanzibar under Colonial Rule,* London, 1991; Muhammad Sani Umar, *Islam and Colonialism: Intellectual Responses of Muslims of Northern Nigeria to British Colonial Rule,* Leiden, 2006; John O. Voll, "A History of the Khatmiyya Tariqah in the Sudan," Ph.D. diss., Harvard University, 1969; Gabriel Warburg, *Historical Discord in the Nile Valley,* London, 1992; G. S. Whitaker, *The Politics of Tradition: Continuity and Change in Northern Nigeria, 1946–1966,* Princeton, 1970; Peter Woodward, *Sudan 1898–1989: The Unstable State,* Boulder, 1990.

On French Islam policies and Muslims in the French colonial territories, see Robert Arnaud, *L'Islam et la Politique Musulmane Française en Afrique Occidentale Française,* Paris, 1912; Lucy C. Behrman, "French Muslim Policy and the Senegalese Brotherhoods," in D. F. McCall and N. R.

Bennett (eds.), *Aspects of West African Islam*, Boston, 1971, 185–208; Marcel Cardaire, *L'Islam et le terroir africain*, Dakar, 1954; Julia A. Clancy-Smith, *Rebel and Saint: Muslim Notables, Popular Protest, Colonial Encounters (Algeria and Tunisia, 1800–1904)*, Berkeley, 1994; William B. Cohen, *Empereurs sans sceptre. Histoire des administrateurs de la France d'outre-mer et de l'école colonial*, Paris, 1973; Michael Crowder, *Senegal: A Study in French Assimilation Politics*, London, 1967; Donal B. Cruise O'Brien, "Towards an Islamic Policy in French West Africa 1854–1914," JAH 8.2 (1967): 303–16; Donal B. Cruise O'Brien, "Le 'contrat social' sénégalais à l'épreuve," *Politique Africaine* 45 (1992): 9–20; Alphonse Gouilly, *L'Islam dans l'Afrique Occidentale Francaise*, Paris, 1952; Sean Hanretta, *Islam and Social Change in French West Africa: History of an Emancipatory Community*, Cambridge, 2009; Christopher Harrison, *France and Islam in West Africa, 1860–1960*, Cambridge, 1988; Wesley G. Johnson, *Naissance du Sénégal contemporain: Aux origines de la vie politiques modernes (1900–1920)*, Paris, 1991; Robert Launay and Ben Soares, "The Formation of an Islamic Sphere in French Colonial West Africa," *Economy and Society* 28.4 (1999): 497–519; Roman Loimeier, *Säkularer Staat und islamische Gesellschaft. Die Beziehungen zwischen Staat, Sufi-Bruderschaften und islamischer Reformbewegung in Senegal im 20. Jahrhundert*, Hamburg, 2001; Paul Marty, *Études sur l'Islam maure. Cheikh Sidia—Les Fadelia—les Ida ou Ali*, Paris, 1916; Paul Marty, *Études sur l'Islam au Senegal*, 2 vols., Paris, 1917; Paul Marty, *L'Emirat des Trarzas*, Paris, 1919; Paul Marty, *Études sur l'Islam et les tribus maures: Les Braknas*, Paris, 1921; Ali Merad, *Le reformisme musulman en Algérie de 1925–1940*, Paris, 1967; Brian J. Peterson, *Islamization from Below: The Making of Muslim Communities in Rural French Sudan, 1880–1960*, New Haven, 2011; Alain Quellien, *La politique musulmane dans l'Afrique Occidentale Francaise*, Paris, 1910; David Robinson, "Beyond Resistance and Collaboration: Amadou Bamba and the Murids of Senegal," JRA 21.2 (1991): 141–71; David Robinson, "Malik Sy: un intellectuel dans l'ordre colonial au Sénégal," ISSS 7 (1993): 183–92; David Robinson, "An Emerging Pattern of Cooperation between Colonial Authorities and Muslim Societies in Senegal and Mauritania," in David Robinson and Jean-Louis Triaud (eds.), *Le temps des marabouts. Itinéraires et stratégies islamiques en Afrique occidentale française v. 1880–1960*, Paris, 1997, 155–80; David Robinson, "The Murids: Surveillance and Collaboration," JAH 40 (1999): 193–213; David Robinson, *Paths of Accommodation: Muslim Societies and French Colonial Authorities in Senegal, and Mauritania, 1880–1920*, Oxford, 2000; Jean-Louis Triaud, "Islam in Africa under French Colonial Rule," in Nehemia Levtzion and Randall L. Pouwels (eds.), *The History of Islam in Africa*, Oxford, 2000, 169–88; Jean-Louis Triaud, *La Legende Noire de la Sanūsiyya: Une confrerie musulmane saharienne sous le regard francais (1840–1930)*, 2 vols., Paris, 1995.

On German Islam policies, see Carl Heinrich Becker, "Materialien zur Kenntnis des Islam in Deutsch-Ostafrika," *Der Islam* 2 (1911): 1–48; Carl Heinrich Becker, *Islamstudien: Vom Werden und Wesen der islamischen Welt*, vol. 1, Leipzig, 1924; L. H. Gann and Peter Duignan, *The Rulers of German Africa, 1884–1914*, Stanford, 1977; Rebekka Habermas, "Islam Debates around 1900: Colonies in Africa, Muslims in Berlin and the Role of Missionaries and Orientalists," Chloe-Beihefte Zum Daphnis 46 (2012): 123–154; John Iliffe, *Tanganyika under German Rule 1905–12*, Cambridge, 1969; August H. Nimtz, *Islam and Politics in East Africa*, Minneapolis, 1980; Richard Reusch, *Der Islam in Ost-Afrika mit besonderer Berücksichtigung der muhammedanischen Geheim-Orden*, Leipzig, 1931; Holger Weiss, "German Images of Islam in West Africa," SA 11 (2000): 53–94.

On Italian colonialism and Muslims in the Italian colonial territories see Ruth Ben-Ghiat and Mia Fuler (eds.), *Italian Colonialism*, New York, 2005; Cesare M. Buonaiuti, *Politica e religione nel colonialismo italiano (1882–1941)*, Varese, 1982; Angelo del Boca, *La guerra d'Etiopia: L'ultima impresa del colonialismo*, Milano, 2010; Angelo del Boca, *Gli Italiani in Africa Orientale, Vol. 1: Dall'unità alla marcia su Roma*, Milano, 1992; Angelo del Boca, *Gli Italiani in Africa Orientale, Vol. 2: La conquista dell'impero*, Milano, 2001; Angelo del Boca, *Gli Italiani in Libia*, 2 vols., Milano, 1993, 1994; Gian Paolo Calchi Novati (ed.), *L'Africa d'Italia: Una storia coloniale e postcoloniale*, Roma, 2011; Matteo Dominioni, *Lo sfascio dell'impero: gli italiani in Etiopia, 1936–1941*, Roma, 2008; Nicola Labanca, *Oltremare: storia dell'espansione coloniale italiana*, Bologna, 2002; J. J. Miège, *L'imperialismo coloniale italiano dal 1870 ai giorni nostri,* Mailand, 1968; Jonathan Miran, *Red Sea Citizens: Cosmopolitan Society and Cultural Change in Massawa,* Bloomington, 2009; Giorgio Rochat, *Le guerre italiane 1935–1943: Dall'impero d'Etiopia alla disfatta,* Torino, 2005; Eric Salerno, *Genocidio in Libia. Le atrocità nascoste dell avventura coloniale italiana (1911–1931),* Roma, 2005; Alberto Sbacchi, *Ethiopia under Mussolini: Fascism and the Colonial Experience,* London, 1985; Bahru Zewde, *A History of Modern Ethiopia, 1855–1991,* Oxford, 1991. Ruth Ben-Ghiat's and Mia Fuler's edited volume also contains a comprehensive bibliography of works on Italian colonialism.

For an impressionistic glimpse on colonial realities, see Amadou Hampaté Bâ's novel *L'étrange destin du Wangrin ou les roueries d'un interprète africain* (trans. as *The Fortunes of Wangrin*), Paris, 1973.

On Muslims in postcolonial Africa, see Cheikh Anta Babou, *Fighting the Greater Jihad: Amadou Bamba and the Founding of the Muridiyya of Senegal, 1853–1913,* Athens, 2007; Mamadou Diouf, *Histoire du Sénégal,* Paris, 2001; Mar Fall, *Sénégal: L'État Abdou Diouf ou les temps des incertitudes,* Paris, 1986; Sean Hanretta, *Islam and Social Change in French West Africa: History of an Emancipatory Community,* Cambridge, 2009; Klaus Hock, *Der Islam-Komplex. Zur christlichen Wahrnehmung des Islams und der christlich-muslimischen Beziehungen in Nordnigeria während der Militärherrschaft Babangidas,* Hamburg, 1996; Samuel Huntington, *The Clash of Civilizations and the Remaking of World Order,* New York, 1996; Hans Krech, *Der Bürgerkrieg in Somalia (1988–1996),* Berlin, 1996; Nehemia Levtzion, "Slavery and the Slave Trade in the Early States of the Bilād al-Sūdān," in N. Levtzion (ed.), *Islam in Africa and the Middle East: Studies on Conversion and Renewal,* Aldershot, 2007; Roman Loimeier, "Die Dynamik religiöser Unruhen in Nord-Nigeria," *Afrika Spectrum* 1 (1992): 59–80; Roman Loimeier, *Islamic Reform and Political Change in Northern Nigeria,* Evanston, 1997; Roman Loimeier, *Säkularer Staat und Islamische Gesellschaft—Die Beziehungen zwischen Staat, Sufi-Bruderschaften und Islamischer Reformbewegung in Senegal im 20. Jahrhundert,* Hamburg, 2001; Roman Loimeier, "Nigeria: The Quest for a Viable Religious Option," in William Miles (ed.), *Political Islam in West Africa: State-Society Relations Transformed,* Boulder, 2007a, 43–72; Roman Loimeier, "Perceptions of Marginalization: Muslims in Contemporary Tanzania," in R. Otayek and Ben Soares (eds.), *Islam and Muslim Politics in Africa,* London, 2007b, 137–56; Roman Loimeier, "Dialectics of Religion and Politics in Senegal," in M. Diouf and M. Leichtman (eds.), *New Perspectives on Islam in Senegal: Conversion, Migration, Wealth, Power and Femininity,* New York, 2009, 237–56; Ken Menkhaus, *Somalia: State Collapse and the Threat of Terrorism,* London, 2004; Charlotte Pezeril, *Islam, mysticisme et marginalité: les Baay Faal du Sénégal,* Paris, 2008; Gérard Prunier, *Darfur: Der „uneindeutige" Genozid,* Hamburg, 2006; Christian Roche, *Histoire de Casamance: Conquête et résistance, 1850–1920,* Paris, 1985; Ben Soares (ed.), *Muslim-Christian Encounters in Africa,* Leiden, 2006; Yusuf Bala Usman (ed.), *Studies in the History of the Sokoto Caliphate,* Lagos, 1979; Gabi Warburg, *Islam, Sectarianism and Politics in Sudan since the Mahdiyya,* Madison, 2003; C. S. Whitaker, *The Politics of Tradition: Continuity and Change in Northern Nigeria,* Princeton, 1970.

Conclusion

Danièle Hervieu-Léger, *Religion as a Chain of Memory,* Cambridge, 2000 (published in French as *La religion pour mémoire,* Paris, 1992); Mervyn Hiskett, *The Development of Islam in West Africa,* London, 1984.

Appendix

On the development of text production in sub-Saharan Africa, see Carl Heinrich Becker, *Materialien zur Kenntnis des Islam in Deutsch-Ostafrika, Der Islam* 2 (1911): 1–48; A.D.H. Bivar and Mervyn

Hiskett, "The Arabic Literature of Nigeria to 1804: A Provisional Account," BSOAS 25 (1962): 104–149; Carl Brockelmann, *Geschichte der Arabischen Literatur,* 5 vols., Leiden, 1937–1942; 'Abdallāh Ṣāliḥ al-Farsy, *Baadhi ya Wanavyuoni wa Kishafi wa Mashariki ya Afrika,* Mombasa, 1972; Jack Goody, *Literacy in Traditional Societies,* Cambridge, 1975; John O. Hunwick, *A Contribution to the Study of Islamic Teaching Traditions in West Africa: The Career of Muhammad Baghayogho,* ISSS 4 (1990): 149–66; John O. Hunwick, (ed.), *Arabic Literature of Africa II: The Writings of Central Sudanic Africa,* Leiden, 1995; John O. Hunwick (ed.), *Arabic Literature of Africa IV: The Writings of Western Sudanic Africa,* Leiden, 2003; Shamil Jeppie and Souleymane Bachir Diagne (eds.), *The Meanings of Timbuktu,* Cape Town, 2008, 45–58; Jan Knappert, *Swahili Islamic Poetry,* 3 vols., Leiden, 1971; Robert Launay, *Beyond the Stream: Islam and Society in a West African Town,* Berkeley, 1992; Robert Launay, *Pedigrees and Paradigms: Scholarly Credentials among the Dyula of the Northern Ivory Coast,* in D. Eickelman and J. Piscatori (eds.), *Muslim Travellers: Pilgrimage, Migration, and the Religious Imagination,* London, 1994, 175–99; Roman Loimeier, *Between Social Skills and Marketable Skills: The Politics of Islamic Education in Twentieth Century Zanzibar,* Leiden, 2009; Louis Massignon, "Une bibliothèque Saharienne," *Revue du Monde Musulmane* 8 (1909): 409ff.; Khadim Mbacke and Thierno Ka, "Nouveau Catalogue des Manuscrits de l'IFAN Cheikh A. Diop," ISSS 8 (1994): 165–99; Sean R. O'Fahey (ed.), *Arabic Literature of Africa I: The Writings of Eastern Sudanic Africa to c. 1900,* Leiden, 1994; Sean R. O'Fahey (ed.), *Arabic Literature of Africa IIIA: The Writings of the Muslim Peoples of Northeastern Africa,* Leiden, 2003; Sean R. O'Fahey and Ann Biersteker (eds.), *Arabic Literature of Africa IIIB: The Writings of the Muslim Peoples of East Africa* (unpublished manuscript, 2001); Rainer Osswald, *Die Handelsstädte der Westsahara. Die Entwicklung der arabisch-maurischen Kultur von Šinqīṭ, Wādān, Tīšīt und Walāta,* Berlin, 1986; Rainer Osswald, *Schichtengesellschaft und islamisches Recht: Die Zawāyā und Krieger der Westsahara im Spiegel von Rechtsgutachten des 16.–19. Jahrhunderts,* Wiesbaden, 1993; Ulrich Rebstock, *Maurische Literaturgeschichte,* 3 vols., Würzburg, 2001; Stefan Reichmuth, *Islamische Bildung und soziale Integration in Ilorin (Nigeria) seit ca. 1800,* Bayreuth, 1998; Jack D. Rollins, *A History of Swahili Prose: From the Earliest Times to the End of the Nineteenth Century,* Leiden, 1983; Elias Saad, *A Social History of Timbuktu: The Role of Muslim Scholars and Notables 1400–1900,* Cambridge, 1983; Amar Samb, *Essai sur la contribution du Sénégal à la litterature d'expression arabe,* Dakar, 1972; Lamin Sanneh, *The Jakhanke: The History of an Islamic Clerical People of the Senegambia,* London, 1979; Charles C. Stewart, *Islam and Social Order in Mauritania: A Case Study from the Nineteenth Century,* Oxford, 1973.

Index

Italicized page numbers refer to maps or tables.

Abā island, 165
abbaan, 197, 201–202, 206
'Abbāsid caliphate, 29, 41, 43, 88, 135, 139, 212
'Abd al-Ḥamīd b. Muḥammad b. Juma' al-Murjībī (Tippu Tip), 244–47
'Abd al-Karīm Sabun, 87
'Abd al-Mu'min, 47, 201
'Abd al-Qādir Bokar Kan, 116
'Abd al-Raḥmān al-Mahdī, Sayyid, 273, 275
'Abd al-Raḥmān al-Zayla'ī, 202
'Abd al-Raḥmān b. al-Baghdādī, 259
'Abd al-Raḥmān b. Rustam, 41
'Abd al-Raḥmān Zagayte, 92, 95, 106
'Abd al-Ra'ūf al-Singkilī, 251
'Abd al-Wahāb, Muḥammad b., 17
'Abd al-Wāḥid al-Abqālī, 199
'Abd a-Qādir al-Jazā'irī, 282
'Abd a-Qādir al-Jīlānī, 20
'Abdallāb federation, 135, 140–41, 145
'Abdallāh b. al-Ḥājj Muḥammad al-Watarawī, 101–102
'Abdallāh b. Muḥammad, Khalīfa, 165–69, 194, 204, 291
'Abdallāh b. Ṣa'd b. Abī Sarḥ, 137
'Abdallāh b. Yāsīn, 45
'Abdallāh Bā Kathīr al-Kindī, 239, 261
'Abdallāh Jammā', 140, 143
'Abdallāh Niass, 286
'Abdallāh Qāḍī 'Abd al-Salām. *See* Tuan Guru
Abdol Rakiep (b. 'Abd al-Ra'ūf b. Tuan Guru), 256, 260–61
Abdul Logies, 255
'Abidīn Tadiā Yūsuf al-Tāj al-Khalwatī. *See* Shaykh Yūsuf
Abiker Aden Dhurow, Shaykh, 199
Abū 'Abdallāh, 43
Abū 'Anga, 166, 169
Abū 'Inān, Sulṭān, 49–50, 62, 65
Abū Iṣḥāq al-Sāḥilī, 71
Abūbakar Effendi al-Kashnāwī, 256, 258–61
Abunä, 176, 178
Achmat Sadiek Achmat, 254–58, 260–61
adab, 104, 300
Adal, 179–80, 183–84, 186–87, 190
Adamawa, 4, 5, 118, 291
'ādat, 5
Addis Abäba, 172, 194–95
'Aden, 185, 203, 207
Ādrār mountains, 2–3, 12, 55, 57, 105
Adua, 194–95
Adulis, 174, 179, 182
Afar, 7, 183–84
African indigenous religions, 7, 14, 28, 77, 79, 172–73, 297
Afrikaaner/Afrikaans, 248, 250, 252–53, 256–57, 259–60
Agadez, 12, 54, 56–57, 62, 90, 105
Agao, 174–77
Aghlabid, 41, 42–43
Aghmāt, 45, 55
Ahīr (Aïr) Mountains, 3, 12, 54, 56
ahl al-istiqāma, 29, 40. *See also* khārijites
ahl al-kitāb, 38
Aḥmad Abū Adhān, 157
Aḥmad al-Baghdādī, Sharīf, 103
Aḥmad al-Kabīr, 121, 124
Aḥmad al-Kūfī, 137
Aḥmad al-Manṣūr, Sulṭān, 51, 63
Aḥmad b. Furtū, 66, 111
Aḥmad b. Idrīs, 74, 159, 199, 202, 209
Aḥmad b. Sumayṭ, 239, 261, 281–82
Aḥmad Bābā, al-Tinbuktī, 61, 66, 71–72
Aḥmad Bamba, 20, 284–86
Aḥmad Grāñ. *See* Imām Aḥmad
Aḥmad Lobbo, 113, 122–23
Aḥmad Qaramanlı, 51, 69
Aḥmadiyya Sufi order, 198
Aḥmadu b. Aḥmadu, 121, 123–24
Ahmadu Bello, 280–81
'Ajīb al-Kāfūta, 145
Akan, 4
'Alawid dynasty, 48, 51, 67, 69, 73
'Alawiyya, 'Alawī family, 234, 236, 239, 253, 261
Alexandria, 136–37, 140, 174, 176, 178, 185

Algeria: and colonial rule, 267; and disintegration of the bilād al-maghrib, 48–49, 51; and European colonialism, 268, 272, 282–83, 286; and evolution of Muslim societies, 29; and historical patterns of the bilād al-maghrib, 35; and quest for Islamic unity, 42; and Sufism, 74; and trans-Saharan trade, 56, 59, 68, 70
Algiers, 46, 49, 51, 58, 94
ʿAlī b. ʿAbdallāh al-Tilimsānī, 69, 72–73
ʿAlī b. al-Sharīf, 87
ʿAlī b. Ḥamūd, Sulṭān, 278, 281
ʿAlī b. Ḥasan, 220
ʿAlī b. Saʿīd, Sulṭān, 277
ʿAlī b. Tashfīn, 46
ʿAlī Dinār, 88–89, 208
ʿAlī Duure, 199
ʿAlī Khurshid Bey, 156
ʿAllaqī, Wādī, 62, 136, 138, 139
Almohad movement, 47–48, 48–50, 52, 61–62, *131*
Almoravid movement, *131;* and conquest of the bilād al-maghrib, 39; and disintegration of the bilād al-maghrib, 48–49, 52; and diversity of Islam, 11, 16; and historical patterns of the bilād al-maghrib, 37; and Islamic rebellions, 41–42; and quest for Islamic unity, 44–47; and trading empires of the bilād al-sūdān, 79–80, 84; and trans-Saharan trade, 61, 65, 67
ʿAlwa, 13, 136, 140–41, 153
Amadou Ba, Cheikhou, 108, 284
Amadou Seku, 284
ʿAmāra Dūnqas, 141, 143, 147
al-Amawī, Burhān b. ʿAbd al-ʿAzīz, 281–82
al-Amawī, Shaykh ʿAbd al-ʿAzīz b. ʿAbd al-Ghanī, 238
ʿAmdä Ṣeyon, emperor, 176, 178–79
Amharic, xii, 7, 172, 175–76, 182, 189, 300
Amīr, ʿAlī Bey, 224, 225
Anbäsa Weddem, emperor, 174
al-Andalus (Spain), 11, 39, 41, 46–48, 49, 71, 81, 216
Anglo-Egyptian Sudan, 89, 161, 165, 169, 246, 268, 273–76, 279, 290
Anjouan, 219, 220
Ankobär, 174
Anṣā r movement, 162, 164–65, 166, 273, 275–76
Antaimoro, 229
anthropology of Islam, 1–10, 21, 27, 28, 172, 274, 329
ʿaqīda, 19, 22, 104, 105, 300, 309
Aqīt family, 71
Arab Islam, 11, 30, 212, 283
Arabia: and conquest of the bilād al-maghrib, 37; and diversity of Islam, 15, 17–18, 296–97; and Egyptian colonialism, 155, 159, 167; and European colonialism, 289; and evolution of Muslim societies, 30; and geography/ecology of Africa, 7, 9; and historical patterns of Nubia and Funj, 135; and institutions of Islam, 22; and Islam in Ethiopia, 173, 175–76, 181, 183, 190; and Islam on the Cape, 248, 258; and Islam on the East African coast, 210, 212–15, 220, 227; and Islam on the Horn of Africa, 196, 199; and Islamization of the bilād al-sūdān, 78; and religious authority, 25; and the Sinnār-Funj empire, 143
Arabian peninsula, ix, 17–18, 30, 37, 155, 167, 176, 196, 258
Arabic: Arabic literature of Africa (ALA), 299–308; and Egyptian colonialism, 156–57, 166–67; and European colonialism, 289; and evolution of Muslim societies, 27; and geography/ecology of Africa, 9; and historical patterns of the bilād al-maghrib, 35; and institutions of Islam, 23; and Islam in Ethiopia, 177; and Islam on the Cape, 252, 257, 259–60; and Islam on the East African coast, 212–13, 216–17, 229, 235–36, 241; and Islam on the Horn of Africa, 196–97; and Islamic learning, 104, 107; and Islamic rebellions, 42; and Islamization process, 147–49; and Muslims in Asante, 102; and the Sinnār-Funj empire, 144, 147–49, 151; and trading empires of the bilād al-sūdān, 79, 82, 88; and trans-Saharan trade, 58, 64–67
Aragon, 49, 62, 179
Arawān, 55–56, 73
Arbajī, 141–42, 148
Arguin, 55, 63
Arma, 69, 72–73, 109
Armenia, 11, 13, 38, 138, 140, 146, 177, 179
Arnaud, Robert, 283
ʿarūḍ, 104, 300, 309
arwiqa (singular *riwāq*), 11, 84, 183
Asante, 13, 60, 63, 80, 89–90, 94, 99–101, 101–103
Askia Dawūd, 83
Askia Muḥammad (Turé), 71, 79, 83, 112
astrology, 16, 104, 229, 309, 310
astronomy, 16, 28, 41, 229, 309, 310
Aswan, 1, 135–39, 145
Asyūṭ, 57, 87, 139
ʿAtbara, 5, 275
Atlantic Ocean: and geography/ecology of Africa, 2, 3, 5; and jihād in the bilād al-sūdān, 108, 110–11, 114, 128; and trading empires of the bilād al-sūdān, 79, 81; and trading networks, 99–101; and trans-Saharan trade, 54–55, 56, 58, 60–61, 63
Atlas Mountains, 2, 39, 46–47, 49, 54, 58, 67
Augustine order, 225–26

Awash River, 179, 187
Awdaghust, 45, 46, 55, 65, 70
Awjila (Jālū), 57, 62, 76, 87
Āwkār, 80
Awrāba, 41
Awssa, 187, 194, 289
Axum, 6, 13, 78, 136, 172, 173–77, 182–83
'Aydhāb, 137–38, 147
Ayyubid dynasty, 42, 137, 138
Azawād, 55, 106
al-Azhar University: and diversity of Islam, 11, 296; and Egyptian colonialism, 156, 161, 168; and European colonialism, 287; and Islam in Ethiopia, 183; and Islamization of Sinnār-Funj, 148; and trading empires of the bilād al-sūdān, 84
Azna, 33

Bā, Amadou Hampaté, 17
Bā, Mamadou Ceerno Seydou, 285
Baardhere (Bardera), 199–200
Bādī II Abū Diqn, 142, 148–49
Bādī III, 146, 151
Bādī IV Abū Shulūkh, 149, 152–53
Badr, battle of, 20, 113–14, 122, 164
Bagamoyo, 230, 242, 244
Bagauda, 91–93
Bägemdir, 178, 189, 193
Baggāra tribes, 5–6, 8, 158, 162, 165, 168–69
Baghayughu (Baghayogho) family, 71, 100
Baghdad, 23, 41, 43, 49, 64, 137, 181, 206, 219, 238
Bagirmi, 70, 84–87, 109, 170–71
Bahmani kingdom, 213
Baḥr al-Ghazal, 75, 86, 157–58, 165, 170
Bakht al-Rūḍa College, 280
al-Bakrī, Abū 'Ubayd 'Abdallāh b. 'Abd al-'Azīz, 65
al-Balbālī, Makhlūf b. 'Alī b. Ṣāliḥ, 61
Bale, 184, 188–89, 190, 289
Baluchistan, 227, 228, 231
Bamako, 77, 128
Bambara, 4, 17, 101, 109, 116, 120–21, 122
Bambuk, 60, 62–63, 80–81
Banādir coast, 7–8, 196, 199–200, 230, 234, 236–37, 288
Bandiagara, 122, 124, 127
Bani River, 101, 125
Banū Ḥasan, 2
Banū Hilāl, 44, 61, 84
Banū Marīn, 39, 49
Banū Midrār, 39, 40–41
Banū Sulaym, 44, 68, 74
Banū Sulaymān, 74
baqṭ, 137
Barābīsh, 70
baraka, 31, 160, 309
Barghash, Sulṭān, 229–30, 232–33, 238, 244, 277–78
Barghawāṭa, 41–42, 44, 46
Barth, Heinrich, 73, 81, 96, 103, 118
Baṣra, 252
Batavia, 250, 253
Bawol, 109, 284, 286
Becker, Carl Heinrich, 33, 271
Beja. *See* Bīja
Belgium, 246–47, 267–68
Bengal, 213, 249–50, 254
Bengalen, Frans van, 253–56
Benghasi, 57, 74, 76
Benin, 290
Benue River, 98–99, 109, 128, 170
Berber (Sudanese town), 144, 156, 162, 165, 217
Berbera, 7–8, 15, 158, 185, 193, 196, 201–204, 207–208
Berbers. *See* Imasighen
Beta Israel, 176–79
Betsimisaraka, 215
bida', (singular *bid'a*, 16–17, 20, 24, 26, 118, 238, 309
Bīja: and decline of Sinnār-Funj, 151; and Egyptian colonialism, 159, 162, 165, 169; and geography/ecology of Africa, 3, 5–6, 8; and Islam in Ethiopia, 174; and Islamization of Nubia, 139–40; and the Sinnār-Funj empire, 141–42
bilād al-maghrib, *130, 132;* and center-periphery relations, 52–53; disintegration of, 48–52; and diversity of Islam, 11–13, 15–16; and Egyptian colonialism, 159, 166; era of conquest, 37–40; and evolution of Muslim societies, 28, 30; and geography/ecology of Africa, 1–3, 8; historical patterns, 35–37; and institutions of Islam, 22; and Islam in Ethiopia, 190; and Islam on the Cape, 248; and Islam on the East African coast, 210; and Islamic rebellion, 40–42; and Islamization of Sinnār-Funj, 150; and jihād, 112; and Kano, 94, 96; quest for unity, 42–48; and the Sinnār-Funj empire, 142; and Sufism, 74; and trading empires of the bilād al-sūdān, 81–83; and trans-Saharan trade, 54–55, 58–64, 64–66, 68, 71, 72, 77, 98
bilād al-makhzan, 11, 36, 52–53, 142
bilād al-sība: and disintegration of the bilād al-maghrib, 52–53; and diversity of Islam, 11; and European colonialism, 269; and historical patterns of the bilād al-maghrib, 36; and Islam on the Horn of Africa, 196, 198; and jihād in the bilād al-sūdān, 112; and Kano, 94; and the Sinnār-Funj empire, 142; and Sufism, 76; and trading empires of the bilād al-sūdān, 88; and trans-Saharan trade, 73

bilād al-sūdān, *133, 134;* and decline of Sinnār-Funj, 151; development of Arabic literature in, *303, 304;* and disintegration of the bilād al-maghrib, 53; and diversity of Islam, 12–13, 15; and Egyptian colonialism, 159, 161, 166; and European colonialism, 290; and evolution of Muslim societies, 28, 30–32; and geography/ecology of Africa, 2–6, 9; historical patterns of, 35–37, 54, 77–78; and institutions of Islam, 22; and Islam in Ethiopia, 183, 190; and Islam on the East African coast, 210, 215–16, 234, 239; and Islamic learning, 103–107; and Islamization of Nubia, 135; and Islamization of Sinnār-Funj, 150; and jihād, 108–16, 116–19, 119–21; and Kano, 90–96; and Masina, 122–24; networks of traders and scholars, 96–103; and quest for Islamic unity, 44, 46; and religious authority, 24; and Samori Turé, 124–29; and scholarship on Arabic literature, 299–302; and the Sinnār-Funj empire, 141–42, 145–47; and Sufism, 74; trading empires of, 79–90; and trans-Saharan trade, 58–64, 64–67, 67–68, 70–72

Bilma, 2, 57, 67, 68, 75, 85, 170

Bimaal, 8, 200, 206–207

Bina ʿAlī, 121

birni, 91–93

Birnin Gazargamo, 85, 118

Biskra, 56

Blue Nile, 1, 5, 7, 135–36, 140–41, 143

Boni, 33

Borgu, 70, 116

bori, 33, 298

Borku, 2, 75

Bornu: and Egyptian colonialism, 170; and European colonialism, 280; and Islam in Ethiopia, 191; and Islamic learning, 105; and jihād in the bilād al-sūdān, 108–11, 113–14, 116–19, 121; and Kano, 91–93, 95–96; and Muslims in Asante, 102–103; and scholarship on Arabic literature, 300; and the Sinnār-Funj empire, 142–43; and trading networks, 98–99

Boru Meda, council of, 178, 181

Bougis, Jan van, 251, 255

Brakna, 110

Brawa: and diversity of Islam, 15; and Egyptian colonialism, 158; and geography/ecology of Africa, 7, 8, 10; and Islam on the East African coast, 210, 213–18, 220, 223–24, 228, 232, 234, 238, 242; and Islam on the Horn of Africa, 196, 199, 200–201, 206–207

Britain: and colonial rule, 267–68, 270–72, 273–76, 276–79, 279–82, 287–88, 290, 291–92; and Egyptian colonialism, 154, 156–58, 161–62, 165–66, 169, 171; and evolution of Muslim societies, 27–29; and institutions of Islam, 23; and Islam in Ethiopia, 193, 195; and Islam on the Cape, 250, 253, 257, 258–60; and Islam on the East African coast, 224, 226–28, 230–34, 242–43, 246; and Islam on the Horn of Africa, 199, 202–208; and jihād in the bilād al-sūdān, 111, 127–29; and Muslims in Asante, 101–102; and religious authority, 25; and trading empires of the bilād al-sūdān, 89; and trans-Saharan trade, 55, 70

British East Africa Company, 277

Bū Saʿīdī family, 226, 227, 231

Buganda, 210, 241, 242

Bukini, 219. *See also* Madagascar

Bulala, 84–86

Buna, 89–90, 99, 101–102, 127

Bundu, 109, 115, 120–21

Bure, 60, 62–63, 80–81

Burns, Abdol, 249, 260

Bushiri, 272

Buyid dynasty, 219

Byzantine empire, 37–38, 60, 135, 136, 138, 174

Cabo Blanco, 55, 56

Caillié, Réné, 77

Cairo: and disintegration of the bilād al-maghrib, 49; and diversity of Islam, 11; and Egyptian colonialism, 154–56, 165, 170; and evolution of Muslim societies, 31; and institutions of Islam, 22–23; and Islam in Ethiopia, 185, 191; and Islamization of Nubia, 137, 138; and Islamization of Sinnār-Funj, 148; and Kano, 94; and quest for Islamic unity, 44; and the Sinnār-Funj empire, 141, 143; and trading empires of the bilād al-sūdān, 81, 84; and trading networks, 98; and trans-Saharan trade, 63, 72

camels: and geography/ecology of Africa, 1, 3, 5, 8; and Islam in Ethiopia, 186; and Islam on the Horn of Africa, 196, 198, 201, 204–205, 208; and Islamization of the bilād al-sūdān, 77; and the Sinnār-Funj empire, 143; and Sufism, 76; and trans-Saharan trade, 54–55, 57–58, 64, 68

Cap Vert, 56, 286

Cape, the: and diversity of Islam, 15–16; and European colonialism, 268; and geography/ecology of Africa, 10; and Islam in Ethiopia, 185; and Islam on the Cape, 248; and Islam on the East African coast, 223, 243; Nineteenth century Muslim community, 253–58; origin of Muslim

community on, 248–53; and religious disputes, 258–61; and trans-Saharan trade, 56
Cape Bojador, 56
Cape Delgado, 220
Cape Town, 15–16, 248, 249, 251–53, 253–58, 258–61, 296
caravan trade: and decline of Sinnār-Funj, 151; and Egyptian colonialism, 158; and institutions of Islam, 22; and Islam on the East African coast, 243–46; and Islam on the Horn of Africa, 201; and Islamic rebellions, 40; and Islamization of the bilād al-sūdān, 77; and Kano, 93; and quest for Islamic unity, 45; and the Sinnār-Funj empire, 141, 142, 146–47; and Sufism, 75–76; and trading empires of the bilād al-sūdān, 81, 87–88; and trading networks, 98; and trans-Saharan trade, 54–60, 64–65, 68, 72–73
caravanserai, 22, 75
caravels, 55–56, 185, 223
Carpot, François, 285
Casamance, 285, 290–93
cataract, 1, 135–36, 139–40, 142, 145, 157, 246
cattle herding: and Diina's economy, 123; and disintegration of the bilād al-maghrib, 52; and Egyptian colonialism, 156, 164; and European colonialism, 281; and evolution of Muslim societies, 32; and geography/ecology of Africa, 5–6, 8; and Islam in Ethiopia, 194; and Islam on the Horn of Africa, 204–206; and jihād in the bilād al-sūdān, 125; and Kano, 92; and the Sinnār-Funj empire, 146–47; and trading networks, 98
Celebi, Evliya, 143
center-periphery relations, ix–x, 36, 52–54, 94, 172, 174, 269, 274
Cerulli, Enrico, 289
Chad, Lake: and Egyptian colonialism, 170–71; and European colonialism, 291; and geography/ecology of Africa, 3, 5–6; and Islamization of the bilād al-sūdān, 78; and jihād in the bilād al-sūdān, 108, 109, 119; and Sufism, 74–75; and trading empires of the bilād al-sūdān, 83–88; and trans-Saharan trade, 57, 67–68, 70
Chalcedon, council of, 38
China, 9, 23, 104
cholera, 51, 73, 168, 194, 233
Christianity: and conquest of the bilād al-maghrib, 38; and decline of Sinnār-Funj, 153; and discursive tradition of Islam, 19; and diversity of Islam, 11, 13–16; and Egyptian colonialism, 167; and European colonialism, 268–69, 289–90, 292–94; and evolution of Muslim societies, 27–28, 31, 33; and geography/ecology of Africa, 6–7; and historical patterns of the bilād al-maghrib, 36; interaction with Islam in Africa, 297; and Islam in Ethiopia, 172–73, 173–79, 180–84, 185–89, 192, 194; and Islam on the Cape, 248, 250, 254, 257, 260; and Islam on the East African coast, 216, 226, 241; and Islam on the Horn of Africa, 203–204; and Islamization of Nubia, 135–40; and quest for Islamic unity, 46; and religious authority, 25; and scope of research, xi; and the Sinnār-Funj empire, 140–41, 146; and trading empires of the bilād al-sūdān, 87–88, 90; and trans-Saharan trade, 62, 66
Clapperton, Hugh, 23, 118
cloves, 227, 231, 232
cocopalm, 231, 232
coffee, 143, 147, 183, 191, 203, 231
colonial rule: and Anglo-Egyptian Sudan, 273–76; and the arms trade, 97; and Asante, 101; and the Cape, 10, 15, 248, 250, 256; colonial modernity in Africa, 267–73; and East Africa, 210, 214, 224, 227, 233–34, 237, 242; and Ethiopia, 184, 192, 194–95; and historical texts, 299, 301; and the Horn of Africa, 196, 199, 203–205, 207; and indirect rule, 279–84; and Islamic resistance, 25; and Italy, 287–89; and jihād, 108, 110–11, 116, 120–21, 124, 125, 127–29; and Khalīfa ʿAbdallāh, 165–69; legacies of, 289–94; and Mahdī movement, 161–65; and Rābiḥ b. Faḍl Allāh, 169–71; and racial issues, 4; and religious conversion, 27, 33–34; and rinderpest epidemic, 6; and sectarian tensions, 30; and Senegal, 284–87; and Sinnār-Funj empire, 142, 154–58; and Sufi orders, 159–61; and Zanzibar, 276–79
Comoé River, 101, 125
Comoro islands, 10, 181, 214–16, 219–20, 228–29, 231, 236, 239, 292
Congo, 210, 246–47, 267, 268, 276
conversion, religious: and conquest of the bilād al-maghrib, 39; and diversity of Islam, 12, 14, 15, 16; and Egyptian colonialism, 169; and European colonialism, 269; and evolution of Muslim societies, 27–34; and Islam in Ethiopia, 173, 174, 181, 191–92, 194; and Islam on the Cape, 250; and Islam on the East African coast, 211, 214, 216–17, 236, 238, 240, 241–42; and Islamic learning, 106; and Islamization of the bilād al-sūdān, 77–78; and jihād in the bilād al-sūdān, 109, 121, 126–29; and quest for Islamic unity, 45; and the Sinnār-Funj empire, 141, 143; and trading empires of the bilād al-sūdān, 84; and trading networks, 99; and trans-Saharan trade, 66

copal, 231–32
Coppolani, Xavier, 283
copra, 231–32
Coptic Church, 136, 140
Copts, Coptic administration, 154, 156, 162, 166
Cordoba, 32, 42, 65
Côte d'Ivoire, 100, 285, 290
cotton, 155, 231, 245, 274
currency, 59, 63, 148, 167, 183, 294
Cyrenaika, 44, 57, 67, 69, 70, 74–76, 287–89

Däbrä Azbo, 175–76
Däbrä Bizän, 176, 178
Däbrä Libanos, 175, 178
Dagbon, 89
Dagomba, 89, 100, 116
Dahlak islands, 181, 182, 185, 191
Dakar, 184, 283, 285, 286
Damascus, 23, 63
al-Dāmir, 144, 161
Danakil, 7, 158, 182–84, 187, 194, 287
Dār al-ḥiyād, 14
Dār es Salaam, 230, 234, 245
Dār Kuti, 87, 170
Dār Mara, 170
Dār Sila, 87, 170
Dar'a, Wādī, 55, 68, 73
Darb al-arba'īn, 57, 87–88, 139
Dārfūr: and decline of Sinnār-Funj, 152–53; and Egyptian colonialism, 156–58, 162, 165–66, 168, 170; and European colonialism, 274, 293; and geography/ecology of Africa, 5–6; and Islam on the Horn of Africa, 208; and the Sinnār-Funj empire, 142, 144–46; and Sufism, 74; and trading empires of the bilād al-sūdān, 80, 84, 87–89; and trans-Saharan trade, 57
Darood, 8, 197, 199–200
dates and date palms, 59, 143, 147, 213, 227–28, 231
Daura, 90, 109
da'wa, 40, 44, 45–46
Däwaro, 179, 184, 188
Dawit, emperor, 178, 179
Daymān, Awlād, 2, 115
Daza, 2, 96
Delafosse, Maurice, 269
Delhi, 210, 213
Dème, al-Ḥājj Ceerno Aḥmad, 285
Denianke, 80, 115
Depont, Olivier, 283
dhikr, 75, 160, 202, 207, 236–38, 281
dhimmī, 31
dhows, 9, 56, 223, 235, 242
Dia, Diakhanke. *See* Ja; Jakhanke
Digo, 211, 226
Diina, 122–24
Dikwa, 170, 280
Dingiray, 120, 124
Diola, 290, 293
diophysis doctrine, 38, 192
diseases and epidemics: and colonization, 267; and disintegration of the bilād al-maghrib, 50–51; and Egyptian colonialism, 157, 167–68; and geography/ecology of Africa, 5–6; and Islam in Ethiopia, 188, 194; and Islam on the Cape, 249; and Islam on the East African coast, 233; and Islam on the Horn of Africa, 198, 206; malaria, 58, 168, 267; plague, 66, 147; rinderpest, 6; and the Sinnār-Funj empire, 147; syphilis, 66; and trans-Saharan trade, 65–66, 73
divine kingdom, 79, 88, 141, 152
diya, 3, 8, 309
Djado, 57
Djibouti, 158, 193, 287
Dogali, 194
Dogon, 4, 122
Dongola, 13, 136–38, 140, 141, 143–45, 151, 156, 162, 166, 169
droughts, 5, 32, 65, 85, 157, 167, 206
Dulbahante, 201–202, 204–205
Dutch colonies and people. *See* Netherlands
Dutch East India Company, 10

East African Coast, *266;* and diversity of Islam, 15, 18; and Egyptian colonialism, 155, 158; and European colonialism, 276, 292; and evolution of Muslim societies, 34; historical patterns, 210–17; and historical patterns of the bilād al-maghrib, 36; and institutions of Islam, 22; and Islam in Ethiopia, 175, 181, 185, 190; and Islam on the Cape, 250; and Islam on the Horn of Africa, 196, 199, 206; and Kano, 90; and Portugal, 223–27; and religious reform, 234–39; and scholarship on Arabic literature, 299–302; Shungwaya to Kilwa, 217–23; and trans-Saharan trade, 65; and upcountry East Africa, 239–47; and Zanzibar, 227–34
East India Company, 10
Egypt: and colonial rule, 301; and conquest of Sinnār-Funj, 154–58; and conquest of the bilād al-maghrib, 37–38; and disintegration of the bilād al-maghrib, 49–52; and diversity of Islam, 11, 13, 16–18; and Egyptian colonialism, 155; and

European colonialism, 268, 273–76, 279, 290–91; and evolution of Muslim societies, 30–31, 33; and geography/ecology of Africa, 1, 6–7, 9; and institutions of Islam, 22–23; and Islam in Ethiopia, 175–77, 179, 183, 185, 193; and Islam on the Cape, 248, 258; and Islam on the East African coast, 230, 237, 241, 246; and Islam on the Horn of Africa, 199, 208; and Islamic learning, 105; and Islamization of Nubia, 135–40; and Islamization of Sinnār-Funj, 150; and Islamization of the bilād al-sūdān, 77–78; and Khalīfa ʿAbdallāh, 165–69; and the Mahdī movement, 161–65; and quest for Islamic unity, 43–44; and the Sinnār-Funj empire, 141–43, 145–46; and Sudanese conquest, 169–71; and Sufism, 74, 159–61; and trading empires of the bilād al-sūdān, 81–82, 87–89; and trans-Saharan trade, 57, 60, 62, 65–66, 68
Emin Pasha (alias Eduard Schnitzler), 246–47
Ennedi, 2, 75, 96
Ephesus, council of, 38
epidemics. *See* diseases and epidemics
Equatoria, 158, 169–70, 246
Eritrea, 6, 158, 195, 287–88, 296, 301
Estifanos, Abba, 179
Etchäge (position), 176
Europe, relations with: and caravans, 244; cultural influences, 18, 230–31; and diversity of Islam, 16; and epidemics, 51; and Ethiopian Islam, 179–80, 185, 192, 195; and geography/ecology of Africa, 1, 4, 6; and the ḥajj, 23; and the Indian Ocean, 211, 224; and jihād, 108, 115, 118, 129; and plantation agriculture, 212–13; and religious conversions, 27–34; and trade relations, 54, 55, 59–64, 65–66, 70, 81, 89, 90, 96–98, 101, 103, 106, 200, 232, 242, 244; and trans-Saharan trade, 144; and upcountry East Africa, 242–46; and Zanzibar, 230–34. *See also* colonial rule; *specific European countries*
Ewosṭātewos monastic order, 176, 178–79
Ezana, 173

Fada N'gurma, 100
Faidherbe, General Louis, 283
Falémé River, 60, 115
Fandano cult, 192
Faras, 136, 138
Fashi oasis, 57, 75
al-Fāshir, 88
Fāshōda, 164
Fasilädäs, emperor, 192–93
Fäṭägar, 184, 188
Fāṭima, 20, 43
Fāṭimid caliphate: and conquest of the bilād al-maghrib, 39; and disintegration of the bilād al-maghrib, 48, 52; and diversity of Islam, 11; and historical patterns of Nubia and Funj, 135; and historical patterns of the bilād al-maghrib, 35, 37; and Islamic rebellions, 41–42; and Islamization of Nubia, 137; and quest for Islamic unity, 42–43, 43–45; and trans-Saharan trade, 65
Faza, 8, 217, 218, 224, 227
Fāzūghlī, 140, 142, 152
Fazzān: and Egyptian colonialism, 170; and European colonialism, 287–88; and geography/ecology of Africa, 3; and historical patterns of the bilād al-maghrib, 37; and jihād in the bilād al-sūdān, 119; and the Sinnār-Funj empire, 143; and Sufism, 74, 75; and trading empires of the bilād al-sūdān, 83–84; and trans-Saharan trade, 57, 61–62, 67–70
Fes, 12, 22, 39–41, 50, 74, 94, 112, 142
fiqh (jurisprudence): and decline of Sinnār-Funj, 152; and discursive tradition of Islam, 19; and diversity of Islam, 13; and European colonialism, 281; and historical patterns of the bilād al-maghrib, 35; and Islam on the Cape, 251; and Islam on the East African coast, 239; and Islamic learning, 104–105; and jihād in the bilād al-sūdān, 117, 123; and library of Shaykh Sidiyya, 299; and quest for Islamic unity, 48; and scholarship on Arabic literature, 300, 302; and trans-Saharan trade, 72
fitna, 113
Fitri, Lake, 84, 86
Fode Kaba, 108
Fort Jesus, 223, 225–26, 227
France: and colonial rule, 267–72, 278–79, 282–87, 287–88, 290, 292; and disintegration of the bilād al-maghrib, 49, 51; and Egyptian colonialism, 154–55, 158, 171; and geography/ecology of Africa, 4; and historical patterns of the bilād al-maghrib, 37; and Islam in Ethiopia, 179, 185, 193–94; and Islam on the Cape, 253; and Islam on the East African coast, 211, 215, 224, 228, 231; and Islam on the Horn of Africa, 199, 208; and Islamization of the bilād al-sūdān, 77; and jihād in the bilād al-sūdān, 110, 111, 113, 116, 120–21, 124–29; and Kano, 96; and religious authority, 25; and scholarship on Arabic literature, 302; and trading empires of the bilād al-sūdān, 87; and trading networks, 97; and trans-Saharan trade, 55, 66

Franciscans, 143, 203
French West Africa, 128, 272, 283, 286
Friday prayers, 46, 82, 123, 126, 260–61
FulBe (Fulani), 4–6, 70, 80, 115, 123, 281
FulFulde, 4–5, 105, 119, 127
Funj, *262;* decline of Sinnār-Funj, 151–53; and diversity of Islam, 11, 13; and Egyptian colonialism, 154–57, 159, 161; empire of Sinnār-Funj, 140–47; historical patterns of Nubia and Funj, 135; historical patterns of the bilād al-maghrib, 36; and Islamization, 78, 147–50; and trading empires of the bilād al-sūdān, 79, 80, 84–86, 88; and trans-Saharan trade, 60
fuqahā', (singular *faqīh*), 46–47, 71–72, 82, 149–50, 191, 197
al-Fusṭāṭ, 137
Fuuta Jalon, 4, 102, 105, 106, 109–10, 115, 120, 127–28
Fuuta Tooro, 102, 109, 115–16, 119–21, 124, 127, 284

gada, 189–91
Gajaaga, 109, 115
Galam, 80
Gälawdewos, 187
da Gama, Christovào, 187
da Gama, Vasco, 223
Gambia River, 3, 58, 98, 105–106, 109, 294
Gamia Mogamed Achmat, 254–58, 260–61
Gao: and diversity of Islam, 12; and Islam in Ethiopia, 174–77; and Islam on the East African coast, 219; and Islamization of the bilād al-sūdān, 77, 78; and jihād in the bilād al-sūdān, 112; and Kano, 90; and trading empires of the bilād al-sūdān, 80–84; and trading networks, 98; and trans-Saharan trade, 56–57, 62, 65–66, 69–70, 73
Gazi, 226, 228
Gedi, 218
Ge'ez language, 172, 177
Geledi, Sultan of, 200
German East Africa, 268–69, 271–72, 292
German language, xii
Germany: colonial rule, 25, 129; and colonial rule, 268–69, 271–72, 276–78, 282, 287, 290, 292; and Egyptian colonialism, 165, 171; and Islam on the East African coast, 227, 231, 233–34, 244, 246; and Islam on the Horn of Africa, 208; and trading empires of the bilād al-sūdān, 86, 87; and trading networks, 97; and trans-Saharan trade, 59
Gessi Pasha, 158, 170
Ghadāmis, 2–3, 12, 56–57, 90
Ghāna empire: and diversity of Islam, 12–13; and European colonialism, 294; and Islamic learning, 105; and Islamization of the bilād al-sūdān, 77, 78; and Muslims in Asante, 101; and quest for Islamic unity, 45; and trading empires of the bilād al-sūdān, 79–81; and trading networks, 100; and trans-Saharan trade, 55, 60, 61–62, 64–65, 70
Ghardaia, 56
Ghāt, 2–3, 12, 56–57, 90
al-Ghazzālī, Abū Ḥāmid, 46
Gidimaxa, 109, 121
glass, 59, 63, 96, 98
Goa, 185, 223–25, 251
Gobir, 24–25, 109, 111, 117–18
Gojam, 189, 193
gold: and decline of Sinnār-Funj, 151; and Egyptian colonialism, 155, 167; and extent of African trade, 23; and geography/ecology of Africa, 4; and Islam in Ethiopia, 175, 183, 186; and Islam on the East African coast, 212, 217, 220, 223, 231, 241; and Islamization of Nubia, 135–36, 138–39; and Islamization of Sinnār-Funj, 148; and jihād in the bilād al-sūdān, 112; and Kano, 94; and Muslims in Asante, 101–102; and the Sinnār-Funj empire, 146; and trading empires of the bilād al-sūdān, 80–81, 83; and trading networks, 98, 99; and trans-Saharan trade, 58, 60–65, 67, 72
Gold Coast, 63, 101–102
Gondär (Gondar), 90, 169, 172, 182, 192–93
Gondokoro, 157, 241
Gongola, 109
Gonja, 66, 89, 93, 103
Goran, 2
Gordon College, 273–74, 276, 280
Gordon Pasha, General Charles, 158, 165, 273
grain: and decline of Sinnār-Funj, 151; and East African trade, 211–12; and Egyptian colonialism, 168; and Islam in Ethiopia, 175; and Islam on the East African coast, 225, 232; and Islam on the Horn of Africa, 198; and jihād in the bilād al-sūdān, 123; and Kano, 93; and trading networks, 98–99; and trans-Saharan trade, 59, 62
Graziani, General Rodolfo, 289
Great Lakes, 10, 136, 246
Greek culture, 2, 13, 38, 135–36, 146, 155–56, 208
groundnuts, 281, 284–86
Guinea, coast: and European colonialism, 287, 290; and geography/ecology of Africa, 4–5, 9; and Islam on the East African coast, 240; and jihād in the bilād al-sūdān, 125, 129; and scholarship

on Arabic literature, 300; and trading empires of the bilād al-sūdān, 87, 89; and trading networks, 98–103; and trans-Saharan trade, 58, 60–61, 63–64
Gujarat, 9, 185, 213, 228
Gulf region, the: and diversity of Islam, 17; and geography/ecology of Africa, 9; and institutions of Islam, 22; and Islam in Ethiopia, 175, 179, 182; and Islam on the East African coast, 212–13, 219, 226–28; and quest for Islamic unity, 43
gum Arabic, 58, 156, 167
guns, 59–60, 97–98, 155, 170, 194, 204–205, 240, 244, 272
Gurage, 175, 289
Gusau, 280–81
Gyaman, 103

Ḥabesh, pashālik, 191
Ḥabīb Ṣāliḥ Jamal al-Layl, 236, 239
Ḥabshī, 213
Ḥaḍāriba, 140, 141, 151
ḥadd (plural *ḥudūd*), 17, 42
ḥadīth: and decline of Sinnār-Funj, 152; and discursive tradition of Islam, 19; and diversity of Islam, 14; and Islam on the Cape, 251; and Islamic learning, 104–105; and jihād in the bilād al-sūdān, 123; and scholarship on Arabic literature, 300; and trans-Saharan trade, 72
Hadiyya, 175, 179, 184, 188, 191–92
Ḥaḍramawt, 7, 196, 198, 214–16, 220, 228, 231, 236–37, 239
Ḥaḍramī, 186, 190, 196, 198, 213, 215–16, 231, 235
Ḥafsid dynasty, 48–49, 51, 62–64
Haidara, Karamoko Ṣidīq Sharīf, 126
Hailä Selase, Ras Tafari Makonnen, emperor, 195
ḥajj, 23, 258
Halpulaaren, 4, 17, 119, 120, 122–23
Ḥamad b. Muḥammad, Sulṭān, 278
Hamallāh, 285
Hamdallahi, 121–22
Ḥāmid b. Thwaynī, Sulṭān, 238, 277
Ḥammādid dynasty, 44
Ḥanafī school of law, 24, 29, 183, 256, 258–61
Ḥanbalī school of law, 17, 24, 29
Hanse cities, 59, 231
Ḥarär: and Egyptian colonialism, 158; and European colonialism, 289; and Islam in Ethiopia, 179–81, 184, 186–87, 190, 193; and Islam on the Horn of Africa, 196, 198–99, 202; and Kano, 90
Hausa: and diversity of Islam, 13; and European colonialism, 270; and geography/ecology of Africa, 4; and Islamic learning, 105; and jihād in the bilād al-sūdān, 109, 116–19, 120, 127; and Kano, 92–93; and Muslims in Asante, 103; and religious authority, 25; and scholarship on Arabic literature, 300; and scope of research, xii; and trading empires of the bilād al-sūdān, 81, 89–90; and trading networks, 98–99; and trans-Saharan trade, 56, 68
Hausaland: and evolution of Muslim societies, 33; and geography/ecology of Africa, 5; and institutions of Islam, 23; and Islamic learning, 105–106; and jihād in the bilād al-sūdān, 109–11, 113, 116–19; and Kano, 92; and religious authority, 24; and scholarship on Arabic literature, 300; and trading empires of the bilād al-sūdān, 80, 83, 85, 89; and trading networks, 96, 98; and trans-Saharan trade, 56–57, 66, 68
Ḥawwāra, 39–41
Ḥayāt b. Sa'īd, 165, 171
ḥijāb, 18, 168, 199, 205
Ḥijāz: and discursive tradition of Islam, 19; and Egyptian colonialism, 155, 159; and Islam in Ethiopia, 175; and Islam on the Cape, 248; and Islam on the East African coast, 213, 221, 237; and Islam on the Horn of Africa, 206; and Islamization of Nubia, 138; and jihād in the bilād al-sūdān, 119; and the Sinnār-Funj empire, 142, 147; and Sufism, 74
hijra: and colonial rule, 273; and diversity of Islam, 13; and Egyptian colonialism, 163–64, 166; and European colonialism, 268; and Islam in Ethiopia, 182; and Islam on the Horn of Africa, 199; and jihād in the bilād al-sūdān, 113, 120, 122
Hintata, 39
ḥisāb, 76, 104, 300
historical anthropology, x, 172
Hoggar Mountains, 57
Hormuz, 185, 223
Horn of Africa, *265;* and Arabic literature sources, 299–302; climate of, 10; epidemics and diseases, 6; geography of, 7–8; and Islamization, 196–98; and jihād, 202–209; and Muslim emirates, 182–83; and reform movements, 198–202; and rise of Zanzibar, 231; and saint veneration, 190; and segmentary societies, 3; and Shāfi'ī school of law, 104; and stateless societies, 15; tribal populations of, 8
horses, 58–59, 60, 86, 94–95, 98, 143, 145, 201
Hubbu movement, 115, 128
Huntington, Samuel, ix, 290
Ḥusaynid dynasty, 51

Ibāḍī movement (Ibāḍiyya): and European colonialism, 278; and evolution of Muslim societies, 29–30; and historical patterns of the bilād al-maghrib, 35; and Islam on the East African coast, 227; and Islamic learning, 104; and Islamic rebellions, 40; and Islamization of the bilād al-sūdān, 79, 82, 84; and trading networks, 96–97

Ibirri, Awlād, 2, 76

Ibn Baṭṭūṭa, Shams al-Dīn Abū 'Abdallāh Muḥammad, 15, 66, 71, 81–83, 97, 196–97, 213, 220–21

Ibn Ḥawqal, Abū l-Qāsim Muḥammad, 42, 55, 65

Ibn Khaldūn, Abū Zayd 'Abd al-Raḥmān, 50, 53, 66, 139

Ibrāhīm, 'Adlān, 145, 153, 167–68

Ibrāhīm al-Barnawī, Sharīf, 102

Ibrāhīm Niass, 23, 286

Ibrāhīm Sori, 115

'īd al-aḍha, 20

'īd al-fiṭr, 20, 92

'īd al-ḥajj, 20

'īd al-kabīr, 20, 92

Idrīs b. 'Abdallāh, 40

al-Idrīsī, Abū 'Abdallāh Muḥammad, 65, 80, 218

Idrīsid, 39, 41, 50

Idrīsiyya, 159

Ifrīqiyya, 1, 37, 41, 43, 45, 47–48

Ijāzāt (singular *Ijāza*), 19, 72

Ijīl, 63

Ikhwān al-muslimīn, 25, 75

'ilm al-falak, 104–105, 300

Ilorin, 118

Imām, 17, 41, 43, 53, 71, 75, 78, 100–101, 108. *See also specific Imāmates*

Imām Achmat (of Chinsura), 254–58, 260–61

Imām Aḥmad, b. Ibrāhīm al-Ghāzī, 14, 185

Imasighen: and disintegration of the bilād al-maghrib, 48; and diversity of Islam, 16; and evolution of Muslim societies, 30; and geography/ecology of Africa, 2–3, 8; and historical patterns of the bilād al-maghrib, 37–40; and Islamic rebellions, 40–42; and Islamization of the bilād al-sūdān, 77; and jihād in the bilād al-sūdān, 112; and quest for Islamic unity, 45–47; and trading empires of the bilād al-sūdān, 90; and trading networks, 96, 98; and trans-Saharan trade, 55, 58, 71–72

Imerina, 215, 229

India: and Cape Muslims, 248, 249–50, 252–53, 256, 259; and colonial rule, 267; and diseases/epidemics, 6; and East Africa societies, 22, 210, 212–15, 220, 227–28, 230–33; and European colonialism, 269, 273–74, 277–79, 278–79; and the Fāṭimid empire, 43; and Islamic law, 15; and jihād, 185–86, 203, 206, 208; and Portuguese explorers, 223, 225; and slavery, 212, 213; and trade with Africa, 9, 22–23, 143, 147, 175, 181, 183, 185, 200, 203, 206, 227–28, 235, 242–45

Indian Ocean: and East African societies, 7–10, 15, 18, 210–11; and Madagascar, 229; and Oman, 227–28; and Portuguese explorers, 56, 191, 221–22, 223–27; and slavery, 32, 175, 249, 250; and spread of Islam, 217, 239–40, 273; and trade relations, 22, 32, 182, 184–85, 211–12, 214–15, 219, 223, 243

indigo, 93, 99, 127, 156, 231

indirect rule, 271–72, 274, 277, 279–82, 284

Indonesia, 10, 22, 248–49

influenza, 209

Iran: and the Almoravid empire, 46; cultural influence of, 135; and East African coastal history, 214; and Indian ocean trade, 219; and long-distance trade, 9; and naval power, 210; and Nestorians, 38; and Oman, 227; and the Sassanid empire, 37; and Shī'a Islam, 43; trade with Asante, 103

'Irāq, 29, 38, 159, 212, 221, 237

iron, 59, 63, 78, 183, 186, 212, 231

Irshād, 25

Isaaq, 8, 197, 204, 205, 207–208

iṣlāḥ, 18

Islam noir, 282–84

Islamization, process of: and Asante, 101–103; and communal conversion, 30; and cultural distinctions, 17–18; and East African coast, 196, 217; and eras of Islamic influence, 37; historical themes and patterns, 77–78; and the Horn of Africa, 196; and Islamic learning, 103–107; and jihād, 109, 126, 128, 291; and Kano, 90–96; and Nubia and Funj, 135, 140, 141, 147–50, 151–52; and the Oromo, 192; and scholarship networks, 96–101; and scope of research, x; and slavery, 61; and trade, 13, 79–90

Ismā'īl, Khedive, 157–58, 230

Ismā'īlī religious movement, 11, 43

Italy: and colonial rule, 267–68, 271–72, 282, 292; as defender of Islam, 287–89; and disintegration of the bilād al-maghrib, 51; and Egyptian colonialism, 158, 170; and geography/ecology of Africa, 6; and historical patterns of the bilād al-maghrib, 37; and Islam in Ethiopia, 173, 193–95; and Islam

on the East African coast, 234; and Islam on the Horn of Africa, 199, 202, 205–208; and religious authority in Islam, 25; and trading networks, 97; and trans-Saharan trade, 58, 62, 66, 69
ivory: and Egyptian colonialism, 155–56, 167; and Indian Ocean trade, 212; and Islam in Ethiopia, 175, 183; and Islam on the East African coast, 222, 227–28, 230–31, 240, 243–46; and Islam on the Horn of Africa, 198–200; and the Sinnār-Funj empire, 146; and trading empires of the bilād al-sūdān, 87–88; and trans-Saharan trade, 58
Ivory Coast, 100, 105, 129, 282, 287, 290
Iwillimiden, Kel, 70, 73

Ja, 78, 105
Ja'aliyyīn, 5, 156, 169
Jabal Nafūsa, 40, 84
jabarti, 182, 183
Jaghbūb oasis, 74, 75
jāhiliyya, 18
Jakhanke, 89, 99, 105–107, 115, 120, 127
jallāba, 150, 157, 162, 170
jamā'a, 29, 113–14, 117–19, 120, 122, 199–200
Java, 23, 251–52
jazīra region (Sudan), 136, 140, 142, 146, 153, 156–58, 162, 167
Jegunko, 120
Jenné: and disintegration of the bilād al-maghrib, 51; and diversity of Islam, 12; and geography/ecology of Africa, 4; and institutions of Islam, 22; and Islamic learning, 105, 107; and Islamization of the bilād al-sūdān, 77, 78; and jihād in the bilād al-sūdān, 122, 123, 127; and scholarship on Arabic literature, 301; and trading empires of the bilād al-sūdān, 83, 90; and trading networks, 100; and trans-Saharan trade, 69, 72
Jerma, 4
Jerusalem, al-Quds, 20, 23, 137, 174, 230
Jews and Jewish trade: and conquest of the bilād al-maghrib, 38; and diversity of Islam, 11, 16; and evolution of Muslim societies, 31; and geography/ecology of Africa, 2; and Islam in Ethiopia, 172–73, 173–74, 176–78; and Islam on the Cape, 260; and jihād in the bilād al-sūdān, 112; and the Sinnār-Funj empire, 143, 146; and trading networks, 97, 98; and trans-Saharan trade, 59, 72. *See also* Judaism
Jibrīl b. 'Umar, al-Ḥājj, 111
Jidda, 142, 146, 182, 185, 226
jihād: and African indigenous religions, 28; and al-Ḥājj 'Umar Taal, 119–27; and East African coast, 234; and Ethiopia, 14, 172, 180, 184–89, 190, 192; and European colonialism, 268, 273, 282, 284–85, 290–91, 293; and FulFulde-speaking groups, 4; in Hausaland and Bornu, 116–19; and the Horn of Africa, 196–98, 202–209; and Islamic law, 17; and Islamic learning, 300, 301; and Islamization of the bilād al-sūdān, 78, 85, 89, 91, 96, 101, 106–107; legacy of, 127–29; and the Mahdī, 163; and Muslim empires, 295; in Nubia and Funj, 137, 151; patterns in the bilād al-sūdān, 108–16; and rebellion, 36; and religious legitimacy, 20, 24–25; and slavery, 110–11, 114–16, 127–28, 206, 208
Jolof, 80, 109–10, 284
Jongie Siers, 256, 261
Jos plateau, 4, 33, 128
Juba River, 7–8, 197–200, 206–207, 211, 242
Judaism, xi, 14, 16, 19, 172, 176–78. *See also* Jews and Jewish trade
Judar Pasha, 69
Juhayna, 5, 139–40
Jukun, 68, 85, 95–96, 109
juma' prayers, 261
Juula, 4, 89, 99–101, 103, 107, 125, 126

Kaabu, 109
Kaarta, 79, 101, 109, 116, 120–21, 122, 284
Kabābīsh, 5, 158, 169
Kaffa, 7, 175, 191–92
Kajoor, 109, 116
Kalumbardo, 105
Kamba, 9, 242
Kānim-Bornu: and diversity of Islam, 12; and Islamization of the bilād al-sūdān, 77–79; and Kano, 92–93; and trading empires of the bilād al-sūdān, 82–87, 89; and trading networks, 96; and trans-Saharan trade, 57, 60, 67–68
al-Kānimī, al-Ḥājj Muḥammad al-Amīn b. Muḥammad, 85, 111, 113, 118–19
Kankan, 105, 125–26
Kano: and indirect rule, 279–80; and Islamic learning, 12, 22, 301; and Islamization, 77–78, 81, 85, 90–96, 101, 105–106; and jihād in the bilād al-sūdān, 109, 111, 116, 127; language of, xii; and trade, 4, 36, 56, 66
Kanuri, 2, 4, 93, 96, 98
Kanz al-Dawla federation, 138–39
Kararī, 169, 273
Karbalā', 29
Kasan, 22
Kasongo, 246–47

Kassala, 159, 194, 274, 276
Katanga, 221, 244–45
Katsina, 4, 12, 56, 66, 90–91, 95–96, 105, 109, 111–12, 116, 301
Kawār oasis, 57, 67, 85
Kawkaw. *See* Gao
Kebbi, 117
Keira dynasty, 88
Kenya: and colonial rule, 234; and European colonialism, 290; and indigenous religions, 33; and Islamization, 210, 292; and qāt leaves, 203; and social structure, 25; and the Somaal, 197; and Zanzibar, 276, 279
Khālid b. Barghash, Sulṭān, 229–30, 232–33, 244, 277–78
Khalīfa b. Ḥārub, Sulṭān, 278
Khalīfa b. Sa'īd, Sulṭān, 238, 278
Khalīl b. Iṣḥāq, 44, 105
Khalwatiyya, 159, 251–52
khārijites, 29–30, 40–41, 44, 83–84, 97, 203
Khartoum (al-Kharṭūm), 136, 156–57, 162–65, 273, 274–76, 292
Khātimī, 216
Kilwa: and evolution of Muslim societies, 33; and geography/ecology of Africa, 8–9; and Islam on the East African coast, 210–11, 214–15, 217–23, 226, 241–42; and scope of research, xii
Kirdi, 84, 86
Kirk, John (British consul), 233
Kisangani, 246
Kismayu, 7, 158, 196
Kiswahili: and discursive tradition of Islam, 19; and diversity of Islam, 15; and geography/ecology of Africa, 9; and Islam on the East African coast, 210, 214, 216, 219, 221, 236–37, 241, 247; and scholarship on Arabic literature, 300, 302; and scope of research, xii
kola nuts, 93, 98–100, 101, 103
Kong, 89, 99–101, 102–103, 125, 127
Kordofan: and the decline of Sinnār-Funj, 151, 152–53; and Egyptian colonialism, 156, 159, 162, 164, 165, 167, 169–70; and indirect rule, 274; and Islamization, 87–88; and nomadic cultures, 5–6; and the rise of Funj, 142, 146
Kota Kota, 242–43
Kotoko, 85, 109
kramat, 252
Krump, Theodor, 143–44
kufr, 19, 116, 118, 119
Kufra oasis, 3, 12, 57, 74, 76, 288
Kukawa, 87, 103
Kūkiya, 83
Kumasi, 102–103
Kumbi Saleh, 65, 70, 80, 82
Kunta, 2, 73, 76, 106, 124
al-Kuntī, Sīdī Mukhtār, 106
Kush, 135
Kutāma, 39, 42–45
Kwararafa, 68, 89, 95–96, 109

Lalibäla, 172–75
Lamtūna, 45, 46
Lamu: and conversion to Islam, 181; and Islamic scholarship, 22, 33; and Mogadishu, 218; and Portuguese rule, 224–26; and religious reform, 235, 236, 239; and Swahili culture, 217–18; and trade relations, 8–10, 199, 200, 210–15, 242; and Zanzibar, 228, 232, 234
langar, 251, 252, 254–55
Lasta, 174, 193
Lebnä Dengel, emperor, 186–87
Leo Africanus. *See* al-Wazzānī
Leopold II of Belgium, 246, 267, 289
Liberia, 267
Libya, 29, 35, 74, 76, 272, 287–89
Lij Iyassu, 208
literature, Arabic, ix, xiii, 9, 257, 299–302, *303–308*
Lobi, 60, 63
Logone River, 86
Lomami River, 245–47
Lugard, Lord, 271–72
lugha, 104, 300
Luuq, 199–201, 206

Ma Ba Jaxu, 108, 284
Madagascar, 10, 215, 219, 222, 228–29, 231, 249
madḥ, 71, 216, 300
Madina Gounass, 285
madrasa (plural *madāris*), 19, 22, 75, 84, 101, 239, 252, 255–57
al-Maghīlī, Muḥammad b. 'Abd al-Karīm, 83, 91, 112–13, 117
Maghsharen, 70–71
Maguzawa, 33, 93
Mahdalī family, 220
Mahdī, the: and Anglo-Egyptian Sudan, 273, 275, 291; and Dārfūr rebellion, 88; and Egyptian colonialism, 154, 158, 161–65, 165–69; and European colonialism, 291; and the Horn of Africa, 202; and Ibn Tūmart, 47; and Ilyās b. Ṣālih, 41; and Islamic texts, 301; and religiously legitimated rebellions, 24; and Shī'īs, 43

Mahdiyya: Anglo-Egyptian Sudan, 273–75; and Arabic literature, 301; and the East African Coast, 241; and Egyptian colonialism, 154, 161, 166–69, 170; and Ethiopian Islam, 181, 193–94; and the Horn of Africa, 204; and Islamic rebellion, 36; and Islamization of the bilād al-sūdān, 87
Maḥmūd, Karantaw, al-Ḥājj, 107
Maḥmūd, Ka'tī, 107
maḥram, 85
Mai 'Alī Gajindeni, 68, 85
Mai Arki, 67, 84
Mai Dunāma Dibalīmī II., 68, 79, 84
Mai Dunāma I., 68
Mai Ḥummay, 84
Mai Idrīs Aloma, 68, 85
Mai 'Umar b. Idrīs, 85
Majdhūbiyya, 150, 159, 161–62, 169
Mājid, Sulṭān, 229–30, 232
Maji-Maji war, 269, 271–72
Makhzūmī, 184
Makonde, 10
Malal, 31–32, 65
malaria, 58, 168, 267
Malawi, Lake, 10, 222, 231, 233, 241–42, 244–45
Malay culture, 249, 257
Mālī: and diversity of Islam, 12; and European colonialism, 269, 282–83, 284–85, 287, 293; and evolution of Muslim societies, 31; and geography/ecology of Africa, 3; and Islamic learning, 106; and Islamization of the bilād al-sūdān, 77; and jihād in the bilād al-sūdān, 109–10, 116, 124; and Kano, 92–93; and scholarship on Arabic literature, 300; and trading empires of the bilād al-sūdān, 79–83, 85, 87; and trading networks, 97, 99–100; and trans-Saharan trade, 55, 60–64, 65–66, 67, 70–71
Mālik Sy, 115, 286
Mālikī school of law: and diversity of Islam, 15; and evolution of Muslim societies, 29–30; and historical patterns of the bilād al-maghrib, 35; and Islam in Ethiopia, 183; and Islam on the East African coast, 210; and Islamic learning, 104; and Islamic rebellions, 41; and Islamization of Sinnār-Funj, 149–50; and jihād in the bilād al-sūdān, 117, 123; and Kano, 91; and quest for Islamic unity, 43–47; and religious authority, 23–24; and the Sinnār-Funj empire, 142–43; and trading empires of the bilād al-sūdān, 79, 81–84; and trans-Saharan trade, 71–72
Malindi: and geography/ecology of Africa, 8–9; and Islam on the East African coast, 210, 212–15, 217–20, 222, 223–25, 226, 232, 234, 235
Malinke, 4, 70, 99, 120
Mamadou Jahe, 128
Mamadu Lamin Dramé, al-Ḥājj, 108, 111
Mamlūks, 6, 49, 137–40, 154–55, 179, 185, 213
Mamprussi, 89, 100
Manda, 218, 220
Mandara, 85, 109
Mande people, 4, 13, 81, 82, 89–90, 98–101, 103, 105, 107, 124–25
Manga, 235
mangroves, 9, 211–12, 220
Mansā Mūsā, 81
Mansā Sulaymān, 81
Mansā Uli, 71, 81
Manyema, 245–47
Maqarrī, 59
Maqurra, 136–37
Mardycker, 249
Maria Theresien Thaler, 167, 183
Marīnid dynasty, 39, 48–51, 62, 65–66
Marka harbor, 7–8, 196
Marka/Maraka traders: and diversity of Islam, 15; and geography/ecology of Africa, 4, 7–8, 10; and Islam in Ethiopia, 190; and Islam on the East African coast, 217–18, 234, 242; and Islam on the Horn of Africa, 196, 199–201, 206; and Islamic learning, 107; and jihād in the bilād al-sūdān, 120; and trading networks, 98–99; and trans-Saharan trade, 70
Marrākish, 12, 22, 46–47
Marty, Paul, 283
Masina: and diversity of Islam, 17; and geography/ecology of Africa, 5; and Islamic learning, 106; and Islamization of the bilād al-sūdān, 77; and jihād in the bilād al-sūdān, 108–109, 113–14, 117, 119–21, 122–24, 127; and religious authority, 24; and trading empires of the bilād al-sūdān, 79; and trans-Saharan trade, 73
Maṣmūda, 39, 47–48, 49
Masqaṭ, 223, 225, 227, 229–30, 244
Massawa, 6, 157–58, 179, 185, 191, 193–94, 287
Massenya, 86–87
al-Mas'ūdī, Abū l-Ḥasan 'Alī, 64, 217–18
Matteo, Vincenzo, 94
Maudūdī, Abū Ā'lā, 25
Mauritania, 12, 106, 110, 267, 282–83, 285, 293, 299–301
Mawlay Ismā'īl, Sulṭān, 51, 60–61

mawlid al-nabī, 90, 160, 216, 236, 239, 251
mawlid barzanjī, 216, 236
mawlidi ya Kiswahili, 216, 236–37
Mazrūʿī, 226
Mbaruk family, 226
Mecca: and discursive tradition of Islam, 20; and diversity of Islam, 13, 17; and Egyptian colonialism, 155, 159, 164; and institutions of Islam, 23; and Islam in Ethiopia, 173, 182; and Islam on the Cape, 248, 251, 255, 258; and Islam on the Horn of Africa, 199, 202, 205; and Islamic rebellions, 41; and Islamization of Nubia, 138; and jihād in the bilād al-sūdān, 111, 113, 119; and the Sinnār-Funj empire, 141; and trading empires of the bilād al-sūdān, 81
Mecca letter affair, 271
Medina: and discursive tradition of Islam, 20; and diversity of Islam, 13, 17; and Egyptian colonialism, 155; and institutions of Islam, 23; and jihād in the bilād al-sūdān, 111, 113, 119
Mediterranean, the: and diversity of Islam, 18; and Egyptian colonialism, 155, 170; and European colonialism, 273; and evolution of Muslim societies, 28; and geography/ecology of Africa, 2; and Islam in Ethiopia, 174, 176; and Islam on the East African coast, 211; and Islam on the Horn of Africa, 203; and Islamization of Nubia, 138, 140; and Kano, 96; and Muslims in Asante, 101; and the Sinnār-Funj empire, 146; and Sufism, 74, 76; and trans-Saharan trade, 54–56, 58–60, 63, 68, 69
Melayu, 252, 257, 260
Menilek I, 176
Menilek II, emperor, 180–81, 193–94
Meroe, 135, 136, 173
Mijikenda, 211
millet beer, 88, 93, 99
al-Mirghānī, Muḥammad Ḥasan, 159
al-Mirghānī, Muḥammad ʿUthmān, 159–60
al-Mirghānī, Sayyid ʿAlī, 274–75
Mirghāniyya, 150, 159, 301
Mogadishu: and diversity of Islam, 15; and geography/ecology of Africa, 7–8, 10; and institutions of Islam, 22; and Islam on the East African coast, 214–15, 217–18, 223–24, 234, 242; and Islam on the Horn of Africa, 196–97, 199–201, 202, 206
Moghuls, 210
Mombasa: and European colonialism, 276; and geography/ecology of Africa, 8–9; and institutions of Islam, 22; and Islam on the East African coast, 210–11, 213–15, 218–20, 222, 223–26, 227–28, 232, 234–35, 242; and Kano, 90
monasteries and monastic orders, 137–38, 143, 172–79, 186
monophysitism, 38, 136, 176
monsoons, 8–9, 15, 210, 220
Morocco: and conquest of the bilād al-maghrib, 39–40; and disintegration of the bilād al-maghrib, 48–52; and diversity of Islam, 18, 296; and European colonialism, 268; and historical patterns of the bilād al-maghrib, 35; and Islam on the East African coast, 224; and Islamic rebellions, 40–41; and Muslims in Asante, 103; and quest for Islamic unity, 44–45; and the Sinnār-Funj empire, 142; and trading empires of the bilād al-sūdān, 83, 85; and trans-Saharan trade, 55, 56, 61–64, 66, 67–69, 70–71, 73
Mossi, 4, 71, 85, 89, 100, 109, 116
Mozambique: and European colonialism, 268, 292; and geography/ecology of Africa, 8, 10; and Islam on the Cape, 259; and Islam on the East African coast, 222, 223–24, 227, 228, 231, 240–41
Mrima coast, 8, 10
Muḥammad, Prophet: and discursive tradition of Islam, 20; and disintegration of the bilād al-maghrib, 50; and diversity of Islam, 13, 17, 18; and Egyptian colonialism, 160, 163–64, 168; and evolution of Muslim societies, 29, 30; and Islam in Ethiopia, 182; and Islam on the Cape, 260; and Islam on the East African coast, 236, 239; and Islam on the Horn of Africa, 197, 204, 207; and Islamic learning, 104–105; and Islamic rebellions, 40; and Kano, 95; and quest for Islamic unity, 42–43, 44; and religious authority, 26; and scholarship on Arabic literature, 300; and Sufism, 74; and trading empires of the bilād al-sūdān, 80, 90; and trans-Saharan trade, 71
Muḥammad ʿAbd al-Bāriʾ, 252, 254–55
Muḥammad ʿAbdille Ḥasan, Sayyid, 24, 196, 200, 202–209, 288
Muḥammad ʿAbdūh, 25
Muḥammad Abū Likaylik, 152–53
Muḥammad Aḥmad, the Mahdī, 154, 161–65, 273
Muḥammad ʿAlī, 17, 138, 155
Muḥammad al-Khayr ʿAbdallāh Khōjālī, 162, 166
Muḥammad al-Nūr Ḍayf Allāh, 239
Muḥammad al-Sharīf, 87
Muḥammad b. ʿAbdallāh b. Tūmart, 47–48
Muḥammad b. Khalfān, 244
Muḥammad Bello, 119, 121
Muḥammad Dollie, 256, 261

Muḥammad Gulayd, Shaykh, 208–209
Muḥammad Khālid, 166, 168
Muḥammad Ma'rūf, 239
Muḥammad Rumfa, 91, 95
Muḥammad Ṣāliḥ Hendricks, 261
Muḥammad Sharefa, 111
Muḥammad Sharīf Nūr al-Dīn al-Dā'im al-Bashīr, Shaykh, 162
Muḥammad II b. Aḥmad (of Pate), 218
Muḥammad Yūsuf, 87, 165
Muhammedan Shafee Congregation, 255–56
Munzinger Pasha, 158
al-murābiṭūn, 45, 48
Murad Rais (Peter Leslie), 70
Murīdiyya, Murīd, 284–86
Mussolini, Benito, 288
Muṣṭafa al-Ahmar, 70
Mutesa I, Kabaka (Buganda), 241
al-Muwaḥḥidūn. *See* Almohad movement
Mwene Motapa, 10, 23, 220, 221, 241
Mzab, 56, 84, 97

Nabahānī, 215
Nachtigal, Gustav, 87
naḥw, 72, 104, 123, 300
Napoleon and Napoleonic wars, 138, 154, 228, 250
Naqshbandiyya, 253
Nāṣir al-Dīn, 109–10, 113, 115, 162, 257
Nederduitse Gereformeerde Kerk (NGK), 15, 248
Nestorians, 38, 181
Netherlands (and Dutch colonies/people), 15, 55, 185, 224, 249–52, 253, 256–57
de Neveu, Captain, 282
Ngajiza, 214–15
Niger, 33, 34, 287, 290, 291, 293
Niger River: and the 'Alawid dynasty, 51; and colonial rule, 170–71; and European colonialism, 291, 293; and geography of Niger Sudan, 3; and Islamization of the bilād al-sūdān, 78, 80–83, 87, 89–90, 98–99, 101, 102, 105; and jihād in the bilād al-sūdān, 109–10, 114, 117, 120–21, 124–25, 128; and routes across the Sahara, 56; and trans-Saharan empires, 67, 69; and trans-Saharan trade, 54, 55–58, 60–62, 65–66, 70–73
Nigeria: and diversity of Islam, 18; and European colonialism, 268, 270, 272–74, 277, 279–81, 290–93; and jihād in the bilād al-sūdān, 117, 128, 129; and Kano, 93; and religious authority, 25; and scholarship on Arabic literature, 301
Nile River and Valley, *262, 263;* and "African" Islam, 11, 13, 15, 32; and Arabic literature, 300–301, 305; and the bilād al-maghrib, 36; and colonial historiography, 5–7; and ecology of North Africa, 3; and Egyptian colonialism, 159, 161–62, 164–65, 167, 168–71; and European colonialism, 273, 274–76, 291–92; and geography of North Africa, 1; and Islam in Ethiopia, 173–74, 175, 180, 193; and Islam in Nubia and Funj, 135–37, 139–40, 140–43, 146, 149–50, 154–58; and Islam on the East African coast, 210, 241, 246; and Islam on the Horn of Africa, 196; and Islamization of the bilād al-sūdān, 78, 79, 84, 87–88, 90; Kano, 90; and the Sahara as connective space, 57, 60–61, 64, 75
Nioro, 120–21, 124
Niumi, 109
Nobatia, 136–37, 139
Nōl dynasty, 152–53
Nosi-Bé, 228
Nubia: and arrival of Islam, 13, 135–40; and Christianity, 87–88; and decline of Sinnār-Funj empire, 151–53; and Ethiopian Islam, 172, 173–74, 177; and European colonialism, 292; and geography of North Africa, 1; and gold mining, 62; and Islam on the Horn of Africa, 208; and Islamization process, 147–50; and matrilineal inheritance, 33; and Monophysites, 38; and regional trade, 78; and rise of Sinnār-Funj empire, 140–47; and Sufism, 159; tribal groups of, 5–6, 156
numerology, 16, 18, 229, 300
Nūn, Wādī, 55
Nupe, 4, 90
Nūr b. al-Mujāhid, Amīr, 187
Nūr Ḥusayn, Shaykh, 190, 198
Nyamwesi, 9, 233, 242–44
nyika, 9, 15, 211, 224, 240
Nzuwani, 219. *See also* Anjouan

al-Obeid (al-Ubayyiḍ), 164
Ogaden, 7, 194–95, 197, 198, 202, 204–205, 208, 289
Oman: and Islam in Africa, 15, 29; and East African Islam, 210–16, 222, 223, 225, 226–27, 227–29, 230–31, 232, 235–36, 244; and Ethiopian Islam, 181, 186
Omdurman, 165, 166–69, 170, 273
Oromo, 5–8, 173, 183, 184, 188–89, 190–94, 198, 224–25, 234
Orthodox Church: and "African" Islam, 11, 19; and the council of Chalcedon, 38; and Islam in Ethiopia, 172–73, 174, 176–77, 179, 180; and Islam in Nubia, 136–38
Osei Bonsu, Asantehene, 102–103

Ottoman empire: and colonial rule, 267, 275, 288; and disintegration of the bilād al-maghrib, 48–50, 51, 52; and diversity of Islam, 17; and East African Islam, 211, 224, 225; and Egyptian colonialism, 155–57; and Ethiopian Islam, 180, 183, 184–87, 191, 193; and historical patterns of Nubia and Funj, 135; and historical patterns of the bilād al-maghrib, 36–37; and Islam on the Cape, 256–57, 258–60; and Islamization of Nubia, 138; and Kano, 94; and the Sinnār-Funj empire, 142, 143, 145, 148; and Sufism, 74; and trading empires of the bilād al-sūdān, 85; and trans-Saharan trade, 62, 63, 67–70

Palestine, 11, 38, 43, 138, 177
Pangani River, 211
Pate: and geography/ecology of Africa, 8–9; and Islam on the East African coast, 210, 213–16, 217–19, 224–25, 226, 227, 228; and scope of research, xii
paths of accommodation, 25, 124, 268, 270, 273, 282
Pemba, 8, 212, 218, 226–28, 232, 278
pepo, 33
Persia: and diversity of Islam, 15; and geography/ecology of Africa, 7, 9; and historical patterns of the bilād al-maghrib, 37; and Islam in Ethiopia, 173, 175, 183; and Islam on the Cape, 258; and Islam on the East African coast, 212–13, 215, 219, 220, 231; and Islamic rebellions, 41; and the Sinnār-Funj empire, 143
Pir, 105
plague, 50–51, 66, 73, 147, 188, 249
Pokomo, 33, 211
Ponty, William, 128, 283
Portal, Sir Gerald, 277
Portugal and Portuguese people: and colonial rule, 268, 292; and disintegration of the bilād al-maghrib, 50; and geography/ecology of Africa, 10; and Islam in Ethiopia, 179, 180, 184–87, 191, 192–93; and Islam on the Cape, 249; and Islam on the East African coast, 210–11, 216, 219, 221–22, 223–27, 227–28, 229, 240–43; and Islam on the Horn of Africa, 208; and the Sinnār-Funj empire, 142, 146; and trans-Saharan trade, 55–56, 63
possession cults, 27, 33, 174, 237

qabḍ, 23–24
Qādiriyya: on the Cape, 253; and Colonial rule, 281, 282, 285; disputes within, 124; on East African Coast, 234, 236, 237–39; expansion of, 237, 238, 300; and al-Ḥājj Maḥmud Karantaw, 107; on Horn of Africa, 196, 198, 199, 202, 206–207; and Jakhanke scholars, 107, 120; and jihād leadership, 108–109, 119, 301; and Muḥammad ʿAbdille Ḥasan, 202, 206–207; "qabḍ-sadl" disputes, 23; rituals associated with, 236, 237–39, 281; and Samori Turé, 126; and Shaykh Uways, 238; and Sīdī al-Mukhtār al-Kuntī, 106
Qalanbū, 79, 80
Qaramanlı dynasty, 51, 67, 69–70
Qarawiyyīn School, 12
Qarrī, 140, 144, 145
qāt, 202, 203
Qayrawān, 22, 37, 39, 44
al-Qayrawānī, Ibn Abī Zayd, 44, 72, 104, 105
Qirū, 74
Quellien, Alain, 283
Qulunqūl, 198, 202
Qur'ān: of the Barghawāṭa, 42; and the empire of Samori Turé, 126; and Fāṭimid theology, 44; ḥadd regulations of, 17; and the judiciary of the Mahdiyya, 168; Kiswahili translations of, 19; "kusoma Kurani" (healing ceremonies), 18; negotiation of, 20–21; and oath-taking, 102; and ritual practices, 19; and spread of Islam, 22; and Wahhābiyya, 17
qur'ānic schools, 72, 75, 104–105, 113, 126, 161, 198, 256

Rābiḥ b. Faḍl Allāh, 87, 165, 169–71, 245
ramaḍān, 20, 42, 92
Rashīd Riḍā, 25
Rashīdiyya, 159
rātib, 273, 275
Red Sea: and Christian crusaders, 137–38; and the Egyptian empire, 138, 155, 158; and the Ethiopian empire, 146, 173–74, 179, 182, 184; and the Funj, 142, 146–47; and Italian colonialism, 287; and the Nubian empire, 138, 139; and the Ottoman empire, 142, 157, 184, 191; and Portugal, 184, 185, 191; and slave trade, 32, 60, 175; and trade routes, 137, 138–43, 147, 181
reform, movement of, 25–26, 116, 239
Reubeni, David, 143
Rifāʿiyya, 252–53
Rift Valley of Africa, 7
rinderpest, 6, 167, 194, 206
Rinn, Louis, 282–83
riwāq. See *arwiqa*
Rizayqāt, 5, 6, 88, 169, 170
Rodd, Rennell, 277

Roha, 172, 174
Rome and Roman empire, 38, 39
Roscher, Albrecht, 233, 242
Rozwi, 221
Rumaliza. *See* Muḥammad b. Khalfān
Russia, 22, 97, 193, 208
Rustamid dynasty, 39, 40–41, 42
Ruvuma River, 240, 241–42

sabbath and sabbatarians, 177–78
al-Sa'dī, 'Abd al-Raḥmān al-Tinbuktī, 66
Ṣa'did dynasty, 51, 52
sadl, 23–24
Safawid dynasty, 210
Sahara: Arabic sources on, 64–67; and Berbers, 5, 11; desertification of, 1; historical themes and patterns of, 54; in Mesolithic period, 1–2; sāḥil, 9; and Sufism, 12, 74–76; and trade empires, 67–70, 70–73; tribes of, 2–3. *See also* trans-Saharan trade
Saḥnūn, 41, 105
Sa'īd, 'Alawī, Tuan, 252
Sa'īd b. Sulṭān, 227, 229
Sakalava, 215, 222
Salafiyya movement, 25
Salaga, 99
Ṣāliḥiyya, 198, 202–203, 205–206, 209
Sālim b. 'Abdallāh, 242
Saloum, 109, 284, 286
salt: and Bornu, 85; and dynamics of Islamization, 85, 93, 98–99, 100; on the East African coast, 240; and Ethiopia, 183; mines of Taghāzā, 55, 63, 67–68, 71; replaced as exchange currency, 148; trans-Saharan salt trade, 58–59, 60, 62–63, 67, 71
Sammāniyya, 150, 159, 162, 165, 169, 253
Samori Turé, 101, 108–109, 114–15, 124–27
Ṣanghāna, 79
Ṣanhāja: and the Almohad empire, 47; and Almoravid warriors, 46–47; in bilād al-maghrib, 44; and the Fāṭimid dynasty, 42; and the Maghrāwa, 45; and the Mālikī school of law, 45–46; Masūfa-Ṣanhāja federation, 71; territories of, 39; in Timbuktu, 71; in Tunisia, 44
Sankore mosque, 71
al-Sanūsī, Abū 'Abdallāh Muḥammad b. Yūsuf, 22, 252
al-Sanūsī, Muḥammad al-Mahdī, 74, 165, 166
al-Sanūsī, Muḥammad b.'Alī, 74, 75, 159
Sanūsiyya, 74–76, 87, 165, 282, 288
Sao, 85
Sarakolle, 4
Sardauna, 280–81
ṣarf, 123
Särṣa Dengel, 187–88
Sassanid empire, 37, 38, 173
Saudi Arabia, 18, 289
Sayfuwa dynasty, 67–68, 84, 85
Sayyidiyye province, 234, 292
Segeju, 211, 225
segmentation, 3
Segu: and al-Ḥājj 'Umar Taal, 116, 120, 124; conversion to Islam, 121; jihād against, 17; and the Mali empire, 109; and Masina, 77, 121; rebellions in, 120; slave population in, 127, 128; as travel destination, 90
Senegal: and al-Ḥājj 'Umar Taal, 110, 119, 120–21; as center of Islamic learning, 105–106; French colonialism in, 116, 124, 125, 268, 270, 282, 283–87, 290, 291, 293, 294; matrilineal traditions in, 33; principalities in, 109; and trade, 18
Senegal River: ecology of, 5; and gold mining, 60; and Jakhanke families, 106; and kingdom of Takrūr, 65; and Mali empire, 109; and the Portuguese, 56; race relations on, 293; and Senegambian Sudan, 3; and trade, 79–80, 98
Senegal River Valley: economy of, 120; and FulBe pastoralists, 5, 80; and Fuutanke, 124; jihād in, 115–16; Nāṣir al-Dīn's rebellion in, 109; slave trade in, 115; and the Wolof kingdom, 80
Senegambia, 3, 108–11, 113, 120, 291
Senufo, 4, 101
Sereer, 33, 294
Sëriŋ fakk-taal, 113
Sëriŋ làmb, 113
Sewji family, 231–32
al-Shādhilī, Abū l-Ḥasan, 48
Shādhiliyya, 150, 159, 196, 234, 236, 239, 253
Shāfi'ī school of law: and the Cape Muslim community, 259–61; and East African Islam, 210, 220; and Ethiopian trade, 183; and European colonialism, 278; geographic reach of, 15; and Indian Ocean trade, 9; and Islamic learning in the bilād al-sūdān, 104; and Islamization on the Horn of Africa, 196; and jihād movements, 205; and religious authority issues, 24, 29; and Swahili culture, 218
Shā'iqiyya, 5, 151, 156, 162
Shanga, 217
Shankalla, 175
Sharaf al-Dīn al-Ḥasan b. Aḥmad al-Ḥaymī, al-Qāḍī, 193
Shari river, 3, 6, 86, 170

sharī'a: adoption of, 16–17; and colonialism, 270, 278, 280; and the Fāṭimid caliphate, 44; and local practices, 16; and Muḥammad 'Abdille Ḥasan, 205; and Muḥammad 'Uthmān al-Mirghānī, 159; and pre-jihād rulers, 114; and unbelievers vs. Muslims, 117; in Wasulu, 126
sharīf (plural *shurafā'*), 40, 50, 221
Shäwa, 174–75, 183–84, 186, 188, 193
Shaykh Aḥmad b. Muḥammad al-Nūbī, al-Yamanī, 142
Shaykh Yūsuf (Shaykh 'Abidīn Tadiā Yūsuf al-Tāj al-Khalwatī al-Maqassarī), 251, 252
Shebelle River: and East African coastal strip, 211; and rinderpest epidemic, 206; and the Somaal, 197; and terrain on the Horn of Africa, 7–8, 10; and trade, 198, 200, 242
Shendi, 156
Shī'a Islam: and the Almoravid empire, 45; and the bilād al-maghrib, 43–44; and the Buyid dynasty, 219; and the Fāṭimid caliphate, 35; and Imasighen populations, 30; and the jihād of Muḥammad 'Abdille Ḥasan, 202; modern orientations of, 43; origin of, 29
Shilluk, 141, 146, 153
Shinqīṭ, 22, 55, 73
Shiraz, Shirazi, 36, 214, 218–20, 225, 235–37, 239
Shungwaya, 217, 219
Sicily, 41, 44, 62
Sidamo, 175, 188, 189, 194, 289
Sidiyya, Bābā, Shaykh, 106, 299
Siin, 33, 109, 294
Sijilmāsa: and the Almoravids, 46; Banū Midrār dynasty in, 39, 40, 41; and Khārijī trade networks, 84; taxes paid to the Fāṭimid caliph, 65; and trade routes, 45, 46, 55, 59, 97
Sikasso, 125
Silā, 80
Sindh, 213
Sinnār, *262;* and center-periphery relations, 36; and divine kingdom tradition, 79; and Egyptian colonialism, 154–58, 161; and Islam in Nubia and Funj, 135, 140–47, 148, 150, 151, 152; and Kano, 90; and pre-Islamic communal religion, 13; and Sudanese trading empires, 80, 85, 88; and Sufism, 159, 160; and trans-Saharan trade, 60
sīra, 104, 105, 152
al-Sirr, Muḥammad 'Uthmān al-Aqrab Tāj, 160, 161
Siwa oasis, 57, 62
Siyu, 217, 232
Slatin, Rudolph (*known as* Slatin Pasha), 168, 207
slavery and the slave trade: and Abūbakar Effendi, 259; in the bilād al-maghrib, 36, 38; and the Cape Muslim community, 15, 249–52, 253, 257; and East African Islam, 212–14, 215, 216–17; and Egyptian colonialism, 154, 155, 156–58, 169–70; and Ethiopian trade, 175, 183; and European colonialism, 267, 276–78, 279, 284, 291; and ḥaratīn, 2–3; influence in African politics, 295; and Islam in Nubia and Funj, 136–37, 144–46, 149, 151; and Islamization on the Horn of Africa, 198; and jihād movements, 110–11, 114–16, 127–28, 206, 208; and Kano, 94–95; and the Mahdī movement, 161–62, 163–64, 165, 167; and Omani trade, 227–28; raiding of sedentary populations, 6; and reform movements, 200, 234–35, 236–37; and religious authority issues, 24; and religious conversion, 32–34; and social stratification, 4; Sudanese trading empires, 84–89; and trade/scholarship networks, 98, 99, 100, 101; and trans-Saharan trade, 58, 60–61, 67, 70, 72; and upcountry East Africa, 239–40, 243–44, 247; and Zanzibar, 231–33
sleeping sickness, 4, 10, 58, 243, 267
smallpox, 51, 73, 147, 194, 249
Sōba, 136, 140, 144
Socotra, 181
Sofala, 8, 217–18, 220–22
Sokoto, 23, 108, 114, 127–28, 165, 171, 279, 280–81
Sokoto caliphate, 24–25, 96, 110, 117–18, 272, 291
Solomon and Solomonid dynasty, 36, 73, 176–78
Somaal people: and agriculture, 8; and Bīja tribes, 6; and conversion, 7, 18, 183; and FulBe pastoralists, 5; and Islamic learning, 15; and jihād movements, 202, 204–205, 206, 207, 208; and Oromo settlers, 188, 189; and reform movements on the Horn of Africa, 198–201; as segmentary society, 3; and unification of tribal groups, 186; and Zanzibar, 230
Somalia: and Egyptian colonialism, 158; and Ethiopian slave trade, 175; and European colonialism, 267, 272, 287, 288, 289, 292, 293; and Islamization on the Horn of Africa, 196; and jihād movements, 206, 207, 208, 209; and Muslim influence in African politics, 296; and reform movements, 199, 236; and religious authority issues, 24
Songhay empire: and conversion to Islam, 12; and Islamization in the bilād al-sūdān, 77–87; and jihād in the bilād al-sūdān, 116; and river-based

trade, 3; Sudanese trading empires, 89–90; and trade routes, 4; and trans-Saharan trade, 60, 62, 64, 68–73
Soninke, 4, 66, 70, 120
Sonni ʿAlī (Ber), 71, 83, 112
Sonni ʿAlī Kolon, 83
Sonni Sulaymān Dandi, 83
Soudan. *See* Mali
South Africa, 6, 15, 248, 250, 268
Spain and Spanish language, 38, 61, 66, 72, 97, 112, 211, 224, 268. *See also* al-Andalus
Sri Lanka, 9, 249, 253
St. Louis, 116, 283, 285
Stanley, Henry Morton, 246
Suakin (Sawākin), 138, 141–42, 147–48, 157, 165, 189, 191
Sudan (Anglo-Egytian): and conquest of Sinnār-Funj, 154–58; historical themes and patterns, 154; and Khalīfa ʿAbdallāh, 165–69; and the Mahdī movement, 161–65; and Rābiḥ b. Faḍl Allāh, 169–71; and Sufism, 159–61. *See also* bilād al-sūdān
Suez, 185
Suez Canal, 155, 158, 203, 232, 269
Sufism and Sufi orders: and "African" religious practices, 18; and Arabic literature on Africa, 299; in the bilād al-maghrib, 35; and the Cape Muslim community, 252, 253; and discursive tradition in Islam, 19; and Egyptian colonialism, 154; and European colonialism, 274, 281–83, 284–87; and Islam in Nubia and Funj, 150; and Islamic learning in the bilād al-sūdān, 104, 106; and Islamization on the Horn of Africa, 196, 198; and jihād movements, 119, 126, 202, 206; and Kano, 91; and Khalīfa ʿAbdallāh, 169; and the Mahdī movement, 168; and reform movements, 234, 237, 297; and religous authority issues, 23; Sanūsiyya order, 74–76; Sufi orders on the Nile, 159–61; and trans-Saharan trade, 12. *See also specific orders and sects*
Ṣufrī, Ṣufrite, Ṣufriyya, 29, 30, 40–41, 84, 97
sugar cane, 63, 166, 175, 231–32, 235
Sulaymān Solongdungo, 88
Sundiata Keita, 81
sunna of the Prophet, 18, 29, 74, 117, 119, 163–64, 168, 260
Sunni Islam: in the bilād al-maghrib, 35, 43–47; in the bilād al-sūdān, 79, 82–84; and the Fāṭimid caliphate, 11; legal traditions of, 23, 29; origin of, 29; and Shiraz, 219; and Timbuktu, 71; and Wahhābiyya, 17. *See also specific religious orientations*
Sūs valley, 45, 50
Susneyos (emperor), 188, 192
Suwaré, al-Ḥājj Sālim, 105, 125
Suwarian, 105–106, 107
al-Suyūṭī, Jalāl al-Dīn, 72, 104, 106
Swahili. *See* Kiswahili
Sy, al-Ḥājj Malik, 286
Sylla, Yacouba, 285
syphilis, 66
Syria, 37–38, 43, 60, 107, 138, 143, 215, 230

Taʿāishī, Baggāra, 6, 162, 165, 168–69
Taal, Seydou Nourou, 286
Tablīghi Jamāʿat, 24
Tabora, 234, 242, 244–45
Tadamakkat, Kel, 2, 70, 73, 122
Tādmakka, 57, 70–71
Tāfīlālt, 45, 55
tafsīr, 19, 72, 104, 106, 117, 251, 257, 297, 300
Tagant, 110
Taghāzā, 55, 59, 63, 67–68, 71
Tāhart, 40–41
taḥfīẓ, 104
Takedda, 56–57
takfīr, 25, 113, 117–18
Täklä Haymanot order, 175–76, 178, 179
Takrūr, 12, 61, 65, 77, 78, 79–81
ṭalab al-ʿilm, 22, 104, 117, 202
Taleh, 208
Tana, Lake, 7, 172, 174, 178–79, 187–88
Tana River, 10, 197, 211, 217, 242, 252
Tanganyika, Lake, 231, 234, 238, 242, 244–46, 269, 276
Tanīzruft desert, 55, 57
Tanzania, 25, 33, 210, 240, 290, 294
taqiyya, 273
taṣawwuf. *See* Sufism and Sufi orders
Tawdenni, 55, 63
tawḥīd, 17, 19, 35, 47–48, 117, 123, 300
Teda, 2, 68, 70, 74–75, 96
Ténéré desert, 57
Tewodros II, emperor, 181, 193
textiles and textile production, 59, 62–63, 93–94, 96, 98–99, 128, 146, 148, 155, 183, 231, 244–45
Thwaynī, Sulṭān, 229–30
ṭibb (medicine), 35, 300
Tibesti mountains, 2, 57, 68, 70, 74–75, 96
Tigre, 7, 172, 174, 181, 183, 193

Tigriña, 7, 172, 174
Tijāniyya Sufi order: and "échange of services" in Senegal, 284–86; and Egyptian colonialism, 159; and historical development of Arabic literature, 300–301; and Islam of Nubia and Funj, 150; and Islamization of the bilād al-sūdān, 107–108; and jihād in the bilād al-sūdān, 110, 119, 120, 124; and religious authority issues, 23
Tilimsān (Tlemçen): and Islamic learning, 12, 22, 39; and al-Maghīlī, 112; and Moroccan rule, 69, 72–73; and trans-Saharan trade, 40, 59; and the Zayyānid dynasty, 49
Timbuktu: and Arabic literary sources, 299, 301; and gold mining, 62; and Islamic learning, 12–13, 22, 59, 61; and Islamization of the bilād al-sūdān, 81–83, 90, 96, 98, 100, 105, 106; and the Jenné settlement, 78; and jihād in the bilād al-sūdān, 121, 122, 123–24; and Moroccan rule, 51; and slavery, 61; and Sudanic trading empires, 4; and trans-Saharan trade, 54–56, 58, 63, 66, 67–69, 70–73; tribal groups of, 2
Tingeregif, Kel, 70, 73
Tinkasso River, 60
Tippu Tip. *See* 'Abd al-Ḥamīd b. Muḥammad b. Juma' al-Murjībī
Tīshīt, 55, 63, 73
Tivaouane, 286
tobacco, 123, 199, 202, 203
Togo, 13, 271, 272, 290
Tondibi, 69
Topan family, 231, 232, 245, 246
TorodBe, 4, 80
Touba, 285
Touré, Sekou, 286–87, 301
trade. *See* caravan trade; trans-Saharan trade
Transoxania, 37
trans-Saharan trade: and the Almohad empire, 47; Arabic sources on, 64–67; and the bilād al-maghrib, 36, 40, 45–46, 47, 50; and cultural connections, 54–64; East-African trade compared to, 243; and Egyptian colonialism, 155, 170; and Islam in Nubia and Funj, 146; and Islamization in the bilād al-sūdān, 74–76, 77, 79–80, 82–84, 86–87, 96, 99–100, 103; and jihād in the bilād al-sūdān, 103, 110, 128; and Mesolithic period, 2–3; and the Ottoman empire, 50; political importance of, 54; and religious conversion, 28, 31–32; scope of trade, 22; and spread of Islam, 12–13; and Sufism, 12, 74–76; and Timbuktu, 70–73; and trading empires, 67–70
Trarza, 116
Tripoli, 49, 51, 57–58, 67, 69, 103, 288
Tripolitania: and conquest of the bilād al-maghrib, 35; and egalitarian theology, 40; and Italian rule, 287–88; and jihād movements, 119; and Ottoman rule, 51; and political divisions of the bilād al-maghrib, 37; and trans-Saharan trade, 61, 67–70, 83
Tuan Guru ('Abdallāh Qāḍī 'Abd al-Salām), 252, 254–56, 260
Tuareg tribes, 2, 55, 68, 70–71, 73, 86, 96, 120, 293
Tubu, 2
Tukulóór, 5, 108, 110, 115, 119
Tunis, 39, 49, 51, 55, 58, 64, 66, 83, 112
Tunisia: and the Almohad empire, 47; and cultures of the bilād al-maghrib, 35; and Islamic conquest of the bilād al-maghrib, 37; and Islamic learning, 12; and Islamic rebellions, 41; and Ottoman rule, 51, 68; and political fragmentation, 48–49; and struggle for political unity, 42–44; and stuggles over the caliphate, 29; and trans-Saharan trade, 56–57, 61–64
Tunjur dynasty, 86, 87
Tuqqurt, 56
Turkish, 156, 157, 260
Turkiyya, 156, 162, 169
Turks, 143, 146, 154, 156, 162, 186, 208
Tuubenaan movement, 115
Tuwāt oasis, 3, 11–12, 55–56, 63, 68–69, 70, 97, 112

Uganda, 157, 210, 241, 242, 276, 290
Uḥud, battle of, 20
Ujiji, 234, 242, 244–45
'ulamā' (singular *'ālim*), 26, 71–72, 117, 142, 150, 161, 168, 189
'Umar al-Mukhtār, 288
'Umar Taal (al-Fūtī, al-Ḥājj): and European colonialism, 283, 284, 286; and instrumentalization of Islam, 24; and the Jakhanke, 107; and jihād in the bilād al-sūdān, 108–11, 114–16, 117, 119–21, 124, 126, 127
'Umar II. 'Abd al-'Azīz, 39
Umayyad caliphate, 29, 37, 39–42, 137, 148, 174, 182
Unguja, 212, 232, 276, 278
Unguja Ukuu, 218
Union Culturelle Musulmane, 286
United States, 231, 296
Ūnsāb dynasty, 152
Upper Congo, 214, 231, 240, 242, 244, 245–47
'urf, 16–17, 31, 34, 252, 270
Usman dan Fodio, 25, 96, 111, 113, 116–19
ustaarabu, 230

ʿUthmān Diqna, 162, 165, 166
Uways b. Muḥammad al-Barawī, 202, 206–207, 237–38

Venice, 58, 61, 62, 64, 96, 185, 211
Vereenigde Oostindische Compagnie (VOC), 248
Victoria, Lake, 10, 240–42, 244, 256, 258–59
Vogel, Eduard, 86
Volta River, 6, 71, 89, 98–101, 102, 107, 109, 125, 300
Vumba, 218, 226

Wa, 89, 99, 100, 107
Waalo, 109–10
wadaad, 8, 198, 199, 201–202
Wadai: and the baggāra belt, 6; and Egyptian colonialism, 170; and Islamization in the bilād al-sūdān, 79, 80, 84, 85–88, 96; and jihād in the bilād al-sūdān, 109; and the Mahdī movement, 165; and the Sinnār-Funj empire, 142, 145, 146; and trade routes, 57; and a trans-Saharan Sufi order, 74–76
Wadān, 55, 63, 97
Wagadugu, 89, 100
Wahhābiyya movement, 17, 24, 25, 111, 155, 203
Wäj, 184, 188
Wäläshma dynasty, 184
Walāta, 55, 59, 66, 70–71, 73, 81, 97
Wälläga, 175, 189, 191
Wällo, 181, 188–89, 191
Wangarawa, 36, 91–93, 95, 99, 106
al-Wansharīsī, Aḥmad b. Yaḥyā Muḥammad, 112
waqf, 75, 260, 278
Wārjābī b. Rābīs, 79
Wārqala, 56, 69
washenzi, 213, 235–36, 245
Wasulu empire, 125–27
Watara, Seku Keita, 101
Watara family, 89, 100–101
Waṭṭāsid dynasty, 48, 50, 51, 62–64
waungwana, 213–14, 216, 235–36
al-Wazzānī, al-Ḥasan b. Muḥammad al-Zayyātī al-Fāsī al-Gharnātī (alias 'Leo Africanus'), 66
Western Congo, 243
White Flag League, 275
White Nile, 1, 5, 135–36, 146, 157, 162, 164, 168
Wolof, 4, 80, 115–16, 290, 300
World War I, 208, 269, 270, 272, 275, 285, 287–88
World War II, 272, 283, 285

Yaḥyā b. Ibrāhīm, 45
Yao, 9, 222, 241–42, 244
al-Yaʿqūbī, Aḥmad b. Abī Yaʿqūb, 65
Yaʿrūbī family/dynasty, 226, 227
Yatenga, 89, 100
Yekuno Amlak, emperor, 176, 178
Yemen: and construction of Taleh, 208; and East African coastal culture, 213, 231; and Ethiopian Islam, 173, 175, 180, 185–87, 191, 193; and geography of the Nile-Sudan, 7; and Islamization in the bilād al-sūdān, 82, 84; and qāt, 203; and the Sinnār-Funj empire, 147; and Sufism, 159, 196
Yesḥaq, emperor, 179, 191
Yifat, 179, 183–84, 190
Yohannes I, emperor, 180
Yohannes IV, emperor, 165, 181, 193
Yoruba, 4, 13, 14, 99, 116, 292
Yūnus b. Ilyās, 41–42
Yūsuf b. Ḥasan, 225–26
Yūsuf Qaramanlı Pasha, 69–70

Zā dynasty, 83
Zaberma, 89
Zaghāwa dynasty, 65, 84, 96
Zagwe dynasty, 174–77
zakāt, 75, 125, 167
Zämana mäsafent, 181, 193
Zambezi River, 8, 10, 220–22, 231, 241, 273
Zamfara, 66, 109, 111, 117
Zanāta, 39–40, 45–47, 49
Zanj, 212–13, 217–18, 220
Zanzibar: and agricultural trade, 175; and Cape Muslims, 250, 261; and the Comoro Islands, 215; and East African coastal culture, 8, 181, 213–14; and Egyptian colonialism, 158; and European colonialism, 268, 270, 276–79, 279–82, 291; and Islamic learning, 19; and Muslims of upcountry East Africa, 241, 242–47; and Omani trading empire, 227–34; and Portugal/Oman conflict, 225–26; and religious reform, 234–35, 238–39; and Shirazi people, 219; and trade relations, 206, 211, 223
zār cult, 33, 174
Zära Yaʿqob, 179–80
Zaramo, 211
Zaria, 66, 90, 109, 127
Zawīla, 57
zāwiya (plural *zawāya*): and the Cape Muslim community, 253; and community formation, 22; and Khalīfa ʿAbdallāh, 165, 169; and the Mahdī movement, 162; and Muḥammad ʿAbdille Ḥasan, 202; and the Sanūsiyya, 74–75; and Sufism on the Nile, 159–60; and warrior tribes, 2, 106

Zaylaʿ, 8, 158, 179, 182–83, 185–86, 193, 196–97, 202
Zaytūna, 12
Zayyānid dynasty, 39, 48–49, 51, 62–63
zikri ya dufu, 12, 236–38
zikri ya kukohoa, 236, 238
Zimba, 222–25, 241
Zimbabwe, 10, 23, 221–22, 223–25, 241
Zīrīd, 44
ziyāra, 22, 82, 159–60
zongos, 98–99
Zubayr Pasha, Raḥma al-Manṣūr, 88, 157, 170

PROFESSOR ROMAN LOIMEIER (b. 1957 in Passau) has held academic positions at the University of Bayreuth, the Centre of Modern Oriental Studies in Berlin, and the University of Florida (Gainesville). He currently teaches at the University of Göttingen. Since the early 1980s, he has done research in Senegal, northern Nigeria, and Tanzania. His major fields of interest are the history of Muslim societies in Africa, historical anthropology, maritime anthropology, as well as the anthropology of catastrophe.